Africa as known to Europeans in the
mid-eighteenth century.

From J. D. Fage, An Atlas of African History *(London:
Edward Arnold Publishers Ltd.)*, © *J. D. Fage 1958.*

THE UNCOMMON MARKET

Essays in the Economic History of the Atlantic Slave Trade

Edited by

HENRY A. GEMERY

JAN S. HOGENDORN

Department of Economics
Colby College
Waterville, Maine

ACADEMIC PRESS   New York   San Francisco   London
A Subsidiary of Harcourt Brace Jovanovich, Publishers

This volume was prepared with the support of National Science Foundation grant No. SOC70-02316 A04. Any opinions, findings, conclusions, or recommendations expressed herein are those of the authors and do not necessarily reflect the view of the National Science Foundation.

ACADEMIC PRESS, INC.
111 Fifth Avenue, New York, New York 10003

United Kingdom Edition published by
ACADEMIC PRESS, INC. (LONDON) LTD.
24/28 Oval Road, London NW1

Library of Congress Cataloging in Publication Data

Symposium on the Economic History of the Trans-Atlantic
    Slave Trade, Colby College, 1975.
    The uncommon market.

    Symposium sponsored by the Mathematical Social Science
Board.
    Includes bibliographical references and index.
    1. Slave–trade––Economic aspects––History––Congresses.
I. Gemery, H. A. II. Hogendorn, Jan S. III. Mathe–
matical Social Science Board. IV. Title.
HT1322.S95 1975   382'.44'09   79–294
ISBN 0–12–279850–3

PRINTED IN THE UNITED STATES OF AMERICA

79 80 81 82   9 8 7 6 5 4 3 2 1

To Pam and Dianne

Contents

Contributors and Participants   xiii

Preface   xv

1   Introduction   1
  Henry A. Gemery and Jan S. Hogendorn

African Perspectives on the Atlantic Slave Trade   3
Atlantic–American Perspectives on the Slave Trade   9
Further Directions for Research   18

I   AFRICAN PERSPECTIVES

2   The Trans-Saharan Slave Trade: A Tentative Census   23
  Ralph A. Austen

The Evidence and Its Manipulation   26
Direct Evidence: The "Medieval" Period, 700–1700   30
Direct Evidence: Egypt and the Nilotic Sudan, 1700–1880   32
Direct Evidence: Libya, 1700–1900   36
Direct Evidence: Tunisia, Algeria, Morocco, 1700–1890   37
Indirect Evidence: Northern African Census Data
    and Slavery   43
Indirect Evidence: Black Servile Military Forces   51
Indirect Evidence: Chronological Synthesis   58
Conclusions: A Global Estimate   65

Appendix. Slave Prices in the Medieval Muslim
   Consumer Market   69
References   72

3 Some Aspects of the Commercial Organization of
   Slaving at Luanda, Angola—1760–1830   77
      Joseph C. Miller

   The Angolan Merchants   80
   The Slaves' Lot   94
   Conclusions: A Constraining Economic Structure   106

4 The Slave Trade in the Bight of Benin, 1640–1890   107
      Patrick Manning

   Resources for the Study of Dahomean History   109
   Place Names   113
   How Many Slaves?   116
   Ethnic Origins of the Slaves   125
   The Interpretation of the History of the Bight of Benin   129
   Appendix 4.1. Chronology of European Trade in the Bight
      of Benin   135
   Appendix 4.2. Slave Exports to Brazil   136
   Appendix 4.3. English Slave Exports   138
   Appendix 4.4. Dutch Slave Exports   138
   Appendix 4.5. Spanish and American Slave Exports   139

5 The Economic Costs of West African Participation in
   the Atlantic Slave Trade: A Preliminary Sampling for
   the Eighteenth Century   143
      Henry A. Gemery and Jan S. Hogendorn

   Methodology   145
   The Evidence   148
   Conclusions   160

6 The Delivery of Slaves from the Central Sudan to the
   Bight of Benin in the Eighteenth and Nineteenth
   Centuries   163
      Mahdi Adamu

   Acquisition of Slaves   166

11 The Direction and Fluctuation of the Transatlantic
    Slave Trade, 1821–1843: A Revision of the 1845
    Parliamentary Paper   273

        D. Eltis

    Statistical Sources   274
    The British Foreign Office   275
    Available Data   276
    Slave Imports by Region   277
    Estimate Series   289
    Data for Other Variables: Losses in Transit
        and Ship Tonnage   291
    Impact of British Policy on the Trade   296
    Conclusion   297

12 West African Consumption Patterns and Their
    Influence on the Eighteenth-Century English
    Slave Trade   303

        David Richardson

    Reassessment of the West African Role in the Trade   304
    British Exports to West Africa, Eighteenth Century   305
    Variations in African Consumption Patterns   311
    English Trading Activity   321
    Foreign Competitors   324
    English Efforts at Expansion   327
    A New Approach   330

13 The Triangular Trade Revisited   331

        Walter E. Minchinton

    The Evidence   334
    Conclusions   351

14 The Dutch Participation in the Atlantic Slave Trade,
    1596–1650   353

        Ernst van den Boogaart and Pieter C. Emmer

    The Beginnings of the Dutch Slave Trade in the Atlantic   353
    The Beginnings of the Slave Trade to Dutch Brazil   357
    Buying Slaves in Guinea   359
    Buying Slaves in Congo and Angola   361
    The Sex Ratio and Age Composition of the Slaves from
        Guinea and Angola   365

Transport of Slaves   172
Conclusion   178

7 Slavery in West Africa   181
   Martin Klein and Paul E. Lovejoy

Kinship and Slavery   184
West African Slavery and the External Slave Trade   198
Slavery as a Mode of Production   207

8 Slave Marketing in West Africa   213
   Paul E. Lovejoy and Jan S. Hogendorn

The Patterns of Slave Marketing   217
Conclusion   232

II ATLANTIC–AMERICAN PERSPECTIVES

9 Mortality in the Dutch Slave Trade, 1675–1795   239
   Johannes Postma

Stages in the Ordeal   240
Mortality in the Initial Stages   241
The Middle Passage   246
Sex and Age Ratios in Mortality   254
Mortality in the Later Stages   256
Crew Mortality   259
Conclusions   260

10 A Note on Mortality in the French Slave Trade
   in the Eighteenth Century   261
   Herbert S. Klein and Stanley L. Engerman

Sources   262
Mortality and Crowding   263
Mortality and Voyage Length   267
Disease, Sanitation, and Provisions   270
Conclusions   272

The Middle Passage and Mortality   365
The Selling of Slaves in Recife   368
The Shift of the Dutch Slave Trade from Brazil to
    the West Indies   371

15 The Adoption of Slave Labor in British America   377
    Richard N. Bean and Robert P. Thomas

The Nature of the Problem   378
Analytical Framework   379
Existing Explanations   380
An Alternative Explanation   387
The Productivity of Labor   388
Prices of Labor   390

16 The Economic Considerations Behind the Danish
    Abolition of the Negro Slave Trade   399
    Svend E. Green-Pedersen

Structure of the Trade   400
Danish Attitudes toward Slavery   402
The Negro Trade Commission   403
The Representation   404
Scholarly Accounts   408
Pragmatic Aspects of Abolition   414

17 British Repression of the Illegal French Slave Trade:
    Some Considerations   419
    Serge Daget

Questions Raised by the 1845 List   419
The International Situation   423
British Policy toward French Slave Trade   425
Conclusions   439
Appendix. Number and Size of British Repression Patrols   440

Index   443

Contributors and Participants

Numbers in parentheses indicate the pages on which the contributors' chapters begin.

MAHDI ADAMU (163), Department of History, Ahmadu Bello University, Zaria, Nigeria

RALPH A. AUSTEN (23), Committee on African Studies, University of Chicago, Chicago, Illinois 60637

STEPHEN BAIER, African Studies Center, Boston University, Brookline, Massachusetts 02146

RICHARD N. BEAN (377), Department of Economics, University of Houston, Houston, Texas 77004

PIERRE A. BOULLE, Department of History, McGill University, Montreal, Quebec, Canada

PHILIP D. CURTIN, Department of History, Johns Hopkins University, Baltimore, Maryland 21218

SERGE DAGET (419), History Department, National University of the Ivory Coast, Abidjan, Ivory Coast

D. ELTIS (273), Department of Economics, Algonquin College, Ottawa, Ontario, Canada

PIETER C. EMMER* (353), Center for the History of European Expansion, University of Leiden, Leiden, The Netherlands

STANLEY L. ENGERMAN (261), Departments of Economics and History, University of Rochester, Rochester, New York 14627

HENRY A. GEMERY (1, 143), Department of Economics, Colby College, Waterville, Maine 04901

SVEND E. GREEN-PEDERSEN (399), Institute of History, Aarhus University, Aarhus, Denmark

* Present address: Churchill College, Cambridge University, Cambridge, England.

JAN S. HOGENDORN (1, 143, 213), Department of Economics, Colby College, Waterville, Maine 04901

JOSEPH INIKORI, Department of History, Ahmadu Bello University, Zaria, Nigeria

HERBERT S. KLEIN (261), Department of History, Columbia University, New York, New York 10027

MARTIN KLEIN (181), Department of History, University of Toronto, Toronto, Ontario, Canada

FRANKLIN W. KNIGHT, Department of History, Johns Hopkins University, Baltimore, Maryland 21218

PAUL E. LOVEJOY (181, 213), Department of History, York University, Toronto, Ontario, Canada

DONALD N. McCLOSKEY, Department of Economics, University of Chicago, Chicago, Illinois 60637

PATRICK MANNING (107), Department of History, Cañada College, Redwood City, California 94061

MICHAEL MASON, History Department, Loyola Campus, Concordia University, Montreal, Quebec, Canada

JOSEPH C. MILLER (77), Department of History, University of Virginia, Charlottesville, Virginia 22903

WALTER E. MINCHINTON (331), Department of Economic History, University of Exeter, Exeter, Devon, England

NIZAR MOTANI, Department of History, Western Michigan University, Kalamazoo, Michigan 49001

JOHANNES POSTMA (239), Department of History, Mankato State University, Mankato, Minnesota 56001

PATRICK M. REDMOND, Bayero University, Kano, Nigeria

DAVID RICHARDSON (303), Department of Economic and Social History, University of Hull, Hull, England

RICHARD ROEHL, Department of Economics, University of Michigan at Dearborn, Dearborn, Michigan 48128

PATRICIA ROMERO, Department of History, Johns Hopkins University, Baltimore, Maryland 21218

SIMON ROTTENBERG, Department of Economics, University of Massachusetts, Amherst, Massachusetts 01002

VERA RUBIN, Research Institute for the Study of Man, 162 E. 78th Street, New York, New York 10021

BARBARA L. SOLOW, Department of Economics, Boston University, Boston, Massachusetts 02215

RICHARD SUTCH, Department of Economics, University of California, Berkeley, California 94720

ROBERT P. THOMAS (377), Department of Economics, University of Washington, Seattle, Washington 98195

ARTHUR TUDEN, Department of Anthropology, University of Pittsburgh, Pittsburgh, Pennsylvania 15260

ERNST VAN DEN BOOGAART (353), Center for the History of European Expansion, University of Leiden, Leiden, The Netherlands

Preface

The chapters in this volume are the product of a conference on the economic history of the Atlantic slave trade held at Colby College on August 20–22, 1975. Thirty-three scholars from the United States and abroad met to present and discuss 18 papers over the course of the 3-day period. All of the historians and economists who were present shared a research interest in the trade and either a disciplinary interest in or tolerance for quantitative approaches to the topic. Further details are included in the Introduction.

Our indebtedness to others is substantial. The conference itself was made possible by a grant from the Mathematical Social Science Board of the National Science Foundation. Two members of that Board, Charles Tilly and Richard Easterlin, deserve especial thanks for their aid, which extended from the initial application to publication. In like fashion, Philip D. Curtin and Stanley L. Engerman supplied valuable comment and suggestion throughout the project. They, together with the editors, made up the committee that selected the papers. The editors also had the further advice and assistance of Donald N. McCloskey, Pieter Emmer, Joseph Miller, and A. G. Hopkins. At Colby, funding for secretaries and editorial assistants was provided by the Social Science Research Fund. The Director of Special Programs, Robert Kany, brought coherence to the physical arrangements of the conference. Martha Nist and Sarah Vetault provided capable editorial aid and Joanne LaBombard typed the manuscript copy with a good-humored acceptance of the inevitable "final" changes. The assistant for indexing and proofreading was Joanne Lynch of Colby College.

Our major indebtedness is clearly to the conference participants who not only produced the content of the conference and this volume, but did so in a fashion that eased the organizing and editorial burdens. They cheerfully acceded to changes of schedule, and to the occasional difficulties in making plane connections to Maine. It was the unstinting cooperation of the participants that made it possible for the organizers to survive the effort with a minimum of psychic harm.

Waterville, Maine
February 2, 1979

1

Introduction

HENRY A. GEMERY
JAN S. HOGENDORN

The tragedy of the slave trade was that it was not uncommon. Only the perspective of the twentieth century allows that title to be given to this volume. A pervasive feature of economic activity over the course of three centuries, the trade's scope and persistence can be understood only by a detailed examination of the motivations and mechanisms that supported it. That is the task of this volume.

The chapters assembled here stem from a conference on "The Economic History of the Transatlantic Slave Trade" held at Colby College, August 20–22, 1975, under the sponsorship of the Historical Advisory Committee of the Mathematical Social Science Board. Two premises dictated the organization of the conference. They were, first, that the combined efforts of historians and economists are essential to any full exploration of a phenomenon as wide-ranging as the transatlantic slave trade; and second, that quantitative data are critical in understanding the operation, dimensions, and impact of the trade. Neither premise can be regarded as exceptional, given the direction and methodology of current research in economic history; yet joint ventures on this topic are rare. The papers given at

1

sessions on the history of the slave trade at the Sixth International Conference for Economic History in Copenhagen in August, 1974, and now published as a special number of *Revue française d'histoire d'outre-mer*, should be cited as an earlier, significant example; but it remains true that the merger of historians' and economists' approaches to the study of the slave trade is unique.[1] The gains to be derived from such a disciplinary mix were clearly demonstrated to conference participants and it is hoped that they will be apparent to readers of this collection as well.

The trade, in leaving its imprint on African, European, and American societies, left equally wide opportunities for research. This volume reflects that breadth in its structure, which is designed to provide perspectives on African supply conditions as well as Atlantic–American market patterns. In keeping with one objective of the conference, the chapters do have a common methodological link in that all are, to a degree, quantitative.

In a sense, quantitative research on the slave trade is not new. Some of the earliest abolitionist studies relied on arguments supported by data;[2] but thereafter, through the remainder of the nineteenth century and most of the twentieth century, little quantitative work on the slave trade was done.[3] The hiatus continued until the publication of Philip Curtin's *The Atlantic Slave Trade* in 1969, the first systematic attempt at a census of the slave trade.[4] The trade itself presents sizable barriers to the employment of quantitative methods—there is a reluctance to attach sterile numbers to a human tragedy of enormous magnitude, there are few written records for the African portion of the trade, and there is a daunting diversity of languages and sources to be sifted when following the trade's range across four continents. The impetus to overcome barriers of this sort probably came from the increasing general use of quantitative methods in historical research, most

[1] *La traite des noirs par l'Atlantique: Nouvelles approches* (Paris, 1976), a slightly revised version of a special issue of the *Revue française d'histoire d'outre-mer*, nos. 226–227, 1975. Joint efforts by historians and economists will probably not be as permanently unique as J. C. Miller has suggested. In a postconference discussion, Professor Miller observed that this was not only the first occasion on which historians and economists gathered to address this topic but, given the increasing specialization of the disciplines, may have been the last as well.

[2] Thomas Clarkson's assembly of data on crew mortality in the English slave trade is perhaps the most famous example. See T. Clarkson to Lords of Trade and Plantation, 27 July 1788, *Board of Trade Report,* Part 2.

[3] Quantitative research was not wholly absent, as the work of Rinchon, Martin, and—more peripherally—Higham will testify. D. Rinchon, *Le trafic négrier, d'après les livres de commerce du capitaine gantois, Pierre-Ignace-Lievin van Alstein,* vol. 1 (Paris, 1931); G. Martin, *Nantes au XVIIIᵉ siécle: L'ère des négriers (1714–1774)* (Paris, 1931); C. S. S. Higham, *The Development of the Leeward Islands under the Restoration 1660–1688* (Cambridge, 1921).

[4] P. D. Curtin, *The Atlantic Slave Trade: A Census* (Madison, 1969), hereafter cited as *Census.*

notably in studies of slavery in the American South.[5] With the publication of the Curtin work and with the example of the research on the American South, it was perhaps natural that research on the Atlantic slave trade would take a quantitative turn.

Quantitative historical research can be broadly divided into two stages. The first is concerned with the generation of usable data—its unearthing, assembling, checking for validity. The second involves its processing in some statistical form and in accord with some applicable notion of theory—economic, demographic, or other. The second stage cannot proceed without the first and indeed the development of a "mere" series of numbers may require by far the largest investment in research time.[6] These chapters illustrate research occurring at both levels, but their intellectual debt to the first systematic data compilation on the numbers and flows in the trade is obvious from the footnotes where references to the work of P. D. Curtin occur repeatedly.[7] A thorough transformation in the empirical content of research on the slave trade has resulted largely from Curtin's pioneering studies. The extent of that transformation will be discussed in the remainder of this introduction and its ongoing progress will be apparent from the chapters themselves.

AFRICAN PERSPECTIVES ON THE ATLANTIC SLAVE TRADE

The chapters collected here demonstrate the several sorts of quantitative research being undertaken by the economic historians of Africa.[8] Such

[5] Quantitative studies on slavery in the American South are usually dated from the well-known essay by A. H. Conrad and J. R. Meyer, "The Economics of Slavery in the Ante-Bellum South," *Journal of Political Economy*, vol. 66, 1958, pp. 95–130. For a critical assessment of the literature on quantification in history, see C. Erickson's review article, "Quantitative History," *American Historical Review*, vol. 80, no. 2, 1975, pp. 351–365. See also R. W. Fogel, "The Limits of Quantitative Methods in History," *American Historical Review*, vol. 80, no. 2, 1975, pp. 329–350.

[6] Note R. W. Fogel's comments on counting. Fogel, "Limits," p. 337.

[7] The bulk of such references will be to Curtin's *Census*.

[8] See the survey article by Joseph P. Smaldone, "Quantitative Research in African History," *Historical Methods Newsletter*, vol. 10, no. 1, December 1976, pp. 20–28. A number of recent works complement the studies in this volume on the status of slavery and the slave trade within Africa itself. Included are the essays in Claude Meillassoux, ed., *L'esclavage en Afrique pre-coloniale* (Paris, 1975); in Suzanne Miers and Igor Kopytoff, eds., *Slavery in Africa* (Madison, 1977); and papers by Marion Johnson and B. K. Drake in Roger Anstey and P. E. H. Hair, eds., *Liverpool, the African Slave Trade, and Abolition*, (Bristol, 1976). Various papers on the subject were given at the conference on Islamic Systems of Slavery held at Princeton University, June 1977. See also Paul E. Lovejoy, "The Plantation Economy of the Sokoto Caliphate,"

research is commonly bifurcated between those who depend primarily on archival source material and travelers' accounts, and those who depend on oral data. Several authors draw liberally on *both* written and oral data.

The most obviously quantitative of the efforts are those by Ralph A. Austen (Chapter 2) presenting a census of the trans-Saharan slave trade, by Joseph C. Miller (Chapter 3) on Portuguese and Brazilian slaving in the South Atlantic basin, by Patrick Manning (Chapter 4) on the numbers involved in the Dahomean slave trade, and by Henry A. Gemery and Jan S. Hogendorn (Chapter 5) on the costs of the slave trade to West Africa. Austen's pioneering attempt to reconstruct the quantitative aspects of trans-Saharan slave movements draws almost entirely on published sources, with heavy dependence on Arab authors. Although Austen does not claim that he is the "Curtin of Arabia," he does cast grave doubt on some recent claims that the scope of the trans-Saharan trade was small. Indeed, his estimate of 10 million slaves moved during the history of the desert trade is approximately the same as Curtin's findings for the transatlantic traffic, although the Saharan trade covered a far longer time span.

Austen's methodology is to identify all extant estimates of the numbers of slaves moved during a time period in a given geographical area, then to eliminate or modify those contradicted by internal or external evidence, and finally to establish overall estimates by a process of what might be called "educated averaging." In his collection of data, Austen has utilized some previously neglected sources which cast substantial new light on the scope of the desert trade. For example, the accounts of Emmanuel Piloti de Crete, covering the relatively long period of 1396–1438, necessitate substantial changes in earlier estimates of slave movements in the medieval period.[9] Edrisi, ibn Battuta, and other Arab observers provide further data drawn on by Austen for his medieval estimates. For the later period of the Saharan commerce (eighteenth and nineteenth centuries), there is a relative wealth of consuls' reports, diplomatic despatches, and eyewitness accounts by travelers and merchants.

On the whole, Austen's work shows the possibilities for breaking new

---

Journal of African History, forthcoming; Polly Hill, "From Slavery to Freedom: The Case of Farm-Slavery in Nigerian Hausaland," *Comparative Studies in Society and History,* vol. 18, no. 3, 1976, pp. 395–426; Jan Hogendorn, "Slave Acquisition and Delivery in Precolonial Hausaland," in R. Dumett and Ben K. Schwartz, eds., *West African Culture Dynamics: Archaeological and Historical Perspectives* (The Hague, forthcoming); Jan Hogendorn, "Economics of Slave Use on Two Plantations: Biye and Hanwa, of the Zaria Emirate of the Sokoto Caliphate," *African Historical Studies,* vol. 10, no. 3, 1977, pp. 369–383; and the articles and theses listed in the footnotes to the Lovejoy–Hogendorn and Klein–Lovejoy chapters.

[9] See Emmanuel Piloti de Crete, *L'Egypte au commencement du xve siècle* (Cairo, 1950, P. H. Dopp, ed.).

ground in the quantitative economic history of Africa by a careful sifting of the available primary sources.[10]

In its employment of data, Chapter 3 by Joseph C. Miller on Portuguese slaving in the South Atlantic bears a close relationship to the Austen effort. Making liberal use of unpublished source material in the Arquivo Histórico de Angola and the Arquivo Histórico Ultramarino at Lisbon, Miller shows that in southern waters the shipping of slaves and the supplying of imported goods used for payment was basically a Brazilian enterprise. Scholars will find, through Miller's work, access to several accounts of the southern trade hitherto unfamiliar to those not fluent in Portuguese, including those of Luis António de Oliveira Mendes (1812), João Carlos Feo Cardoso de Castello Branco e Torres (1825), and Accursio das Neves (1820s). The remarkable variability in the quantities of slaves shipped annually in the southern trade is emphasized in the chapter, as is the relatively sophisticated commercial structure of the commerce at Angolan points of embarkation.

Inland from the coast, the Angolan system of slave supply as described by Miller differed substantially from that found in most of West Africa. *Sertanejos,* "backwoodsmen" who traveled far afield by caravan in search of slaves for sale, carried the European presence much further into the interior than was generally true in West Africa. The activities of the *sertanejos* and their bondage to a complicated system of credit, including a selection of quantitative data, have been compiled by Miller from material in the Angolan archives. In concluding, Miller proposes that the slave trade in southern waters involved a high degree of risk, with debt-ridden firms struggling to stay solvent in an economic environment where government monopolies and restrictions limited the alternatives open to entrepreneurship. With profits restricted and capital short, slaves in transit were often underfed and poorly quartered, arriving at Brazilian ports in a much debilitated state. Such conditions were predictable, according to Miller, because of the economic organization of the Angolan trade itself.

Chapter 4 by Patrick Manning is quantitative in providing estimates of the number of slaves shipped from the Bight of Benin, estimates that modify somewhat those advanced originally by Curtin. The number of slaves exported to Brazil has been reconstructed by Manning through Pierre Verger's recent research.[11] English exports are estimated from the Curtin data but are modified for the period 1680–1700 by utilizing Royal

---

[10] Ralph Austen, "Dutch Trading Voyages to Cameroon, 1721–1759: European Documents and African History," *Annales de la Faculte des Lettres et Sciences Humaines, Universite de Yaounde,* vol. 6, 1975, pp. 5–27.

[11] Verger's calculations can be found in *Flux et reflux de la traite des nègres entre le golfe de Benin et Bahia de Todos os Santos du 17ᵉ et 18ᵉ siècles* (The Hague, 1968).

African Company import statistics to Ardra and Whydah. Curtin's estimates for the French trade are followed but extended into the period before 1710, whereas the new figures on the Dutch trade are based on the recent research of Johannes Postma as interpreted by Manning.[12] These revisions result in the conclusion that approximately one and three-quarters million slaves were exported from the Bight of Benin during the period of the slave trade.

Following a discussion of the ethnic origins of Dahomean slave exports, Manning calls attention to the pervasive influence of Archibald Dalzel's 1793 book, *The History of Dahomy*, on almost all subsequent writers on the area's economic and social history.[13] The suggestion is made that this has resulted in substantial stereotyping of Dahomean historiography, and is accompanied by a plea for further research efforts to test Dalzel's conclusions.

A considerable difference in methodology marks Chapter 5 by Gemery–Hogendorn, which is an attempt to show that even under the most favorable assumptions the eighteenth-century Atlantic slave trade subjected West Africa to long-term economic losses even if the enormous social costs of the trade are not considered. The model followed is one of total economic welfare, with estimates of the production lost to West Africa through the export of slaves compared to the value of imported goods obtained through the sale of those slaves. Production loss is estimated by referring to the amount of food needed to maintain, in Marvin Miracle's phrase, a "minimum physiologic level of living."[14] This figure is then multiplied by prices prevailing in various markets and at various time periods in order to establish a long-term average cost for subsistence over wide areas of West Africa. Information on costs is obtained from a variety of secondary sources (including Philip Curtin's *Economic Change in Precolonial Africa*, Marvin Miracle's *Maize in Tropical Africa*, E. P. LeVeen's University of Chicago doctoral thesis, "British Slave Trade Suppression Policies 1821–1865: Impact and Implications," and primary sources [William Bosman, John Barbot, Heinrich Barth, and others]). The suggested minimum subsistence diet is tested for calorie content using FAO data.

Gemery and Hogendorn then attempt a measure of the economic gains from West African participation in the slave trade by calculating the quantity of imported goods that could be purchased because of the slave exports. Here the data employed are the quantity of slaves exported as estimated in

[12] Johannes Postma, "The Dimension of the Dutch Slave Trade from Western Africa," *Journal of African History*, vol. 13, no. 2, 1972, pp. 237–248.

[13] A. Dalzel, *The History of Dahomey, an Inland Kingdom of Africa* (London, 1967).

[14] M. Miracle, "Subsistence Agriculture: Analytical Problems and Alternative Concepts," *American Journal of Agricultural Economics*, May 1968, pp. 195–196.

Curtin's *Atlantic Slave Trade* and revised by Roger Anstey, and the average coastal price of slaves presented in Richard Bean's University of Washington doctoral thesis, "The British Trans-Atlantic Slave Trade, 1650–1775,[15] and the LeVeen doctoral thesis just cited.

Based on these two sets of calculations, losses in terms of output sacrificed by the removal of population, and gains in terms of command over imported goods, Gemery and Hogendorn conclude by stating the near certainty of a net economic loss to West Africa from the eighteenth-century slave trade.

The remaining chapters that consider the African side of the slave trade share a different orientation toward the use of source materials. All depend to some large extent on oral testimony collected in relatively recent times. Economic historians, historians, sociologists, anthropologists, and the like have shared in a revolution in oral data collection. Equipped with small, portable cassette tape recorders in place of the "field notebooks" of former years, they have embarked on wide-ranging programs of data collection utilizing the new techniques of oral history.[16]

In Chapter 6, "The Delivery of Slaves from the Central Sudan to the Bight of Benin in the Eighteenth and Nineteenth Centuries," Mahdi Adamu has attempted a study of the slave supply mechanism operating between Hausaland and the Atlantic coast during the era of the slave trade. The treatment covers both slave acquisition and delivery, and a number of the central conclusions of the chapter are based on collected oral data. The oral data chiefly relied upon is Adamu's own, based on field work for his Birmingham University doctoral thesis, "The Hausa Factor in West African History."[17]

The supply system according to Adamu was based on capture by large government-sponsored expeditions raiding into source areas, with an ultimate division of the spoils among the Emir, his military officers, and platoon leaders. Thence to the coast the system of disposal operated in a relatively complex manner. Beginning with the purchase of captured slaves from the officials in the raiding armies, under the auspices of a government appointee at the main market of Zaria (the *sarkin dillalin bayi*) or private entrepreneurs elsewhere, the slaves entered the transport system. The details of the transport arrangements are an interesting contribution of the Adamu chapter. Export regulations were avoided by the simple tactic of using slaves as porters, with two uses for slaves in this regard—either as permanent

---

[15] Now published under the same title by Arno Press (New York, 1975).

[16] For a concise survey of the techniques for the collection of oral data see Paul E. Lovejoy and Jan S. Hogendorn, "Oral Data Collection and the Economic History of the Central Savanna," *Savanna*, vol. 7, no. 1, forthcoming.

[17] Forthcoming. (London and Zaria). 1978.

members of the porterage system or as temporary members destined eventually for export.

Attention is called to the relay centers where slaves changed hands on the way to the coast, and to the *zango* rest stops where food and secure sleeping arrangements could be had. Many of the slaves delivered through this mechanism actually served in the coastal economies. Here was a parting of the ways, with many slaves kept permanently in local use while others were sold for export at the coast. A main conclusion is that the delivery mechanism flowed both ways, with commodities, livestock, and imported manufactured goods flowing inland as the quid pro quo for slave exports.

Chapter 7 by Klein and Lovejoy is also based to a large extent on collected oral data. One source is field work by Klein and Lovejoy in rural Senegal and Nigeria respectively, during 1975, but the greater part of their oral material is contained in the answers to a series of questionnaires completed by all French commandants in French West Africa early in the year 1904, a time when the colonial authorities had decided to review their policy toward indigenous slavery.

The intent of Klein and Lovejoy is to redefine the place of slavery as it existed within West Africa. For purposes of discussion, Klein and Lovejoy divide the slave population of the Western Sudan into three groups—trade slaves captured during their own lifetime and subject to sale and export, slave warriors attached to important offices or royal lineages, and domestic slaves attached to households. They estimate that 30–50% of the population in the Western Sudan belonged to one or another of these slave categories. It has been commonplace to argue that after a slave's initial capture there began a process of assimilation with the owning family that protected the slave against further sale. The two authors take issue with this position, and give evidence that such assimilated slaves might indeed still be sold under a variety of circumstances. They are also critical of the view that a slave and a family dependent occupied the same social and economic position. Although a slave could accumulate property and take a second wife, Klein and Lovejoy believe that further similarities between slaves and dependents exist, as they say, "largely in the eyes of the outsider."

In several sections that consider the position of the domestic slave in the family, the means and frequency of manumission, the extent and severity of mistreatment, and the place of the slave in the producing system, Klein and Lovejoy add to our knowledge of indigenous West African slavery. Perhaps the most interesting (and controversial) element in the chapter is the claim that several recent works on slavery in Africa underestimate the economic base of slavery. In particular, their identification of certain areas where slave labor was used to produce exports (millet, cotton cloth) on a profit-maximizing basis will be of significant interest to economic historians.

Chapter 8 by Paul E. Lovejoy and Jan S. Hogendorn on "Slave Marketing in

West Africa" is an effort to call attention to the different forms of slave marketing as they existed in four distinct geographical areas: the savanna from the Senegambia basin to Lake Chad, the coastal forest states along the Bight of Benin and the Gold Coast, the area between the Benue valley and the Bight of Bonny, and the littoral from the southern Ivory Coast to Guinea. For their evidence, much of which is originally oral in nature, Lovejoy and Hogendorn depend on data collected in recent years by specialists working in each of the main areas surveyed. The collections of E. A. Oroge, Polly Hill, Claude Meillassoux, Mahdi Adamu, Stephen Baier, R. C. C. Law, J. B. C. Anyake, A. J. H. Latham, F. I. Ekejiuba, David Northrup, S. C. Ukpabi, K. O. Ogedengbe, S. J. S. Cookey, and others provide the base for the Lovejoy–Hogendorn synthesis.

The basic theme of the chapter is that various barriers to entry were typical in the intra-African slave trade.[18] Attention is first called to the restriction of access to supply at the source. In a number of the areas considered, slavery was not at all a private activity in a legal sense, and private efforts would risk the penalty of law.

Restriction of access to long-distance transport is also emphasized. Solutions ranged from diaspora organizations through private or semiprivate commercial societies, to explicit state management of transport. Finally, consideration is given to restrictions on credit. Slaving could consume a good deal of capital, and a steady supply of imported goods was also required, so that credit availability became a restriction on entry. In the state-trading systems (Oyo, Dahomey, Asante) credit was advanced to governments or through government auspices. In the private or semiprivate organizations, credit might be limited by religious and social factors—as exemplified by the Agalawa, Tokarawa, Kambarin Baribari, and Jahanke of the savanna, or the Jukun oracle, Ekpe society, and Aro system inland from the Bight of Bonny. On the coast institutions such as the Canoe House in the Niger Delta were also important in channeling credit and policing defaulters.

The conclusion drawn by Lovejoy and Hogendorn is that barriers to entry were a relatively common feature in the mechanism for slave supply.

ATLANTIC–AMERICAN PERSPECTIVES ON THE SLAVE TRADE

When they follow the course of the slave trade beyond the African continent, economic historians continue to face questions of the trade's

---

[18] A position also taken by T. C. I. Ryan in his unpublished doctoral dissertation, "The Economics of Trading in Slaves" (M.I.T., 1975).

structure and its impact on the societies and economies it touched. Only one wholly new issue appears—the nature, effectiveness, and consequences of abolition and emancipation—and that because its origins lay outside Africa. Though the questions remain largely the same, the type of data available to researchers changes dramatically. The European market patterns that dominated the non-African portion of the trade left a legacy of numbers, fragmentary and of variable quality, but sufficient to tantalize scholars with the prospect of posing and testing hypotheses within a quantitative framework. That prospect is common ground to the chapters that consider the Atlantic–American slave trade.

The degree to which the numbers available both constrain and advance our knowledge of the trade is most evident in the study of mortality patterns. Chapter 9 by Johannes Postma, which draws its data largely from the records of Dutch trading companies now housed in the archives of the Netherlands, makes it clear that only two stages of slaving, coasting and the middle passage, offer the substantial empirical evidence necessary to estimate mortality.

The research of the last two decades has succeeded in reducing the variance in mortality estimates, and something of a consensus has tended to emerge.[19] Postma's calculations of mortality (16.8% and 17.4%), his findings that the length of voyage was correlated with mortality, and his observation that mortality differed by sex are all results consistent with other research utilizing other data. There is an interesting absence, however, of any long-term trend in Postma's mortality calculations, which sets the Dutch evidence somewhat apart from the English and French sources that generally show a secular decline in the mortality of slaves in passage. The explanation may lie in the fact that the Dutch data are limited to the latter part of the seventeenth century and the eighteenth century, whereas the English and French evidence cover a longer span.[20]

[19] For a discussion of this literature, see P. D. Curtin's "A Postscript on Mortality" in *Census,* pp. 275–286. See also M. Craton's expression of caution regarding the "average mortality" concept in *Sinews of Empire* (London, 1974), pp. 96–97. Recent research on the mortality question includes H. S. Klein, "The Trade in African Slaves to Rio de Janeiro, 1795–1811: Estimates of Mortality and Patterns of Voyages," *Journal of African History,* vol. 10, no. 4, 1969, pp. 533–549; Sv. E. Green-Pedersen, *Om forholdene pa danske slaveskibe, med sverlig benblik pa dodeligheden, 1777–1789* (Alborg, 1973); R. Anstey, "The Volume and Profitability of the British Slave Trade, 1761–1807," in S. L. Engerman and E. D. Genovese, eds., *Race and Slavery in the Western Hemisphere: Quantitative Studies* (Princeton, 1975), pp. 25, 26; and H. S. Klein and S. L. Engerman, "Shipping Patterns and Mortality in the African Slave Trade to Rio de Janeiro," *Cahiers d'études africaines,* vol. 15, 3ᵉ Cahier 1975, pp. 381–398. See also Part 3 of the Ryan doctoral thesis.

[20] Curtin, *Census,* and Craton, *Sinews of Empire.* See also M. Goulart, *Escravidão africana no Brasil (das origenes a extingão)* (São Paulo, 1949), p. 278, and Jean Mettas, "Pour une histoire de la traite des Noirs francaise: Sources et problèmes" in *Revue française d'histoire d'outre-mer,* nos. 226–227, 1975, pp. 19–46.

Isolating the actual determinants of mortality calls for more formal procedures for testing relationships, and this is the task undertaken by Herbert S. Klein and Stanley L. Engerman in Chapter 10, "A Note on Mortality in the French Slave Trade in the Eighteenth Century." The major data source for Klein and Engerman is the information compiled by Dieudonné Rinchon for Nantes in the eighteenth century. Their most striking finding (also arrived at in the Postma chapter) is the absence of a relationship between overcrowding and slave mortality on the Atlantic passage. Although this should be interpreted with the same caution the authors themselves adopt, the similar conclusion of the two chapters implies that passage times and location of port of exit may explain more than does crowding. The exact manner in which length of passage and port of exit influenced mortality remains open to a number of interpretations, and the current state of historical knowledge does not yet permit an informed choice among them.[21] Does the location of the port of exit, for example, serve as a proxy for the epidemiological environment in that portion of Africa? In what ways did the length of travel from inland sources or the nature of "storage" before shipment affect mortality?

The fact that further questions remain, however, should not obscure the magnitude of the new contribution. Average mortality levels have been specified for another component of the trade and, given the separate data bases for the Postma and Klein–Engerman chapters, convincing doubt has been cast on overcrowding as a significant determinant of mortality.

The "point of departure" estimates provided by Curtin's overall survey of the volume and flow of the trade have been modified in part by the subsequent work of Roger Anstey and Johannes Postma, work that Curtin has discussed and incorporated into his results.[22] Chapter 11 by David Eltis is a further step in this revision.

Drawing on Foreign Office correspondence to extend the reporting coverage of slaver voyages, Eltis reconstructs slave import series for the period 1821–1843. The methodology in itself is of note, for it essentially

[21] One interesting interpretation is given by P. D. Curtin, *Census*, p. 282.

[22] Anstey, "Volume and Profitability"; J. Postma, "The Origin of African Slaves: The Dutch Activities on the Guinea Coast, 1675–1795"; and P. D. Curtin, "Measuring the Atlantic Slave Trade," all in Engerman and Genovese, *Race and Slavery*, pp. 3–32, 33–50, and 107–130. J. E. Inikori has commented critically on present estimates in "Measuring the Atlantic Slave Trade: An Assessment of Curtin and Anstey," *Journal of African History*, vol. 17, no. 2, pp. 197–223. The Inikori paper was originally presented at the Colby conference but had been committed earlier for publication in the *Journal of African History*. Curtin has replied in his "Measuring the Atlantic Slave Trade Once Again: A Comment by Philip D. Curtin," *Journal of African History*, vol. 17, no. 4, 1976, pp. 595–605, and there is a rejoinder by Inikori in the same issue, pp. 607–627. See also the essays in Part 1 of *La traite des noirs*, and R. Anstey, "The Slave Trade of the Continental Powers, 1760–1810," *The Economic History Review*, 2nd series, vol. 30, no. 2, May 1977, pp. 259–268.

involves the rewriting of the 1845 Parliamentary Paper of the British Foreign Office on the basis of material available to, but unused by, the authors of that document. The returns to such an intensive working of primary source material are evident in the additional detail offered and in the revised aggregate import series developed. The average annual flow of slaves indicated by Eltis's series is nearly the equal of that which occurred at the peak of the trade in 1761–1780. Such results raise obvious questions as to the effectiveness of British suppression policies and open for reexamination the conclusions of studies based largely on the published Parliamentary Paper.[23]

Accumulating detail on the conduct of the trade has reinforced the picture of a well-organized responsive market dealing in slave labor.[24] The flexibility characterizing this market has been remarked on and has been incorporated as a feature of the more general economic models of the trade.[25] The adaptability of participants in the market is given more precise historical definition in Chapters 12, 13, and 14 by Richardson, Minchinton, and van den Boogaart and Emmer, respectively.

Richardson utilizes data taken from merchant invoices to infer regional differences in African tastes. These differences underlie the variations in demand for trade goods, the data on which illuminate the nature of market opportunities offered to European and American traders. A trader's ability to earn profits was dependent on his success in:

1. Choosing a cargo assortment that closely matched the tastes of the intended markets.

---

[23] E. P. LeVeen, "A Quantitative Analysis of the Impact of British Suppression Policies on the Volume of the Nineteenth Century Atlantic Slave Trade," in Engerman and Genovese, *Race and Slavery*, pp. 51–82. Eltis has a paper, "The Export of Slaves from Africa 1821–1843," *Journal of Economic History*, vol. 37, no. 2, 1977, pp. 409–433, which is related to the one published here.

[24] That point appears well established with regard to European and New World participation in the trade; the nature of African participation is more open to debate. For a concise delineation of the issues involved in adopting a market framework in the African context, see A. G. Hopkins, *An Economic History of West Africa* (New York, 1973), pp. 4–6. A specific test for an African market response appears in E. P. LeVeen, "The African Slave Supply Response," *African Studies Review*, vol. 18, no. 1, 1975, pp. 9–28.

[25] See S. L. Engerman's reaction in "Comments on the Study of Race and Slavery," in Engerman and Genovese, *Race and Slavery*, p. 496. General economic models of the slave trade are found in LeVeen, "Supply Response"; R. P. Thomas and R. N. Bean, "The Fishers of Men: The Profits of the Slave Trade," *Journal of Economic History*, vol. 34, no. 4, 1975, pp. 885–914; H. A. Gemery and J. S. Hogendorn, "The Atlantic Slave Trade: A Tentative Economic Model," *Journal of African History*, vol. 15, no. 2, 1974, pp. 223–246; and T. C. I. Ryan, "Economics of Trading."

2. Sorting out the regional markets in a fashion that achieved the most favorable rates of exchange for the cargo components.

3. Acquiring access to a low cost supply of major trade goods.[26]

Possession of an advantageous trade good, one with unusually favorable rates of exchange for European and American traders, generally insured a profit if disasters in shipping and mortality were avoided.[27] As with most market opportunities, both entrepreneurial skills and market circumstances played a part.

The complexity of the African trade is also apparent from Richardson's discussion. "Reading the market" was no simple task. Ship captains had to manipulate local units of account, goods assortments, the local prices of the goods, and the prime costs of the goods bartered. African traders did essentially the same, though their limited ability to move from market to market restricted their leeway in bargaining.[28] The complexity of the market faced by Europeans may have been more apparent than real, however, since gross margins may have been sufficiently large and the coastal markets sufficiently imperfect to allow even inept traders a profit. If market sophistication should not be too quickly inferred from Richardson's chapter, the significance of market information can be validly inferred. Among the reasons why slaving tended to concentrate in particular ports was the external economy of available market knowledge generated by the continuous return flow of slaving captains. Such information played an evident part in the strategy of cargo choice that Richardson details.

The triangularity of flows in the slave trade has been a long-accepted image. Goods preferences, specie shortages, and traders' desires to carry profitable cargo on each leg of a voyage were all reasons for the development and persistence of trade routes with three (or more) points. Two

[26] Robert Stein has suggested a similar but shorter prescription for profits based on his research on the Nantes slave trade. "The critical components of success were not by any means exotic or peculiar to that trade; the keys to success were to obtain merchandise cheaply and to sell in sufficient volume" [pp. 789–790]. See R. Stein, "The Profitability of the Nantes Slave Trade, 1783–1792," *Journal of Economic History,* vol. 35, no. 4, 1975, pp. 779–793.

Contemporaries had a longer list of the requisites for success. For one example, see John Atkins' 1735 discussion as quoted in E. Donnan, *Documents Illustrative of the History of the Slave Trade to America,* vol. 2 (Washington, 1930–1935), pp. 273–283.

[27] For a calculation of average profitability and a review of the profitability question, see Anstey, "Volume and Profitability," pp. 14–24. See also Stein, "Profitability." For trading on the African coast see B. K. Drake, "The Liverpool–African Voyage c. 1790–1807: Commercial Problems" and Marion Johnson, "The Atlantic Slave Trade and the Economy of West Africa," in Roger Anstey and P. E. H. Hair, eds., *Liverpool, the African Slave Trade, and Abolition* (Bristol, 1976), pp. 126–156 and 14–38.

[28] See the M. Adamu and P. Lovejoy–J. Hogendorn chapters included in this volume.

questions have been raised in regard to these patterns: (1) How important was triangular trade relative to other overseas trade? (2) Was the trade indeed triangular in the sense of carrying cargo on all three legs of a route, in particular the route England–West Africa–Caribbean (or mainland colony) and return? This latter question is examined in the Minchinton chapter. Shipowner correspondence and naval office shipping lists provide the data necessary for assessing both intent and actual practice. Minchinton's finding that slave vessels continued to be engaged in a triangular trade—defined as cargo-carrying on all three voyages—despite the incursions of a direct sugar trade on the Caribbean–England leg, suggests that earlier scholarship that emphasized triangularity was, in the main, correct. Despite the difficulties encountered by slave ships in obtaining return cargo from the Caribbean, they did largely avoid returns in ballast. On the definitional ground Minchinton selects, triangularity persisted.

The contribution to profit stemming from success in acquiring Caribbean cargoes was probably modest. Anstey's conclusions on the profitability of the late eighteenth-century trade are thus not likely to be altered.[29] Of note, however, is the insight into entrepreneurial behavior. The effort and time spent in obtaining return cargoes does imply some appreciation for incremental costs and revenues on the part of shipowners. Given the hazards of the trade, such a concern may appear to be of negligible value but it is no doubt one of the reasons why the slave trade was as flexible and responsive as it was. Since risk of disaster was ever-present, entrepreneurs could do no more than adopt precautions and then assume that risk could be offset by aggressively turning a profit wherever market opportunities appeared. The acquisition of return cargo, however marginal the profit, was one such opportunity.

The role of national traders is critical to an assessment of particular periods of the trade. The Dutch participation during the first half of the seventeenth century is one example, since that period saw the introduction of sugar and plantation slavery into the British Caribbean, a pivotal event in both Caribbean history and the development of the slave trade. Chapter 14 by van den Boogaart and Emmer attempts to piece together details of this early Dutch trade, involving both African coastal activity and activity in the Americas. The archival source material they employ can, at this stage, yield only glimpses of the trade patterns, but these are sufficient to provide further detail on the geographical sources of slaves, relative prices, age and sex composition, and the mortality experience of the middle passage. The Dutch slave imports to Brazil are specified and a crude estimate of the direct costs and revenues of that trade is made. The Dutch data on both mortality

---

[29] Anstey, "Volume and Profitability," pp. 14–24.

and profitability indicate conclusions not far different from those derived for other national trades in other time periods. Mortality averages of 18% (slaves taken aboard in Guinea) and 15.5% (loadings in Angola) are found and again the absence of a relationship between crowding and mortality is observed.[30] Though only a rough calculation is possible, profits appear to be nonexistent for the years over which van den Boogaart and Emmer aggregate costs and revenues, 1637–1645. This level of performance is not dissimilar to that of other monopoly (and nonmonopoly) companies in the trade.[31]

Properly assessing the Dutch role during this period calls for further comparative work on the question of slave flows to Brazil and on the relative shares provided to the Caribbean by Dutch and British traders. Since interlopers represented a sizable component of the Caribbean trade, full answers may be beyond reach.

The appearance of slavery in British America was so clearly linked to sugar production and the plantation system that the temporal association is frequently transmuted into a causal one. Yet slavery also appeared in nonsugar and nonplantation surroundings, a fact that suggests a more basic underlying rationale for slavery. For the New World, that rationale is most frequently taken to be, following Nieboer, a high land–labor ratio.[32] Abundant land places a premium on the scarce factor, labor, while simultaneously giving labor unlimited opportunity for agricultural self-employment. For an employer to retain labor then, free (or near free) land must be eliminated or, alternatively, labor must be made unfree. Though plausible for the New World in general, the "open resource" hypothesis is of no value in discriminating between cases of slavery in the New World. The question posed in Chapter 15 by Bean and Thomas, Why did the transition to slave labor

[30] See the J. Postma and H. Klein–S. Engerman chapters in this volume.

[31] The Royal Company of Adventurers, the Royal African Company, and the Middleburg Company may serve as comparative examples. In the latter case, R. Anstey's calculations from Unger's data indicate a return of +1.43% for the 1761–1800 period, and +2.58% for the 1741–1800 period. "Volume and Profitability," Table 7. See also G. F. Zook, "The Company of Royal Adventurers Trading to Africa," *Journal of Negro History,* vol. 4, 1919, pp. 134–231, and K. G. Davies, *The Royal African Company* (London, 1957).

[32] H. J. Nieboer, *Slavery As An Industrial System,* revised ed. (The Hague, 1910). See also E. D. Domar, "The Causes of Slavery or Serfdom: A Hypothesis," *Journal of Economic History,* vol. 30, no. 1, 1970, pp. 18–32, and S. Engerman, "Some Considerations Relating to Property Rights in Man," *Journal of Economic History,* vol. 33, no. 1, 1973, pp. 43–65.

Though Nieboer was the most prominent exponent of an explicit land–labor ratio theory, the concept received detailed consideration in earlier work. P. D. Curtin has pointed out that a group called Colonial Reformers, centered around E. Gibbon Wakefield, discussed many of the ideas associated with the theory in the 1830s and 1840s. Herman Merivale's *Lectures on Colonization and Colonies* (reprint, New York, 1967, originally published, London, 1841) is representative of that body of thought. See in particular his Lectures 9–11.

occur in the Chesapeake region a half century after it occurred in the West Indies? cannot be answered by resort to Nieboer.

Bean and Thomas frame their analysis in the strict analytical context of least-cost production theory and, within that, attempt to derive an answer from the admittedly fragmentary data available. Though other treatments of the issue, most notably E. S. Morgan's discussion of the Virginia case, have suggested that relative prices played some role in the transition to slavery, no formal empirical tests of that or other hypotheses have been advanced.[33] For an issue as complex as the origins of American slavery, the Bean and Thomas approach has the virtue of clearly delineating the mechanisms, and to a degree, the motivations involved. In concluding that the role of relative labor prices was prime, they reject two other hypotheses that have considerable currency. The first may be termed "plantation per se" causality; the second postulates a demographic causality, that is, that a general mortality decline in mid-to-late seventeenth-century Virginia made slaves (who obviously served a longer term) a better buy.[34] Neither of these hypotheses survives the scrutiny of Bean and Thomas. If they similarly fail the tests of other historians, economists, and demographers, the history of the origins of American slavery will have to be written with an altered perspective.

The forces giving rise to the abolition of the slave trade can be, and have been, dichotomized into ones of pure humanitarian impulse and pure economic advantage.[35] Despite its restrictive title, Chapter 16 by Green-Pedersen on Danish abolition considers both forces and maintains a balanced view between them. That balance may be more readily achieved in Danish circumstances since Denmark was a peripheral participant in both the slave trade and plantation slavery. It thus lacked the degree of dependence on a "slave system" that has given such force to the Williams thesis in the British case.[36] The objectivity, however, is not due solely to the differing historical context; it is also attributable to Green-Pedersen's knowledge of the structure of the trade and its relationship to domestic political considerations.

Unlike the situation in Great Britain, Danish conditions bred neither

[33] E. S. Morgan, *American Slavery, American Freedom* (New York, 1975), pp. 295–315. Relative labor prices are noted. "A dwindling supply of willing servants may have forced a switch to slaves," but Morgan sees mortality decline as "probably of greater consequence [p. 299]." For the role of relative labor prices in a more general framework see Gemery and Hogendorn, "The Atlantic Slave Trade."

[34] E. S. Morgan, *American Slavery*, p. 299.

[35] Roger Anstey's brief review of abolition historiography illustrates that division. See R. Anstey, "Capitalism and Slavery: A Critique," in *The Economic History Review*, 2nd series, vol. 31, 1968, pp. 307–320.

[36] E. Williams, *Capitalism and Slavery* (Chapel Hill, 1944).

religious nor secular abolitionist movements. The impetus for abolition came from political leadership, thus allowing Green-Pedersen to avoid several elements of the complexity in analysis that marks the British case.[37] The weight he assigns to the role of a simple demographic analysis is indicative of the clearer context of the Danish debate and of the rationality (cum faith?) that reinforced humanitarian concerns. In his discussion of British abolition, Michael Craton noted that "the Enlightenment had to demonstrate that slavery was not indispensable before idealism could come closer to success."[38] The demographic argument of the Great Negro Trade Commission provided just such a demonstration that the slave trade was not indispensable and thus provided the basis for Denmark's withdrawal from the trade.

Chapter 17 by Serge Daget, "British Suppression of the Illegal French Slave Trade: Some Considerations," represents a substantial advance in the amount of quantitative information available on the French slave trade. Building on earlier studies by the late Jean Mettas, whose work Daget is presently editing, the chapter is an attempt to free students of the French traffic from an unavoidable but somewhat embarrassing reliance on various older accountings such as Gaston Martin's. The main target of Daget's analysis is the 1845 British parliamentary report (also discussed in detail by David Eltis in this volume). Daget suggests a staggering number of omissions in the parliamentary report's listing of French slaver voyages, with perhaps as many as 700 voyages missed by the compilers of the report between the close of the Napoleonic Wars and the mid-1840s.

One purpose of the chapter is to provide a more refined time scale for the French trade in the nineteenth century, which appears to have peaked in the period 1817–1831 (719 listings out of a total of 763). The striking volume of activity during these 15 years tells us a good deal about the continued vitality of French slaving ports, in particular that of Nantes. The fact that the period of peak activity was so brief requires an explanation. Daget rejects convincingly the effect of the British antislavery squadrons as a cause. Their activities cost French slavers no more than an acceptable 8% loss rate. The explanation must be sought instead in France itself, where the decline in the slave trade coincided with a growing opposition to the regime of the restored Bourbons, culminating in the July Revolution and the accession to power of a new kind of bourgeoisie opposed in principle to slavery.

[37] Michael Craton, though, has written an excellent, concise outline of British abolition. See his Chapter 5 in *Sinews of Empire*. More detailed treatment is found in R. Anstey's *The Atlantic Slave Trade and British Abolition 1760–1810* (London, 1975). An encompassing discussion of the British and American experience is D. B. Davis's *The Problem of Slavery in the Age of Revolution 1770–1823* (Ithaca and London, 1975).

[38] Craton, *Sinews of Empire*, p. 254.

FURTHER DIRECTIONS FOR RESEARCH

The overall intent of this volume has been to combine the analytical abilities of economists and historians, to further the use of quantitative techniques in studies of the slave trade, and to attempt a broad geographical coverage that includes the three great segments of the trade—supply in Africa, transport to the Americas, and demand derived from the production of crops in the New World. The chapters themselves reflect this intent to a degree that has hitherto been unusual in studies of the slave trade.

Even so, it is clear that the volume represents no more than one step in what amounts to a continuing attempt to give further definition to our knowledge of the mechanisms of the Atlantic slave trade. Ample research tasks remain. Promising directions for future work include these:

1. Further historical definition and testing of existing economic hypotheses regarding the trade. A considerable barrier to productive research on slavery and the slave trade remains. Historians with their methodological tools and familiarity with original source materials are too often unacquainted with recent economic model building. Meanwhile, economists are often not sufficiently conversant with the progress of historical research to test adequately their own models. Organized interchange between the two groups should prove seminal and productive.

2. The extension of studies that explore the impact of slavery on society. Here there is room for a wide range of additional research. We know little about the origins of slavery in sub-Saharan Africa, and little concerning the domestic use of slaves in Africa before the growth of the transatlantic trade. The early development of trans-Saharan slave exports, and the reactions to it in African society, are certainly open to further exploration. There is surprisingly little work on the economic role of slaves retained in Africa during the heyday of the trade, and good studies of the institution of slavery itself in its African settings remain rare. Further research into the motivations behind the trade and its economic, social, and psychological consequences for the New World (especially the impact on the black populations of the United States, the West Indies, and Brazil) would be welcome, as would organized discussion of recent statements and critiques of the Williams thesis. Finally, the linkage effects of slavery in Africa and the Americas, including its relation to subsequent economic and social developments, could receive further investigation. For Africa in particular, the tracing of such linkage effects is virtually in its infancy.

3. The identification of African political, military, and economic initiatives and responses to the slave trade, and the inclusion of these within the framework of appropriate models. P. D. Curtin's ventures into historical

anthropology show the directions such research might take, but much remains to be done in tracing the demographic effects of the slave trade, the impact on state formation, the imperial expansion of states, changes in the structure of military establishments, and the rise of military elites.

4. The construction and testing of hypotheses that explain the role of technical change in the promotion and eventual decay of the slave trade. Little research has been directed toward this question, which may well contain revealing explanatory factors in the choice of slave labor over other competing alternatives.[39]

Common as the slave trade was, its operations comprised a most uncommon market. Coercion was an essential component, and political and economic factors intertwined in a complex circle of causation. The analytical tools of the economist are not fully appropriate to the case of coerced labor, nor can political or military analyses provide a satisfactory framework for explaining the nature of the trade. Deficient as the market model may be, it possesses the widest applicability of any single organizing principle; yet, perhaps more than in any form of commerce, the nature of the slave trade makes it mandatory that no single discipline be solely relied on for explorations of the topic. The chapters contained in this volume and the suggested avenues for further research illustrate the advantages, real and potential, of a cross-disciplinary effort.

[39] An initial effort in this direction is H. A. Gemery and J. S. Hogendorn, "Technological Change, Slavery, and the Slave Trade," in C. J. Dewey and A. G. Hopkins, eds., *The Imperial Impact: Studies in the Economic History of India and Africa* (London, 1977).

I

AFRICAN PERSPECTIVES

2

The Trans-Saharan Slave Trade: A Tentative Census

RALPH A. AUSTEN

Invidious comparisons between Europeans taking Africans across the Atlantic and Muslims using routes across the Sahara Desert (as well as the Indian Ocean) for similar purposes have long been a staple of slave trade historiography. Now that Philip Curtin has provided us with the basis for calculating the demographic impact of the Atlantic slave traffic,[1] it would appear appropriate to attempt something similar for the forced movement into the Islamic world. As will soon become obvious, however, the author of the following chapter can make no claim to being the Curtin of Arabia. In the first place the data examined is limited to the Saharan trade (extended so as to include the Nile Valley; see Figure 2.1 for relevant locations), thus allowing only secondary reference to the important East African–Indian Ocean commerce. Second, the effort is only a very preliminary one, limited to published sources (Curtin did the same but with more justification) and not entirely exhaustive of these. Most important of all, the data generated

[1] Curtin, 1969.

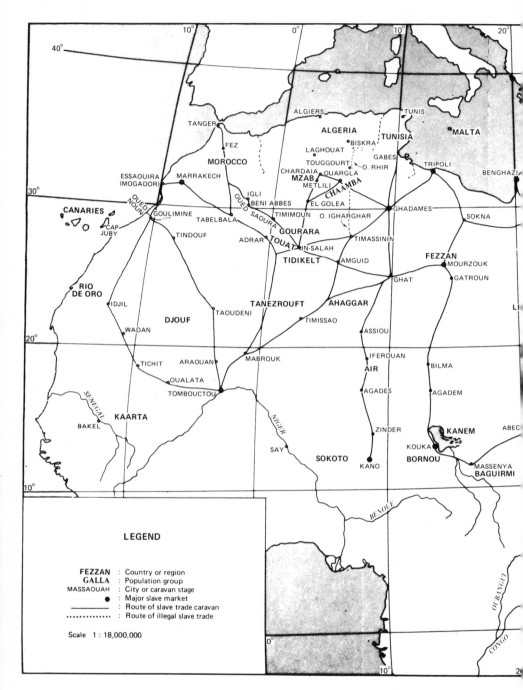

Figure 2.1. Map of northern Africa and the Middle East: Second half of the nineteenth century. [From Francois Renault, *Lavigerie, l'Esclavage Africain, et l'Europe* (Paris, 1971). Reprinted by permission of Syndicat des Missionnaires Africains.]

24

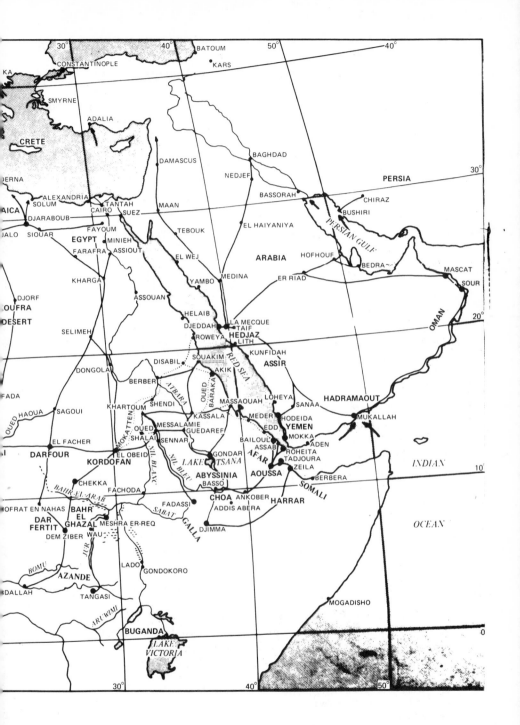

by the trans-Saharan slave trade simply do not lend themselves to the kind of sophisticated analysis applied by Curtin and others to the Atlantic.

An exercise of this kind can still make claim to some utili on both methodological and substantive grounds. First of all it offers a critique of the existing, largely polemical, literature comparing the two slave trades. The first lesson of such a critique is that the whole debate may not be as significant as has often been thought. Numbers of people, as Curtin points out in his own conclusion, do not necessarily provide a measure for the historical impact of a phenomenon such as the slave trade.[2] Furthermore, it is not so easy to treat the Atlantic and Saharan slave trades as entirely distinct developments. Much of the demand for slaves in the Mediterranean was generated or at least sustained by European as well as Islamic markets.[3] The systems of slave supply in the critical Sudanic and Middle Belt regions of West Africa also linked together Atlantic and Saharan markets, so that the two slave trades were often complementing, as well as competing against, one another.[4]

Despite all these qualifying considerations, there was a movement of slaves northward out of tropical Africa which has not been accounted for in the researches of Curtin and others working on the Atlantic. This chapter will indicate how the work of those who have presented approximations of the trans-Saharan slave trade fall short of the possibilities of even the unsatisfactory data available. It is hoped that the discussion of what *can* be done with such data will represent a positive contribution to the methodology of quantitative history in general and a specific stimulus to further exploration of sources relevant to this topic. Finally, the substantive results to be presented here should, tentative as they are, represent an improvement over existing estimates of the number of slaves involved in the desert trade.

THE EVIDENCE AND ITS MANIPULATION

The previous historiography of slave trade studies suggests that both direct and indirect evidence may be useful in determining the dimensions of such a traffic. The ideal direct sources are the continuous working records of either merchants engaged in the slave trade or government bodies supervising it for fiscal or other purposes. A less reliable category of direct evidence consists of literary records compiled by travelers, diplomats, or

[2] Curtin, 1969, pp. 269f.

[3] The quantities of medieval European demand for trans-Saharan African labor supplies have not yet been established but for a general picture see Verlinden, 1955, 1966. See further discussion of this point to follow.

[4] Curtin, 1975; Lovejoy and Baier, 1974.

other outside observers who either witnessed the trade or questioned those involved in it. Indirect evidence derives from factors of supply and demand in the societies sending and receiving slave shipments. The best quantitative indicators here are census statistics on slave populations in the receiving societies. Other information about prices and competition in slave markets and political conditions along the trade routes can serve as a check upon demographic estimates.

The published literature on the trans-Saharan slave trade relies almost entirely upon literary records for its quantitative analysis. It is easier to note the shortcomings of such a method than to provide any alternative approach. The observations from literary sources are discrete (usually involving only one year or even one caravan) rather than serial in their scope. They report, at best, information at one remove from the actual operation of the trade. Even when slave traders are directly quoted they cannot be trusted to be making real calculations of annual averages as opposed to what Curtin has called "capacity estimates" of how much the trade should carry under optimal conditions.[5] Historians can at least evaluate from independent evidence the reliability of various literary sources, but this is difficult to transpose into an adjustment of the resulting figures.

Working records would thus be far preferable to literary ones but unfortunately these are practically nonexistent for the trans-Saharan slave trade. The only extensive sets of mercantile documents available for the Islamic world before the modern time are the eleventh- through thirteenth-century Cairo Geniza documents. These derive from a Jewish community that did not, at that time, participate in the slave trade.[6] Even if a similar set of materials for slave traders had been preserved, it is unlikely that they would supply us with information of the continuous sort available to students of the Atlantic slave trade because, as the Geniza documents and other sources indicate, the organizational structure of medieval caravan trade did not lend itself to such record keeping.[7] For similar reasons, as well as because of their own limited bureaucratic powers, the governments responsible for the areas into which the caravans entered could not keep accurate track of their cargoes.

The problem of historical documentation gives us an important insight into the substantive historical distinctions between caravan and ship trade.

[5] Curtin, oral communication. In his own work Curtin has found the variance between data derived from working records and literary estimates to be somewhere in the neighborhood of 20%.

[6] Goitein, 1967, passim; 1973, p. 16; on the lowly and poorly documented position of the Egyptian and Sudanese *jellaba* traders who did specialize in slave importing during the eighteenth and nineteenth centuries see Baer, 1969, p. 174; and Raymond, 1973, 1, pp. 161–162, 527, 609.

[7] This point has never been fully developed in any literature although it is consistent with assertions in Goitein, 1967, pp. 229ff.; Steensgaard, 1975; Udovitch, 1970.

Even in the medieval or nineteenth-century Muslim world, we have relatively good accounts of slave trade carried out by ship, whether from North Africa to the Eastern Mediterranean[8] or, more significantly, from the Black Sea to Turkey and Egypt.[9] Trade on the high seas (as opposed to the small dhows used to run back and forth in front of the Indian Ocean monsoons) provides us with detailed statistical records because the unit of transport is a relatively large, compact entity which is incorporated into the accounting systems of merchant firms as a major fixed capital investment. It also becomes subject to government surveillance by nature of its visibility and need to load and unload at relatively fixed points.

Caravans, by contrast, were rather ephemeral entities, formed for the immediate convenience of whatever merchants happened to be sending cargoes between any two points along a major route, but almost always dividing and/or taking on new units at each of the stops between their sub-Saharan starting point and their first destination in North Africa.[10] Over the 11 or so centuries during which such trade flourished in the Sahara it was impossible to make improvements in the technology of camel transport that would have allowed or encouraged merchants to treat this part of their enterprise as a fixed capital investment over which it might have been worthwhile to exercise fuller control. Instead, the camels and the land through which they traveled always "belonged" to the Bedouin inhabitants of the Sahara, who made a series of short-term arrangements with merchants for services and protection. Under such conditions the partnerships of trans-Saharan merchants tended to be the kind of one-shot affairs indicated in the Geniza correspondence and not the long-lived corporate entities that give us so much better data on the Atlantic. Finally, the very routes used by Saharan caravans were constantly shifting, due to the intractable instability of the desert frontier between the two *sahels* of the Maghreb and the Sudan, so that, far from finding government records at the crucial ports of entry to the north, one is often hard pressed to find a government.[11]

Given this limited base of evidence, it is not surprising that existing estimates of the trans-Saharan slave trade are not very impressive. As with Curtin's Atlantic "numbers game."[12] however, the arbitrary and careless

[8] Boahen, 1964, p. 128, n. 2.

[9] Inalcik, 1975.

[10] Boahen, 1964, pp. 103–121, provides the best general description of these routes although any attempt to summarize their patterns cannot do justice to the complexities and insecurities revealed in the travel literature and such sources as Goitein, 1967, pp. 212–280.

[11] Egypt is a partial exception to this rule, as will be noted in the following; but even here the southern frontiers, including especially their customs administration, were particularly vulnerable to any general disintegration of political authority. See the following and d'Esteve, 1822, pp. 144–145.

[12] Curtin, 1969, pp. 3–13.

manner with which historians have compiled overall figures deserves to be criticized.

The first serious attempt to estimate the populations involved in this traffic was made in 1840 by the abolitionist Thomas Fowell Buxton.[13] Basing his calculations on an industrious, if uncritical, survey of available travelers' accounts, Buxton concluded that the average annual figure for at least the early nineteenth-century trans-Saharan slave trade was about 20,000.

In more recent times the Ghanaian historian A. Adu Boahen has undertaken a general study of British interests and African commerce in the Sahara during the first two-thirds of the nineteenth century.[14] Boahen examined far more travel literature and diplomatic correspondence on the desert slave trade than any previous scholar; however, he is still far from exhausting the material available (particularly from the very rich French sources), nor does he lay out for his readers a breakdown or critique of the specific contemporary statistics upon which his own aggregate estimate is based. Boahen's reading of Buxton hardly inspires confidence in the methods he may have used to analyze more obscure and disparate sources. Boahen claims that his own figure of 10,000 slaves passing annually across the Sahara into the area between Libya and Morocco represents a halving of Buxton's 20,000. Buxton estimated, however, that only 7000 slaves entered the Maghreb each year whereas 13,000 or more reached Egypt, partially from West Africa but mainly from the Nilotic Sudan and Ethiopia. Thus Buxton and Boahen are probably in agreement since both recognize that a portion of the slaves entering Libya passed on into Egypt.

The only historian to hazard an estimate of the entire course of the trans-Saharan slave trade is the French scholar Raymond Mauny.[15] Mauny does use some data from the nineteenth century (although less than even Buxton, who, along with Boahen, is not cited) and also places the annual figures for this period at 20,000. In his 1961 work, which quotes some not-very-indicative figures (see pp. 68–69) for the medieval period, Mauny assumed that the rate of 20,000 applied throughout the history of the trans-Saharan trade, which thus exported 2,000,000 people per century. In 1971, however, without any explanation, he altered this projection to show that lower rates prevailed before 1400 and arrived at a total figure for 13 centuries of 14,000,000.

As in the case of pre-Curtin Atlantic slave trade studies, the work on specific regions of the trans-Saharan is better than the overall estimates. Thus, impressive evaluations of data on nineteenth-century Morocco and

---

[13] Buxton, 1840, pp. 65–70.
[14] Boahen, 1964, pp. 127–128.
[15] Mauny, 1961, pp. 377–379; 1971, pp. 240–241, 279.

Egypt are made, respectively, by Jean-Louis Miege and Gabriel Baer, whose work will be discussed. Neither of these two authors, however, nor Nehemiah Levtzion, in his careful account of the medieval western Sudan,[16] attempt a systematic synthesis of his tabulations.

The use of indirect evidence as a proxy for, or check upon, information about the slave trade has been only suggested rather than undertaken by previous authors. Thus Samir Amin and A. G. Hopkins note that the numbers of black Africans or their descendants found in the present-day Mediterranean Muslim world are too few to lend credence to the vast numbers attributed by historians such as Mauny to the trans-Saharan traffic.[17] Basil Davidson has undertaken a brief investigation of slave uses and prices in the medieval Muslim economy and concluded that slaves represented a highly expensive consumer luxury which could not have been imported in large quantities.[18]

Records of Muslim populations and markets before the modern period—particularly concerning black slaves who were not much in the public eye—also present difficulties to the researcher. They are in fact more accessible than slave trade statistics. The present chapter will therefore attempt to show how such material, which is becoming increasingly available through research in Ottoman and Egyptian archives, might be used to control direct but limited or unreliable evidence on the slave trade itself. Before embarking upon this somewhat more adventurous methodological exercise, however, it is necessary to review, in a more systematic way than has been done before, the direct evidence.

DIRECT EVIDENCE: THE "MEDIEVAL" PERIOD, 700–1700

The difficulties of a medievalist scholar such as Mauny in estimating slave trade quantities can be appreciated when it is recognized how few numerical data are yielded by sources for this period. Literary records studied by Mauny and others[19] do describe a regular slave trade across the Sahara, but can this be quantitatively specified from the spotty figures cited here? (See Table 2.1.)

On the basis of figures alone, this question must be answered in the negative, especially when the individual observations are analyzed more closely. Only 5 out of the 12 citations concern the kind of commercial transactions in slaves that would be assumed to provide the most regular

[16] Levtzion, 1973, pp. 176–177.
[17] Amin, 1972, p. 109; Hopkins, 1973, pp. 82–84. Hopkin's comment is particularly directed at an absurd figure of 12,000,000–15,000,000 slaves passing through Cairo in the sixteenth century, projected from a Polish traveler's account by Lewicki, 1967.
[18] Davidson, 1971, pp. 57–61; see Appendix, pp. 69 ff.
[19] Lewicki, 1969, passim.

TABLE 2.1

"Medieval" Slave Trade

Date	Quantity[a]	Situation	Source
1. 650–circa 1250	400–500	*Baqt* tribute paid by Nubian rulers to Egypt	Rotter, 1967, p.38
2. Circa 800	5000+	Tunisian ruler Ibrahim I purchases military slaves (specified) and an unspecified number of domestic slaves as cover	Talbi, 1966, p, 136
3. 977	1000	Dahlak governor (Sudan) to Yemen	Hasan, 1967, p. 49
4. 1016+	30,000	New Tunisian regime purchases military slaves	Idris, 1962, 2, p. 530
5. Circa 1061–1071	2000	Purchased for Almoravid (Morocco) army	ibn Idhari, 1961, pp. 56–57
6. 1100–1150	"Camel files"	Mali to Maghreb.	Edrisi, 1969, pp. 7/v
7. 1275	10,000	Sudanese sold in Egypt after military expedition	Maqrizi (Quatremere, 1837, 1, 2, p. 131)
8. 1353	600 (single caravan)	Takedda (in Sahara)	ibn Battuta, 1929, p. 337
9. 1396–1438	1000–2000	Maghreb to Alexandria by sea	Piloti, 1950, p. 57
10. 1455	800–1000	Diverted by Portuguese from western Morocco to Arguin	Ca da Mosto, 1966, pp. 26–27
11. 1583	130	Cargoes of ships from Tripoli to Levant	Pozzo in Pignon, 1964, p. 106
1585	300		
1634	650 (including Berbers)		
12. 1598	1200	Despatched to Moroccan Sultan by his commander at Timbuktu	El-Ifrani in Delafosse, 1923, p. 6
		Projection: Approximate annual averages	
		Minimum 1000+	
		Maximum 6000+	

[a] Unless otherwise specified, all the slaves referred to in this and the other eight tables are black peoples of sub-Saharan Africa.

basis for such a traffic. Of these, only 2, Items 9 and 10, give any indication of annual averages. Piloti's description of the seaborne traffic to Egypt is potentially of great value since its author was a Cretan merchant who had worked for many years in Egypt. His accuracy, however, has been questioned in an authoritative recent work.[20] Ca da Mosto may be more reliable but he is describing a relatively marginal trade route. The single caravan in Item 8 and the ships in Item 11 may or may not be representative. Edrisi's "camel files" (Item 6) at least echoes the language of traders and makes ibn Battuta's one caravan appear more significant.

The rest of the figures are derived from official transactions that, except for the Sudan–Egyptian *baqt* (Item 1), did not repeat themselves on any regular basis. Such data are overrepresented here because the available sources place more emphasis on political than on economic chronology. For this reason the numbers they use may be suspect (particularly Item 4) as metaphorical rather than statistical figures. Nonetheless, expeditions and gifts of this kind did take place even more often than indicated here and thus constitute an important, if highly irregular, factor in the slave trade.

The most that can be disclosed from this table as it stands, therefore, is a set of approximate minimal and maximal limits to the annual traffic of slaves across the Sahara before 1700. The lowest possible figure would have to be somewhere above 1000, given the *baqt* and the commercial data as indicators of some kind of normal base. Occasional disruptions would at least be compensated for by the irregular political procurements of slaves. If it is assumed that there is much more regular trade than indicated here (and the descriptive literature does suggest this, particularly for routes from the Central and Nilotic Sudan) and that the figures for irregular procurement are also understated, it is possible to entertain an annual figure exceeding 6000.

A proper evaluation of such limited data, however, requires a wider perspective. Although the period treated here covers the longest time span of the entire trans-Saharan trade, it can be fully analyzed only after some basis of estimation is obtained from the better direct evidence of the eighteenth and nineteenth centuries and a consideration of indirect evidence.

DIRECT EVIDENCE:
EGYPT AND THE NILOTIC SUDAN, 1700–1880

For the slave trade of the eighteenth and, even more, the nineteenth century, the amount and quality of direct quantitative evidence improve

---

[20] Ashtor, 1971, p. 93.

vastly (see Table 2.2). The main reason for this change is the increased presence in the Middle East of Europeans who were generally (although not always) more concerned with statistics than Muslim writers and took an entirely unprecedented interest in the slave trade because of the great ideological fervor aroused by this issue in their home countries.

Egypt attracted a particularly numerous and talented group of European observers in this period. Valuable information on the slave trade of this country has been provided by explorers, members of Napoleon's 1798–1800 expeditionary force, diplomats, and foreign employees of the Egyptian government. Such investigators also profited from the fact that the compact character of settlement on the lower Nile and the well-established indigenous and Ottoman traditions of central administration provided some control over the importation of slaves into Egypt with the resulting production of at least a few working records (see Item 5). Egypt, furthermore, received a greater number of slaves from sub-Saharan Africa than did any other single Muslim country, so that the data generated here are very significant for the trade as a whole.

From the figures listed (which do not include a few available but obviously inaccurate estimates) it is possible to construct some general set of totals. These, too, will later be reviewed in the light of indirect evidence.

For most of the eighteenth century we have only "capacity estimates" made by slave dealers to French observers in the 1790s. It can be assumed that the 1790s figures represent a decline and are also themselves somewhat too low, since they only cover slaves passing through the Cairo market, thus omitting those sold in upper Egypt and/or purchased by state officials who did not use the market or pay customs. Moreover, the numbers reported (Items 6, 8, 9) in the caravans from Darfur—the most important source of Egyptian slaves in this period—are at odds with the low general estimates, although many of the accounts note that the supply from this region fluctuated greatly. We can therefore accept only the lowest pre-1790 average of 3000 per annum and raise that of the next period to 2000. Item 10 suggests a recovery along the Sennar route, which was reduced to near zero in the 1790s, so that this decade can be returned to the eighteenth-century norm of 3000. The 1820s document (Item 11) shows both a lively trade from Sennar and the direct capture of many Sudanese slaves by the invading Egyptian armies, to which must be added a continuing trade from Darfur. Similar factors are described by Bowring (Item 13) so that Pruner's estimate for 1830 (Item 12) looks far too low. For the two decades we can thus project an annual average only slightly below Bowring's lowest figure. The 1840s and 1850s seem to have experienced a decline in slave imports but for the latter decade the lower British diplomatic figure (Item 17) appears more reliable than von Kremer's uniquely low estimate (Item 16). For the 1860s, which is clearly the highest of all decades, the figures in Item 19

TABLE 2.2

Egyptian Slave Imports from the Nilotic Sudan: Eighteenth and Nineteenth Centuries

Date	Quantity[a]	Situation	Source
1, 1700s	3000–4500	Norm for entire country	Dogereau and Breton in Raymond, 1973, 1, p. 160
2. 1768–1798	3000–4000	Norm for entire country	Frank, 1807, p. ccxi (based on consultation of Cairo slave market overseers and clerks)
3. 1783–1785	1000–1200	Sennar caravan	Volney, 1788, 1, p. 207
4. 1788	20,000[a]	Projection for entire country	Ledyard reporting information from Venetian Consul Rosetti in Hallat, 1964, p. 60
5. 1790–1792	1260 per annum	Cairo market	Girard, 1824, p. 383 (based on inspection of customs records)
6. 1796	5000	Darfur caravan (at departure)	Browne, 1799, p. 298 (eyewitness)
7. 1798–1800	1200 per annum	Total Cairo arrivals	Frank, 1807, p. ccxi
8. 1799	5000–6000	Darfur caravan (arrivals at Asyut)	Girard, 1824, p. 282 (eyewitness)
1799	150	Sennar caravan	Girard, 1824, p. 93
9. 1799–1800s	1000–10,000	Darfur caravan (at departure)	Jomard/al-Tunisi, 1845, in Sedillot, 1846, p. 535
10. 1814	1500	Shendy (Sennar) market destined for Egypt (+3500 destined for Red Sea and Sudan-Dongola)	Burckhardt, 1822, p. 290 (eyewitness)
11. 1822	4000	Total Shendy market	Cailliaud, 1826, 2, p. 115 (eyewitness; also notes enslavement by Egyptian military)
12. 1830	3000	Total for Egypt	Pruner, 1847, p. 68 (long-resident physician but estimate appears casual)
13. 1830s	10,000–12,000	Total for Egypt	Bowring, 1840, p. 400 (reputable British scholar on official mission)
14. 1840s	5000	Total for Egypt	Pruner, 1847, p. 68 (appears more sure than previous estimate)

No.	Date	Quantity	Region / Description	Source
15.	1850	945	Darfur caravan (arrival at Asyut after particularly heavy losses en route)	d'Escayrac, 1850
16.	1850s	1000	Total for Egypt	von Kremer, 1868, 1, p. 86 (casual projection from Pruner's figures for previous decade)
17.	1850s	3000–4000	Total for Egypt	British diplomatic despatch in Baer, 1969, pp. 171–172
18.	1850s	"A few thousand"	Southern Sudan	Gray, 1961, pp. 44–45
19.	1860	25,000–30,000	Total for Egypt	British diplomatic despatch in Baer, 1969
20.	1860–1871	12,000–15,000	Darfur	Schweinfurth, 1874, 2, p. 430
21.	1860	2000	Kuka, Southern Sudan	Gray, 1961, pp. 53, 68
	1860–1871	2000	Southern Sudan river routes	Gray, 1961
22.	1800–1860s	13,000–17,000	Ethiopia to Sudan	Pankhurst, 1964, pp. 226–227
23.	1870s	1500	Nile Valley	British diplomatic despatch in Baer, 1969, pp. 171–172
24.	1870s	80,000	Capture and sale in Southern Sudan Bahr-l-Ghazal region	Gessi, 1892, pp. 386–387
25.	1876	8000	Southern Sudan	General Gordon in Gray, 1961, p. 127

Projections

Decades	Annual average	Subtotal	Decades	Annual average	Subtotal
1700–1790	3000	270,000	1840–1850	5000	50,000
1790–1810	2000	40,000	1850–1860	3000	30,000
1810–1820	3000	30,000	1860–1870	20,000	200,000
1820–1840	8000	160,000	1870–1880	2000	20,000

total 800,000

a Although referring only to one year, this figure represents total imports over a two- to four-year period.

seem somewhat out of proportion with the estimates from the Southern Sudan and Darfur (Items 20 and 21), the main sources of slaves. It is difficult, however, to know what to make of the high figures quoted from various sources (including Schweinfurth) in Item 22 for the Ethiopia–Sudan trade in this same period. Probably most of the slaves involved were exported via the Red Sea port of Suakin, but a certain number must have gone north to account for the 25,000–30,000 Egyptian total in Item 19, which need therefore only be reduced to 20,000. For the 1870s the various sources (Items 23–25) are seriously at odds, but at least a "depression" 2000 figure does not seem unrealistic.

The statistics by themselves thus suggest that over three-quarters of a million slaves were imported into Egypt along the Nilotic desert routes. It remains to be seen from indirect evidence whether Egypt could possibly have received such a large number of servile immigrants (plus those arriving via Libya, as seen in the following) and whether the supply conditions in the Sudan were consistent with such a heavy outflow.

DIRECT EVIDENCE: LIBYA, 1700–1900

Although Libya in the eighteenth and nineteenth centuries was, as it is now, a thinly populated and arid country with limited possibilities for taking in new immigrants, this territory received a very large percentage of the slaves sent across the Sahara to the Maghreb. Slaves arrived in the Libyan desert-side cities of Murzuk, Ghadames, Ghat, and (beginning in the mid-nineteenth century) Kufra, from where they often continued on a diagonal route to either Tunisia or Egypt. A major portion of the slaves arriving at the northern Libyan ports of Tripoli and Benghazi were also exported, in this case by sea, to points further east.

The reputation of Libya (then called the Regency of Tripoli) as a major slave trading entrepôt attracted considerable attention from nineteenth-century European observers, including explorers, British consuls, and French Algerian colonial officials, many of whom traveled directly into the southern portions of Tripolitania, Cyrenaica, and the Fezzan, to gather the relatively voluminous data that are presented here (see Table 2.3). The connection with Egypt and the shipping factor in Tripoli provided additional opportunities for locating data.

The evaluation of the available statistics on the Libyan slave trade remains highly speculative, particularly because the counting at the various points of entry in the south as well as at the northern receiving points is difficult to collate. Again, the results arrived at here will have to be checked against indirect evidence explaining plausibility and fluctuation.

The single entry here for the seventeenth century (Item 1) is insufficient to provide an estimate for this whole period except to support loosely an argument to be developed, in the following, that the trade was of a similar magnitude to that of the 1700s. The figure for Egyptian trade via Libya (Item 2) fits the various descriptions of this route in the discussions of Egypt in the late eighteenth century, all indicating that it was extremely irregular. Items 3–5 provide the best overall indications of Libyan trade in this period, assuming Item 4 to be an exaggerated or atypical figure and Items 3 and 5 to be close to accurate for the portions of the trade they report. Thus, an estimate of 1000 slaves annually passing into Libya during the 1700s seems reasonable.

In the nineteenth century all accounts suggest that this figure had gone up considerably just as it did in Egypt. The figures given, however, for specific times and places, show considerable variation which reflects both the irregularity of the trade and a degree of unreliability in the observations. Boahen (Item 24) takes 5000 as a figure for most of the century, but apart from the absence of precise calculations his estimate seems to double count much of the trade from Ghadames that was destined for Tunisia, where it is again listed. If we assume that Murzuk regularly received something less than the 5000 reported in Items 7 and 8 for the period of its greatest activity, and that the emergence of the Wadai–Cyrenaica route more or less compensated for the decline of Murzuk after 1840, we can take 4000 as a reasonable average for all the years up to 1870. After that the trade began to be restricted essentially to the Cyrenaica route with a few hundred only from the Fezzan and Tripolitania (Item 29) so that the totals are halved up to 1890. The slave trade in Cyrenaica appears, from Items 30 and 31 as well as various nonquantified descriptions,[21] to have continued for at least another decade at something like the rate indicated here of circa 1000 per annum.

DIRECT EVIDENCE: TUNISIA, ALGERIA, MOROCCO, 1700–1890

The countries immediately to the west of Libya received relatively few slaves from across the Sahara during the period for which we have our best data (see Table 2.4). Indeed, rather than exporting slaves as did Libya and, to some extent, Egypt, Tunisia and Algeria seem to have received most of their black servile population as secondary imports from neighboring North African countries. Moreover, in both these states the pressure of European control (in Algeria after 1830, actual colonization) was sufficient to produce

[21] Boahen, 1964, p. 158; Valensi, 1967, p. 1283.

TABLE 2.3

Libyan Slave Imports: Eighteenth and Nineteenth Centuries

Date	Quantity[a]	Situation	Source
1. 1686	500–600	Borno slaves from Fezzan to Tripoli	French Consul Lemaire in Masson, 1903, pp. 177–178
2. 1702	2500	Fezzan to Egypt (caravan lost and is first in 12–15 years)	Egyptian archives in Raymond, 1973, p. 163
3. 1700s	700–800	Borno–Murzuk	Emerit, 1954, pp. 44–45
4. 1766	2500	Fezzan–Tripoli	French Consul de Lancey in Masson, 1903, p. 605
5. 1779	700–800	Fezzan slave tribute to Tripoli in major of three annual caravans	French Consul d'André in Masson, 1903, p. 607
6. 1818	1300	Arrive Tripoli	United Kingdom Consul Warrington in Bovill, 1966, 2, p. 541
7. 1819	5000–5500	Murzuk	Lyon, 1821, pp. 188–189 (estimate from short visit)
8. 1819	5000	Murzuk	Ritchie, 1820, p. 228 (companion of Lyon, better observer but died at Murzuk)
9. 1843	2200 ⎫		Reports by United Kingdom Consul
10. 1844	1200 ⎬	Murzuk	Gagliuffi in Richardson,
11. 1845	1100 ⎭		1848, 2, p. 323
12. 1846	1000	Kano to Ghat Caravan	Richardson, 1846, 2, pp. 115, 310 (estimate of annual arrivals; part go on to Murzuk)
13. 1846	800	Kano–Ghat caravan	Prax, 1850, p. 84
14. 1846	2000	Waday–Benghazi caravan	Richardson, 1846, 2, p. 324
15. 1846	ca. 2500	Tripoli arrival (various sources including Benghazi)	Valensi, 1967, pp. 1275–1276
16. 1846	500	Waday–Benghazi caravan	Fresnel, 1848 (eyewitness)
17. 1849	1200	Waday–Benghazi caravan	Vice-consular report in Boahen, 1964, p. 151
18. 1840s	2500–3000	Murzuk	Duveyrier, 1846, p. 254 (estimate of trade *before* visit)
19. 1853	400–500	Borno–Murzuk caravan	Vogel in Mauny, 1961, p. 378 (eyewitness)

No.	Date	Quantity	Location	Source
20.	1858	3000–4000	Ghat	Bouderba, 1860, p. 184
21.	1854	10,000–15,000	Fezzan as whole	Rohlfs, 1868b, p. 7
22.	1865	4408	Murzuk alone	Rohlfs, 1868b (Rohlfs got this second figure fron a Turkish corporal stationed at the main Murzuk entry gate; the sources of the larger Fezzan figure are not given)
23.	1860s	5000–8000	Fezzan	Nachtigal, 1879, pp. 132–133 (estimate made some years later)
24.	Up to 1870s	5000	Regency of Tripoli	Boahen, 1964, p. 128
		2500	Shipped by sea from Tripoli	
		2000	Waday–Cyrenaica	
		1500	Murzuk	
		4500	Ghadames	
25.	1869	1700–2600	Fezzan	Nachtigal, 1879, pp. 132–133 (estinae made during short visit)
26.	1871	2000	Waday–Cyrenaica–Cairo	Schweinfurth, 1874, 2, p. 428 (eyewitness)
27.	1870s	2000	Western Desert to Egypt	British diplomatic despatch in Baer, 1969, p. 171
28.	1874–1875	500	Ghadames	Largeau, 1881, p. 246
29.	1878	1000–1200	All of Tripolitania	Rohlfs, 1881, p. 83
30.	1890	1400–1500	Benghazi	Consular report in Parliamentary Papers, 1893–1894, p. 243
31.	1891	770+	Part of year's arrivals in Benghazi	Parliamentary Papers, 1893–1894, pp. 245–246

Decades	Projections Annual average	Subtotal
1700–1800	1000	100,000
1800–1870	4000	280,000
1870–1890	2000	40,000
1890–1900	1000	10,000
	total	430,800

TABLE 2.4

Tunisian, Algerian, and Moroccan Slave Imports: Eighteenth and Nineteenth Centuries

Date	Quantity	Situation	Source
Tunisia			
1. 1788	Few	Ghadames to Tunis	Nyssen in Monchicourt, 1929, pp. 23–24
2. 1789	1000	Ghadames (200–300 also sold there) to Tunis	United Kingdom Consul Train in Hallet, 1964, p. 83
3. 1808	600 or less	Ghadames to Tunis	MacGill, 1811, p. 148
4. Circa 1810	1000–1200	Ghadames to Tunis	Frank, 1856, p. 115
Algeria			
1. 1815–1825	Small	Various routes	Shaler, 1826, pp. 80, 89
2. 1820s	500	Touggart	Emerit, 1949, pp. 32ff.
3. 1844	500	Touggart	Emerit, 1954, p. 39
4. late 1840s	3300	Oran (mainly)	Julien, 1964, p. 348
5. 1874	1500–2000	Mzab region from southwest	Soleillet, 1877, pp. 164, 273–274 (eyewitness)
6. 1880	450	Wargla	Rabourdin, 1882, pp. 31–33
Morocco			
1. 1789	3000–4000	Timbuktu to Morocco and Algeria	United Kingdom Consul Metra in Hallet, 1964, pp. 80–81
2. 1790–1791	4000	Timbuktu to Morocco as well as rest of Maghreb	Lempriere, 1814, p. 78
3. 1798	700	Timbuktu (single caravan, considered small)	Jackson, 1814, p. 287
4. Early 1830s	4000	Tuat to northern Morocco	Graberg, 1833, p. 10
5. Circa 1810	2000	Timbuktu	Sidi Hamet single caravan in Riley, 1817, p. 345

			Reference
6. 1830–1844	Up to 7000–8000	Various routes	Miege, 1961, 2, p. 151
7. 1840–1850	3500–4000	Various routes	Miege, 1961, 3, p. 92
1858	3000 (diminished over previous years)	Various routes	Godard in Miege, 1961, 3, p. 151, n. 2
8. 1864	500–1000	Timbuktu–Tuat	Rohlfs, 1868a, pp. 119–120
9. 1865–1870	3000–4000	Timbuktu	Beaumier in Miege, 1961, 3, p. 29
10. 1872–1878	500	Timbuktu	Ollivet in Miege, 1961, 3, p. 29
11. 1870s–1880s	500–1000 (plus unknown quantities)	Timbuktu	Miege, 1961, 3, p. 363
12. 1883	1248–1540	Sold on various urban markets	Parliamentary Papers, 1883, 66, p. 66

Projections

Decades	Annual average	Subtotal
Tunisia		
1700–1800	500	50,000
1800–1850	1000	50,000
	total	100,000
Algeria		
1700–1880	250	25,000
1800–1890	500	45,000
	total	70,000
Morocco		
1700–1800	2500	250,000
1800–1850	4000	200,000
1850–1870	3000	60,000
1870–1890	500	10,000
	total	520,000

an early and (at least in Tunisia) apparently effective abolition of the slave trade. The information on both countries is sparse but fairly reliable.

Tunisian imports before 1800 are indicated by only one numerical statement (Item 2). On the assumption, however, that here, as elsewhere, the firmer early nineteenth-century statistics represent an increase over previous trade (for reasons to be examined via indirect evidence) and that one-shot consular sources tend to be "capacity estimates," we can assign to this period a figure far below the statement reproduced and even slightly below the lowest figure given for the nineteenth century. For the next 45 years Frank's estimate is to be preferred to that of McGill, who visited Tunis only briefly, whereas Frank not only spent a considerable time there as physician to the Bey but had already demonstrated his serious interest in the slave trade through the study made while accompanying the Napoleonic expedition to Egypt.[22] After 1850 when the Tunisian slave trade had been officially abolished, there is little point in projecting any figures since even the earlier slaves entering the country had partly been secondary imports from Libya.

Algeria appears at all times to have been involved only very marginally in the trans-Saharan slave trade. For the totally undocumented eighteenth century we can project half of the subsequent average figure. In this later period Emerit's average of 500 (Item 3) seems preferable to the more recent assertion of Julien, an equally authoritative scholar, simply because the former is in accord with Shaler's nonenumerated observation (Item 1) and also takes into account the necessity of not double counting secondary imports from Morocco and Libya. It is also not entirely clear what sources Julien relies upon. The observations in the Mzab of 1874 (Item 5) are unusually large; they reflect considerable secondary imports from Morocco and also count slaves who remained at the northern desert edge and will thus be tabulated in a separate percentage adjustment of the present estimate. Nevertheless this figure and the one in Item 6 from Wargla (by now a much less important commercial center than the points farther west) suggest that Algerian slave imports did remain at about the same level until the French moved directly into the Sahara in the 1890s.

For Morocco in the eighteenth century there are only three sources. On the assumption that Items 1 and 2 are somewhat exaggerated capacity estimates, both including explicitly some slaves who would figure in the Algerian count, an average of 2500 during the whole period appears close to accurate. For the nineteenth century Miege, in his monumental study, has examined and analyzed a great deal of documentation on the slave trade. His own estimate for the earlier decades (Item 6) is somewhat higher than

----

[22] Frank, 1807.

his sources (including the highly respected Swedish–Italian scholar–diplomat in Item 4), largely because he wishes to add to them the slaves retained at the desert edge and thus not observed by witnesses at the northern markets. In order to remain consistent with the system of tabulations being used here it is therefore necessary to lower Miege's first set of figures. We can accept the sources he cites for the 1840–1870 periods at more or less face value (Items 7–9). For the 1870–1890 period, the figures in Item 12 and the report of Soleillet for southwestern Algeria (Algeria Item 5) indicate that the highest range of estimates cited by Miege for Morocco (Item 11) is more reliable than the lower one (Item 10).

INDIRECT EVIDENCE: NORTHERN AFRICAN CENSUS DATA AND SLAVERY

Census data on the black slave populations of northern Muslim countries would provide the best of all possible supplements to the limited and unreliable direct statistics of the trans-Saharan trade. Unfortunately, for the period up to 1700, which is most in need of such help, there are no systematic census counts of any kind. During the eighteenth and nineteenth centuries some population surveys were made in Egypt and various parts of North Africa. Even these, however, are far from trustworthy and must be used with extreme caution. Thus, before analyzing the census indications that are available, we must discuss the general occupational and demographic situation of blacks in premodern Muslim society.

Urban domestic service was the role in which black slaves were most regularly visible to observers of the Islamic world. Although it is also probably true that the majority of Africans brought across the Sahara entered this occupation, it is not clear by what percentage domestic servants outnumbered other groups of black slaves who, as will be seen, have a tendency to be overlooked in much of the literature. The purchase of a domestic servant for an urban household can be categorized as an investment in luxury consumption, even conspicuous consumption, as opposed to the capital investment represented by an American plantation hand. The assumption underlying Davidson's argument, that luxury commodities are necessarily rarer than capital goods is not, however, justified. After all, luxury goods—including the sugar produced by West Indian black slaves—were the mainstay of virtually all trade between Europe and the tropics up to the nineteenth century. Davidson's attempts to demonstrate that slaves were such an extraordinarily expensive luxury that only small numbers of them could have arrived in any one year is more logical, but based upon misleading price data and a totally untenable calculation of the modern "buying power" equivalent of the medieval gold dinar. Given what we know about the distribution of disposable income in the medieval and early modern Islamic world, the purchase of a slave does not seem to have been prohibitively expensive for a fairly large sector of the urban population.[23]

The demographic significance of the tendency for free Muslims to enfranchise and even assimilate their black slaves has been largely misinterpreted by historians of the invidious comparison school. The formula seems to be that harsh treatment and large numbers of imports are both bad, so they must be found in the same system, whereas mild treatment must accompany smaller imports. The opposite is probably the case. The nineteenth-century southern United States, which most rigidly blocked black slaves from enfranchisement and assimilation could, *for this very reason* (among others), maintain a servile labor force with virtually no fresh imports.[24] The Islamic world needed large numbers of imports, first of all, because of the wasteful cruelty of transportation across the Sahara.[25] Second, the very tendency to free slaves, either as a pious act or because they (if female) had borne children to their masters or simply earned their own price (more common even in New World urban than rural settings), meant that they had to be replaced more regularly than groups under comparable conditions who retained their status over lifetimes and even generations. Finally, the fact that females outnumbered males in this urban servile population[26] partially answers Hopkins's, Amin's, and Lewicki's question about the progeny of this immigration: The fathers, in a very large number of cases, were not black, so that the children became genetically mulatto but socially "white." There is probably no way of projecting the results of such miscegenation into an African percentage of the general Middle Eastern gene pool so that modern urban populations in this region give us little indication of the scale of earlier enslavement. Indeed, a geographer more familiar with North African physical typologies than, at least, Hopkins or Lewicki, has, in an equally casual manner, argued that the large number of mulattos in local cities suggests a slave trade of many millions over the centuries.[27]

[23] See Appendix.

[24] Curtin, 1969, pp. 72–75, pp. 88–93; Fogel and Engerman, 1974, 1, pp. 20–29.

[25] All nineteenth-century travelers noted the sharp contrast between the sufferings of slaves in transit across the Sahara and the relatively favorable conditions under which they lived with their eventual owners. For estimates of mortality in the caravans, see the concluding section.

[26] This is the one consistent and verifiable result of all inquiries into the trans-Saharan trade populations and prices; the disproportion in favor of females also confirms the dominance of urban occupations for the slaves, since males would be preferred for military or rural labor roles. A closer examination of such statistics, in comparison with those for labor-oriented, male-dominated slave systems, might establish more precisely the degree of this bias.

[27] Capot-Rey, 1953, p. 216.

The frequency of manumission and the imbalanced sex ratio thus suggest a very high replacement rate required to maintain an Islamic domestic slave population at any given level. This factor is augmented by information about the disproportionately high death tolls among black Africans who had already been brought across the Sahara into Egypt or North Africa. One should expect such a phenomenon not only as an aftereffect of the brutal desert crossing but also as a result of the change in climate, diet, and disease ecology experienced in the new setting. These factors are noted, without statistical specification, by Frank in his studies of early nineteenth-century Egypt and Tunisia.[28] They are also supported by several reports of plague deaths in Egypt.[29] In all these counts blacks appear in far greater proportions than their representation within the general population.

Apart from their role as urban domestic servants, black slaves were also found in the Islamic world as military forces and rural laborers of various kinds. Military service, as already indicated in Table 2.1, constitutes a major category of procurement and deployment which has left behind relatively extensive statistics. These will have to be examined separately in the next section.

Evidence of black slaves in the Islamic rural labor force is often treated by historians as so exceptional as to be statistically insignificant. It is certainly true that the Muslim economy had no equivalent of the New World plantation system. Land, not labor, was the scarce commodity in most times and places in Muslim history so that cultivation of the richest countryside did not call for the importation of alien servile gangs. Slaves, however, were important in exploiting various marginal regions of the Islamic rural world and these were sufficiently critical and numerous so as to involve an important—if poorly tabulated—slave work force.

Much of the rural employment of black slaves took place in areas that would have brought most of their servile labor from East Africa and thus added relatively little to the demands on the trans-Saharan trade. This is suggested by the very term, *Zenj,* applied to the tens of thousands of slaves used for clearing agricultural land and mining saltpeter in southern Iraq during the latter ninth century. We know more, however, about this group than others like it because of the massive slave rebellion that broke out here. From the resulting documents it is clear that a considerable number of the slaves involved originated in the Nilotic and Central Sudan, although even these may have reached Iraq via the Red Sea.[30] The same is probably true of the 30,000 black slaves (an implausible number) reported as agricul-

---

[28] Frank, 1807, pp. ccxivff.; 1856, pp. 115ff.

[29] Ibn Taghri Birdi, 1957, p. 66 (1913 slaves out of 7717 reported victims in 1419); Burckhardt, 1822, p. 307 (8000 slave victims in 1815); Collucci Bey, 1862 (blacks 9% of victims in 1850, 1855 cholera plagues).

[30] Nöldeke, 1892, p. 153; Rotter, 1967, pp. 62–63.

turalists from the Carmathian community of Bahrain in the eleventh century[31] and a fortiori the African servile workers in date and coconut plantations, docks, sailing ships, and pearl fisheries encountered throughout the
Red Sea–Indian Ocean–Persian Gulf area.[32]

Slaves more heavily drawn from the trans-Saharan trade were employed
by Arab migrants in the northern Nilotic Sudan between the ninth and
fourteenth centuries for mining gold and precious stones.[33] In Egypt, the
classic land of overcrowded and exploited peasant holdings, slaves apparently never worked the land before the nineteenth century. After 1800,
however, when ambitions and opportunities for agricultural expansion temporarily exceeded population growth, slaves were employed in considerable
numbers, first to grow sugar and then to assist with the great 1860s cotton
boom.[34]

Finally, the largest "exception" to the alleged nonuse of Africans for
Islamic rural labor is located at the very frontier of the Sahara. Various
literary sources and government statistics show a major concentration of
blacks in this region; and the findings are consistent with the large Negro
element in contemporary local populations, and also with recent studies of
the organization of labor in both the northern and southern desert edges.[35]
The free populations in these areas are not, of course, very dense, so that an
extensive use of servile blacks for working fields and salt mines or tending
herds need not imply a large slave trade. The steadiness of this demand,
however, and the constant need to replace laborers in a situation that was
and is both unhealthy and unattractive suggests that a significant percentage
must be added to the total of those slaves who appear in the commercial and
demographic records, such as they are, of the lands further north and east.

The figures in Table 2.5 are intended as a check upon the unsatisfactory
commercial data presented in earlier sections. It will soon become obvious,
however, that the statistical projections made here are even more speculative than their predecessors. The sources for this table are, at least, independent of those used earlier and thus do provide some test for the
plausibility of the former results even if they give no precise alternative
indications. The methods used here may also suggest to other scholars an
approach by which better understanding may be achieved, of both the
trans-Saharan slave trade and related questions of Islamic and comparative
social history.

[31] Nassiri Khosrau, 1881, p. 227.

[32] Harris, 1971, pp. 39ff.

[33] Hasan, 1967, pp. 44–58.

[34] Rivlin, 1961, pp. 149, 338; Baer, 1969, pp. 165–166; Parliamentary Papers, 1883, 83, p.
91; 1887, pp. 177–178.

[35] Valensi, 1967, pp. 1278ff., Lovejoy and Baier, 1976; Rabourdin, 1882, pp. 33–36. See
also Table 2.5.

The notes related to each section of the table indicate the reliability of the original observations from which these statistics are taken. It should be noted that almost all the figures refer only to slaves recruited for civilian occupations; evidence dealing with the military will be presented separately in Table 2.6. The Egyptian data in Part A do not give as much information about slave populations on the desert edge (i.e., Nubia in Item 2) as do the subsequent entries for the southern Maghreb (Part B, Items 1, 5, 8), but all of these figures provide only very general indications of the importance of involuntary black immigrants to the populations of this zone. Also, except for Item 8 in Part A, none of the figures or projections take epidemiology into consideration as a factor in shifting ratios between slave and free populations.

As indicated in the fourth column heading, the information upon which this table is based often uses some permutation of the black–slave categories that does not indicate directly how many black slaves were present in the society described. Because of this and other instances of incomplete or often simply absent statements of the main statistic being sought, it has been necessary in most of the observations tabulated here to project the size of black slave populations. The figure of 4% as a normal proportion of black slaves to general urban populations is derived from the relatively solid census data for eighteenth-century Cairo and is consistent with other essays in premodern Middle Eastern demography.[36] The same proportions are not relevant to national figures since in rural areas slave and free populations tend to grow in inverse ratio to one another (e.g., latter nineteenth-century Egypt versus Maghreb desert edge as indicated here). It has also been assumed that: (*a*) urban black slaves were mostly female (therefore Item 2); (*b*) about 80% of all blacks listed in Egypt were slaves, since there is little indication of free blacks maintaining any clear identity in the urban population; (*c*) in the Maghreb only 50% of blacks listed were slaves since one source (Item 7) says so explicitly, and most of the descriptive literature does note communities of nonservile sub-Saharan immigrants who would have been conspicuous enough to be counted in any census; (*d*) finally, over 90% of the population listed as urban slaves in any of these sources were black Africans since the descriptive literature again states that whites from the Caucasus or elsewhere had become rare in any but military servile roles by the fourteenth century in Egypt and by the eighteenth century in the Maghreb.

The most controversial projection in this table must be the use of 15% as the rate by which new slaves had to be brought into these societies in order to maintain any given level of the servile population. The figure is certainly no more than an educated guess which, in mathematical terms, assumes that

[36] Barkan, 1958, p. 222.

TABLE 2.5

Slave Populations in Receiving Societies

Place	Date	General population	Black slave population reported (B = all blacks; BS = black slaves; S = all slaves; FB = free blacks)	BS projections Population (4% general urban population)	Annual replacement (15% BS population)
A. Egypt					
1. Cairo	1300s	500,000	2000 (gang of runaway and enfranchised blacks at large in city)	20,000	3000
2. Cairo	1400s			No projections	
3. Cairo	1516		12,000 (male slaves recruited as auxiliaries into army)	20,000	3000
4. Cairo	1798	260,000	12,000 B	10,000	1500
5. Country	1822		40,000 BS		6000
6. Country	1830	2,213,110	18,000 B	15,000	2250
7. Country	1838–1877	3,000,000–6,000,000	20,000–25,000 BS		3000–3750
8. Cairo	1840	250,000	14,000 BS	20,000	2100
9. Country	1840	3,000,000	24,000 B	20,000	3000
10. Cairo	1850–1855	261,724	11,500 B	10,000	1500
11. Country	1877–1889	6,500,000–7,000,000	22,200 (slaves officially manumitted)	37,000	5500 (?)
12. Nubia	1810s	?	12,000 BS employed in agriculture		
B. Maghreb: Libya					
1. Cyernaica desert oasis	1883		2000 BS		300
2. Country	1891	750,000–800,000	6000 S	5500	800
Tunisia					
3. Country	1860	1,000,000	6000–7000 B (minus major cities)	7000 (with cities) 10,000 (1850)	1500
4. Country	1845		30,000 B		1500
5. Southern region	1848	346,000	86,500 B		4500

Algeria				
6. Country	1844	2,200,000–2,500,000	10,000 BS	1500
7. Country	1844		8000 B 4000 BS	600
8. Southern region	1840s	625,000	Circa 125,000 B	

Sources (Part A):

1. Abu-Lughod, 1971, p. 37 (this carefully researched historical geography also validates the population figures in Item 4 and suggests that Cairo did not grow substantially again until after 1850).

2. Lapidus, 1967, p. 171 (citing various Arabic chronicles).

3. Ben Joshua, 1967, 1, p. 48 (account by Jewish physician of Genoa circa 1550).

4. Jomard, 1829, pp. 363ff. (impressive effort at tabulation).

5. Cailliaud, 1826, 2, p. 117 (secondhand account by explorer of Nile Valley).

6. Cadalvene, 1836, pp. 103–104 (scholarly French traveler).

7. Baer, 1969, pp. 167–168 (estimates based on contemporary documents, not all of which were available to the present author).

8. Bowring, 1840, p. 10 (fairly creditable estimate based on house count).

9. Clot Bey, 1840, 1, p. 168 (general population estimate here is considered by scholars as exaggerated in order to flatter Muhammad Ali, the ruler of Egypt and the author's employer; but the same motives are less likely to produce an overestimate of slaves).

10. Colucci, 1862, pp. 604–605 (relatively low estimate probably reflects effect of cholera epidemics which the author describes as particularly severe among blacks).

11. Parliamentary Papers, 1883, 83, p. 91; 1889, p. 44 (a large but indeterminate proportion of the slaves in Egypt were manumitted without the official procedures recorded here).

12. Burckhardt, 1822, p. 307 (rough estimate by scholarly traveler).

Sources (Part B):

1. Duveyrier, 1884, pp. 21–22 (describing main lodge of Senussi brotherhood).

2. Parliamentary Paper, 1893–1894, p. 245 (Benghazi consular report).

3. Valensi, 1967, p. 1278 (based on registers for taxes not paid at Tunis and Kairouan).

4. Emerit, 1949, p. 39 (no source given).

5. Capot-Rey, 1953, pp. 163–175 (author insists that many of these "blacks" are the descendants not of slaves but of indigenous Saharan negroid groups).

6. Carette in Carette and Roget, 1856, pp. 158–159 (projection from circumscribed military census).

7. Emerit, 1949, pp. 30–31 (based on documents and contemporary discussion of same census as preceding).

8. Capot-Rey, 1953, pp. 163–175.

the average service life of a slave was slightly under seven years. The demographic assumptions upon which this figure is based are (*a*) a high death rate of slaves during their first years of settlement in the Middle East and also during any subsequent epidemics; (*b*) the manumission of more than half the surviving slaves within 10 years of their entry into service; (*c*) a virtually zero reproduction rate among slaves—they bore few children who survived and among those who did extremely few remained as slaves; (*d*) that the only substitute for the services of a manumitted or deceased slave was a newly purchased slave.

Obviously, all the preceding points are open to question and could be explored further through evidence already known to be available (e.g., epidemiological and immigration data from New World slave societies, slave records in the Ottoman archives,[37] comparisons of slave prices and wage rates in Cairo and other Middle East urban centers. All that is contended, for the present, is that the method proposed here is, in a general sense, useful, and that the resulting figures are not unreasonable given the sources so far consulted.

If we compare these results to the figures derived from direct commercial evidence it will be seen that some useful indications are provided. The fourteenth-century Egyptian data are a bit thin (Items 1–3) but are at least consistent in their indications and suggestion of a bias toward the upper bounds of the projections made for the trade figures of this period in Table 2.1. Item 4 is very close to the trade data for eighteenth-century Cairo in Table 2.2. Items 5–9 suggest much lower trade figures than did Table 2.2 for Egypt in the earlier nineteenth century, which may cast some suspicion on the estimates used there; however, it must be remembered that military recruitment, which is not indicated here, accounted for a large part of such slave imports. Item 10 is again close to the figures in Table 2.2. In Item 11 the projection of total to officially manumitted slaves is based upon a proportion established by Baer[38] to calculate from a less accurate statement of the number of slaves manumitted. The method is questionable, except that the result suggests that earlier estimates of the actual slave population in Egypt (Item 7) may have been too low because they did not take into account the large proportion of rural servile laborers revealed in the manumission figures. The projected import figures attached to this observation probably mean little since it is clear that rural slavery in Egypt grew rapidly during the 1860s and ceased growing with the indigenous population explo-

---

[37] Inalcik, 1975 (in an oral communication Professor Inalcik has also cited material from the Ottoman archives that supports the notion that manumitted slaves in Istanbul usually abandoned the households of their masters and thus would have to be replaced by new slaves).

[38] Baer, 1969, p. 168.

sion and renewed entry of United States cotton onto the world market in the next period.

For the Maghreb, the Libyan population figures are probably inadequate indicators of imports since the sample of the desert edge (Item 1) is too limited and the coastal observation (Item 2) does not take into account the fact that a large proportion of the slaves entering Libya were to be exported elsewhere. Nonetheless they do suggest that the latter figures in Table 2.3 are not exaggerations.

The Tunisian figures are complicated by the fact that they were compiled in an incomplete census 10 years after local slave trading had effectively ceased. It has been assumed that the black population was larger in the earlier period although by much less than the 15% replacement rate, since the death rates were highest precisely among newly arrived slaves. Even if Item 4 is thus rejected as unrealistically high, Item 3 yields more slaves imported annually than had been indicated in Table 2.4. All of this discrepancy may be accounted for by secondary imports as well as by slaves retained on the desert edge (and producing part of the black populations in Items 5 and 8) none of which formed part of the Tunisian total in Table 2.4. For Algeria the figures in Item 7 are consistent with Table 2.4 and probably more reliable, for other reasons, than those in Item 6.

In general, then, the population data used here lend some degree of plausibility to the trade figures previously cited. Some major questions, however, are raised concerning Egypt, little information is presented for the medieval period, and no population data are available at all for the second largest (according to trade figures) importing country, Morocco. Fortunately, the military demography to be presented next addresses itself precisely to these lacunae.

INDIRECT EVIDENCE:
BLACK SERVILE MILITARY FORCES

The most densely concentrated populations of black slaves in the Islamic world were to be found in the ranks of various professional military formations. Servile armed forces dominated much of medieval and early modern Islamic military and political history, but in most cases their membership was drawn from the white peoples of East and Southeast Europe and Central Asia. Black Africans did, however, supply a portion of such forces at almost all times and, as Table 2.6 indicates, constituted the main standing armies for a number of important regimes. Jere Bacharach has recently demonstrated that black soldiers generally suffered from an identification with infantry units, usually held in lower esteem than mounted troops, and

TABLE 2.6

Black Servile Military Forces in Metropolitan Muslim States

Regime	Date	Numbers	Situation	Source
Iraq				
Abbasids				
1.	833–842	?	"Raven" contingents of Al-Mu'tasim	Rotter, 1967, p. 67
2.	869–883	"Many"	Black troops fight Zenj rebellion	Nöldeke, 1892, pp. 153–167
3.	930	Sizable	Entire infantry black, attacked by Turkish cavalry	Rotter, 1967
4.	936	3000	Black infantry used against Buyyids, who then eliminate black troops in East	Rotter, 1967
5.	941		Black troops brought by ibn Ra'iq from Egypt	Bacharach, 1975
Egypt				
Tulunids				
6.	877–904	12,000	Assessment by historian Qalashandi (died 1418)	Rotter, 1967, p. 69
7.	879	10,000	Army brought to Libya by Abbas b. Tulun	Talbi, 1966, p. 349
8.	884	45,000	Report of Ahmad b. Tulun's estate at death	Hasan, 1967, p. 487
Ikhshidids				
9.	935–968	"Many"	General use of black troops	Hasan, 1967, p. 48
10.	945	(3000)	Black and other slave troops if estate of Muhammed ibn Turhy-l-Ikhshid	Bacharach, 1975
11.	Circa 968	(4000)	Black and other slave troops under black regent, Kafur	Bacharach, 1975
Fatimids				
12.	990	(4000)	Black and other slave troops in estate of ibn Killis	Bacharach, 1975
13.	1046	30,000+	Author saw but did not personally count troops	Nassiri Khosrau, 1881, p. 138
14.	1062	50,000	Battle between black and Turkish troops	Hasan, 1967, p. 48
15.	1149	10,000+	Civil war among black troops	Bacharach, 1975
16.	1169	50,000	Battle with white troops of Saladin (Ayyubid regime)	Lewis, 1971, p. 74

	Number	Description	Reference
Mamluks			
17. 1287	?	Used in expedition into Sudan	Maqrizi (Quatremere, 1840, 2, 1, p. 90)
18. 1497–1498	500	Black arquebus corps established, quickly suppressed	Ayalon, 1956, pp. 68–71
19. 1516–1517	?	Black arquebus corps reestablished and popular but too little, late to avert defeat by Ottomans	Ayalon, 1956, pp. 83–86
20. 1800	"Few"	Present in last stages of Mamluk rule	Frank, 1807, p. ccxliv
Muhammad Ali			
21. 1822–1823	30,000	First large recruitment for new black army	Hill, 1959, p. 25
22. 1823	8000	Present at Syene training camp	Mengin, 1823, 2, p. 251
23. 1837	8000	Active black regiments (about four times this number are reported dead since recruitment)	Duhamel in Cattaui, 1935, II, 2, pp. 396–397
24. 1840	2500	Active black troops	Bowring, 1840, p. 10
Tunisia/Libya			
Aghlabids			
25. Circa 800	5000+	Ibrahim I purchases military slaves (specified) and an unspecified number of domestic slaves as cover	Talbi, 1966, p. 136
Zirids			
26. 1016+	30,000	Slaves purchased to create black corps	Idris, 1962, 2, p. 530
27. 1062–1108	Negative	Recruitment of black troops disrupted by Hilali invasions of Maghreb	Idris, 1962, 2, p. 531
Hafsids			
28. Early 1300s	"Small"	"Probably rather small" black corps	Brunschvig, 1947, 2, p. 80
29. 1500s	?	"Veritable garde negre" used by Sultan	Brunschvig, 1947, 2, pp. 80–81
Qaramanlids			
30. ?	"Small"	Black troops observed accompanying Prince Yusuf Qaramanlis in Tripoli	Vadala, 1919, pp. 190–191

(continued)

TABLE 2.6 (continued)

Regime	Date	Numbers	Situation	Source
Morocco				
Almoravids				
31. Circa 1061–1071		2000	Slaves purchased for black army	Levtzion, 1973, p. 176
32. 1086		4000	Battle of Zallaga	Rotter, 1967, p. 74
Almohades				
33. 1145–1248		? (few)	Vague documentation of military forces	Hopkins, 1954, pp. 98–99
Alawites				
34. 1670s		8000	Report of Christian slave	Mouette, 1710, p. 101
35. Circa 1680		14,000	Moulay Ismail army after initial stages of recruitment	En-Nasiri, 1906, pp. 77
36. 1721		15,000–20,000	Report of British ambassador's aide	Windhus, 1725, p. 475
37. 1727		150,000	Traditional Moroccan estimate of army at Moulay Ismail's death	En-Nasiri, 1906

38. 1727	50,000	Modern estimate of same	Morsy, 1967, pp. 102–103
39. 1789	13,000	Surviving numbers of black army	United Kingdom Consul Metra in Hallet, 1964, p. 81
40. Circa 1804	10,000	Mostly black Moroccan royal guard	Ali Bey, 1814, 1, p. 311
41. 1808	18,000	Black contingent in 36,000-man total army	Burel in Caille, 1953, p. 59
42. 1904	4000	Troops available from black Boukhari military "Tribe"	Aubin, 1904, p. 187
Spain			
Ummayads			
43. 970s	Circa 1000	Black infantry, cavalry, and messengers used by Hakam II	Levi-Provencal, 1953, 2, pp. 29, 177–178; Rotter, 1967, p. 74
44. 981–1002	Circa 1000+	Expansion of existing troops	Levi-Provencal, 1953, 2
Hummudids			
45. Circa 1020	? (few)	Small Umayyad successor state uses black troops	Rotter, 1967, p. 74

were also victims of violent political conflicts with other ethnic contingents.[39] It remains clear, however, that black servile troops were a major factor in Muslim society and that the demand for such forces provided a critical incentive for the trans-Saharan slave trade.

It is difficult to project the statistical data available on black military forces into estimates of slave import quantities. First, as already noted, numbers cited in relation to early Muslim armies are often difficult to treat as statistics (e.g., Item 37 in Table 2.6). Second, the recruitment patterns over the life cycles of various military formations are not yet clear, although some progress may eventually be expected in this area from studies of white janissary and mamluk forces which can then be compared to the less amply documented black armies.[40] At present, all that is evident are large figures for the periods of initial formation, some indication of the sizes maintained by various units over their lifetimes, and then suggestions that they ceased recruiting new members when, often quite abruptly, they fell out of favor with the ruling authorities. Whatever its shortcomings, however, the data presented here do provide another independent check upon the direct slave trade evidence.

Each geographical and political subdivision within Table 2.6 suggests a time and place when black military forces were of prominence and also indicates an order of magnitudes that is relevant to the general demand for slaves. Thus the section on Abbasid Iraq (Items 1–5) establishes a limited but consistent use for about one century. The Egyptian use of black troops (Items 6–24) was the heaviest of all, particularly in the ninth through twelfth and again in the nineteenth centuries (the figures for the latter period, incidentally, are fairly reliable and give us some check upon the other numbers). Even in the thirteenth- through eighteenth-century period dominated by Turkish, Circassian, and Balkan mamluk and janissary troops, blacks continued to form a minor part of the Egyptian military establishment.

In North Africa black troops were employed by Tunisian regimes (Items 25–29) at an obviously heavy rate during the ninth and eleventh centuries, more lightly in the thirteenth through sixteenth centuries, and possibly, rarely, in the other periods. Morocco (Items 31–41) engaged limited amounts of black troops in the eleventh and twelfth centuries and possibly very heavy amounts in the late seventeenth–early eighteenth centuries. The figures for this era and the early nineteenth century are in some dispute, as indicated in the table. It appears that not only the traditional Islamic peak of

[39] Bacharach, 1975.
[40] Ayalon, 1956; Ashtor, 1971; and Inalcik, 1975 suggest that reasonably accurate estimates of white military slave recruitment are possible from both commercial and army records.

150,000 (Item 37) is unrealistic but that even Morsy's reduction to 50,000 (Item 38) is somewhat inflated. On the other hand, the lower Moroccan estimate (Item 35), based on a detailed accounting of the stages of recruitment, is roughly in accord with those of the two contemporary European observers (Items 34 and 36), as well as representing a more plausible relationship to the figures for the eighteenth–early nineteenth century figures in Items 39–41. Possibly the account by Burel (Item 41) is the most reliable of all since the author was a military officer sent to Morocco by Napoleon to study precisely this kind of question.

We thus have fairly precise ideas of the size of the Moroccan black army but unfortunately cannot tell to what extent it was recruited via the slave trade. All accounts of Moulay Ismail insist that he took most of his military slaves from among blacks already present in Morocco, although there are a few references to purchases in the Sudan.[41] Possibly the distinction between the two forms of recruitment is not terribly relevant for measuring the long-term slave trade impact of this formation, since the slaves tabulated here would simply have entered the country earlier (and the numbers include not only the male troops listed but also an equivalent number of black women to whom Moulay Ismail married them) and were presumably replaced in the civilian sector once the Sultan had appropriated them for his military purposes. The declining size of the black army after 1727, however, suggests that it was surviving mainly on the basis of natural increase (including marriage of the Negro soldiers to Moorish women, according to Item 40). By the beginning of the twentieth century, when the Moroccan slave trade had come virtually to an end according to all accounts, the group from which the black army was mobilized became the equivalent of a "Makhzen tribe" (i.e., an indigenous descent group in alliance with the government to provide troops in return for tax exemptions and other favors). Thus the Moroccan military need for slaves would not seen to have induced as massive a slave trade as was the case in Egypt, particularly under Muhammad Ali.

The data from Muslim Spain (Items 43–45) indicate a minor, if not totally insignificant, employment of black troops in a context where the major servile forces were Slavs and West Europeans. Some of the black troops in Spain were taken over from other Muslim regimes in North Africa although they are not accounted for in any of the available statistics for these areas and should thus be treated as evidence of additional trans-Saharan imports.

Rather than analyzing at this point the relationship between military demands for blacks and direct evidence on the slave trade, it seems best to

[41] Delafosse, 1923; Morsy, 1967.

postpone this exercise for the general collation of slave supply and demand factors to be undertaken in the next section.

INDIRECT EVIDENCE:
CHRONOLOGICAL SYNTHESIS

In order to make the fullest possible use of the indirect evidence available on the trans-Saharan slave trade, the data discussed in the previous two sections, both tabulated and untabulated, have been inserted into a single chronological table (see Table 2.7). This exercise provides only a very limited check upon direct commercial evidence, since the numbers used here are either less precise than when originally presented in the preceding or simply not available except in the form of general verbal formulations. The comparison, however, of a similar range of supply and demand factors across the entire time span of the trade may allow for the establishment of some order of magnitude between periods with varying qualities of direct evidence.

The table thus begins with the nineteenth century, for which we know the most. This period has been assigned an index number of 10 so as to function as a base for comparison with earlier centuries. The numbers assigned to these earlier centuries are based upon an evaluation of the relevance to the slave trade of the six factors presented for each period. Before discussing the entries for each century, it is necessary to explain what some of these factors mean.

Items 1 and 2 require no explanation since they are simply summaries of information from Tables 2.5 and 2.6. Item 3 refers to the general prosperity of the Middle East, but more particularly Egypt, as described in various secondary works.[42] The statements are imprecise because, for the most part, the documentation and analysis in this secondary literature lack precision. It is assumed, however, that any increase in Middle East wealth would raise the demand for black slaves as domestic servants in urban households. This demand, moreover, would not be limited to Egypt and the Maghreb but would also affect the shipment of slaves farther east, a process for which we have only the kind of spotty direct documentation indicated in Item 11 of Table 2.1. Column 4 here attempts to account for slaves employed outside urban households, but the data on this subject are particularly deficient.

Item 5 indicates the degree of competition for black African slave

---

[42] The major works are Cook, 1969; Issawi, 1966; Labib, 1965; Richards, 1970. See also Eliyahu Ashtor, *A Social and Economic History of the Near East in the Middle Ages* (London, 1976).

supplies created by the Atlantic slave trade as well as the availability of white slaves on Mediterranean markets as an alternative to blacks. In general it does not appear that either of these factors played too great a role in determining the magnitude of the trans-Saharan slave trade since the population pools from which such slaves were drawn were either too far from the Atlantic or too numerous to suffer much from European competition. The one area where the two trades did converge and sometimes compete was the Western Sudan, especially around Senegambia. Slaves from the Caucasus (usually Circassians) did fill some of the domestic servant roles also associated with blacks, but they tended to be quite expensive in Egypt or the Maghreb and thus compete only marginally with blacks. The shifts in availability, however, of such slaves farther east and north to both Muslim and Christian households may have determined the total quantities of Africans shipped out of northern Africa.[43]

Finally, the Sudanic political situation summarized under Item 6 refers to the most immediate supply factor in the slave trade. It has been assumed here, on the basis of broadly consistent literary evidence, that slave exports were at their peak either during an extended invasion–occupation of the Sudanic–Sahelian zone by Mediterranean armies or under the rule of a strong local state that could capture slaves and maintain the local stability required for regular caravan trade. Generally it is the Nilotic and Central Sudanic situation that provides the crucial indicators of slave trade volume since slaves were the main trans-Saharan export here, as opposed to the gold of the Western Sudan.

Apart from more precision in the evaluation of the factors already listed, this effort would benefit from a chronology of the droughts and famines that periodically disrupted (sometimes for several years) commercial life in the Sudan. For present purposes these natural–epidemiological catastrophes have been treated as coincident with the low points of local political order.[44]

All available evidence, both direct and indirect, suggests that the nineteenth century witnessed the highest annual rate of slave trading in the history of trans-Saharan commerce. This is evident from the civilian slave population figures of Column 1 as well as the reliably documented use of large numbers of black slaves in the Egyptian army (especially since we know that many more slaves were recruited than the number who survived to make up the active members in this force). We also know that the Middle East in general experienced a high degree of prosperity during this period, accounting for the ability to bring slaves into all urban areas. Possibly more

[43] On Christian demand for black slaves in this period see Verlinden, 1955, passim; Heers, 1958; Heers, 1961, pp. 404–495 passim.

[44] On droughts and famines see Cissoko, 1968; Tymowski, 1974, pp. 126ff.; Lovejoy and Baier, 1974, Appendix.

TABLE 2.7

Chronology of Trans-Saharan Slave Supply and Demand Factors

Period	1. Egyptian BS population	2. BS military use	3. Middle East economic conditions	4. Agricultural, mining use of BS	5. Competing slave trades	6. Sudanic political situation	Magnitude index
1800s	25,000–35,000	Egypt: large Morocco: small	Booming	Egypt: very strong Libyan desert edge: strong	Atlantic: strong to 1850 Caucasus: closed	Nilotic: strong plus Egyptian occupation Central: very strong Western: moderate to very strong	10
1700s	Cairo circa 10,000 (plus smaller rural number)	Egypt: very small Morocco: large but decline Libya: small	Declining	Weak all over	Atlantic: very strong Caucasus: weakening	Nilotic: strong Central: weakening West: weak	5
1600s	Unknown	Egypt: small Morocco: small to large	Stagnant	Weak	Atlantic: strong Caucasus: strong	Nilotic: strong Central: moderate West: Moroccan occupation	5
1500s	Circa 20,000 in Cairo (?)	Egypt: small Tunisia: small	Egypt: declining Ottoman East: prosperity	Weak	Atlantic: growing Caucasus: strong	Nilotic: moderate Central: very strong West: very strong	4
1400s	Sizable	Egypt: small	Egypt: sharp decline East: prosperity	Weak	Atlantic: very small Caucasus: strong but closed to Europeans	Nilotic: weak Central: disorder West: very strong	3

1300s	No direct data	Egypt: small Tunisia: small	Peak and then sharp decline	Last stage of Sudan mining	Caucasus: strong Asia: closed	Nilotic: weak Central: weak West: very strong	4
1200s	No data	Egypt: small	Prosperous	Sudan mines	Caucasus: strong Central Asia: strong	Nilotic: Egypt Central: very strong West: strong	4
1100s	No data	Egypt: large Morocco: small	Prosperous	Sudan mines	Caucasus: strong Central Asia: strong	Nilotic: stable Central: strong West: disorderly	4
1000s	No data	Egypt: large Tunisia: large Morocco: moderate Spain: moderate	Increasingly prosperous	Sudan mines	Caucasus: strong Central Asia: strong	Nilotic: stable Central: strong West: Almoravid invasion	6
900s	No data	Egypt: large Tunisia: large Spain: moderate	Prosperous	Sudan mines	Caucasus: strong Central Asia: strong	Nilotic: stable Central: Strong West: strong	6
800s	No data	Iraq: small Tunisia: large	Prosperous	Sudan mines Iraq: Zenj	Caucasus: strong Central Asia: strong East Africa: major Iraq supplier	Nilotic: stable Central: weak West: moderate	2
600–700s	No data	Little or none	Disorderly	Southern Maghreb cities founded	Insignificant	Invasions of Nilotic, Central and West Sudan–Sahara by early Muslim armies West Sudan: moderate	1

research into the rural history of regions other than Egypt and Libya would add some evidence to the two indications in Column 4 concerning agricultural employment of black slaves. The Atlantic slave trade is shown by Curtin and, even more, by David Eltis in this volume, to have been operating at a very high level during the first half of the century; possibly its cessation after 1850 had some influence on the continued flow of slaves across the Sahara despite some efforts at prohibition by European-pressured local governments. The closing of the Caucasus came about by a combination of Russian expansion into former Muslim slave trading domains and the conversion of the most important of these, Circassia, to Islam, thus rendering its population immune from enslavement. Finally, the Sudan during this period was in a situation particularly conducive to slave trading: First, the extensive Egyptian occupation of the northern Nilotic Sudan and the expansion of slave traders from the region into the southern Sudan were completely unprecedented developments; second, the autonomous states extending westward from the Nile, such as Darfur, Waday, Borno, Zinder–Damagaram, the Hausa–Fulani Sokoto Caliphate, Macina, and the Tokolor empire, all exhibited great political strength throughout most of the century. Despite moments of decline and occasional disruption of caravan routes (but never by drought), the very conflicts of these states with one another and their jihadist assaults on peoples at their frontiers are a major factor in explaining the large scale of the nineteenth-century slave trade.

For the eighteenth century, Columns 1 and 2 indicate a lower civilian and military slave population in Egypt, although Moroccan demands for troops may have been fairly high (if not comparable to those of nineteenth-century Egypt) at the beginning of the century. For the Middle East as a whole this period represents an economic nadir during which relatively few slaves would have been used in domestic service and virtually none as productive labor. The descriptions of Egyptian slave trading during the Napoleonic period also indicate the downward spiraling effects of such conditions upon commerce as noted in other accounts of earlier periods of decline. The government tried to increase its own share of declining revenue by raising customs duties (compounded by the competing demands of various factions within the divided military administration), thus further discouraging merchants from investing in caravan undertakings.[45] The Atlantic slave trade was also at its height during this entire century while, until the Russian advances of the last decades, the Caucasus continued to supply white slaves. Supply conditions in the Nilotic Sudan were favorable to a fairly regular output of slaves—the Funj Sultante of Sennar had entered a fatal decline

---

[45] Frank, 1807, p. ccxl; d'Esteve, 1822, pp. 144–145; Shaw, 1962, p. 322.

but Darfur was at its peak. Farther west, however, Waday was not very strong and Borno had gone into partial decline, with resulting effects upon the security of desert routes. The Hausa states were prosperous but politically divided and the western Sudanic savanna was dominated by Bambara states that did not very effectively control the desert edge. Several droughts, including one extending nearly 10 years, are reported. Despite all these factors pointing to a much smaller trade for the eighteenth than the nineteenth century, the direct commercial data, which seem to be consistent with civilian and military population figures, suggest a ratio of only 2:1 between the two periods (see Table 2.8 and the following for fuller explanation). Thus the eighteenth century is assigned an index number of 5. The relationship of general factors to trade differentials in this relatively well-documented set of centuries will be used to construct the index figures for earlier periods in which all that can be compared are general conditions.

Thus, in the seventeenth century, there is some indication of a rise in military slave demands by Morocco (especially if one assumes that a large part of the slaves comprising Moulay Ismail's army entered the country before his reign). The economic conditions and resulting government effects upon commerce were probably slightly better than in the next century. Atlantic competition was considerably less than in the 1700s, and Caucasian imports slightly higher. Along the Nile the Funj Sultanate was more effective as a trading partner, but Darfur was just becoming organized. Borno and Hausaland may have been more orderly than in the eighteenth century. In the western Sudan there was no stable indigenous state, but the Moroccan garrison at Timbuktu, ineffective as it may have been, probably provided rather steady slave exports to the north. Thus, on the whole, the period would appear to have maintained a slave trade at about the same level as the eighteenth century.

For the 1500s we have an indirect indication of a rather large slave population in Cairo (itself undoubtedly bigger than two centuries later). On the other hand, there is no evidence of a major military demand for blacks or an economic situation any better than in the next century for Egypt, although military expansion by the Ottomans to the east created some demand for domestic slaves. The Atlantic offered only limited competition to the Saharan slave trade in this period, but the availability of Caucasian slaves undoubtedly affected the demand for Africans in the east. Sudanic supply factors are again fairly positive as the Funj Sultanate had become established on the Nile, whereas Borno in the Central Sudan and Songhai in the West Central region were at the height of their powers during this time. On the basis of a diminished demand for slaves in Morocco, we may assume an overall downward movement from the subsequent century, yielding an index figure of only 4.

The fifteenth century appears to represent a continuation of the weak demand already noted for the next period in the areas immediately bordering the Sahara. The fall of Constantinople, however, and general expansion of Ottoman power and wealth, created problems of slave supply for Europeans in the Mediterranean, which were met partially by resort to trans-Saharan sources, although this expansion also accounted for the opening of Atlantic trade at points that were directly competitive with trade to North Africa and Egypt.[46] The Nilotic Sudan lacked any strong state at this time although the presence of Arab tribes in the north may have promoted a continuation of the slave trade. To the west, the disintegrating Kanem empire had not yet been transformed into the Borno state. Farther west, Songhai was still in a very strong position. Overall factors in this period thus suggest a degree of decline from the subsequent century as indicated in the index number.

The first three-quarters of the 1300s were a period of prosperity for Egypt and the rest of the Islamic world, although there are no direct indications of large use of black slaves in any civilian or military occupations. The closing of Central Asia as a source of slaves had little direct relation to Africa since the Turkic peoples of the area supplied mainly male cavalry troops. To the degree, however, that female domestics were also purchased from this source and a greater pressure generally placed on the remaining Caucasian supply regions, a somewhat increased demand for black Africans may have resulted. The Nilotic Sudan in this period was in disorder and the Kanem empire in the Central Sudan was beginning to disintegrate. In the west the Mali empire was at its peak of local control and involvement in trans-Saharan trade. Thus, overall conditions for the slave trade were probably better than in the subsequent century.

In the thirteenth century there is evidence of somewhat greater demand for black slaves in military and mining functions north of the Sahara. The invasions of the Nilotic Sudan by Egyptian mamluk armies also increased the immediate flow of slaves northward. Farther west, Kanem reached the high point of its power in both the Sudan and Sahara while the Mali empire was beginning to form. Thus overall trade was again at the same level as in the preceding period.

Between 900 and 1300 the demand for black troops in various Muslim states appeared to have achieved a point probably superior even to that of Egypt in the early 1800s. Domestic slavery also must have flourished in the general urban prosperity that accompanied the trade boom of the Crusades era. On the Nile the Christian kingdoms appear to have been on good terms with the various Egyptian Muslim regimes that relied upon them precisely

[46] Ca da Mosto, 1966, pp. 26–27; Heers, 1958; Labib, 1965, p. 271.

for the supply of military as well as mining manpower. Farther west, Kanem was just emerging into power, and the Ghana empire, after a period of prosperity that probably emphasized gold trading very heavily, fell to Almoravid invaders who clearly could make good use of slave captives. Thus the level of slave trade here must have been, at least in the earlier two centuries, somewhat higher than that of the 1700s.

The ninth century was a period of decreased although still discernible demands for black troops. The cities of the Islamic world were in their golden age and black slaves were also being used in mining and agricultural enterprises. The supplier areas were also well organized for delivering slaves except for the critical Central Sudan, which lacked any strong political center. A large portion, however, of the slaves used for both military and agricultural purposes, were found in Iraq, and it is likely that the majority of these came from East Africa, as implied in the term *Zenj* for the labor force in the Basra salt flats. Thus the general flow of trans-Saharan slave trade was probably lower than for most medieval periods.

Evidence on the slave trade in the seventh and eighth centuries is particularly hard to come by. No precise data on demand factors are available although the founding of new Muslim cities inland from the Mediterranean littoral, particularly Qayrawan in Tunisia and Tahert in Algeria, would have required a considerable addition of black slaves as both urban servants and agricultural laborers. The invasion of the Nilotic Sudan by Arab armies from Egypt in this period led to the establishment of the *baqt* whereby local Christian states promised regular deliveries of slaves. Likewise, the invasions of the Sahara, which extended a considerable distance southward, by the Arab armies of Uqba b. Nafi and his successors, are reported to have brought back huge numbers of captives, although the details of these campaigns, including the race and real quantity of those enslaved, are extremely vague. In any case it is clear that regular trading relations between the Maghreb and Gao on the Niger, as well as Ghana in the far Western Sudan, were well established by this time and included some regular purchases of slaves.[47] Assigning an index figure to this period is almost impossible although we may assume that the numbers involved were considerably smaller than in any of the subsequent centuries.

CONCLUSIONS: A GLOBAL ESTIMATE

The figures for specific periods and places of the trans-Saharan slave trade have already been shaky enough; their projection into a census of the traffic

[47] Levi-Provencal, 1954; Lewicki, 1969, pp. 24–27, 66–68.

as a whole can be presented only with the greatest hesitation. Nevertheless it is necessary to see how the results of even an effort such as this compare with the figures published by others. Moreover, only by seeing where the present method finally leads can any appreciation be made of its usefulness.

The figures entered in Table 2.8 are derived from a combination of the direct evidence in Tables 2.2–2.4 and the relationship of these to the general conditions expressed in the magnitude index of Table 2.7. This means that direct evidence has accounted for only a little more than 25% of the total estimate. Table 2.1, which presented the available statistics on the slave trade before 1700, was used directly only for the period 650–800. Of the six subsequent entries only that for 800–900 falls into a position roughly halfway between the extreme projections drawn from Table 2.1. The entries for 1100–1700 are all at, or slightly beyond, the upper end of the predicted scale, whereas those for 900–1100 go far beyond the entire scale.

TABLE 2.8

Global Estimate of Trans-Saharan Slave Trade

Period	Index number	Place	Subtotal	Annual average	Total (all numbers minus last 000)
650–800	1.0			1.0	150
800–900	2.0			3.0	300
900–1100	6.0			8.7	1740
1100–1400	4.0			5.5	1650
1400–1500	3.0			4.3	430
1500–1600	4.0			5.5	550
1600–1700	5.0			7.1	710
1700–1800	5.0			7.1	715
		Egypt	290		
		Libya	100		
		Tunisia	50		
		Algeria	25		
		Morocco	250		
1800–1880	10.0			14.5	1165
		Egypt	510		
		Libya	300		
		Tunisia	50		
		Algeria	40		
		Morocco	265		
1880–1900	1.5			2.0	40
				total estimate	7450
				plus 5% desert edge retention	7822
				plus 20% mortality en route	9387

This relatively high estimate for the "medieval" slave trade is based first of all upon the conviction that the figures for the 1700s are fairly reliable and that the conditions of this period were conducive to slave trading within a range that was often equaled and at some points exceeded by the previous centuries. It is necessary, however, to return to the data in Table 2.1 so as to see whether it is at least compatible with such a sharp upward revision of its accompanying projections.

First, it has already been noted that the commercial data in Table 2.1 are biased toward the Western Sudan, a zone mainly engaged in exporting gold (and therefore drawing the attention of contemporary writers) but less prominent in the slave trade. Egyptian trade with the Nilotic Sudan, which must account for a large part of the black military forces employed by the Tulunids, Ikhshidids, and Fatimids, is indicated only by the *baqt* figure. Trade with the Central Sudan, probably the major supplier of slaves up to the seventeenth century and always more important than the West after that, is not directly referred to at all. The figures, however, for seaborne traffic of Piloti (Item 9) and Pozzo (Item 11) probably represent a portion of the slaves entering Libya from the zones directly to its south and thus give some indication of how large such a trade might have been.

The entries in Table 2.8 for 1700–1800 are most convincing in the case of Egypt, somewhat less so for Morocco, and rather thinly based for Libya, Tunisia, and Algeria. If they err, however, it is probably on the conservative side, as the decisions were always to reduce capacity estimates and assume a generally lower figure than for the most active period in the nineteenth century.

The period 1800–1900 has been broken into two portions with only the first 80 years providing the base for the index figure of 10. The extension of European influence and/or rule in all of Africa during the last two decades of the century clearly imposed a very radical reduction upon the slave trade. No estimate has been given for the twentieth century, although the slave trade certainly continued during this period, because its numbers would not appear to add anything significant to the total for the preceding 1250 years.[48]

The adjustment at the end of the table for slaves retained at the northern desert edge rather than reaching the Mediterranean zone has already been explained in several places. The percentage used is somewhat arbitrary although deliberately set below the estimates for such slaves given in Footnote 35 and Items 5 and 8 in Part B of Table 2.5. The estimate for

---

[48] Mauny, 1971, p. 241 argues that 300,000 slaves were shipped out of Africa in the twentieth century, but apart from its general vagueness (probably the routes referred to are mainly East African) this figure does not seem to fit the descriptions of more contemporary African slavery in Derrick, 1975, passim.

TABLE 2.9

East African Slave Trade Estimates

Number of slaves per annum		Total number of slaves	Source
Red Sea Coast			
800–1800	2000	2,000,000	Pankhurst, 1961, pp. 380–388; Harris, 1971, pp. 43ff.
1800–1890	12,000	1,000,000	Pankhurst, 1964, pp. 224–228; Harris, 1971
Swahili Coast			
800–1700	1000	900,000	Harris, 1971
1700–1800	2000	200,000	Sheriff, 1971, pp. 45–46; Alpers, 1975, pp. 151, 191–193
1800–1850	3000	150,000	Sheriff, 1971, pp. 157–170, 302; Alpers, 1975, pp. 191–193
1850–1875	1000 (local use)	25,000	Sheriff, 1971, pp. 439–469
1800–1875	10,000	750,000	Sheriff, 1971
		total 5,000,000	

mortality in transit routes comes from Boahen's evaluation (p. 129) of British consular information, referring mainly to Libya. Some accounts suggest that the death rate was even higher along the Nile Valley routes.[49]

Once a total figure for the trans-Saharan trade has been derived, it seems appropriate to add at least some kind of estimate of the closely linked Red Sea–Indian Ocean traffic. The sources cited in Table 2.9 are all secondary works. No effort has been made to compile an independent list of direct evidence or to check this against any kind of indirect indications. Even more than with the trans-Saharan trade, the bases here for the pre-1800 period are very unreliable, especially since Pankhurst and Harris draw no general conclusions from the various scattered statistics they quote, thus indicating only that there was a quite regular human export from the Horn of Africa. Their figures for the nineteenth century have been revised downward because of what appears to be a tendency to evaluate upward from existing data. This is shown more clearly by the careful way in which Alpers and Sheriff have reduced the figures for the Swahili coast, given by both Harris and such earlier abolitionist scholars as Coupland. The figure of 5 million here is thus a fairly conservative result.

The combined results of the two tables come out as virtually identical with Mauny's 1971 figure of 14 million. This outcome, however, is little more than a coincidence, since the method of calculating here has been very

---

[49] Bowring, 1840, p. 84; d'Escayrac, 1850.

different from that of Mauny and the results for specific centuries do not match at all.[50]

More interesting is the comparison with Curtin's figures for the Atlantic slave trade. Even if, as the result of research by Eltis and others, Curtin's 11 million plus for the Atlantic traffic is revised upward, it will probably remain slightly short of the total calculated here for Muslim exports. The pace of exportation across the Sahara and Indian Océan, however, was certainly lower, and the contrast in conditions of social integration at the point of reception still remains broadly valid. The statistics thus undermine beliefs that the Muslim slave trade was either very much worse (i.e., greater) or very much milder (i.e., smaller) than the European demand for African labor. Invidious comparisons between the two historical encounters with sub-Saharan Africa may still be made, but if this chapter has any validity all partisans will have to be more cautious about invoking the support of numbers.

APPENDIX. SLAVE PRICES IN THE MEDIEVAL MUSLIM CONSUMER MARKET

The question raised by Davidson concerning the prices of slaves as an indicator of their probable quantity in the Muslim world raises issues that are far too complicated to be resolved here or, perhaps, anywhere. It is, however, possible to present some better data on the prices of slaves, the meaning of these prices in terms of the prevailing gold standard, and a comparison with prices of other commodities (see Table 2.10). This information can be related to prevailing salaries so as to gain some idea of the disposable income likely to be invested in slaves.

The unit of price used in these evaluations is the gold dinar, whose weight in true gold varied from 3.45 to 4.72 grams throughout the medieval history of Egypt and Muslim Spain but was restricted to the upper level of this range in the Maghreb (Hinz, 1955). One way to transform this value into modern terms is to use the dollar value of gold; Popper (1957, p. 44) thus determined the dinar to be worth $2.35–3 (at pre-1934 gold values), but perhaps a more realistic figure (if there is anything "real" about a gold monetary standard) would be something like $12–16 (taking the value of gold as an arbitrary $100 per ounce). This is still very far from Davidson's unexplained $100 dinar.

---

[50] The distribution in Mauny is

A.D. 600–700:	100,000	900–1300:	2,000,000
700–800:	200,000	1300–1400:	1,000,000
800–900:	400,000	1400–1900:	10,000,000
		1900–:	300,000

TABLE 2.10

Prices of Slaves and Other Medieval Islamic Commodities and Wage Figures[a]

Region	Centuries (A.D.)	Prices			Living costs	Salaries (monthly)		
		Slave	Horse	House[b]		Worker	Bureaucrats[c]	Military[c]
Iraq	8–11	20–30	60	30–35	2–3	.2–2	10–25	10–20
Egypt	8–10	20–30	7	40–140	2–5	2	25–30	?
Egypt	10–13	20	16–30	?	2–3	1–2	5–10	—
Egypt	13–15	20	15	30	1–4	2–3	6–7	10–100
Muslim Spain Maghreb	12–14	18–20	?	50–60	—	—	—	7–15

[a] All figures are gold dinars.
[b] Medium urban housing.
[c] Middle range bureaucrats and low-ranking military officers.

As indicated in Table 2.10 the price of slaves in the relevant regions seemed to remain somewhere around 20 dinars (i.e., $240–320 if one wants to use the adjusted form of Popper's system). The alternative buying power of such a sum is, however, difficult to judge. By looking at the indications of subsistence costs in the table one might be tempted to agree with Davidson that a given weight of gold had far more buying power in the medieval Middle East than it does today. When looked at in relation to salaries, however, basic living costs in this society simply appear to represent a smaller tax on disposable income than in our own situation, thus liberating a greater part of this income for the purchase of consumer luxuries such as domestic servants. Moreover, compared to other major consumer purchases such as urban housing and horses, slaves do not seem extraordinarily expensive. The fact that their prices appear somewhat more stable than the other items despite inflationary trends in the economy might also suggest something about their supply, although here the shortage of data and my own ignorance of economic theory become overwhelming. Finally, the evidence of distribution of incomes suggests that a fairly sizable elite class was sufficiently affluent so as to afford even the quite costly luxury of owning (and frequently manumitting) large numbers of domestic slaves. It should also be noted that merchants, who constituted a major group of domestic slave purchasers, are not included here because their incomes, while often extremely high, were neither sufficiently regular nor well enough known to contemporary observers to be assigned any specific figure.

The military in Egypt was always very large, especially in the Mamluk (thirteenth to fifteenth centuries) period. Popper estimates (1955, pp. 86–87) between 2000 and 10,000 "Sultan's Mamluks" (i.e., the class receiving the upper range of salaries on Table 2.10), and some 4000 mamluks under the emirs, receiving the lower range of salaries.

It should perhaps have been noted in the body of this text that black slave prices in the nineteenth century were lower than those proposed here for the Middle Ages (i.e., averaging about $100 in Egypt or the Maghreb). This itself may indicate a larger supply than in the earlier period, explicable by the situation of Sudanic states geared to external trade who now needed to substitute slaves for their diminished gold exports. A later version of this study may attempt to analyze the more plentiful but less conveniently assembled data on prices and wages in Middle Eastern countries during the sixteenth through nineteenth centuries.

ACKNOWLEDGMENTS

Apart from the written and oral sources cited here and in the bibliography I would like to acknowledge the scholarly advice and technical assistance provided for this chapter by Professor John Coatsworth and Ms. Polly Thomason, both of the University of Chicago.

REFERENCES

Abbreviation: BSG = *Bulletin de la Société Géographique*, Paris

Abu-Lughod, Janet L., *Cairo: 1,001 Years of the City Victorious*, Princeton 1971.

Ali Bey el Abbassi, *Voyages en Afrique et en Asie . . . 1803 . . . 1807*, Paris 1814.

Alpers, Edward A., *Ivory and Slaves. Changing Patterns of International Trade in East Central Africa to the Later Nineteenth Century*, Berkeley 1975.

Amin, Samir, "Underdevelopment and Dependence in Black Africa: Historical Origin," *Journal of Peace Research*, 9, 1972.

Ashtor, Eliyahu, *Histoire des prix et des salaires dans l'Orient Medieval*, Paris 1969.

Ashtor, Eliyahu, *Les métaux precieux et la balance des payements du Proche-Orient à la Basse Epoque*, Paris 1971.

Aubin, Eugene, *Le Maroc d'aujourd'hui*, Paris 1904.

Ayalon, David, *Gunpowder and Firearms in the Mamluk Kingdom*, London 1956.

Bacharach, Jere, "The Use of Black Troops in Medieval Egypt and Iraq," American Historical Association Meetings, 1975.

Baer, Gabriel, *Studies in the Social History of Modern Egypt*, Chicago 1969.

Barkan, Omer Lutfi, "Essai sur les données statistiques des régistres de recensement dans l'Empire Ottoman au XVe et XVe siècles." *Journal of the Economic and Social History of the Orient*, 1, 1958.

Barth, Heinrich, *Reisen und Entdeckungen in Nord-und Central-Afrika*, 3 vols., Gotha 1857.

ibn Battuta, *Travels in Asia and Africa* (H. A. R. Gibb, ed. and trans.), London 1929.

Bennett, Norman R., "Christian and Negro Slavery in Eighteenth Century North Africa," *Journal of African History*, 1, 1, 1960.

Boahen, A. Adu, *Britain, the Sahara, and the Western Sudan*, Oxford 1964.

Bouderba, I., "Voyage à R'at [Ghat]," *BSG*, 4th series, 20, 1860.

Bovill, E. M., *Missions to the Niger*, 3 vols., London 1966.

Bowring, J., *Report on Egypt and Candia*, London 1840. (Also in *Parliamentary Papers*, 21, 1840.)

Browne, W. G., *Travels in Africa, Egypt and Syria*, London 1799.

Brunschvig, Robert, *La Berberie Orientale sous les Hafsides*, 2 vols., Paris 1947.

Burckhardt, John Lewis, *Travels in Nubia*, London 1822.

Buxton, Thomas Fowell, *The African Slave Trade*, London 1839.

Buxton, Thomas Fowell, *The African Slave Trade and Its Remedy*, London 1840.

Ca da Mosto, Alvise, *La Navigazioni Atlantiche* (Tullia Gasparrini Leporace, ed.), Rome 1966.

Cadalvene, de and J. de Brevery, *L'Egypte et la Turquie de 1829 à 1836*, Paris 1836.

Caille, Jacques, *La mission du Capitaine Burel au Maroc en 1808*, Paris–Rabat 1953.

Cailliaud, Frederic, *Voyage à Meroe . . . 1819 . . . 1822*, Paris 1826.

Capot-Rey, Robert, *Le Sahara français*, Paris 1953.

Carette, E. and Roget, *Algerie*, 1856.

Cattaui, René, *Le règne de Mohammed Aly d'après les archives russes en Egypte*, Rome 1935.

Cissoko, Sekene-Mody, "Famines et épidemies à Timbouctou et dans le Boucle du Niger du XVIe au XVIIIe siècle," *Bulletin de l'Institut Fondamentale de l'Afrique Noire*, 30, 3, 1968.

Clot-Bey, Alphonse B., *Apercu general sur D'Egypte*. Paris 1840.

Colluci-Bey, M. J., "Quelques notes sur le cholera," *Mémoires ou travaux originaux presentés et lus a l'Institut Egyptien*, 1, Paris 1862.

Cook, M. A., *Studies in the Economic History of the Middle East*, London 1969.

Curtin, Philip, *The Atlantic Slave Trade: A Census*, Madison 1969.

Curtin, Philip, *Economic Change in Precolonial Africa: Senegal in the Era of the Slave Trade*, Madison 1975.

Davidson, Basil, "Slaves or Captives? Some Notes on Fantasy and Fact," in Nathan Huggins et al., ed., *Key Issues in the Afro-American Experience*, 1, New York 1971.

Delafosse, Maurice, "Les debuts des troupes noires du Maroc." *Hesperis*, 3, 1923.

Derrick, Jonathan, *African Slavery Today*, New York 1975.

Duveyrier, Henri, *Exploration du Sahara: Les Touaregs du Nord*, Paris 1846.

Duveyrier, Henri, *La confrererie musulmane de Sidi Mohammed Ben Ali Es Senousi*, Paris 1884.

Edrisi, Abou-Abdallah Mohammed, *Description de l'Afrique et l'Espagne* (P. A. Dozy and J. De Goeje, trans.), Paris 1969.

Emerit, Marcel, "L'abolition de l'esclavage," in M. Emerit, ed., *La Revolution de 1848 en Algerie*, Paris 1949.

Emerit, Marcel, "Les liasons terresteres entre le Soudan et l'Afrique du Nord au XVIIIe et au debut du XIXe siècle," *Travaux de l'Institut de Recherches Saharienne*, 11, Université d'Alger 1954.

En-Nasiri es-Slaani, Ahmed ben Khaled, *Chronique de la dynastie Alooui du Maroc* (Eugen Fumey, trans.), Paris 1906.

d'Escayrac de Lauture, Stanislas, "Extrait d'un memoire sur le commerce du Soudan Orientale," *BSG*, 3rd series, *14*. 1850.

d'Esteve, "Mémoire sur les finances de l'Egypte," *Description de l'Egypte*, 12, Paris 1822.

Fogel, Robert, and Engerman, Stanley, *Time on the Cross*, 1, Boston 1974.

Frank, Louis, "Mémoire sur le commerce des Nègres au Caire . . ." appendix to Denon, Vioanto *Voyage dans le Basse et le Haut Egypte*, 2, London 1807.

Frank, Louis, *La Tunisie*, Paris, 1856.

Fresnel, Fulgence, "Notice sur le Waday," *BSG*, 3rd series, *9*, 1848.

Genovese, Eugene, "The Treatment of Slaves in Different Countries: Problems in the Application of the Comparative Method," in Laura Foner and E. Genovese, eds., *Slavery in the New World: A Reader in Comparative History*, Englewood Cliffs, N. J. 1969.

Gessi, R., *Seven Years in the Sudan*, London 1892.

Girard, P. S., "Mémoire sur l'agriculture, l'industrie et le commerce de l'Egypte," *Description de l'Egypte*, 29, Paris 1824.

Goitein, S. D., *A Mediterranean Society. Jewish Communities in the Arab World, Vol. 1, Economic Foundations*, Berkeley 1967.

Goitein, S. D., *Letters of Medieval Jewish Traders*. Princeton 1973.

Graberg di Hemsö, *Prospetto del Commercio dell'Impero di Marocco*, Firenze 1833.

Gray, Richard, *A History of the Southern Sudan, 1839–1889*, London 1961.

Hallet, Robin, *Records of the African Association*, London 1964.

Harris, Joseph E., *The African Presence in Asia. Consequences of the East African Slave Trade*, Evanston 1971.

Hasan, Yusuf Fadl, *The Arabs in the Sudan*, Edinburgh 1967.

Heers, Jacques, "Le Sahara et le commerce méditerranée à la fin du Moyen Age," *Annales de l'Institut d'Etudes Orientales*, 16, Université d'Algers 1958.

Heers, Jacques, *Genes au XVe siècle*, Paris 1961.

Hill, Richard, *Egypt in the Sudan*, London 1959.

Hinz, W., *Islamische masse und gewichte*. Göttingen 1955.

Hopkins, A. G., *An Economic History of West Africa*, London 1973.

Hopkins, J. F. P., "The Almohade Hierarchy," *Bulletin of the School of Oriental and African Studies*, 16, 1954.

ibn Idhari al-Marrakushi, "Un fragmento inedito de Ibn Idari sobre los Almoravides," *Hesperidis-Tamuda*, 1961, 2, 1 (ed. Ambrosio Huici Miranda).

Idris, Roger Hady, *La Berberie Orientale sous les Zirides*, 2 vols., Paris 1962.

Inalcik, Halil, "Slave Labor and Slave Trade in the Ottoman Empire," University of Chicago Social History Workshop, 1975.

Issawi, Charles, *The Economic History of the Middle East, 1800–1941*, Chicago 1966.

Jackson, James Grey, *An Account of the Empire of Morocco*, London 1814.

Jackson, James Grey, *An Account of Timbuctoo and Hausa*, London 1820.

Jomard, E., "Description de la ville et la citadelle au Caire," *Description de l'Egypte*, 18, 2, 1829

ben Joshua ha-Kohen, Joseph, *Divre ha-yamim le-malkhe Tsarefat*, Jerusalem 1967.

Julien, Charles André, *Histoire de l'Algerie contemporaine*, Paris 1964.

Klein, Herbert, *Slavery in the Americas*, Chicago 1966.

Kremer, Alfred von, *Aegypten*, Leipzig 1863.

Labib, Subhi Y, *Handelsgeschichte Ägyptens im Spätmittelalter*, Wiesbaden 1965.

Lane, Frederic, *Venice: A Maritime Republic*, Baltimore 1973.

Lapidus, Ira, *Muslim Cities in the Later Middle Ages*, Cambridge, Massachusetts, 1967.

Largeau, V, *Le Sahara algerien*, Paris 1881.

Lempriere, William, "A Tour from Gibraltar to . . . Morocco, in John Pinkerton, ed., *A General Collection of the Best and Most Interesting Voyages and Travels*, London 1814.

Levi-Provencal, E., *Historie de l'Espagne muslamane*, Paris 1953.

Levi-Provencal, E., "Un nouveau récit de la conquète de l'Afrique du Nord par les Arabes," *Arabica*, 1, 1954.

Levtzion, Nehemiah, *Ancient Ghana and Mali*, London 1973.

Lewicki, Tadeusz, "Arab Trade in Negro Slaves up to the end of the Sixteenth Century," *Africana Bulletin*, 6, 1967.

Lewicki, Tadeusz, *Arabic External Sources for the History of Africa South of the Sahara*, Warsaw 1969.

Lewis, Bernard, *Race and Color in Islam*, New York 1971.

Lovejoy, Paul E, "Interregional Monetary Flows in the Precolonial Trade of Nigeria," *Journal of African History*, 15, 4, 1974.

Lovejoy, Paul, and Baier, Stephen, "The Desertside Economy of the Central Sudan," University of Wisconsin African Economic History Workshop, 1974.

Lovejoy, Paul, and Baier, Stephen, "Gradations in Servility at the Desert Edge (Central Sudan), in I. Kopytoff and S. Miers, *Slavery in Traditional African Society*, Madison 1976.

Lyon, George F., *A. Narrative of Travels in Northern Africa in the Years 1818, 1819 and 1820*. London 1821.

MacGill, Thomas, *Account of Tunis*, Glasgow 1811.

Masson, Paul, *Histoire des establissements et du commerce français dans l'Afrique barbarèsque (1560–1793)*, Paris 1903.

Mauny, Raymond, *Tableau Géographique de l'Ouest Africain au moyen age*, Dakar 1961.

Mauny, Raymond, *Les siècles obscurs de l'Afrique noire*, Paris 1971.

Mengin, Felix, *Histoire de l'Egypte sous le gouvernement de Mohammed Aly*, Paris 1823.

Miege, Jean Louis, *Le Maroc et l'Europe*, 4 vols., Paris, 1961.

Monchicourt, C, *Relations inédites de Nyssen, Fillippi, et Calligaris*, Paris 1929.

Morsy, Masali, "Moulay Isam'il et l'armée de métier," *Revue d'Histoire Moderne et Contemporain*, 14, 1967.

Mouette, "Travels of the Sieur Mouette in the Kingdoms of Fez and Morocco during his Eleven Years Captivity in those Parts," in *John Stevens Collection of Voyages and Travels*, London 1710.

Nachtigal, Gustav, *Sahara und Sudan*, 3 vols. published separately, Berlin, Leipzig 1879, 1881, 1889.

Nassiri Khosrau, *Sefer Nameh*, (Ch. Shefer, trans.), Paris 1881.

Newbury, Colin, "North African and Western Sudan Trade in the Nineteenth Century: A Re-evaluation," *Journal of African History*, 7, 2, 1966.

Nöldeke, Theodore, *Sketches from Eastern History*, London 1892.

O'Fahey, R. S., and Spaulding, J. L., *Kingdoms of the Sudan*, London 1975.

Pankhurst, Richard, *An Introduction to the Economic History of Ethiopia*, London 1961.

Pankhurst, Richard, "The Ethiopian Slave Trade in the Nineteenth and Early Twentieth Centuries: A Statistical Inquiry," *Journal of Semitic Studies,* 9, 7, 1964.

Parliamentary Papers (Great Britain, House of Commons): 66, "Reports on the State of the Slave Trade in Morocco," 1883.

Parliamentary Papers, 83, "Reports . . . Egypt," 1883.

Parliamentary Papers, 59, "Reports . . . Egypt," 1887.

Parliamentary Papers, 87, "Reports . . . Egypt," 1889.

Parliamentary Papers, 85, "Reports . . . Benghazi," 1893–1894.

Pignon, Jean, *Un document inédit sur la Tunisie au 17e siècle,* Tunis n.d. circa 1964.

Piloti de Crete, Emmanuel, *L'Egypte au commencement du XVe siècle* (P. H. Dopp, ed.), Cairo 1950.

Popper, William, *Egypt and Syria under the Circassian Sultans,* 2 vols. published serially, Berkeley 1955, 1957.

Prax, "Carte de la Regence de Tripoli et les principales routes commerciales de l'intérieur de l'Afrique," *BSG,* 3rd series, *14,* 1850.

Pruner, F, *Die Krankheiten des Orients,* Erlangen 1847.

Quatremere, Etienne, *Histoire des sultans Mamlouks de l'Egypte,* Paris 1837–1840.

Rabourdin, Lucien, *Algerie et Sahara,* Paris 1882.

Raymond, Andre, *Artisans et commerçants au Caire au XVIIIe siècle,* Damascus 1973.

Renault, François, *Lavigerie, l'Esclavage Africain et l'Europe.* Paris 1971.

Richards, D. S., *Islam and the Trade of Asia,* Oxford 1970.

Richardson, James, "Report on the Slave-Trade of the Great Desert," *The Anti-Slavery Reporter,* NS 1, 9–11, 1846.

Richardson, James, *Travels in the Great Desert of the Sahara,* 2 vols., London 1848.

Riley, James, *An Authentic Narrative of the Loss of the Brig American Commerce . . . ,* New York 1817.

Ritchie, Joseph, Correspondence cited in editorial, *Quarterly Review,* 45, 1820, p. 228.

Rivlin, Helen Anne B, *The Agricultural Policy of Muhammad Ali,* Cambridge, Mass. 1961.

Rohlfs, Gerhard, *Reise durch Marokko,* Bremen 1868a.

Rohlfs, Gerhard, *Reise durch Nord-Afrika,* Gotha 1868b.

Rohlfs, Gerhard, *Kufra,* Leipzig 1881.

Rotter, Gernot, "Die Stellung des Negers in der Islamisch-Arabische Gesellschaft bis zum XVIe Jahrhundert," doctoral dissertation, Bonn 1967.

Schweinfurth, Georg, *The Heart of Africa,* 2 vols., New York 1874.

Sedillot, "Notice sur *Voyage au Darfour* par le Cheykh Mohammed-ebn-Omar-el-Tounsy," *Journal Asiatique,* 4th series, 7, 1846.

Shaler, William, *Sketches of Algiers,* Boston 1826.

Shaw, Stanford, *The Financial and Administrative Organization and Development of Ottoman Egypt,* Princeton 1962.

Shaw, Stanford, *Ottoman Egypt in the Age of the French Revolution,* Cambridge, Mass. 1964.

Sheriff, Abdul Mohamed Hussein, "The Rise of a Commercial Empire: An Aspect of the Economic History of Zanzibar, 1770–1873," doctoral dissertation, London University, 1971.

Soleillet, Paul, *L'Afrique occidentale: Algerie, Mzab, Tildeket,* Paris 1877.

Steensgaard, Nels, *The Asian Trade Revolution of the Seventeenth Century,* Chicago 1975.

ibn Taghri Birdi, Abu l-Mahasin, *History of Egypt, 1382–1469 A.D.,* Part 3 (William Popper, trans.), Berkeley 1957.

Talbi, Mohamed, *L'Emirat Aghlabide,* Paris 1966.

Tambo, David Carl, "The Sokoto Caliphate Slave Trade in the Nineteenth Century," Master's thesis, Madison 1974.

Tomiche, Nada, "Notes sur la hierarchie sociale en Egypte à l'époque de Muhammad Ali," in P. M. Holt, ed., *Political and Social Change in Egypt,* London 1968.

el-Tounsy, Mohammed ibn Umar, *Voyage au Ouaday,* Paris 1851.

Tymowski, Michel, *Le développement et la regression chez les peuples de la boucle du Niger a l'époque précoloniale,* Warsaw 1974.

Udovitch, Abraham L, *Partnership and Profit in Islam,* Princeton 1970.

Vadala, A., "Essai sur l'historie des Karamanlis, pachas de Tripolitaine de 1714 à 1835," *Revue d'Histoire des Colonies Françaises,* 7, 1919.

Valensi, Lucette, "Esclaves chrétiens et ésclaves noirs à Tunis au XVIIIe siècle," *Annales,* 22, 4, 1967.

Vatikiotis, P. J., *A Modern History of Egypt.* London 1969.

Verlinden, Charles, *L'esclavage dans l'Europe medievale,* Bruges 1955.

Verlinden, Charles, "L'esclavage noir en France meridionale," *Annales du Midi,* 78, 1966.

Volney, M. C. F., *Travels through Syria and Egypt. 1783–1785.* London 1788.

Windhus, John, "A Journey to Mequinez," in John Pinkerton, ed., *A General Collection of the Best and Most Interesting Voyages and Travels,* London 1725.

Ziadeh, N. A., *Sanusiyah.* Leiden 1958.

3

Some Aspects of the Commercial Organization of Slaving at Luanda, Angola—1760–1830

JOSEPH C. MILLER

Portuguese merchants in Angola established themselves as increasingly autonomous participants in the commerce of the southern Atlantic during the period of "free trade" in slaves between 1760 and 1830. Royal decrees of 1758 and 1761 for the first time allowed merchant firms at Luanda and Benguela, the two major commercial centers of the Portuguese colony, to trade directly in slave-producing areas inland from the coast and encouraged the growth of local commercial independence in ways not possible in the preceding period of domination of civilian and military royal appointees. The end of legal slaving in 1830 changed the course of economic development in Angola yet again, leaving the decades from 1760 to 1830 as a transitional period in the history of Angolan commerce, during which local merchants gradually surmounted a variety of obstacles to financial autonomy. Especially during the earlier years of the period, merchants at Luanda complained of elements in the structure of the trade that thwarted optimal use of the profits they derived from slaving—uncontrollably irregular practices in the marketplaces of the interior, financial domination by

Brazilian capital, inadequate commercial institutions in Angola, and, during the years before 1808, superior foreign competition outside the two Portuguese entrepôts.

Whatever the difficulties perceived by traders at Luanda and Benguela—and the list may be expanded to include epidemic disease among their slaves, official incompetence and venality, and a fair amount of sharp dealing with one another—the merchant communities as a whole showed signs of increasing strength by the end of the period. Perhaps the steady growth in the volume of the southern Atlantic slave trade during this period, and the increasing share of it in the hands of Portuguese, contributed to these apparent achievements. Shipments of slaves increased through the 1820s at the larger of the two ports, Luanda, whereas the quantities of slaves leaving Benguela, the smaller southern port, rose to record heights in the mid-1790s before slipping into a gradual decline that continued until 1830. At the same time, aggregate volume continued to rise as Portuguese and Brazilian slaving became significant on the coasts north of Luanda, in the lower Zaïre River, and along the Loango coast.[1] A corollary expansion marked the African side of the Angolan slave trade, as itinerant traders extended the commercial hinterlands of the two coastal towns farther and farther to the east in search of black hands to satisfy the growing demand of planters, miners, merchants, and townspeople in Brazil.[2]

The economics of the slave trade in Angola remain obscure, compared to those of the well-documented mercantile systems of British and French slavers or to the sophisticated new studies of West African economic history.[3] Unofficial descriptions and government documents, however, yield a rough and unquantified, but still revealing, picture of the strategies and practices of Angolan Portuguese participants in the slave trade at this time. The same sources tentatively suggest how the organization of the trade may have contributed to its destructive effects on the lives and health of the persons enslaved. The most clearly delineated aspects of the trade center on late eighteenth-century Luanda; its least-known features, in com-

---

[1] I have summarized trends in volume and direction in "Legal Portuguese Slaving from Angola—Some Preliminary Indications of Volume and Direction, 1760–1830," *Revue française d'histoire d'outre-mer,* vol. 62, nos. 226–227, 1975, pp. 135–176.

[2] Joseph C. Miller, "The Slave Trade in Congo and Angola," in Martin Kilson and Robert I. Rotberg, eds., *The African Diaspora: Interpretive Essays* (Cambridge, Mass., 1976), pp. 75–113.

[3] Herbert S. Klein, "The Portuguese Slave Trade from Angola in the Eighteenth Century," *Journal of Economic History,* vol. 32, no. 4, 1972, pp. 894–918, contains notes on an Angolan merchant of the 1720s. The papers of Francisco Pinheiro, a Lisbon merchant of the early eighteenth century, recently published in Luis Lisanti, ed., *Negócios Coloniaes,* 5 vols. (Marília, 1974), although not consulted in the preparation of this study, should prove valuable in this connection.

mon with records of the Atlantic slave trade elsewhere, relate to the experience of the slaves themselves.[4]

Even though the southern Atlantic slave trade between 1760 and 1830 acquired a limited unity owing to its nominal regulation by the decrees of 1758 and 1761,[5] wider diplomatic and political factors stimulated a number of changes, including the rise in Portuguese exports of slaves from Angola. The Napoleonic Wars led to effective termination of French competition for slaves along the southwestern African coast in 1791. The contemporaneous British effort to end slaving in the Atlantic was also important, since it ended virtually all non-Portuguese trading in Angola after the 1808 outlawing of British participation. In Brazil, the European conflicts contributed to surges in sugar and cotton exports from the northern parts of the colony, Bahia and Pernambuco; these surges, combined with growing coffee production in the southern captaincies of São Paulo and Rio de Janeiro, kept demand for Angolan slaves on the increase. When the Portuguese royal court fled the wars in Europe and took refuge in Rio de Janeiro in 1808–1809, events led to the opening of Brazilian ports to British and other foreign commerce, and exports of Angolan slaves rose again. Cruisers of the Royal Navy brought Britain's campaign against the slave trade to West African waters after 1810, allowing Angola—assisted by Mozambique, Portugal's other major African possession—to become the major remaining supplier of slave labor for the Americas. Brazilian independence in 1822 divided the loyalties of Angolan merchants, suddenly made obedient to a restored Portuguese government in Lisbon but still subject to economic conditions regulated by a different regime in Rio de Janeiro. Shipments of Angolan slaves continued to rise during the 1820s, as growing diplomatic pressure on both Brazilian and Portuguese authorities to end the slave trade caused buyers of slaves in Brazil to increase their purchases in anticipation of the cutoff of legal imports that finally came in 1830.[6] The post-1830 illegal slave trade may be presumed to have been conducted rather differently from that of the years of legal and "free" slaving.[7]

[4] Mortality in the Angolan slave trade has been investigated by Herbert S. Klein, "The Trade in African Slaves to Rio de Janeiro," *Journal of African History*, vol. 10, no. 4, 1969, pp. 533–550; and by H. S. Klein and Stanley L. Engerman, "Shipping Patterns and Mortality in the African Slave Trade to Rio de Janeiro, 1825–1830," *Cahiers d'études africaines*, vol. 15, no. 59, 1975, pp. 381–398.

[5] Published in part in Antonio Carreira, "As Companhias Pombalinas de Navegação, Comércio, e Tráfico de Escravos entre a Costa Africana e o Nordeste Brasileiro," *Boletim Cultural da Guiné Portuguesa*, vol. 24, no. 93, 1969, pp. 388–390.

[6] For the ending of legal slaving in the southern Atlantic, see Leslie Bethell, *The Abolition of the Brazilian Slave Trade* (Cambridge, 1970).

[7] As is apparent from Mary Karasch, "The Brazilian Slavers and the Illegal Slave Trade, 1836–1851," Master's thesis (University of Wisconsin, 1967).

THE ANGOLAN MERCHANTS

Throughout these political changes, the basic economic problem facing the dozen or more influential merchants handling slaves at Luanda or the four or more major trading firms at Benguela remained that of finding an autonomous position between pressures exerted by Brazilian merchants and the unpredictable dealings of bush traders in the Angola interior. Most Angolan firms tended to restrict their functions to the warehousing and distribution of imports, to direct buying of slaves in the city or, later, in a few regulated marketplaces in the interior, and to the bulking and housing of slaves in preparation for their embarkation on slave ships in the harbors.[8] Facing east from Luanda and Benguela, they left to highly specialized operators of slave caravans and to bush traders their commercial linkages to sources of slaves scattered throughout the small area administered directly by Portuguese authorities and in a ring of perhaps two dozen African slave-trading states surrounding it. Of even less immediate concern to the traders of the towns were hundreds or thousands of Africans, petty slave traders, thugs and bandits, lineage elders and headmen, and more distant political authorities, who initiated the myriad processes of enslavement that ultimately fed labor to the cities, mines, and plantations of Brazil.

On the seaward side, Angolan merchants dealt face-to-face with dozens of captains and supercargoes who handled the off-loading of trade goods and the embarkation of slaves. Their direct commercial contacts also extended to Brazil where, for most of the period before 1830, merchants in Rio de Janeiro, Pernambuco, and Bahia maintained a firm grip on their contacts with commercial houses in metropolitan Portugal and, beyond them, with British and French mercantile and financial interests that, already in the eighteenth century, occupied strong positions in the commerce of Lisbon and Porto.[9] These European Portuguese merchants, protected under mercantilist decrees regulating the trade of scattered Portuguese possessions in Asia, America, and Africa, asserted exclusive rights to supply Brazil and Angola with manufactured wares; but they failed to establish these claims

---

[8] See Arquivo Histórico de Angola (AHA), códice 3259, passim. Some of the larger firms of the 1770s–1780s may have operated plantations to supply foodstuffs required by slave caravans leaving their branches in the interior; they must also have kept artisans to repair buildings and equipment and to fabricate stocks and other slaving equipment. Jean-Baptiste Douville, *Voyage au Congo et dans l'intérieur de l'Afrique equinoxiale*, 3 vols. (Paris, 1832), vol. 1, p. 92, described merchant-owned plantations along the lower Bengo river in 1828.

[9] Dauril Alden, "Manoel Luis Vieira: An Entrepreneur in Rio de Janeiro during Brazil's XVIIIth Century Renaissance," *Hispanic–American Historical Review*, vol. 39, no. 4, 1959, p. 524.

over geographical and economic forces that left Portugal excluded from a semiindependent commercial system in the southern Atlantic.

Aside from the fact that all slaves, Angola's overwhelmingly dominant export, were legally bound for Brazil, winds and currents in the southern Atlantic reinforced Angola's ties with the American colony. In the broadest terms, these formed a large counterclockwise-moving circle revolving around a dominant ridge of high pressure located over the ocean between Brazil and Angola. Vessels setting out from Portugal for Africa had virtually to pass Brazil to reach Angola. Africa-bound ships out of the northern Brazilian ports sailed southward along the coast, to be joined by others from Rio, before swinging out to sea on the westerly trade winds of the higher southern latitudes. Merchants in Brazil took advantage of their relative proximity to establish closer relations with traders in Angola than metropolitan competitors could achieve.[10]

If the origins of slave ships arriving in the ports of Angola accurately indicated the locations of Angolan traders' commercial correspondents, nearly all of Benguela's and about half of Luanda's contacts resided at Rio. The destinations of the remaining slave ships outbound from Luanda fluctuated from decade to decade but in the long run amounted to about one-fourth to Pernambuco and one-fifth or less to Bahia. Although records show only the proximate origins of ships calling in Angola and thereby render difficult the identification of their home ports, frequencies of arrival may show the extent to which the slave trade was also Brazilian in terms of maritime movement. Relatively few ships, presumably Brazilian, shuttling between Angola and Brazil, carried a large share of the slaves, whereas ships appearing only once or twice, only some of which need have been out of Lisbon or Porto, accounted for a much smaller proportion of arrivals. A sample of Angolan shipping between 1780 and 1830 showed, for example, that the one-tenth of all vessels appearing more than 10 times in Angolan harbors accounted for a disproportionately large 42% of all slaving voyages; 79% of the entries were made by ships that called there more than twice. European ships that put in at Brazilian ports and then continued on to Angola would have figured, along with Brazilians only occasionally participating in the trade, among the 45% of the vessels that appeared only once in the sample, or perhaps among the slightly more than half that showed up only once or twice. Such infrequent callers took only a minor

[10] José Accursio das Neves, *Consideraçpes politicas, e commerciaes sobre os descobrimentos, e possessões dos Portuguezes na Africa, e na Asia* (Lisbon, 1830), p. 240, remarked, if somewhat obscurely, that by the 1820s "some commercial firms of Portuguese origin" still remained in Angola but there was only one factor employed by a European Portuguese trading house.

share of the slave trade, for they made only 21% of all slaving voyages in the sample.[11] Voyages direct to Portugal were virtually nonexistent, and only about 10% of the ships entering Luanda or Benguela came straight from Europe.[12]

The commodities exchanged for slaves in Angola were more diverse in origin, consisting of a mixture of manufactured wares from Europe, textiles woven in Asia, and the products of Brazilian agriculture. An observer listed imports during the 1780s as textiles, presumably Asian as well as European;[13] Portuguese wines, firearms, powder, lead shot, ironware, and beads.[14] Government statistics for selected years 1812–1823 showed that textiles accounted for up to three-fourths of Angolan imports in some years, with the coarse sugar brandies known as *cachaça* or *bagaço* in Brazil and as *gerebita* in Angola, the second largest component at 10–23% of the yearly totals by value.[15] Though only 1.6–4.4% of the totals in the data for 1812–1823, rice, wheat flour, dried meat, and manioc flour, and other foodstuffs occupied a prominent position among the products destined for consumption in the port towns. Brazilian hides, construction timber, and naval supplies filled out the cargoes of vessels entering Luanda and Benguela.[16] Small quantities of Brazilian tobacco (never more than 1.3% for known years between 1812 and 1823) joined the other commodities destined for the

[11] Since changes in the names of vessels cannot be distinguished from new ships, these estimates may not be precise. Allowing for bias of this sort would strengthen the general argument, as the method employed yields the maximum possible number of metropolitan vessels by taking each new name (of which some must have been renamed Brazilian slavers) as an occasional arrival from Portugal.

[12] The statistics are derived from unpublished data in the AHA, códices 314, 315, 316, 725, 726, and 727; also Arquivo Histórico da Câmara Municipal de Luanda (AHCML), códice 27.

[13] Ships bound for Lisbon with Asian textiles at some times smuggled cargoes directly into Brazil and Angola. See Ralph Delgado, "O Governo de Sousa Coutinho em Angola," *Studia,* vol. 3, no. 6, 1960, p. 42; and Carlos Couto, "O Pacto colonial e a interferência brasileira no domínio das relações econômicas entre Angola e o reino no século XVIII," *Estudos Históricos* (Marília), vol. 10, 1971, pp. 27–29.

[14] Lists of imports appear in Luis António de Oliveira Mendes, "Discurso academico . . .," *Memórias Econômicas da Academia das Ciências de Lisboa,* vol. 4. (Lisboa, 1812), p. 21, reprinted as doc. ZC in Carreira, "Companhias pombalinas, vol. 24, 1969, pp. 422–423 (1780s); AHA códice 3259, docs. 59, 69 (1790s); João Carlos Feo Cardoso de Castello Branco e Torres, *Memórias contendo . . . A Descripção geographica e politica dos reinos de Angola e de Benguella* (Paris, 1825), p. 336 (1817–1819); Accursio das Neves, *Considerações sobre as possessões portuguezas.* p. 233 (1820s).

[15] Manuel dos Anjos da Silva Rebelo, *Relações entre Angola e Brasil 1808–1830* (Lisboa, 1970), Quadros 2–5, following p. 179.

[16] Sources cited in n. 13; and Elias Alexandre da Silva Correa, *História de Angola,* 2 vols. (Lisboa, 1937), vol. 1, p. 50; José Honório Rodrigues, *Brazil and Africa* (Richard A. Mazzara and Sam Hileman, trans., Berkeley and Los Angeles, 1965), pp. 33–34.

African interior but did not assume the importance of Bahian tobacco in the slave trade from the Gulf of Benin.[17]

Captains bound for Angola aimed to strike the African coast well to the south of Benguela and then ride the north-flowing currents and winds off the Angola shore down to Benguela or on to Luanda.[18] Before the elimination of foreign competition after 1808, few if any Portuguese ships continued on to the northern slaving ports of Cabinda, beyond the mouth of the Zaire River, or even to the Ambriz area between Luanda and the Zaire, where Dutch, French, and British slavers direct from Europe generally excluded Portuguese and Brazilians approaching from the opposite direction. Cabinda's relative remoteness from Brazil may have supplemented the high prices of Portuguese merchandise as a cause of the weak Portuguese commercial presence to the north of the nearer southern Angola ports.

Benguela, the smaller of the two, with perhaps 2000 or so inhabitants at this period, of whom censuses recorded 60 or 70 as "whites" (i.e., more or less European in culture), attracted primarily vessels from Rio. Four large mercantile firms there ran the slave trade during the 1780s as they wished, trading on their own account (*"de effeitos próprios"*).[19] This meant that they purchased wares in Rio de Janeiro with their own funds, paid freight charges (*fretes*) to shippers for transportation to Benguela (unless, as seems unlikely, they owned their own sailing vessels at that time), and incurred similar charges for the transportation of their slaves back to Rio. Although financial structures and modes of commercial organization are not clearly documented for eighteenth- and early nineteenth-century trading firms in Angola, observers seem to have made a fundamental distinction between merchants who traded *de effeitos próprios* and others known as *negociantes comissários,* or commission agents. The latter owned relatively few of the slaves who passed through their slave pens but, rather, acted as agents on behalf of Brazilian correspondents who retained ownership of the goods sent to Africa and of slaves on their way to America. Individual firms probably did business in both modes, but merchants would have striven to build up the capital required to operate as traders on their own accounts.

The dominance of these four firms, reported only for the 1780s, may have declined as the volume of slave exports at Benguela rose at the end of the century, since, in 1796, 19 traders, of whom no less than 9 were wealthy

[17] Cf. Pierre Verger, *Flux et reflux de la traite des nègres entre le golfe de Benin et Bahia de Todos os Santos du dix-septième au dix-neuvième siècle* (Paris, 1968).

[18] Silva Correa, *História de Angola,* vol. 1, p. 19; Henry Chamberlain to Viscount Castlereagh, 27 April 1816, Public Record Office, London (PRO), FO63/193, folio 36.

[19] Silva Correa, *História de Angola,* vol. 1, p. 39.

enough to occupy the large dwellings known as *sobrados*,[20] were reported active at Benguela. The Benguela merchant firms may also have shown a tendency after 1800 to expand their operations from the town into the highland areas to the east.[21] This movement toward the interior, although unknown in extent, presumably indicated growing wealth as coastal merchants assumed direct control over the operation of caravans between the port and points in the interior where slaves were bulked for despatch to the coast.

The larger and more diversified slave trade at Luanda included a dozen or more large firms, some trading on their own account—although to an unknown extent—and others primarily *negociantes comissários*, along with a horde of part-time petty slave dealers among the city's population of about 4000. The slave merchants probably came mainly from the 400 or so "whites" in the city or from an equivalent-sized community of Afro–Portuguese Angolans.[22] In addition, supercargoes, paid agents of Brazilian firms aboard ships in the harbor, and the masters of the slave ships sent by Brazilian or Portuguese venturers without established commercial contacts at the main Angolan port, participated in slaving there.[23] The greater diversity and number of merchants active at Luanda seem to have been reflected in the division of Luanda's trade among all three of the major Brazilian ports; occasional participants in the slave trade would have been more likely to find a commission agent to handle their goods, or a local trader who would make a direct exchange of imports against slaves, at Luanda, than in the tightly controlled market at Benguela during the 1780s.

By the 1790s, the majority of Luanda trading houses had already established subsidiaries in the Portuguese marketplaces, military posts, and settlements east of Luanda. Most of these registered only one or two branches; the largest claimed five such affiliates and slightly less than a third had no formal branches in the interior at all. At least 11 mercantile establishments made Dondo, just below the head of navigation on the lower Kwanza River, the most important of the inland slaving centers. The Dondo firms, 8 of

---

[20] Ralph Delgado, *O Reino de Benguela* (Lisboa, 1945), p. 381. A report of an 1816 dispute over the regulation of the slave trade in Benguela listed seven merchants by name and alluded to the presence of others; Silva Rebelo, *Relações entre Angola e Brasil,* p. 78.

[21] Ralph Delgado, *A Famosa e histórica Benguela: Catálogo dos Governadores* (Lisboa, 1940), p. 57.

[22] Feo Cardoso, *Memórias,* p. 348; Douville, *Voyage au Congo,* vol. 1, p. 39; Ilidio do Amaral, *Luanda (estudo de geografia urbana)* (Lisboa, 1968), pp. 50, 51, 54. The number of merchants is inferred from Oliveira Mendes, "Discurso academico, in Carreira, "Companhias pombalinas," vol. 24, 1969, pp. 427–428, and roughly matches the total of 15 different firms registered between 1788 and 1797, AHA, códice 2653.

[23] Carreira, "Companhias pombalinas," vol. 24, 1969, p. 85, divides Angolan merchants into *"contradores fixos"* (evidently the established firms), *"compradores de ocasião"* (apparently unspecialized merchant venturers engaging in slaving only on occasion), and ship captains.

which were subsidiaries of Luanda houses, depended for the most part on merchants of the capital. Dondo served as a jumping-off place for caravans destined both north and south of the river, but the town was known especially for its connections with slave sources to the south.[24] Four or more Luanda merchants, all with operations at Dondo, also maintained branches at Massangano, perhaps 15 kilometers downstream. This clustering of trading firms along the lower Kwanza indicated the extent to which the river served as a major artery of the slave trade in Angola.

Slaving elsewhere in the hinterland of Luanda was theoretically concentrated in *feiras*, or officially recognized marketplaces near major suppliers of slaves. In areas north of the Kwanza under Portuguese control these functioned in the shadow of fortified government positions at Ambaca (Lucamba), Pungo Andongo (Pedras and Beja), and Encoje. Other *feiras* operated well beyond the range of Portuguese cannon, south of the Kwanza in Libolo (or Haco), in the east at Bondo, and in Holo and Kasanje, the major slave-trading states of the Kwango River valley. Repeated government attempts to police these *feiras* produced only limited results as slavers spread their trading outside the specified localities, ignored fixed price scales, and altered the weights and measures in use.

The *feiras* at Dondo and Ambaca appeared to be the home bases of at least one large firm not registered at Luanda, and two or three others seem to have concentrated their activities in the easternmost marketplaces in the Kwango valley. These, and the widespread branches of the merchants headquartered at Luanda, indicated a movement inland that preceded the parallel development at Benguela after 1800. The precise arrangements by which firms without a base at Luanda sold their slaves in the port city are not known. They either could have been commission agents specialized in collecting and despatching slaves from the interior to correspondents at the coast or could have themselves been traders *de effeitos próprios* who employed exporters in the city as their agents.[25]

Late eighteenth-century merchants in Luanda, in apparent contrast to those in Benguela, complained that they were deeply indebted to mercantile firms located in Brazil.[26] In the absence of direct evidence on the

[24] Feo Cardoso, *Memórias*, p. 354.

[25] AHA, códices 2653 and 3259. This paragraph can do no more than approximate the mercantile structure of the interior, as registration of firms was irregular at best. The documentation omits firms active at Kasanje, the major market of the interior at this period.

[26] Silva Correa, *História de Angola*, vol. 1, pp. 51–52, 57. Carreira, "Companhias pombalinas," vol. 23, 1968, p. 25, affirms the indebtedness of the Luanda merchants and indicates that similar conditions existed at the beginning of the eighteenth century; but Klein, "Portuguese Slave Trade," implies that indebtedness was not significant in the 1720s. One may compare the tactics used by the large Brazilian firm of Fonseca in the 1840s to indebt the merchants it dealt with; Karasch, "Brazilian Slavers," pp. 26–34.

financial condition of individual Brazilian or Angolan firms, the credit arrangements in force and the directions of credit flows cannot be spelled out in detail, but three methods of financing the slave trade may be presumed to have been present.[27] Local firms short on capital purchased commodities in Rio, Pernambuco, or Bahia on credit given against the future delivery of slaves to the *negociantes comissários* who handled transactions for them in Brazil. In addition, some Brazilian merchant houses operated directly in Angola through supercargoes or through agents permanently located in Luanda and Benguela, whereas other Brazilian firms engaged Angolan commission agents to handle goods and slaves on their behalf. Although the exact shares of the trade conducted in each of these modes are not known, all involved the extension of Brazilian merchant control to Angola.

Brazilian merchants employing the latter two sorts of arrangement seem to have come into open conflict with Angolan firms of the first category during most of this period and to have taken a variety of steps to hinder the development of competitive and debt-free trading by Angolans. Brazilian financial interests had obtained an initial advantage under the 1758 and 1761 decrees establishing the regime of "free trade."[28] By the terms of these laws regulating the order in which slave ships might depart the ports of Angola, vessels that had arrived *"de effeitos próprios"* were entitled to preference in clearing for Brazil. Since prompt loading and departure significantly reduced the expenses of a slaving voyage, this provision favored Brazilian merchants owning vessels laden entirely with their own commodities and discriminated against Angolan merchants who appear to have imported and exported at that time aboard ships belonging to Brazilians. These conditions may have been most onerous for Luanda merchants during the earlier years of "free trade." One method used by Brazilians to keep Angolan traders dependent, best documented in the case of Brazilian holders of contracts for the collection of royal duties on Angolan slaves during the 1760s, hinged on paying sellers of slaves with unbacked notes (*livranças*) convertible to currency only in Brazil. Payment in this form forced Angolans trading on their own account to accept notes of limited negotiability which the issuers of the *livranças* paid only at their own option. Delays compelled Luanda merchants, whose working capital was tied up in worthless *livranças*, to accept further shipments of trade commodities on credit and thus converted some of the strongest firms into debtors.[29] Angola

---

[27] As they were in West Africa; C. W. Newbury, "Credit in Early Nineteenth Century West African Trade," *Journal of African History,* vol. 13, no. 1, 1972, pp. 81–96.

[28] Silva Rebelo, *Relações entre Angola e Brasil,* p. 197.

[29] Delgado, "Governo de Sousa Coutinho," no. 6, 1960, pp. 33, 36–38; Couto, "Pacto colonial," p. 26n.

remained chronically short of currency, and attempts by holders of these bills to convert them into a more negotiable form foundered on the large discounts at which they circulated outside of Angola.[30] Most independent Luanda traders, even if they showed an accounting profit,[31] thus found themselves drawn into the debt of Brazilian merchant firms and unable to export profits realized in Angola except at ruinous discounts.

The balance of credit may have shifted in favor of Angolan merchants after 1800, however, since by 1820 a group of traders in Luanda had acquired sufficient capital to purchase sailing vessels and to fill their holds with slaves and commodities carried on their own account.[32] In that year they requested that they receive the same rights of precedence granted to Brazilian ships sailing *de effeitos próprios* by the decrees of 1758 and 1761. Aside from the petition's implicit confirmation that the earlier decrees had favored the merchants of Brazil, it evoked anguished protests from some Brazilian firms, which also showed the extent to which Brazilians had been accustomed to finance the Angolan slave trade. Extending Brazilian privileges to the Luanda firms, one American representative argued, would render Brazilian commerce totally "passive," that is, the Brazilians recognized that they faced the threat of being reduced to commission agents without capital involved in slaving and thus subject to the same domination that they had once exercised over the Angolans. The 1820 petition may also have been a subterfuge, as other Brazilians alleged, on the part of still undercapitalized Angolans hoping to front for British, French, or metropolitan Portuguese capital.[33] Several large and independent slave exporters were certainly present in Luanda by the 1840s[34] and had probably first appeared some years earlier.

An apparent high rate of turnover among the firms comprising the Luanda merchant community may provide another indication of the slight extent to which local Angolan capital financed the slave trade before the last years of legal slaving. On the assumption that adequately capitalized firms

[30] Silva Correa, *História de Angola,* vol. 1, pp. 51–52, 180n.

[31] Dom Miguel António de Mello, "Relatorio," *Archivo das Colonias,* vol. 5, no. 29, 1930, pp. 139–140, also published as "Angola no começo do século (1802)," *Boletim da Sociedade de Geografia de Lisboa,* vol. 5, 1885, pp. 548–564, stated that the slave trade was almost always profitable, presumably with reference to the local Angola merchants rather than their Brazilian counterparts, but cf. Silva Correa, *História de Angola,* vol. 1, p. 174n, who specified that profits came from importing trade wares rather than exporting slaves. The question depended largely on the cost accounting techniques used.

[32] Silva Rebelo, *Relações entre Angola e Brasil,* pp. 199–202.

[33] Allowed to trade in overseas Portuguese ports by decrees of 1808–1811; see Olga Pantaleão, "Aspectos do comércio dos domínios portugueses no período de 1808 a 1821," *Revista de História* (São Paulo), no. 41, 1960, pp. 91–104.

[34] Karasch, "Brazilian Slavers," pp. 22–26.

would tend to survive from one generation to the next,[35] financially solid merchant firms would have appeared in successive lists of traders in Luanda, either under the same name or under names including the designation (or its equivalent) ". . . and sons," or with surnames suggesting inheritance by a son or nephew.[36] Few such indications of local wealth appear in three lists from 1764, the 1790s, and 1810. Of 16 merchants registered as principal traders in Luanda, the name of only 1 (possibly[37]) appeared in a register of 22 firms extending credit to bush traders during the 1790s.[38] Hardly more than a decade later, 3 of those 22 (and none of the original 16) turned up in a report listing 12 of the major merchants of Luanda in 1810.[39] The disappearance of at least some may be attributed to indebtedness, which apparently broke up many firms as creditors pressed for liquidation of their debts at the deaths of their principal partners. Firms therefore tended not to survive beyond a single merchant's career, short enough under the high mortality rates prevailing among the European-born in Angola, and sons infrequently salvaged enough of their father's assets to preserve the firms in their own names.[40] The slightly greater continuity evident between the later two lists (14% as against 6%) may have resulted in part from the shorter lapse of time separating them (15–20 years rather than 25–30); but growing financial autonomy among traders in Luanda could also have increased stability, since one merchant in the 1810 list was described as the "wealthiest man south of the equator."

Still, in the earlier years, merchants unable to export their gains had a choice of either converting their profits into additional trade goods and thus expanding their trading operation in Angola or accepting consumer imports from their Brazilian creditors. The latter alternative was accompanied by the retention of assets in the form of slaves not exported and produced the faintly opulent style of living characteristic of Luanda bourgeois society in

[35] The validity of this assumption depends in part on the procedures used to dispose of the assets in estates of deceased merchants.

[36] This method cannot identify sons-in-law and will underestimate continuity to the extent that businesses went to married daughters of the deceased merchants.

[37] Uncertainty of the identification stems from what appears to be a variant record in the 1790s of the name that appeared in 1764 as Manuel José da (Rocha e) Silva.

[38] Delgado, "Governo de Sousa Coutinho," no. 6, 1960, p. 20; AHA, códices 2653 and 3259. The two lists may fail to reveal some of the continuity actually present since they refer to slightly different groups. The 1764 list may have excluded Brazilian-owned factories that would have appeared in the 1790s register of firms employing bush traders, whereas the later list would have omitted important local firms present also in 1764 but not entrusting goods to bush traders during the 1790s.

[39] Silva Rebelo, *Relações entre Angola e Brasil*, pp. 43–45.

[40] This argument may be qualified by a reported tendency for successful merchants to transfer their wealth to Brazil or Portugal; Silva Rebelo, *Relações entre Angola e Brasil*, p. 43.

the days of slaving—oversize and inappropriately elegant houses (*sobrados*), more slave retainers than seemed necessary or economical, and apparent profligacy.[41] Funds generated by profitable slaving probably flowed also into expanded networks of subsidiaries, evident east of Luanda by the 1790s. This course had its limitations, since rapid growth threatened to reduce future gains through an inflationary flooding of the market with textiles, spirits, and other imports.[42]

Brazilian domination also contributed to an apparent overextension of credit from merchants to the caravan operators, or *sertanejos*, and others who brought slaves down from the interior to Luanda or Benguela. To these *sertanejos*, also known as *aviados*, or *funantes*, they sold trade commodities on credit to be repaid in slaves upon their return to the coast 6–8 months or even years later. Ownership of both goods and slaves resided with the *sertanejos*, and the Luanda merchants, either as principals or as agents, purchased the slaves from them after their arrival on the coast. This system operated at most times in an extremely disorderly manner, by the standards of the merchants in the towns. These backwoodsmen seem to have been independent minded and resourceful; accordingly, they were known as "lawless" and "disreputable" by the bourgeois traders of Luanda, who saw the relatively reliable commercial organization prevailing between Brazil and the Angolan ports, break down into chaos in the interior of the colony. More order must have prevailed than appears in the merchants' complaints that constitute the only surviving record of the conduct of the caravan operators, but the *sertanejos'* preferred practices are now difficult to perceive through the haze of mercantile and official condemnations. The Luanda exporters strove sporadically to impose an order congenial to their own interests, in part by fixing prices and procedures at the government-authorized *feiras* and in part by keeping the caravan operators permanently in debt to them.[43]

---

[41] Douville, *Voyage au Congo*, vol. 1, p. 52; Silva Correa, *História de Angola*, vol. 1, p. 82; Anne Stamm, "La société créole à Saint-Paul de Loanda dans les années 1838–48," *Revue francaise d'histoire d'outre-mer*, vol. 59, no. 4, 1972, p. 581, no. 217, describes similar conditions for the 1840s but elsewhere (p. 579) suggests, although without citing evidence on the methods employed, that merchants were able to export wealth to Brazil in this later period.

[42] Silva Correa, *História de Angola*, vol. 1, pp. 49–51, and a variety of indirect evidence concur in suggesting that short-term supply responses were inelastic and that greater quantities of goods merely inflated the exchange ratios of goods to slaves.

[43] Evidence of the *sertanejos'* collective indebtedness pervades the documentation on trade at this period; AHA, códice 3259, docs. 2 (1759), 10 (1762), 64, 65 (1792), etc. The registry of goods entrusted to *sertanejos* between 1788 and 1797 (AHA, códice 2653), while a far-from-perfect record of the dealings of the merchants with the caravanners, probably gives a fair idea of the proportions of this debt. The total amount owed at the conclusion of a slaving journey to the interior, for those cases where the figure can be calculated, amounted to nearly 48% of the

The keystone of the *sertanejos'* indebtedness to the Luanda traders lay in the merchants' valuation of the goods that they sold to the operators of the caravans and of the slaves that they received in return. Merchants at Luanda set goods-to-slaves ratios at levels that approximately doubled the currency cost of their imports.[44] Although they apparently kept their accounts and dealt with Brazilian correspondents in terms of *mil-réis*, transactions with the *sertanejos* were negotiated in terms of *banzos*, units of account that facilitated the linkage of European to African economies in Angola very much as did trade ounces and bars in West Africa.[45] The *banzo* was a constantly varying assortment of goods deemed equivalent to the value of a prime male slave, or *peça;* a standard scale of lesser grades expressed the value of individuals actually produced for sale in terms of *peça-* and *banzo-*equivalents.[46] The *banzo* was usually thought of as a basic assortment of textiles filled out at Luanda with *gerebita*, firearms, and other imports; the Benguela *banzo* may have contained a greater proportion of beads. Sea salt from evaporation pans near both Luanda and Benguela supplemented the imported goods in most *banzos*.[47]

The assortment bargaining must have been extremely complex, but once completed the *banzo* offered a simple and straightforward accounting system suitable to a stage in the slave trade where few participants possessed more than the rudiments of literacy and where account books must have been virtually unknown.[48] When the *sertanejo* accepted an assortment of

---

value of the goods originally loaned. Only 5 of 58 individuals had no outstanding debts listed against their names, and these instances were probably all accounts not yet reckoned at the time the registry was abandoned, rather than successful ventures. These debts undoubtedly tied up a large portion of merchant capital in Angola, preventing investment in agriculture or other enterprises; Accursio das Neves, *Considerações sobre as possessões portuguezes*, p. 231, stressed shortages of capital.

[44] Accursio das Neves, *Considerações sobre as possessões portuguezes*, p. 231, stated that European slavers took a "profit" of 100%, an alternative phrasing of the point.

[45] The *mil-réis* (written 1$000) was the basic Portuguese currency of the eighteenth century, although very little specie circulated in Angola at that time. The Portuguese *cruzado* (S400 = 1 *cruzado*) was also apparently used as a currency of account; AHA, códice 3259, doc. 44 (1789). AHA, códice 3259, doc. 10 (1762), implied that the merchants clearly perceived the impossibility of conducting the trade of the interior in terms of money accounting.

[46] The components of the *banzos* varied in value according to the remoteness of the *feira* to which the imports were destined, probably in reflection of the differences in goods–slaves ratios; slaves would have been cheaper in the most distant *feiras* in Holo, Kasanje, Haco, and so on.

AHA, códice 3259, doc. 59, specified the grades of slaves recognized at Kasanje in 1792: *peça de India* (prime adult male), *molecão* (healthy male youth), *molecana* (healthy and attractive female), *molecão de seis palmas* (boy?), and all others of inferior stature, health, etc.

[47] Accursio das Neves, *Considerações sobre as possessões portuguezes*, pp. 196–197.

[48] On eighteenth-century Portuguese accounting, Dauril Alden, *Royal Government in Colonial Brazil* (Berkeley and Los Angeles, 1968), pp. 287–294ff.

goods evaluated in terms of *banzos*, the one-to-one correspondence of *banzos* to *peças* told him in advance exactly how many slaves he had obligated himself to repay. The *sertanejo* could then estimate whether his trades were proceeding satisfactorily by placing a rough *peça* evaluation on each slave that he would take back to the city. Allowing for renewed bargaining, in which his merchant creditor would try to place as low an evaluation on the slaves as he could, and barring higher-than-anticipated deaths among the slaves during the westward march or exceptionally numerous escapes and injuries, an experienced caravan operator could accurately anticipate the likely returns from his journey. Still, these costs were likely to compound, leaving the *sertanejo* permanently in debt to the merchants of the city.

Merchants wielded the indebtedness of the *sertanejo* to wed him to future dealings with themselves rather than with their competitors. The common method required the *sertanejo* to accept more *banzos* on the promise that he would return with slaves sufficient to discharge both current and prior debt. Commission agents supplemented this tactic by deducting their commissions from the next lot of goods that each returning caravan operator virtually obligated himself to accept from the merchant.[49] The system did not work entirely according to the creditors' designs during most of the 1760–1830 period, since the *sertanejos* expertly fended off insolvency by means of a straightforwardly fraudulent practice known as a *reviro*. Since *sertanejos* took full title to their trade goods, they also owned the slaves for which they exchanged them and could pass title to them to anyone they chose. In a *reviro*, *sertanejos* returning with too few *peças* to pay off what they owed, surreptitiously sold their slaves not to their creditor but to one of his competitors who would offer a more liberal evaluation of the *peça*-equivalency of his slaves.[50] The competitor could afford to buy the slaves at premium rates because the *reviro*, in effect a direct barter, avoided the bad debts inherent in the normal arrangements as well as the risky and long-term credit involved in financing *sertanejos'* lengthy journies. For the *sertanejo*, a favorable *reviro* would restore depleted working capital and enable him to return to the interior with new trade goods where, with a bit of luck, more successful transactions might enable him to return eventually to his original sponsor and to liquidate, more or less, his debt.

Although merchants constantly complained of *reviros* throughout the later eighteenth century, none could avoid the practice so long as any one of them persisted. Growing Brazilian demand for slaves may have encouraged

[49] Silva Correa, *História de Angola*, vol. 1, p. 32.

[50] Silva Correa, *História de Angola*, vol. 1, p. 36; AHA, códice 3259, passim, but especially docs. 21 (1764), 27 (1765), 37 (1775), 44 (1790), when *reviros* were said to have been on the increase, 64 (1792), and 66 (1792). For Benguela, Delgado, *Famosa e histórica Benguela*, p. 44 (1801) and p. 75 (1820).

reviros by providing quantities of trade commodities at Luanda and Benguela in excess of short-term supplies of slaves. Merchants with more goods than they could sell resorted to irregular means of obtaining slaves; meanwhile their pressure on their own *sertanejos* produced willing accomplices for other traders with the same surplus. Under the guidance of governors concerned with imposing a degree of order on the colony's irregular commercial practices, merchants occasionally defined elaborate but futile regulatory schemes. Intense competition, however, hindered implementation of their plan, and even if the merchants had somehow concerted their efforts to end *reviros* at Luanda, the *sertanejos* could have intensified their *reviros* with British and French slavers who bought slaves at bays all along the Angolan coast until 1808 or with Brazilian smugglers thereafter.

A variety of less reputable characters sold slaves on the fringes of the official system. Dozens of petty traders frequented the environs of the harbor, begging sufficient trade goods to support a quick trip to the interior where they hoped to pick up a slave or two; others hawked profitable deals to be made somewhere in the maze of paths and huts that hid uncounted stolen captives in the African parts of the town. Sailors off the ships in the port bought, borrowed, or took their pay in trade commodities and tried their hand at this sort of slave trading. Some contacted black marketeers known as *comboladores* who specialized in handling *reviros* and also sold slaves too weakened physically to find a buyer through respectable channels. *Adelos*, or "junk dealers," bought and sold the most decrepit of the slaves on infinitesimal margins, and these last were the ones who had developed to a fine art the disguising of physical defects and the misrepresentation of the origins of slaves who came from regions not favored by the current market.[51] Luanda was not a town in which the unwary amateur could hope to turn a profitable trade.

Sertanejos appear to have experienced a strong cost squeeze in the late eighteenth and early nineteenth centuries, if the prevalence of *reviros* was an accurate indicator of their plight. In addition to the exploitive terms imposed by creditors in Luanda, they faced a variety of other extortions and expenses before they ever arrived at the slave *feiras* in the interior. Transportation of the imported wares, given the virtual absence of draft animals in Angola, meant that caravan operators had to engage bearers; and *sertanejos* attempted ideally to build up working capital in the form of slaves who head-loaded their merchandise from the ports and river towns to its point of sale. In the unlikelihood of making the consistent profits that would protect such an investment, they more often than not found themselves forced to hire bearers from military officials (*capitães-mores*) or civilian

[51] Silva Correa, *História de Angola,* vol. 1, pp. 125–126.

regentes whose charge of the government posts in the interior empowered them to raise corvée labor from the African population under their command. These positions tended to fall, it appears, to some of the largest slave dealers of the interior, and the fortunate nominees, although technically constrained by the terms of their appointments, did little to facilitate the enterprises of *sertanejos* who were, in effect, their competitors.[52]

Sertanejos also had to bear the expense of tolls at river ferries, losses by theft and accident, ordinary living expenses, and depletion of their investments in slaves through escape and deaths. The costs of running slave caravans mounted even higher for *sertanejos* who ventured beyond the Portuguese-administered areas to trade with independent African authorities who exacted a variety of tolls and taxes as part of the price of doing business with them. By the time a *sertanejo* reached the more remote markets of the Kwango valley, exchange ratios of goods against slaves had fallen by one-half below those prevailing in Luanda, with the difference going to cover the costs of transportation of his wares.[53]

A persistent shortage of bearers—not entirely an artificial creation of the *capitães-mores*—acted as one of the major constraints on the ability of *sertanejos* to deliver goods to interior markets and to escort slaves to Luanda.[54] In these circumstances, large-scale Portuguese military expeditions added little to the volume of slaves exported, since an army in the field diverted so many potential bearers into the army's supply train that trade threatened to grind to a halt.[55] Large slave dealers played on the chronic shortage of bearers by attempting to engage, in advance of their real needs, as much labor as they could. By cornering the supply of transportation in a region, they could buy slaves there at lower prices, as their competitors were unable to deliver merchandise or slaves. Care and maintenance of the slaves thus obtained presumably provided productive occupations for the labor that they had engaged. Strict rules—usually ignored in practice—condemned this tactic. The constant demographic drain of the slave trade,

[52] Carlos Couto, *Os Capitães-mores em Angola no século XVIII* (Luanda, 1972), pp. 181–239. Also Silva Correa, *História de Angola,* vol. 1, p. 37; AHA, códice 3259, docs. 6, 10 (1760s); Arquivo Histórico Ultramarino (AHU), Lisbon, códice 1627, folios 2–3 (1790); Delgado, *Famosa e histórica Benguela,* p. 69 (1817).

[53] AHA, códice 3259, doc. 6, gives an example from 1761, when goods valued at 40$000 in Luanda were said to be worth 80$000 in the far interior. This was probably a statement in terms of currency values that the *banzo* equivalent to a *peça* consisted of half as many goods there as in the city.

[54] Silva Correa, *História de Angola,* vol. 1, p. 27 (1780s), complained of labor shortages with regard to ivory, which could not be transported from the interior for want of bearers to carry it. Douville, *Voyage au Congo,* vol. 1, p. 310, passed through Ambaca, a major point of departure for caravans heading east, and noticed the absence of population in the region in 1828–1829.

[55] AHU, códice 1633, folio 2 (example from 1796).

intensified by emigration to avoid the forced labor and other prestations to which Africans living under Portuguese control were subject, together with easy access to sanctuary in nearby African states, lurked as causes behind the inadequate supplies of head-bearers in Angola.

The strategies of all participants in the Angolan slave trade pivoted on minimization of maintenance and transportation costs, beginning with the large and specialized monopolist African suppliers—kings in Kasanje, Jinga, Holo, Mbondo, Bihe, Mbailundo, and elsewhere. Even lacking comprehensive evidence on their practices, the economics of their role in the trade explain why Kasanje kings made every effort to avoid supporting a large population of slaves awaiting sale at their marketplaces. They kept as small an inventory of captives as possible, preferring to wait for the arrival of a *sertanejo* before bringing more into the town. They would first accept the *sertanejo*'s goods on the promise to provide an agreed number of *peças* and then despatch messengers throughout their kingdom and beyond in search of people to be sold. As slaves gradually trickled into the royal residence in response to these directives, they were handed over as quickly as possible to the *sertanejo*, thereby making their maintenance his responsibility. A *sertanejo* could refuse immediate possession of the slaves only at the risk of inviting the king to deliver his prisoners to a competitor and forfeiting whatever goodwill he might have built up with his monopolist trading partner. The collection of a full coffle of slaves (*libambo*, or *quibuca*, as it was sometimes known in Angola)[56] involved weeks and months of delay for the *sertanejo*, as he waited for a return on the loan he had extended to the king, watched the expenses of maintaining a half coffle of slaves rise,[57] and paid higher and higher prices to an African monopolist who understood very well his haste to complete his business.[58]

THE SLAVES' LOT

Once a *sertanejo* had completed his exchanges of goods for slaves—probably calling at more than one marketplace and perhaps acquiring some

[56] Silva Correa, *História de Angola*, vol. 1, pp. 50–51, uses *libambo*, as do numerous documents. Oliveira Mendes, "Discurso academico," p. 21, terms the lot of slaves a *mampa* and identifies the *libambo* as the chain that bound them together. AHA, códice 3259, doc. 41, used *quibuca*.

[57] AHA, códice 3259, doc. 15, contains an explicit statement on the importance of haste in forwarding slaves of deceased *sertanejos* to creditors in Luanda; the creditors' concern must have derived from the desire to avoid expensive maintenance costs.

[58] The details of slave trading in African kingdoms are only obliquely documented; the reconstruction given here is based on complaints of merchants in Luanda about conditions primarily in the late eighteenth-century *feira* at Kasanje.

of his *libambo* from local bush traders (*pumbeiros*) who took his wares on credit and returned with small lots of slaves from locations too remote or insignificant to attract operators of the large caravans[59]—the *sertanejo* bulked a coffle of about 100 slaves, and the entire party set out for the lower Kwanza or marched directly toward Luanda. The *sertanejos* organized the returning caravans to minimize operating expenses at every opportunity. Slaves were fed only the cheapest rations available, often spoiled, and each carried his or her own provisions, mainly maize, beans, and manioc flour. The caravan's stores did not include salt or water, since water weighed too much to carry, and salt, which circulated as a currency in some parts of the interior, was too valuable to allot for slaves' consumption. Leaders under-staffed their caravans to save labor costs, and the few guards accompanying a *libambo* kept their slaves securely bound at all times and subjected them to harsh discipline apparently designed to break the will to escape or revolt.[60] The *sertanejos* and their personal slaves were heavily outnumbered, and they behaved cruelly, frightened men that they were. The slaves bore the consequences, or absorbed the costs, of short-run efficiencies of this sort, in the form of physical debilitation and psychological shock.

The size of the slave coffles provided yet another issue setting city merchants against the *sertanejos*. Merchants in 1790–1791 recommended that *libambos* not exceed 30–50 slaves, a size that seemed intended to ensure a smooth flow of slaves into Luanda and thus reduce merchants' maintenance costs in the town; they urged the *sertanejos* not to exceed in any case a maximum of 100 captives in a coffle.[61] The self-serving effect of the recommendation is obvious, assuming that some economies of scale occurred in the operation of larger slave caravans. Limiting the size of the *libambo* forced the caravan operators to spend more time per slave sold in traveling between Luanda and the slave *feiras*. At the same time, it assured a steady flow of slaves compared to the gluts and scarcities caused by irregular arrivals of fewer but larger caravans. In a year in which 10,000 slaves passed through Luanda, at least 100 coffles of the maximal size (not allowing for slave deaths and slaves retained in the city) would have come down from the interior at a rate of approximately 2 per week.[62]

---

[59] For the distinction between *sertanejo* and *pumbeiro*, AHA, códice 3529, docs. 23, 27 (1765), 66 (1792). Douville, *Voyage au Congo*, vol. 1, p. 62n, gives *pumbeiro* the significance here assigned to *sertanejo*. The distinction may not have been as rigid in practice as that assumed here for purposes of clarity in expression.

[60] Oliveira Mendes, "Discurso academico," in Carreira, "Companhias pombalinas," vol. 24, 1969, pp. 422–426.

[61] AHA, códice 3259, docs. 48, 49.

[62] This calculation oversimplifies, since slaves also arrived by launch from the trading stations on the Kwanza and from outlying bays along the coast.

The facilities provided for slaves when they finally reached Luanda were hardly better than the conditions they had endured en route. They waited in floorless, roofless pens until their owners found space aboard a vessel whose officers had received permission to take on slaves and to clear the port. Salt was relatively abundant and inexpensive in the city, and the slaves' basic diet continued to consist of maize and beans, supplemented by a small, oily fish plentiful in the nearby sea but unsalable to the free population of the city. Water was generally very scarce.[63]

Shortages of food and water were often acute in Luanda and created a persistent bottleneck in the movement of slaves toward Brazil. The city and its immediate environs chronically failed to provision the 4000 or so inhabitants and the slaves who were, each year, several times this number, and who had to be nourished while imprisoned in the city's baracoons and then supplied with foodstuffs for the ocean crossing.[64] Owing to the cost and difficulty of transporting provisions from the distant interior to the coast, Luanda drew its food mainly from plantations accessible by water, mainly in the lower Bengo and Kwanza valleys. The drain on local labor supplies—both by exports of slaves and by the employment of so many of the people remaining in one connection or another with slaving—also left agricultural labor in short supply. In consequence, Luanda was only intermittently self-sufficient in food. Merchants from time to time cornered supplies of essential commodities, and the supply of beans, manioc flour, and maize in the city market remained one of the most sensitive issues in the town.[65] Water shortages stemmed from Luanda's location in a sandy semidesert where, although a few wells in and around the city yielded reasonably fresh water, infrequent rains and inadequate ground water perennially taxed both the ingenuity of governors trying to remedy the situation and the pocketbooks of residents compelled to purchase notoriously filthy river water brought by boat from the Bengo.[66]

Some slavers avoided scarcities by importing provisions for their slave cargoes, including fresh water, from Brazil.[67] The seasonality of the food

[63] Oliveira Mendes, "Discurso academico," in Carreira, "Companhias pombalinas," vol. 24, 1969, p. 427.

[64] Silva Correa, *História de Angola*, vol. 1, pp. 46–47. AHA, códice 3259, doc. 26 (1765), mentions food imported from Benguela. Most lists of Brazilian exports to Angola (n. 14–15 preceding) included staple foods. AHU, códices 1634–1635, contain documentation of the efforts of one governor to alleviate a famine in 1791–1795 by securing imports of food from Brazil.

[65] For example, measures taken by a governor in the 1760s–1770s; Delgado, "Governo de Sousa Coutinho," vol. 10, 1962, pp. 28–29.

[66] Silva Correa, *História de Angola*, vol. 1, pp. 144–145; Douville, *Voyage au Congo*, vol. 1, · pp. 9–11, 46–49; Accursio das Neves, *Considerações sobre as possessões portuguezes*, pp. 191–193.

[67] Oliveira Mendes, "Discurso academico," in Carreira, "Companhias pombalinas," vol. 24,

shortages, although tempered by imported Brazilian rice, wheat, and manioc, influenced the tendency of ship departures to cluster in the dry months beginning each May. The rate of slave purchasing would have declined in the last months of each rainy season as the previous year's harvest was consumed, as prices of remaining supplies rose, and as shippers resisted buying food at hungry-season prices. They would then have rushed to leave after the new crop began to reach the market in May and during the succeeding months of the harvest season. According to one knowledgeable estimate, provisions for 8000 slaves in the 1780s required 15–19% of the manioc flour offered on the Luanda public market, 30–54% of the beans, and 24% of the maize. Yearly exports of slaves from the 1790s onward often exceeded that level by 50–100% and must have strained local food resources accordingly.[68] Scarcities may have moderated at least temporarily around 1819 when a brisk trade in provisions was reported flowing from Luanda to the northern ports of Ambriz, Zäire, and Cabinda.[69]

No matter how carefully slavers planned their departures from Luanda, the availability of slaves for sale often delayed captains hastening to clear port. Since merchants kept as few slaves as possible on hand in Luanda, and since the slaves reached the city in small lots spread throughout the year (although in somewhat larger numbers during the dry season months of improved food supplies and easier traveling in the interior), most ships spent 2–3 months or more acquiring a full cargo of slaves. In a typical year, in which 10,000 slaves left Luanda, they would have entered the city at a mean rate of less than 30 each day,[70] and an average of five ships competing to purchase them would have lain at anchor in the bay. A captain did well, therefore, if he could acquire slaves at the rate of a half dozen each day until he made up the 400–600 that he would need before he would leave.[71] The costs of lying at anchor mounted steadily without offsetting revenues, since the ship operators were paid a flat rate for each slave they transported safely to Brazil.[72] They rightly regarded time in port as unproductive—"barco ancorado, não ganha frete" was the saying[73]—and competition between

---

1969, p. 450. For Benguela in 1812, see Silva Rebelo, *Relações entre Angola e Brasil*, p. 212. Also undated general reference in Rodrigues, *Brazil and Africa*, p. 106.

[68] Silva Correa, *História de Angola*, vol. 1, pp. 50–51n, 115–117.

[69] Silva Rebelo, *Relacões entre Angola e Brasil*, p. 207.

[70] That is, 30 who would eventually leave the city alive. Deaths in Luanda meant that the total number of slaves entering the city would have been higher; cf. n. 93 to follow.

[71] The irregularity with which *sertanejos* in fact arrived caused ship captains to bid furiously for lots sufficient to complete their cargoes; Silva Correa, *História de Angola*, vol. 1, p. 50.

[72] Silva Correa, *História de Angola*, vol. 1, pp. 46–47; Carreira, "Companhias pombalinas," vol. 23, 1968, p. 67, prints instructions, given to a captain destined for Luanda, that reveal a buying strategy designed to minimize the costs of maintaining a partial load of slaves.

[73] Rough paraphrase: the ship at anchor earns no return.

captains rushing to buy slaves, purchase provisions, and clear port, constantly threatened to become disorderly and violent.

An elaborate set of rules technically regulated the order in which captains provisioned, loaded, and made sail; but knowledgeable masters avoided these regulations, often with official tolerance. Few government officials cared to resist the blandishments of shippers and merchants who monopolized space on outgoing vessels and who did not hesitate to refuse passage home to uncooperative government employees at the end of their appointments to Angola.[74] Ambitious Portuguese officials regarded Luanda as a dead end and must have felt that bending the rules was a small price—aside from whatever remuneration might also have been involved—for an eventual ticket back to what they regarded as civilization in America or Europe.

Merchants at both Luanda and Benguela, whether owning slaves or acting as commission agents on behalf of correspondents in Brazil, tried to distribute remittances of slaves over as many different ships as possible. The optimal strategy balanced risks of catastrophic mortality aboard a single ship struck by an epidemic or by delays at sea against the added costs of maintaining slaves in the town until additional vessels might arrive.[75] Because the distinction between ships arriving *de effeitos próprios* and those coming with goods belonging to several merchants referred only to incoming wares, it did not discriminate against ships carrying slaves belonging to several merchants.[76] Nor, since freight rates were fixed, did price differences encourage merchants to concentrate their shipments in particular vessels.

The multiplicity of ownership of the slaves on board each ship did, however, force merchants to take precautions against falsification of the identities of the slaves each owned. Unscrupulous captains smuggled inferior slaves aboard their ships and substituted them for the captives whom merchants had carefully selected from among the many offered for sale on the Luanda market. Owners limited the incidence of such thefts by branding their slaves with distinctive markings indicative of ownership; each successive owner of a slave—*sertanejos*, merchants, and masters—burned his mark into the flesh of their captive, and some slaves bore several such marks on their right and left breasts.[77] So important was branding to the orderly

---

[74] Silva Correa, *História de Angola,* vol. 1, p. 56, describes some of the tactics employed. See also Silva Rebelo, *Relações entre Angola e Brasil,* p. 80.

[75] Silva Correa, *História de Angola,* vol. 1, p. 50; and Oliveira Mendes, "Discurso academico," in Carreira, "Companhias pombalinas," vol. 24, 1969, p. 427, emphasized this strategy.

[76] Silva Correa, *História de Angola,* vol. 1, pp. 46–47, echoed the distinction.

[77] Oliveira Mendes, "Discurso academico," in Carreira, "Companhias pombalinas," vol. 23, 1968, pp. 362–363.

conduct of the trade that when a liberalized code governing sale and shipment of slaves eliminated the practice in 1813, Angolan merchants ignored the offending provisions and then managed to have those clauses of the decree modified in 1818.[78]

Two metropolitan Portuguese chartered companies that entered the slave trade in Angola for a few years during the 1770s and 1780s constituted an exception to the practice of distributing slave shipments over several vessels. The companies did not prosper in the Angolan trade, if their modest volume and early withdrawal accurately indicated their degree of success; and reasons for the company directors' disillusionment with Angola may have included their inability to duplicate the strategy of the local merchants. By investing in entire shiploads of slaves, they not only raised their risks of catastrophic loss at sea, but they also upset the delicately balanced relationships of buyers and sellers in Luanda. They did not carry slaves belonging to local traders and so had to buy every slave they loaded on the open market; the added demand raised local prices for slaves, unless—as seemed to be the case—company agents accepted inferior slaves for whom other buyers would not bid, slowed the company's rate of purchases, and correspondingly raised their costs of maintaining the slaves already purchased and awaiting embarkation.[79] In addition, the companies incurred the active opposition of local merchants and government officials who resented the facts that they bypassed many established merchant houses and flooded the market with cheap wares imported direct from Portugal.[80]

Significant diseconomies of scale must have affected the maritime segment of the Angola–Brazil slave trade, given the irregularities in the availability of slaves at Luanda and high costs for food and other provisions, as well as delays in the repair of ships in the harbor and, doubtless, many other inefficiencies apparent in the organization of slave trading. These occurred less in the economics of sailing ships on the high seas than in the inability of the Angola market to absorb the cargoes of large inbound vessels and in difficulties experienced in preparing and loading them for departure.[81] The local merchant community dreaded the arrival of large ships, especially those of the two Pombaline chartered companies. The sheer quantities they disgorged produced an inflation that drove upwards the ratio of goods to slaves for all. Rising slave prices in turn slowed the rate

---

[78] Silva Rebelo, *Relações entre Angola e Brasil,* pp. 75–79.

[79] Carreira, "Companhias pombalinas," vol. 23, 1968, pp. 349–350, 353.

[80] The Companhia Geral de Pernambuco e Paraiba may have employed a local merchant, Raimundo Jalamá, as its factor in Luanda; cf. Delgado, "Governo de Sousa Coutinho," no. 6, 1960, p. 20; and Oliveira Mendes, "Discurso academico," in Carreira, "Companhias pombalinas," vol. 23, 1968, pp. 46–47.

[81] The decree of 11 January 1758 recognized this aspect of slaving by granting marginal departure priorities to larger ships.

of slave purchasing, as shippers delayed in the hope of buying later at lower rates; and the queue of vessels waiting in the bay lengthened. When the turn of the large ships finally came up, they required longer to provision and to fill with slaves, so that others behind them in the order of preference found their expenses mounting, slave deaths increasing, and their purchases of slaves slowing while they waited.[82] Even the owners of the large ships were unlikely to have profited under such circumstances, since the chartered companies failed to maintain their initially intensive trading at Luanda; and the sizes of the vessels employed in the slave trade showed a tendency to decline between 1780 and 1830 as shippers evidently responded to these conditions by utilizing smaller craft. These efficiencies proceeded apace with the early nineteenth-century evolution of specialized merchant vessels out of the undifferentiated eighteenth-century military–mercantile corvette and the diversion of small Brazilian coastal craft into slaving after 1808. Reduced turnaround times and shortened rates of round trip voyages were apparent by the 1820s.[83]

Economies achieved in transporting slaves contributed heavily to ship overloading but probably only indirectly to the adverse effects on slave lives and constitutions, stressed by the critics of the slave trade. Slave ships leaving Angola nearly always declared cargoes at or near their authorized maximum, largely to lower the unit costs of transporting their cargoes. Brazilian venturers, who hoped to make trading gains as well as to recover transporting charges, generally calculated over 60% of their investment in a slaving voyage as transportation expenses, if late eighteenth-century estimates from Bahia and Rio de Janeiro were representative of the Angola trade as a whole.[84] Their profits therefore appeared more sensitive to efficiencies in transportation than to the cost of goods exchanged for the slaves, which, since the Angolan merchants and the *sertanejos* both took 50% margins to cover their own expenses, would have amounted to only one-fourth of their total investment in the slaves (FOB Luanda), exclusive

[82] Silva Correa, *História de Angola*, vol. 1, pp. 49–56.

[83] Unpublished analysis of data from the Public Record Office and the Biblioteca Nacional do Rio de Janeiro, the latter kindly provided by Professor Harold B. Johnson. See also Klein, "Trade in African Slaves"; and Klein and Engerman, "Shipping Patterns and Mortality." Conditions altered after 1836, when large vessels apparently became economical; Karasch, "Brazilian Slavers," p. 17.

[84] "Discurso preliminar, histórico, introductivo. . . . da comarca e cidade de Bahia (1790?)," *Anais da Biblioteca Nacional do Rio de Janeiro*, vol. 27, 1905, p. 342. Silva Rebelo, *Relações entre Angola e Brasil*, p. 88, reproduces a comparable estimated breakdown of the cost of a typical slave from Angola in the early nineteenth century. Cf. Francis E. Hyde, Bradbury B. Parkinson, and Sheila Marriner, "The Nature and Profitability of the Liverpool Slave Trade," *Economic History Review*, vol. 5, 1953, pp. 371–372, who indicate a similar ratio.

of transportation costs from Angola to Brazil.[85] They therefore tried to spread the costs of running the slave ships over the greatest possible number of slaves, filling the last places in the holds of their ships even at the cost of paying premium prices for the final slaves purchased. In effect, slaves were cheap to buy but costly to deliver.

Common carriers, who had a less direct financial stake in the welfare of their slave cargoes,[86] depended entirely on savings in transportation to return a profit. Lacking figures for the economics of sailing vessels in the southern Atlantic, no explanation for the treatment of slaves in terms of the costs of their transportation is conclusive; but the general pattern is clear by analogy with shipping elsewhere. Captains would have balanced the fixed costs of a voyage against the variable expenses involved in loading additional slaves relative to the *fretes*. If, as appears to have been the case, fixed costs for salaries, insurance, depreciation, and berthing and other charges exceeded expenses for slaves' food, supervision, and medication, common carriers would have derived the same incentive to pack their holds tightly in order to spread the fixed costs more widely.[87]

Transportation costs aside, factors that should have encouraged better treatment of slaves during the middle passage also entered into the calculations of merchants in Brazil and Angola. They must have taken into account the fact that every slave who died at sea represented the loss of an asset that could also be valued at the much higher sale price that he or she might bring in Rio, Pernambuco, or Bahia. Slave owners, however, seem to have been unable to control the slaving captains, who persisted in behaving with disregard for the slaves' chances for survival.[88] Other considerations that might have been decisive in producing the lethal conditions experienced at sea included the owners' and captains' inability to control the most common causes of slave deaths. Mortality at sea resulted in significant part from the deteriorated physical condition of slaves who, by the time they reached the African coast, had already lost too much strength to repay expensive medical attention. Slavers may also have calculated on the basis of expected death rates lower than those that actually occurred; sheer unfounded optimism, in fact, found some support from the patterns of mortality at sea,

[85] I am indebted to Dr. David Whynes of the University of York for pointing out to me the implications of the high transportation costs relative to goods costs.

[86] Silva Correa, *História de Angola,* vol. 1, p. 48, indicates that even they had some stake, since shippers were paid only for slaves they landed alive in Brazil. The entire matter of freighting and freight charges requires clarification.

[87] No precise calculation in support of this argument has been made, but the case rests on the analogy with shipping in the North Atlantic; Douglas C. North, "Sources of Productivity Change in Ocean Shipping, 1600–1850," *Journal of Political Economy*, vol. 76, no. 5, 1968, pp. 953–970.

[88] Silva Correa, *História de Angola,* vol. 1, pp. 172–173n.

since the most common mortality rates per voyage were significantly below the mean rate for all voyages. For example, rates half as great as the most commonly experienced ones still occurred frequently enough to have stirred hopes that each individual voyage might be more fortunate than proved to be the case in the aggregate. At some periods more deaths resulted from uncontrollable epidemics than from conditions that shippers could remedy, and wise captains responded to sickness in one of the African ports by seeking slaves elsewhere rather than by boarding fewer of them or providing larger stocks of food and water.[89] Finally, the medical knowledge of the time was too rudimentary to reduce death rates significantly, even if systematically applied. Many slavers carried medical practitioners, but experience showed some, at least, that African remedies were to be preferred over the bleedings given by European surgeons.[90]

Captains facing a trade-off between loading additional slaves and carrying supplies of food and water in the limited space at their disposal, disregarding as they did the discomfort attending crowded conditions below deck, apparently laid in provisions adequate to cover delays of only about half again the predicted voyage duration. Delays beyond that limit therefore occasionally produced disastrous results.[91] The chronic shortages of food and water at Luanda undoubtedly contributed also to the well-known lack of provisions for slaves at sea, since some slavers would have chosen to risk slave malnutrition rather than pay high prices in Luanda. Others would have brought few of the high-bulk, low-value foodstuffs from Brazil, if higher value commodities of lower bulk could be sold at a profit in Angola. Under either calculation, periods of high or increasing volume, like the 1780s–1830s, would have strained Angolan resources and the capacity of Brazilian shipping and thus contributed to worsening conditions on the returning slave ships at sea.

The art of smuggling slaves out of Angola, barely documented in the surviving records, may have exacerbated overloading and shortages of provisions, if practices commonly resembled one instance in Benguela in about 1816. Officers and crew of the slave ship *Livramento* concealed on board their vessel 158 slaves of a quality inferior to those legally boarded by

[89] Unpublished analysis of the distribution of mortality rates aboard Rio-bound vessels, 1795–1830.

[90] Oliveira Mendes, "Discurso academico," in Carreira, "Companhias pombalinas," vol. 24, 1969, pp. 447–449.

[91] Silva Correa, *História de Angola,* vol. 1, p. 56; Klein and Engerman, "Shipping Patterns and Mortality." For descriptions of conditions on board the slave ships, see Silva Correa, *História de Angola*, vol. 1, p. 57; Mello, "Relatorio," *Arquivos de Angola*, 1st series, vol. 2, no. 14, 1936, n.p.; Oliveira Mendes, "Discurso academico," in Carreira, "Companhias pombalinas," vol. 24, 1969, pp. 428–430.

merchants of the town. Food and water would have been loaded in proportion to the smaller number of authorized slaves. The smugglers intended to substitute the inferior slaves for those legally consigned to correspondents in Brazil while at sea and to dispose surreptitiously of the better slaves to their private advantage.[92] The ports of Cabinda, Zaïre, and Ambriz lacked effective government regulation and thus attracted slavers seeking to fill their holds beyond their authorized capacities, since the course of most Brazil-bound vessels took them close along the shores north of Luanda before they headed directly west and out to sea. Both these tactics limited the space available for provisions and courted disaster if the ship should encounter delays on its way to Brazil.

The arrival in Brazil of each shipload of slaves, the surviving remnants of much larger numbers of people originally sold and kidnapped in central Africa,[93] exhausted and sickened by a year or more of enforced existence at the minimum of physical subsistence, finally allowed merchants in Rio, Bahia, Pernambuco, Luanda, and Benguela to liquidate investments in trade goods and transportation that they had made anywhere from 1 to 2 years previously. Sale of the lot of slaves usually brought currency, promises, and bills of exchange.[94] Bills redeemable in Europe or Brazil against future purchases of manufactures, Asian textiles, and Brazilian produce closed a circle of reinvestment in the slave trade. Sales, however, often left the financial position of Angolan merchants far from liquid, even assuming that the venture had yielded a paper profit, if indebtedness was as extensive as appears to have been the case. Firms with large outstanding credits in their favor could afford to withdraw only at the cost of forfeiting most of the

[92] Silva Rebelo, *Relações entre Angola e Brasil*, p. 78. The *Livramento* was recorded as reaching Rio de Janeiro on 21 September 1816 with 515 slaves aboard; Henry Chamberlain to Viscount Castlereagh, 25 January 1817, PRO, FO63/202, folios 76–78. Judging from later arrivals in Brazil by the *Livramento,* the ship's authorized capacity was 541; if so, the smuggled slaves represented an overload of just under 30%.

[93] Solid estimates of the numbers who died before embarkation are not available, but one apparently knowledgeable observer (Raimundo Jalamá, cf. n. 80 preceding) of conditions during the 1780s used as working estimates death rates of 50% during the slaves' march to the coast and 40% (of the remainder) in Luanda; Oliveira Mendes, "Discurso academico," in Carreira, "Companhias pombalinas," vol. 24, 1969, pp. 427, 443–446. Early nineteenth-century merchants counted at 10–15% the value of slaves lost to deaths, flight, and trading losses taken on resale of slaves in Luanda; Silva Rebelo, *Relações entre Angola e Brasil*, p. 88. The discrepancy between the two figures may not have been as great as appears, since the latter estimate applied only to the period between their purchase of the slaves in the ports of Angola and the embarkation. Deaths occurring in Luanda or Benguela before purchase by Brazilian interests, presumably included in the estimate for the 1780s, would not have counted in the 10–15%.

[94] Oliveira Mendes, "Discurso academico," in Carreira, "Companhias pombalinas," vol. 24, 1969, pp. 430–434.

funds owed them by their own illiquid debtors. Nor was a debt-ridden firm likely to face foreclosure by its creditors, who knew that excessive pressure could lead only to bankruptcy for the debtor and losses for themselves.[95] Still, indebtedness did not imply unprofitability, and, if vague indications in the sources have been read correctly, at least the larger firms returned profits sufficient to support their owners in relative ease.

For many people, the central fact about the Angolan slave trade, as indeed for any trade in slaves, was the hardship that it imposed on the people enslaved. Abuses in this case resulted in part from a commercial and financial structure that included many expensive intermediate links between the initial captors of an individual in Africa and his or her final sale as a slave in Brazil. Under eighteenth-century limitations on the technology of administration, transportation, and communications, sequential ownership may have represented efficient commercial organization from the point of view of the consumers of slave labor; but the passage of the slaves through the hands of numerous small specialists in Brazil and Angola meant that none of the slaves' successive owners incurred responsibility for their long-term welfare. Slaves were expensive to maintain and tended to succumb rapidly to the effects of the treatment they had received at the hands of previous owners. As a result, each merchant, caravan operator, or shipper tried to maintain them in a physical condition minimally sufficient to allow quick resale. These practices left the buyers, who as a rule were also creditors of the sellers, to restore the sickest of the slaves to health. The effect was to repay debts in debased currency.

None among the dealers in slaves had much reason to undertake responsibility for their welfare, and some even ignored incentives for better care and demonstrations that improved treatment could lead to overall higher returns.[96] Although the full reasons for such apparent intransigence cannot now be divined, some inferences flow logically from the structure of the trade. The fact that transportation and maintenance costs equaled or exceeded the value of a slave in goods must have encouraged investors to risk the survival of their assets in order to lower the costs of bringing them to the point of sale in Brazil. In addition, many *sertanejos* and merchants in Luanda could not afford the additional investment necessary to provide better facilities or to improve their treatment of slaves, since they operated with working capital barely sufficient to keep ahead of their most pressing

---

[95] Silva Correa, *História de Angola*, vol. 1, pp. 38n, 51–52, mentions instances prior to 1789 in which firms attempted to liquidate and found themselves unable to realize more than one part in nine of what was owed them. Silva Rebelo, *Relações entre Angola e Brasil,* pp. 211–212, 573–574, cites a similar case in 1815.

[96] Silva Correa, *História de Angola,* vol. 1, pp. 172–173n; see also Oliveira Mendes, "Discurso academico," in Carreira, "Companhias pombalinas," vol. 24, 1969, pp. 447–449.

debts.[97] Merchants might have seen further that one firm could command premium prices in Brazil by improving the conditions in which it kept its slaves; but if all acted simultaneously they would merely raise costs, tighten the squeeze on provisions in Angola, and, by providing more expensive slaves to the final buyers in Brazil, risk reducing the number of healthier slaves that they might transport and sell—a prospect that must have looked unpromising to all but the most enlightened. Phrased in other terms, as long as no one sold slaves in better health, buyers would have to accept slaves in whatever condition they were offered. The slaves' welfare did not enter the picture, and merchants and governments gained from the increased volume. Viewing this process in terms of the physical condition of the slaves, an analogous effect worked in the opposite direction. Each owner passed the lots of slaves on to the next buyer in ever-worsening condition, accepting the deterioration in slaves' health and a certain number of deaths as a normal operating expense.[98] So long as he rid himself of the debilitated survivors as rapidly as possible, he was unlikely to experience unbearable losses to slave morbidity or mortality. Only the final purchasers of slaves in Brazil had no similar option, and they absorbed the consequences of prior mistreatment as a normal expense of employing slave labor, part of the well-known process of "seasoning."

Several aspects of the Angolan slave trade suggest that its participants may have seen the gains realized from transportation and maintenance of slaves as at least as important as the trading profits that have captured the attention of later analysts. Merchants paid so little for a slave in relation to the money price brought for her or him in Brazil that their profits depended as much on minimizing unit delivery expenses as on their slave-trading skills. This led to overcrowding of slave ships, shortages of provisions, and other strategies designed to increase volume at the expense of slaves' health or lives. In pursuing greater numbers, their interests coincided with the concerns of officials responsible for regulating the trade, since duties on both exports from Angola and imports to Brazil were levied on the basis of volume rather than the value of the slaves; the more captives that passed through the ports, in whatever condition short of dead, the greater the revenues flowing into royal coffers.[99]

[97] The demonstration of improved returns from better treatment of slaves was conducted by one of the Pombaline companies and was explicitly rejected by the local merchants as inapplicable to their circumstances. The company's longer-term interest in its slaves, as well as its better capitalization, must have figured in the indifference of the merchants to the results of the experiment.

[98] Silva Correa, *História de Angola*, vol. 1, p. 174n, noted that deaths were expected.

[99] Silva Correa, *História de Angola*, vol. 1, pp. 51–52, implies that some eighteenth-century traders recognized (and deplored) this effect of royal taxation.

CONCLUSIONS: A CONSTRAINING
ECONOMIC STRUCTURE

Late eighteenth- and early nineteenth-century slave traders in Angola faced significant restrictions on their ability to invest elsewhere than in local slaving. Royal decrees and Brazilian merchants hindered the movement of funds out of Angola, retarded the development of an autonomous Angolan merchant marine, and kept merchant capital from flowing into agricultural or other enterprises not directly related to slaving. Merchants who built up wealth at Luanda seem, first, to have invested in consumer imports, then to have expanded their slaving operations within Angola, and only belatedly to have found ways to purchase ships or begin selling in Brazil on their own account. Short-term inelasticities in the supply of slaves in the highly competitive environment of Luanda slaving limited the amount of funds that could usefully be applied to expanded slaving, since the common results were only inflation and risky loans of trade goods to bush traders. The persistent complaints of Angolan merchants during the decades before 1800 or so were symptoms of an economic structure that was also retarding diversification of the Angolan economy beyond its narrow concentration on the export of African labor. The expanding slave trade also braked economic diversification by reducing local labor supplies until government military expeditions lacked logistical support and local agriculture failed to feed the city of Luanda. These constraints, however, were not absolute. After the opening of Brazilian ports to foreign commerce, the merchants of Angola showed increasing signs of a financial independence that may eventually have supported economic reform that followed the end of legal slaving, later in the nineteenth century.

4

The Slave Trade in
the Bight of Benin, 1640-1890

PATRICK MANNING

Between 1727 and 1890, scores—probably hundreds—of Europeans
were invited to make the 90-mile journey by hammock from Ouidah to
Abomey, where they witnessed the Annual Customs of the kings of
Dahomey. There they were treated to several days of parades and specta-
cles, involving considerable human sacrifice, great displays of wealth, and
the adulation of the king by all his subjects. Meanwhile, throughout the
eighteenth century, directors of the English, French, and Portuguese forts
sat on the coast in Ouidah, attempted to increase the flow of slaves to their
nations' colonies, and took part in intrigues involving each other and a
variety of factions in the states of the region.

All eighteenth-century observers recognized Dahomey to be part of a
larger grouping, known variously as the Costa da Mina, Bight of Benin, or
Slave Coast, extending from Keta to beyond Lagos.[1] They remained,

[1] More recently, I. A. Akinjogbin has called this area the "Yoruba–Aja Commonwealth,"
including the northern and western Yoruba and all the Aja peoples. With the partition of the
area by the British and French, ties throughout the larger area were deemphasized for many
years.

nonetheless, fascinated with the kingdom of Dahomey and transfixed by their experiences at the Annual Customs and in the forts at Ouidah.

Accordingly, eighteenth-century writers developed two main aspects to the interpretation of Dahomey: a fascination with the power of the king, and an emphasis on slave trade as the key factor in Dahomean political history.

These two themes have remained dominant in the interpretation of eighteenth- and nineteenth-century Dahomey to this day. In the hands of various authors they sometimes coexist and at other times conflict, but the two are invariably present. The first theme has made Dahomey into a commonly cited example of African absolutism. The second has fueled an approach to African history that may be called "trade determinism."

Archibald Dalzel made a key contribution to the infamy of Dahomey by drawing together the writings of earlier observers and publishing *The History of Dahomy* in 1793.[2] Dalzel tied together the events recorded from the forts in Ouidah and on the road to Abomey with chronicles of an endless stream of wars and executions. So brutal and despotic is Dalzel's history that it might well have served as the source for Professor Trevor-Roper's conclusion, some years back, that African history was no more than the "picturesque but unrewarding gyrations of barbarous tribes."

The image of Dahomey created by the experiences in Abomey and Ouidah is so strong, especially as presented by Dalzel, that it shows up in all later writings.[3] That same image has also attracted writers with an axe to grind—writers who hoped to harness the strong symbolic content of the Annual Customs and the slave trade to the demonstration of the validity of their point of view. Many writings on the history of Dahomey are largely polemical. To cite three prominent examples, Dalzel himself wrote with the intention of defending the slave trade, Akinjogbin has bent much of his effort to refuting Dalzel, and Polanyi chose Dahomey as a society that would help validate his approach to institutional economics.[4]

By any standard, the interpretations given thus far, to the history and economic history of Dahomey, are inadequate. They are based on insufficient source materials, they include numerous errors, and they are limited to a narrow set of foci. They chronicle wars, they describe the

---

[2] Dalzel, *The History of Dahomy, an Inland Kingdom of Africa* (London, 1967).

[3] The French and English left the coast of Dahomey in 1797 and 1812 respectively, but when they returned in roughly 1840, they again saw Dahomey through the Annual Customs and from coastal forts and factories. Now, however, they were trying to restrict rather than expand the slave trade.

[4] Dalzel, *History;* I. A. Akinjogbin, *Dahomey and its Neighbours, 1707–1818* (Cambridge, 1967); Karl Polanyi, *Dahomey and the Slave Trade, an Analysis of an Archaic Economy* (Seattle, 1966).

institutions of the kingdom, and they trace disputes among European and Dahomean merchants and political figures over privileges in trade.[5]

From the viewpoint of the Dahomean historian, two types of work are needed to break out of this stereotyped historiography: first, a complete review of the historical record of the Bight of Benin beginning at least with the seventeenth century (and that historical record, as I attempt to indicate in the following, is more ample than is generally acknowledged); and second, a far more rigorous approach to the concepts used in interpreting history. An excellent way to begin an improvement of the concepts used in Dahomean history would be to make explicit those that have been used in the past. Thus, a thorough historiography of published works on the Bight of Benin from before Dapper to the present would be most illuminating.[6]

One aspect of the review of Bight of Benin history will be to study the slave trade, to confront questions of its nature, its magnitude, and its role in politics and society. Responses to these questions will also be of interest to students of slavery and the slave trade, not only because of the famous image of Dahomey, but also because some 1.9 million slaves from the Bight of Benin appear to have landed in the New World during the course of the trade.

The present study, after a few words on sources and geography, concentrates on a preliminary estimate of the number of slaves shipped from the Bight of Benin, some investigation of their ethnic origin, and a comparison of the slave trade estimates with interpretations given in several historical works.

RESOURCES FOR THE STUDY OF DAHOMEAN HISTORY

Since historians of Dahomey are to be faulted for failure to use all available resources, and since a wide range of resources is available, a review of the source materials may help indicate the degree to which the role of

[5] The biggest step toward the development of an adequate interpretation of the history of the area is the publication of Pierre Verger's *Flux et reflux de la traite des nègres entre le golfe de Bénin et Bahia de Todos os Santos du 17ᵉ et 18ᵉ siècles* (The Hague, 1968). Two recent and important studies are Robin Law, *The Qyǫ Empire, c. 1600–c. 1836* (Oxford, 1977), and Werner Peukert, *Der Atlantische Sklavenhandel von Dahomey* (Wiesbaden, 1978). In addition, David Ross's study of the Fon kingdom in the nineteenth century will be published soon.

[6] Beninois have unfortunately been left out of many discussions of Dahomean history. Several Beninois scholars are now preparing theses that will correct this imbalance. Past contributions of Dahomean authors may be found in *Etudes dahoméennes* (both the old series and new series). See also, for example Honorat Aguessy, "Le Dan-Homê du XIXᵉ siècle, était-il une société esclavagiste?" *Revue française d'études politiques africaines*, no. 50, February 1970, pp. 71–91.

slavery and slave trade in Dahomean history may eventually be elucidated. These are discussed in the following five categories.

The first category consists of a few well-known reports on Dahomey. These have been widely read and have often been the sole basis for studies of Dahomey which have become quite influential. Among the major reports are those of Dapper (based on observations from roughly 1600 to the 1660s), Barbot (based on observations up to 1682), Bosman (based on observations up to 1702), Labat (based on observations in 1725–1726), Snelgrave (based on observations up to 1732), Norris (based on observations up to 1772), Dalzel (1793), Duncan (1847), Forbes (1851), Burton (1864), and Skertchly (1874).[7]

Second, there are an immense number of additional reports, especially for the nineteenth century, which are less well known and less accessible than the preceding. Some of them, such as those of Pruneau de Pommegorge and Pires, are as extensive as the better-known reports.[8] Many others are useful in a variety of particulars. In the aggregate, they ought not to be ignored. A good start in the location of these works may be obtained by consulting the bibliography in Cornevin and that prepared by Da Silva.[9]

The third category is archival holdings. A great variety of archives have material on the history of Dahomey, and some of these holdings are extensive. What follows is a brief listing showing which authors have consulted which archives. None of these archives has been studied so thoroughly that it does not merit much more work. Reference to the works cited in this listing may, however, indicate what sort of information is to be found in each set of archives.

[7] O. Dapper, *Description de l'Afrique* (Amsterdam, 1682)—published in Dutch in 1668, also published in English as John Ogilby, *Africa: Being an Accurate Description . . .* (London, 1670); John Barbot, *A Description of the Coasts of North and South Guinea,* in Awnsham Churchill, ed., *A Collection of Voyages and Travels* (London, 1732), vol. 5, pp. 1–668; William Bosman, *A New and Accurate Description of the Coast of Guinea* (London, 1967); Jean Baptiste Labat, *Voyage du Chevalier des Marchais en Guinée, isles voisines et à Cayenne fait en 1725, 1726 & 1727,* vol. 2 (Paris, 1730); Capt. William Snelgrave, *A New Account of Guinea and the Slave Trade* (London, 1754); Robert Norris, *Memoirs of the Reign of Bossa Ahadee, King of Dahomy* (London, 1968); Archibald Dalzel, *The History of Dahomey* (London, 1967); John Duncan, *Travels in Western Africa in 1845 and 1846,* 2 vols. (London, 1847); Frederick E. Forbes, *Dahomey and the Dahomans,* 2 vols. (London, 1851); Richard Burton, *A Mission to Gelele, King of Dahome,* 2 vols. (London, 1864); J. A. Skertchly, *Dahomey as It Is* (London, 1874).

[8] Pruneau de Pommegorge, *Description de la Nigritie* (Paris, 1789); Vincente Ferreira Pires, *Crônica de una embaixada luso-brasiliera à Costa d'Africa* (São Paulo, 1957).

[9] Robert Cornevin, *Histoire du Dahomey* (Paris 1962); Guillaume da Silva, "Contribution à la bibliographie du Dahomey," *Etudes dahoméennes,* n.s., vol. 2, no. 12, June 1968, pp. 9–129, and vol. 3, no. 12, January 1969, pp. 9–162.

Lisbon: Pierre Verger has consulted these archives on Dahomey, mostly for the eighteenth century.[10]

The Hague: Johannes Postma has studied the Dutch slave trade, mostly for the period 1675-1794. Verger has dipped into these archives for the same period.[11]

Madrid: Labouret and Rivet retrieved documents on Ardra in the seventeenth century.[12]

Rome: David Ross has looked at missionary work in the nineteenth century. Earlier missionary records may await discovery.[13]

London: Davies, Akinjogbin, and Verger have studied the records of the Royal African Company. Records of the Foreign Office and the Colonial Office in the eighteenth and nineteenth centuries have been studied by Newbury, Akinjogbin, Coquery-Vidrovitch, Verger, and Ross.[14]

Paris: For the eighteenth century, Berbain, Akinjogbin, and Verger have studied archives of the Ministry of Marine and Colonies. For the nineteenth century, Schnapper, Coquery-Vidrovitch, Newbury, and Ross have studied archives of the Ministry of Marine and Colonies, and the latter three have also studied archives of the Ministry of Foreign Affairs.[15]

French Departments: These archives have been studied to a degree, especially the municipal archives of eighteenth-century Nantes, which have been studied by Martin, Berbain, and Akinjogbin. Other departmental archives studied include La Rochelle, Gironde, Loire-Atlantique, Seine-Maritime, Charente-Maritime, and Bouches-

---

[10] Verger, *Flux et reflux.*

[11] Johannes Postma, "The Dimension of the Dutch Slave Trade from Western Africa," *Journal of African History,* vol. 13, no. 2, 1972, pp. 237–248; Verger, *Flux et reflux.*

[12] Henri Labouret and Paul Rivet, *Le royaume d'Ardra et son evangelisation au XVIIᵉ siècle* (Paris, 1929).

[13] David Ross, "The Autonomous Kingdom of Dahomey, 1818–1894," doctoral dissertation (University of London, 1967).

[14] K. G. Davies, *The Royal African Company* (London, 1967); Akinjogbin, *Dahomey;* Verger, *Flux et reflux;* C. W. Newbury, *The Western Slave Coast and Its Rulers* (Oxford, 1961); Catherine Coquery-Vidrovitch, "Le blocus de Whydah (1876–1877) et la rivalité franco-anglaise au Dahomey," *Cahiers d'etudes africaines,* no. 77, 1962, pp. 373–419; Ross, "Autonomous Kingdom."

[15] Simone Berbain, *Le comptoir français de Juda au XVIIIᵉ siècle* (Paris, 1942); Akinjogbin, *Dahomey;* Verger, *Flux et reflux;* Bernard Schnapper, *La politique et le commerce français dans le Golfe de Guinée de 1838 à 1871* (Paris, 1961); Coquery-Vidrovitch, "Le blocus"; Newbury, *Slave Coast;* Ross, "Autonomous Kingdom."

[16] Gaston Martin, *L'Ere des Négriers* (Paris, 1931); Berbain, *Le comptoir;* Akinjogbin, *Dahomey;* Schnapper, *La politique.*

du-Rhône.[16] The late Jean Mettas undertook a monumental study of the French slave trade based on local and provincial archives; his work is being edited by Serge Daget.

Bahia: Verger has studied these archives in depth for the seventeenth through nineteenth centuries, and has reproduced many documents.[17]

Rio: Goulart has worked on the slave trade in the eighteenth and nineteenth centuries. Verger has also looked at these archives.[18]

French West Africa: Schnapper, Newbury, and Ross have worked on the last half of the nineteenth century.[19]

Porto-Novo: Newbury and Verger have studied the late nineteenth century.[20]

Ibadan: Newbury and Verger have studied the late nineteenth century.[21]

Missionary archives: Akinjogbin looked at the Church Missionary Society archives; he, Newbury, and Ross looked at the Methodist archives; and Schnapper looked at the archives of the Pères du Saint-Esprit.[22]

Marseille: Schnapper looked at the archives of the Marseille Chamber of Commerce.[23]

The fourth major group of sources consists of oral traditions. These have been collected by a wide variety of authors since the beginning of the colonial period, but most significantly by Le Herissé, Johnson, Herskovits, Dunglas, and Akindélé and Aguessy.[24] Although these traditions provide, to a large degree, an independent source on the history of the Aja and Yoruba peoples, none of them have been collected scientifically. That is, one cannot distinguish the tradition itself from modifications given to it by the researcher, nor can one separate the tradition from material and ideas gathered by the researcher from published materials such as Dalzel's his-

[17] Verger, Flux et reflux.

[18] Mauricio Goulart, Escravidão Africana no Brasil (São Paulo, 1950); Verger, Flux et reflux.

[19] Schnapper, La politique; Newbury, Slave Coast; Ross, "Autonomous Kingdom."

[20] Newbury, Slave Coast; Verger, Flux et reflux.

[21] Ibid.

[22] Akinjogbin, Dahomey; Newbury, Slave Coast; Ross, "Autonomous Kingdom"; Schnapper, La politique.

[23] Schnapper, La politique.

[24] Auguste Le Herissé, L'ancien royaume du Dahomey (Paris, 1911); Samuel Johnson, The History of the Yorubas (Lagos, 1921); Melville J. Herskovits, Dahomey, an Ancient West African Kingdom, 2 vols. (New York, 1938); Edouard Dunglas, "Contribution à l'histoire du Moyen-Dahomey," Etudes dahoméennes, nos. 19–20, 1957; A. Akindélé and C. Aguessy, Contribution à l'étude de l'histoire de l'ancien royaume de Porto-Novo (Dakar, 1953).

tory. It remains possible to do a more scientific job of collecting the traditions, which have not disappeared, though they have surely been distorted with the passage of time.[25]

The fifth and final group of sources is the information that may become available through the study of social anthropology, linguistics, and archaeology. A great deal of work has been done on Dahomey by anthropologists, especially on religion and divination, but including some on social structure.[26] This type of work could be applied to historical enquiry. The languages of the area have been well studied, though the research is dispersed in a variety of small publications; it would be possible to study aspects of the economic history of the Bight of Benin through linguistics. Virtually no iron-age archaeology has been done in Dahomey. Such work could be quite useful for an understanding of the last few centuries, as in reconstructing the ethnic and political map, trade patterns, and systems of production. The European forts and factories could be excavated.

In sum, the sources on Dahomey since 1600 are relatively rich, although digging out the material, assembling it, and interpreting it will be a laborious task. The point, however, of this emphasis on the wealth of sources is to urge that, henceforth, historians desist from interpreting and reinterpreting the history of Dahomey through the same few sources only, as, for example, Karl Polanyi has done.[27]

PLACE NAMES

The literature on the seventeenth, eighteenth, and even nineteenth century in Dahomey contains much confusion on the names of towns and ethnic groups. This geographical confusion has led in turn to confusion of the political and economic history of the area. Virtually every author writing on the Bight of Benin has included a section locating the towns. Yet in virtually every case significant errors remain, and insufficient attention has

[25] For some recent work with oral traditions, see Peter Morton-Williams, "The Oyo Yoruba and the Atlantic Trade, 1670–1830," *Journal of the Historical Society of Nigeria,* vol. 3, no. 1, December 1964, pp. 25–46; and Jacques Lombard, "Contribution à l'histoire d'une ancienne société politique au Dahomey: La royauté d'Allada," *Bulletin de l'IFAN,* vol. 29, 1967, pp. 40–66.

[26] For example, Herskovits, *Dahomey*; Bernard Maupoil, *La géomancie à l'ancienne Côte des Esclaves* (Paris, 1943): Pierre Verger, *Notes sur le culte des Orisa et Vodun* (Dakar, 1957); Paul Hazoumé, *Le pacte du sang au Dahomey* (Paris, 1937).

[27] Polanyi, *Dahomey*. Some of the studies based on limited sources are sophisticated and informative. For example, W. J. Argyle, *The Fon of Dahomey* (Oxford, 1966) and Jacques Lombard, "The Kingdom of Dahomey," in D. Forde and P. M. Kaberry, eds., *West African Kingdoms in the Nineteenth Century* (London, 1967). Nonetheless, they tend to reinforce the stereotyped themes in Dahomean history.

been called to the discrepancies among various authorities.[28] My own impression is that there has been great stability in the towns and, to a lesser degree, in the location of ethnic groups. Unquestionably, however, the names given to towns and peoples by Europeans changed radically with passage of time. Rather than attempt to unravel the errors in the literature step by step, I will present an interpretation of the location of coastal towns in the seventeenth through nineteenth centuries (see Figure 4.1).[29]

Going from west to east, Keta, Little Popo (Anecho) and Grand Popo have been identifiable since 1600. At some points, authors confused Little Popo and Grand Popo or assumed that they had a single king. Grand Popo is also often reported to have been an island, but probably it was always the long peninsula it is today, perhaps with a marshy area in the peninsula. Allegations by seventeenth-century writers that Little Popo, Grand Popo, and Ouidah were ruled earlier by Ardra are backed by no specifics and may just as well be disbelieved.

In the Hueda kingdom, the capital was at Savi, 10 kilometers inland, and so too were the European factories from the 1680s to the 1720s. Ouidah (Whydah to the English, Glehoue to the Hueda) was known to the Dutch of the 1650s as Foulaan and later as Fida. The town, 4 kilometers from the beach, was the site of the forts built beginning 1701. Akinjogbin gives the Yoruba name of Igelefe to Ouidah town.

Three main towns have been identified by European writers in the kingdom of Ardra, all known since the early seventeenth century. Ardra itself (Great Ardra) is the modern town of Allada. Jakin, the port town, is the modern Godomey. It is distant from the beach by 5 kilometers. Offra, the town where the Dutch and English factories were first set up, is the modern town of Abomey-Calavi, 7 kilometers inland from Godomey. Writers and mapmakers often confused Offra and Jakin. The name of Little Ardra was given at various times to Godomey, to Godomey beach, and to Abomey-Calavi, in the period during which the kingdom of Ardra existed.

Cotonou did not become a port or a town until the 1840s, when it became an entrepôt in the palm oil trade.

---

[28] A significant clarification of place names for the seventeenth century, at least, has been achieved through two recent articles: Pierre Verger, "Les côtes d'Afrique occidentale entre Rio Volta et Rio Lagos, 1535–1773," *Journal de la société des africanistes,* vol. 38, no. 1, 1968, pp. 35–58; and Yves Person, "Dauma et Danhome," *Journal of African History,* vol. 15, no. 4, 1974, pp. 547–561. See also Yves Person, "La toponymie ancienne de la côte entre la Volta et Lagos," *Cahiers d'E:udes Africaines,* vol. 15, no. 60, 1974, pp. 715–722.

[29] A complete review and correction of names of towns and ethnic groups will ultimately have to be done. Since I could find no halfway point, I have not cited references for the statements in the rest of this section. This section and the accompanying map are intended primarily as a guide to those wishing to read the sources and authorities on the history of the Dahomean coast.

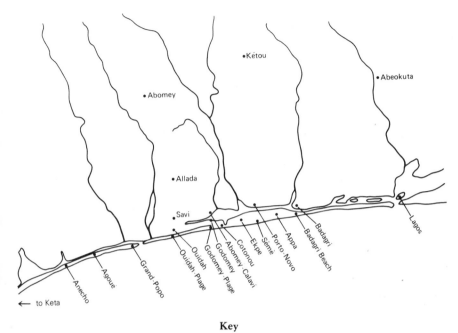

Key

Current name	Other names given (century)
Keta	Coto (17th–18th), Quittah (18th–19th)
Anecho	Petit Popo (Little Popo), Popo (17th–18th)
Agoué	Founded 19th
Grand Popo	Popo (17th–18th)
Ouidah-Plage	
Ouidah	Foulaan (17th), Fida (17th–18th), Whydah (17th–20th), Glehoue (in Hueda and Fon), Igelefe (in Yoruba)
Savi	(Mostly destroyed 1727)
Allada	Ardres (17th–18th), Ardra (17th–18th), Great Ardra (17th–18th)
Godomey-Plage	Little Ardra (17th–18th)
Godomey	Jakin (17th–18th), Little Ardra (17th–18th)
Abomey-Calavi	Offra (17th–18th), Jakin (17th–18th)
Cotonou	Founded 19th
Ekpe	Epe (17th–19th), Apa (18th–19th), Appi (17th–19th)
Sèmè	Porto-Novo (18th), Little Ardra (18th), Porto-Novo-Plage (19th)
Porto-Novo	Little Ardra (18th), Great Ardra (18th), Porto-Novo (19th)
Appa	
Badagri Beach	
Badagri	
Lagos	Onim (18th–19th)

Figure 4.1 Map of the Bight of Benin in the seventeenth through the nineteenth centuries, locating coastal towns.

Ekpe was the next port east. It, too, is 4 kilometers inland. This port seems rarely, if ever, to have been under the control of any but its own king, and it was known from the seventeenth century. Because of the many ways in which the town's name was spelled (often Epe or Appi), it can easily be confused with Appa, to the east.

The ports east of Ekpe seem to have gone virtually without visits from merchant ships until at least the 1730s. Badagri and Lagos began to be noted as ports for the slave trade in the 1730s and 1740s, and Porto-Novo in the 1750s.

Porto-Novo traded sometimes by communication through the lagoon to Lagos, to Ekpe, or to Porto-Novo beach (now Sèmè), 12 kilometers south of Porto-Novo. In the mid-eighteenth century some writers called Porto-Novo Little Ardra, in contrast to Great Ardra (Allada). Later in the century, Porto-Novo came to be called Ardra or Great Ardra, and Sèmè was called Little Ardra or, more frequently, Porto-Novo. Modern Porto-Novo itself (Hogbonou in Gun, Ajashe in Yoruba) has been the capital and the main town of the kingdom since it was founded. Akinjogbin's assertion that the capital was 25 miles inland at a place called Ajashe-Ipo is without foundation.

Appa entered the trade in the late eighteenth century and was never very important. It can easily be confused with Ekpe.

Badagri traded either by communication through the lagoon to Lagos, or at the beach 5 kilometers south of the town.

Lagos, known as Onim to the Brazilians, was known to navigators from the earliest days but did not become a place of significant trade until the late eighteenth century.

HOW MANY SLAVES?

Table 4.1 gives estimates of the number of slaves exported, by decade and by exporting nation, for the coast from Little Popo through Lagos. It is based on the approach and the estimates of Curtin, but it includes figures revised from or in addition to Curtin's estimates, and it includes some guesses I have concocted in order to fill in the table.[30]

In addition to the normal error that might be expected from such estimates (±20%, according to Curtin), the factor of mortality introduces a

[30] Philip D. Curtin, *The Atlantic Slave Trade: A Census* (Madison, 1969). A major updating of the figures in this work is given in Curtin, "Measuring the Atlantic Slave Trade," in Stanley L. Engerman and Eugene D. Genovese, eds., *Race and Slavery in the Western Hemisphere: Quantitative Studies* (Princeton, 1975), pp. 107–128.

TABLE 4.1
Estimated Slave Exports from the Bight of Benin

Decade	Brazil[a]	English[b]	French[c]	Dutch[d]	Spanish and American[e]	Total
1641–1650	3000	—	—	9000	—	12,000
1651–1660	3000	—	—	6000	—	9000
1661–1670	5000	—	—	12,000	—	17,000
1671–1680	10,000	5000	5000	12,000	—	32,000
1681–1690	17,200	22,800	5000	10,200	—	55,200
1691–1700	60,800	18,500	10,000	15,600	—	104,900
1701–1710	86,400	47,400	15,000	12,500	—	161,300
1711–1720	67,200	55,800	16,700	13,700	—	153,400
1721–1730	63,400	30,200	18,200	8400	—	120,200
1731–1740	49,000	27,300	32,100	9600	—	118,000
1741–1750	39,200	26,800	4100	—	—	70,100
1751–1760	34,400	12,000	23,600	500	—	70,500
1761–1770	36,000	26,700	40,000	—	—	102,700
1771–1780	30,000	24,800	35,300	600	—	90,700
1781–1790	32,700	54,700	65,700	—	—	153,100
1791–1800	53,100	7300	8600	—	5000	74,000
1801–1810	72,400	3900	—	—	5000	81,800
1811–1820	59,000	—	—	—	24,800	83,800
1821–1830	51,800	—	—	—	25,700	77,500
1831–1840	54,800	—	—	—	50,900	105,700
1841–1850	63,000	—	—	—	18,000	81,000
1851–1860	10,000	—	—	—	38,200	48,200
1861–1870	5000	—	—	—	19,100	24,100
1871–1880	—	—	—	—	—	—
1881–1890	—	—	—	—	—	5000[f]
1641–1700	99,000	46,300	20,000	64,800	—	230,100
1701–1800	491,400	313,000	259,300	45,300	5000	1,114,000
1801–1890	316,500	3900	—	—	181,700	507,500
1641–1890	906,900	363,200	279,300	110,100	186,700	1,851,200

[a] See Appendix 4.2 for details.

[b] See Appendix 4.3 for details.

[c] For 1711–1800, estimates of Curtin, pp. 170, 200. For 1671–1710, my guesses.

[d] See Appendix 4.4 for details.

[e] See Appendix 4.5 for details.

[f] My guess, based on Newbury, *Slave Coast,* p. 130, and Archives nationales du Bénin (Porto-Novo), Registres de Correspondance, 1880–1893.

significant ambiguity into these calculations. Most of the studies on which
Table 4.1 is based are estimates of the number of slaves disembarked in the
New World. A few studies, such as Postma's on the Dutch trade, are
estimates of the number of slaves embarked in Africa. Other studies are
ambiguous and include elements of both approaches. The difference between the two approaches is the slave mortality during the crossing from the
Bight of Benin to the New World, which ranged generally from 10% to
20%. Table 4.1, which includes elements of both approaches, is therefore
best seen as a low estimate of the number of slaves embarked in Africa.

The estimates for exports to Brazil are based on shipping data given by
Verger, and follow assumptions Verger has laid down (see details in Appendix 4.2).[31] For the eighteenth century, these estimates are slightly
smaller than those of Goulart, which Curtin has used.[32]

The English estimates for 1681–1700 are based on data given by Davies
for the value of imports by the Royal African Company to Ardra and
Whydah (see Appendix 4.3).[33] The English estimates for 1701–1810 are
those of Curtin, as he revised them based on Anstey's work. It should be
noted that Curtin's estimates are derived by estimating a total amount for
the English trade to the West Indies, and then apportioning it among
regions in Africa according to relative percentages given by various authorities. These are, of course, subject to a margin of error. In particular, it
may be that to apply the percentage for 1711–1720 to the period 1701–
1710 results in too high an estimate of the English trade on the coast of
Dahomey in that period.[34]

The French estimates from 1711 are those of Curtin, based on shipping
data from Martin and Rinchon.[35] These figures may be expected to be
superseded in the near future by data provided by the late Jean Mettas and
Serge Daget. Estimates for the period before 1710 are my own guesses,
based on the knowledge that the French were there, and the belief that the
volume of their trade was well below that of the English.[36]

The Dutch trade has been studied in some detail by Postma. The preliminary estimates given in Appendix 4.4 are based on his two summary
articles.[37]

[31] Verger, *Flux et reflux*, pp. 651–669.

[32] Goulart, *Escrividâo*, pp. 203–209; Curtin, *Census*, p. 207.

[33] Davies, *Royal African Company*, pp. 233, 236–237, 357.

[34] Curtin, "Measuring," p. 123; Roger Anstey, "The Volume and Profitability of the British
Slave Trade, 1761–1807," in Engerman and Genovese, *Race and Slavery*, pp. 3–31.

[35] Curtin, *Census*, pp. 170, 200.

[36] For ninteenth-century French trade see Chapter 11 in this volume.

[37] Postma, "Dimension," and "The Origin of African Slaves: The Dutch Activities on the
Guinea Coast, 1675–1795," in Engerman and Genovese, *Race and Slavery*, pp. 33–49.

The American and Spanish trade, notably to Cuba but also to the Gulf Coast and Puerto Rico, is known to have taken place from the Napoleonic Wars to the abolition of slavery. David Eltis's revision of the 1845 Parliamentary Paper clarifies this trade for the period 1821–1843; otherwise I have relied on Curtin's estimates.[38] Details of these estimates are given in Appendix 4.5.

In addition, other elements of this region's slave trade surely await discovery. For example, several hundred slaves are known to have been purchased by the Danes at Grand Popo in the 1770s.[39]

A second sort of information on the volume of slave trade consists of many isolated estimates recorded by observers on the African coast. These estimates seem to be far less dependable than the shipping and import data cited previously. Especially in the seventeenth and early eighteenth centuries, they are much higher than the figures in Table 4.1.

The earliest published estimate of the volume of the slave trade from the Bight of Benin is d'Elbée's assertion in 1670 that 3000 slaves were sold each year at Offra to the Dutch and English.[40] The implied figure of 30,000 per decade is well above the 17,000 I have estimated for 1661–1670, especially when it is considered that d'Elbée included only one port and only two of the three slave-trading nations. In 1678 the Royal African Company factor at Offra reported that 6000–7000 slaves per year were available there.[41] That would imply up to 70,000 slaves per decade, again from one port, as opposed to my estimate of 32,000 for the whole coast, 1671–1680.

Shipping records for the Portuguese, English, and Dutch become much more reliable than previously in the 1680s, and they indicate a total export of some 5000 slaves per year. Barbot, however, reported, based on observations in 1682, that the Dutch bought 3000 slaves per year at Offra, and that Ouidah could provide another 1000 slaves per month—an implied total of at least 15,000 slaves per year for the whole coast.[42] The figure of 1000 slaves per month from Ouidah was repeated by two other observers in the 1690s, Bosman and D'Amon.[43] Ducasse gave fairly comprehensive estimates for the year 1687: 300 per year total from Little Popo and Grand

[38] Curtin, *Census,* pp. 234, 237.

[39] See Svend E. Green-Pedersen, "The History of the Danish Negro Slave Trade, 1733–1807," *Revue française d'histoire d'outre-mer,* vol. 62, nos. 226–227, 1975, pp. 196–220.

[40] D'Elbée, as quoted in Labat, *Voyage,* vol. 2, p. 321.

[41] Davies, *Royal African Company,* p. 228.

[42] Barbot, *Description,* pp. 326–327, 350. Barbot also claimed that 40–50 ships per year came to Ouidah (p. 335).

[43] Bosman, *Description,* p. 343; Le Chevalier D'Amon, "Relation du voyage de Guynée fait en 1698," in Paul Roussier, *L'Etablissement d'Issiny, 1687–1702* (Paris, 1935), pp. 82–83.

Popo to the English and Dutch, 4000–5000 per year from Offra to the
Dutch, 14,000–15,000 per year from Ouidah to the English, and 600–700
per year from Ouidah to the French.[44] This estimate means, at maximum,
21,000 slaves per year and cannot be supported by shipping evidence. It
may be noted that all the preceding observers have ignored the Portuguese
trade, although it was perhaps the largest. It is a puzzling omission.

For the period after 1700, Berbain retrieved a document from the French
archives dividing up the Ouidah trade in 1716 as follows: 5000–6000 per
year to the French, 6000–7000 per year to the English, 1000–1500 per year
to the Dutch, and 6000–7000 per year to the Portuguese, a total of
18,000–21,500.[45] According to Table 4.1, however, the trade for the whole
coast averaged 15,000 per year in that decade, and Ouidah was not the only
port. Labat gives figures of 16,000–18,000 per year for Ouidah in the
period 1725–1726.[46] Perhaps a more dependable observer was the slave
ship captain Atkins, who estimated that the trade of Ouidah had been about
half that of the whole Guinea coast for the period roughly from 1710 to
1727, that the figure had hit 20,000 exports in certain years, and that 40–50
ships per year visited the port.[47]

Akinjogbin has noted several fragmentary estimates of the slave trade.
He cites a 1744 statement that Little Popo, Ekpe, and Badagri each exported more slaves than Ouidah.[48] For 1750 he cites a statement that 9000
slaves were sold annually at Ouidah, 4000 to the Portuguese and 5000 to
the French.[49] Patterson has cited a French document showing 10,900 exports from the whole coast in 1765, 5000 from Ouidah.[50] Norris gives a
figure of 5000–6000 slaves per year from Ouidah in 1772.[51] Labarthe gives
figures of 10,150 slaves from Ouidah in 1776, and a decrease to 3605 slaves
from Ouidah in 1787.[52] Donnan gives estimates for 1789 for the whole
coast: 100 from Grand Popo, 4500 from Ouidah, 3500 from Porto-Novo
and Badagry, and 3500 from Lagos and Benin, for a total of 11,600.[53] Each

[44] Jean-Baptiste Ducasse, "Relation du voyage de Guynée fait en 1687. . .," in Roussier,
Issiny, pp. 14–15.

[45] Berbain, *Le comptoir*, p. 52.

[46] Labat, *Voyage*, vol. 2, p. 103.

[47] John Atkins, *A Voyage to Guinea, Brasil, and the West-Indies* (London, 1737), pp. 111, 157,
172. Snelgrave (*New Account*, p. 2) asserted that over 20,000 slaves were exported yearly from
Ouidah "and the neighbouring Places."

[48] Akinjogbin, *Dahomey*, p. 115.

[49] Akinjogbin, *Dahomey*, p. 134.

[50] K. David Patterson, "A Note on Slave Exports from the Costa da Mina, 1760–1770,"
Bulletin de l'IFAN, vol. 33, no. 2, 1971, p. 255.

[51] Norris, *Memoirs*, pp. 62, 147.

[52] As cited in Newbury, *Slave Coast*, p. 26.

[53] E. Donnan, *Documents Illustrative of the History of the Slave Trade*, vol. 2 (Washington,
1931), p. 598.

of these estimates is conceivably valid for the given year, but they are generally too large by some 50% to be consistent with the figures in Table 4.1.

For the nineteenth century, few global estimates of the slave trade of the Bight of Benin have been published. Cruickshank estimated that Dahomey exported 8000 slaves in 1848, and the British navy in the 1840s estimated 10,000 slaves per year for the Bight of Benin.[54] The 1848 British Foreign Office estimates of the nineteenth-century slave trade, which became quite influential, have been shown by Curtin to be exaggerated.[55] On the other hand, Eltis has used Foreign Office records to reconstruct detailed estimates, slightly higher than Curtin's, of African exports and New World imports for 1821–1843.[56]

All in all, the makers of isolated estimates on the African coast, especially in the early years, overstated the volume of the slave trade. As Curtin has suggested, they tended to see a "normal" year as one in which the trade was at·a high level.[57] They also confused the actual volume of trade with the volume of trade they thought attainable. Or, as seems to be the case for Ducasse in 1687, they would exaggerate the trade of other nations in order to get more support for the trade from within their own nation.

Information on the relative contribution of various ports to the slave trade is of great interest to historians. Unfortunately, it is hard to come by, especially since the most systematic estimates of the volume of the trade come from New World shipping and import data. Nevertheless, some estimates of the volume of trade by port have survived, and it is possible to fill them out, to a degree, with qualitative impressions from the literature.

By the 1650s the Dutch and Portuguese knew and visited the ports of Keta, Little Popo, Grand Popo, Ouidah, Jakin, and Ekpe. The Portuguese gained passports from the Dutch at Elmina to visit Grand Popo, Ouidah, Jakin, and Ekpe. Jakin was apparently the most significant slave port. English merchants had come to Jakin and Offra by the 1670s, and French merchants followed them to the coast. During the 1680s, Ouidah surpassed Jakin as the principal slave port of the coast. Whereas writers of the 1670s and before had given most of their attention to the kingdom of Ardra, writers of the 1680s and after gave more attention to the Hueda kingdom.[58] Slave trade continued, meanwhile, at Grand Popo and Ekpe; it has been poorly recorded partly because it was of a smaller volume, and partly

---

[54] Newbury, *Slave Coast*, pp. 10, 51.

[55] Curtin, *Census*, pp. 233–235.

[56] See Chapter 11 in this volume.

[57] Curtin, *Census*, p. 17.

[58] Compare the emphasis of Dapper and d'Elbée on Ardra with the emphasis of Barbot, Bosman, and Labat on the Hueda kingdom.

because the weaker political authorities there did not merit much diplomatic attention.

From the 1690s through the 1720s, Ouidah continued to be the principal port, and Jakin presumably was in second place, perhaps a distant second. With the Dahomean conquest of Ardra in 1724, the town and factories of Offra were destroyed. Dahomey traded in slaves through Jakin, which it did not at first rule directly. In 1727 Dahomey conquered the Hueda kingdom and destroyed the town and factories of Savi. The slave trade henceforth was organized around the European forts at Ouidah. In 1732–1734 Dahomey conquered Jakin and destroyed the Dutch and other factories there. Trade at Jakin then ceased, and virtually all trade of Dahomey went through Ouidah.[59]

Slave traders complained of the decline in the slave trade following the Dahomean conquest to the coast, though the figures in Table 4.1 do not suggest a sharp decline for the whole coast. It may be that the slave trade of Grand Popo increased, beginning 1730, as the expelled Hueda dynasty fought for decades to regain its patrimony, from an area north of Grand Popo, and in alliance with the rulers of Grand Popo and Little Popo.[60] Similarly, it may be that the trade of Ekpe increased at the same time— partly as a result of trade by exiles from Jakin, as well as the Weme to the north across the lagoon, and partly through slaves sent down from Oyo.

In the 1730s and 1740s new ports to the east began to open up. Badagri and Lagos were opened up, apparently, by Brazilian and Dutch merchants. Porto-Novo is mentioned, beginning in the 1750s.[61] This opening of new ports is usually explained through their alliance with Oyo, which apparently sought to market slaves at Porto-Novo since the terms there were better than in Dahomey, where they had previously marketed slaves at Cana and at Offra.[62]

Three separate estimates of the slave trade in the latter part of the eighteenth century are summarized by port in Table 4.2. The first and third

[59] Akinjogbin, *Dahomey,* pp. 68–100. Postma ("Origin," p. 48) gives the following list for Dutch West Indies Company "lodges" on the Slave Coast:

Offra	1660s–1724
Ouidah	1670s–1734
Jakin	1726–1734
Appa (Ekpe)	1732–1736; 1742–1749; 1754–1755
Badagri	1737–1744; 1748
Popo	1738–1740; 1744; 1752–1760

[60] Hueda raids on Ouidah continued into the 1780s and then appear to have ceased.

[61] Verger, *Flux et reflux,* pp. 207–208; Akinjogkin, *Dahomey,* pp. 105–115; and see n. 59 preceeding.

[62] Morton-Williams, "The Oyo Yoruba."

TABLE 4.2

Estimated Slave Exports, by Port

Port	Total trade, 1765 (French estimate)[a]		Brazilian trade 1760–1770[b]		Total trade, 1789 (British estimate)[c]	
Keta	800	(7%)	—		—	
Little Popo	100	(1%)	—		—	
Grand Popo	2000	(18%)	—		100	(1%)
Ouidah	5000	(46%)	8754	(39%)	4500	(39%)
Ekpe	600	(6%)	3716	(17%)	—	
Porto-Novo	1200	(11%)	3756	(17%)	3500	(30%)
Badagri	800	(7%)	5058	(22%)		
Lagos	400	(4%)	984	(4%)[d]	3500	(30%)[e]

[a] Paris, Archives nationales (about 1765), as quoted in Patterson, "Slave Exports," p. 255.
[b] Lisbon, Arquivo Histórico Ultramarino, as quoted in Patterson, "Slave Exports," p. 253.
[c] Privy Council, as quoted in Donnan, *Documents,* Vol. 2, p. 598.
[d] Includes 285 slaves from "Betam" (Benin?).
[e] Lagos and Benin.

are estimates of the entire trade for the coast. The second is a complete record of Brazilian ships that stopped at Principe on the way back to Brazil (Patterson estimates that these account for two-thirds of the Brazilian ships trading to the Costa de Mina).[63] The differences among the estimates may be an indication of the reliability of the estimates, the fluctuating nature of the trade, or both. The apparent move of the slave trade to the east in the 1780s is consistent with other evidence. By the 1780s, with the wars in Oyo, more and more slaves came to be exported from Porto-Novo, Badagri, and Lagos. This occasioned a series of wars and raids on the coast as the kings of Dahomey attempted to suppress these ports.[64] The eastern ports seem, however, to have maintained their new significance.

From the 1790s, all but the trade to Brazil seems to have fallen sharply. The French ceased slave trading in 1794 with the Revolution. Napoleon reinstituted the slave trade in 1804, but this does not seem to have led to significant French slave trading on the coast of Dahomey. The English trade ended definitely in 1808 but had been at a low ebb for years previously. Brazilian traders, however, maintained their trading posts all along the coast.

Under the terms of a special agreement, the Portuguese continued to trade legally in slaves at Whydah until 1815.[65] Elsewhere after 1808, and

[63] Patterson, "Slave Exports," p. 256.
[64] Akinjogbin, *Dahomey,* pp. 146, 164–170.
[65] Verger, *Flux et reflux,* pp. 294–299.

everywhere after 1815, the illegal and clandestine trade began. Now slaves had to be moved rapidly to chosen points on the coast and loaded before the slave squadron could seize the ships. In this period, the slave trade was dominated by great Brazilian merchants, notably Francisco Felix de Souza and later Domingo Martins. They set up factories at various points on the coast from Agoué to Lagos, and succeeded in exporting large numbers of slaves from the coast as long as there was a demand.[66]

Additionally, slaves were purchased by Spanish and American ships in this period. A number of Spanish had settled on the coast, but no Americans are known to have done so. Few details are known of this trade, but it appears from contemporary accounts to have been quite significant.[67]

In 1851 the slave trade was abolished in Brazil. In the same year, the British established effective control of Lagos. The result was to cut off the main source of demand and one major outlet for supply on the coast. Trade continued to Brazil and Cuba, but on a sporadic basis. The real end to the slave trade in the Bight of Benin came in 1862–1863 with the abolition of slavery in Brazil and the clear turning of the American Civil War.[68]

After that, nonetheless, a few slaves continued to be sold on the coast of Dahomey. The French protectorate of Porto-Novo in the 1860s and the British westward movement from Lagos cut off all ports but Ouidah and Grand Popo. Such slaves as were exported after 1880 seem to have gone to other African colonies, such as São Thomé and Kamerun. In particular, sales of slaves by Dahomey to the Germans have been documented for the years 1889–1892.[69]

As a summary of these estimates of slave exports from the Bight of Benin, Table 4.1 gives totals of the estimates for each importing nation and for the seventeenth, eighteenth, and nineteenth centuries. The total of nearly 1.9 million slaves exported between 1640 and 1890 from Little Popo to Lagos in certainly a very large number.[70] Over half of the slaves exported, both overall and in each century, appear to have gone to Brazil. For the

[66] David A. Ross, "The Career of Domingo Martinez in the Bight of Benin, 1833–64," *Journal of African History,* vol. 6, no. 1, 1965, pp. 79–90.

[67] For example, Duncan, *Travels,* vol. 1, pp. 110–118. See also Christopher Lloyd, *The Navy and the Slave Trade* (London, 1949), pp. 163–183.

[68] "The last slave ship appears to have left Dahomey in 1865." Ross, "Autonomous Kingdom," p. 179.

[69] Newbury, *Slave Coast,* p. 130. A Dahomean shipment of 500 slaves from Avrekete to German Kamerun was noted in 1892, shortly before the Franco–Dahomean war broke out. (Archives nationales du Bénin, Porto-Novo, Q-129-A, Maison Fabre—Montaignnai to Ballay, 7 May 1892).

[70] If estimates of slave mortality during the Atlantic crossing were included systematically in these calculations, the estimated total of slave exports would probably be somewhat higher. Additional slave deaths occurred while they awaited shipment, etc.

entire eighteenth century, an average of over 11,000 slaves appear to have been exported every year. The high point of the trade was from 1700 to perhaps 1725, with another great peak of exports in the 1780s. The nineteenth-century slave trade was not as great in volume as that of the eighteenth century, though it was greater than for any other region of West Africa.[71]

ETHNIC ORIGINS OF THE SLAVES

Beyond the quantity of slaves exported and the point of export, a full assessment of the slave trade and its impact would require information on the ethnic origins of the slaves. Although evidence on this topic is scattered and quite impressionistic, a comparison of observations made on the African coast with records on slaves in the Americas can at least raise some of the major questions about ethnic origins of slaves from the Bight of Benin. At a broad level, an attempt may be made to classify slaves as belonging to the Aja peoples, the Yoruba peoples, or other groups such as the Nupe, the Hausa, or the Voltaic peoples of northern Benin. In some cases, especially within the Aja peoples, more specific identification of ethnic origin is possible.

For the seventeenth century, Dapper remarked that a large quantity of slaves were brought from Ulcami (meaning either Oyo or Yoruba generally), to Jakin, where they were sold to the Dutch and the Portuguese.[72] D'Elbée stated that some of the slaves sold at Offra in 1670 were prisoners of war, some were contributions of nearby kingdoms dependent on Ardra, and others were criminals from Ardra.[73] Barbot noted that among the slaves sold at Ardra and carried to America "there are many of the *Oyeo* and *Benin Blacks,* implacable enemies to those of *Ardra.*"[74] Whereas Dapper and Barbot have emphasized the number of Yoruba and possibly even Benin slaves sold by Ardra, d'Elbée emphasized the sale of Aja slaves.

Evidence from the New World tends to support d'Elbée's view. A sample of 402 slaves in Mexico at the end of the seventeenth century showed 36 from the eastern Guinea Coast.[75] Of these, 6 were listed as "Arara" and 9 as "Arda," both apparently signifying Aja peoples. The remainder were 6 "Carabali," 14 from São Thomé (meaning that they were transshipped

---

[71] Eltis has shown slave exports from the Bight of Biafra to have exceeded those of the Bight of Benin for the period 1821–1840, but the Bight of Benin trade went on for another 20 years.

[72] Dapper, *Description de l'Afrique,* p. 307.

[73] D'Elbée, as quoted in Labat, *Voyage,* vol. 2, pp. 321–322.

[74] Barbot, *Description,* p. 327.

[75] Curtin, *Census,* p. 113.

there, probably from the Bight of Benin), and 1 from "Terra Nova." No
Yoruba slaves can be identified in this group, though they might be hidden
under a nomenclature that often confuses point of exit with point of origin.
A more detailed sample is Debien's report of the slaves on a French Guiana
sugar plantation in 1690. It shows 33 of the 65 slaves to have originated in
the Bight of Benin. Their origins are summarized as follows:[76]

"Foin" (Fon)	12
"Arada"	7
"Juda" (Ouidah)	7
Popo	6
"Ayo" (Oyo Yoruba)	1

The slaves in this sample often gave the village of their origin, and Debien
has attempted to place them on the map. This evidence shows that the terms
"Arada," "Arda," "Popo," "Foin," etc., overlap to a considerable degree,
and all refer to Aja peoples of the Bight of Benin. This evidence also
shows, incidentally, that the Fon kingdom was well known by 1690, though
the name of Dahomey is not used. Finally, only a single slave of Yoruba
extraction was found on the plantation. Thus, although Oyo slaves and Oyo
traders were clearly involved in the seventeenth-century trade, the number
of each appears to have been small. Nor is there any indication as to
whether the Oyo traders were acting on behalf of the Alafin.

For the eighteenth century, Labat gives the most complete published
account of the ethnic origins of slaves. He remarked that the slave traders of
Ardra and the Hueda kingdom sold their countrymen only rarely, as when
the king inflicted a punishment. Slaves came from the environs of these
kingdoms but also from "400–500 lieues dans les terres"—hence some 500
kilometers.[77] Labat also gives a classification of slaves by ethnic group, which
may be summarized as follows: (a) Aradas—these are not to be confused
with natives of Ardra. They come to Juda (Ouidah) from 50–100 leagues
(50–100 kilometers) to the northeast; (b) Nago—these are little different
from the Aradas; (c) Foin—these make bad slaves, as they tend to kill
themselves. They have scars on the temples; (d) Tebou—even worse slaves
than Foin, they have scars on their cheeks; (e) Guiamba—these are so like
the preceding two they can almost be seen as one. They have the same
marks as the Tebou; (f) Mallais—slaves brought by the Mallais (i.e., Hausa),
but who are not themselves Mallais. They come from as much as 3 months
inland; (g) Ayois—these are hard workers. They have lines from their eyes to
their ears; (h) Minois—from Elmina; (i) Aqueras—these make good slaves.

---

[76] Curtin, *Census,* p. 189; G. Debien, "Les origines des esclaves des Antilles," *Bulletin de
l'IFAN,* vol. 26, 1964, pp. 167–181.

[77] Labat, *Voyage,* vol. 2, p. 124.

They often have designs on their back and chest in the form of lizards and snakes; (j) *Juda* and *Jakin*—they have scars on their cheeks.[78]

Labat thus demonstrates the variety of ethnic origins of slaves, though considerable confusion remains. Presumably there is clear identification of the Foin (Fon), Ayois (Oyo), Juda (Hueda), and Jakin (Hueda from Godomey). Arada appears to mean Aja peoples outside the major kingdoms. Nago probably means southwestern Yoruba, though it is not clear in what sense Labat meant they were almost like the Arada. Similarly, if Tebou and Guiamba are almost like the Foin, they would be seen as Aja peoples, perhaps the Mahi. More likely they are Voltaic peoples from northern Dahomey. The slaves brought by the Mallais (Hausa) are not described; they might include people from any or all the ethnic groups. Minois presumably means the Gen and Hula peoples of Little Popo and Grand Popo. Aqueras cannot yet be identified.

As a further aside, Labat gives a long description of Mallais merchants that shows them to be Hausa Muslims. They arrived in Ouidah in 1704 but had traded in Ardra before that time. They brought slaves, ivory, and cotton cloth, which they exchanged for liquors and cowries.[79]

Akinjogbin notes that in the early 1750s the slaves sold at Ouidah were Fon, Whydah, Allada, and Anago. The Portuguese, he says, bought Aja slaves but not Yoruba, to a total of 4000 out of 9000 slaves sold.[80] This may indicate that a large number of Yoruba slaves were being sold on the coast at that early date. It also indicates, however, that a large number of Aja slaves were sold at Ouidah, and does not exclude the possibility that many of these were from the Fon kingdom itself. Adams, speaking of the 1790s, says that the slaves obtained at Lagos came from Ijebu to the northeast and from Porto-Novo and Badagry. The slaves at Porto-Novo came from the Oyo, Hausa, Dahomey, Mahi, and Gun. Slaves from Hausa were brought to Porto-Novo by Oyo traders and sold to European or black traders from Lagos and Badagry.[81]

Curtin has summarized the work of Debien, showing ethnic origins of slaves in Saint-Domingue in the last four decades of the eighteenth century. The results, reorganized somewhat, are shown in Table 4.3. The table shows the Aja peoples to have been consistently the predominant group exported from the Bight of Benin by the French, with slaves of the Yoruba and Voltaic peoples approaching them in numbers only in the 1770s. These data may be contrasted with Akinjogbin's implication, noted previously,

---

[78] Labat, *Voyage,* vol. 2, pp. 125–130.
[79] Labat, *Voyage,* vol. 2, pp. 273–283.
[80] Akinjogbin, *Dahomey,* p. 134.
[81] Captain John Adams, *Remarks on the Country Extending from Cape Palmas to the River Congo,* London, 1966; (originally published London, 1823), pp. 220–222.

TABLE 4.3

Ethnic Composition of Saint-Domingue Slaves

	1760s		1770s		1780s		1790s	
	Number	Percentage	Number	Percentage	Number	Percentage	Number	Percentage
Arada	29	15.4	17	9.8	107	18.8	63	11.1
Foeda (Ouidah)	1	.5	2	1.1	5	.9	2	.4
Adia (Aja)	1	.5	6	3.4	10	1.8	12	2.1
Fon	—	—	1	.6	—	—	—	—
Subtotal: Aja peoples	31	16.4	26	14.9	122	21.5	77	13.6
Nago (Oyo Yoruba)	11	5.9	25	14.4	41	7.2	53	9.3
Ada and Attanquois (Otta or southwest Yoruba)	1	.5	1	.6	—	—	—	—
Subtotal: Yoruba	12	6.4	26	15.0	41	7.2	53	9.3
Thiamba (Chamba, Gurma)	6	3.2	14	8.0	15	2.6	17	3.0
Cotocoli (Tem)	1	.5	4	2.3	11	1.9	7	1.2
Barba (Bariba, Bargu)	1	.5	3	1.7	3	.5	3	.5
Samba (Somba)	—	—	—	—	—	—	1	.2
Subtotal: Voltaic	8	4.2	21	12.0	29	5.0	28	4.9
Tacoua, Tapa, Taquoa (Nupe)	1	.5	—	—	4	.7	7	1.2
Hausa and Gambary	—	—	—	—	—	—	10	1.8
Total: Bight of Benin	52	27.7	73	42.0	196	34.5	175	30.7
Grand total	188	100	174	100	568	100	570	100

Source: Curtin, pp. 192–197.

that the French bought predominantly Yoruba slaves, and with the common impression that the number of Yoruba slaves increased in the late eighteenth century.[82] The term *Arada,* as before, appears to be a generic term for Aja peoples. The term Nago, previously and subsequently applied to the southwestern Yoruba only, seems in this period to have been applied to Oyo. The term Gambary was used in Dahomey and elsewhere to refer to the Hausa.

The only comprehensive estimate of the ethnic origins of nineteenth-century slave exports from the Bight of Benin is that which Curtin and Vansina have developed from the 1848 Sierra Leone census and the accompanying work of the linguist Koelle.[83] From the census, the following numbers of recaptives from the Bight of Benin were found.

Popos (Fon, Gun, etc.)	1075
Yoruba	7114
Nupe	163
Benin	107
Hausa	657

These came to 68% of the total recaptives enumerated in the census.[84] Koelle's list of languages shows representatives from each major group among the Aja, Voltaic, and Yoruba peoples. The significance of Yoruba slaves in the nineteenth-century trade is emphasized by the strong Yoruba cultural tradition surviving in Brazil and Cuba—as, indeed, the survivals of Aja culture in Haiti may be traced to the large-scale imports of Aja slaves up to the eve of the Revolution.

THE INTERPRETATION OF THE HISTORY OF THE BIGHT OF BENIN

The history of Dahomey, as seen from the coast, is divided into several clear periods. The history of the Bight of Benin, moreover, with the exception of the wars in nineteenth-century Yoruba, has tended to be organized around the history of Dahomey. The first period, up to 1724, is a period of preconditions. In this period the literature covers the dynastic origins of the Aja states, the arrival of European merchants, and the question of whether political collapse was imminent. The second period,

---

[82] Akinjogbin, *Dahomey,* p. 134; Morton-Williams, "Oyo Yoruba."

[83] Philip D. Curtin and Jan Vansina, "Sources of the Nineteenth-Century Atlantic Slave Trade," *Journal of African History,* vol. 5, 1964, pp. 185–208; Curtin, *Census,* pp. 244–249.

[84] Curtin and Vansina placed Hausa slaves in the category of exports from the Bight of Biafra. Surely some were exported on either side of the Niger, but I have assumed here that the eighteenth-century pattern persisted.

1724–1735, covers the Dahomean conquest to the coast and the establishment of the new system. The questions considered for this period are why
Dahomey wanted to conquer to the coast and what objectives the king set
for the new system. The long period from 1735 to the 1830s is treated as
one in which Dahomey attempted to maintain the system set up after the
conquest. The question for this period is whether that attempt led to
success or tragic failure. From the 1830s to the 1860s, historians have
concentrated on the change from slave trade to palm oil trade, and on
conflicts between those who favored the continuation of slave trade and
those who opposed it. The period from the 1860s through the 1880s was
another time of maintenance of the established order in Dahomey, now in
the face of growing European pressure. Finally, Dahomey fought two losing
wars against the French from 1889 to 1894, and the colonial period then
began. Descriptions of Dahomean institutions—ministers, war, the Annual
Customs, the Amazons—were recorded during each of the periods, though
there has been very little study of the way in which these institutions may
have changed over time.

The "conquest to the coast" has consistently been the most interesting
period to historians.[85] Did Dahomey conquer to the coast to gain control of
this profitable trade (Dalzel), to cut the amount of the slave trade (Atkins),
or simply as part of its destiny (Le Herissé)? A wider variety of interpretations is given for the objectives of the new system. Some hold that the
objective was to maximize war and the slave trade, which could be turned
variously to royal revenue, to guns, or to captives for sacrifice. Others hold
that the objective was to limit the slave trade, for the security of the
country. Still others hold that the objective was to carry out the critical
minimum of slave trade required for royal revenue, guns, or sacrifices.

By choosing various permutations from the positions outlined in the
preceding, historians of Dahomey have been able to enjoy considerable
controversy without having any basic difference in approach. All assume
that slave trade was the key to the policy of the kingdom, and they vary only
in their description of the nature of the key. All accept the central role of
the king, and they vary only in the way he is combined with the other
elements of the interpretation. The canons for the history of Dahomey were
firmly set by the time of the appearance of Dalzel's *History of Dahomy* in
1793, and we have yet to venture beyond them.

Dalzel held to the theory that African nations were inherently given to
war and slaughter, and that the slave trade provided a means for drawing off
prisoners of war and saving them from execution. He explicitly opposed

---

[85] An analogous "conquest to the coast" theme also exists for Oyo. See Morton-Williams,
"Oyo Yoruba."

the thesis that the slave trade had induced more wars in Africa. Following Snelgrave, he compared Dahomey to the Aztecs, whom he took to be the epitome of sanguinary barbarism.[86]

Snelgrave, Dalzel's source for 1724-1732, emphasized the bloodshed in the conquest and further emphasized the sharp decline in the slave trade caused by the Dahomean conquests, despite Agaja's initial attempts to establish good terms for the trade. Atkins, another slaver, chose to interpret the Dahomean conquests as a purposeful attempt to limit, if not abolish, the slave trade. He also went to great lengths to contradict Snelgrave's assertion that the Dahomeans were cannibals.[87]

Among the nineteenth-century visitors to Dahomey, Forbes and Burton wrote the most historically oriented accounts, and they followed the general approach laid down by Dalzel.[88] The difference was that they were opposing the slave trade, but they railed against the excesses of the king of Dahomey much as Dalzel had done. Nevertheless, Forbes and Burton were favorable to Dahomey, in comparison with the Church Missionary Society and Baptist missionaries in Abeokuta who, beginning in the 1840s, sought to protect Egba interests in the face of Fon invasions.[89]

The first pro-Dahomey study of the kingdom was that of Le Herissé.[90] As administrator in Abomey for several years, he became an admirer of the Fon ruling elite, though he had no doubt that the French were now in charge. His is still perhaps the best collection of the traditions of Abomey. He presents a narrative that emphasizes the inexorable growth of the kingdom, and its objective of uniting all the Aja peoples into a single political unit.

Herskovits arrived in the 1930s to do an ethnological study of an African society from which many slaves were taken to the Americas.[91] He took a pro-Fon position similar to that of Le Herissé. Rather than emphasize a historical narrative, however, he emphasized a cross section of institutions

---

[86] Dalzel, *History;* Snelgrave, *New Account.* See also Loren K. Waldman, "An unnoticed aspect of Archibald Dalzel's *The History of Dahomey," Journal of African History,* vol. 6, no. 2, 1965, pp. 185–192; Akinjogbin, "Archibald Dalzel: Slave Trader and Historian of Dahomey," *Journal of African History,* vol. 7, no. 1, 1966, pp. 67–78; and J. D. Fage, Introduction to the 1967 reprint of Dalzel.

[87] Snelgrave, *New Account*; Atkins, *Voyage.*

[88] Forbes, *Dahomey;* Burton, *Mission.* More recent interpretations of this period have followed an approach based heavily on the politics of trade. See Schnapper, *La politique,* and Coquery-Vidrovitch, "De la traite des esclaves à l'exportation de l'huile de palme et des palmistes au Dahomey: XIXe siècle," in C. Meillassoux, ed., *The Development of Indigenous Trade and Markets in West Africa* (London, 1971), pp. 107–123.

[89] Ross, "Indigenous Kingdom," pp. 55–223.

[90] Le Herissé, *L'ancien royaume du Dahomey.*

[91] Herskovits, *Dahomey.* Argyle's *The Fon of Dahomey* is intended, in turn, as a corrective to Herskovits.

and thus gave the most detailed description of the powers of the royal hierarchy. At the same time, Herskovits also gave the first thorough description of the lineage structure. His work can thus be used to emphasize either the power of the king or the limits on his influence.

Karl Polanyi's *Dahomey and the Slave Trade* appeared in 1966.[92] The book is an attempt to apply his concepts of economic history, which spring in turn from his utopian scoialist views—a way of working out his reaction against industrial capitalism and his search for a critical social analysis and program different from that of Marxism.[93] For all its theoretical pretensions, it conforms faithfully to the canons laid down by Dalzel. Polanyi argues that Dahomey was trapped by its geographic fate, lying in the Benin Gap through which slaves would inevitably be funneled from the interior. The kingdom had no choice but to take up the slave trade. It protected itself, however, from the ill effects of this politico–economic necessity through a special institution, the "port of trade," in which the slave trade was sealed off from other affairs of the kingdom. Although the book is full of broad assertions, no real attempt is made to prove them.

Akinjogbin's interpretation of eighteenth-century Dahomey may be seen as an attempt to refute Dalzel.[94] Contesting Dalzel's assertion that Dahomey depended upon and encouraged slave trade, Akinjogbin accepted Atkins' thesis that Dahomey hoped to reduce or eliminate the slave trade. As no alternative means, however, of supporting the state could be found, he argues, Dahomey was drawn into a tragic dependence on the slave trade, compounded by an inability to make the trade flourish. In contrast to the notion that Dahomey was strong, Akinjogbin argues that it was often militarily weak and at times threatened with extinction.

Akinjogbin's interpretation is little more than another permutation of the elements provided by Dalzel, but his work provides advances in two main areas: He investigated English and French archives, and he included the interactions of Dahomey with Oyo. In fact, he has used this as a springboard from which to offer interpretations of Oyo history.[95]

[92] It appeared posthumously, and in collaboration with Abraham Rotstein.

[93] As an economic historian, Polanyi was most concerned with exchange, whereas Marx was most concerned with production. George Dalton, Polanyi's most faithful follower, has written an obsequious but comprehensive presentation of Polanyi's ideas that shows how Dahomey— or Polanyi's contorted conception of it—came to play a key role in his view of the world. George Dalton, ed., *Primitive, Archaic and Modern Economies: Essays of Karl Polanyi* (New York, 1968), pp. ix–xlvi. I hope to present, in another context, some consideration of the fascinating intellectual historical questions raised by Polanyi's work and its reception by other scholars.

[94] Akinjogbin, *Dahomey.*

[95] Akinjogbin, "The Oyo Empire in the Eighteenth Century—A Reassessment," *Journal of the Historical Society of Nigeria,* vol. 3, no. 3, December 1966, pp. 449–461. See the able review of Old Oyo history by J. A. Atanda, *The New Oyo Empire* (London, 1973), pp. 1–44.

Although the interpretations of Dahomean history are built around the slave trade, it is not yet easy to test them against figures for slave exports. If the estimates developed in Table 4.1 were broken down by port and by year, it would be easier to test interpretive statements. The more fundamental problem, however, is that the interpretive statements are not generally in a testable form. Polanyi, for example, simply asserts that Dahomey was dependent on the slave trade. No attempt is made to document the statement, and no way is provided to verify it.[96] Elsewhere, however, Polanyi asserts that a "rush" of slave trade began on the Dahomean coast in the 1670s.[97] This does, in fact, seem to coincide with the rapid growth in slave exports indicated in Table 4.1 for the last half of the seventeenth century.

Several sources imply that slave trade in the area reached a peak in the years just before the Dahomean conquest to the coast.[98] According to Table 4.1, however, a record-high level of slave exports was maintained for a full two decades before the 1720s.

Did the sharp decline in slave trade bemoaned by Snelgrave actually take place after 1727? The 1720s and 1730s each show a decline over the previous decade, but the trade was hardly cut off. Here it would be helpful to have a breakdown of the trade by port.

Akinjogbin gives various ups and downs in the volume of the slave trade for the eighteenth century. These are generally asserted for various individual ports, and there is no reason to expect that a change in the trade of one port should be reflected in the trade of the whole coast, although Ouidah generally exported nearly half of the slaves for the Bight of Benin.

The sharp increase in the slave trade estimated for the 1780s is, however, of interest. It coincides with the wars of the end of the reign of Abiodun in Oyo, and with the pro-slave trade policies of Kpengla in Dahomey.[99] Akinjogbin's assertion of a long-term decline in the slave trade of Dahomey, beginning in 1767, is not matched by a decline in the estimates of total slave exports from the Bight of Benin.[100] It could, of course, be explained by a shift in trade from Ouidah to other ports, presumably Porto-Novo, Badagry, and Lagos.

Although the estimates of the nineteenth century are less dependable than before, it is interesting to note a fairly steady level of slave exports from the whole coast. This does not correspond to Akinjogbin's assertion

[96] Polanyi, *Dahomey*, pp. 5–6.
[97] Polanyi, *Dahomey*, pp. 17–21.
[98] Snelgrave, *New Account*, pp. 1–2; Atkins, *Voyage*, p. 157; Akinjogbin, *Dahomey*, pp. 39–67.
[99] Akinjogbin, *Dahomey*, pp. 164–168.
[100] Akinjogbin, *Dahomey*, p. 209.

that Adanzan encouraged little slave trade, whereas Gezo brought a big increase in slave trade beginning with his accession in 1818.[101] Ross has contested these assertions, arguing that any decline in the slave trade of Ouidah must have ended at least as early as 1810.[102] Ross argues that Ouidah's slave trade fell sharply in the 1830s, with the collapse of Francisco Felix de Souza's trading empire, but that the slave trade of Lagos was at its zenith in the 1830s and 1840s. The slave trade of Dahomey did not increase until 1846.[103] These assertions, while plausible, cannot be tested in detail with the figures in Table 4.1.

The development of estimates of slave exports and their comparison to existing historical interpretations is suggested as one step toward breaking out of the stereotypes of Dahomean historiography. Some steps in other directions may also be suggested. First, a critique of the assumptions made by major authors is in order. What, for example, do the authors assume to be the social structure of the Aja and Yoruba peoples? What sort of differences do they assume to exist between the major states and the areas outside such states? Why is trade seen as such an important factor in the policy of kingdoms? What is the reason for concentrating studies on the policies of kings? For that matter, how can one do useful studies of the policies of kings or nations if it is not clear what their fundamental interests are?

As a second step, then, some serious study is in order to determine the nature of the fundamental interests of the Aja and Yoruba peoples. Presumably there were varying and conflicting interests, and presumably many of these were related to people's roles in the process of production. In short, an analysis of the social structure and its economic functions is needed.

A third step is for historians of the Yoruba and Aja peoples to make much more systematic efforts to include the peoples in between the major states as part of their analysis, in hopes of achieving greater analytical and historical validity. Similarly, historians should make a greater effort to consider more than one or two of the conventional periods in Dahomean history.

As an example of a slightly different way to think about the economic history of the area, consider cowries. Cowries, as is generally known, were the money of the Yoruba and Aja peoples, as well as of the Hausa trading area. What is not generally realized is that there was a steady import of cowries to the Bight of Benin since the mid-seventeenth century, at least. In

[101] Akinjogbin, *Dahomey*, pp. 193–201.
[102] Ross, "Autonomous Kingdom," pp. 2–3.
[103] Ross, "Autonomous Kingdom," pp. 50–57.

the seventeenth and eighteenth centuries the rule of thumb was that one-third of the value of any purchase of slaves was to be made in cowries. Now, why should anyone want to sell valuable human beings for money? Why exchange slaves for money rather than useful goods? Of course, from the point of view of any individual seller of slaves, the money can be used to buy other goods. The situation is clearly analogous to that of Europe, which sold goods to get gold at the same time. In the aggregate, however, the Bight of Benin gave away thousands upon thousands of productive human beings for cowries. Is this sort of behavior an argument for the existence of a class of some sort, present through the area, which benefited preferentially from the slave trade? That is, can the import of cowries tell us anything about the social structure of the area?

In order to develop a workable interpretation of the economic history of the Bight of Benin, it will be necessary to overcome the stereotypes of the past but also to learn what is valid in them. If Archibald Dalzel's image of Dahomey has been sufficient to raise that kingdom to a position of such infamy then perhaps, with some imagination, that same image can be used to attract to Dahomey the scrutiny necessary to clarify the basic issues in its economic history.

APPENDIX 4.1. CHRONOLOGY OF EUROPEAN TRADE IN THE BIGHT OF BENIN

Early seventeenth century. Portuguese trade between Ardra and São Thomé.

1637. Dutch capture of Elmina, after which Portuguese trade to Grand Popo, Ouidah, Jakin, and Ekpe only with Dutch permission.

1640s. Dutch trade begins at Ardra, then extends to Grand Popo and Ekpe.

1660s. English merchants come to Ardra.

1669. French mission to Ardra, aimed at opening trade.

1671. French and English establish factories at Ouidah.

1670s. Portuguese trade becomes dominated by ships from Bahia rather than ships from Lisbon.

1702. English build Fort William at Ouidah.

1704. French build Fort Saint-Louis at Ouidah.

1721. Portuguese build Fort São Jorge de Ajuda at Ouidah.

1727. Dahomey conquers Ouidah, Dutch are expelled.

1732–1734. Jakin destroyed and trade halted there. Dutch remain at Grand Popo and Ekpe.

1730s. Badagri begins slave trade.

1750s. Porto-Novo begins slave trade.
1794. French abandon slave trade.
1797. French abandon Fort Saint-Louis.
1805. Portuguese abandon fort. It is taken over by Francisco Felix de Souza.
1808. British cease slave trade.
1812. British abandon Fort William.
1808–1815. Brazilians continue slave trade legally.
1800–1860s. Spanish and American slave traders frequent Southern Dahomey.
1838. Thomas Hutton establishes palm oil factories on coast.
1841. Victor Régis establishes palm oil factory in French fort at Ouidah.
1851. Brazilian abolition of slave trade. British intervention at Lagos.
1860s. French protectorate of Porto-Novo.
1870s. German merchants to the coast.
1889–1894. French conquest of Dahomey.

APPENDIX 4.2. SLAVE EXPORTS TO BRAZIL

Slave exports from Costa da Mina to Bahia are estimated, based on shipping data given by Verger (pp. 651–667). I have neglected slave exports from Costa da Mina to other areas of Brazil. The outlines of the calculations are presented in Table 4.4.

The estimates in Table 4.4 may be compared with the estimates of Goulart and with estimates gathered by Verger from a variety of sources (see Table 4.5). Eltis (personal communication) has estimated exports from the Bight of Benin to all of Brazil at 50,000 for 1821–1830 and at 41,000 for 1831–1840.

For the period before 1680, Verger concludes (p. 667) that there were an additional 100 vessels (which, at 400 slaves each, means 40,000 slaves) that traveled to Bahia from Costa da Mina before 1678. His reasoning, based on a comparison to Goulart, is faulty, but it might be taken to represent his feeling, based on his reading of the archives, that a sizable trade existed before 1678. It amounts to one ship per year for 40 years. Nevertheless, I have guessed that a smaller number of slaves was exported, beginning in the 1640s.

Both Verger and Goulart cease counting slave exports after 1851, but Verger gives the impression that some clandestine trade continued. David Ross shows that many more slaves were exported in the 1850s than reached their destination. I have guessed that some trade continued until the early 1860s, when slaves were emancipated in Brazil.

TABLE 4.4

Slave Exports from Costa da Mina to Bahia

Years	Ships	Slaves
1681–1690	43	17,200[a,b]
1691–1700	152	60,800
1701–1710	216	86,400
1711–1720	168	67,200[c]
1721–1730	159	63,400
1731–1740	123	49,000
1741–1750	98	39,200
1751–1760	101	34,400[d]
1761–1770	120	36,000
1771–1780	100	30,000
1781–1790	109	32,700
1791–1800	177	53,100
1801–1810	243	72,900
1811–1820	192	59,000[e,f]
1821–1830	148	51,800[g]
1831–1840	218	54,800[h,i]
1841–1850	299	63,000

[a] 1678–1815—ships departing Bahia for Costa da Mina, carrying tobacco (Verger, *Flux et reflux*, pp. 653–654). I have assumed that each ship returned with a slave cargo in the same year that it left.

[b] Assuming 400 slaves per ship for the years up to 1756 (Verger, *Flux et reflux*, p. 666).

[c] Figures for ship departures are missing for the years 1715–1725 and 1734–1738. Verger has suggested a total of 200 ships for those years, or 12.5 ships per year with 400 slaves per ship. I have placed this average amount in each of the years lacking data (Verger, *Flux et reflux*, pp. 653–654, 666).

[d] Assuming 300 slaves per ship for the period from 1757 through 1815 (Verger, *Flux et reflux*, p. 666).

[e] 1815–1830—ships departing Bahia for Costa da Mina carrying tobacco (Verger, *Flux et reflux*, p. 655).

[f] Assuming 350 slaves per ship for the period from 1816 to the end of the trade (Verger, *Flux et reflux*, p. 667).

[g] Figures for departures are missing for the years 1828–1837. For 1815–1827, 158 ships departed (12 per year), and for 1838–1851, 377 ships departed (29 per year). Interpolating, I have assumed 20 ships per year for each of the years lacking data (Verger, *Flux et reflux*, pp. 655–657, 666–667).

[h] Adding vessels destined for the southern hemisphere which went instead to Costa da Mina, and subtracting vessels engaged in legitimate trade, Verger estimated that 600 vessels traded in slaves between 1815 and 1851, which is 80% of the total estimated departures of 757 from 1815 to 1851 (Verger, *Flux et reflux*, pp. 666–667). One could assume 80% of the departures each year represent slaving vessels, or, as I have done here, assume 100% of the vessels, 1815–1833, were slavers, and 60% of those 1834–1851 were slavers, the rest trading in palm products.

[i] 1831–1850—passports to ships departing Bahia for Costa da Mina (Verger, *Flux et reflux*, p. 657). These figures are 50–70% of the equivalent figures given by the British consulate, which are also listed by Verger.

TABLE 4.5

Comparison of Three Estimates of the Bahia Trade

Decade	Goulart (as given by Curtin, p. 207)	Estimates collected by Verger (pp. 664–665)		Estimates based on Verger's shipping data
1681–1690	—	—	—	17,200
1691–1700	—	—	—	60,800
1701–1710	83,700	—	—	86,400
1711–1720	83,700	—	—	67,200
1721–1730	79,200	—	—	63,400
1731–1740	56,800	47,500	—	49,000
1741–1750	55,000	41,468	(9 years)	39,200
1751–1760	45,900	24,615	(6 years)	34,400
1761–1770	38,700	19,267	(6 years)	36,000
1771–1780	29,800	15,554	(6 years)	30,000
1781–1790	24,200	12,234	(6 years)	32,700
1791–1800	53,600	40,842	(8 years)	53,100
1801–1810	54,900	38,339	(8 years)	72,900
1811–1820	—	55,352	(8 years)	59,000
1821–1830	—	72,066	—	51,800
1831–1840	—	—	—	54,800
1841–1850	—	—	—	63,000

APPENDIX 4.3. ENGLISH SLAVE EXPORTS

For the period after 1700, I have followed Curtin's estimates, as he revised them based on Anstey's findings (Curtin, "Measuring the Atlantic Slave Trade," p. 123). For the period from 1681 to 1700 I have estimated slave exports from import values given by Davies, with a guess added for interlopers in the 1690s (see Table 4.6). For the 1670s I have made a guess.

Royal African Company (RAC) cowrie exports (Davies, *Royal African Company*, p. 357) correlate very well with RAC exports to Ardra and Whydah. It may be assumed that most of the cowries exported went to Ardra and Whydah. The low figures for cowrie exports in the 1670s, therefore, indicate very little RAC trade with Ardra and Whydah. This is the basis for my guess of the low figure of 5000 slaves exported by the English in the 1670s.

APPENDIX 4.4. DUTCH SLAVE EXPORTS

Postma ("Dimension," pp. 239–246) gives estimates for the whole Dutch slave trade. These are not broken down by regions, except that he has assumed two-thirds of the trade to be from Guinea, and one-third to be

TABLE 4.6

English Slave Exports, 1681–1700

Year	Royal African Company exports to Ardra and Whydah (pounds)[a]	Price (pounds)[b]	Estimated slave exports
1681	8275	3	2758
1682	10,633	3	3544
1683	14,097	3	4699
1684	6869	3	2290
1685	16,974	3	5658
1686	—	—	—[c]
1687	—	—	—
1688	6607	3	2202
1689	1266	3	422
1690	3550	3	1183[d]
1691	—	—	—
1692	5940	4	1485
1693	9414	4	2353
1694	3864	4	966
1695	2303	4	576
1696	5126	4	1282
1697	1979	4	495
1698	5231	4	1308
1699	—	—	—[e]
1700	—	—	—[f]

[a] From Davies, *Royal African Company*, p. 233.

[b] Prices are my guesses, based on Davies, *Royal African Company*, pp. 236–237. If higher prices were used, estimated slave exports would decrease.

[c] No returns are available for 1686 and 1687.

[d] The total of slave export estimates for 8 years in the 1680s is 22,800. I have used this as the estimate.

[e] No returns are available for 1699 and 1700.

[f] The total of the slave estimates for 7 years in the 1690s is 8500. I have added a guess of 10,000, partly on the strength of D'Amon's statement (Roussier, p. 106) that English interlopers accounted for 10% (presumably of the entire trade). This gives an overall estimate of the English trade of the 1690s, of 18,500 slaves.

from Angola and Loango. I have assigned to the Bight of Benin portions of Postma's estimated Dutch exports from West Africa, as indicated in Table 4.7.

APPENDIX 4.5. SPANISH AND AMERICAN SLAVE EXPORTS

The estimates in Table 4.8 are based on Eltis's figures for slave exports from the Bight of Benin to Cuba and Puerto Rico for 1821–1843 (personal

TABLE 4.7

Dutch Slave Exports

Years	Total slaves	West Africa (two-thirds of total)	Bight of Benin
1630–1674	70,000	46,200	—
1675–1680	18,302	12,079	—
1630–1680	—	—	39,000[a]
1681–1690	15,437	10,188	10,188[b]
1691–1700	23,155	15,282	15,282
1701–1710	23,822	15,723	12,500
1711–1720	23,624	15,592	13,700
1721–1730	32,639	21,542	8400
1731–1740	47,794	31,544	8600[c]
1741–1750	55,243	36,460	—[d]
1751–1760	51,350	33,891	500
1761–1770	62,921	41,528	—
1771–1780	40,300	26,598	600

[a] For the period 1630–1680, I took two-thirds of the total for West Africa and apportioned it arbitrarily, following qualitative indications given by Postma ("Dimension," p. 240), as follows:

1641–1650	9000
1651–1660	6000
1661–1670	12,000
1671–1680	12,000

[b] For the period 1681–1730, I have assigned to the Bight of Benin the portions of West African exports indicated by Postma ("Origin," Table 2, p. 43). The portions are, 100% (1681–1690), 100% (1691–1700), 80% (1701–1710), 88% (1711–1720), and 39% (1721–1730).

[c] Postma enumerated 7600 slave exports from the Bight of Benin, 1730–1735 ("Origin," p. 43). To this I have added a guess of an additional 2000 for the period 1736–1740.

[d] Estimates for the period beginning 1741 are based on Postma's Table 3 ("Origin," pp. 44–47). Recorded Bight of Benin exports are taken as a portion of total recorded West African exports, and this factor is multiplied by estimated total West African exports for the decade.

communication), and on Curtin's estimates for Cuban slave imports, derived from figures on the rate of Cuban slave population growth (Curtin, *Census*, p. 234).

I have assumed that 31% of the Curtin's slave imports to Cuba came from the Bight of Benin: Curtin developed this figure from the 1848 Sierra Leone census and Foreign Office records (Curtin, *Census*, p. 247). Eltis, however, has assumed that the proportion of Cuban and Puerto Rico slave imports from the Bight of Benin ranged from 18.7% to 28.3% in the years 1821–1840.

TABLE 4.8

Slave Trade between Bight of Benin and Cuba

Decade	Benin exports to Cuba (Eltis)	Cuban imports[a]	Benin exports (31% Cuban imports)
1811–1820	—	79,900	24,800
1821–1830	25,679	112,500	34,900
1831–1840	50,912	126,100	39,100
1841–1850	11,020[b]	47,600	14,800
1851–1860	—	123,300	38,200
1861–1870	—	61,500	19,100

[a] From Curtin, *Census*, p. 234. I have chosen Curtin's figures as the preferred estimates for 1811–1820 and 1851–1870, and Eltis's figures as preferred for 1821–1840. For 1841–1850 I added 7000 to Eltis's estimate for 1841–1843. In addition, I have guessed that a trickle of this trade began in the years before 1811.

[b] 1841–1843 only.

ACKNOWLEDGMENTS

I wish to express my gratitude to those who have given me useful commentary and suggested corrections to an earlier version of this chapter: David Eltis, Serge Daget, Johannes Postma, Philip Curtin, Arthur Tuden, Sv. E. Green-Pedersen, Pierre Boulle, David Ross, and Paul Lovejoy.

5

The Economic Costs of West African Participation in the Atlantic Slave Trade: A Preliminary Sampling for the Eighteenth Century

HENRY A. GEMERY
JAN S. HOGENDORN

Little empirical evidence has been brought to bear on discussions of the slave trade's impact within West Africa. Except for estimates of population loss, most writing on the question exhibits virtually no recourse to data.[1] For a subject in which the intangible social costs bulk so large, it may appear quite reasonable to dismiss the relevance of empirical data. Yet such a dismissal may be premature, given the growing body of African historical research, together with economic historians' use of social saving and cost of war analyses.[2] Studies attempting to assess particular costs (and benefits) associated with an historical event, though admittedly incomplete even in

---

[1] See the discussions appearing in J.F.A. Ajayi and M. Crowder, eds. *History of West Africa,* Vol. 1 (New York, 1972), pp. 391, 392; B. Davidson, *A History of West Africa* (New York, 1966), pp. 293–300; L. H. Gann and P. Duignan, *Africa and the World* (San Francisco, 1972), Chapter 25; A. G. Hopkins, *An Economic History of West Africa* (New York, 1973), pp. 119–123. Population estimates appear in J. D. Fage, *A History of West Africa,* (Cambridge, 1969), pp. 84–89.

[2] Citations for both social saving and costs-of-war analyses appear in the methodological section following.

data-rich time periods, have provided illuminating insights into those events. Africa's participation in the eighteenth-century trans-Atlantic slave trade has now been detailed to a point where similar insight might be hoped for in imposing an analytical construct on existing data. This chapter ventures such an effort and offers some controlled speculations on the "economic" costs of West African participation in the Atlantic slave trade.[3]

It seems self-evident that when all costs are counted—the intangible costs of disruption with all of their social, political, and psychological ramifications—the welfare of West African society as a whole deteriorated over the centuries of its involvement in the trade. These intangible costs are not susceptible to measurement and loom so large that Gann and Duignan are doubtless correct in their statement that "no balance sheet can ever present the full debt account of the slave traffic."[4] There remains, however, the possibility that market data can be used as evidence in examining a narrower question, and in focusing on a cost–benefit framework that is partial in nature. If we arbitrarily assume that the costs of the trade are confined to the direct consequences of population loss on production, and similarly assume that benefits derived are the total value of import goods received, what then were the implications for West Africa of its participation in the eighteenth-century slave trade?

Implicit in the formulation of the question are two positions which should be underscored at the outset:

1. West Africa is viewed as a single economic and social entity for purposes of measurement and it is this "unit" whose total welfare is the question at issue. Analytically, it is debatable whether one should employ a total or a per capita measure in assessing the impact of population losses. Lacking adequate population data on which a per capita measure depends, this chapter of necessity employs a total measure; however, discussion of the debate on an appropriate measure appears in the methodological section.

2. A very restricted definition of costs and benefits will be followed, and this imparts an intended bias to the methodology. Costs are deliberately not fully defined and thus are understated. The exclusions are major ones. No provision is made for intangible social costs of whatever form though it is obvious that the capture and forcible removal of prime-age Africans imposed sizable costs on the affected society. No indirect costs are included

---

[3] All costs associated with a choice are properly the province of economics; however, the difficulty of measurement in the absence of market prices has meant that economic analysis has been largely constrained to the use of market-related costs where direct application or imputation of market prices is possible. This chapter falls victim to such a limitation and the quotation marks about economic are meant to convey the incomplete (but unfortunately commonplace) definition of costs being followed.

[4] L. H. Gann and P. Duignan, *Africa and the World*, p. 339.

(i.e., the multiplier effects that stemmed from production declines in areas subject to enslavement or the increased defense costs in those same areas). The benefits of the trade, though they also are defined without intangible or indirect components, are overstated by the assumption that all imported goods purchased via the exchange of slaves represented gains from the trade. Firearms, a significant portion of imports, are illustrative of this upward bias. To the extent firearms were used in slave gathering or defense against enslavement, they are properly a cost of the trade and not a benefit. The specific biases introduced into these measures serve an intended purpose. Net gains from the trade, if they occurred, would be most apparent in an approach that overstates benefits and understates costs. If the calculations based on this methodology result in net economic gains that are modest or nonexistent, the validity of the "self-evident" judgment that West African welfare deteriorated during the slave trade would seem strong indeed.

In the sections that follow, the underlying theory of the measurement used is defined, the evidence is reviewed, and an assessment is made of the economic costs of the eighteenth-century trade.

METHODOLOGY

Fully measuring the impact of the slave trade would require the contrast of a hypothetical "West African economy" that did not engage in the trade, with the existing "economy" that did.[5] Such a counterfactual construction, though conceivable in later time periods when ample data within defined national boundaries are obtainable, is impossible in the case of the slave trade. A narrower measure may be employed, however, and this chapter draws on international trade theory in an attempt to measure "gains from

[5] Social saving models, in attempting to assess the economic impact of an innovation, adopt such an approach. A historical economy is contrasted with a hypothetical one, the latter alike in every respect except that it is denied the use of the innovation in question. An extensive literature exists, beginning with the original social saving studies of Robert Fogel and Albert Fishlow. See R. Fogel, *Railroads and American Economic Growth* (Baltimore, 1964), and A. Fishlow, *American Railroads and the Transformation of the Ante-Bellum Economy* (Cambridge, Mass., 1965). An excellent survey of the concept and the controversy over its use appears in G. Gunderson, "The Nature of Social Saving," *Economic History Review*, second series, vol. 23, no. 2, 1970, pp. 207–219. In estimating the economic impact of war losses on an economy, a somewhat related methodology may be used. See, for instance, Claudia D. Goldin's approximation of the costs of the Civil War in "The Economics of Emancipation," *Journal of Economic History*, vol. 33, no. 1, March 1973, pp. 66–86. Considerably greater detail appears in C. D. Goldin and F. D. Lewis, "The Economic Cost of the American Civil War: Estimates and Implications," *Journal of Economic History*, vol. 35, no. 2, June 1975, pp. 299–326.

trade," if such existed. Gains from trade are traditionally given classroom exposition by illustrating the extent to which a country advances beyond its domestic production possibility frontier to a new and higher frontier and community indifference curve. Though gaining and losing sectors within a country are recognized, it is the ability of the gainers to compensate the losers and still retain some gains that results in the general conclusion that an economy is, in the normal case, a net gainer from participation in trade.[6] By adopting the fiction of a West African society, the gaining and losing portions of that society can be examined as if the gainers were to be placed in the position of compensating losers.

The gaining sectors of the assumed West African society were clearly the slaver groups of whatever form who would have faced a choice of essentially the type shown in Figure 5.1. Slaves could presumably have been "produced" for internal use at any time resources were directed to that end; contrarily, the production of other types of economic goods could have claimed resources, as shown along PP. The intruding demand of the Atlantic slave trade, in offering the prospect of trading slaves for other goods on terms better than the internal transfer of resources allowed, motivated these groups to "produce" more slaves (moving from A to B) for export (X), thus acquiring other goods (M) to an extent greater than their preexisting internal capability. The new trade-created position of C is on a community indifference curve CIC_2 higher than the pretrade position on CIC_1. Though gains from trade cannot be directly measured, M can be estimated and used as a proxy. As the diagram makes clear, doing so overstates the probable real gains from trade. For the purposes of this analysis, that inflated measure is acceptable since it provides a high-range estimate of the amount from which compensating payments might have been drawn.

Enslaved groups suffered unambiguous losses since their production possibility frontier "imploded" as the lost labor input affected virtually all production choices. (Subsistence goods production versus other goods production is taken as an illustrative choice in Figure 5.2.) The movement in Figure 5.2 from D on CIC_1 to E on CIC_2 indicates the reduction in welfare occurring. Again, direct measurement of a welfare loss is not possible and resort to a proxy is necessary. The reduction in subsistence goods production capability, shown by F, is a crude proxy which, appropriately for the purposes here, represents a total less than true costs. The understatement occurs for two reasons. No attempt is made to measure the destruction of capacity to produce "other goods" on the X axis, and even the estimate of F itself is reduced by our decision to measure the decrease in the output of

[6] For an illustrative treatment, see H. Robert Heller, *International Trade* (Englewood Cliffs, New Jersey, 1973), Chapter 11.

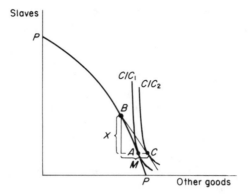

Figure 5.1. An upward-biased M is counted as the probable real gain from trade.

food, clothing, and shelter by assuming that the enslaved (or deceased) Africans produced only at subsistence levels.

In a simple analytical model, then, an upward-biased M is counted as the entire gain from trade whereas a downward-biased F is counted as the sole loss. In the case at hand, both M and F are estimated as long-period averages in an effort to make them more representative of an extended process and to avoid the necessity of present-value calculations (with the dilemma of interest rates) if a single time period were chosen.

The model developed here adopts explicitly the view that total economic welfare is a more appropriate measure than per capita welfare, for cases involving mass removals of population. As this assumption is debatable, the justification for it is presented below.

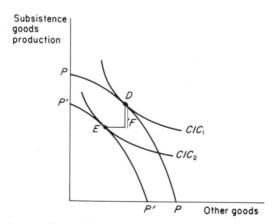

Figure 5.2. A downward-biased F is counted as the total loss from trade.

Most economists would agree that under ordinary circumstances, per capita figures should be relied upon. James Meade, now a proponent of abandoning the per capita measure in cases of large population loss, favored its retention in his earlier work.[7] As the current Meade argument suggests, however, the conclusions that follow from the choice of welfare per head are unacceptable when applied to population decreases as significant as those that accompanied the slave trade.[8] For example, suppose the existence of two countries A and B, quite independent of one another but with A somewhat richer than B. Then suppose that B's population is obliterated by plague, genocide, or by export into slavery. Use of a per capita measure would imply that the arithmetical calculation of real income for country A in its "world" of A and B had increased.

Unwillingness to accept this logic has led to a preference for a total welfare measure whenever large-scale population losses are suffered.[9] For the purposes of this chapter, the choice of total welfare instead of a per capita concept involves one particular advantage of especial importance. The methodology involved here does allow for a rough estimation of the slave trade's impact on total West African economic welfare, but it cannot be used to estimate such changes on a per person basis, because of the inadequacies in the available data.

THE EVIDENCE

Following the logic of the first section, an assessment of the economic costs imposed on West Africa as a whole by the Atlantic slave trade involves an estimate of lost productive capacity. We do not know the sum total of production lost to Africa from the export (or death) of each individual

[7] J. E. Meade, *An Introduction to Economic Analysis and Policy,* 2nd ed., (London, 1937), Part 4, Chapter 2.

[8] J. E. Meade, *Trade and Welfare* (London, 1955), Chapter 6.

[9] See for example C. P. Kindleberger, *Economic Development*, 2nd ed., (New York, 1965), p. 5. Meade puts the case for a total welfare measure convincingly, arguing that it is "improper to take the maximization of welfare per head as the ultimate objective [p. 87]" when plague–genocide–slave export is the cause of welfare improvement among the survivors. See Meade, *Trade and Welfare*, pp. 83, 87–93, and Appendix 1. Awareness of the per capita versus total debate is apparent with a number of other authors, perhaps none more clearly than C. D. Goldin and F. D. Lewis in "Economic Cost of the American Civil War." They point out that

It is important to note that the method of evaluating war deaths and war wounds depends critically on how the war cost estimate is to be applied. A human capital approach appears justified if one wants to know the extent to which gross national product or some other measure of economic activity was reduced as a consequence of the war. But if one is considering the losses experienced by those who survived the war, inclusion of the full marginal products of those who did not would be unjustified [p. 302].

caught up in the slave trade. A second best approach is possible, however, because sufficient fragmentary evidence exists to allow an estimate of the cost of subsistence in several areas of the slave trade. Subsistence has proven to be a slippery concept, as shown by Marvin Miracle.[10] Following Miracle, one can conceive of a minimum physiologic level of living (MPL) or a minimum desired level of consumption (MDL). Either formulation could be labeled "subsistence." For the purposes of this chapter, the former definition (MPL) is employed throughout. Subsistence is assumed to be that minimum quantity of food, housing, and clothing necessary to sustain life under conditions of rural agricultural labor. Whatever figure is determined to be the average value of subsistence (MPL) for West Africa must then also be a minimum figure for production per person lost to West Africa from the slave trade.[11] Although food clearly forms the highest proportion of MPL, the need for shelter and clothing is not so negligible in tropical conditions as might be assumed. Heavy rainfall, mosquito and tsetse infestation, extreme temperatures, and bright sunlight all presumably mean that shelter and clothing must be included in MPL.

In almost every case, the actual evidence for MPL presented in this

[10] M. Miracle, "Subsistence Agriculture: Analytical Problems and Alternative Concepts," *American Journal of Agricultural Economics,* May 1968, pp. 195–196.

[11] The postulated minimum subsistence output is equivalent to the value of the average physical product of labor. It would be analytically more convincing to measure marginal product instead of average product. This route, however, is foreclosed by absence of data for the eighteenth century. The danger in using average product as a substitute for marginal product arises from the possibility, frequently found in the economic development literature, that a surplus of labor will drive labor's marginal product far below its average product, perhaps even to zero. (The two most familiar models of surplus labor are those of W. A. Lewis, "Economic Development with Unlimited Supplies of Labor," *The Manchester School,* May 1954, pp. 139–191; and Gustav Ranis and J. C. H. Fei, *Development of the Labor Surplus Economy: Theory and Policy* [Homewood, Ill., 1964].)

Indeed, had eighteenth-century West Africa been overpopulated in the sense that the marginal product of labor was low or zero, the use of an average value for subsistence to measure costs of population removal would introduce significant error. Few observers, however, contradict the standard assertion that Africa was a land surplus economy, not only during the slave trade, but even today in most areas. (The point is made by A. G. Hopkins, *Economic History*, pp. 15–17; G. K. Helleiner, "Typology in Development Theory: The Land Surplus Economy (Nigeria)," *Food Research Institute Studies*, vol. 6, no. 2, 1966, pp. 181–194; and J. S. Hogendorn, "Economic Initiative and African Cash Farming: Precolonial Origins and Early Colonial Developments," in P. Duignan and L. H. Gann, *Colonialism in Africa*, vol. 4 (Cambridge, 1975). A condition of surplus land suggests a marginal product of *land* that is very low or zero, and implies a marginal product of labor approximately equal to its average product. (See the discussion of symmetry in linear, homogeneous production functions undertaken by any standard text, for example, C. E. Ferguson, *Microeconomic Theory*, rev. ed., (Homewood, Ill., 1969). Thus the choice of average subsistence value, in any case the only measure of product available for the eighteenth century, is an appropriate approximation of marginal product.

chapter is for a basic ration of one staple foodstuff, millet or maize. The figure of MPL thus derived must almost always be an understatement of its real value because other foods are excluded, as are housing and clothing. In short, the level for subsistence utilized in the following is a minimum figure that ordinarily would have been exceeded in practice.

There are a number of diverse sources that can be drawn upon to illustrate in money terms the amount of staple foodstuffs that would suffice for subsistence. These sources are unavoidably spotty in their geographical coverage, but fortunately they cover a reasonably wide selection of regions and also appear to include data for West Africa's lowest-cost producing area. What seems to be the most accurate information is derived from the accounts of the slave traders themselves. Philip D. Curtin's monumental new study of the Senegambian economy shows that the standard slave ration for slaves in storage or transit was approximately 1 kilogram of millet per day. Millet alone would make for a poor diet, so that other foods would be used to some extent as a supplement. Nevertheless, 1 kilogram of millet may be taken as a standard for subsistence.[12] Millet prices in the vicinity of St. Louis, a large grain-producing area, ranged in the 1750s from a low £2.60 per metric ton in a very good year to £19.50 per ton in a very bad year. In an ordinary year, the rough average was £6.80 per ton. Curtin states that there is no reason to suspect that this average price differed very substantially over much of the eighteenth century.[13]

Calculating from these figures, in an ordinary year the millet ration for an individual would cost about £2.50 per person per year, whereas, under the very best crop conditions, the millet ration would cost almost exactly £1 per person per year.[14] Recall that other food, housing, and clothing all represent extra costs of subsistence.

An independent check on these calculations may be found in the accounts of slave transport on the Senegal River in 1785, which have been discovered by Curtin.[15] Lots of 100 slaves were shipped on the 2-month trip from

[12] Philip D. Curtin, *Economic Change in Precolonial Africa* (Madison, 1975), Chapter 4, p. 169. According to modern studies made by the FAO, millet contains 3410 calories per kilogram. See FAO and US Department of HEW, *Food Composition Table for Use in Africa* (Bethesda, Md., 1968), p. 17. This amount of calories looms large in comparison with estimates for average adult requirements in Africa and other tropical areas, which tend to fall in the range of 2300–2500 per day. These figures, however, do not include manual work, and every agricultural activity whose caloric requirements were measured in 1954 by P. G. Phillips adds at least 1000 calories and often more to the daily adult requirement. See P. G. Phillips, "The Metabolic Cost of Common West African Agricultural Activities," *Journal of Tropical Medicine and Hygiene*, vol. 57, 1954, Table 2.

[13] Curtin, *Economic Change*, p. 169.

[14] The actual calculation in the first case would be .365 kilogram × £6.80 per metric ton = £2.48 per person per year. In the second case it is .365 × £2.60 = £.95.

[15] See Curtin, *Economic Change*, p. 279.

Maxana to St. Louis, at a total food ration cost of 1000 livres tournois. In 1785, the exchange rate was 28.5 livres tournois to £1. Thus for 2 months, 100 slaves were fed for £35. The cost for 1 year works out to £210, or £2.10 per person per year for food alone.

A third cost calculation may be based on data for the Gold Coast and nearby regions of the Guinea Coast. Here the data apply to maize as well as millet. According to Marvin Miracle, a standard daily slave ration of maize was of the same weight as Curtin reports for millet, namely 1 kilogram.[16] William Bosman reports in his work of 1705 that one bushel of shelled maize (he calls it Turkish millet) ordinarily sold at a harvest price of £.05, whereas between harvests, maize prices would usually rise about four times, to a high of about £.20.[17] The resulting calculation shows a daily slave ration costing £.73 at harvest, rising to £2.92 before the next harvest.[18]

Bosman also allows us to calculate the value of a 1-kilogram daily ration of millet on the Gold Coast. Millet was about 50% more expensive than the equivalent amount of maize. One standard bushel of millet weighs about 22 kilograms. A metric ton at harvest would thus cost £3.41, and the annual ration works out to .365 × £3.41 = £1.24.

A fourth calculation of subsistence food costs comes from an altogether different source: the expenses incurred by slave ship captains who victualed their vessels in Africa for the trip to the Americas. Here, the figure used by E. P. LeVeen for the late legitimate trade is treated by him as relatively constant over a very long time period at about 5 U. S. cents per day.[19] Using a dollar–pound exchange rate of $5 = £1, this comes to an annual ration cost of about £3.65 per year. This time all food is included, but again housing and clothing are not.

Although the century is different, the voluminous research undertaken by Heinrich Barth in the early 1850s is the best evidence available for food

[16] Marvin P. Miracle, *Maize in Tropical Africa* (Madison, 1966), p. 91. According to the FAO, 1 kilogram of maize contains sufficient calories (3570) for subsistence of an agricultural laborer. See FAO and US Department of HEW, *Food Composition Table for Use in Africa*, p. 12.

[17] William Bosman, *A New and Accurate Description of the Coast of Guinea*, 4th English ed. (New York, 1967, original edition, 1705), p. 297. Also see Miracle, *Maize*, p. 91, which draws on data gathered by John Barbot in the eighteenth century.

[18] Bosman's bushel is presumably the old English Winchester bushel, fortunately the exact equivalent of today's standard United States measure. One standard bushel of maize weighs about 25 kilograms. (See *Webster's New International Dictionary*, 2nd ed. (Springfield, Mass., 1953), p. 362.) As a result a metric ton of maize would cost £2 at harvest, and a 1-kilogram slave ration per day would cost annually .365 × £2, or £.73. Prices would rise following harvest to an ordinary maximum of £8 per metric ton, giving an annual slave ration cost of .365 × £8 = £2.92.

[19] E. P. LeVeen, "British Slave Trade Suppression Policies 1832–1865: Impact and Implications," unpublished doctoral thesis, (University of Chicago, 1971) pp. 170, 175–177.

costs in the interior regions. Barth notes that millet was the least expensive grain available in Bornu, where "the necessaries of life are cheaper . . . than in any other place which I have visited in Central Africa, almost half as cheap again as in Katsena and Sokoto, a third cheaper than in Kano, and about a fourth cheaper than in Timbuktu."[20] Barth states that three ox-loads of millet could be purchased for a dollar in Bornu.[21] Converting this to the measures used earlier in the chapter involves several different steps as explained in note 22. The result is that a 1-kilogram per day slave ration would be worth £.30 annually in Central Africa's cheapest market area, Bornu. Utilizing Barth's comments on prices elsewhere the same 1-kilogram grain ration would be worth approximately £.40 in Timbuktu, £.46 in Kano, and £.60 in Katsina and Sokoto. Once more other food, clothing, and housing are not included.[22]

One other passage in Barth is illustrative. In describing the Kano area, he points out that a family (meaning a nuclear family of perhaps four or five people) can live on £4 or £5 per year, "including every expense, even that of their clothing.[23] Given this data, annual per capita subsistence costs would range between £.80 at the lowest to £1.25 at the highest. (Barth's reference to "every expense," when compared to his data for a millet ration mentioned previously, implies that other food, housing, and clothing could be obtained for £.35–.80 in the Kano area.)

Most of the evidence collected here thus far refers to settled areas with relatively stable government, protected by more or less well-organized armed forces, and not specifically subject to constant slave raids. It is reasonable, however, to suppose that in areas raided for slaves, sheer survival would require that safety be valued above agricultural productivity.

[20] Heinrich Barth, *Travels and Discoveries in North and Central Africa,* vol. 2, centenary ed. (London, 1965), p. 56.

[21] Barth, *Travels and Discoveries,* pp. 56–57.

[22] First, the dollar referred to is the Maria Theresa dollar, a silver coin equivalent to approximately £.21 in the Sokoto Caliphate during the 1850s. (Paul E. Lovejoy, "Interregional Monetary Flows in the Precolonial Trade of Nigeria," *Journal of African History,* vol. 15, no. 4, 1974, p. 584). Estimating an ox load is more difficult. We know that the standard donkey load was about 55 kilograms (Paul E. Lovejoy, "The Hausa Kola Trade (1700–1900) a Commercial System in the Continental Exchange of West Africa," unpublished doctoral thesis [University of Wisconsin, 1973]). Oxen carried somewhat more, but the nineteenth-century African pack-ox was small and light. Barth reports that a very good ox weighed only about 600 pounds (Barth, *Travels and Discoveries,* p. 57). It seems safe to suggest that an ox load would weigh perhaps half again as much as a donkey load; here the figure of 82 kilograms is utilized. (A standard ox load in North Africa is about 95 kilograms at the present time, but this involves heavier oxen. Our thanks to Professor Raouf Hanna of Eastern Michigan University for this information.) Employing this estimate, a Maria Theresa dollar would buy 82 × 3 = 246 kg of millet. This is the equivalent of $4.1 per metric ton, in turn equal to £.80 per ton in sterling.

[23] Barth, *Travels and Discoveries,* vol. 1, pp. 511–512.

Poorer land in more defensible hill country would come under cultivation, thus raising the real costs of output. Compensating for the less-than-ideal agricultural conditions, some peoples subject to slave raiding adopted patterns of settlement with permanent cropping, use of fertilizer, hillside terraces and other capital-using improvements. A good example of this is the Mandara Uplands along the Nigeria–Cameroun border.[24] In many other areas, rural populations tended to seek safety in nucleated villages, rather than dispersing through their croplands (e.g., in northeastern Iboland and along the northern fringe of the Benue valley). "Foothill refuges" such as those inhabited by the Voltaic Talensi, the Atacora Range of Togo and Dahomey, and the Ari, Ningi, Burra, Warji, Birom, and Hill Angas of the Jos Plateau, must almost always have involved a penalty in terms of reduced output per acre.[25] As a result, it is very likely that the real costs of grain production in areas commonly victimized by slave raids would exceed those found in the "grain belts" of Kano, Bornu, etc.

Based on the foregoing evidence, a range of £.80–1.20 per person per year has been selected to represent the subsistence costs of food, housing, and clothing in eighteenth-century West Africa. Intentionally, this chosen magnitude errs on the conservative side. Grain alone cost much more than this in a good many of the areas noted, and as just explained, higher real production costs must have affected any regions where defensive measures against slavers were necessary.

From this point we employ the estimate that the permanent removal of one person from his native habitat, either by export to the Americas or by death during capture or transit, would mean lessened annual African production of £.80–1.20 during the eighteenth century. Any production over and above subsistence needs carried on by the individual in question would of course mean greater economic losses, but these are disregarded here. It should be noted that few—perhaps no—West African peoples appear to have been living on the very margin of subsistence during the eighteenth century; research almost always seems to disclose some surplus output and some interregional trade even in the most isolated areas. To the extent that

[24] See A. G. Hopkins. *Economic History,* pp. 35–36.
[25] For details see W. B. Morgan and J. C. Pugh, *West Africa* (London, 1969), pp. 27, 41, 230–231, 242, 429, and 465. Morgan and Pugh give a vivid picture of the capital–intensive agriculture employed by some of these refugees.

The magnificence of the terracing could be described as being in reverse ratio to the power and importance of the tribe responsible. Usually the terracing is seen on steep hill-sides or scarps, and it may run from top to bottom of a scarp, as it does near Kwong, on the southeast side of the Jos Plateau. . . . The districts concerned are usually refuge areas to which have fled small, weak communities, individual tribes today often numbering only a few thousand. A weak group of this type had no choice of farming sites [p. 230].

this is so, production losses would exceed the posited £.80–1.20 per person per year by some unknown but probably large amount.

There is a further consideration that tends to make the selected figure an underestimate. To the extent that slavers captured the younger and more productive portion of the labor force, the actual output loss would be greater than an overall average for subsistence. Koelle's data for age distribution, reproduced elsewhere as Table 5.1, shows that over 70% of the former slaves in his sample had been captured before their thirtieth year. Furthermore, the sex ratio in the Atlantic trade was approximately two men shipped for each woman.[26] If agricultural productivity was higher for the male labor force—understandable in western farming but sometimes not so in Africa, where many women still serve as full-time cultivators—then the production loss from the slave trade would exceed the average for subsistence. As we have no way to determine the magnitude of either of these two factors, no account is taken of them in establishing the range of £.80–1.20.

The next question to consider is, how many years' worth of production would on average be lost from the export of an individual? The answer requires some knowledge of life expectancy in Africa during the era of the slave trade. According to A. G. Hopkins, the "average expectation of life at birth was probably around thirty-five years, much as it was in medieval Europe."[27] This does not, however, mean that the average adult could not expect to survive his thirties. Very high infant and childhood mortality was primarily responsible for the quoted low life expectancy, and as in medieval Europe or ancient Rome a young adult could look forward to attaining his forties or even fifties as a normal matter of course. European merchants exporting slaves from the Senegambia put the upward age limit on a "standard slave of full value" at 35, and for men this limit was sometimes raised to 40.[28] There is certainly no indication from this that the average adult died in his thirties or early forties.

The best available information on the age of slaves at capture comes from Koelle's informants, as shown in Table 5.1. Given these percentages, the authors believe that on average each person enslaved could have expected to have a working life at home in Africa of at least 15 years. Even if productivity ended as early as age 40, this figure would be reasonable given Koelle's age distributions. It is likely that 15 years is a conservative figure and that 20 years may be closer to actuality. It will minimize the chance for error, however, if the 15-year span is adopted.

[26] Curtin, *Economic Change,* Chapter 4, p. 176.

[27] A. G. Hopkins, *Economic History,* p. 17.

[28] Curtin, *Economic Change,* Chapter 4, p. 175. The standard *peça das Indias* had an upward age limit of 36, and older slaves had a market value until about 45, according to Lars Sundstrom, *The Exchange Economy of Pre-Colonial Tropical Africa* (New York, 1974), p. 77.

Table 5.1
Sample of 164 Ex-slaves Showing Age of First Enslavement

Age	Percentage of total
Under 20	22
20–24	25
25–29	24
30–39	23
Over 40	5

Source: P. E. H. Hair, "The Enslavement of Koelle's Informants,"
Journal of African History, vol. 6, no. 2, 1965, p. 194.

The third and last question on the side of costs is, how many people were removed from production? The best available evidence at present is provided by Curtin and Anstey as shown in Table 5.2. 4.25 million slaves were exported from West Africa from 1701 to 1800, including an addition of 10% for mortality on the sea voyage.[29] Note three important considerations, however, all of which raise the effective total of losses over and above the figure for exports. First was mortality during the process of capture. If the slave acquisition was part of a war or *razzia* involving armed conflict, Curtin may be correct in suggesting that a price in deaths would be exacted "that was inevitably several times the number of captives enslaved and shipped to the coasts."[30] Even raids undertaken because of the profit motive could be sanguine. Second, it was not uncommon to kill the older men who were unsalable as slaves, even though they would have contributed to local agricultural productivity if left alive.[31] People wounded in slave operations but left behind might not recover fully. Finally, there would be fatalities on the trek to a coastal point of export, and during storage there. The effect of the endemic diseases of the rain forest on those not acclimated, unsuccessful attempts to escape, and the psychic malaise of enslavement itself, would all have taken a toll. Curtin speculates that deaths between capture and American delivery may have been about equal to the numbers that eventually survived the transatlantic voyage even in the more peaceful forms of slave acquisition such as judicial condemnation or kidnapping.[32]

Given the uncertainty of the evidence in this area, only the reasonably hard coastal export figure of Table 5.2, including 10% for ocean mortality, plus an additional 10% as an estimate for fatalities during capture, interior

[29] The figure of 10% is conservative. Hopkins suggests 15% (*Economic History*, p. 101), and Morgan and Pugh also use 15% (*West Africa*, p. 424).

[30] Curtin, *Economic Change*, Chapter 4, p. 182.

[31] E. W. Bovill, *The Golden Trade of the Moors*, 2nd ed. (London, 1968), p. 247.

[32] Curtin, *Economic Change*, Chapter, 4, p. 182.

Table 5.2
Value of Slave Exports[a]

(1)	(2)	(3)	(4)	(5)	(6)
		Percentage of		Average	Value of slave
		slaves exported	Slave exports	coastal	exports from
	Slave exports	from West	from West	price,	West Africa,
Years	from Africa	Africa	Africa	pounds	pounds
1701–1710	457,000	74	339,000	12.6	4,271,400
1711–1720	483,000	81	391,000	16.8	6,568,800
1721–1730	440,000	71	312,000	14.2	4,430,400
1731–1740	580,000	65	377,000	20.2	7,615,400
1741–1760	1,316,000	60	790,000	17.7	13,983,000
1761–1770	753,000	66	497,000	20.0	9,940,000
1771–1776	760,000	60	456,000	21.0	9,576,000
1777–1780	400,000	60	240,000	11.4	2,736,000
1781–1790	1,050,000	48	504,000	29.1	14,666,400
1791–1800	800,000	43	344,000	25.3	8,703,200
Total			4,249,000		79,754,600

Sources: Column 2, E. P. LeVeen, "The African Slave Supply Response," paper delivered at the African Studies Association, Syracuse, N.Y., November, 1973, Table 2, p. 9. Data taken from P. D. Curtin as corrected by R. Anstey and containing a 10% addition for ocean mortality.

Column 3, calculated from Curtin, *Atlantic Slave Trade*, Table 63, p. 211.

Column 5, for years 1701–1776, see Richard Bean, "The British Trans-Atlantic Slave Trade, 1650–1775," unpublished doctoral dissertation (University of Washington, 1971), pp. 71–72 and Appendix A.

For other years, from LeVeen, "African Slave Supply Response," Table 1, p. 9.

[a] The average prices have been raised by 50% above those quoted in these sources to convert from European prime cost to African coastal prices. See Bean, "Slave Trade," pp. 125–127. They have also been reduced by .157 to adjust from the prices of prime male slaves to the prices of all slaves. See Bean, "Slave Trade," pp. 132–134. The necessity for making these adjustments was called to our attention by Professor Bean at the 1974 meeting of the African Studies Association.

transit, and coastal storage, has been taken to represent the numerical loss to West Africa. Our mortality supplements, 20% in all, are deliberately set far lower than the 50% used by Miracle,[33] the 100% employed by Curtin when slaves were acquired on kidnapping raids, Curtin's much greater figure ("several times the number . . . enslaved") when war was the producer of slaves, and the highest figure we have seen, 1000%, used by Morgan and Pugh.[34] Utilizing a conservative 20% addition, the number of people lost to West Africa in the eighteenth century would have been not

[33] Miracle, *Maize,* p. 91.
[34] Curtin, *Economic Change,* Chapter 4, p. 182. Morgan and Pugh, *West Africa,* p. 424.

less than 4.67 million. Inclusion of a higher figure for losses in the process of capture and inland transit (e.g., Miracle's or Curtin's) would of course inflate the figure substantially.

The three estimates of manpower lost, annual value of lost subsistence output, and number of working years lost per person removed from production may now be combined in a calculation of the slave trade's economic costs to West Africa—a figure that in many ways is minimal, as already noted, and that includes no increment whatever for the enormous social costs of the trade. Lost manpower has been calculated previously at 4.67 million for the period 1701–1800. The average annual production loss to West Africa, obtained from data on subsistence output, is estimated in the range of £.80–1.20. The number of working years of productive labor that could have been expected from each person lost by death or export through the slave trade is estimated at 15. The *total* production loss to West Africa, would thus appear to range from a low of 4.67 million × £.80 × 15, all of which equals £56.0 million; to a high of 4.67 million × £1.20 × 15, which equals £84.1 million.

Unfortunately, there is a statistical complication that requires an adjustment to be made to these figures. Some lost production that was actually due to slave exports occurring before 1701 affected West Africa during the eighteenth century. Conversely, some production was lost after 1800 (outside this chapter's frame of reference) even though the slave exports that caused the losses occurred during the eighteenth century. The most agreeable solution to this problem was to calculate the additional production loss occurring after 1701 but due to slave exports before that date and include it in the century's total. Then the loss accruing after the century's end from exports before that date was calculated, and the result subtracted from the century total. These adjustments are shown in Table 5.3. The outcome is a positive adjustment ranging from a low of £2.3 million to a high of £3.5 million for the period 1701–1715, and a negative adjustment in the range of £3.8–5.8 million for the period 1801–1815. The resulting net negative figures (£1.5–2.3 million) must then be subtracted from the unadjusted cost range (£56.0–84.1 million) presented in the preceding.

The final result ranges from a low of £54.5 million to a high of £81.8 million. This range is used henceforth as our proxy for the economic costs to West Africa of the slave trade.

The economic benefits accruing to West Africa in the eighteenth century because of the Atlantic slave trade may be measured in monetary terms by the value of slave exports. The calculation is less complicated than the determination of costs in the last few pages. Necessary data are the number of slaves exported from West Africa, 1701–1800, including deaths in ocean transit, and the average coastal sale price in Africa. Multiplying the two

Table 5.3
Adjustments for Production Losses Extending into and Continuing after the
Eighteenth Century

(1)	(2) Man-years of production lost in 1701–1715 from slave export of year shown	(3)	(4) Man-years of production lost in 1801–1815 from slave exports of year shown
Year		Year	
1686	23,900	1786	55,400
1687	47,700	1787	110,900
1688	71,600	1788	166,300
1689	95,400	1789	221,700
1690	119,300	1790	277,200
1691	145,400	1791	226,600
1692	167,100	1792	264,600
1693	191,000	1793	302,400
1694	214,800	1794	340,200
1695	238,700	1795	378,000
1696	262,600	1796	415,800
1697	286,400	1797	453,600
1698	310,300	1798	491,400
1699	334,200	1799	529,200
1700	358,000	1800	567,000
Total	2,866,000		4,800,000

Sources: Column 2: Calculated from slave exports times the number of working years beyond 1700 given the assumption of a 15-year work life. Slave export figures from P.D. Curtin, *The Atlantic Slave Trade,* Table 34, p. 119. The slave export figures were adjusted by minus 18% to correct for slaves exported from areas other than West Africa, then by 10% for ocean mortality (per LeVeen) and a further 10% for intra-African mortality.

Column 4: Calculated as the preceding. Slave export figures from Table 2, Column 4, increased by 10% for intra-African mortality.

gives the value of slave exports, which value represented a command over imported goods. Trade was ordinarily accomplished via the direct exchange of imported goods for slaves. Even when slaves were sold for cash in the form of metal bars, cowries, or gold that continued as a circulating medium, however, this also represented real imports with real value—for these items were a large portion of West Africa's money supply during the eighteenth century.[35]

It should be recalled that command over imports as a measure of the

[35] Around 1720, about one-third by value of all goods imported to West Africa were cowries destined for use as currency. See Marion Johnson, "The Cowrie Currencies of West Africa, Part 1," *Journal of African History,* vol. 11, no. 2, 1970, pp. 21–22.

benefits of the slave trade does to some extent overstate those benefits. For example, a proportion of the firearms, powder, flints, and lead imported found their chief employment in the wars and raids that generated slaves. As noted in the first section, they are properly a cost of the trade, not a benefit, and could legitimately be subtracted from the total import bill.[36] Once again, however, the preferred route is to maximize any benefits and minimize any loss, so as to bias the measurement against the appearance of net losses. Hence no such subtractions are made, and the entire value of slave exports, representing command over imported goods, is expressed as the benefits to West Africa from the slave trade.

On this basis, Table 5.2 calculates the value of those benefits. Column 2 shows total slave exports 1701–1800 by decennial periods to the Americas from all of Africa. Column 3 is the percentage of these exports derived from West Africa. Column 4 shows slave exports from West Africa alone. The information shown in both Columns 2 and 4 includes a markup of approximately 10% for ocean mortality, following LeVeen. Column 5, price, is the average African coastal price during the time period shown. Column 6 is the product of Columns 4 × 5 and represents the value of slave exports in the decennial periods. The total of £79.8 million for 1701–1800 is considered here to be a measure of the benefits accruing to West Africa from the slave trade.[37]

In summary, the suggested economic cost in money terms of the slave trade during the eighteenth century was in the range of £54.6–81.8 million, whereas the suggested money benefit during the same time period was on the order of £79.8 million.

[36] In "Dutch Trading Voyages to Cameroon, 1721–1759: European Documents and African History," *Annales de la Faculté des Lettres et Sciences Humaines*, University of Yaounde, vol. 6, 1974, pp. 5–27, Austen refers to firearms and their accoutrements as "destructive capital," in contrast to other imports of consumer goods and productive capital. The same logic is utilized in the preceding text. There are some rough indications of the magnitude of the subtraction if firearms, powder, ball ammunition, and the like are counted a cost and not a benefit of the slave trade. P. D. Curtin states that such weaponry accounted for 10% of Senegambia's import bill in an average year of the eighteenth century. (Curtin, *Economic Change*, pp. 318, 321). Basil Davidson notes that Birmingham alone was exporting 100,000–150,000 muskets per year to Africa at the peak period of the eighteenth century. (See his *Black Mother* [Boston, 1961], p. 242). As the cost of muskets in Africa was relatively constant during the eighteenth century at about £.50–1.00 each, this suggests a subtraction of perhaps as much as £90,000 annually from the total of imports financed by slave exports (about £798,000 annually as noted later in this chapter). Of course, some use of firearms had no connection with the slave trade, as in hunting animals or protecting crops against animal predators. Thus the actual diminution of welfare would be less than the figure utilized in the preceding.

[37] The total is not too far from J. D. Fage's estimate of £66,000,000, a figure obtained in a very different manner in Fage's *History of West Africa* (Cambridge, 1969), p. 91.

CONCLUSIONS

The measure developed here is sufficiently artificial to warrant the recitation of several caveats before conclusions are drawn. They are as follows: (1) a purposefully narrow definition of economic cost is employed; (2) a hypothetical economy, West Africa, is the locus of both costs and benefits; (3) costs and benefits are oversimplified to the point of viewing them as a stark trade-off between imports of trade goods and slave exports with no political causality; (4) empirical data are extended to diverse regions of West Africa and through considerable time.

Such violence to historical reality is only justifiable if the construct generates additional worthwhile insights not apparent in the detail of the period and the trade.

In fact, a major insight does seem to appear. Even when assumptions are made that tend to maximize the economic benefits of the slave trade, these benefits are fairly minimal. The net gain over the course of the eighteenth century approximates £25.2 million when the low cost range for subsistence production is chosen (£.80). Such gains are almost certainly illusory, however, even in our construct, which ignores any and all social costs and measures only private, economic costs. Calculating from the figures contained in the previous section, any gains would disappear in their entirety and be replaced by a net economic loss to West Africa under any one of the following conditions:

1. If the minimum level of subsistence production exceeded £1.14 per person per year. Most of the figures reported in the paper do exceed that level.
2. If the population lost to West Africa via the slave trade had been producing an average surplus of £.34 or more per person per year over and above subsistence requirements.
3. If the working life of those enslaved were an additional 21.7 years instead of the 15 years utilized in the chapter. As noted earlier, a figure of 20 years does not appear unreasonable.
4. If mortality during slave acquisition and delivery to the coast were 56% of the slaves eventually shipped overseas instead of the postulated 10%. Recall that a figure of 50% has been quoted by Miracle, and 100% by Curtin.
5. If the enslaved Africans, in being taken from the younger and more active portion of the labor force, were more productive than the average, thus raising costs sufficiently to offset the benefits. (No numerical calculation of this productivity differential is possible because the distribution of population between those enslaved and those remaining is not known.)

As noted, any one of these independent factors 1–5 would in itself convert the net impact of the slave trade into an economic loss for West Africa. The implication is overwhelming that when these factors are taken in combination, the economic costs of the trade exceeded its gains on an overall basis. Let us reemphasize that this conclusion is reached without any reference to the massive intangible costs of the trade. It is altogether unlikely that large additional benefits have been overlooked, or that costs were significantly lower than those posited here. We may conclude that the overseas slave trade had a detrimental economic impact even without considering its social costs.

A further conclusion may be inferred. The fact that voluntary trade with Europeans occurred despite a negative economic impact on West African society as a whole suggests that, because decision making occurred within relatively narrow geographic bounds, calculations of cost and benefit were made on a level more consistent with private than social perceptions. At that level, capture costs were the only relevant private costs and social costs were perceived as nonexistent or were, at best, severely underestimated. Political fragmentation and the resulting dominance of a private cost–benefit calculus thus explains the continuance of trade despite the adverse bargain.

ACKNOWLEDGMENTS

A preliminary version of this chapter was presented at a panel of the African Studies Association, Chicago, October 1974. We are indebted to Ralph Austen, Richard N. Bean, Heywood Fleisig, Gerald Gunderson, A. G. Hopkins, and Richard Roehl for assessments and incisive questions. They are, of course, neither responsible for the analytical direction we chose nor for the errors that may be present. Those remain the responsibility of the authors.

6

The Delivery of Slaves from the Central Sudan to the Bight of Benin in the Eighteenth and Nineteenth Centuries

MAHDI ADAMU

Slavery and the slave trade are very old social and economic institutions in West Africa even though their importance within that area has not yet been given due prominence in recent research. Nobody has yet tried seriously to trace their developments before the era of the Atlantic slave trade. Although the beginning of the slave trade in West Africa is not yet satisfactorily probed, the export of slaves[1] from the region across the

[1] It should be noted that the terms *slave* and *slavery* had different connotations for the majority of West Africans than for the American plantation owners. In most parts of West Africa, though in theory the slave belonged to the lowest level of the social hierarchy, and could be treated as the owner's chattel and therefore disposed of at will, he had a certain amount of respect given to him as a human being, which was not so in any part of the Americas. For instance, in some parts of West Africa, particularly away from the slave ports, a domestic slave might be given a public appointment carrying high responsibility (see text), he could own property (including slaves) separate from that of his master, and when he died his children would inherit part of the wealth. Depending on his personal character, he could be treated as a member of the family of his owner. Should the master decide to sell him, he reserved the right, bestowed on him by the society, at least in Central Sudan, to choose his next master, for his

Atlantic Ocean, as we all know, is fairly well documented.[2] It is worth noting, however, that the export of slaves from West Africa developed in phases, the first being the export from the interior to the Saharan and North African markets; the second from the coastal areas and their immediate hinterlands to the overseas markets, particularly the Americas; and the third phase from the interior, via the coast, also to the Americas. How early the first phase initially developed cannot be said with much certainty, but it antedated the Muslim conquest of North Africa at the end of the seventh century A. D. Most of the slaves exported were used as domestic slaves in Arabian homes, and also as soldiers and guards. The second phase was first developed by the Portuguese from the beginning of the sixteenth century. The slaves exported were mainly used on sugar cane and tobacco plantations and also in the mines of the Americas.[3] The third phase, as the work of Philip Curtin shows,[4] developed largely during the second half of the eighteenth century, as an expansion of the second phase; and by the middle of the last century, the two, already merged into one, had completely dried up. This third phase is basically the same as what Verger calls the Bight of Benin cycle (of African immigration at Bahia) between 1770 and 1851.[5] The Saharan slave trade lingered on to the end of the nineteenth century. This chapter is concerned with the third phase.

In the last 4 years there has been much discussion of the economic conditions underlying and molding slave delivery within Africa. The initial attempts were painted with a broad brush and were incidental to other aspects of the slave trade. Examples include Philip Curtin's "The Slave Trade and the Atlantic Basin: Intercontinental Perspectives," Marion Kilson's "West African Society and the Atlantic Slave Trade," Basil Davidson's "Slaves or Captives? Some Notes on Fantasy and Fact," and Philip Curtin's

---

acceptance of the buyer was necessary before the purchase was effected. Nowhere in the New World was a slave given this type of humane treatment.

[2] See the following references in particular: Philip D. Curtin, *The Atlantic Slave Trade: A Census* (Madison, 1969); P. D. Curtin, *Africa Remembered: Narratives by West Africans from the Era of the Slave Trade* (Madison, 1967); A. G. Hopkins, *An Economic History of West Africa* (London, 1973); Centre of African Studies, Edinburgh, *The Trans-Atlantic Slave Trade from West Africa* (Edinburgh, 1965); J. D. Fage, "Slavery and the Slave Trade in the Context of West African History," *Journal of African History*, vol 10, no. 3, 1969, pp. 393–404; C. W. Newbury, *The Western Slave Coast and Its Rulers* (Oxford, 1961); Pierre Verger, *Flux et reflux de la traite des nègres entre le golfe de Bénin et Bahia de Jodos os Santos du 17ᵉ et au 19ᵉ siècle* (Paris, 1968).

[3] See Verger, *Flux et reflux* and Curtin, *The Atlantic Slave Trade*.

[4] Curtin, *The Atlantic Slave Trade*, pp. 188ff.

[5] Pierre Verger, *Bahia and the West Coast Trade, 1549–1851* (Ibadan, 1964). Verger, however, looks at the cycles from the American end, so it was the cycles of African immigration into Bahia that he describes, whereas the phases I am talking about here refer to slave emigration from the Central Sudan.

"The Atlantic Slave Trade, 1600–1800."[6] Two stimulating doctoral theses have investigated prices and quantities of slaves along the coast: E. Phillip LeVeen's "British Slave Trade Suppression Policy" and R. N. Bean's "British Trans-Atlantic Slave Trade."[7] The first was a detailed study of coastal prices, whereas the second used price data to estimate elasticity of slave supply, which LeVeen discovered to be relatively high compared to other forms of labor used in the New World. Recently, H. A. Gemery and J. S. Hogendorn (in *Journal of African History*, 1974) argued that one of the responses to high slave demand and prices in the Americas was innovation in the delivery mechanism, and that the mechanism was responsive to price differentials in such a way as to make the labor supply elastic.[8] The two authors, in another essay[9] go on to examine this theory in more detail, but still in a way that is very general, covering the whole of West Africa.

Another article, by R. P. Thomas and Richard N. Bean has gone so far as to claim that the delivery system in West Africa was highly competitive, resulting in the elimination of potential monopoly profits.[10] In response to their article, P. E. Lovejoy and J. S. Hogendorn have employed a model emphasizing the short-term tendency for monopoly influence in the slave delivery mechanism to break down over time in overseas exporting under the pressure of competitive forces. The evidence they bring to bear covers a wide spectrum of case studies in West Africa.[11]

To date, however, no specific full-length study has yet been written that puts a particular West African delivery system into the context of the more general studies noted previously. Such an approach has indeed been called

[6] Philip D. Curtin, "The Slave Trade and the Atlantic Basin: Intercontinental Perspectives," in N. Huggins, M. Kilson, and D. Fox, *Key Issues in the Afro–American Experience* (New York, 1971); Marion D. d.B. Kilson, "West African Society and the Atlantic Slave Trade 1441–1865," in Huggins, Kilson, and Fox, *Key Issues;* Basil Davidson, "Slaves or Captives? Some Notes on Fantasy and Fact," in Huggins, Kilson, and Fox, *Key Issues;* Philip D. Curtin, "The Atlantic Slave Trade 1600–1800" in J.F.A. Ajayi and M. Crowder, eds., *History of West Africa,* vol. 1 (New York, 1972).

[7] E. Phillip LeVeen, "British Slave Trade Suppression Policies, 1821–1865: Impact and Implications," unpublished doctoral thesis (University of Chicago, 1971); Richard N. Bean, "The British Trans-Atlantic Slave Trade, 1650–1775," unpublished thesis, (University of Washington, 1971).

[8] H. A. Gemery and J. S. Hogendorn, "The Atlantic Slave Trade: A Tentative Economic Model," *Journal of African History,* vol. 15, no. 2, 1974, pp. 223–246.

[9] H. A. Gemery and J. S. Hogendorn, "Technical Change, Slavery and the Slave Trade," in C. J. Dewey and A. G. Hopkins, *The Imperial Impact: Studies in the Economic History of Africa and India* (London, 1978).

[10] R. P. Thomas and Richard N. Bean, "The Fishers of Men," *Journal of Economic History,* vol. 34, no. 4, 1975, pp. 885–914.

[11] See Chapter 8, "Slave Marketing in West Africa," in this volume.

for by George Shepperson in his article entitled "Comment."[12] This chapter attempts to provide such a study, concentrating on one delivery system, from the Central Sudan to the Bight of Benin. The primary aim in writing it is to show the amount of economic processing that normally went into the delivery of slaves from the Central Sudan to the Bight of Benin during the last hundred years of the Atlantic slave trade (middle of the eighteenth century to the middle of the nineteenth).

ACQUISITION OF SLAVES

There are a number of ways in which people in the different parts of West Africa acquired slaves, but as far as the Central Sudan was concerned—and this excludes those parts of the present Republics of Nigeria and Benin that were south of the latitude of the Niger-Benue confluence—the following seem to be the main ones:

1. capture
2. as payment of tribute[13]
3. purchase
4. gifts

It is not intended here to go into the mechanics of each of these, but to merely note who did what, and to whose economic advantage.

Capture fell basically into two categories, the legal and the illegal. Legal capture was an act whereby a person was made a prisoner of war following a battle or a punitive expedition, whereas illegal capture was kidnapping.

By virtue of the fact that the maintenance of law and order was solely the responsibility of the government—indeed, its prime responsibility to the people—it was only during military expeditions organized by the government or any of its agencies that slaves could be acquired through legal capture. In such cases, they were brought to the war camps first as prisoners of war,[14] and then those who were not ransomed by their relatives (the

[12] George Shepperson, "Comment," in S. L. Engerman and E. O. Genovese, *Race and Slavery in the Western Hemisphere: Quantitative Studies* (Princeton, 1975).

[13] There is a difference between tribute and taxes. The latter was levied on the people by the government of the land, and the former was a levy paid annually by one government to a superior king.

[14] In the "Hogendorn Collection," Tape 3, there are details of how prisoners of war were often policed during the march from the battlefield. The "Hogendorn Collection" of tapes containing oral information was recorded in Zaria and Kano emirates during the 1974–1975 academic session. The tapes have been transcribed and copies have been deposited with the Northern Nigeria History Research Scheme, Department of History, Ahmadu Bello University, Zaria, Nigeria.

majority were not) were converted into slaves.[15] In theory, all the prisoners of war captured during any military engagement should be surrendered to the head of the army who would arrange their sharing out in the usual (Islamic) way. One-fifth would go to the *Sarki* (the territorial chief, the king) and the rest would be shared by the officers who took part in the campaign. This division of booty was called *humusi* in Hausa. In practice, however, individual platoon commanders kept a few of their captives whom they later appropriated as their personal slaves on the grounds that they were private booty. The enslavement of prisoners of war was the most common way in which slaves were acquired in the Central Sudan;[16] and since wars, most of which were launched for purely political reasons, were frequent,[17] this system of acquiring slaves had become a continuing feature of the economy. Allan and Humphrey Fisher argue that this system of acquiring slaves was extremely uneconomic on the grounds that the resources expended to capture the slaves—that is, human lives lost during the encounters; arms and ammunition, bows, arrows, and spears used; horses lost; food consumed—often added up to more than the market value of the slaves that eventually reached the base camp.[18] It is important, however, to note that with regard to the purpose for which most of the military campaigns were launched (in nearly all cases politics was the cause), any slaves that the army came back home with were a sort of economic gain and should be deemed as forming part of the war indemnity that the captors appropriated to reduce their material losses.

The kidnapping of people for enslavement could take place anywhere, anytime. There were cases of people kidnapped while working on their farms, or simply when one or two of them had strolled out of the town and had the misfortune of coming across a concealed group of kidnappers. This

[15] Traditionally in the Central Sudan, sons of the *Sarakuna* (the nobility) were not enslaved by territorial chiefs. If they were captured in a battle they would be given differential treatment and sent back home. The prince was expected to send to his captors, through the escort that took him home, a handsome present in appreciation of the gesture. Princesses captured were often persuaded to, or even coerced into, marrying the captor chief or any of his sons. Royal musicians were also treated differently; they were often set free but incorporated with the musical band of the chief who captured them.

[16] It should be noted, however, that even though the society in Hausaland and in Borno was basically Islamic, the Islamic principles on enslavement were not followed. Even war captives who were Muslims were enslaved, contrary to the social laws of Islam that say that believers in the faith should not be enslaved. See Abdullahi ibn Fodiyo, *Duya al-Siyasa.*

[17] For a brief discussion on the major political wars in the Central Sudan, reference may be made to Adeleye for the seventeenth and eighteenth century wars and D. M. Last on the nineteenth. R. A. Adeleye, "Hausaland and Bornu 1600–1800" in Ajayi and Crowder, *History of West Africa*, vol. 1; D. M. Last, *The Sokoto Caliphate* (London, 1967).

[18] Allan G. B. Fisher and Humphrey J. Fisher, *Slavery and Muslim Society in Africa* (London, 1970), pp. 76–82.

type of kidnapping is called *samame* in Hausa. Victims of *samame* simply disappeared from their homes without any notice or trace. There was also the case of people kidnapped on the highways. Such incidents often followed violent highway robberies organized to rob merchants of the goods they were carrying. Highway robbery was known as *fashi*. Even though both *samame* and *fashi* resulted in the seizure of people, they were not the same, for in *samame* the people attacked were the specific targets, whereas in *fashi* it was their property. Any people captured during the *fashi* attack simply provided additional loot and could be ransomed in the same manner as people captured on a battlefield.[19]

Kidnapping of any description was an act of lawlessness, apart from being one of social injustice, and was accordingly condemned by the established authorities.[20] There is nothing to show that the kidnapping of people was rampant in the Central Sudan, and indeed some sources indicate that the majority of kidnapping incidents took place in the border zones where armed merchants occasionally raided small unprotected settlements and captured some able-bodied people to use as porter slaves.[21]

Tributes were annual levies paid to a stronger government by a weaker one as an admission of the former's political hegemony over the latter. In essence, it was to ensure the protection of the recipient in case the payer was threatened with an outside attack.[22] In most cases payment of tribute was made in the most common natural produce of the land, including human beings. Unfortunately, no specific study has yet been made on the quantitative side of tribute in the Central Sudan.[23]

The only legal way in which people who were outside the ruling circle could acquire slaves (other than through free gifts) was by purchase. This might be through the normal buying and selling process, or they might receive the slaves as payment for goods previously bought on credit.[24] The

---

[19] See D. A. Olderogge, *Zapadnyi Sudan* (Moscow, 1960), for cases of victims of *fashi* in Borgu ransomed by their relatives.

[20] See H. Abrahall in *History of Bussa,* a typewritten collection of the history of Borgu (a file at the Nigerian National Archives, Kaduna), where mention is made of expeditions, mounted by the king of Kebbi, sent out specially to capture the highway robbers threatening the Hausa–Borgu route.

[21] See "Hogendorn Collection," Tape 3.

[22] See Y. B. Usman, "A Reconsideration of the History of Relations between Bornu and Hausaland before 1804 A.D.," a paper for the Borno Seminar, 1973, where he discusses tributes in general, and the tributes paid to Borno by the Hausa States before the beginning of the nineteenth century in particular.

[23] It is high time that at least the tribute paid to the Sokoto Caliphate during the nineteenth century be assessed. This is quite possible to do because documentary evidence (mainly letters) on the issue are still extant though not often consulted.

[24] In many instances chiefs in Hausaland and in Borno bought goods on short-term credit. See Lander and Lander, vol. 2, for Yawuri, and Barth, vol. 1 for Kano and Borno. John and

manner in which slaves were bought and sold in the Central Sudan is discussed further.

The export of slaves to places outside the territories in which they were initially captured was not done by the chiefs themselves or their agents, but by traders and merchants who, as discussed later, were almost entirely people of the commoner class (the *talakawa*). The chiefs who acquired the slaves, would, after keeping some for labor, often sell the rest to the traders from whom they would purchase some valuable commodities—luxury consumer goods, such as textile goods and carpets, or military equipment, such as horses, mounted and unmounted swords, and a few firearms. Some slaves were, however, given away as free gifts to favorites who eventually exported some of them.[25] (Thus, for a successful chief, a military campaign served two purposes, reestablishing his political hegemony over an area or over a set of people, and providing the means to acquire more luxury goods and military equipment.)

Before the sale and export of slaves are discussed, it is perhaps better to first examine what general economic and social factors governed the decision to sell and to export slaves, and also determined whom to sell away. A brief survey of the factors is considered necessary because the export of slaves was just one of the numerous ways in which slaves were disposed of advantageously.

Alternative Usage

This included using slaves for farm labor and also for domestic service in the house; as commercial agents and assistants; as porters, soldiers, and guards; as helpers and apprentices in crafts; in public administration; as concubines in wealthy homes; etc.

With regard to farm labor, people who had numerous slaves often settled them on virgin lands and supplied them with the necessary agricultural input—hoes, seeds, and some food. Such slave farm settlements were called *runji* (*rumji, rinji*). At the end of the growing season, the slaves and the masters shared the crops in proportion.[26] Other slave owners preferred

---

Richard Lander, *Journal of an Expedition to Explore the Course and Termination of the Niger, with a narrative . . .* (London, 1832). H. Barth, *Travels and Discoveries in North and Central Africa,* reprint, centenary ed. (London, 1967).

[25] See the journal of Lyons, who met a certain mean Arab who exported the slaves given him in Sokoto. George Francis Lyons, *A Narrative of Travels in Northern Africa in the Years 1818, 19, and 20* (London, 1821).

[26] *Runji* farming is discussed in a number of learned works including Last on Sokoto, and Njeuma and Saad Abubakar on Adamawa; M. G. Smith wrote on Zaria. Also see Clapperton's journal. Last, *The Sokoto Caliphate;* M. Z. Njeuma, "The Rise and Fall of Fulani Rule in Adamawa," unpublished doctoral thesis (University of London, 1969); S. Abubakar, "The

keeping the slaves in their houses and then sending them to their farms daily. The women slaves in the house did most of the errands, general cleaning, and kitchen work. The beautiful ones among them were converted into concubines; their children grew up as free members of the society.[27]

As commercial agents and assistants the slaves would be involved in the business transaction of their masters, and occasionally, if they were trusted, they might be sent on trading missions to buy or sell for the masters.[28] It should however be stated that the use of slaves in commerce was not peculiar to the traders from the interior, for Oroge has also noted the same development with some Yoruba slave owners in the forest belt.[29]

Craftsmen also used slave labor quite extensively. The slaves were either engaged merely to provide manual labor in producing the goods under supervision, or were apprenticed to their masters and taught professional skills and even some business secrets. This included both men and women slaves (the latter particularly engaged in spinning and weaving).[30] Slaves who were apprenticed to their masters were, in most cases, eventually absorbed into the families of their masters, and on the death of the heads of the families a few of them might even step into their masters' shoes if the sons were minors.

Chiefs and other members of the nobility had other ways in which they utilized their slaves. Some of the male slaves were engaged as guards and soldiers, and others were recruited into public service and even given important posts with full responsibilities over free members of the society. The engagement of slaves in public administration is an issue that has already been discussed by a number of people, including Adamu Fika (for Kano Emirate), Louis Brenner (for Borno), and M. G. Smith (for Zaria); and reference to their works may be made for details.[31]

Emirate of Fombina," unpublished doctoral thesis (Ahmadu Bello University, 1970); M. G. Smith, *Government in Zazzau* (London, 1960); H. Clapperton, *Journal of a Second Expedition into the Interior of Africa*, reprint London, 1966 (originally published London, 1829).

[27] Children born of such liaisons were not *cucunawa* (cucunawa were people born in slavery whose fathers and mothers were both slaves).

[28] Kundila of Kano was one of the Hausa merchants who made the most extensive use of slave trading agents during the nineteenth century. Research work is now in progress under Jan Hogendorn and Paul Lovejoy to retrieve material on the principal merchants of Kano, including Kundila.

[29] E. A. Oroge, "The Institution of Slavery in Yorubaland," unpublished doctoral thesis (University of Birmingham, 1970), pp. 204–249.

[30] Clapperton's observations in Sokoto during the second visit, *Second Expedition*.

[31] Adamu Fika, "The Political and Economic Re-orientation of Kano, 1882–1940," unpublished doctoral thesis (University of London, 1973); L. Brenner, *The Shehus of Kukawa* (London, 1973); Smith, *Government in Zazzau*.

Sale and Export

Traditionally, in the Central Sudan—though more so in Hausaland than in Borno—there was (and by and large it is still unchanged) an unwritten societal regulation as to who should take active part in commerce publicly and who should not. Basically, commerce was for the *talakawa* (the com- moners)[32] in the same way that military services were the principal concern of the *masu sarauta* (titled officers, the nobility) and their personal bands. This division of effort is apparently the same in all aristocratic societies, and the Hausa and the Barebari (Borno) societies were, and still are, quite aristocratic.[33] That way why, with regard to the slave trade, the members of the *masu sarauta* group were rarely directly responsible for the export of any slaves that passed through their hands. Except in certain cases of *samame* by passing merchants, slaves were rarely exported by those who initially captured them.

Slaves meant for sale were handled in the same way as all other major commodities were handled, the main channels of distribution being house trading and display in the market squares.

In the Central Sudan, up to the end of the eighteenth century, expensive commodities, including slaves, were rarely taken to the markets. Rather, the traders kept them at home for display and sale to customers.[34] Even in Katsina and Kano, which in the eighteenth and nineteenth centuries were the largest marketing centers in the region, this system was operative. In most of the interior towns slaves were bought and sold in house trade up to the enactment of the Abolition Act by Britain at the beginning of the nineteenth century.[35] Since then, however, there occurred what looked like slave inflation, due probably to three factors. The first was the drying up of the Atlantic slave trade, which followed the British Abolition Act of 1807; and the second was the tremendous slackening in the export of slaves across the Sahara. The third factor was the substantial increase in the number of

---

[32] See Mahdi Adamu, *The Hausa Factor in West Africa History* (Zaria, 1978), Chapter 1.

[33] See the works of M. G. Smith on the Hausa society and those of R. Cohen and L. Brenner on Borno.

[34] The rationale is that the people who could afford slaves considered it beneath their social standing to transact in the market square.

[35] For house trading in slaves and other commodities in the different parts of the Central Sudan, reference may be made to the following works: Polly Hill, "Two Types of West African Hausa Trade" in Claude Meillassoux, *The Development of Indigenous Trade and Markets in West Africa* (London, 1971), pp. 312–314; Polly Hill, *Rural Hausa: A Village and a Setting* (Cambridge, 1972), pp. 319–320; William Allen and T. R. H. Thomas, *A Narrative of the Expedition Sent by Her Majesty's Government*, vol. 1, reprint (London, 1968), p. 401; Barth, *Travels and Discoveries*, vol. 2.

slaves available, most of whom were prisoners of war captured during the numerous Jihad campaigns that followed the Islamic reform movement centered at Sokoto. Slave markets therefore began to emerge. The slave sections that developed in the Zaria and Kano markets were very large. In the former town, for instance, Baikie in 1862 saw up to 4000 slaves displayed in the market.[36] Some years later, Staudinger made a similar remark on the same market;[37] and just before the century ended, Robinson's observation in the same town confirmed both.[38] The slaves awaiting sale were often fed by the market brokers (the dilalai) who also sheltered them. They rarely received humane treatment, especially with regard to accommodation. Unlike other places, in Zaria the marketing of slaves, at least during the second half of the nineteenth century, was controlled by the government through the office of Sarkin Bayi (chief of the slaves).[39]

TRANSPORT OF SLAVES

As indicated earlier, the decision to sell one's slaves was not a straightforward one because there were many other economical ways in which the slaves could be utilized. The decision having been made, however, the slaves might find themselves owned by some merchants who might decide either to sell them through the internal distribution system, or to take them to some places outside the region (i.e., export them). Before the middle of the eighteenth century most of the slaves taken out of the Central Sudan and sold away were, as noted earlier, destined for Saharan and North African markets. After that date export to the Bight of Benin began to be significant. All available information, however, indicates that slave caravans from the Central Sudan providing through transport to the markets along the coast in the south did not exist. Instead, slaves from the Central Sudan reached the coast in the following manner:

[36] W. B. Baikie, "Notes of a Journey from Bida in Nupe to Kano in Hausa Performed in 1862," Journal of the Royal Geographical Society, vol. 37, 1867, pp. 92–107.

[37] P. Staudinger, Im Herzen der Hausalander (Berlin, 1889).

[38] C. H. Robinson, Hausaland: Fifteen Hundred Miles through the Central Sudan (London, 1896).

[39] Sarkin Bayi (Hausa, literally, chief of the slaves), was always a wealthy market broker (dillali) who could afford to buy slaves from desperate sellers and keep them for sale for any length of time. He operated under the control of the Sarkin Kasuwa (chief of the market), the officer who supervised the daily running of the city market. See the tapes in the "Hogendorn Collection." Further details on the marketing of slaves in the Central Sudan may be found in Chapter 8 by Paul E. Lovejoy and Jan S. Hogendorn, in this volume.

1. as porters
2. through a chain of traders
3. from homes in the forest belt where they had been serving as domestic slaves

What probably accounts for the absence of slave caravans to the coast is the fact that the export of slaves from the Central Sudan, particularly from Hausaland, to the forest zone in the south, was prohibited through Islamic-biased government regulations.[40] So people exporting slaves to the south would have to show them as part and parcel of their caravans. Further discussion on the manner of exporting the slaves will be more meaningful if the routes often used by the exporters are discussed.

The most popular routes that merchants from the Central Sudan took to reach the Bight of Benin during the hundred years being studied here (circa 1750–circa 1850) were (*a*) the land route to the Gwanja (Gonja) markets[41] in the present northern Ghana and thence to the Gold Coast; (*b*) the land route through Nupe and Old Oyo and from there to Lagos, to Badagry or to the Dahomean ports; and (*c*) the river Niger route, down to the creeks of the Niger delta, to the coast and from there by lagoons to Lagos and Badagry. These routes have already been discussed in my earlier works.[42] The major towns on the routes will be discussed further. One of the points that should be noted concerning these routes is the relationships they had with the centers of commercial activity in the places through which they passed, for most of the major trading centers located in the different areas were on them. The importance of this for the export of slaves to the south will become obvious when the manner in which slaves were exported to the coast is examined.

Merchants from the Central Sudan (the majority of them were of Hausa, Barebari and Nupe origins) who took the land routes to reach the coast in the south and the Gwanja (Gonja) markets in the southwest, used pack animals (donkeys and mules mainly) and human beings for porterage.[43]

[40] Muhammad Bello, *Infaq al-Maysur* (Cairo, 1965). The export of slaves to the Muslim north was, however, allowed to continue unchecked.

[41] Gwanja (Gonja, Gunja) was a kingdom in the present northern Ghana, and it was in the towns in the kingdom that the traders from the Central Sudan found the kolanuts they had come to buy. The nuts were gathered in the Asante (Ashanti) forest zone. By extension, the whole territory that now constitutes northern Ghana came to be regarded as the Gwanja markets (or Kurmin Gwanja, as Hausa traders called it).

[42] Mahdi Adamu, *The Hausa Factor*, and "The Distribution of Trading Centres in the Central Sudan in the Eighteenth and Nineteenth Centuries," a paper submitted to the Sokoto Seminar, January 1975.

[43] There are quite a number of references on this; the leading ones being the doctoral theses of Paul E. Lovejoy, "The Hausa Kola Trade 1700–1900: A Commercial System in the Continental Exchange of West Africa." (Wisconsin, 1973) and Ogunremi (Birmingham, 1973).

Because of the fatal effects of the tsetse fly in the forest zones, however, those traders who wanted to continue to the coast had to abandon their animals on the northern fringes of the forest belts (of Yorubaland, Dahomey, and Asante) and continue the journey using human porterage only.[44] But since the northern edge of the forest zone, however, was the intended destination of most of the merchants from the interior,[45] this natural limitation on southward penetration did not pose a serious problem to the traders from the Central Sudan. In any case, these interior traders used porters—both free people and slaves—quite extensively.[46]

Policing the slave porters during the journey presented no difficulties because only slaves who had stayed with the merchants for some time were normally used as porters; so they carried their loads without being shackled. Exceptions were the slave porters kidnapped from their villages by passing merchants. Oral information on this shows that such kidnapping incidents were more prevalent in places away from the centers of government and in most cases occurred near the forest zones.[47] Merchants of the *madugu* type who traveled with armed escorts were notorious for this.[48] Such conscripted porters were marched in single lines with armed foot and mounted guards supervising them to prevent them from running away.[49] Those who behaved well during the outward journey were not often sold but were incorporated into the porterage pool of the merchant. In addition to any security checks that merchants might make to prevent their slave–porters from running away, what kept the slaves with their masters during the journey was the realization that once they dropped out of the caravans they were liable to be captured and enslaved again.[50]

[44] Polly Hill, *Studies in Rural Capitalism in West Africa* (Cambridge, 1970), and her *Rural Hausa*. See also Lander in Clapperton, *Second Expedition.*

[45] For commerce along the northern edge of the Asante forest in the eighteenth and nineteenth centuries, reference may be made to the works of Ivor Wilks and Nehemia Levtzion, particularly Wilks' "Asante Policy towards Hausa Trade in the Nineteenth Century" in Claude Meillassoux, ed., *The Development of Indigenous Trade and Markets in West Africa* (London, 1971), pp. 124–141; and Levtzion's *Muslims and Chiefs in West Africa* (London, 1968).

[46] Clapperton, *Second Expedition.*

[47] See tapes of interviews at Zaria in the "Hogendorn Collection."

[48] See the frequent references in Lovejoy's thesis. P. E. Lovejoy, "The Hausa Kola Trade 1700–1900: A Commercial System in the Continental Exchange of West Africa," unpublished doctoral thesis (University of Wisconsin, 1973).

[49] Information supplied by J. S. Hogendorn, Zaria, 1975.

[50] Indeed it was this fear of recapture that had kept many liberated slaves near the coast rather than returning home to the interior. Frederick E. Forbes, *Dahomey and the Dahomans: Being the Journals of Two Missions to the King of Dahomey and Residence at his Capital, in the Years 1849 and 1850,* 2 vols. (London, 1851). See vol. 1, p. 33.

Another way in which slaves from the Central Sudan reached the Coast was through a chain of traders. This is well illustrated by the manner in which a certain cleric–merchant from Kano, named Muhammad Abdullah, who was interviewed in Bahia in 1848 by Francis de Castlenau,[51] was exported to the Coast. His name in Bahia was Manuel. He was captured in Borgu when his Hausa–Gwanja caravan was attacked by highway robbers. After staying for a short while in the custody of his captors, he was sold to Yoruba traders, and after being resold, he was eventually transported to the coast via the river Ogun. Muhammad Abdullah was shipped to Bahia from Lagos. Obviously such slaves who were neither familiar with their new masters nor fully reconciled with their new servile status would need to be closely guarded at all times and even chained if they were difficult during the journey.

Up to the end of the eighteenth century the main trading centers on the way to the coast where commodities, including slaves, changed hands, included Idah south of the Niger–Benue confluence, Rabbah in Nupe, Old Oyo in Yorubaland, and Nikki in Borgu. Further away, there were Benin, Ijebu, Djougou (in southern Borgu), and Abomey in Dahomey. The most important ports for the export of slaves from the interior were Lagos, Badagry, Porto Novo, and Whydah. Since the beginning of the nineteenth century, however, some additional inland entrepôts emerged, including Lokoja[52] at the Niger–Benue confluence, and Ilorin,[53] Ibadan, and Abeokuta in Yorubaland.[54] Old Oyo, however, disappeared after 1836–1837 when it was deserted by the government and the people. With it went Sagudu, its river Niger port.[55] It was principally through these chains of trading centers that slaves (and other commodities) who were "relayed" from the Central Sudan, reached the coast in the Bight of Benin.

The third major way in which slaves from the Central Sudan reached the coast was through serving as domestic help in some homes of the forest belt,

[51] See F. B. de Castlenau, *Renseignements sur l'Afrique Centrale* . . . (Paris, 1851), p. 46 and Verger, *Flux et reflux*, pp. 327–328.

[52] See C. C. Ifemesia, "The British enterprise on the Niger 1830–1869," unpublished University of London doctoral thesis, 1959; and Flint, *Sir George Goldie and the Making of Nigeria*.

[53] Hopkins, *Economic History of West Africa*.

[54] For the rise of Ibadan and Abeokuta as political and commercial centres in the nineteenth centuries, reference may be made to P. C. Lloyd et al., eds., *The City of Ibadan* (Cambridge, 1967); S. O. Biobaku, *The Egba and their Neighbours* (Oxford, 1957); and E. Krapf-Askari, *Yoruba towns and cities* (London 1969).

[55] For commerce in old Oyo in the eighteenth and nineteenth centuries, reference may be made to Robin Law, *The Oyo Empire c. 1600–1836; A West African Imperialism in the Era of the Atlantic Slave Trade* (Oxford, 1977).

and, thence, being sold away at a later time. That there were thousands of slaves from the Central Sudan serving in various homes in Yorubaland in the eighteenth and early nineteenth centuries was attested to by the relative ease with which the *Jamaa* army was raised in Ilorin between circa 1817 and 1823. The *Jamaa* was an army of mainly Hausa-speaking Muslim people, both freemen and runaway slaves, which grew up under Mallam Alimi to assist Kakanfo Afonja to secede from the Empire of Oyo.[56] Prior to the rise of the *Jamaa,* that is, during the eighteenth century, the Hausa slaves serving in Yorubaland occupied very strategic places in the economy of their new country on account of the specialized services that most of them performed for the Yoruba people, which the Yoruba could not perform themselves. These services, which the slaves performed side by side with free immigrants from the north, included tending the numerous horses on which the military power of the Alafinate of Oyo depended,[57] and herding the cattle owned by some of the rich Yoruba people.[58] "Barbers and rope-makers also mostly Hausa and Fulani. These crafts were rarely practiced by Yoruba. On occasion, these Hausa barbers also performed some surgical operations such as cupping, bone-setting, tapping, and hydroceles. Some were even oculists professing ability to operate for cataract."[59] A few of the slaves were also engaged on farms, and others worked as trading agents and assistants for their masters.[60] It was indeed because of the economic useful-ness of the slaves from the Central Sudan that a large proportion of them were retained within the forest zone and not taken to the European slave merchants on the coast. Since it was the usual practice all over West Africa, however, to sell away any slaves that proved difficult to live with, some of the interior slaves serving in homes in the south no doubt found themselves in the slave camps on the coast.

During the journeys to the south, slaves who were engaged as porters were often fed in the same manner as the free porters, from the master's provisions.[61] It is obvious that these slave–porters had to be fed reasonably well in order that they could carry the heavy loads often placed on them. No specific study has yet been made on how the Hausa and Barebari merchants traveling through the forest belt fed themselves; but since the Hausa had a standard pattern of feeding on all the other routes they operated, it is

[56] For details on the formation and the subsequent operation of the *Jamaa* army reference may be made to S. Johnson, *History of the Yoruba* (Lagos, 1956).

[57] Ajayi and Smith, *Yaruba warfare in the 19th century.*

[58] Johnson, *History of the Yoruba*, p. 123.

[59] Johnson, *History of the Yoruba*, p. 123.

[60] On trader–slaves, reference may be made to Oroge, Ph.D., 1970, pp. 204–266.

[61] Olderogge, D. A., *Zapadnyi Sudan* (Moscow, 1960).

reasonable to assume that they behaved in the same way even in the forest zone. Traveling Hausa traders often operated from *zangos*. A *zango* is a resting place, usually on the outskirts of the town, on a major route, where travelers could find ready food and drinks to buy and even shelter for the night in some places. Some Hausas often stayed at the principal *zangos* for long periods to cater to the passing travelers. It was also from these resident *zango* dwellers that the merchants got their information on the commerce of the area (e.g., prices) and also on the security of the roads.[62] In Yorubaland in the course of the nineteenth century, some of the Church Missionary Society Christian missionaries working in the country saw quite a number of traders from the north traveling to and from Ilorin, camping outside the towns.[63] Some of the principal merchants occasionally traveled with their wives and concubines, who cooked for them. It was generally at the catering services along the routes, however, that the travelers fed themselves, their servants, and slaves. Of course one would normally expect the slaves to feed from the leftovers.

There are some oral traditions, however, recorded by this author[64] and corroborated in Nur Alkali's collections,[65] that say that some of the Barebari traders from Borno often carried dried and seasoned food which they would heat whenever they settled down at a *zango*. They carried small metal pots with them and did most of the cooking, for they did not travel with wives as often as did the Hausa. This information, plausible though it may be, seems to contradict what appears to have been an established practice of the Barebari men who were out on military campaign. In Ibn Furtua's history of Mai Idris Aloma of Borno, it is reported that the Barebari soldiers detested cooking for themselves, and it was for this reason that they brought their wives and other women with them whenever they were going out for war. Since traders were essentially on profit-making ventures, however, it should not be surprising if they adopted measures that would cut their spending. Certainly any merchants who had slaves, male or female, would make them their cooks, as was the practice on the trans-Saharan routes.

With regard to custom duties, there is nothing to show that levies were

[62] For further discussion on this, reference may be made to Lovejoy, *The Hausa Kola Trade;* Adamu, *Hausa Factor;* and Olderogge, *Zapadnyi Sudan.*

[63] C.M.S. papers. Could be consulted in the University Library, Ibadan, and the C.M.S. headquarters, London.

[64] Fieldwork, Maiduguri, August, 1972.

[65] Mr. Nur Alkali is a lecturer in Bayero University, Kano. He collected his material from many oral interviews in Western and northern Borno. I am grateful to him for the information.

paid on slaves during the journey to the coast. Traditionally territorial chiefs charged duties only on portable goods, the unit of account being donkey loads or human loads. Though the slaves passing through the forest belt from the Central Sudan were indeed as much trading commodities as, say, the leather and textile goods that the merchants carried, no duties were paid on them because they would pass as part of the mobile household of the masters. This no doubt explains the absence of any mention of duties paid on the slaves transported southward.

The sale of slaves at the coast is an issue that has already received the attention of various writers, both contemporary travelers in the eighteenth and nineteenth centuries and some recent scholars. The slaves were sold mainly in exchange for European goods, such as textiles, drinks, tobacco, firearms, and fanciful objects for decoration and amusement. For further discussion of this point, see the works of A. G. Hopkins and Pierre Verger.[66] In the Central Sudan, however, the slave captors (the chiefs) received principally luxury goods and military (cavalry) equipment.

CONCLUSION

This chapter is intended to give a view of a slave delivery system in operation. Though many writers have talked about the general character of such systems, few if any have actually looked at one in very much detail. In the case of slave delivery from the Central Sudan to the Bight of Benin, the process involved acquisition through capture, usually by the government; sometimes by illegal kidnapping; or through tribute, purchase, or gift. After sale from houses (and later in markets), slaves reached the coast as part of a wider trading mechanism, with merchants involved in the delivery of general merchandise as well as slaves. It is misleading to think of the slave supply system as being separated from the supply of other goods.

The mechanism had little in common with the stereotype of slaves simply marching from where they were captured, through the jungle to a slave port. Rather, there were inland centers for exchange of slaves for merchandise, relay systems for transport, *zangos* for rest and for catering services— all requiring a substantial amount of commercial organization. Slaves were used as porters, and many remained in that occupation.

We do not know how many slaves traveled along this network. It is reasonably certain that a large number never were reexported overseas, because the Yoruba people in the forest zone had for quite some time

---

[66] A. G. Hopkings, *Economic History of West Africa*, Chapter 3; Pierre Verger, *Flux et reflux . . .*

found an equally economical way of utilizing the labor of many of the slaves they received from the north.[67] The appearance of slaves from the latter area in transatlantic shipment, most important during the last quarter of the eighteenth century,[68] is no doubt due to the competition of transatlantic demand with internal demand. The whole question of the relation between the external merchandise trade of the Central Sudan and the slave demand within Africa and overseas is much in need of serious study. As I have indicated in my *Hausa Factor* (pp. 185–186), the second half of the eighteenth century and the first of the nineteenth were a period of economic boom in Hausaland. This was the time when the incoming trade of Hausaland and the export of goods from the country both expanded greatly. Since the export of slaves from Hausaland was always part and parcel of the general foreign commerce of the Hausa and Barebari merchants, an expansion in the latter trade was bound to stimulate the former.

It also happened that at the time the Hausa merchants were intensifying their exports in different directions, one of their trading partners—the Yoruba people—were also intensifying their political expansion southwards. I am referring heie to the southward expansion and consolidation of the Empire of Oyo under Alafin Abiodun (1774–1789). By the time that Abiodun died in circa 1789, the Yoruba people were an effective commercial link between the north and the south, that is, between Nupe and Hausaland and the Bight of Benin.[69] Even though the Oyo Empire declined during the nineteenth century, the trading network connecting Hausaland and the Bight of Benin did not wither away with the decline of the empire because Dahomey was developed by the interior merchants as their new outlet.[70] The export of goods from Hausaland to Yorubaland and Dahomey had, all the time, been controlled by the economic forces in the exporting area. Part of the proof of this is that when, early in the second half of the nineteenth century, the economic situation in Hausaland so decreed, the Central Sudan became an importer of slaves from Dahomey.[71]

---

[67] As an incidental development, this study indicates among other things, that the place of slaves from the interior in the economy of Yorubaland to the beginning of the nineteenth century was something very complex, certainly deserving a separate research exercise. Unfortunately the Ph.D. thesis of Oroge, as far as the interior slaves are concerned, concentrates mainly on the activities of the liberated slaves since the 1840s.

[68] As revealed in Curtin's census of the Atlantic slave Trade referred to in note 3 above.

[69] For the political history of Yorubaland in the eighteenth and nineteenth centuries, reference may be made to R.C.C. Law, *The Oyo Empire*, and Johnson, the *History of the Yoruba*.

[70] Mahdi Adamu, *The Hausa Factor*, pp. 113–123.

[71] See J. A. Skertchly, *Dahomey as is. Being a narrative of eight months stay in that country* (London, 1874), p. 346. Also see Mahdi Adamu, *The Hausa Factor*, pp. 6 and 121.

In summary, the delivery mechanism involved traders from both the Central Sudan and the forest zone. It was highly economical and efficient in operation so far as we can tell; and its methods for care and policing, as well as the use of slaves as porters for other exports, were its outstanding characteristics. It will be most interesting to see the similarities and differences that future research brings to light on the other delivery mechanisms within West Africa.

ACKNOWLEDGMENTS

The draft of this chapter was read at the Social Sciences Seminar of Ahmadu Bello University, Zaria, on 11th June 1975, and I benefited from the comments made there. I however take full responsibility for the interpretations contained in the paper. I wish to take this opportunity to express my gratitude to J. S. Hogendorn who really encouraged me to write this chapter. I found his comments on the draft quite useful. Paul Lovejoy has also read the draft and commented.

7

Slavery in West Africa[1]

MARTIN KLEIN
PAUL E. LOVEJOY

Most of the other chapters in this volume address themselves directly to the trade in slaves between sub-Saharan Africa and the markets of the world. The underlying premise of this chapter is that it is not possible to comprehend fully the range of motivations, economic choices, and methods of acquisition and delivery extant in Africa during the centuries of the transatlantic trade without understanding the role and development of slavery within Africa itself.

To this end, this study attempts to assess the importance of slavery in West African history and to delimit the main theoretical issues.

Two major collections, one edited by Miers and Kopytoff and the other by Meillassoux, as well as numerous other studies, have added considerably to our knowledge of servile institutions and their impact on social and economic structures.[2] Our own study of slavery has been primarily in the

[1] The Social Science Research Council and Canada Council provided various grants that supported the research on which this is based.

[2] S. Miers and I. Kopytoff, eds., *Slavery in Africa: Historical and Anthropological Perspectives* (Madison, 1977); and C. Meillassoux, ed., *L'esclavage en Afrique précoloniale* (Paris, 1975). Also

Senegambia and the Central Sudan and is based on collections of oral data and archival material including the extensive 1904 enquiry by the French colonial administration, as well as on the growing published literature. The following analysis is a synthesis of these materials. In order to keep references within manageable proportions only a few examples from the literature and primary sources are cited for specific points.[3]

Our analysis proceeds from three basic assumptions. First, we make a distinction between the ideology of slavery and the reality of slavery. The institution was conceived of primarily in terms of kinship structures, a perspective most fully explored by Miers and Kopytoff.[4] Their analysis provides valuable insights into marginality as a status variable in the assimilation of slaves, but we are critical of their orientation because it does not provide sufficient explanation for the treatment of many slaves, particularly those who worked in mines or on plantations. In these and other situations kinship had much less influence than in the households where a kin-based system operated.[5] In effect, practice often differed from the theory.

---

see various papers presented at the Conference on Slavery and Related Institutions in Muslim Africa (Princeton University, 1977), especially Bernard Barbour, "The Miʿrāj: A Legal Treatise by Ahmad Bābā on Slavery"; David C. Conrad, "Slavery in Bambara Society: Segou, 1660–1861"; Polly Hill, "Comparative West African Farm-Slavery Systems (south of the Sahel) with Special Reference to Muslim Kano Emirate (N. Nigeria)"; Constance B. Hilliard, "Slave Status among the Futanke: A Preliminary View Derived from the Shaikh Mūsā Kamara Papers"; M. Hiskett, "Enslavement, Slavery and Attitudes towards the Legally Enslavable in Hausa Islamic Literature"; J. O. Hunwick, "Notes on Slavery in the Songhay Empire"; Martin Klein, "Domestic Slavery in the Muslim Societies of the Western Sudan"; Nehemia Levtzion, "Slavery and Islamization in Africa: A Comparative Study"; Paul E. Lovejoy, "The Characteristics of Plantations in the Sokoto Caliphate"; B. G. Martin, "Aḥmad Rāsim Pāshā and the Suppression of the Fazzān Slave Trade, 1881–1896"; L. Sanneh, "Islamic Slavery in the African Perspective"; and J. R. Willis, "The Servile Estate."

[3] For the French reports see Archives Nationales du Senegal (ANS) K18–22. Somewhat less extensive material on the Central Sudan is contained in F. Lugard's memorandum on slavery in 1906 (*Political Memoranda,* London, 1906). For oral data from the Senegambia, M. Klein's interviews are available at the Archives Culturelles in Dakar and the Center for African Oral Data in the Archives of Traditional Music, Indiana University. Oral data relevant to Central Sudan slavery are in the Lovejoy Collection, 1969–1970, Graduate History Room, Ahmadu Bello University, and in various collections of the 1975–1976 economic history project, including those by J. S. Hogendorn, Lovejoy–Maccido, A. B. Umar, Y. Yunusa, O. S. Ahmed, A. Musa, A. Babangida, M. Ahmed, Y. Haruna, A. Alfanda, and O. Adesiyin. The combined project is discussed in P. E. Lovejoy and J. S. Hogendorn, "Oral Data Collection and the Economic History of the Central Savanna," *Savanna,* vol. 7, no. 1, forthcoming. The material is currently being prepared for deposit at Ahmadu Bello University and Indiana University.

[4] For a criticism of the Miers–Kopytoff thesis, see F. Cooper, "Studying Slavery in Africa: Some Criticisms and Comparisons," forthcoming; and M. Klein, "The Study of Slavery in Africa: A Review Article," *Journal of African History,* vol. 19, no. 4, 1978.

[5] We concur with A. G. Hopkins that "there was a long-established labour market in

Second, we consider that the analysis of slavery must be placed within the context of the slave trade, including transatlantic and trans-Saharan exports and the internal supply mechanism within West Africa. Slaves were a commodity that had to be produced, but they were also producers in agriculture, crafts, mineral processing, and domestic activities. The double nature of slaves as an item of production and as an instrument for production demonstrates the fundamental importance of slavery to West African economy and society. Slavery was a changing institution, with great variation over time and place, which cannot be understood without reference to other historical developments.

Finally, we recognize the influential contributions of Terray, Bazin, Meillassoux, and other Marxist scholars.[6] We accept the implications of Terray's hypothesis that a slave mode of production was dominant in parts, if not most, of West Africa, a finding based on his study of Gyaman, a province of Asante. We also follow Bazin in considering the production of slaves and the organization of this business around slave recruits as crucial factors in the slave mode of production. Meillassoux has analyzed similar phenomena for the medieval period when trans-Saharan slave markets were the principal external factor in the development of slavery within the subcontinent. We believe the work of Oroge (Yoruba), N. Klein (Asante), Terray (Gyaman, Asante), Hogendorn (Zaria), Hill (Kano), Lovejoy (Sokoto Caliphate), Mason (Nupe), M. Klein (Senegambia), and various contributions in the Meillassoux and the Miers and Kopytoff volumes allow for confirmation of the Terray–Meillassoux–Bazin model.[7]

Africa," and "that this market took the form of slave labour"; see A. G. Hopkins, *An Economic History of West Africa* (London, 1973), p. 26.

[6] See the contributions to the Meillassoux volume, but also J. Bazin, "War and Servitude in Segou," *Economy and Society*, vol. 3, 1974, pp. 107–143; E. Terray, "Classes and Class Consciousness in the Abron Kingdom of Gyaman," in Maurice Bloch, ed., *Marxist Analyses and Social Anthropology* (London 1975), pp. 85–136; Terray, "Long-Distance Exchange and the Formation of the State: The Case of the Abron Kingdom of Gyaman," *Economy and Society*, vol. 3, 1974, pp. 315–345; and C. Meillassoux, "The Role of Slavery in the Economic and Social History of Sahelo–Saharan Africa," unpublished paper presented at the seminar on the economic history of the Central Savanna (Kano, 1976).

[7] In addition to the contributions to the Miers–Kopytoff and Meillassoux volumes, see A. E. Oroge, "The Institution of Slavery in Yorubaland with Particular Reference to the Nineteenth Century," unpublished doctoral thesis (University of Birmingham, 1971); N. Klein, *Inequality in Asante*, forthcoming, (we wish to thank Professor Klein for showing us a copy of this manuscript); Terray, "Classes and Class Consciousness," pp. 85–136; Terray, "Long Distance Exchange," pp. 315–345; J. S. Hogendorn, "The Economics of Slave Use on Two 'Plantations' in the Zaria Emirate of the Sokoto Caliphate": *International Journal of African Historical Studies*, vol. 10, no. 3, 1977, pp. 369–383; Polly Hill, "From Slavery to Freedom: The Case of Farm-Slavery in Nigerian Hausaland," *Comparative Studies in Society and History*, vol. 18, no. 3, 1976, pp. 395–426; P. E. Lovejoy, "Plantations in the Economy of the Sokoto Caliphate," *Journal of African History*, vol. 19, 1978; M. Mason, "Captive and Client Labour and the

KINSHIP AND SLAVERY

Curtin has considered slaves within a basically assimilationist framework in which slaves acquired "subordinate membership" in their adopted society, "including a fictitious quasi-kinship relationship to the master's lineage."[8] We can accept this view as the fundamental tenet in the ideology of slavery. Kopytoff and Miers have elaborated on this concept in their discussion of slavery as institutionalized marginality. They consider slavery to have been essentially an instrument for incorporating aliens into lineage structures by reducing their marginal position.[9] In their perspective, slaves sought to "belong" rather than to escape, and this aim reinforced kinship structures. They see this as the essence of lineage slavery, but this approach fails to explain why slavery lasted longer in Africa than virtually anywhere else in the world. It seems clear that there was a direct relationship between the continued importance of lineage cohesion and the general level of insecurity in Africa, which in turn directly related to war and enslavement. The emphasis on "belonging" is indeed revealing, precisely because people could not seek to be "free." As Wright has also shown in her analysis of the lives of three women in Central Africa, dependency was usually essential to survival.[10].

We recognize a distinctive category of lineage slavery, but we believe that emphasis on its "assimilationist" tendencies misrepresents the condition of many slaves in the past. Kopytoff and Miers's transition from marginality to full "belonging" took place in many societies, but it usually involved generations and there was frequently a vast differential in status and material well-being between master and slave, and between the master's children and slave children. It is likely that transformation did in fact occur over time. The status of slaves "born in the house" was always better than that of newly enslaved. Established second-generation slave villages needed less management, and obligations shifted towards tribute arrangements. When pay-

---

Economy of the Bida Emirate," *Journal of African History*, vol. 14, no. 3, 1973, pp. 453–471; Mason, "Trade and State in Nineteenth-Century Nupe," Kano Seminar, 1976; M. Klein, "Slave Systems in the Western Sudan," forthcoming; M. G. Smith, "Slavery and Emancipation in Two Societies," in M. G. Smith, *The Plural Society in the British West Indies* (Berkeley, 1965), pp. 116–161; and M. G. Smith, "Introduction," in Mary Smith, *Baba of Karo* (New York, 1955), pp. 11–34.

[8] P. D. Curtin, *Economic Change in Precolonial Africa. Senegambia in the Era of the Slave Trade*, (Madison, 1975), vol. 1, pp. 34–35, 155.

[9] Miers and Kopytoff, "Introduction: Slavery as Institutionalized Marginality," in Miers and Kopytoff, *Slavery in Africa*, pp. 7–66.

[10] Miers and Kopytoff, "Introduction," pp. 10–24; Marcia Wright, "Women in Peril: A Commentary on the Life Stories of Captives in 19th Century East Central Africa," *African Social Research*, vol. 20, 1975, pp. 800–819.

ments became standardized, the pattern resembled serfdom.[11] It was similar, perhaps, to what Olderogge describes for sixteenth-century Songhai. There, early forms of slavery were modified so that

> we can see that feudal relationships were gradually developing in the Songhai kingdom, and that feudal patterns of land tenure were emerging. The status of slaves who were settled on the land did not differ in an economic respect from that of serfs. They differed from the rest of the population only in a legal sense.[12]

Whether or not the parallel with feudalism will hold up under further examination is uncertain, but it is clear that situations varied and the institution was very complex. In fact the many types of slaves and the different uses to which they were put reveal a fundamental contradiction between ideology and practice. It remains to examine this contradiction in order to evaluate historical change and to elucidate the position of slavery within West African economy and society.

Although one fundamental distinction was between slaves in Islamic societies and those in non-Muslim areas where lineage structures were more pervasive, other differences were crucial, particularly that between slaves who were born into captivity and those who were recently acquired. Thus we can detect several categories based on the degree of assimilation: captives, purchased slaves, and those born in the household.

The first category was the captives.[13] These were people who were newly enslaved and essentially in transit. They had to be moved away from areas where escape would be easy and where they had kinship ties. They had virtually no rights, lacked a social identity, and were in effect mere chattel. It was at this stage that treatment was worst. The importance of captives dates back to the medieval period. Indeed, for virtually all West African

[11] W. Derman, *Serfs, Peasants, and Socialists* (Berkeley, 1973), pp. 27–30, uses "serf" to describe servile agricultural workers in a stable, hereditary relationship. The problem with this definition is that a serf is usually tied to the land. In Africa, however, it was the person of the subordinate individual that was controlled. The slave was owned. Thus, informants in Sudanic societies frequently speak of slaves being property like their cattle. Also see Marion Johnson, "The Economic Foundations of an Islamic Theocracy—The Case of Masina," *Journal of African History,* vol. 17, no. 4, 1976, pp. 481–496, but again there is a major conceptual problem in the analysis, since Johnson considers that serfdom is established in the first generation of servility, without the crucial tie to the land.

[12] D. A. Olderogge, "Feodalizm v Zapadnom Sudane v 16–18vv," *Sovietskaya etnografia,* vol. 4, 1957, pp. 91–103; summarized in *African Abstracts,* vol. 10, 1959, pp. 11–12.

[13] There is some ambiguity in the use of the term "captive." During the early colonial period, it was often used by administrators trying to differentiate between the relatively benign household institution and the harsh treatment dealt to those we have labeled "captives." We, however, do not see a better term for those who had been taken by force from one society and not yet inserted into another.

states in all periods, raiding and war were major factors in the production of slaves. Asante, Dahomey, mercenary bands under Aro direction, and Islamic states relied upon raiding for the acquisition of slaves, either directly, or indirectly through tribute payments. Hence the enslavement of the vast majority of slaves appears to have been closely associated with political history. It is the pool of captives recently enslaved and lacking any social identity, that was tapped by the Atlantic and trans-Saharan slave trades.[14]

From the moment a slave entered a new society, his status changed. He took on a new name, assumed a recognized status in the host society, and became a subordinate member of a kinship group. These slaves have often been referred to as "trade slaves" even after they were no longer in transit. They could be sold and often were, if their behaviour did not conform to the expectations of their owners or if they tried to escape. The newly enslaved were often poorly treated and generally given harsher tasks than those more fully incorporated, but they had a social identity and the process of assimilation had begun. Three crucial changes occurred for these slaves. First, with time, many learned the master's language, developed affective ties, and reconciled themselves to the new society's ways. This assimilation was obviously most complete with those enslaved as children and is a reason why children were preferred to adult men. Second, they were married either to another slave or, in the case of attractive females, to a member of the master's family. Third, and perhaps most important, they had children, which created a strong tie, especially in the case of women. In practice, however, this may not always have been effective. French reports in the last decades of the nineteenth century, at least, are full of accounts of freed slaves trying to claim or redeem children, mothers, husbands, and wives.[15]

Although there was a tendency toward assimilation, practice often depended upon the relative numbers of slaves in a society. High concentrations were common around cities and near the centers of strong states, including Asante, Dahomey, Oyo, Benin, the Aro-dominated confederation, and the Muslim empires of the savanna. On the peripheries of these states, in acephalous societies, and in times of economic collapse, patterns of slavery differed. In some cases, there were radical variations in the percentage of slaves in different communities within the same kingdom.

---

[14] Numbers can occasionally be estimated because the sudden increase in slave exports at the coast often reflected outbreaks of war. Many other times, however, their number remains unknown, especially with respect to the nineteenth-century *jihads* when many people were enslaved. For efforts to correlate changes in the interior with exports, see Philip D. Curtin, *The Atlantic Slave Trade. A Census* (Madison, 1969).

[15] These exchanges are widespread in local correspondence. See Archives Nationales du Sénégal, K18–22. See also J. L. Boutillier, "Les captifs en A.O.F. (1903–1905)," *Bulletin de l'IFAN*, vol. 30, no. 2, series B, 1968, pp. 513–535.

Where concentrations were lower, the possibilities of assimilation were much greater. Clearly, any detailed treatment of the institution must take these factors into account.[16]

Those born into slavery often could be sold, at least in most periods and places, but the tendency everywhere was for their absorption into the household and by extension into the larger society. In the early eighteenth century, for example, the slave merchant, Francis Moore, commented on the influence of public opinion in restraining masters from selling slaves born into the household:

> And tho' in some parts of Africa they sell their slaves born in the Family, yet in the River Gambia they think it a very wicked thing; and I never heard of but one that ever sold a Family-Slave, except for such crimes as would have made them to be sold had they been free. If there are many Family Slaves and one of them commits a Crime, the master cannot sell him without the joint consent of the rest, for if he does, they will all run away, and be protected by the next kingdom to which they fly.[17]

In fact, however, as the French Administrator, Brevié, noted in his report of 1904, Soninke custom also forbade the sale of slaves born into captivity, "but no sanctions existing, the master violates it [custom] as soon as he has sufficient interest."[18]

Domestic or household slaves, in either Islamic or lineage situations, lived in the master's compound, usually in a special section; but even slaves who inhabited a separate village, which characterized areas with large slave populations, were still considered members of the household in theory. In many places, as, for example, in the nineteenth-century Yoruba states, farming hamlets were used during the growing season, after which the slaves returned to the larger and safer walled settlements of their masters. Domestic or household slaves had obligations similar to other dependents, especially with regards to farming, when for brief periods time was very valuable. Young slaves worked alongside their age-mates. When they were old enough to farm for themselves, they were given their own plots, on which they worked evenings and free days. This division of labor between the master's lands and the slave's own plot seems to have been true in all areas.[19]

[16] Much of these data is in the 1904 Franch enquiry. See also Klein, "Slave Systems." For two case studies, see Edmond Bernus, "Kong et sa région," *Etudes Eburnéennes,* vol. 8, 1960, p. 253; and J. L. Boutillier, "La ville de Bouna de l'époque précolonial à aujourd'hui," *Cahiers ORSTOM,* vol. 6, 1969, pp. 9–10. There was also an earlier inquiry on slavery in the French Sudan, Archives Nationales du Sénégal, K14.

[17] Francis Moore, *Travels into the Inland Parts of Africa* (London, 1738), p. 33.

[18] Brevié, report on Bamako, Archives Nationales du Sénégal, K19.

[19] For Yoruba areas, see Oroge, "Slavery," Chapter 3. In the western Sudan, the labor obligation of the male slave was usually 5 days, generally from shortly after sunrise until early

In places with high slave concentrations, however, slaves worked longer hours, were supervised more closely, and in most cases, worked only with other slaves. This tendency demonstrates that practice could often diverge from theory. Still, young slaves could save the product of their own land, buy livestock, and own tools; but it is probable that most produce went toward subsistence or savings for marriages. In this the difference between slave and free dependent was only one of degree. In areas with low slave densities, slaves worked with the master and his offspring and participated more fully in the master's culture than in areas of greater slave concentrations. In artisan households, a slave might be an apprentice and participate in family activities. In low density societies, the slave was often initiated with his or her free counterparts. In some places, he received a religious education; though generally, he only learned a few prayers, if he were Muslim, or local rites, if he were not, and enough education to participate in the community's religious life in a subordinate capacity.

The head of the house was obligated to clothe slaves, which meant that one or two garments were provided each year, but slaves often worked in leather loincloths, in the savanna at least. In high density areas, feeding seems to have been fairly strictly controlled, but the theory was that household members ate from the same pot during times of cooperative activity. Slaves received one or two meals a day when they worked for the master, just as the master's children did. If a man had a wife, she cooked for him at other times, and his own garden was expected to meet these needs. He could probably count on help during periods of hardship, but the distribution of food was clearly an area where economic rationalization operated to the disadvantage of the slaves. This is most striking in reports on Soninke areas. Slaves interviewed by Brevié in 1904 complained of underfeeding, and those who sought their freedom at French posts were often emaciated.[20]

The master's responsibility for finding wives for male slaves related to his interest in keeping all dependents satisfied and in maximizing the reproductive capacity of females. Most of those newly enslaved were women and children. In societies with a rapidly expanding slave population, female slaves often outnumbered males 2:1. This meant that there were enough females to meet the demand for concubines and to provide wives for male slaves. Recent captives and unassimilated slaves may not have married as early as others, but most slaves eventually did so. Masters generally pre-

---

afternoon prayer (2:00 P.M.). This left the slave evenings and 2 days per week for his own fields. There was, however, considerable regional variation both in the length of the working day and in the number of days the slave had for his own fields. See Klein, "Slave Systems."

[20] Bamako report, Archives Nationales du Sénégal, K19.

ferred that slaves remain within their households, but where someone sought a spouse from outside, either exchange or purchase was possible. If this was not done, the wife usually lived with her husband but continued to work for her master, unless a regular payment was made. The wife's master had rights to children. The owner of the hen, it is said in the Senegambia, is the owner of the chicks. Marriage between male slaves and free women was very rare.[21]

With marriage, slave couples became more autonomous, especially after the birth of one or more children. The Wolof use the word *beru* for this autonomy, but the slave's *beru* differed from that of the free man in that he never became economically independent.[22] These slave couples did, however, have a substantial amount of autonomy. They could move away from the master's compound, they worked their own fields in exchange for certain fixed dues, and a man could take another wife, if he could afford to. He could also accumulate property, though possibilities were limited by his financial obligations, by the fortunes of the weather, and by disease and accident.

If the two major stages in the slave's integration were marriage and parenthood, the absence of legal paternity constituted the essence of the slave's subordination in the household, despite the use of kinship terminology.[23] Slave children inherited their mother's status and belonged to their mother's owner, unless freed. Personal acquisitions seem to have been generally respected, but slaves usually could not bequeath property to their children. In practice, masters often permitted children to inherit a part of the father's wealth, but, when they did so, it was not a right but an act of generosity. Similarly, the master could claim the services of the slave child, in some places after he had lost his baby teeth, in others after circumcision. The age and the extent of the child's service probably varied. In some areas, children seem to have worked largely on the slave father's plot, but the master could claim his labor for other activities. Essentially, the father played the paternal role only in the education of the child. When the child was old enough, he related directly to the head of the household. Another way this dependence was expressed was the custom of attaching slaves,

[21] David Ames, "Plural Marriage among the Woloj in the Gambia," unpublished doctoral dissertation (Northwestern University, 1953), p. 14.

[22] See Klein, "Slave Systems." A similar type of relationship developed among the Hausa (Smith, *Slavery and Emancipation,* pp. 116–161) and the Kanuri (R. Cohen, "Slavery in Africa," *Trans-Action,* vol. 4, 1967, pp. 48–50) and seems to be common elsewhere as well. Also see Miers and Kopytoff, "Introduction," p. 27.

[23] Meillassoux, "Etat et conditions des esclaves à Gumbu (Mali) au XIXᵉ siècle," in Meillassoux, *L'esclavage,* p. 224. Also see Paul Riesman, *Société et Liberté chez les Peul Pjelgôbé de Haute Volta* (Paris, 1974), p. 88.

usually children, to bride-price payments. This meant that the young slave often moved to the master's compound and could be permanently separated from his parents.

The final stage in the integration of a slave came with manumission. It is difficult to evaluate the extent of this practice, but various forms are widely reported from different parts of the savanna and forest, and the likelihood is that it was common in most periods. In the first instance, Islam sanctioned manumission and self-purchase (Hausa: *murgu*), while in forest societies kinship ideology encouraged full assimilation, even if it took place over the course of a generation or two. Manumission, therefore, altered the status of the slave to one of client or junior kinsman, very much as Kopytoff and Miers have argued, for the position of an individual alone in society was a difficult one.[24] It is unlikely that the slave capable of buying his own freedom had ties elsewhere. It is equally unlikely that he was capable of forming a fully independent household of his own.[25]

Former slaves usually maintained some kind of tie with the household, sometimes because those freed were elderly or trusted retainers. Meillassoux has described the position of a freedman among the Soninke of Gumbu, where the *woroso,* or domestic slave, became a *kome xoore* who no longer owed regular dues to the master and who could bequeath to his offspring.[26] He still remained a client of his former master, however. He gave gifts and presided over certain family ceremonies, was the messenger when there was a death, and distributed kola at baptisms. The *kome xoore* could no longer be sold, but he could not move from Gumbu nor could he marry a free-born person. Monteil's description of Bambara practice in the 1890s further demonstrates this promotion to the status of artificial kinsman:

> The link is not severed, and the freed man is a kind of relative. He is interested in everything that happens in his master's community and is present on all important occasions, never coming with empty hands. Reciprocally, he is never treated like a stranger by the master. The master contributes to every event concerning him: he helps him get his sons married and established. . . .[27]

Once a slave was permitted to farm his own land full-time, his major obligation was an annual payment to the head of the household. This seems

[24] Miers and Kopytoff, "Introduction," pp. 26–27. For a discussion of *murgu* and similar patterns of emancipation, see Smith, "Slavery and Emancipation," pp. 116–161.

[25] According to Richard Roberts, "The Maraka and the Economy of the Middle Niger Valley 1790–1908" (Unpublished Ph.D. thesis, University of Toronto, 1978), slaves of the Maraka preferred to buy slaves rather than their freedom, the latter being of limited value in an insecure world (personal communication).

[26] Meillassoux, "Gumbu," pp. 238–242.

[27] Charles Monteil, *Les Bambara du Ségou et Kaarta* (Paris, 1923), p. 193.

to have varied in amount. Yoro Dyao gave the Wolof slave's obligation as 35 kilograms of millet, whereas Meillassoux evaluated the Soninke slave's obligation at 337 kilograms per year.[28] In the upper Niger area, the norm seems to have been closer to Meillassoux's figure, though this probably depended on rainfall, quality of soil, and the degree of economic rationalization. The chief problem in evaluating the figures is in determining the value of a *muude*, the measure used for grain. Meillassoux uses 2.24 kilograms.[29] If this is correct, the usual obligation was somewhere between 200 and 300 kilograms per year. Monteil would thus be correct in writing that a slave could free himself from other obligations by paying "a certain number of measures (moudd) of millet, approximately enough to feed an adult for a year."[30] Meillassoux estimates the productivity of the average male at Gumbu at a little over a ton, which may be high but was certainly possible for a healthy and hard-working man. Pollet and Winter use 300 muude, which would be a good bit lower.[31] If the latter are correct, the slave diet was sparse and there was relatively little food for the unproductive young and old. The obligation of a woman or a child was about half that of an adult male. These data are for the nineteenth century; the situation is unclear for earlier periods and many places.

Concubines varied from other household slaves in their path to freedom. Once they bore children for their master they were freed, as were their children. As Cooper has pointed out, this was a fundamental distinction from slavery in the Americas.[32] When a slave woman bore the child of a free man other than her master that child inherited the mother's status. The slave concubine was not married in any formal sense. She was simply moved in and would be sent away at her master's whim. Only when she bore a child did she achieve status. Several factors made a slave concubine desirable. She had no family, there was no bride-price, and she was totally dependent. Offspring of slave women were probably a significant factor in population growth.

Assimilation was most pronounced in some forest zone societies and in

[28] R. Rosseau, "Le Sénégal d'autrefois. Etude sur le Oualo. Cahiers de Yoro Dyao," *Bulletin du comité d'études historiques et scientifiques de l'A.O.F.*, vol. 12, 1929, pp. 189–194; Meillassoux, "Gumbu," p. 236.

[29] This was a measure of volume, which did not have the same value in all areas. Curtin gives it as 1.75 liters; *Economic Change*, vol. 2, pp. 57–61. Meillassoux's estimate of the weight of a *muude* is low. Most administrators gave it as 3 kilograms. A slave owed 150 *muude* in Gumbu, 100 at Nioro, 90 at Bandiagora; ANS, K19. Where slaves wove, they also owed a certain amount of cloth. In areas with a high degree of market developments, slaves spent the full dry season weaving. ANS, K19; and Richard Roberts, personal communication.

[30] Monteil, *Bambara*, p. 191.

[31] Eric Pollet and Grace Winter, *La Société Soninke (Dyahunu, Mali)* (Brussels, 1971), p. 239.

[32] Cooper, "Studying Slavery."

some of the less differentiated Sudanic societies, where practice remained closer to the classical lineage model. Not only were children of slave concubines assimilated, but other slaves were largely absorbed into the lineage in one to three generations.[33]

In Asante where slaves sometimes formed junior branches of the master's lineage, it was illegal to mention a person's origins, but most people knew the truth. Sublineages of slave descent were distinct from the free, so that questions of rights to titles, inheritance, control of land, ritual responsibilities, and payments of tribute were kept clear. This suggests the presence of large concentrations of slaves, sometimes in such disproportion that it became possible for slaves to become heads of villages and shrine priests.[34]

Slave soldiers were found in almost all states and were dominant in many. In general they "belonged" to the royal office or to royal lineages in much the same way as agricultural slaves. The importance of slaves as soldiers lay in their kinlessness and hence their lack of status outside the master–slave relationship.[35] Many states gave important military and civil responsibilities to slave warriors precisely because they could be trusted. They often contributed to cohesion within the royal lineage. Normally, households tended to split after becoming large, but when power was contested between several opposing lineages, the members of different factions had an incentive for cooperation. Slave warriors promoted the dominance of the *geej* matrilineage within Kajoor and they, in turn, sometimes controlled its leaders.[36] Similarly, the Bambara *tonjon* could make or break candidates for

[33] N. Klein, *Inequality in Asante;* R. S. Rattray, *Asante Law a Constitution* (London, 1929), Chapter 5; Oroge, "Slavery," Chapter 3; E. Terray, "La Captivité dans le royaume abron du Gyaman," in Meillassoux, *L'esclavage,* pp. 389–454; Claude Perrot, "Les captifs dans le royaume anyi du Ndényé," in Meillassoux, *L'esclavage,* pp. 351–358; C. Meillassoux, "Introduction," in *The Development of Indigenous Trade and Markets in West Africa* (London, 1971), p. 63; but see K. Nwachukwu-Ogedengbe, "Slavery in Nineteenth-Century Aboh," in Miers and Kopytoff, *Slavery in Africa,* pp. 148–149, who notes that slaves in Aboh comprised a separate stratum; and Svend E. Holsoe, "Slavery and Economic Response among the Vai (Liberia and Sierra Leone)" in Miers and Kopytoff, *Slavery in Africa,* pp. 287–303.

[34] N. Klein, *Inequality in Asante;* Rattray, *Asante Law,* Chapter 5; and Ivor Wilks, *Asante in the Nineteenth Century* (London, 1975), p. 86.

[35] See Jean Bazin, "Guerre et servitude à Segou," in Meillassoux, *L'esclavage,* pp. 135–182; and Michel Izard, "Les captifs royaux dans l'ancien Yatenga" in Meillassoux, *L'esclavage,* pp. 281–295; M. Klein, "Servitude among the Wolof and Sereer of Senegambia," in Miers and Kopytoff, pp. 344–345, and Roberta Dunbar, "Slavery and the Evolution of 19th-Century Damagaram (Zinder, Niger)," in Miers and Kopytoff, *Slavery in Africa,* pp. 170–171; Humphrey J. and Allan G. B. Fisher, *Slavery and Muslim Society in Africa* (Garden City, New York, 1971), pp. 154–163.

[36] Vincent Monteil, "The Wolof Kingdom of Kayor," in Daryll Forde and P. M. Kaberry, eds., *West African Kingdoms in the Nineteenth Century* (London, 1967), pp. 260–279; Lucie Colvin, "Kajor and Its Diplomatic Relations with Saint Louis du Senegal, 1763–1861," doctoral thesis (Columbia University, 1972).

royal office in the nineteenth century.[37] What slavery involved for these privileged groups was a commitment to the interests of the royal lineage, which they, in turn, could help define and influence. During the period of the Atlantic slave trade, warrior-dominated forces tended to become hereditary. Official positions were often restricted to descendants of slaves of the state's founder or some early important ruler.[38]

In many slave-producing societies, there was no distinction between fighting slaves and farming slaves. The slave warrior also farmed, albeit sometimes reluctantly. In these societies, there was often an opposition between the slave-producing and slave-exploiting sectors, which was coterminous with the opposition that Meillassoux has underlined between the warrior and the trader.[39] It was the trader who bought the slaves "produced" by war or kidnapping and it was the trader who exploited slave labor. The military state assimilated new slaves only as warriors. In the nineteenth century this changed as new states emerged largely out of the market-oriented sector or adapted to the decline of the export trade. It is at this point that the distinction between farming slaves and fighting slaves became important.

Slaves involved in craft production and trade also tended to fit into the household model. Textile production was probably the most important single industry in the Sudan, and many slaves were involved in production. In areas of low slave density, slave and free both seem to have woven, but weaving was largely a slave occupation in much of the Western Sudan, at least.[40] In some communities, production was for the needs of the household, but in others, they produced for sale and worked systematically for at least 4 months, from the time when the cotton was ready until the time before the rains came when they had to start clearing the fields. This meant that in communities where weaving was important, slaves were kept busy virtually all year long. There was a brief slack time between the last weeding and the harvest and another after most of the crops came in, when there were many weddings and other festivities.

In a few areas, smiths and leather-workers seem to have also been slaves, most notably in Fuuta Jallon.[41] Smiths, leather-workers, and griots often bought slaves or received them as a reward for services. These slaves were

---

[37] Bazin, "Segou," p. 168; Monteil, *Bambara*, p. 329.

[38] Bernus, "Kong," p. 253; Michel Izard, "Les captifs royaux dans l'ancien Yatenga," in Meillassoux, *L'esclavage*, pp. 281–296; and for the Wolof kingdom of Saalum, see interview, Malik Sarr, Kahone, 6 April 1975 (see note 3 above).

[39] Bazin, "Segou," pp. 135–181; and Meillassoux, "Introduction," *Trade and Markets*, p. 55.

[40] Frederic Carrère and Paul Holle, *De la Senegambie Francaise* (Paris, 1855), p. 53; Klein, "Slave Systems"; Meillassoux, "Gumbu," pp. 224, 249–250; and personal communication from Richard Roberts.

[41] Derman, *Serfs*, pp. 37–39; and Mamadou Saliou Baldé, "L'esclavage et la guerre sainte au Fuuta-Jalon," in Meillassoux, *L'esclavage*, p. 202.

then taught the craft and worked in the master's workshop. Members of the craft castes were sometimes taken prisoner and forced to enter the service of their captors.

Slaves also had divers obligations within commercial households, which were subject to the highest degree of economic rationalization. The majority divided the year between agriculture and weaving, but some participated in trading expeditions either as porters or drivers. Trusted slaves often became pedlars, were given trading missions, and could assume important responsibilities in the household firm. These slaves were the commercial counterpart of the slave official in the noble household. Like the slave chief, their value was rooted in their dependence, and they could achieve a very comfortable position if they served well.[42] As Boutillier has noted in describing the commercial center at Bouna, slaves

> serve as cheap and docile labor in trading activities as porters, caravaneers, petty traders, or purchasing agents. Once freed, they are often installed in other market cities where they serve as agents for their former masters, the relationship modified into a link of clientship.[43]

Still, if traders were away during the rainy season, it was important that they find full granaries on their return home. This meant that many slaves did not have the opportunities of the select few.

If the ideology and the divers uses to which slaves were put promoted assimilation, other forces, particularly the development of plantation agriculture and the use of slaves in mines, operated on the institution so that practice did not always measure up to theory. This contrast between theory and practice is common to all institutions, but in the case of West African slavery many analysts have either ignored it or favored interpretations that more closely coincide with the theoretical perspective. This idealized version of slave status arises from a superficial reading of the sources; the version often describes a rather blissful situation where master and slave spent most of their time sitting in the shade and awaiting nature's bounty. Most colonial administrators, for example, were loath to establish otherwise, largely because they were concerned to prove to superiors in Dakar, Paris, or London that African slavery was a mild and beneficent institution best left alone. Lord Lugard, one of the most important of such writers, revealed why this should be so, when in 1906 he dispatched his famous memorandum on slavery to his subordinates in Northern Nigeria:

[42] Stephen Baier, "African Merchants in the Colonial Period: A History of Commerce in Damagaram (Central Niger), 1880–1960," unpublished doctoral thesis (University of Wisconsin, 1974), pp. 187, 192–203.

[43] Boutillier, "Ville de Bouna," pp. 9–10.

If, however, slaves were to be encouraged to assert their freedom unnecessarily in large numbers, or if those so asserting it, by leaving their masters without some good cause, were indiscriminately upheld in their action by Political Officers, a state of anarchy and chaos would result, and the whole social system of the Mohammedan States would be dislocated. It might even become necessary to legalise the institution under some other name.[44]

It is significant that this memorandum, which was so influential in the treatment of the slavery question, was purposely not forwarded on to London, where it was likely to have met strong disapproval.

The reality was in fact often harsh for those slaves who lived in areas with a strong market orientation and a high percentage of slaves. Soninke slaves, for example, complained that they received as little as a fifth of what the French considered a normal daily ration for a working male.[45] They worked longer, were usually fed less, and were often treated more harshly than slaves in many other places. Similarly, Paul Guebhard contrasted Fulbe slavery in Fuuta Jallon with that of the neighbouring Malinke: Among the Fulbe, plantation slaves were

poorly nourished, poorly treated and poorly regarded . . . they only work as long as their masters are present to watch them, as a result of which the latter are forced to remain close to them, seated under a tree reading the Quran or chatting with friends. . . . With the Malinke there is no visible difference between master and slave, no disdain of the one for the other, no rancor, they eat the same food and work side-by-side.[46]

It was among plantation slaves that the most dramatic movement toward emancipation occurred under the early French regime. In 1895, the French thwarted a massive movement by Soninke slaves north of Bakel to leave their masters.[47] In 1905 Marka slaves at Banamba sought their independence. Confronted with a small-scale class war, the local administrator persuaded the slaves to return to the fields and convinced the masters to ease their labor demands. A year later, however, the slaves were ready to go again, and this time, William Ponty, the highest authority in the French Soudan, acquiesced in their departure. From Banamba, the movement spread through Marka and Soninke areas to other parts of the western savanna zone.[48] The British faced similar mass escapes in the first few years of their occupation of the Sokoto Caliphate, and it was precisely this threat that led Lugard to institute a series of measures designed to discourage the

[44] Lugard, *Political Memoranda,* p. 136.
[45] Brevié, report on Bamako, ANS, K19.
[46] ANS, 7 G84, report of tour, 15 July 1903.
[47] ANS, 13G, 197–199, 395.
[48] ANS, 15G, 170, K24, K26. See also political reports in series 2G.

flight of slaves.[49] Earlier, the British advance into the interior of Lagos had encouraged slave escapes of similar proportions.[50]

By the nineteenth century, plantation slavery was found over large parts of West Africa, and it largely coincided with areas of relatively dense population, especially in the savanna. Plantations or slave villages were concentrated in the centers of the Islamic states and around most towns. The important town of Bouna, for example, was surrounded by about 100 plantations, whereas beyond this area of intensive cultivation lived the Koulango, where, as Boutillier has shown, slave conditions conformed more to a lineage model and the population density was quite low.[51] Bissandougou, the capital of Samory's first empire, was surrounded by a 15-kilometer belt of plantation settlements, and cities like Banamba, Kong, Kankan, and others were similar.[52] Lamine Sanneh presents estimates for the slave population dependent on Touba, the important clerical town in Fuuta Jallon, as high as 11,000 or 12,000. The Jaxanke, who inhabited this and other centers and who were noted for their scholarship and teaching, were dependent upon the output of plantation agriculture.[53] Gumbu, the importance of which lay in its desert-side position, fit into the same pattern. It produced millet, sold to Mauritanian pastoralists, and large amounts of cotton cloth. All of the cloth and most of the millet were produced by slaves, who made up about half of the population. A number of major families had between 100 and 300 slaves each.[54]

The plantation economy was perhaps most developed in the Sokoto Caliphate, where political consolidation and expansion were accompanied by the massive transfer of people, as slaves, to areas near the emirate capitals.[55] Often plantations had as many as a few hundred slaves, although many merchants, lesser members of the aristocracy, and craftsmen had smaller estates with only a few score slaves. The largest holdings were

[49] See interviews in the Hogendorn Collection, 1975; Lovejoy–Maccido Collection, 1975–1976; and Yunusa Collection, 1975.

[50] Oroge, "Slavery," pp. 360–375.

[51] Jean-Louis Boutillier, "Les trois ésclaves de Bouna," in Meillassoux, L'esclavage, pp. 268–269.

[52] Yves Person, Samori, une revolution Dyula, vol. 2 (Dakar, 1968), pp. 837–839; Peroz, Au Soudan français (Paris, 1889), pp. 353; Emile Baillaud, Sur les routes du Soudan (Toulouse, 1902), p. 294; Bernus, "Kong," p. 266; René Caillié, à Journal d'un voyage Tombouctou et à Jenne dans l'Afrique Centrale (1824–28), vol. 1, (Paris, 1829), p. 281.

[53] Lamine Sanneh, "Slavery, Islam and the Jakhanke People," Africa, vol. 46, 1976, p. 84; see also "The History of the Jakhanke People of Senegambia: A Study of the Clerical Tradition in West African Islam," unpublished doctoral thesis (University of London 1974).

[54] Meillassoux, "Gumbu," p. 225.

[55] Lovejoy, "Plantations in the Sokoto Caliphate"; Lovejoy, "Characteristics of Plantations"; and Hogendorn, "Two Plantations."

owned or controlled by the aristocracy and were usually centered around walled towns or capital cities. This pattern of slave use and agricultural development was actively promoted by the Caliphate government and applied to all parts of the empire, from areas to the west of the Niger River to southern Fombina in the Cameroon highlands. Production was geared in part at least for market exchange, principally the provision of cotton and indigo for the important export-oriented textile industry, the supply of grain for the desert-side sector and the cities, and the maintenance of armies which were crucial to the enslavement of people and the continued supply of slave labor.

In the forest areas, too, large-scale production was common by the nineteenth century. Plantations were found around Kumasi in Asante, and many thousands of slaves were used in gold mining.[56] Although the dominant ideology encouraged assimilation into matrilineages, this did not prevent the state and its officials from using large numbers of slaves for their own purposes. Lineages held slaves as collective property, to assist in porterage, kola gathering and processing, and other activities. In Dahomey and the Yoruba states, the government was equally involved in large-scale production that depended upon slave labor in both agriculture and trade. The creation of palm plantations in Dahomey was instrumental in the development of the export industry in palm oil and kernels.[57] In the Biafran hinterland, a slightly different pattern developed, but there, too, slaves were used in large numbers as porters and to man canoes. Palm production appears to have depended more on household output, but in the new agricultural lands of northeastern Igboland, yam plantations were common. As the central Igbo country was planted with palm trees, the northern frontiers became an important source for foodstuffs.[58] A similar pattern emerged in the immediate hinterland of Calabar and may also have developed elsewhere in the region.[59]

The process of slave accumulation was stimulated in the nineteenth century by a drop in the price of slaves as foreign markets were closed off. At the same time, the demand for various products both within and outside Africa was increasing, and better weapons facilitated the slavers' task. The

[56] Wilks, *Asante*, pp. 93–94, 177, 675; and N. Klein, "Asante."

[57] Catherine Coquery-Vidrovitch, "De la traite des esclaves à l'exporation de l'huile de palme et des palmistes au Dahomey: XIXe siècle," in Meillassoux, *Trade and Markets,* pp. 118–119; Oroge, "Slavery," Chapter 3. See also E. Oroge, "The Political Factor in the Growth of Slavery in West Africa: The Case of the Yoruba," forthcoming.

[58] David Northrup, "Patterns of Nineteenth-Century Slavery and Economic Growth in Southeastern Nigeria," unpublished paper presented at the African Studies Association (Boston, 1976).

[59] A. J. H. Latham, *Old Calabar, 1600–1891* (London, 1973), pp. 48, 91–93; and Northrup, "Slavery."

biggest slavers of the nineteenth century differed from their predecessors in that they came out of the Muslim commercial community or the increasingly bourgeois class of the coast. Rooted in two distinct traditions, they used slave warriors and they exploited slave labor on estates. It was a continuation of earlier patterns but the scale was larger than ever before.

The development of more intensive slave use involved a breakdown in face-to-face ties, a limitation on the process of assimilation, harsher treatment, and more rational exploitation. The separate slave settlement was the basis of this transformation. These settlements were not new. They existed in the medieval empires and during the era of the overseas slave trade. The change in residential patterns did not necessarily bring a change in the organization of work. In some areas, gang labor systems evolved,[60] but in others, early forms of work organization persisted.[61] There does seem to have been a tendency toward longer hours and more collective work, however. Although this is a subject that needs much more research, it seems clear that while the plantation system of the Americas was undergoing drastic transformation as a result of the collapse of plantation slavery there, the situation in West Africa involved the expansion of such a system until the colonial period enforced a radical transformation to new types of exploitation.

WEST AFRICAN SLAVERY AND THE EXTERNAL SLAVE TRADE

Scholars have disagreed over the extent of the influence of the export trade on West African slavery, but we are convinced that any discussion of the institution must start from the assumption that there was a strong impact. Walter Rodney, for example, has argued that West Africa lacked extensive social stratification until the external demand for slaves introduced forces that encouraged enslavement and the reduction of people to servile status. At the beginning of the Atlantic slave trade

> Europeans had noticed some West African kings with numbers of servants who were not entirely free, while a few persons actually belonged to a master and worked as agricultural serfs. But that was all—there was no large slave class, such as could be found in West Africa at the end of the Atlantic slave trade. There were large numbers of slaves working in West Africa in the late eighteenth and nineteenth centuries because Africans who obtained captives to sell to the Europeans usually kept some for their own purposes. Naturally, it was the ruling class which came to own slaves, while among the tribes which

---

[60] Lovejoy, "Plantations in the Sokoto Caliphate"; Lovejoy, "Characteristics of Plantations"; Hogendorn, "Two Plantations."

[61] Derman, *Serfs,* pp. 37–39.

sold the most slaves to the Europeans one also found the greatest number of slaves used for local purposes.[62]

Although many scholars have accepted his conclusions for the upper Guinea Coast, which was relatively insignificant in terms of export supply, they have rejected them for other areas. Instead, evidence has been put forth to demonstrate that slavery was in existence before Europeans began to purchase slaves. This argument is convincing, since savanna states had long supplied the Islamic world, and indeed Sudanic political economy was geared to this trade with local society already strongly influenced by Islamic patterns of slave use.[63] Thus states were organized along structural lines that enabled the enslavement of people and the exploitation of their labor through military service, administrative duties, agricultural labor, domestic activities, and the like. Even along the coast, the Portuguese first became involved in the slave trade as middlemen for internal West African demand.

Nevertheless, the impact of the Atlantic trade was profound. Although savanna patterns were initially unaffected, except for the Senegambia region which was within the orbit of both trans-Saharan and transatlantic markets, the implications of Rodney's argument cannot be easily dismissed. Kopytoff and Miers miss the point when they reduce Rodney's proposition to one of supposed simplicity where slavery "sprang forth only under the impetus of extra-continental, and never internal demand for people."[64] The question is how internal and external demand were related and what impact this had on slavery and other institutions. Similarly, in dismissing the violent context of enslavement and the significance this had, they fail to appreciate the long-term interaction between an oppressive political economy and the social system. Thus they see "the roots of these 'servile' institutions in the need for wives and children, the wish to enlarge one's kin group, and the desire to have clients, dependents, servants, and retainers."[65] This functionalist interpretation divorces the discussion from historical reality. The external slave trade existed, it changed over time, and for a significant period it was on such a scale that African institutions were strongly influenced by it.

The dramatic increase in overseas slave exports, especially after the middle of the seventeenth century, was reflected in major political and

[62] Walter Rodney, "West Africa and the Atlantic Slave Trade," Pamphlet of the Tanzanian Historical Society, 1967, p. 17. Also see Rodney, "Slavery and Other Forms of Social Oppression on the Upper Guinea Coast in the Context of the Atlantic Slave Trade," *Journal of African History*, vol. 7, no. 4, 1966, pp. 431–443.

[63] Meillassoux, "Role of Slavery"; Ralph Austen, "The Trans-Saharan Slave Trade: A Tentative Census," Chapter 2 in this volume.

[64] Miers and Kopytoff, "Introduction," p. 67.

[65] Miers and Kopytoff, "Introduction," p. 67.

economic adjustments in coastal society and its hinterland. Scholars argue whether political or economic factors were more profound in enslavement,[66] but recent analysis of technological change, the organization of structures, and the development of oligopolistic marketing arrangements for slaves should leave no doubt that a strong correlation existed between external demand and West African supply.[67] It is also likely that an equally strong influence developed between these factors and the institution of slavery.

In order to appreciate this impact, a distinction must be made between the production of slaves for market and the production of other commodities. Slaves were both a form of labor and an item of exchange, so that the multiplier effect of producing slaves for export was far less than for other goods. Indeed, as Hopkins has argued, net economic gains were very low, if not negative, in the case of slave exports.

> Although the more extreme claims regarding the destructive effects of Atlantic and Saharan commerce have yet to be proved, it is quite clear that international trade, though long established and efficiently organised, failed to act as an engine of growth in West Africa. The export sector, besides being comparatively small, established few beneficial links with the rest of the economy. The result was that the gains from international trade were severely limited, quantitatively, geographically and socially. Export growth produced a type of "enclave" development, which had few connections with the domestic economy.[68]

One must qualify this last statement: There were few *positive* connections. The withdrawal of people from the economy, including able-bodied men, women of childbearing age, and children, had to affect other forms of production; and slaves themselves had to be produced. It retarded overall production and limited growth possibilities, and the cost of labor was kept at a minimum. Hence the development of alternate forms was inhibited, although there was some free migrant labor; and kinship obligations were used as a mobilizing force. Furthermore, the purchasing power of the lower orders was kept down, so much so that it has often appeared to scholars as if West Africa were at a subsistence level where market forces did not operate. The development of this myth is an excellent indicator of the extent to which the market for slaves did in fact affect economic conditions.

A pattern of slavery that was derived from Islamic tradition developed in

---

[66] Curtin, *Economic Change*, vol. 1, pp. 156–168.

[67] H. Gemery and J. S. Hogendorn, "Technological Change, Slavery and the Slave Trade," in C. J. Dewey and A. G. Hopkins, *The Imperial Impact: Studies in the Economic History of India and Africa*, London, 1978; and Paul E. Lovejoy and Jan S. Hogendorn, "Slave Marketing in West Africa," Chapter 8 in this volume.

[68] Hopkins, *Economic History*, 122.

the savanna and southern Sahara long before the Atlantic slave trade influenced the West African economy. As Meillassoux has demonstrated, the extension of Islam into the savanna and sahel was closely related to the export of slaves from this region and the emergence of a militaristic, aristocratic elite which was necessary for the production of slaves for export.

> The evidence gives the picture of a slavery linked with these aristocratic forms of society; court slavery, military slavery, plantation slavery, devoted to the reproduction of the dominant class and its means of domination: war and the administration of war.[69]

Even the collapse of Songhai in the 1590s, before the dramatic increase in overseas exports, did not basically alter this pattern. Instead

> slavery ceased to be the privilege of sovereigns and court personnel. It extended to the rest of the population, each community being capable of becoming an employer of slaves, whose product they released onto the markets. What one sees emerging then, in step with the weakening of the empires, is a mosaic of chiefdoms and mercantile towns of variable size, a diffusion of productive slavery among the peasant communities, a substitution of the trade in products for the trade in men.[70]

This development extended productive slavery along both sides of the desert edge, but it still depended upon the constant renewal of the slave population.

West Africa resembled other Muslim frontiers in the maintenance of distinct domestic and export markets for slaves.[71] The proximity to point of enslavement and the participation of states in the production of slaves helped keep slave prices low and account for the tendency toward extensive slave use. Domestic employment of slaves became pegged to the existence of the foreign market and its supply. This relationship between internal consumption and export demand was a pattern that later extended to the non-Muslim areas near the coast.

With the reorientation of coastal political economy toward slave production and trade in the sixteenth and early seventeenth centuries, slave prices were again maintained at deflated levels, relative to other forms of labor. Increased involvement in intercontinental exchange tended to modify existing social relationships to allow for the large-scale capture, import, and reexport of slaves. In this case, however, Islam did not have the deciding influence, either legally or religiously. Instead slavery was more firmly embedded in kinship structures, although state participation in the Euro-

---

[69] Meillassoux, "Role of Slavery."
[70] Meillassoux, "Role of Slavery."
[71] M. Bloch, *Feudal Society* (Chicago, 1970), vol. 1, pp. 3–7.

pean trade often resulted in the concentration of large numbers of captives in the hands of the government or its officials. The trend over the 300-year period of Atlantic slave exports was for increased exploitation of slaves within these societies, with both the incidence of slavery and size of holdings rising.

The seventeenth-century origins of the forest state system were closely related to the growth in that century of the transatlantic slave trade. Whereas Benin, at least, had existed as a important state before this period, it was not long a major slave exporter. The states of Oyo, Akwamu, and Denkyira, however, were all committed to the overseas market, although in the case of the latter two gold was also a significant export. Despite the fact that slave prices did not rise during this period, slave quantities increased sevenfold.[72] Competition between states intensified enslavement and kept prices stable, and technological and political innovations transformed small states into large-scale producers of slaves. Similarly, oligopolistic practices emerged in the marketing sector, as states and their new elites sought to control foreign markets to maximize their revenues and access to imports, which soon included firearms and ammunition. At this time Europeans were confined to coastal entrepôts or "ports of trade" along the Gold Coast, Oyo developed commercial links with the coast, and the Niger Delta and Calabar commercial networks were converted to the slave traffic.[73] Polanyi and his associates have used developments in this period to demonstrate the nature of non-market-oriented economies, but the concepts of "administered trade" and "ports of trade" which characterize this analysis, only highlight the restrictive practices in the export sector and serve to establish the direct connection between the production of slaves for export and political change.[74] The parallel with the savanna should be clear, but the growth of a foreign market not connected to the Islamic world permitted the consolidation of a system that retained its base in a lineage-dominated social order.

[72] Richard Bean, "A Note on the Relative Importance of Slaves and Gold in West African Exports," *Journal of African History*, vol. 15, no. 3, 1974, pp. 351–356; and H. A. Gemery and J. S. Hogendorn, "Elasticity of Slave Labor Supply and the Development of Slave Economies in the British Caribbean: The Seventeenth Century Experience," in Vera Rubin and Arthur Tuden, eds., *Comparative Perspectives on Slavery in New World Plantation Societies*, special issue, *Annals of the New York Academy of Sciences*, vol. 292 (New York, 1977), pp. 72–83.

[73] Lovejoy and Hogendorn, "Slave Marketing"; Peter Morton-Williams, "The Oyo Yoruba and the Atlantic Slave Trade, 1670–1830," *Journal of the Historical Society of Nigeria*, vol. 3, no. 1, 1964, pp. 25–45; R. C. C. Law, *The Oyo Empire: c. 1600–1836, A West African Imperialism in the Era of the Slave Trade* (Oxford, 1977); K. Y. Daaku, *Trade and Politics on the Gold Coast, 1600–1720* (London, 1970); Latham, *Old Calabar,* Chap. 2; and E. J. Alagoa, "Long-Distance Trade and States in the Niger Delta," *Journal of African History*, vol. 11, no. 3, 1970, pp. 319–329.

[74] K. Polanyi, *Dahomey and the Slave Trade* (Seattle, 1966); and K. Polanyi, C. M. Arensberg, and H. W. Pearson, eds., *Trade and Market in the Early Empires* (Chicago, 1957).

The dichotomy between an Islamic system and another based in lineage structures largely coincided with different ecological regions, the first centered in the savanna and southern Sahara and the second concentrated along the coast and the forest–savanna divide. Despite this basic social contradiction within West Africa, there were strong connections between the two regions and important exceptions within both. First, trade between regions had existed for centuries before the advent of the Atlantic slave trade, and it continued and indeed increased thereafter. Muslim merchants operated into the forest areas or close by, and they exerted considerable influence on local developments. Second, lineage structures existed in the savanna and southern Sahara, particularly among aristocracies that dominated the political economy and along the desert-side sector where nomadic society was organized along segmentary lineage principles. Hence, the fundamental contradiction between Islamic and lineage patterns should be seen in dialectical terms. The interaction was between the two, they were not isolated from each other, and even in the Muslim model, lineage structures were often important.

The balance between the two social formations may have become more equal in the eighteenth century, when severe economic dislocation resulting from the Great Drought of the 1740s and early 1750s upset the savanna and southern Sahara at the very time when rapid expansion of Atlantic slave exports was reaching unprecedented levels further south.[75] The climatic crisis of the mid-eighteenth century probably increased the patriarchal tendencies within Islamic savanna society, at least temporarily. People needed patrons as a form of insurance in these bad times, as people were forced to migrate, population was reduced by famine and epidemics, and the possibilities of trade were temporarily depressed.

Despite the collapse, the Sudanic pattern of slave use and supply entered a new phase in the late eighteenth century, and this became more pronounced in the nineteenth. Already the western Sudan was marked by a high degree of market development, long-distance trade, and economic specialization; and market cities scattered throughout the savanna were centers of trade and production. A series of revolutionary uprisings based on Islam intensified this pattern. These *jihads* ushered in a new series of empires and further interaction between military and commercial elites, which, in Meillassoux's terms, continued to be "both solidary and antagonistic." The warriors of Islam needed the traders to provide luxury goods and basic supplies, to sell prisoners taken in war, and to organize production and

[75] P. E. Lovejoy and S. Baier, "The Desert-Side Economy of the Central Sudan," *International Journal of African Historical Studies,* vol. 8, 1975, pp. 551–581; Curtin, *Economic Change,* vol. 2, p. 4; Sékéné Mody Cissoko, "Famines et épidémies à Tombouctou et dans la Boucle du Niger du xvie au xviiie siècle," *Bulletin de l'IFAN,* vol. 30, 1968, pp. 806–821.

distribution. The traders needed the protection of the new aristocracies but feared the disorder and danger that war brought.[76]

The growth of the commercial sector and the expansion of the new states resulted in a situation where two different types of savanna slavery emerged. The two differed in pattern of residence, in demographic structure, and in the degree of economic rationality. The first, based on a high density of slave population, involved communities in which slaves lived in separate villages or plantations where they made up a large part (usually a majority) of the total population, and where slave labor was exploited in a systematic manner. These communities seem to have been almost all Muslim. Although Islam as such did not cause the more intensive exploitation of this labor, it tended to be the religion of those more oriented to the market, which in turn was the most important factor in the increased exploitation.

The second included areas with a low density of slave population and was characteristic of agricultural societies less oriented to the market, in part, at least, because they were politically isolated by the *jihads.* In these communities slaves made up a small part, often under 10%, of the total population, lived in household units with their masters, participated fully in the master's culture, and engaged in daily face-to-face relations with the master and his family. (This pattern was most similar to lineage-based slavery, but was less affected by the transatlantic market.) In these societies there was less of a tendency toward intensified use of slaves for domestic purposes.[77]

If the eighteenth century was the period of relative collapse in the savanna, it was a time of extensive development within the forest zone. Eighteenth-century European slave demand resulted in the accumulation of vast numbers of slaves in the forest states and among the Aro, a development that undermined the lineage base of the institution and promoted a more systematic exploitation than was possible within lineage structures.[78] Thus slaves were settled on plantations and used in mines in Asante; became porters for Aro merchants, manned the canoes of Niger Delta firms; and staffed the administrative, military, and commercial establishment of Oyo. Greater concentration of slaves probably increased their alienation from lineage members and thereby reduced the possibility of assimilation, so that it was necessary to develop more coercive methods of social control. The Aro achieved this through the promotion of their oracle at Aro Chukwu, which sanctioned the judicial and religious "sacrifice" of slaves through export.[79]

[76] Meillassoux, "Introduction," *Trade and Markets,* p. 55.

[77] For a fuller discussion, see Klein, "Slave Systems."

[78] Northrup, "Slavery"; Northrup, "Trade Without Rulers: Pre-Colonial Economic Development in the Biafran Hinterland," unpublished doctoral thesis, (University of California at Los Angeles, 1974), Chapter 5.

[79] N. Klein, *Inequality in Asante;* Wilks, *Asante,* pp. 93–94, 177, 675; G. I. Jones, *Trading*

Efforts at control were not always so successful, however. The Oyo Empire faced collapse after a successful slave uprising and *coup d'état* in c. 1817, when slave soldiers of northern origin united under the flag of Islamic *jihad* to seize power.[80] Only in the Niger Delta and the Aro-dominated hinterland did it prove possible to accommodate lineage ideology with the existence of a substantial number of slaves in the population; and even here institutions like the Ekpe secret society, the Aro Chukwu oracle, and the canoe-house significantly altered lineage structures.[81] This trend towards greater alienation of slaves from kinship systems paralleled the already established pattern in the savanna, but it lacked the ideological framework of Islamic law and society. Islam was a factor in Asante and Oyo, but only as a dimension of an emergent slave consciousness and not as the basis for legitimizing slavery as an institution.[82]

The progressive withdrawal of European countries from the slave trade after 1807 intensified the contradiction between ideology and practice, for it released many slaves into the domestic economy at the same time that the number of slaves became a serious threat to the established ruling classes. The challenge to society was already well pronounced, however, and the response in many areas was to emphasize more fully the lineage basis of slavery. Shifts in production strategies differed within the forest zone, but in many cases, lineage-controlled production became more pronounced. There were few economies of scale in the production of the new crops of the nineteenth century. Small-holder production for the market increased, and profits were often invested in buying a slave or two.[83] In the Biafran hinterland, slaves were still used by Aro and other merchants as porters, but many more were incorporated into relatively small households to assist in agricultural production.[84] In Dahomey, the royal family promoted plantation agriculture,[85] a system that was deliberately dismantled in Asante to avoid the dangers of slave revolt in the capital territory around Kumasi. Instead, Asante redistributed its slaves to the lineages to encourage kola production for northern export, although large numbers of slaves were still used in the gold mines.[86] Oyo's collapse in the early nineteenth century had

---

States of the Niger Delta (London, 1963); Alagoa, "Long-Distance Trade," pp. 319–329; Oroge, "Slavery," Chapter 1; and Oroge, "Political Factor."

[80] Oroge, "Slavery," pp. 88–90.

[81] Latham, *Old Calabar,* pp. 37–39; Alagoa, "Long-Distance Trade," pp. 319–329; Jones, *Trading States,* pp. 51–62; Northrup, "Trade Without Rulers," Chapter 5.

[82] Wilks, *Asante,* pp. 254, 263; Oroge, "Slavery," pp. 88–90.

[83] M. A. Klein, "Slavery, the Slave Trade and Legitimate Commerce," *Etudes d'histoire africaines,* vol. 2, 1970, pp. 5–28.

[84] Northrup, "Slavery"; and Northrup, "Trade Without Rulers," Chapter 5.

[85] Coquery-Vidrovitch, "La traite," pp. 107–123.

[86] Wilks, *Asante,* pp. 93–94, 177, 264, 675; P. E. Lovejoy, *Caravans of Kola. Hausa Trade with Asante, 1700–1900* (London and Zaria, forthcoming).

a similar impact. Such successor states as Ibadan and Abeokuta depended upon slave labor to a large extent, but the Oyo aristocracy no longer dominated slave supplies. Instead, the military elite of the nineteenth century was more dispersed. Each new city had its own leadership which controlled thousands of slaves who farmed, filled administrative, domestic, and military ranks, and were used in trade. As in Dahomey, plantations were common; they depended upon slave labor, but control of these plantations was sometimes lineage based.[87]

The abolition of the Atlantic slave trade had a profound impact on West African society, but the adjustments that occurred intensified slave use in the domestic economy. It could hardly have been otherwise, since the collapse of the foreign market maintained slave prices at a low level throughout the century, and the continued domination of the political economy by a military elite prevented the radical transformation of society, which would have been necessary to alter a mode of production based on a constantly replenished slave supply. "Legitimate" trade, therefore, only intensified the use of slaves, even as the slave system of the Americas was gradually undermined.

The savanna region also experienced this extension of slave use in the nineteenth century, and, to some extent, for the same reasons. The peanut belt of the Senegambia fit into the new pattern of overseas export-oriented agricultural production and relied, at least in part, on slave labor.[88] The *jihads* of the nineteenth century, which led to the foundation of empires comparable in size to those of medieval times, forced the resettlement of large numbers of people, usually as slaves. In the Sokoto Caliphate, which was founded between 1804–1808 but continued to expand even after mid-century, slaves were settled around towns and cities as agricultural workers, whose production was destined for both the domestic market and export.[89] Similarly in the Caliphate of Hamdullahi, in the states founded by Al-Hajj ʿUmar, Samori, Rabeh, and the *juula* cities, slaves played a major role in the military, agriculture, and other parts of the economy.[90] Furthermore, these new, larger Islamic states continued to supply trans-Saharan slave markets, which were not affected by European pressure to end the traffic until the last third of the century. Perhaps more important savanna

[87] A. G. Hopkins, "Economic Imperialism in West Africa: Lagos, 1880–1892," *Economic History Review*, vol. 31, 1968, pp. 580–606; and Oroge, "Slavery."

[88] M. A. Klein, "Social and Economic Factors in the Muslim Revolution in Senegambia," *Journal of African History*, vol. 13, 1972, pp. 419–441.

[89] Lovejoy, "Plantations in the Sokoto Caliphate."

[90] William Brown, "The Caliphate of Hamdullahi, ca. 1818–1864," unpublished doctoral thesis (University of Wisconsin, 1969), pp. 114–116, 124, 134–136; Boutillier, "Trois esclaves," pp. 268–269; and Meillassoux, "Introduction," *Trade and Markets,* p. 57.

slave supplies increasingly went toward the coast to satisfy demand emanating from "legitimate" trade. This pattern had begun in the last decades of the eighteenth century but became especially pronounced in the nineteenth. Exports south probably kept the price of slaves down; and by impeding the transition to other forms of labor, the pattern marked a continuation of the dual market structure of earlier times. Thus more than a third of the population of Abeokuta, a city of perhaps 100,000 people at mid-century, were slaves, mostly of northern origin.[91] In the nineteenth century slaves moved north and south, for there were two belts of economic expansion, one related to overseas demand for tropical products in the forest, and the other to savanna urbanization and regional integration centered on the *jihad* states.

It is clear, therefore, that slavery was widespread in West Africa for centuries before 1900. Although exact figures will never be possible, it appears that the incidence of slavery was very high, with perhaps a substantial majority of people in the late nineteenth century being slaves or the descendants of slaves. Even if freedmen are excluded, slaves still probably constituted half the total population, and in some areas even more.[92]

SLAVERY AS A MODE OF PRODUCTION

In spite of the vast numbers of slaves and their importance in economic and political institutions, most analysts have been reluctant to accept the fundamental significance of slavery. For functionalists like Miers and Kopytoff, there has been an unwillingness to appreciate the economic basis of social relations and the importance of slavery as a source of labor. The result is that not only do Miers and Kopytoff minimize the economic functions of slavery, but they tend to minimize the importance of the institution itself.

Even more surprising, most Marxist writers have denied the existence of a slave mode of production. For example, Jean Suret-Canale writes in a classical statement of the Marxist position,

> The condition of the captive, although widespread in Africa, has essentially a juridical quality and does not involve the defined role in production which characterises a class.

[91] Oroge, "Slavery," p. 167.

[92] French estimates of the servile population in 1904 ran as high as two-thirds of the population in the more market-oriented areas such as the Fuuta Jallon and near the Juula cities; ANS, K18–22. Estimates were also as high for the Sokoto Caliphate; see figures summarized in Polly Hill, *Rural Hausa. A Village and a Setting* (London, 1973), pp. 40, 319. For the Yoruba area, see Oroge, "Slavery," pp. 158–178. High estimates for Asante and the Igbo areas also exist; see Northrup, "Slavery"; and N. Klein, *Inequality in Asante.*

The fundamental exploited class is the working peasantry, including at the same time tribute-paying free men and slaves; the dominant class is the combination of aristocracies—tribal, military, administrative—including certain categories of royal slaves entrusted with public responsibilities.[93]

Similarly, Rodney rejects the idea that a slave mode of production exists, and even Meillassoux is circumspect.[94] Only Terray recognizes the crucial role of slavery. In his discussion of Gyaman, a province of the Asante empire, Terray distinguishes

two modes of production in the Abron social formation, one of a lineage and tributary character, the other slave. We now see that the functioning of the former is subordinated to the requirements for the reproduction of the social relations that constitute the latter. It can be concluded that the Abron social formation is dominated by this slave type of mode of production. . . . The relations of servitude are based on the use of force; and the nature of the state, like the status of the (peasant) communities, is determined by the exigencies of this use of force.[95]

The presence of Muslim merchants and planters in Gyaman adds another dimension to this analysis, for they operated their plantations more rationally than did the aristocracy or the free peasantry. The role of Islam was more contained here than in the *jihad* states, but Islamic patterns of slave use existed alongside a slave system embedded in kinship structures.

It is clear from many of the studies in the Meillassoux volume and the Miers and Kopytoff compendium that slavery was indeed basic to the economy of many West African societies, and that these were the most expansive and the most populous states in the nineteenth century. Where slaves comprised one-half to three-quarters of the total population, it is hard not to speak of a "slave mode of production." In these societies, the position of the slave was different from that of Suret-Canale's tribute-paying peasant. The slave's work was distinct from that of the free man; he entered into relatively few face-to-face relations with his master, and his labor was organized in an increasingly rational way. This situation certainly prevailed in much of the Sokoto Caliphate, in the Fuuta Jalon, around the Juula cities, in Asante and Dahomey—indeed, in the heart of the largest and most expansive states.

[93] Jean Suret-Canale, "Les societés traditionalles en Afrique Tropicale et le concept de mode de production asiatiques," in Centre d'Etudes et de Recherches Marxistes, *Sur le mode de production asiatique* (Paris, 1969), pp. 101–133.

[94] Rodney, "West Africa and the Atlantic Slave Trade"; Meillassoux, "Introduction," *L'esclavage,* pp. 18–21.

[95] Terray, "Classes and Class Consciousness," p. 129; also see Terray, "Long-Distance Exchange," pp. 331–333. For a similar analysis, see Mason, "Trade and State in Nineteenth-Century Nupe."

The concept of "slave mode of production," however, is applicable for two other reasons. It was a mode of production that was self-perpetuating, for it was based on enslavement as an institutionalized process.[96] It was therefore related to a different mode of production, a slave-producing mode. The functioning of the slave-producing state was based on the export of slaves either within Africa or outside. It "produced" slaves through war, kidnapping and the distortion of the judicial process.[97] In this system of production, control was confined to a relatively small class of people who directed the military and headed the states that negotiated exports. Before the nineteenth century, the slave "producers" were often not slave exploiters. They absorbed slaves largely as warriors and not as farm labor, and sold the majority to traders. It was within this commercial sector that nineteenth-century slave-exploiting states emerged.

Second, slaves were essential to the reproduction of society.[98] In acephalous or minimally differentiated societies, where lineage organization was most influential, slaves were often sought largely for their numbers. By their presence, they increased the power and the reproductive potential of the assimilating kinship group. In these small-scale societies, the work they did was often the same as that done by the free, and their offspring frequently had a status similar to that for free-born. Nevertheless, these societies sought slaves, albeit in smaller numbers than the market-oriented states of the Sudan and forest; and they did so largely for their reproductive capacity. Even in more complex societies the reproductive factor remained important.

Assimilation through control of reproduction was, of course, also an important element of social control. It assured that the powerful and wealthy who dominated West Africa reproduced at a disproportionately higher rate in terms of the population as a whole. As an institutionalized method of assimilating slaves, children of slave mothers and free men were either free or at least much higher in status than children of slave fathers. Whereas Islam required that the children of concubines, and indeed the concubines themselves, be free, lineage structures guaranteed that elders and the wealthy acquired most women, slave and free, and that offspring were absorbed within the family.

[96] This point is emphasized by Meillassoux, "Role of Slavery," and is also discussed in Cooper, "Studying Slavery."

[97] Bazin, "Segou," pp. 107–143, and Terray, "Classes and Class Consciousness," pp. 120–122, explore the relative impact both of the importance of slave production and of an economy based on slave labor.

[98] Miers and Kopytoff, "African Slavery," pp. 7–24; Meillassoux, "From Reproduction to Production," *Economy and Society,* vol. 1, 1972, pp. 93–105; and Meillassoux, "Introduction," *Trade and Markets,* pp. 20–21.

Another important element in social control was slave domination of the military, where they received special benefits and often formed elite corps. Administrative positions especially reserved for slaves or recently freed men were also crucial in undermining the development of slave consciousness as a class and thereby maintaining slave resistance within manageable bounds.

Beyond these forms of social control were others, moreover. If either the native society or the one receiving the trade slave practiced scarification, he always stood out as a person of foreign origin. He also had different ways and spoke a foreign language or an easily recognizable dialect. The possibility of resale was a major sanction that could be brought to bear on him, and he could be whipped or placed in irons. Given the wide network of kin and clan ties everywhere, it is likely that ransoming took place for significant numbers of prisoners whose families could afford it and who could make contact with the slavers. As Jean Bazin has argued, a large percentage of those moved into trade at any time were probably already in slavery, that is to say, they were simply being reenslaved.[99]

To argue that the dominant mode of production in nineteenth-century West Africa was based on slavery does not mean that other modes did not exist—they did. First, lineage-based production and redistribution, as Terray and N. Klein have shown, had a strong influence in forest regions and the southern savanna.[100] This system was based on kinship networks, which included extensive reciprocity. The tendency was towards a nonmarket economy that provided insurance for members and assimilated outsiders. It was based on egalitarian principles that identified power and influence with age and sex, not class. Polanyi, Dalton, and other substantivists, who also accept the idea of an economy based on nonmarket principles, would agree with much of Marxist analysis on the nature of lineage-based production.[101] Their concepts of reciprocity and redistribution are based on the supposition that nonmarket forces governed most exchange.

Capitalist features also affected West African development, however, and were intimately connected with an expanding capitalist system based on increasing rationalization of the world market. Genovese has argued that the American South developed a peculiar plantation economy and society that were dependent on the bourgeois world but that were still distinct and

[99] Bazin, "Segou," pp. 107–143.

[100] Terray, "Class and Class Consciousness," pp. 120–129; Terray, "Long-Distance Exchange," 315–345; N. Klein, *Inequality in Asante.*

[101] K. Polanyi, C. M. Arensberg, H. W. Pearson, eds., *Trade and Market in Early Empires* (Glencoe, 1957); George Dalton, "Karl Polanyi's Analysis of Long-Distance Trade and his Wider Paradigm," in J. A. Sabloff and C. C. Lamberg-Karlovsky, eds., *Ancient Civilization and Trade* (Albuquerque, 1975), pp. 63–132.

in basic contradiction with the capitalist mode of production.[102] A similar argument can be made for West Africa, where capitalist influences also had an important effect. West Africa first supplied manpower for American plantations and mines, but in the nineteenth century, it switched to the supply of raw materials produced by its own slave labor. Like the American South, West Africa remained on the periphery of the industrial capitalist world, but it was being incorporated into the world market economy and was influenced increasingly by fluctuations in price in the industrial West. The West African economy did not, however, become capitalist, though the commercial sector of West African societies was stimulated, and "proto-capitalist" institutions expanded. The function of capitalism in West Africa, as in other peripheral areas, was to exploit and expand precapitalist modes of production and to intensify extractive elements that already existed. Slavery was antithetical to capitalism; and yet, on the periphery, capitalism fostered the expansion of slavery, both for export to other peripheral areas and for production of those goods European and American industry wanted from Africa.[103]

Over the course of the three centuries of the Atlantic slave trade, slavery strongly influenced all aspects of West African society and economy. As Cooper has noted,

> Slavery, then, must be studied both from the top and the bottom and over time. We must examine the objectives slaveowners might have and the means they have to fulfill them—in relation to specific historical situations and to the entire structure of society. And we must examine the behavior of slaves in terms of the options they had, and remember that they could affect the way a slave system developed. And it is not sufficient to catalogue the variations. Slavery was not just shaped by other elements of the social structure; it shaped them too.[104]

Thus, the position of women, children, and other dependents tended to deteriorate when the numbers of slaves were greatest and the degree of market development most extensive; and in different places and periods the opposite proved the case. In these situations slavery was softened as an institution by the assimilationist tendencies of lineage structures and by the egalitarian principles of Islam. These themes must be explored in much greater detail but are beyond the scope of this analysis. Nevertheless, an

---

[102] Eugene D. Genovese, *The Political Economy of Slavery* (New York, 1965), pp. 13–39.

[103] Immanuel Wallerstein, "The Three Stages of African Involvement in the World-Economy," in P. C. W. Gutkind and I. Wallerstein, eds., *The Political Economy of Contemporary Africa* (Beverly Hills, 1976), pp. 30–57. We revise Wallerstein's thesis to take account of the intensive use of slaves in West Africa. This suggests that the process of "peripheralization" was more advanced in the eighteenth and nineteenth century than Wallerstein allows.

[104] Cooper, "Studying Slavery."

attempt has been made here to correct the basically functionalist approach
of Kopytoff and Miers and to contribute to the historical approach of
Meillassoux and his collaborators. Seen from a chronological perspective,
the dialectical nature of slavery as an institution becomes apparent. Islamic
and lineage slavery developed in opposition but with similar results, and
both were strongly influenced by international market forces. It remains to
explore these interconnections for each region within West Africa for
specific historical periods.

ACKNOWLEDGMENTS

We wish to thank Allen Isaacman and Patricia Romero for their comments.

8

Slave Marketing in
West Africa

PAUL E. LOVEJOY
JAN S. HOGENDORN

The economic history of slavery and the Atlantic slave trade has advanced on a very broad front during the last two decades. New light has been shed on a wide variety of issues, ranging from the profitability of slave use within the Americas,[1] to studies of the transatlantic commerical mechanism for moving slaves to the New World.[2] In one major aspect, however, this mass

[1] See especially R. W. Fogel and S. L. Engerman, *Time on the Cross: The Economics of American Negro Slavery* (Boston, 1974); and their essay "The Economics of Slavery" in *The Reinterpretation of American Economic History* (New York, 1971); A. H. Conrad and J. R. Meyer, *The Economics of Slavery*, (Chicago, 1964); R. Sutch, "The Profitability of Ante-Bellum Slavery—Revisited," *Southern Economic Journal*, vol. 31, 1965, pp. 365–377; S. L. Engerman, "The Effects of Slavery upon the Southern Economy," *Explorations in Entrepreneurial History*, second series vol. 4, no. 2, winter 1967, pp. 71–97; and H. G. J. Aitken, *Did Slavery Pay*, (Boston, 1971).

[2] P. D. Curtin, *The Atlantic Slave Trade: A Census* (Madison, 1969); R. N. Bean, "The British Transatlantic Slave Trade, 1650–1775," unpublished doctoral dissertation (University of Washington, 1971); E. P. LeVeen, "British Slave Trade Suppression Policies 1821–1865," unpublished doctoral dissertation (University of Chicago, 1971); essays by R. Anstey, E. P. LeVeen, P. D. Curtin, and J. Postma in S. L. Engerman and E. D. Genovese, eds., *Race and Slavery*

of new work on the economics of slavery and the slave trade has failed to illuminate adequately a most important aspect of the Atlantic slave system—namely, the market mechanism for slave delivery within Africa itself.

To be sure, a number of scholars have described slavery and the slave trade within specific areas of West Africa.[3] Modern studies, however, which deal explicitly with internal slave marketing mechanisms as economic phenomena, can still claim pioneer status. Among these are the initial descriptive efforts of the slave trade era provided by Basil Davidson, P. Curtin, M. D. Kilson, A. J. B. Fisher and H. J. Fisher, and D. P. Mannix;[4] the study of slave prices in the Sokoto Caliphate by D. Tambo;[5] the valuable

---

in the Western Hemisphere: Quantitative Studies (Princeton, 1975); S. Rottenberg, "The Business of Slave Trading," *The South Atlantic Quarterly*, vol. 66, no. 3, Summer 1967; works by H. S. Klein on slave mortality during the Atlantic passage; and papers presented at the 1975 Mathematical Social Science Board Conference at Colby College by J. Inikori, W. E. Minchinton, J. C. Miller, P. C. Emmer, D. Eltis, D. Richardson, S. L. Engerman and H. S. Klein. The Inikori paper has appeared in the *Journal of African History*, vol. 17, no. 2, 1976, pp. 197–223. The others are included in this volume.

[3] E. A. Oroge, "The Institution of Slavery in Yorubaland," unpublished doctoral thesis (University of Birmingham, 1971); M. Klein, "Slavery, the Slave Trade, and Legitimate Commerce in Late Nineteenth Century Africa," *Etudes d'histoire africaine*, vol. 2, 1971, pp. 5–28; and his "Social and Economic Factors in the Muslim Revolution in Senegambia," *Journal of African History*, vol. 13, no. 3, 1972, pp. 419–441; M. Mason, "Population Density and 'Slave Raiding'—the Case of the Middle Belt of Nigeria," *Journal of African History*, vol. 10, no. 4, 1969, pp. 551–564; M. Adamu, "Aspects of the Economics in the Export of Slaves from the Central Sudan to the Bight of Benin in the Eighteenth and Nineteenth Centuries," Ahmadu Bello University Social Science Seminar Paper, 11 June 1975, and included in this volume; W. Rodney, "African Slavery and Other Forms of Social Oppression on the Upper Guinea Coast in the Context of the Atlantic Slave Trade," *Journal of African History*, vol. 7, no. 3, 1966, pp. 431–443; P. Hill, "From Slavery to Freedom: The Case of Farm-slavery in Nigerian Hausaland," *Comparative Studies in Society and History*, vol. 18, no. 3, 1976, pp. 395–426; S. Miers and I. Kopytoff, eds., *Slavery in Africa: Historical and Anthropological Perspectives* (Madison, 1977), Chapter 2 by R. A. Austien, Chapter 4 by P. Manning, and Chapter 7 by M. Klein and P. Lovejoy, included in this volume; and C. Meillassoux, ed., *L'Esclavage en Afrique Précoloniale* (Paris, 1975).

[4] B. Davidson, *Black Mother* (Boston, 1961); B. Davidson, "Slaves or Captives? Some Notes on Fantasy and Fact" in N. I. Huggins, M. Kilson, and D. M. Fox, *Key Issues in the Afro-American Experience* (New York, 1971); P. D. Curtin, "The Slave Trade and the Atlantic Basin: Intercontinental Perspectives" in Huggins, Kilson, and Fox, *Key Issues*; and "The Atlantic Slave Trade 1600–1800" in J. F. A. Ajayi and M. Crowder, *History of West Africa*, vol. 1 (New York, 1972); M. D. d. B. Kilson, "West African Society and the Atlantic Slave Trade, 1441–1865," in Huggins, Kilson, and Fox, *Key Issues*; A. J. B. and H. J. Fisher, *Slavery and Muslim Society in Africa* (London 1970); and D. P. Mannix with M. Cowley, *Black Cargoes: A History of the Atlantic Slave Trade 1518–1865* (New York, 1962).

[5] D. Tambo, "The Sokoto Caliphate Slave Trade in the Nineteenth Century," *African Historical Studies*, vol. 9, no. 2, 1976, pp. 187–217.

estimates of high supply elasticity made by E. LeVeen;[6] the use of a vent-for-surplus model to explain this high elasticity by H. Gemery and J. Hogendorn; and an effort by the same authors calling attention to technological change as a factor in the supply mechanism.[7]

One conclusion that tends to emerge rather generally from these works is that throughout the era of legal slave shipments, the delivery mechanism was characterized by a relatively high degree of competition. For example, Gemery and Hogendorn argue that "local monopoly never achieved significant long run restriction of supply . . . because of the entrance of new sellers into the market. This involved the geographical extension of competition and brought many coastal ports into the trade to break the grip of the older established sellers."[8] Similar points of view have been expressed by M. D. d. B. Kilson, Basil Davidson, and other writers attempting a broad description of the slave-supply mechanism.[9]

Recently a hypothesis has been advanced by R. P. Thomas and R. N. Bean that argues even more strongly that the trade was basically competitive. In their stimulating paper, "The Fishers of Men: The Profits of the Slave Trade," Thomas and Bean contend that slaves were "supplied in substantial measure from markets organized like a contemporary high seas fishery. . . . The African slaver was a fisher of men."[10] Fishing on the high seas is the economist's standard example of an industry where economic profit cannot achieve permanence because entry to the industry is unimpeded by the presence of property rights.[11] As Thomas and Bean put it, "to the degree that slaving was actually carried on as an economic activity, similar in organization to a modern fishery, . . . profits were likely to have been dissipated by excess entry into the industry. This is the result that would be expected with the extensive exploitation of a common property resource such as an ocean fishery."[12]

These theses of highly competitive markets, ease of entry, and little or no

---

[6] LeVeen, "British Slave Trade"; and "The African Slave Supply Response," paper delivered at the conference of the African Studies Association (Syracuse, New York, 1973).

[7] H. A. Gemery and J. S. Hogendorn, "The Atlantic Slave Trade: A Tentative Economic Model," *Journal of African History,* vol. 15, no. 2, 1974, pp. 223–246, and "Technological Change, Slavery, and the Slave Trade," in C. J. Dewey and A. G. Hopkins, eds., *The Imperial Impact: Studies in the Economic History of Africa and India* (London, 1978).

[8] Gemery and Hogendorn, "Atlantic Slave Trade," p. 241.

[9] M. D. d. B. Kilson, "West African Society," pp. 45–51; B. Davidson, "Slaves or Captives," p. 69.

[10] R. Thomas and R. Bean, "The Fishers of Men: The Profits of the Slave Trade," *Journal of Economic History,* vol. 34, no. 4, 1974, p. 885.

[11] Economic profit is defined here as returns to entrepreneurship over and above what could be obtained in the next best alternate use.

[12] Thomas and Bean, "Fishers of Men," p. 888.

economic profit present a challenging problem to African economic historians. To what extent can this view be verified or contradicted by historical evidence? Thomas and Bean state frankly'that their evidence "on the way that slaves were actually supplied from the interior of Africa is much weaker" than that for other stages of the trade.[13] Indeed, very little research has been directed to the question of the competitive or noncompetitive structure of African slave delivery systems. The present essay is an attempt to rectify this omission. It surveys a number of the principal interior–coastal delivery systems, scrutinizing each one to ascertain its geographical extent, its chief characteristics, the changes that occurred in it over time, and in particular the degree of competition that existed within it, as well as between it and other such systems.[14]

It is obviously difficult to examine the competitive or noncompetitive nature of slave marketing when quantifiable data on price, transfer cost, elasticity, etc., are scarce. Nevertheless, it is possible to collect a surprisingly large amount of qualitative information on the various marketing systems. Such information relates to the regulation of commerce, transport, and credit, and demonstrates that cartel-like restrictions against new entry to the "industry" were not uncommon. These restrictions might be legal, involving state regulation of the trade, or they might be economic, including limited access to capital.

The degree of imperfection in slave marketing systems cannot be measured in any standard way. Even the existence of imperfection in delivery does not mean that this activity was profitable—competition at the point of capture may have meant that no abnormal profits could accrue within the transport network. Little progress, however, will be made in analyzing the economic effects of the slave market structure until that structure is described in far more detail than has been hitherto available. Such a description is the main purpose of this chapter.[15]

[13] Thomas and Bean, "Fishers of Men," p. 888.
[14] There is of course a very extensive literature on the problems of testing for noncompetitive behavior in industry and marketing. For excellent short surveys see Leonard Weiss, "Quantitative Studies of Industrial Organization" in M. D. Intriligator, *Frontiers of Quantitative Economics* (Amsterdam, 1971); Leonard Weiss, "The Concentration–Profits Relationship and Antitrust" in H. J. Goldschmid, A. H. Mann, and J. F. Weston, *Industrial Concentration: The New Learning* (Boston, 1974). This literature is reflected today in any standard text in industrial organization such as J. S. Bain, *Industrial Organization* (New York, 1968); or F. M. Scherer, *Industrial Market Structure and Economic Performance* (Chicago, 1970); and indeed in undergraduate microeconomics texts such as E. Mansfield, *Microeconomics,* 2nd ed. (New York, 1975).
[15] A superficial reading of this introduction might lead a reader to suppose that the dichotomy discussed is between the substantivist school exemplified by the works of K. Polanyi and G. Dalton; and the formalist interpretations advanced by H. Schneider, R. Firth,

THE PATTERNS OF SLAVE MARKETING

The marketing of slaves in West Africa tended to fall within several different patterns that have only recently become apparent. These patterns can be identified within at least four regions in West Africa: first, the savanna from the Senegambia basin to Lake Chad, which was by far the largest region; second, the coastal forest states along the Bight of Benin and the Gold Coast; third, the area between the Benue valley and the Bight of Bonny (Biafra); and finally, the area along the littoral from the southern Ivory Coast through Liberia, Sierra Leone, and Guinea. Between 1650 and 1850, the main period of slave exports, a minimum of 5 million slaves were shipped from these regions, with most exports passing through ports along the coast from the Gold Coast to the Bight of Bonny. Over 4.0 million of these exports occurred in the century 1711–1810.[16]

The Savanna

The early slave trade, especially before 1600, largely satisfied savanna and North African markets, although the Senegambia basin was one of the earliest regions in Africa to be drawn into the Atlantic trade. Not until the late eighteenth century did slaves from the central savanna appear in European ledgers, and slaves from northern savanna areas seem never to have been as significant as those from places nearer to or within the forest region. Consequently, it is difficult to estimate overseas exports from the savanna,

---

W. Jones, and most notably in A. G. Hopkins, *An Economic History of West Africa* (New York, 1973). (Substantivists contend that noneconomic forces are paramount in explaining the patterns of exchange and trade, whereas formalists argue that much standard economic theory is applicable to the African experience.)

Most emphatically in its structure this chapter does not pose a choice between a substantivist and a formalist interpretation. The case of the formalists is now much too strong for serious challenge. Indeed, a finding that slave marketing was often accomplished under conditions of imperfect competition in no way hints that economic incentives were inoperative or unimportant. As Adam Smith once warned so vividly, the lure of higher profits (that economic incentive *par excellence*) may make every social gathering of entrepreneurs an occasion for planning a "conspiracy against the public, or in some contrivance to raise prices. . . ." *The Wealth of Nations,* vol. 1 (Cannan edition, London, 1961), p. 144.

[16] For estimates of slave exports from West Africa, see Curtin, *Atlantic Slave Trade.* Recent research has modified some of Curtin's figures for slave exports. See especially Curtin's "Measuring the Atlantic Slave Trade," in Engerman and Genovese, *Race and Slavery*; J. Inikori, "Measuring the Atlantic Slave Trade: An Assessment of Curtin and Anstey," *Journal of African History,* vol. 17, no. 2, pp. 197–223; Curtin's measured reply, "Measuring the Atlantic Slave Trade Once Again: A Comment by Philip D. Curtin," *Journal of African History,* vol. 17, no. 4, 1976, pp. 595–605; and Inikori's riposte, "Measuring the Atlantic Slave Trade: A Rejoinder by J. E. Inikori," in the same issue, p. 605.

and the necessary research on trans-Saharan shipments is only now underway. Nevertheless, trade in slaves was always crucial to savanna economies.

By the fifteenth century, Muslim merchants, centered in the savanna and
often urban-based, dominated slave marketing in most parts of West Africa.[17] They controlled trade in the Senegambia basin, the central savanna,
the Niger bend, Mossi country, and even operated in such southern regions
as the Akan forests, where they are reported as early as the sixteenth
century, before the creation of the major states there. These commercial
organizations are often referred to as Juula (Dyula), Hausa, Yarse, Jahanke,
Kanuri, or Wangara, depending upon their area. Some names, such as Juula,
Wangara, or Kambari, meant "merchant," whereas others, including Hausa
and Kanuri or Beriberi, referred to a metropolitan culture with which
merchants identified. The merchants themselves had diverse origins, frequently associated with the desert-side economy; but all were similar in that
they relied upon a series of dispersed commercial settlements, sometimes
referred to as a commercial diaspora, which permitted member merchants
to travel between communities and employ associates as agents.[18]

---

[17] The literature on savanna trade is very extensive, but see Adamu, "The Export of Slaves;"
Adamu, "The Hausa Factor in West African History," unpublished doctoral thesis (University
of Birmingham, 1974); Stephen Baier, "African Merchants in the Colonial Period: A History
of Commerce in Damagaram (Central Niger), 1880–1960," unpublished doctoral thesis (Uni-
versity of Wisconsin, 1974); Philip D. Curtin, "Pre-Colonial Trade Networks and Traders: The
Diakhanke," in Claude Meillassoux, ed., *The Development of Indigenous Trade and Markets in
West Africa* (London, 1971), pp. 228–239; Curtin, *Economic Change in Precolonial Africa.
Senegambia in the Era of the Slave Trade* (Madison, 1975); Fisher and Fisher, *Slavery and Muslim
Society;* Michael Izard, "Les Yarse et le commerce dans le Yatenga pré-colonial," in Meillas-
soux, *Trade and Markets,* pp. 214–227; Paul E. Lovejoy, "The Hausa Kola Trade, 1700–1900:
A Commercial System in the Continental Exchange of West Africa," unpublished doctoral
thesis (University of Wisconsin, 1973); Lovejoy, "Interregional Monetary Flows in the Pre-
colonial Trade of Nigeria," *Journal of African History,* vol. 15, no. 4, 1974, pp. 563–585;
Lovejoy, "The Kambarin Beriberi: The Formation of a Specialized Group of Hausa Kola
Traders in the Nineteenth Century," *Journal of African History,* vol. 14, no. 2, 1973, pp.
633–652; Lovejoy, "The Role of the Wangara in the Economic Transformation of the Central
Sudan in the Fifteenth and Sixteenth Centuries," *Journal of African History,* vol. 19, no. 2,
1978, pp. 173–193; Lovejoy and Baier, "The Desert-Side Economy of the Central Sudan,"
African Historical Studies, vol. 8, no. 4, 1975, pp. 551–581; C. Meillassoux, "Introduction," in
Meillassoux, *Trade and Markets,* pp. 49–90; Meillassoux, "Le commerce pre-colonial et le
developpement de l'esclavage à Gumbu du Sahel (Mali)," in Meillassoux, *Trade and Markets,*
pp. 182–195; C. C. Stewart with E. K. Stewart, *Islam and Social Order in Mauritania* (London,
1973); Tambo, "Sokoto Caliphate Slave Trade;" Ivor Wilks, "The Mossi and Akan States,
1500–1800," in J. F. A. Ajayi and M. Crowder, *History of West Africa* (London, 1971).

[18] The term *diaspora* has been advanced by Abner Cohen but it is also used by many
scholars. For Cohen's initial conception, see his theoretical discussion, "Cultural Strategies in
the Organization of Trading Diasporas," in Meillassoux, *Trade and Markets,* pp. 266–284. For
modifications in the concept, see Lovejoy, "Kambarin Beriberi;" Lovejoy, "Hausa Kola
Trade"; Lovejoy and Baier, "Desert-Side Economy;" and Curtin, *Economic Change,* Chapter 2.

A diversified mix of products passed along the routes—including live-stock, gold, textiles, kola nuts, various salts, North African and northern Saharan imports, and leather goods, as well as slaves. Animal transport, particularly donkeys within the savanna and camels between the desert and savanna, was important within these commercial systems, although slave porters were sometimes used and river transport was significant on the Senegal, Gambia, Niger, and Benue rivers. Highly organized caravans of merchants, slaves, and livestock constituted temporary cartels that con-trolled prices en route and that provided insurance against robbery and ambush. These caravans, sometimes consisting of over 1000 people, often involved the delegation of authority to buy and sell en route to the caravan leader and his assistants. This miniature monopsony–monopoly on the move cut costs of provisioning and freed caravan members from otherwise inevitable cutthroat competition.

The Muslim diaspora organizations were grounded on control of credit, although the control was somewhat unusual in often having a social and religious character. Only Muslims could secure credit, and therefore it was essential to establish Islamic credentials by acculturation to the middle-class commercial culture of diaspora communities. Associations of merchants, like the Agalawa, Tokarawa, Kambarin Beriberi, and Jahanke, could coun-teract this limited access to credit through close cooperation and manage-ment, but in all cases the availability of credit was essential to commercial operations. This can be seen in relation to the landlord–brokerage system, in which short term credit was important to the successful completion of business deals in distant towns. Often transactions were multilateral, involv-ing many commodities and several buyers and sellers in any given transac-tion. In this situation an established resident broker was essential to assure that credit was honored. This was particularly so in transactions involving expensive items like slaves, where many products had to be sold before transactions could be completed. Similarly, merchants who disposed of war captives for Islamic governments advanced goods on credit to officials, in lieu of future payment in slaves. This effectively eliminated smaller mer-chants who were unable to tie up capital for months or even years.

The centers of economic activity for the Muslim diasporas were most often savanna empires and commercial emporia along the desert edge and Niger Valley.[19] For the seventeenth and eighteenth centuries, there were

Curtin notes that commercial diasporas in West Africa, which he terms acephalous diasporas, were comparable to the diasporas created by Greek, Phoenician, and others in the Mediterra-nean, the Lombard banks and Hanseatic League of Europe, as well as similar phenomena elsewhere. In all cases monopolistic or oligopolistic tendencies are common. Curtin is cur-rently engaged in preparing a full-length comparative study of commercial organizations.

[19] For a summary of political events in this period, see John Ralph Willis, "The Western Sudan from the Moroccan Invasion (1591) to the death of al-Mukhtar al-Kunti (1811)," in

no large savanna empires for much of West Africa, at least not on the scale of earlier Songhay, Mali, and Ghana. Only Borno (Bornu) in the Lake Chad basin had a major political influence over large-scale international trade, so that Borno was a major slave exporter across the desert and took an active role in other branches of international trade, particularly the export of various desert salts and livestock.[20] Because of the relative weakness of political structures in this era, the diasporas assumed an international orientation that maintained a strong element of political neutrality in local affairs. This international orientation promoted the development of a West African merchant class, Islamic in dedication, which transcended regional differences in culture and loyalty.

In the eighteenth century, however, Islamic upheavals hit key areas and influenced the pattern.[21] Beginning in the Senegal River valley and spreading to the Futa Jallon highlands, new governments that were dedicated to Islam came to power. Strongly supported by Muslim merchants, these governments initiated an ideological campaign against unbelievers that provided the rationale for large-scale enslavement. By the nineteenth century, this pattern became especially pronounced, as major empires were created on the scale of the medieval states. The new Sokoto Caliphate, for example, became the center of dramatic economic growth, in part at the expense of Borno but also because large areas were incorporated into one political system for the first time. The expansion of Hausa commerce, Sokoto political influence, and Islam proceeded together, so that previously inde-

J. F. A. Ajayi and M. Crowder, *History of West Africa*, vol. 1 (London, 1971), pp. 411–484; and R. A. Adeleye, "Hausaland and Bornu, 1600–1800," in Ajayi and Crowder, *History of West Africa*, vol. 1, pp. 485–530.

[20] We follow the suggestion of the 1973 Ahmadu Bello University seminar on Borno in adopting the spelling with an "o."

[21] For a summary of the various jihads, see the relevant chapters in Ajayi and Crowder, *History of West Africa,* particularly Murray Last, "Reform in West Africa: The Jihad Movements of the Nineteenth Century," vol. 2, pp. 1–29; R. A. Adeleye, "The Sokoto Caliphate in the Nineteenth Century," vol. 2, pp. 57–92; Yves Person, "The Atlantic Coast and the Southern Savannahs, 1800–1880," vol. 2, pp. 263–307; also see M. A. Al-Hajj, "The Meaning of the Sokoto Jihad," and Omar Jah, "The Relationship between the Sokoto Jihad and the Jihad of Al-Hajj Umar: A New Assessment," both of which were presented at the Sokoto Seminar, Departments of History, Ahmadu Bello University (Sokoto, 1975). For a discussion of the economic dimensions of the Sokoto *jihad,* see Lovejoy, "Hausa Kola Trade," Chapter 3; Adamu, "Hausa Factor," Chapter 4; Adamu, "Distribution of Markets in the Central Sudan in the 18th and 19th Centries," Sokoto Seminar, unpublished; Saad Abubakar, "The Finance of the Eastern Emirates," Sokoto Seminar, unpublished; and Yusufu Usman, "The Transformation of Katsina, circa 1796–1903: The Overthrow of the *Sarauta* System and the Establishment and Evolution of the Emirate," unpublished doctoral thesis (Ahmadu Bello University, 1974); and Tambo, "Sokoto Caliphate Slave Trade." For a discussion of official control of trans-Saharan slave exports from Borno in the nineteenth century, see Louis Brenner, *The Shehus of Kukawa: A History of the Al-Kanemi Dynasty of Bornu* (London, 1973), p. 115.

pendent Muslim merchants became more and more closely attached to government interests. Trade in slaves and the settlement of large numbers of slaves within the central areas of the various emirates of the Sokoto Caliphate reflected this new alliance between merchants and politicians, and the spread of jihad to other parts of West Africa extended it elsewhere. Thus the new states founded by Ahmed of Hamdullahi, Al-Hajj Umar, Samori, Rabeh, and others, promoted the enslavement of people, helped maintain slave supply, and increased the demand for slaves needed to settle the metropolitan regions of the new polities. Slaves were used in these areas for public works and in agricultural production of grains, particularly millet and sorghum, and other goods. Much of this output was destined for market exchange, grains being important in desert-side commerce, whereas cotton, indigo, onions, and other goods were needed for local industry and export. In parts of these states more than half the rural population was usually slave. Hence slavery and the procurement of slaves were central to economic and military policy in the savanna.[22]

The Coastal Forest: Bight of Benin to Gold Coast

The emergence of coastal states between the Niger Delta and the Akan forests of southern Ghana provided the first major modification in the commercial pattern established by the Muslim merchants, and this development is closely associated with the growth of slave exports after the middle of the seventeenth century. State formation, political power, improved military technology, and the overseas slave trade were closely related. First, except for Benin, states were very small before the seventeenth century and the growth of slave exports.[23] Second, the consolidation of

[22] The authors are currently engaged in a study of slavery in the Sokoto Caliphate, but see Tambo, "Sokoto Caliphate Slave Trade;" Michael Mason, "Population Density and 'Slave Raiding'—The Case of the Middle Belt of Nigeria," *Journal of African History*, vol. 10, no. 4, 1969, pp. 551–564; Mason, "Captive and Client Labour and the Economy of the Bida Emirate, 1857–1901," *Journal of African History*, vol. 14, no. 3, 1973, pp. 453–471; Allan Meyers, "Slavery in the Hausa–Fulani Emirates," in D. McCall and N. Bennett, eds., *Aspects of West African Islam* (Boston, 1971), pp. 173–184; and S. Baier and P. E. Lovejoy, "Gradations in Servility at The Desert-Edge (Central Sudan)," in Miers and Kopytoff, *Slavery in Africa* (Madison, 1977).

[23] For a summary of political events, see Wilks, "Mossi and Akan States," and J. A. Akinjogbin, "The Expansion of Oyo and the Rise of Dahomey, 1600–1800," in Ajayi and Crowder, *History of West Africa*, vol. 1, pp. 344–386, 304–343, respectively. Also see Ivor Wilks, *Asante in the Nineteenth Century* (London, 1975), R. C. C. Law, "The Oyo Empire: The History of a Yoruba State, Principally in the Period c. 1600–c. 1836," unpublished doctoral thesis (University of Birmingham, 1971); Edward Reynolds, "The Rise and Fall of an African Merchant Class on the Gold Coast, 1830–1874," *Cahier d'études africaines*, vol. 14, 1974, pp. 253–264; Kwame Daaku, *Trade and Politics on the Gold Coast, 1600–1720* (London, 1970);

powerful states depended upon imported military technology, including firearms for seventeenth-century Akwamu and eighteenth-century Dahomey and Asante. Oyo required horses from the north to make her imperial fortune, and after 1730 she too imported firearms to keep abreast of the coastal states.[24] These military imports could not have been financed without slave exports, although for the Akan states gold also was a major export, sometimes exceeding the value of slaves. Gradually Muslim traders were restricted in their movements and activities, whereas European merchants were confined to coastal entrepôts once the overseas trade became important. States such as Akwamu and Oyo in the late seventeenth century, and Oyo, Dahomey, and Asante in the eighteenth century, assumed a major role in procuring and marketing slaves.

Oyo prevented northern merchants from passing through her territories by imposing differential turnpike fees but allowing unrestricted access to markets for government traders. Rivalries within Oyo appear to have centered on control of trade, with the Alafin and his court dominating the export of slaves and the nobles of the Oyo Mesi dominating the military and hence the "production" of slaves. Successive Alafin promoted royal trade (1) by establishing a series of commercial towns along routes to the coast, all within the important southwestern province of Egbado; (2) through the appointment of palace slaves to administer the provinces, collect turnpike fees, and thereby limit commercial opportunities for freemen; (3) by discriminatory turnpike fees, from which palace traders, many of whom were women, were exempt; and (4) through levying heavy tribute obligations on coastal dependencies. Oyo policy towards ports on the Gulf of Guinea constantly played on local political and economic rivalry, alternately encouraging Allada, then Dahomey, then Porto Novo, and finally Lagos. The division between the military and state-controlled commercial bureaucracy resulted in the collapse of the empire in the first quarter of the nineteenth

---

Daaku, "Trade and Trading Patterns of the Akan in the Seventeenth and Eighteenth Centuries," in Meillassoux, *Trade and Markets,* pp. 168–181; I. A. Akinjogbin, *Dahomey and Its Neighbours, 1708–1818* (London, 1967); C. S. Newbury, *The Western Slave Coast and its Rulers* (London, 1961); W. B. Dickson, "Trade Patterns in Ghana at the Beginning of the Eighteenth Century," *The Geographical Review,* vol. 56, no. 3, 1966, pp. 417–431. It should be noted that Benin was never important in the slave trade, primarily because foreign merchants were confined to the port of Ughoton, because other products, such as ivory and pepper were available, and because the Oba of Benin placed a long-lasting embargo on the sale to Europeans of male slaves, for which European demand was greatest. Even after 1720, when this embargo was lifted, the sale of male slaves remained a closely policed royal prerogative; see Alan Ryder, *Benin and the Europeans, 1485–1897* (London, 1969), pp. 88–93, 168, 196, 198. Also see Obaro Ikime, *Niger Delta Rivalry: Itsekiri–Urhobo Relations and the European Presence, 1884–1936* (London, 1969), pp. 50–59.

[24] Gemery and Hogendorn, "Technological Change"; and Law, "Oyo Empire," pp. 354–355.

century.[25] The collapse was probably related to changes in the slave export market, first shaken by the Napoleonic wars and then made increasingly more uncontrollable with the British blockade along the "Slave Coast."

Further west, Dahomey developed as a state in the early eighteenth century with a strong commitment to official control of slave exports and slave procurement. The first administration even imposed a successful boycott of slave exports that forced prices up, and thereafter she continued to ration slave exports in order to influence price. As with the case of Oyo, on which state Dahomey was dependent until the early nineteenth century, foreign merchants, whether Muslims from the north or Europeans on the coast, were restricted in their internal movements.[26]

Asante pursued policies equally restrictive to those of her eastern neighbors. The emergence of the Asante empire after 1700 had the effect of eliminating all the earlier states in the region, including Denkyira and Akwamu; and the monopolistic practices that these earlier, small states had attempted to implement were pursued with greater force in the eighteenth century. First, Asante inherited control of the European commercial entrepôts on the coast, with the authorities at Kumasi continuing to demand rental fees for coastal establishments and prohibiting European operation in the interior. The Asante government dominated trade, often operating through a single factor on the coast; and this domination extended to all export markets as Asante expanded into the gold- and kola-producing regions to the northwest of Kumasi. Slave supply was enhanced since conquered provinces and tributary states were expected to provide annual slave quotas to the central government. Beginning in the eighteenth century, Muslim merchants were confined to northern Asante towns; and local merchants within Asante were similarly restricted in their activities through the imposition of discriminatory inheritance taxes and commercial regulations that provided first access to markets for government traders.[27]

---

[25] Law, "Oyo Empire," pp. 113–118, 156–166, 350–391; Peter Morton-Williams, "The Oyo Yoruba and the Atlantic Trade, 1670–1830," *Journal of the Historical Society of Nigeria,* vol. 3, no. 1, 1964, pp. 25–46.

[26] Law, "Oyo Empire," pp. 374–384; Akinjogbin, *Dahomey,* pp. 75–80, 151–164, 208–212.

[27] For Asante trade, see Ivor Wilks, "Asante Policy towards the Hausa Trade in the Nineteenth Century," in Meillassoux, *Trade and Markets,* pp. 124–141; Wilks, *Asante,* pp. 267–269, 276, 697–680, 690; Lovejoy, "Hausa Kola Trade," Chapter 2; Reynolds, "African Merchant Class"; Kwame Arhin, "The Financing of Ashanti Expansion (1700–1820)," *Africa,* vol. 38, no. 1967, pp. 283–291; Arhin, "Aspects of the Ashanti Northern Trade in the Nineteenth Century," *Africa,* vol. 40, no. 4, 1970, pp. 363–373; and Daaku, "Akan Trade." In this context, it should be noted that Asante exports of kola nuts and gold were also tightly controlled by the government. These products were of major importance to the Asante economy, with gold sometimes exceeding slaves in export value. Estimates for kola exports are more difficult to acquire, but this product, too, was crucial to Asante, especially in the

The nineteenth century brought changing export patterns to the area of the Gold Coast and the Bight of Benin. Asante redirected its economy to take into account the European boycott of slave sales. Muslim merchants were pushed further north, by breaking the ties with Kong and confining Hausa and Yarse traders to Salaga, a new market town northeast of the middle Volta bend. This promoted kola production, maintained control of kola prices, and enabled the state to export gold as needed, primarily to Europeans in order to compensate for the loss of slave sales. Asante, however, continued to acquire slaves in large quantities, via tributary arrangements and wars, and through purchases from Muslim merchants in the north. Instead of reexporting these slaves across the Atlantic, they were absorbed into the Asante economy to be used in kola harvesting, gold mining and head portage.[28]

Oyo failed to make the economic adjustment that characterized Asante's nineteenth-century economic policies. Instead she became embroiled in civil war, which resulted in a slave revolt, a Muslim coup d'état, and the incorporation of the Oyo heartland into the Sokoto Caliphate as the Emirate of Ilorin.[29] This development opened the area to Muslim merchants from the north, so that, unlike in Asante, the area of Muslim operation actually expanded. Within the Yoruba and Dahomey region as a whole, slave exports continued to be important, despite the British blockade. Civil strife resulting from the Oyo collapse, the jihad in the north, and a general exodus of people to new towns and into more defensible forest positions laid the foundation for major economic changes, including, from the 1840s, development of the palm oil industry for export overseas. As in the case of Asante, however, much of this new development was state enterprise and involved widespread use of slave labor, both in production and in transport. Thus, even as slave exports dwindled, slave imports from the north for use in Yoruba cities and farms assumed major importance. State control was much weaker in the Yoruba cities than in Dahomey and Asante, but Muslims were still largely confined to Ilorin. European traders were also restricted. They strongly influenced the economy through their purchase of palm products, but they rarely left Lagos or other coastal posts. Repatriated Yoruba ex-slaves from Sierra Leone (called Saro) and from Brazil acted as intermediaries between Europeans and the local economy, so that state

---

nineteenth century. For a general discussion of the relative importance of slaves, gold, and other exports, see Richard Bean, "A Note on the Relative Importance of Slaves and Gold in West African Exports," *Journal of African History*, vol. 15, no. 3, 1974, pp. 351–356.

[28] Wilks, "Asante Policy"; Wilks, *Asante*, pp. 264–269; Lovejoy, "Hausa Kola Trade," Chapter 2.

[29] Law, *Oyo Empire*, pp. 46, 419 ff; Oroge, "Yoruba Slavery," p. 88; Robert S. Smith, *Kingdoms of the Yoruba* (London, 1969), pp. 133–145.

control was not as strong as it formerly had been under Oyo domination. Nevertheless, the pattern of state influence continued, both at Abeokuta where the Saro took over the government itself, and at Ibadan, where the major warlords dominated trade, agricultural production, and the military.[30]

From the Benue to the Bight of Bonny (Biafra)

The third region considered here consisted of the Benue River valley southwards to the Cross River basin and the Niger Delta. In the seventeenth and eighteenth centuries the northern parts of this region were dominated by Jukun merchants, who controlled most salt production in the many locations that stretch from the Gongola basin across the Benue valley southward to the northern Igbo country. By the eighteenth century, however, Jukun domination of river and overland trade in this area was challenged from the north by Muslim merchants and in the south by Aro merchants and Tiv regiments.[31] The region as a whole may not have been a major slave exporter to American markets until the 1730s, a development that is in sharp contrast to other areas where transatlantic slave exports were important from about 1650 or even earlier for trans-Saharan shipments.[32]

Ethnic federations governed most of this area, with the Jukun controlling the Benue basin in the seventeenth and eighteenth centuries and the Aro dominating the south in the eighteenth and nineteenth. Commercial associations similar to the Jukun pattern of dispersed settlement with strong links to a religious oracle continued to be standard. The area as a whole can be considered to have constituted a segmentary political and economic system, in which the commercial organizations were able to assert political control over large areas through the manipulation of their economic position and their guardianship of religious shrines.

As slave exports to the Americas grew from the middle of the eighteenth century, the Bight of Bonny became the largest single exporter in the period 1750–1850. This remarkable growth was related to four internal developments: (1) the modification and expansion of Niger Delta city states and the commercial houses that were the backbone of their economies; (2) the

[30] Oroge, "Yoruba Slavery," pp. 91–95, 101–112, 131–137, 146–211; Smith, *Yoruba Kingdoms*.

[31] We wish to thank J. Sterken, University of Lagos, for information on the Jukun, although the interpretation here is entirely our own. Mr. Sterken is currently completing research for a doctorate.

[32] Curtin, "Measuring the Atlantic Slave Trade." Also see David Northrup, "Trade Without Rulers: Pre-Colonial Economic Development in the Biafran Hinterland," unpublished doctoral thesis (University of California at Los Angeles, 1974), pp. 91–93, for slight modifications in Curtin's figures.

introduction of the Ekpe society at Calabar, which established and enforced commercial laws and guaranteed the payments of debts; (3) the consolidation of the Aro marketing system between the Cross River, Niger Delta, and northern grasslands; and (4) the division of Niger River trade into segments dominated respectively by Ijaw, Aboh, Igala, Awka, and Oguta merchants.[33] These developments established localized monopolies over trade, so that all slave exports passed either down the Niger or along Aro-controlled trade routes to the Niger Delta and Calabar. The growth of these commercial systems, which succeeded in exporting at least 2 million people in less than 100 years, is even more impressive when the fact of nineteenth-century British naval intervention is taken into account.

The coastal cities, especially Bonny and Calabar, successfully established themselves as the ports through which most slaves were exported. The general tendency was for the two major ports to increase in importance at

[33] Sources for trade in the Bight of Bonny interior include: E. J. Alagoa, *A History of the Niger Delta* (Ibadan, 1972); Alagoa, "Long Distance Trade and States in the Niger Delta," *Journal of African History*, vol. 11, no. 3, 1970, pp. 319–329; J. B. C. Anyake, "The Coastal States of South-Eastern Nigeria, 1891–1939," doctoral thesis, forthcoming (University of Ibadan); G. I. Jones, *The Trading States of the Oil Rivers* (London, 1963); A. J. H. Latham, "Currency, Credit, and Capitalism on the Cross River in the Pre-Colonial Era," *Journal of African History*, vol. 12, no. 4, 1971, pp. 599–601; Latham, *Old Calabar, 1600–1891. The Impact of the International Economy upon a Traditional Society* (London, 1973); A. E. Afigbo, "The Aro of Southeastern Nigeria: A Socio-Historical Analysis of Legends of Their Origins," *African Notes*, vol. 6, no. 2, 1971, pp. 31–46; vol. 7, no. 1, 1971–1972, pp. 91–106; Afigbo, "Trade and Trade Routes of Nineteenth Century Nsukka," *Journal of the Historical Society of Nigeria*, vol. 8, no. 1, 1973, pp. 77–90; Afigbo, "Pre-Colonial Links between Southeastern Nigeria and the Benue Valley," unpublished paper, Niger–Benue Valley Seminar (Jos, 1974); E. M. Chilver, "Nineteenth Century Trade in the Bamenda Grassfields, Southern Cameroons," *Afrika und Ubersee*, vol. 44, no. 4, 1961; F. I. Ekejiuba, "The Aro Trade System in the Nineteenth Century," *Ikenga*, vol. 1, no. 1, 1972, pp. 11–26; Ekejiuba, "Igba Ndu: An Igbo Mechanism of Social Control and Adjustment," *African Notes*, vol. 7, no. 1, 1971–1972, pp. 9–24; David Northrup, "The Growth of Trade among the Igbo before 1800," *Journal of African History*, vol. 13, no. 2, 1972, pp. 217–236; Northrup, "Trade Without Rulers"; S. C. Ukpabi, "Nsukka before the Establishment of British Administration," *Odu*, vol. 6, 1971, pp. 101–110; Lovejoy, "Interregional Monetary Flows"; K. O. Ogedengbe, "The Aboh Kingdom of the Lower Niger, c. 1650–1900," unpublished doctoral thesis (University of Wisconsin, 1971); S. J. S. Cookey, "An Igbo Slave Story of the Late Nineteenth Century and Its Implications," *Ikenga*, vol. 1, no. 2, 1972, pp. 1–9; Lawrence Offie Ocho, "A Short History of Aku before the Establishment of British Rule," *Okikpe, a Publication of the Aku Undergraduates' Union (Nsukka)*, vol. 1, 1974, pp. 1–29; David Northrup, "New Light from Old Sources: Pre-Colonial References to the Anang Ibibio," *Ikenga*, vol. 2, no. 1, 1973, pp. 1–5; N. Uka, "A Note on the 'Abam' Warriors of Igbo Land," *Ikenga*, vol. 1, no. 2, 1972, pp. 76–82; F. I. Ekejiuba, "The Aro System of Trade in the Nineteenth Century, Part II," *Ikenga*, vol. 1, no. 2, 1972, pp. 10–21; Saad Abubakar, "The Middle Benue Region up to c. 1850," unpublished paper, Niger–Benue Valley Seminar (Jos, 1974).

the expense of smaller rivals. In the nineteenth century when palm products began to replace slaves as the main export, these two cities continued their domination, although with the effective British blockade of Bonny, slave exporters operated through the more remote town of Brass, and after 1870 Opobo succeeded Bonny as the major port when many Bonny merchants deserted the city as a result of civil strife.

Throughout the Delta, commercial developments of a capitalist nature reduced competition, so that local politics as well as the economy were dominated by the wealthiest merchants. Local lineage structures, especially at Bonny, were modified into corporate firms that successfully assimilated slaves and other subordinates within business establishments, often referred to as canoe-houses. This institution was centered around the trade canoe, an increasingly large vessel which by the late eighteenth century could transport as many as 120 people and provisions in a single voyage. Canoes, some of which were 80 feet long, were well armed, many with cannon fore and aft, for commercial rivalry and military confrontation went hand in hand in the establishment and maintenance of an oligopoly position.[34] Bonny was connected by various estuaries to the important Aro commercial fair at Bende and with Aboh on the Niger, so that Bonny merchants were able to dominate both markets. The canoe-houses were staffed by oarsmen, brokers, guards, and merchants who lived and worked together as a corporate unit under the direction of a manager, often of slave origin. Canoes were then associated in larger corporations under the founder or inheritor of major establishments, only one of which was aristocratic in origin. This structure permitted the tight control of credit, which was extended by European merchants to the heads of the major canoe organizations. This effectively ensured that defaulters could be prosecuted and that advances could be guaranteed, and consequently credit was extended in large amounts for periods of one or more years.[35]

An infusion of European credit on a massive scale was the basis of Calabar's trade as it was in the Delta. As at Bonny, Calabar merchants restricted access to this credit by systematically eliminating their rivals in the Cross River area, so that by the last third of the eighteenth century they were predominant as the largest exporters in the eastern Bight of Bonny. The ability of Calabar businessmen to attain an oligopolistic position was directly related to the introduction and development of the secret Ekpe society, which became the effective judicial and law enforcement agency at

[34] Robert Smith, "The Canoe in West African History," *Journal of African History*, vol. 11, no. 4, 1970, pp. 518, 524–527; Jones, *Oil Rivers*, p. 55; Alagoa, "Trade and States," pp. 322, 324; Cookey, "Igbo Slave Story," p. 4.
[35] Jones, *Oil Rivers*, pp. 96–97; Dike, *Trade and Politics*, pp. 108–127.

Calabar and which the largest merchants controlled. Ekpe's key role in commerce can be seen by the list of sanctions it could impose for failure to honor commercial obligations:

> First it could boycott a person, by having *Ekpe* "blown" against him, which would prohibit anyone from trading or having any other dealing with the offender. Secondly, it could place a mark on someone's property which prevented its being used until the mark had been removed. Thirdly, it had the power to impose fines. Fourthly, it could arrest an offender and detain him or hand him over to the person with whom he was at odds. Fifthly, it could execute an offender, either by decapitation, or by tying him to a tree in the bush with his lower jaw removed. Sixthly, it could confine people to their quarters by hoisting a yellow flag. And lastly it could destroy or destrain a man's property.[36]

Such an institution as Ekpe permitted the Calabar merchants to adjust to changing export demands, so that the shift from slave sales to palm oil in the 1820s and 1830s hardly affected the Calabar monopoly.[37]

The growth of the Aro commercial network between the Cross River, the Delta, and the northern grasslands appears to be directly related to developments in the export trade in slaves. The origins of the Aro Chukwu settlements date to the seventeenth century, but a major change occurred before the mid-eighteenth century, when the area was invaded by mercenaries armed with firearms, reportedly the first firearms used inland from the Bight of Bonny. The mercenaries, who were called Akpa, came from the Calabar region and probably were equipped from Calabar in order to provide slaves for export. They formed the nucleus of one of the Aro lineages, Ibom Isii. By the end of the eighteenth century, moreover, the Aro had developed a marketing system that extended north into the grasslands, east into the Ibibio country and west to the Niger. Besides their successful use of firearms, the Aro also adopted the 12 grades of the Ekpe society so that their commercial operations were governed by rules similar to those at Calabar. This facilitated the extension of credit from Calabar to the Aro and ultimately throughout the Igbo country and its complex of market places. In addition the Aro promoted the fame and influence of a religious oracle at Aro Chukwu, Ibinukpabi, which sanctioned the movement of Aro traders and assured prompt retaliation for any transgression against Aro property or lives. Under the authority of this oracle and other, perhaps subordinate, ones, the Aro hired their own mercenaries, Abam, Ohafia, and Edda, just as they appear to have been originally hired by Calabar merchants. This alliance with selected villages crisscrossing the Igbo country provided the protection that centralized states normally extended

---

[36] Latham, *Old Calabar,* p. 38; and for a general discussion of Ekpe, pp. 35–41.
[37] Latham, *Old Calabar,* pp. 55–66.

to merchants, and permitted the Aro to dominate the economy of the Igbo country.[38]

Aro marketing arrangements centered on the operations of two 24-day fairs, one at Bende, connecting with Bonny and Calabar to the south, and one at Uburu near an important salt lake further north. These two fairs were functionally integrated and scheduled at 24-day intervals. The 12 days between the fairs were enough to allow merchants to travel between the two, allowing for a few days of rest. Around each fair was organized a series of periodic markets. These market rings were based on contracts between Aro merchants and local authorities, whereby the Aro established and enforced market rules, under the direction of the Ekpe society and with the assistance of their own police, and wherein local authorities were assured a monopoly of accommodation and storage facilities. Contracts were consummated with ritualized ceremonies and involved regular payments to the Aro for the business opportunities. In return local villages promised not to allow other merchants, except craftsmen and local farmers, to operate at market sites.[39]

The Aro received payment for slaves in both currency and goods, though they preferred commodities. Dealers were entitled to a present of about 20–25%, added to their accounts, for every slave sold. Gifts of gin, tinned fish, or other assorted goods were also given to regular and prominent customers. Coastal merchants' advances of goods on credit were made only to the Aro trading partner or to his close associates. Other traders desiring commercial relations with the coastal broker were required to obtain an introduction by the Aro traders, who acted as his bond. In recompense, the Aro bondsman would take from the coastal trader both the dash and the additional commission (called "topside" on the coast) ordinarily due on a transaction. "The guarantor also got a commission of 15 brass rods per slave from the new trader, as the Aro guarantor was responsible to the coastal broker for the new trader's debts, the dash, commission, etc., acted as surety to the guarantor and helped him to liquidate any outstanding debt."[40] The Aro worked to preserve their tight control of interior trade via the establishment of colonies outside their immediate homeland. Spheres of influence based on the pioneering ventures of individual traders were

[38] Northrup, "Trade without Rulers"; Ekejiuba, "Aro Trade," pp. 13–15; Afigbo, "Nsukka," p. 77; Afigbo, "Aro," pp. 41, 45; Latham, *Old Calabar*, pp. 26, 28; Ukpabi, "Nsukka before the British," p. 107; Northrup, "Igbo Trade," pp. 233–236. The Aro Chukwu oracle was recognized at Bonny. See Cookey, "Igbo Slave Story," p. 5.

[39] See Northrup, "Trade without Rulers," Ekejiuba, "Aro Trade," pp. 16–25; Ekejiuba, "Igba Ndu"; pp. 9–24; Ukpabi, "Nsukka Before the British," p. 107. For the commodities in Aro trade, see Ekejiuba, "Aro Trade," Part 2, pp. 10–11.

[40] Ekejiuba, "Aro Trade," Part 2, p. 16.

passed on to descendants. Competition among the Aro themselves was thus closely delimited. The Aro-Obinkita

> established several settlements in the Ibibio region as well as at Itu, Opobo and Bonny and controlled the trade route from Itu and Bende to Azumini and Akwette; Umunka-Aro (Worsu Tostis family and Ndoti Aro) said to have migrated from Ngwa and Olokoro area established settlements in the Ngwa territory around Aba; Uguakuma (a section of the Akpa-Aro) established several settlements to the east of the Cross River and controlled the land route via Biakpan, Uwet, Akpankpa to Calabar.[41]

Merchants who violated the boundaries of these spheres of influence were severely punished, and one function of the Aro central council was to deal with such cases.

The Aro also developed a system for employing mercenary soldiers, responsible for the original acquisition of slaves. The Aro mercenaries were usually members of the Ohafia, Abam, Abiriba, and Nkporo-Edda clans of Ohafia division. The Aro determined the "targets," acted as guides, and paid the bills for services rendered with deliveries of war caps, heads of tobacco, cases of liquor, money, and sometimes slaves. The societal relations of the mercenaries encouraged the military life—those who did not participate in raiding were punished and ridiculed, their property could be confiscated, and their wives mistreated.[42]

The Niger River pattern was based on short-distance monopoly of river transport and most commercial activity. Delta merchants controlled the stretch as far as a fair south of Aboh,[43] whereas Aboh merchants operated as far north as Onitsha, whence Igala merchants, centered at Idah, controlled the river as far as the Niger–Benue confluence. Nupe merchants (Kakanda and Kede) dominated the Niger from the confluence to Bussa, and Jukun and Idoma traders controlled the Benue. The Anambra River basin was a subsystem of the Niger trade that penetrated the Igbo country from the west. Igala, Aboh, Awka, and Oguta traders dominated this trade, and it served as an alternate outlet to the Aro overland routes. Merchants other than those who held special privileges could travel on different stretches. Hausa and Kakanda traders, for example, are reported to have operated from the Niger–Benue confluence downstream and through lagoons to Lagos by the eighteenth century, whereas Igbo merchants traveled on the Benue; but these exceptions did not alter the basic control of river trade and transport. Credit along the river tended to flow upstream, from

---

[41] Ekejiuba, "Aro Trade, p. 18; also see Northrup, "Trade without Rulers."

[42] Uka, "Abam Warriors," pp. 76–81.

[43] Ohambele town refused to trade directly with Europeans in 1887 because of a pact with Bonny. The pact was an old one dating at least as early as the first years of the nineteenth century. See Ekejiuba, "Aro Trade," Part 2, p. 17.

the Niger Delta, but also from the ivory- and slave-rich emirates of the southeastern Caliphate. The river system was upset in the nineteenth century, first by the activities of a few American and Brazilian slave traders who bought slaves as far north as the confluence, but more importantly by the activities of river steamers after mid-century. This last development did not at first affect slave movements, for the Europeans were not involved in slave marketing at this time; but ultimately it broke the monopoly of river transport in many other products, particularly palm oil and kernels.[44]

The Western Forest Zone (Ivory Coast to Guinea)

Large parts of the last geographical area to be considered, the region of southern Ivory Coast, Liberia, Sierra Leone, coastal Guinea, and Guinea-Bissau, were of only minor importance to the overseas slave trade. The coast was generally dangerous for ships, with high breakers, and few lagoons or harbors. The interior was an important kola-producing region, but this tied the area to the savanna and not the coast. Some slaves were purchased along the coast, while ivory and foodstuffs for slave ships were also exported. Total slave exports for the whole period of the trans-Atlantic trade probably did not reach 1 million; and this figure is somewhat deceptive, for it reflects large exports from three different parts of the coast for three different periods. Eighteenth-century exports from Sierra Leone largely related to the *jihad* and later expansion of Futa Jallon, exports reaching a peak of over 112,000 for the decade of the 1760s. For the Ivory Coast and Liberia, where close to 600,000 slaves were exported in the eighteenth century, there were two peaks, each identified with widely separated parts of the coast and different political eruptions. The first occurred between the 1720s and 1740s and was probably related to the eastward expansion of the Kuranko and the extension of Malinke *juula* trade south from Konyan. The second route, further east in the Bandama River valley, was also related to Muslim commercial activities, in this case Malinke *juula* from Boron. The peak in exports was reached in the 1760s and was closely connected with the flight of Baule refugees from Asante, who pushed westward into country inhabited by Senufo and Guro. Hence, this region had some similarities with savanna patterns, particularly the Senegambia area, where Muslim diasporas controlled trade.[45]

The relative unimportance of the western forest region, except for the local variations, highlights one significant conclusion of this paper, that

[44] Northrup, "Igbo Trade," p. 221; "Trade without Rulers"; Afigbo, "Nsukka," p. 77; Ogedengbe, "Aboh Kingdom"; Lovejoy, "Interregional Monetary Flows," pp. 569, 574–575.
[45] Curtin, "Measuring the Atlantic Slave Trade," pp. 117–121; Rodney, "Slavery," pp. 434, 436.

competition was not unrestricted in West Africa. The constraints here appear to have been shipping risks, perhaps less population, and the late development of commercial links with the far interior which could have supplied coastal slave ports on a regular basis. For purposes of analysis, the Senegambia region, continguous in the north, can be included, although it has previously been considered in relation to savanna patterns. As in the western forest region, however, slave exports from Senegambia, numbering only a few hundred thousand for the whole slave trade era, were never as crucial as elsewhere in West Africa, in part because gold, hides and skins, gum arabic, beeswax, and other exports often equaled or exceeded slave values, and in part because the population density in the Senegambia area was also low. Thus, the effective commercial watershed for slave exports to the coast and slave exports to North Africa and elsewhere in the Sudan was east of the Senegambia headwaters. At that point merchants could profitably ship slaves in any direction, but the numbers were relatively small, particularly after Futa Toro prohibited the export of its settled slaves in the eighteenth century. Futa Toro, the most densely populated state on the Senegal River, was able to enforce this policy because of its alternate exports, and this action helped limit the trade in slaves.[46]

Thus, European merchants were not faced with a perfectly competitive supply situation. Sources from the Gold Coast through the Bight of Benin before 1740, and to the Bight of Bonny after 1740, were the only consistent suppliers in sufficient quantities; and the relative proximity of this region to many parts of the Americas provided a competitive advantage over other parts of Africa that would have served as alternate sources. Only when the British blockade raised prices did southeast Africa and Angola take up the slack. Earlier Angolan exports were largely destined for Brazil, and East African exports were marginal at that time.

CONCLUSION

This essay has set out to survey the general structure of slave delivery mechanisms in West Africa. A major finding has been that a characteristic of that mechanism was the existence of restrictive trade associations and practices, sometimes official, sometimes private, and sometimes involving collaboration between the two. Muslim diasporas that acted as marketing cartels, Asante and Dahomey state traders, the Jukun merchants, the Delta canoe-houses, the Ekpe Society, the Aro commercial network, and many others all engaged in a multiplicity of restrictive practices.[47]

[46] Curtin, *Economic Change,* vol. I, p. 183.

[47] The best compendium of West African states and traders engaging in restrictive practices

It is true enough that these marketing organizations and associations often differed from one another to a very great degree. The economic historian with an interest in slave marketing must be impressed even more, however, by the similarities. In every one of the examples cited, entry to trade was strictly limited with access to the marketing mechanism vouchsafed only to those with the proper religious beliefs, social position, entree to the state trading system, or some combination of these.[48]

As the examples cited demonstrate, these restrictive practices were neither static nor immutable. Leadership and membership changed, geographical coverage expanded or contracted, the relative importance of slaves to other products varied, and the restrictive arrangements themselves underwent frequent alteration.[49] In spite of a changing nature, however, some type of cartel or state trading was very likely to be encountered at any time in almost every region in which slave marketing was undertaken.

"Membership" in such systems, however defined, was likely to encompass significant economic advantages. An individual trader's operations would thereafter be supported by an organic and often powerful commercial structure. He would usually find easier access to credit, important for successful trade when working capital is short. He might depend on an already established convoy system, involving the provision of foodstuffs and

---

can be found in Chapter 2 of Lars Sundstrom's *The Exchange Economy of Pre-Colonial Tropical Africa* (New York, 1974). Sundstrom catalogues the references in the literature to the settlement by trading groups of "colonies" in other states (p. 46), to the "middleman monopoly" achieved by many trading groups astride the lines of transport (pp. 50–53), and to the numerous royal monopolies on trade (p. 61). His biographical references cover 31 cases of middlemen with monopoly power and 25 cases of royalty holding monopoly power or a dominant position in external trade.

[48] As has been noted previously in several places, slaves were only one of many products exported from West Africa. These other items included maize, palm oil, yams, gum arabic, ivory, gold, pepper, textiles (often for resale elsewhere in Africa), groundnuts, beeswax, hides, and skins. Foodstuffs were primarily exported to supply slaves ships, but other products could be locally very important. Only the "Slave Coast" in the Bight of Benin and the Bight of Bonny area relied overwhelmingly on slave exports. Elsewhere, slaves were only one of many products and often formed less than half the total value of exports. This point has been most recently argued by Bean, "Slaves and Gold." Because of the diversity of exports, a thorough analysis of marketing in West Africa would have to go far beyond the preliminary treatment of slave marketing presented here. Lack of space has prevented an examination of other export marketing, but it is suggested that our general conclusions may apply to these other commodities. Many of the same merchants and governments also dominated other sectors, but this means that the restrictive practices in slave marketing were most likely to be followed with other commodities as well.

[49] Similarly, most modern industrial cartels—the Stehlwerksbund, The Association of Licensed Automobile Manufacturers, The Rhenische Gesellschaft—altered their tactics and membership over time to accord with economic and political pressures. The wholly static cartel, while no doubt desirable for the profit-maximizer, is a myth.

shelter at halting places, and the existence of intermediaries and middle-men, dealing with storage, currency exchange, liaison with local officials, and the like. If he were not always licensed to or by state officials, he would at least be represented by the authorities of the trade association. Without their support, his "capital equipment," particularly firearms and other weapons, horses, porters, donkeys, and large canoes might be difficult or impossible to acquire. Finally, access to the imported goods needed to pay for slaves (textiles, salt, metal goods, firearms, powder, money currency such as cowries) was often made much easier.

No claim is made that *all* slaves were transported via the sort of market-ing organizations described here. Detailed studies of the numbers involved lie in the future, if indeed they are possible. The evidence is strong, however, that the major slave-exporting regions were among the most highly organized and the most restrictive in their marketing practices. In view of this, it is difficult to see West African slave marketing as the preserve of the rugged individualist and thousands like him operating in a milieu of open commercial rivalry. Hypotheses of highly competitive deliv-ery systems within Africa must thus be modified to take account of the imperfections in marketing discussed here.

A final question remains to be discussed. What implications does the present paper carry for analyses of the slave trade's profitability? Several interesting corollaries may indeed follow.

Most recent authors (e.g., Thomas and Bean, as well as Gemery and Hogendorn) have agreed that coastal competition between marketing sys-tems would make it difficult for these various domestic "cartels" to have earned long-run monopoly profits from European buyers. The existence of restrictive arrangements may then imply the following conclusions.

1. *That long-run abnormal profit was indeed eliminated, but that short-run profit could be significant.* Such a situation is possible, given lack of perfect knowledge, attempts by Europeans to keep foreigners out of their own coastal spheres of commercial influence, and the real costs of movement to other stretches of the coast (tying up the ship and crew for longer periods; trade goods especially selected for a certain sector of the coast; "sunk costs" involving dash, duties, pilot fees on occasion, and unloading charges, all of which may have been incurred before the slave price was finally deter-mined).

2. *That monopoly profit may have been eliminated in transactions with Euro-pean buyers, but still accrued within the domestic protected market for slaves.* Most slave-exporting societies were themselves users of slaves in the domestic economy, often on a large scale. In almost every case, slaves could be exported or retained as market conditions dictated. If we assume that it was easy for slave ships to hoist anchor and transfer their custom to another

seller, nonetheless, competition from other suppliers had always to be reckoned with in the overseas trade. Internally, however, a "cartel" might face far less overt competition. Supported and sustained by religious authority, military strength, economic power, or all three, it might be very long-lasting indeed, with a life of decades or even centuries, as seen in this chapter.[50] Though economic profit might be eroded in the overseas trade, profits could still be earned in the protected market area. They might accrue through high-priced sales to domestic consumers, or through low-price delivery of slaves to "cartel" members for use in domestic productive activity. (This aspect appears to have been important in the palm oil trade. It resembles the potential profitability of vertical integration in a modern industrial cartel. The possibility of internal profits accruing in a protected market area, together with highly competitive market conditions outside the protected area, is familiar to students of international trade. The German steel cartel at the turn of the century, or the United States pharmaceutical industry today, are cases in point.)[51]

We do not in this chapter take a definite stand with regard to the two alternatives just noted, and further work to uncover evidence of abnormal profit in the African portion of the slave trade will be undertaken subsequently by the authors. There does seem to be evidence of conspicuous consumption among the major slave-trading groups, involving expensive houses, fancy firearms, and other luxury imports. This, however, is a topic for the future. The main aim of the present chapter is simply to demonstrate that competition in slave marketing was considerably more imperfect than is sometimes assumed. Restrictive practices were common and long-lasting, though subject always to social, political, and economic evolution. The widespread occurrence of these restrictive systems, and their remarkable longevity, is in our opinion a most important element in understanding the mechanism for slave supply.

[50] It should be remembered that European interlopers, who broke the Royal African company's monopoly and other companies' as well, had far greater freedom to compete on the high seas than did African interlopers on the patrolled paths of the coastal forests. Furthermore, the penalties enforced against illegal competitors were very much harsher within Africa than they were in the maritime trade.

[51] Note that neither of these two alternatives alters in any important way the general conclusion that the supply of slaves to buyers in the New World was significantly more elastic than the supply of competing forms of labor.

II

ATLANTIC–AMERICAN PERSPECTIVES

9

Mortality in the Dutch Slave Trade, 1675–1795

JOHANNES POSTMA

The loss of life in the massive forced migration from Africa, the Atlantic slave trade, has long been a matter of conjecture, and few efforts have been made to examine this complex problem. A recent synthesis of literature on the subject revealed that mortality estimates have ranged from 13–30% of the total number of slaves exported from Africa,[1] and these figures apply to the Atlantic crossing or "middle passage" only. An important reason for this wide range in estimates and the dearth of scholarly studies on the subject is the lack of reliable and readily available data. Some of the essential statistics are available but to gather, organize, and analyze the data meaningfully requires patience, time, and often special expertise.[2]

This chapter is one of the products of 2 years of archival research,

---

[1] Philip D. Curtin, *The Atlantic Slave Trade: A Census* (Madison, 1969), p. 276.

[2] Herbert S. Klein and Stanley L. Engerman have pioneered in this subject. See their unpublished paper "Shipping Patterns and Mortality in the African Slave Trade to Rio de Janeiro, 1825–1830," Annual Meeting of the African Studies Association, Syracuse, 1974. Also see Herbert S. Klein, "The Trade in African Slaves to Rio de Janeiro, 1795–1811," *Journal of African History,* vol. 10, 1969, pp. 533–549.

producing a vast quantity of statistical information on nearly 1200 slaving voyages of the Dutch merchant marine involving the transportation of circa 500,000 slaves from Africa.[3] In addition to an assessment of middle passage death rates this chapter will examine mortality shortly before embarkation in Africa and after disembarkation in the Western Hemisphere. Also significant in this study are the analysis of sex and age ratios in mortality, as well as the relatively early period, late seventeenth and early eighteenth centuries, not covered in previous studies on this subject.

STAGES IN THE ORDEAL

Most references to the mortality of the Atlantic slave trade are primarily concerned with the middle passage. The obvious reason for this is that the highly organized maritime aspect of the migration has left behind a select but quantifiable record. This fact should not lead to the misconception, however, that the middle passage was the only nor the most costly aspect of the trade in terms of its heavy toll on human lives. For purposes of analysis one might divide the ordeal of the slaves, between enslavement in Africa and adjustment to their new environment in the Americas, into the following categories. (Note that what is generally referred to as the middle passage has been subdivided into two separate categories.)

1. Enslavement
2. Journey to coast
3. Awaiting shipment
4. Coasting ⎫
5. Ocean crossing ⎬ Middle passage
6. Sale and transfer
7. Seasoning

Not all slaves, not even those who survived the whole ordeal, were subjected to all these categories, but some may have had to undergo the same experience more than once. The sale and transfer in the West, for example, often involved a second ocean voyage in transfer from a Caribbean island depot to the mainland or another plantation island.[4] On the other hand,

---

[3] For an overview of the volume of the Dutch slave trade see Johannes Postma, "A Quantitative Assessment of the Dutch Slave Trade," in S. L. Engerman and E. O. Genovese, eds., *Race and Slavery in the Western Hemisphere: Quantitative Studies* (Princeton, 1975).

[4] This is particularly true for the Asiento (contract with the Spanish Crown for the importation of slaves into the Spanish colonies by foreign subjects) slaves from islands such as Curaçao and Jamaica.

some slaves went directly to their destination. Others were born into the state of slavery and were spared the ordeal of capture in a slave raid or tribal war. Still others were fortunate enough to avoid the often dreadful waiting period before departure (in sight of the African coast). Depending on weather and market conditions these various legs of the migration differed greatly in length, but they were rarely very short.

As in previous studies on slave trade mortality, the focus of this chapter will be on the ocean crossing and coasting, often combined and called the middle passage. Some qualitative statements will be made and statistics cited about the waiting period in Africa and the sale and transfer in the West, but the lack of sufficient data will not allow for a systematic analysis of these phases of the migration. Dutch documents provide hardly any information on the process of enslavement and the march to the coast of Africa, preventing an examination of those aspects.[5] The loss of life in those legs of the journey may forever remain a mystery. The slaves' adjustment to the American environments is actually beyond the scope of this study but offers an intriguing challenge to future scholarly exploration.

MORTALITY IN THE INITIAL STAGES

Of those enslaved Africans who survived the often long march to the coast, many died before embarking on European ships. Both pyschological and physical factors contributed to an apparent high death rate among the slaves awaiting embarkation. Here they first came in contact with Europeans and Africans who had been exposed to diseases to which Africans of the interior had not yet developed immunities. The "white man's grave," the Guinea Coast so dreaded by Europeans, posed a threat to Africans of the interior as well.[6] Added to the danger of contracting a strange disease were the squalor of their existence and the uncertainty of their future. The initial sight of the ocean, alone, might have been traumatic, particularly when this reinforced the rumor that the "white savages" were going to eat them on the

---

[5] Of considerable interest on this subject are the following articles: Albert VanDantzig, "Effects of the Atlantic Slave Trade on Some West African Societies," and Joseph C. Miller, "The Portuguese Slave Trade in the Southern Atlantic, 1780–1830," in a special issue of the *Revue française d'histoire d'outre-mer*, no. 226–227, 1975, pp. 252–269 and 135–176.

[6] Philip D. Curtin, "The White Man's Grave: Image and Reality, 1780–1870," *Journal of British Studies*, vol. 1, 1961, pp. 94–110; "Epidemiology and the Slave Trade," *Political Science Quarterly*, vol. 83, 1968, p. 205.

other side of the water.[7] Humiliating physical examinations and the branding with a red-hot iron further heightened their agony.[8]

Before 1730, when the WIC (Dutch West India Company) had a
monopoly on the slave trade and employed larger ships in the so-called
"castle trade,"[9] slaves were kept (or stored) for several weeks or even
months until a company vessel arrived. On the Slave Coast (Togo,
Dahomey, and Western Nigeria) slaves were generally housed in barracoons or stockades (*tronks,* they called them) on the beach. At Elmina, on
the Gold Coast (Ghana), a portion of the storage space in the castle was
utilized for housing slaves, and the documents also refer to a so-called "slave
hole" or dungeon, where slaves were kept until embarkation was possible.[10]
This dungeon could accommodate 300 slaves but often as many as 400 were
packed into the place.[11]

Many slaves lost their lives in these storage areas; on the Slave Coast 43
died at Ouidah in 1724 and 80 at Epee in 1735.[12] The Dutch exported
approximately 1200 and 1800 from this area during these two respective
years, which would put the death rate at 4%. It is not certain, however, that
these were the only slaves who died during the wait, nor is it known if these
mortality figures are representative for other years. At Elmina slaves were
put to work during the waiting period because this was regarded better for
their health than "sitting" in confinement.[13] One WIC director at Elmina
expressed his concern about the irregular arrival of slaving vessels and the
possible consequences as follows:

> [I] recommend that you space the arrival of ships better for we cannot purchase large
> numbers of slaves if no ships are on the [African] coast or due to arrive, because if slaves
> have to wait a long time they run a great risk of dying and also cost a great deal to feed.[14]

---

[7] J. A. de Marree, *Reizen op en beschrijving van de Goudkust van Guinea,* vol. 2 (The Hague,
1817–1818), p. 248.

[8] For a more detailed description of the treatment of the slaves see my dissertation, "The
Dutch Participation in the African Slave Trade; Slaving on the Guinea Coast, 1675–1795"
(Michigan State University, 1970), pp. 200–202.

[9] On methods of slaving see Postma, "Dutch Participation," Chapter 3.

[10] The Castle at Elmina does not have the remains of a slave dungeon as does the English
castle at Cape Coast. Marree, *Reizen op en beschrijving,* p. 248, confirms the presence of a
dungeon, but whether the dungeon has been eliminated or the space referred to was used for a
low-grade storage area is not certain.

[11] Archive of the Tweede West Indische Compagnie (WIC), The Hague, vol. 487, p. 35;
Archive of the Nederlandse Bezittingen ter Kuste van Guinea (NBKG), vol. 7, Minutes 27
January 1737.

[12] WIC, vol. 486, pp. 491–492; vol. 488, pp. 92–94.

[13] NBKG, vol. 24, Correspondence 25 June 1774.

[14] WIC, vol. 55, Correspondence 30 March 1705.

At times slaves were boarded before a ship was ready to sail because the fresh sea air was regarded better for their health than the stale air of the slave hole.[15]

Information regarding preembarkation mortality is somewhat enhanced by the record-conscious WIC officials who required for bookkeeping purposes that a death warrant (*attestatie*) had to be signed for every slave who died, including infants.[16] Several of these documents have been preserved among WIC papers but their number is not sufficient or representative enough to provide a sound basis for calculating an average death rate. They do confirm, however, that mortality among waiting slaves was occasionally high. In 1705, for example, out of a group of approximately 650 slaves at Elmina, 95 died. For one 8-month period (1734 and 1735) at least 50 death warrants were preserved, and for the years 1728 and 1729 at least 95 such documents have been located.[17] During those last two years the WIC exported between 3000 and 4000 slaves from the Guinea Coast, which would put the average at less than 3%; this is assuming that 95 is the complete mortality figure for those years. For the year 1725 only 25 death warrants have been located,[18] a year in which the WIC exported at least 2000 slaves from Guinea. If this is a complete record the death rate would be barely above 1%. It is possible that a combination of favorable ship arrival spacing and the absence of epidemics could produce such a low rate; however, this low figure would be offset by the high rate of 15% in the sample just cited for 1705.

Since there are no complete statistics available on either the total number of deaths or the waiting period, one is once more left to conjecture. For the WIC trade I would venture an estimate of 3–5% as a mortality rate for slaves waiting for embarkation. For the free trade during the last three-quarters of the eighteenth century the estimated death rate for waiting was undoubtedly lower. Far fewer records are available for this trade but the smaller ships and the frequent arrivals and larger volume of the trade would almost certainly lower the death rate for that phase of the slave trade to half the figure estimated for the WIC.

The conclusion should not be drawn, however, that slaves were better off during the free trade period, for what they may have gained in shorter

---

[15] NBKG, vol. 6, Minutes 22 March 1730.

[16] See Postma, "Dutch Participation," for the record-consciousness of the WIC. Appendix E of the dissertation is a translation of an attestatie. An infant is the subject of the document in WIC, vol. 180, p. 192.

[17] Most of the attestaties are located in WIC, vols. 107 and 108. See also WIC, vol. 99, pp. 199–205.

[18] WIC, vol. 107, pp. 322–341.

onshore waiting was balanced by a longer coasting period. The ship trade (also called interloper trade)[19] replaced the so-called castle trade, which had been practiced widely by the WIC.[20] Instead of stopping exclusively at WIC trading factories, the free traders anchored at several places along the coast for the purchase of slaves, thereby extending their stay on the African coast. Although they might buy slaves at the WIC factories, it was no longer an operation under the same commercial umbrella.

An analysis of 70 free trade slaving voyages of the MCC (Middelbursche Commercie Compagnie), the largest of the Dutch free trading companies, shows that the average stay on the African coast was 7.5 months, or 288 days. The longest time spent to obtain a cargo of slaves by one ship was 18 months and the shortest, 2 months.[21] Another sample, not including MCC ships, puts the average coasting period at 249 days, or more than 8 months (see Table 9.1). These favorable MCC statistics, reflected in other elements of the operation as well, may have been the reason for the company's success.

These long periods of coasting obviously contributed to the mortality rate on the slave ships. The manner in which death rates were recorded, however, makes it often difficult to determine which slaves died off the African coast and which died during the middle passage. Documents of both the WIC and the free trade generally do not distinguish between the two, leaving the impression that all the slaves died during abnormally long crossings. In actuality, however, the coasting period was nearly always much longer than the middle passage. The MCC sample cited previously shows an average length of 62 days for the middle passage, which is nearly one-fourth of the coasting period for the same ships.[22]

The average period spent by WIC ships to complete a slave cargo was much shorter than for the free trade. The statistical basis for calculating an average is complex and weaker, but the average can be estimated at about 60 days.[23] One reason for this striking contrast of 60–228/249 for coasting

[19] See Postma, "Dutch Participation," Chapter 3, for an assessment of the methods of slaving.

[20] The WIC rapidly withdrew from participation in the Atlantic slave trade at the end of the 1730s, and only a few WIC slavers went to the West after 1740. The company continued to manage the trading castles, however, and remained active in the slave trade in an intermediary or middleman capacity.

[21] W. S. Unger, "Bijdragen tot de geschiederis van de Nederlandse slavenhandel, II," *Economisch-Historisch Jaarboek*, vol. 28, 1958–1960, p. 39. These averages were based on a sample of 70 MCC ships. See Table 9.2.

[22] Unger, "Bijdragen tot de geschiederis," pp. 39 and 50.

[23] Based on a sample of 50 WIC voyages the period for coasting and the middle passage averages out to 132 days. Many of the dates used in this sample commence with the death of the first slave, which easily could have happened 1 or 2 months after arrival on the African

TABLE 9.1

Duration Middle Passage

	General	WIC	Free trade	MCC[a]
Combined				
Average days	78.5	83.5	69.4	62.0
Voyages	(142)	(93)	(51)	(70)
Guinea				
Average days	80.9	84.5	73.6	—
Voyages	(133)	(91)	(44)	—
Loango–Angola				
Average days	43.0	41.5	43.4	—
Voyages	(9)	(2)	(7)	—
Single voyages				
Longest	—	230	183	135
Shortest	—	24	34	45
Coasting				
Average days	—	60[a]	249	228
Voyages	—	(33)	(27)	(70)

Sources: Postma Data Collection; Unger, "Bijdragen tot de gesdriederis," pp. 39, 50.
[a] This is a speculative estimate; see text.

is that many WIC coastal vessels (employed for service on the African coast) were used for the slave trade when there was an oversupply of slaves at Elmina; such vessels required no coasting period at all, which lowered the average considerably.[24] The shortest times registered for ordinary WIC slavers completing their slave cargo were 23 and 27 days.[25] A few WIC ships spent at least 6 months on the African coast before starting the Atlantic crossing.

Table 9.2 illustrates the sad tale of how often slaves succumbed in sight of the African coast. The 17 WIC ships listed in the table may have been recorded because they were severe cases, but they were certainly not the only ones with high death rates off the African coast. Given the much longer coasting period for free traders, their mortality rates for that leg of the slaves' journey must have been considerably higher than for the WIC.[26]

---

coast. Then one has to subtract the period required for the middle passage, which took an average of 81.5 days (see Table 9.1).

[24] See Postma, "Dutch Participation," pp. 98–99.

[25] WIC, vol. 180, p. 59; vol. 486, p. 365. These were the ships *Duynvliet* in 1723, and the *Europe* in 1688, respectively.

[26] A careful reexamination of the WIC data used by Unger should eventually provide us with a better picture of that situation.

TABLE 9.2

Slave Mortality at Various Stages

Ship	Year MP[a]	Cargo	MP[a] deaths	Africa coast	Port America	Shore
Graf van Laarwijk	1701	488	150	91	—	—
De Son	1703	513	134	—	—	—
Vriendschap	1704	393	72	23	7	—
Quinera	1706	547	?	45	—	—
Justitia	1707	740	152	48	9	1
Catharina Christina	1709	509	?	50	—	—
Amsterdam	1710	520	?	30	—	—
Carolus Secondus	1710	510	32	18	0	—
St. Clara	1710	517	?	17	—	—
Akredam	1713	596	?	51	—	—
Guntersteyn	1715	541	?	29	—	—
Duynvliet	1723	340	27	—	—	49
Akredam	1725	643	32	—	2	3
Amsterdam	1726	466	178	14	—	12
Leusden	1727	748	66	25	—	10
Beekesteyn	1733	866	?	57	—	—
Rusthof	1734	716	345	Many	—	43
Beschutter	1735	768	?	13	—	—
Stad en Lande	1735	760	349	Many	—	34
Jonge Daniel	1736	469	58	1	—	5

Sources: Postma Data Collection.

[a] MP means middle passage.

THE MIDDLE PASSAGE

The ocean crossing, although one of the shorter legs of the Atlantic slave trade, continues to be associated most closely with mortality. This is partly due to the organization and administration of the trade, but also because the crowded conditions on the relatively small sailing ships produced a dreadful experience—beset with all sorts of dangers such as shipwreck, calms, pirates, lack of water and food, storms—that easily could result in the death of slave and sailor alike. The length and route of the ocean crossing (often referred to as the middle passage) depended on a variety of factors involving winds and currents, places of origin and destination, and faulty navigation. Looking at the map one must be careful not to equate air mileage with sea mileage, in that seasons, winds, and currents often necessitated long delays and roundabout routes. Except for Senegambia, ships loading on the Guinea Coast could not sail directly westward but had to sail east and southward first before they could find and "run" the westerly winds. This made the voyage from Guinea, though actually closer to the Western Hemisphere, often as long as from Angola.[27] Both Curtin and Unger confirm this fact.[28]

A careful analysis of Dutch data on the length of middle passage voyages produced a significant surprise. Not only were the voyages from the two regions similar in distance but, contrary to appearances, Angola voyages were much shorter, requiring little more than half of the time (43 compared to 81 days) required for the middle passage from Guinea.[29] This finding is quite contrary to some of the qualitative documentary evidence. By citing an extreme case, West Indian planters urged the WIC to avoid Angola voyages because that route was much longer and costly.[30] The real motive for the allegation was undoubtedly the dislike of Angola slaves by Surinam planters.[31]

After land was sighted in the West the problems were usually far from over. Slavers headed for plantation colonies in Surinam or the Guianas frequently bypassed their river of destination and were then unable to turn about. This meant either proceeding to a different destination or ferrying the slaves back and up the river in small boats, which was often costly in time, expense, and human lives.[32] Worse yet was the danger of running ashore and getting shipwrecked; the Guiana Coast seems to have been particularly hazardous in that respect. Records of about a dozen such incidents have been unearthed and some of the most serious ones have been listed in Table 9.3. One of these, the shipwreck of the ship *Leusden* in 1737, may well have been the most tragic catastrophe in slave trade history. Only 16 of the original cargo of 716 slaves survived, because they were fortunate enough to be working on deck when the ship ran on the shoal. When called upon to account for the enormous financial loss, surviving crew members testified that they had closed the hatches when the ship was making water and they heard slaves attempting to scramble out of the hold, knowing that the ensuing battle for life boats might result in the death of everyone. Thus, while waiting out the storm for the next few days, they heard the slaves slowly suffocate and drown below decks.[33]

---

[27] Actually this refers to the area north of the Congo River, often referred to as the Loango Coast, where the Dutch obtained approximately one-fourth of their slaves. See J. Postma, "A Quantitative Assessment of the Dutch Slave Trade," *Revue francaise d'histoire d'outre-mer,* no. 226–227, 1975, pp. 232–244.

[28] Curtin, *Atlantic Slave Trade,* p. 279; Unger, Bijdragen tot de geschiederis," p. 50.

[29] See Table 9.3. The longest and shortest voyages took 230 and 24 days, respectively.

[30] WIC, vol. 619, 22 April 1726; vol. 1140, doc. 36. The ship *Beekesteyn* was used as an example because it took 22 months to sail from Holland via Africa to Surinam.

[31] WIC, vol. 1138, 16 February 1707.

[32] For such incidents see WIC, vol. 1139, 10 February 1719; vol. 1026, doc. 20.

[33] WIC, vol. 1141, doc. 169.

TABLE 9.3
Catastrophic Voyages

Ships	Year	Length MP (days)	Cargo	Deaths	Survive	Loss (percentage)	Post-MP deaths
Epidemics							
Stad Moscow	1706	(121)	572	261	311	46	
Carolus Secondus	1707	(78)	425	254	171	59	
Wapen van Holland	1701		664	211	453	31	
Rusthof	1733	(90)	716	345	371	48	
Adrichem	1715		717	344	475	48	
Phenix	1728		783	281	502	36	
Stad & Lande	1732	(91)	439	307	132	70	
Stad & Lande	1735	(94)	760	349	411	46	22
Leusden	1735	(122)	687	408	279	59	
Beekesteyn	1731	(206)	755	238	417	32	51
Watervliet	1747		Circa 600	Majority			
Nicolaas Theodorus	1772		350	150	200	43	
Jonge Jan	1763		?	(50%+)	180	50+	
Nooitgedacht	1773	(183)	157	140	17	89	
Sarinaamse Welvaar	1773	(140)	290	210	80	72	
Zeemercuur	1789	(70)	272	174	98	64	
Shipwrecks and groundings							
Roosenburg	1709		390	95	295	24	
Nieuwe Post	1719		535	344	191	64	
Akredam	1727	Exploded at Angola					
Leusden	1737		716	700	16	98	
Bassienburg	1744		?	?	20	?	
Belisarius	1772		190	154	36	81	
Goede Verwachting	1767		?	?	28	?	
Slave rebellions							
De Son	1703		513	100	?	20	
Vreybeid	1734		647	1	543		
Middelburgs Welvaren	1751		260+	230+	30	88	
Johanna Cores	1763		?	22	270		
Vliegende Faam	1758		281	7	199		
Armina Elisabeth	1775	Fate unknown		11	109		
Vigilantie	1781			?	18		
Neptunis	1785	Exploded Guinea			8		

Sources: WIC, vols. 200, 206, 1140–1142; S. Sur., vols. 406–415; AAC, vol. 1212.

The *Leusden* was one of the last large WIC slavers to cross the Atlantic; only two others completed the voyage that had already been commissioned or started before this incident. Whether the shipwreck of the *Leusden* influenced this change in policy is not known, but the strange coincidence would clearly be in harmony with the preponderance of financial concerns on the part of the company directors.

Slave rebellions aboard ships could also lead to enormous loss of life. Fewer than 20 serious slave rebellions have been found recorded in Dutch documents, and most of these were easily suppressed by the crew; however, in a few instances the consequences were disastrous.[34] In the case of the *Neptunis* in 1785 the slaves gained control of the ship, but it exploded shortly thereafter when an English slaver coming to the rescue of the crew accidentally hit the powder chamber with a cannon ball. Only eight slaves of an undetermined number of slaves and crew survived the explosion.[35] In another incident, involving the ship *Middelburgs Welvaren* in 1751, the crew opened fire on the revolting slaves and killed all but 30 of the cargo numbering more than 260.[36] The slaves on the ship *Vigilantie* in 1780 also managed to capture control of the vessel, forcing the crew to flee in life boats with 18 of the slaves. Eventually the ship ended up in English hands, but it is not known what happened to the 183 slaves that remained on board at the time of the revolt.[37]

Crowding or "packing" slaves in the small sailing ships used for the slave trade has often been regarded as a factor contributing to the death rate.[38] This study confirms, however, what has been asserted by Klein and Engerman,[39] that crowding appears not to have raised the death toll, at least not as an independent factor. Dutch free trade data contain two types of measurement for ship capacity, tonnage (*last*) and fees paid for the right to purchase slaves in Africa. Employing both as a basis for determining cargo density and correlating this with the mortality rate of the same cargo, the results fail to show any relationship. In fact, some of the more crowded cargoes often had relatively low mortality rates (see Figure 9.1).[40] Since few ship measurements are available for the WIC ships a separate method of

[34] See Table 9.3, and Postma, "Dutch Participation," pp. 207–210.

[35] Amsterdamse Admiraliteits College (AAC), vol. 1212, Shiplog of the *Pollux*. The Captain of the *Neptunis* also survived as he happened to be ashore during the incident.

[36] Societeit Suriname (S. Sur.), vol. 409, 11 February 1751. S. Sur. is a large documentary collection, the survival of the early charter government of the plantation colony of Surinam.

[37] S. Sur., vol. 416, 11 October 1780 and 23 January 1781.

[38] Daniel P. Mannix and Malcolm Cowley, *Black Cargoes: A History of the Atlantic Slave Trade, 1518–1865* (New York, 1962), pp. 105–106.

[39] Klein and Engerman, "Shipping Patterns," p. 9.

[40] I gratefully acknowledge the assistance and advice of Dr. Duane Braaten of the Computer Science Program at Mankato State University in analyzing the data for this project.

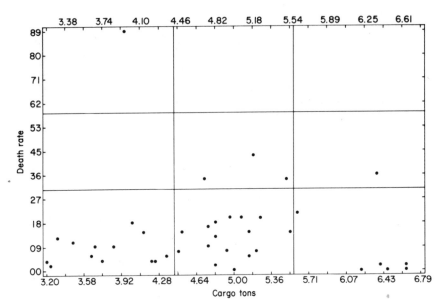

Figure 9.1. Scattergram testing the correlation between cargo crowding and mortality.

paired comparison has been employed to test the correlation between crowding and mortality. The mortality rates of the largest and the smallest cargoes were compared and more than half of the matches showed a higher rate of death among the less crowded cargoes.[41]

The duration of the middle passage provides the most systematic explanation of mortality patterns (see Figure 9.2). This has been confirmed by earlier studies,[42] and it also holds true for the Dutch slave trade. As was noted before, for the Dutch slavers the voyages from Angola tended to be considerably shorter than those from the Guinea Coast. This is reflected in the respective mortality rates from the two regions. In the case of the free trade the Guinea death rate was nearly double (17.4% compared to 10.6%) that of the Angola traffic. For the WIC the differences are not as large but they are nonetheless significant (see Tables 9.4–9.5). The impact of longer voyages may also be evident in the fact that the majority of cargoes having disastrous mortality rates originated from the Guinea Coast. Whereas the disasters could generally be attributed to independent factors, particularly epidemics, long voyages seem to have complicated such conditions and contributed to the higher death rates through shortages of food and water (see Table 9.6 for breakdown of percentiles for death rates).[43]

[41] Of the 21 matches only 9 showed a higher mortality rate for the more crowded cargoes.
[42] Curtin, *Atlantic Slave Trade*, p. 282; Klein and Engerman, "Shipping Patterns," p. 10.
[43] Mortality rates of more than 25% have been designated as disasters in this study. More than 85% of the Dutch slaving voyages had death rates below 25%.

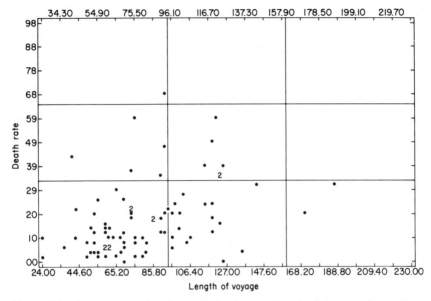

Figure 9.2. Scattergram testing the correlation between length of voyage and mortality.

Correlating mortality with the major points of destination of Dutch slaving vessels produced the suprising result of unusually low death rates on ships bound for St. Eustatius, although the island is actually no farther away from Africa than Surinam and Curaçao. Although the location of and route to St. Eustatius may have had some impact on these statistics, a closer examination revealed that the largest portion of the slavers bound for St.

TABLE 9.4
Mortality Rates by African Origins

	Combined		Guinea		Angola	
	Percentage (voyages)		Percentage (voyages)		Percentage (voyages)	
WIC						
All known						
cases	16.2 (244)		16.9 (128)		13.3 (33)	
Exclusive of	11.1 (132)		11.3 (103)		10.2 (29)	
disasters[a]			(−25 = 19.5%)		(−4 = 12.1%)	
Free Trade						
All known						
cases	15.5 (121)		17.4 (87)		10.6 (32)	
Exclusive of	8.9 (100)		10.1 (71)		5.7 (27)	
disasters[a]			(−16 = 18.3%)		(−5 = 15.6%)	

Source: Postma Data Collection.
[a] Cargoes with more than 25% mortality.

TABLE 9.5
Mortality Rates by Caribbean Destination

	Complete sample	25% up excluded	
	Percentage (voyages)	Percentage (voyages)	Disasters[a]
WIC	16.3 (174)	11.2 (143)	−31 = 17.8%
Curaçao	16.8 (56)	12.0 (45)	−11 = 19.6%
St. Eustatius	9.8 (15)	9.8 (15)	0 = 0%
Surinam and Guiana	16.3 (96)	10.8 (78)	−18 = 18.7%
Free Trade	16.7 (125)	9.2 (103)	−22 = 17.6%
Curaçao	15.3 (10)	9.1 (8)	−2 = 20.0%
St. Eustatius	10.8 (12)	6.5 (11)	−1 = 8.3%
Surinam and Guiana	17.9 (97)	9.1 (79)	−28 = 28.8%

Source: Postma Data Collection.
[a] Cargoes with more than 25% mortality.

Eustatius came from Angola rather than from the Guinea Coast,[44] which confirms the lower mortality rates for cargoes originating in Angola.

Disastrous mortality rates were nearly always associated with middle passages of above average length.[45] Short voyages, however, were no guarantee against high death rates. The WIC ship *Justitia,* for example, had a short crossing of 55 days (not the shortest on record, but certainly far below the WIC's average) in 1708, but still had a mortality rate of 26% because of a smallpox epidemic on board.[46]

Contagious diseases were almost invariably the cause of mortality disasters. Several cases have been documented as such. Most common among the epidemics were scurvy, dysentery, and smallpox. Scurvy, perhaps the most notorious of the killers, was the cause of one of the major free trade disasters as late as 1772.[47] Shortage of food and water, often caused by unexpectedly long voyages, would often complicate epidemics. This was the case with the disastrous voyage of the *Beekesteyn* in 1731, in which were lost at least 150 slaves through scurvy.[48]

It has been suggested that seasonal variations influenced the mortality

[44] See Table 9.5. Notice that only one of the St. Eustatius-bound ships fell into the disaster category, which underscores the significance of the length of voyage. Eleven of the 15 WIC slavers to St. Eustatius came from Angola, even though the WIC generally sent only one-fourth of its ships there.
[45] See Table 9.3. Only 1 of the 11 voyages listed with a known voyage length fell below the average voyage length.
[46] WIC, vol. 1138, 22 August 1708.
[47] S. Sur., vol. 415, 25 April 1773. This was the slaver *Nooitgedacht,* in which only 17 slaves out of a total of 157 survived the voyage.
[48] WIC, vol. 1140, 13 July 1731.

TABLE 9.6
Mortality Rates in Percentiles

Percentage mortality	WIC			Free trade		
	Ships	Percentage total	Cumulative percentage	Ships	Percentage total	Cumulative percentage
0	4	2.2	2.2	1	.8	2.2
1–5	25	13.8	16.0	34	25.6	26.3
6–10	41	22.7	38.7	25	18.8	45.1
11–15	35	19.3	58.0	28	21.1	66.2
16–20	23	12.7	70.7	11	8.3	74.4
21–25	20	11.0	81.8	11	8.3	82.7
26–30	10	5.5	87.3	4	3.0	85.7
31–40	12	6.6	93.9	5	3.8	89.5
41–50	6	3.3	97.2	4	3.0	92.5
51+	5	2.8	100.0	10	7.5	100.0
Total	181	(=59.5% of known WIC voyages)		133	(=16.2% of known free traders)	

Source: Postma Data Collection.

rate.[49] Correspondence from the West Indies, for example, blames the high death rate of one slaver on its arrival during the wet season.[50] Sailing during wet and stormy weather prevented the slaves from leaving the closed holds, which also contributed to the death rate in one instance.[51] A systematic analysis of Dutch slave trade data shows that the rate of arrivals in the West Indies was lower in the February–March and September–October periods, whereas they were higher at midyear and during the change of the year (see Figure 9.3).[52] An analysis of death rate by season, however, produced no conclusive trends, particularly not when the WIC and free trade statistics were compared (see Table 9.7).

Taken in its entirety the Dutch slave trade mortality rate was approximately 17%, slightly lower for the WIC and slightly higher for the free trade (see Table 9.8). Whereas there were substantial fluctuations between the various decades, there is no discernible trend toward decrease or increase in the overall pattern for the period of 1680–1795. If any change occurred at all there was a slight increase during the free trade period, perhaps attributable to the longer coasting periods of the free traders.

[49] Klein and Engerman, "Shipping Patterns," pp. 9–10. This study tends to place the emphasis on the slaves' journey in the African interior rather than on the middle passage itself.

[50] WIC, vol. 56, p. 144.

[51] WIC, vol. 1144, 29 June 1721.

[52] The statistics are based on West Indian arrivals rather than African departures because the sample of the former is substantially larger.

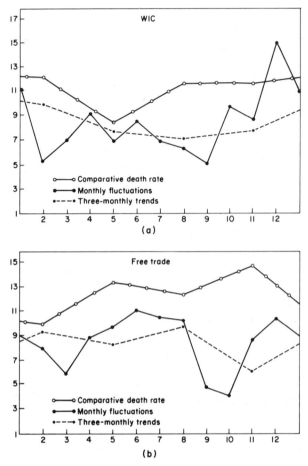

Figure 9.3. Seasonal fluctuations in the slave trade, plotted for (a) the WIC and (b) the free trade. (From Table 9.7 and the Postma Data Collection.)

Exceptionally high mortality rates during specific decades, particularly in the 1730s, were generally the result of several disastrous voyages. There may also have been a correlation between high mortality and escalation of the volume of the slave trade, as the decades of the 1730s, 1740s, and 1760s would indicate.

SEX AND AGE RATIOS IN MORTALITY

Slave trade mortality affected men and women with quite different degrees of severity. Data preserved in the Dutch archives are adequate so that

TABLE 9.7
Mortality by Season

	Complete sample Percentage (voyages)	25% up excl. Percentage (voyages)	Disasters
WIC	16.0 (163)	10.2 (133)	−30 = 18.5%
December–February	17.1 (51)	10.2 (40)	−11 = 22.5%
March–May	13.4 (35)	10.3 (31)	−4 = 11.4%
June–August	16.8 (36)	9.7 (27)	−9 = 25.0%
September–November	16.3 (41)	13.5 (35)	−6 = 14.6%
Free trade	17.7 (105)	9.5 (84)	−21 = 20.0%
December–February	15.0 (28)	9.5 (23)	−5 = 17.9%
March–May	18.4 (27)	8.4 (21)	−6 = 22.2%
June–August	17.7 (28)	9.1 (22)	−6 = 21.4%
September–November	20.0 (22)	11.0 (18)	−4 = 18.2%

Source: Postma Data Collection.

a comparison of both sex and age groups is possible. For more than 70 WIC slave cargoes, statistics on sex distinctions have survived, and similarly for age groups for a somewhat smaller number of ships. More than 50 of the cited number have also left records of deaths broken down by sex, and for a slightly smaller number, by age groups. Based, therefore, on samples of thousands of slaves, an estimated 70% of the WIC slaves were males and 30% were females. Of this number nearly 13% were youths between the

TABLE 9.8
Mortality Rates by Decades

	Ship sample	WIC percentage mortality	Ship sample	Free trade percentage mortality
1680–1689	(6)	6.0		
1690–1699	(10)	11.4		
1700–1709	(45)	16.6		
1710–1719	(34)	22.4		
1720–1729	(44)	13.5		
1730–1739	(38)	27.0		
1740–1749	(5)	20.5	(20)	21.3
1750–1759			(23)	14.6
1760–1769			(30)	19.7
1770–1779			(42)	14.1
1780–1789			(10)	21.6
1790–1795			(5)	18.6
Overall	(182)	16.8	(130)	17.4

Sources: Principally the archives of the Second WIC, the MCC, and the S. Sur. The statistics are part of the Postma data collection; individual references are too numerous to be listed.

approximate ages of 2 and 15; nearly 75% of the youths were boys. As the eighteenth century advanced there was a trend toward larger percentages of both women and youths, as free trade statistics indicate (see Table 9.9).

Men seemed to die at a considerably higher rate than women—19% as compared to 14.7% respectively (see Table 9.10).[53] The fact that youths died at nearly the same high rate as males may be explained in part by the high percentages of boys among them. The statistical significance of this imbalance between males and females is strengthened by the fact that on more than three-fourths of the ships in the sample men died at higher rates than women.

No documentary evidence can be marshaled to explain the causes of this sexual disparity, nor is there evidence to indicate that contemporaries were aware of this fact. The basic reason may be that women were stronger in the battle against the new diseases encountered in the migration. It is also possible, because women were generally a minority and less feared for their physical strength than men, that they received favorable treatment. Sexual exploitation may also have been a reason for this. There are indications, for example, that women were not chained to each other or the ship,[54] which would have given them both a physical and a psychological advantage over men. Because women frequently had children or babies with them they had a greater psychological will to live and apparently received better food rations.[55] Women may also have assisted in the preparation of food, which undoubtedly produced extra morsels essential to survival.[56] Finally, women may also have been accustomed to a greater degree of bondage than men, giving them more stamina to survive the humiliations and hardships of the slave trade.

MORTALITY IN THE LATER STAGES

After arriving in the western hemisphere the danger to life was hardly passed for the slaves. Ships often had to wait for several days before slaves were allowed to disembark. First the captain of the slaver had to promise under oath that there was no contagious disease on board, which was then verified by a medical team of the WIC.[57] The disembarkation itself could

---

[53] It is unfortunate that the MCC records have not yet been analyzed for differences in mortality rates.

[54] Mannix and Cowley, *Black Cargoes,* p. 116.

[55] WIC, vol. 1141, Document 35. Comments concerning shortage of food on the ship *Rusthof* in 1734 implied that women with babies required special dietary treatment.

[56] WIC, vol. 180, p. 151.

[57] S. Sur., vol. 410, 30 November 1753. This source concerns a captain of a slaver who refused to swear the oath and was therefore not allowed to land his slaves in Surinam.

TABLE 9.9
Slaves by Sex–Age Categories

	WIC (1675–1740)			Free trade (1730–1795)		
	Slaves	Ships	Percentage	Slaves	Ships	Percentage
Males	22,682	73	69.6	11,488	90	59.1
Females	10,132	73	30.4	8135	90	40.9
Adults	32,813	73	100	25,051	90	100
Youths	3343	56	12.6	5428	90	21.7
Boys	2442	53	73.7	3314	90	61.0
Girls	865	53	24.4	2114	90	39.0
Total youths	3307	53	100	5428	90	100

Sources: WIC: Postma Data Collection; Unger; "Bijdregen tot de geschiederis," p. 49.

take several days.[58] At Surinam the waiting period often lasted more than a week, and when an epidemic was on the ship this would last much longer because the planters feared that such an epidemic might spread to the colony.[59] One captain complained that the waiting period would make the slaves "listless" and the crew "restless," and that many of the slaves would die because of the inaction.[60] For 34 WIC ships that reported harbor deaths, an average of five slaves died after the middle passage and before disembarkation.[61]

Once on land slaves had to undergo additional physical examinations and another branding (in Curaçao at least), and finally were sold to new owners. In Surinam and other colonies in the Guianas they were sold directly to the planters, but in Curaçao and St. Eustatius the vast majority of the slaves were reexported to Spanish and French colonies, which meant another ocean voyage. There was another waiting period between disembarkation and the sale which lasted, on the average, 1–2 weeks, and in some cases much longer. In a sample of 49 WIC ships, an average of 18.6 slaves died during this interlude. If there had been an epidemic on board and the waiting period before sale was long the death rate might well exceed that of the middle passage. In 1700 on the *Brandenburg,* for example, of the cargo of 450 slaves, 131 died at sea and 64 more died within a period of 10 months.[62] In 1727, the ship *Rusthof* had 74 casualties on the middle passage,

[58] WIC, vol. 1138, 22 September 1706. The procedure described here refers to Surinam; methods differed slightly in other colonies.

[59] WIC, vol. 1140, doc. 74.

[60] WIC, vol. 1138, 26 June 1706.

[61] Since high rates may well have been the reason for recording these statistics, the actual average is undoubtedly lower.

[62] WIC, vol. 1026, pp. 26, 36, and 44.

TABLE 9.10
Mortality by Sex–Age Categories, 1680–1735

	Males	Females	Youths[a]
Rate of deaths (percentage)	19.0	14.7	17.4
Sample specific	13,360	5968	1671
Total sample	19,328	19,328	13,925
Ships in sample	43	43	28

Sources: Postma Data Collection.
[a] Youths were approximately 2–14 years of age; they are included in their respective sex categories.

but within 4 months after arrival in St. Eustatius 263 additional slaves died while another 148 could not be sold because of illness.[63]

No complete record of slaves dying during this transition period has been preserved, and it is therefore impossible to make a systematic appraisal of their mortality rate. A nearly complete record of deaths at Curaçao during the first decade of the eighteenth century, however, gives us some basis for speculation. Of the 11 WIC slave cargoes included in the records, 376 slaves died before they were sold and transshipped to the Spanish colonies, either illicitly or in accordance with the Asiento contract (see Table 9.11).[64] A few years later, during a 16-month period (1712–1713), the deaths of 60 slaves, belonging to 4 different cargoes were recorded.[65] These deaths occurred even before the second ocean voyage of the slaves had started. Where this transition stage was present in the slave trade it would therefore not be unreasonable to assume that an additional 10% of the slaves succumbed in the process.

Not all slaves were reexported. In Surinam and the Guianas most slaves were sold directly to planters. Curaçao was not a plantation colony but a slave depot; however, some slaves were kept there for service to the WIC. As with "trade slaves" mentioned previously, an incomplete record of the mortality of company slaves has been preserved, and it indicates that at least 119 of these slaves died during the first decade of the eighteenth century.[66] This seems to suggest that slaves continued to die at high rates even after they had been in the New World for some time. A noteworthy record of 1715 relates how the WIC sold 38 of the oldest company slaves in order to

[63] WIC, vol. 619, pp. 373 and 388. In this case, a modest middle passage death rate of 11.5% was followed by an additional 50% death rate after arrival.
[64] It should be mentioned that this was a period of international turmoil and confusion in the Asiento trade agreement, with the Dutch having at best only a small share in it.
[65] WIC, vol. 205, pp. 348–349.
[66] See Table 9.11. The WIC generally had a few hundred slaves in regular service. In 1700 there were 118 company slaves at Curaçao and 137 at Bonaire. See WIC, vol. 200, pp. 13–20.

TABLE 9.11
Slave Mortality at Curaçao

Periods	Days	Trade slaves	Ships	Company slaves
1700–1709				
1/ 1/1700– 7/ 1/1700	(182)	—	—	21
8/31/1701–11/19/1701	(79)	76	(2)[a]	—
11/11/1701– 3/25/1702	(134)	45	(5)[a]	5
4/ 3/1702– 6/ 9/1702	(67)	16	(4)[a]	4
11/ 3/1702– 3/ 1/1703	(150)	40	(1)	—
6/ 1/1702– 2/ 9/1703	(252)	19	(2)	10
1/17/1703– 6/18/1703	(152)	15	(2)	4
7/—/1703–12/—/1703	(150)	19	(2)	—
1/10/1704– 3/16/1705	(65)	5	(2)	27
8/ 4/1705–12/18/1705	(108)	—	—	13
4/10/1706– 5/17/1707	(37)	73	(1)	2
		31[b]		
2/ 4/1708– 5/—/1708	Circa (140)	Circa 20	(2)	Circa 7
5/27/1708– 1/27/1709	(244)	24	(1)[a]	—
2/ 3/1709– 5/19/1709	(105)	8	(1)	3
6/26/1709–10/ 4/1709	(100)	16	(2)	12
1716–1719				
3/13/1716– 6/ 3/1716	(82)	23	(2)	4
6/13/1716– 1/31/1717	(232)	43	(2)	—
8/24/1716– 3/13/1717		—	—	11
3/26/1718– 7/11/1718	(107)	17	(1)	—
2/—/1719– 6/—/1719		—	—	12

Source: WIC, vols. 200–206, 560.
[a] Includes also a few slaves from other cargoes.
[b] From cargoes other than the one listed.

scale down its expenditures. Judging by their identifying brand marks, these slaves must have arrived in Curaçao between the 1670s and the beginning of the eighteenth century.[67] These "oldest slaves of the company," depending on their age at arrival, could hardly have been very old.

CREW MORTALITY

A study of slave trade mortality would not be complete without some reference to the toll of the white crews. Unfortunately, the large amount of data collected for this study throw little additional light on this problem,

[67] WIC, vol. 206, doc. 85. The cargoes of each slaver arriving at Curaçao were branded with the same iron, either in a succession of the letter of the alphabet or with numbers to 100.

primarily because nearly all of the WIC slave ship logs have been lost. An assessment of the MCC records puts the crew mortality rate at 17.9% as compared to 12.3% for the slaves.[68] This extremely high toll of the slave ship crews has been confirmed by others as well.[69]

No systematic record on crew mortality has been preserved for the WIC. In light of the short coasting period and the more highly organized system of trading it is quite possible that the WIC toll was lower than the free trade. There is no doubt, however, that many WIC crew members died on the slaving voyage. In one catastrophic case 67 crew members died, leaving only 19 (many of whom were ill) to navigate the ship.[70] Of the 239 WIC captains whose identity is known, at least 20 have been reported dying on their voyage; the actual figure is undoubtedly higher.[71] Due to the fact that sailors lacked some of the comforts enjoyed by officers, it would seem reasonable that the death rate of the crews in general would have been higher than that of captains. It is also interesting to note that MCC records indicate a higher death ratio for crew members than for slaves transported by them.

CONCLUSIONS

In summary, this study implies that the death toll of the Atlantic slave trade may well have been higher than recent scholarship has suggested. A careful analysis of stages other than the middle passage may confirm this. The 17% mortality rate calculated for the middle passage could easily double before the survivors were permanently established in the New World. This position should be tempered, however, by the fact that the Dutch slave trade was not representative of the whole Atlantic slave trade. The origin and destination of the slaves, largely because of the length of the journey and voyage, has clearly become established as a primary determinant of mortality. Next to duration of the voyage, contagious diseases were significant in determining mortality, albeit less predictable in systematic analysis. Crowding the slaving ships was clearly not a significant determinant in death rates. Perhaps the more or less crowded conditions added little to generally unhygienic conditions on board ship. Men appeared to die at much higher rates than women during the middle passage, but the reasons for this remain speculative.

[68] Unger, "Bijdragen tot de geschiederis," pp. 26–27.
[69] See Curtin, *The Atlantic Slave Trade*, pp. 282–283.
[70] WIC, vol. 1140, docs. 223 and 224.
[71] These data are part of the computerized package collected by myself and are drawn from such a variety of sources that documentation would be too tedious for this study.

10

A Note on Mortality in the French Slave Trade in the Eighteenth Century[1]

HERBERT S. KLEIN
STANLEY L. ENGERMAN

In this chapter our intention is to evaluate the role of several frequently discussed factors in the determination of mortality on slave ships.[2] Factors frequently discussed include the extent of crowding (based on the number

[1] This is a revised and expanded version of our paper, "Facteurs de mortalité dans le trafic français d'esclaves au XVIIIᵉ siècle," *Annales: Économies, Sociétés, Civilisations,* vol. 31, no. 6, 1976, pp. 1213–1224. The first, second, and fourth parts are abridged from that article, whereas the third part is newly written, replacing the earlier discussion of mortality in the Portuguese trade. Financial assistance was provided by the National Science Foundation under Grant GS-27262.

[2] For recent statistical material on mortality in the slave trade, see, in particular, Philip Curtin, *The Atlantic Slave Trade: A Census* (Madison, 1969); Herbert S. Klein, "The Trade in African Slaves to Rio de Janeiro, 1795–1811: Estimates of Mortality and Patterns of Voyages," *Journal of African History,* vol. 10, no. 4, 1969, pp. 533–549; Herbert S. Klein and Stanley L. Engerman, "Shipping Patterns and Mortality in the African Slave Trade to Rio de Janeiro," *Cahiers d'études africaines,* vol. 15, no. 3, 1975, pp. 381–398; Sv. E. Green-Pedersen, "Om forholdene pa danske slaveskibe med soerlig henblik pa dødeligheden, 1777–89," *Handels-og Søfartsmuseets årbog,* 1973, pp. 27–76; Roger Anstey, *The Atlantic Slave Trade and British Abolition, 1760–1810* (London, 1975), pp. 414–415; and Herbert S. Klein and Stanley L. Engerman, "Slave Mortality on British Ships, 1791–1797," in Roger Anstey and P. E. H. Hair, eds., *Liverpool, the African Slave Trade and Abolition,* (Bristol, 1976), pp. 113–125; and Chapter 9 by Postma in this volume.

of slaves shipped per ton) and the African regions of supply, as well as the length of time the slaves were involved in internal transit to African ports, the time between arrival at port and ship's departure, and the length of the voyage from Africa to the New World. In the materials used here, unfortunately, data relating to aspects of the time in transit between capture and departure from the African coast are not available, but we can examine the impact of the African source of supply, of the duration of the "middle passage," and of the number of slaves carried per ton.

SOURCES

The basic source for this study is a survey of the eighteenth-century Nantes slave trade undertaken by D. Rinchon, which is available in published and, for earlier years, manuscript form.[3] There is a basic listing of over 1300 French slave ships that sailed from Nantes between 1697 and 1793, of which 794 have complete data for the period 1712–1777.[4] Given

[3] The published lists of Nantes slave ships from 1748–1792 are found in Dieudonne Rinchon, Le trafic négrier, vol. 1 (Paris, 1938), pp. 248–301. We are indebted to Professor Philip Curtin for the use of his codebook and punched dataset of these materials. The unpublished collection of recordings of Nantes slave ships that Rinchon made for the period 1697–1747 are to be found in Le Centre de Recherces sur l'Histoire de la France Atlantique (Nantes), Fonds Rinchon, Boîtes 10 à 12.

[4] The Rinchon manuscript listing contains some 400 voyages from which 45 were eliminated either because of incomplete recordings or because the figures gave zero mortality rates. The printed list starts in 1748 and contains 910 ships, of which, for the same reasons, only 428 were retained. Also, in dealing with crew mortality there is a further reduction because of the frequent lack of such data. Within the period 1711–1777 there are years in which no sailings whatsoever were reported, 1723–1725 and 1756–1762; and none were reported between 1778 and 1784. Although slave mortality data are available for a few years in the late 1780s and 1790s, we have decided not to include this data. Although an extremely active trade existed after 1777, with the annual number of ships being higher between 1785 and 1792 than before (see Jean Meyer, "Le commerce négrier nantais [1774–1792]," Annales E. S. C., vol. 15, no. 1, 1960, pp. 120–129), changes in legislation on colonial shipping in 1785 create problems with the tonnage data. It has been argued that this new legislation possibly brought new types of ships into the slave trade (see J. Everaert, "Les fluctuations du trafic négrier Nantais [1763–1792]," Les cahiers de Tunisie, no. 43, 1963, pp. 54–55). The late Professor Jean Mettas in a personal communication (7 October 1974) argued that Rinchon made errors of judgement in identifying African ports, as well as some simple arithmetical errors that appear in the printed sources. Until his recent and untimely death, Professor Mettas was engaged in a major reanalysis of the French Atlantic slave trade and had begun to explore the trade of other ports aside from Nantes; see his study "Honfleur et la traite des Noirs au xviiie siècle," Revue française d'histoire d'outre-mer, vol. 60, no. 218, 1973, pp. 5–26. At the same time Professor Serge Daget has been generating a major new data set on the nineteenth-century slave trade of France. See "Catalogue des navires . . . de participation au trafic négrier atlantique entre 1814 et 1833," mimeo (Abidjan, December 1973). Also see his study, "L'abolition de la traite des

the fact that Rinchon made errors of designation in his listing of African ports, and failed as well to include any data on time of middle passage, we have supplemented these data with an alternative dataset generated by Robert Stein from the same listing of ships. Although the Stein dataset includes only 501 ships for the years 1713–1777, there are data on voyage length for many of these ships, unlike the information in Rinchon's more summary recordings. The smaller Stein dataset, which agrees in all basic aspects, such as numbers shipped and mortality at sea, with the two Rinchon datasets, has been used only for analysis of the impact of sailing time and African port on mortality. Whereas it is probable that current research will lead to a great expansion in the quantity and quality of available data, we believe that the general trends and patterns indicated in the present materials will prove to be valid for all subsequent additions to the Nantes listings of Rinchon, and will also appear in other slave trades.

MORTALITY AND CROWDING

As is evident from Figure 10.1, the annual average mortality experience of ships that departed from Nantes in the period between 1712 and 1777 shows a sharp year-to-year fluctuation as well as a mild downward trend in the rate of mortality over the century.[5] The period 1772–1777 had a mortality experience below that of previous periods, only 5 of the previous 47 years having a mortality rate below that of the highest in this 6-year period. This reduction was not due to shifts in African ports of departure, nor to marked variation in ships' tonnage, carrying rates, or sailing time. Rather, the decline characterized all African regions and cannot be explained in terms of any of the expected variables. A long-term decline similarly characterized the mortality experience of the crews, and the determinants of these declining rates remain an issue for further examination.[6] Looking at the distribution of mortality by ships (Figure 10.2), one sees the wide range of experience in the trade as well as the occurrence, although infrequent, of the very high mortality that has been frequently pointed to in the literature. It is not that no slave ships experienced high mortality but rather that this was not typical of the middle passage.

Noirs en France de 1814 a 1831," *Cahiers d'études africaines,* vol. 11, no. 1, 1971, pp. 14–58.

[5] The particularly high mortality suffered by slaves in the year 1730 was largely due to the fact that 4 of the 12 ships had death rates of 60% and above.

[6] Average crew mortality on 439 ships that had data for both crew and slave mortality was 18.3%. When the large sample of ships that had crew mortality data (with or without slave mortality information) was analyzed, the crew mortality was slightly lower than this figure, but still higher than the slave mortality rate.

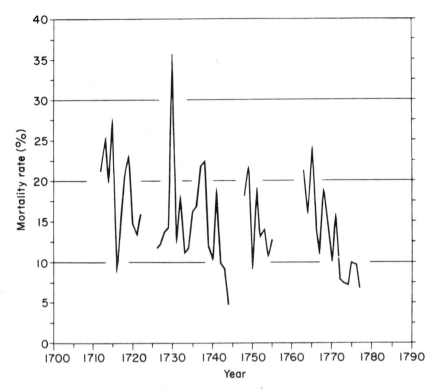

Figure 10.1. Average annual slave mortality by ships, 1712–1777.

In trying to analyze the possible determinants of this mortality pattern, we used as an index of overcrowding, the number of slaves shipped per ton of vessel. It was anticipated, given the debates on so-called "tight-packing," that mortality would be highest where the number of slaves per ton was greatest. As seen in Table 10.1, such a pattern did not occur. Rather, the mortality rate appeared to be independent of the number shipped per ton.[7] Of course, in general, slave ships carried more individuals per ton than did other vessels. Within the range carried, however, the degree of crowding did not seem to affect mortality.

There is, however, some difficulty in the relationship between the measured slaves per ton and the degree of crowding suggested by the material in Table 10.2, for it seems that the numbers of slaves per ton were highest on vessels of 100–149 tons, falling quite markedly on ships of greater tonnage. Yet, as seen in Table 10.2, these smaller vessels had mortality experience

[7] The simple correlation between slaves per ton and slave mortality is −.0158.

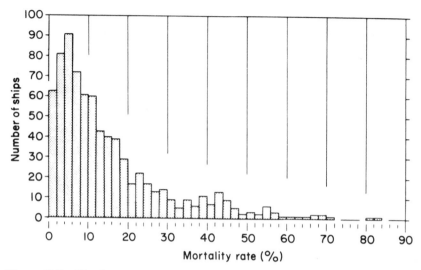

Figure 10.2.   Distribution of slave mortality rates, by number of ships.

similar to those of larger ships.[8] The reason for the negative relationship between slaves per ton and tonnage is not clear.[9] Given this relationship, however, the most appropriate test of the crowding argument and its impact on slave mortality would be to examine the relationship, within a given tonnage group, between the number of slaves per ton and the mortality rate. This comparison, however, indicates that the extent of crowding on ships of a given size did not appear to affect the mortality.[10] Thus, the best indication at present is that, within the range observed, the degree of crowding in itself did not significantly affect mortality. Most ships fell within the range of 1.39–2.88 slaves carried per ton, a range that includes the maximum allowed by both English and Portuguese regulations.[11] The relatively narrow range, and the limited effect upon mortality, suggests that economic considerations may have been the important determinant of the

[8] The correlation of slaves per ton with tonnage is −.3767; and of slave mortality with tonnage is −.0052.

[9] Note that the British law of 1788 permitted a higher ratio of slaves per ton on smaller vessels. For a discussion of this law and its impact, see Klein and Engerman, "Slave Mortality."

[10] See Table 4 in our *Annales* article, which, however, inadvertently omits several ships with higher number of slaves per ton.

[11] For the Portuguese data, which indicated a variation of 2–3 slaves per ton depending on construction, see Herbert S. Klein, "The Portuguese Slave Trade from Angola in the Eighteenth Century," *Journal of Economic History*, vol. 32, no. 4, 1972, p. 902n. For the British, see Klein and Engerman, "Slave Mortality."

TABLE 10.1
Average Slave Mortality per Ship, by Slaves per Ton per Ship

Range of slaves per ton	Average mortality (percentage)	Number of ships
Less than .88	19.2	16
.88–1.389	15.1	70
1.39–1.639	16.8	51
1.64–1.889	13.3	98
1.89–2.139	15.7	120
2.14–2.389	15.1	117
2.39–2.639	12.6	98
2.64–2.889	13.6	83
2.89–3.139	17.4	45
3.14–3.389	17.0	38
Above 3.39	15.6	27
Total	14.9	763

degree of crowding, considerations that no doubt were then reflected in the codes regulating the trade.[12]

Regression analysis of the 763 ships similarly points to this interpretation. The correlations are poor, neither tonnage nor slaves per ton, alone, accounting for even 1% of the variation in mortality rates. Moreover, as shown by the following multiple regression, where M is mortality rate, T is tonnage, and SPT slaves per ton, both together still fail to account for 1% of the variation (standard errors in parentheses).

$$M = 16.25 - .0024T - .4253SPT \qquad R^2 = .00039$$
$$(.0071) - (.8060)$$

The explanatory power of the regression is increased somewhat (but R^2 remains below .01) when allowance is made for differences in African ports of departure, there being apparent some differentials in mortality from the different African ports.

It is important to note, also, as shown in Table 10.3, that the ships with high slave mortality were also ships with the heaviest mortality of the crew.[13] The data indicate also that, overall, the mortality of the crew exceeded that of the slaves, although on the middle passage itself that of

[12] Although it is correct that the expected mortality experience in transit would affect the prices paid for slaves in Africa, after purchase it was economically desirable for captains to achieve a low mortality rate. Thus, as discussed in the following, "excessive" crowding need not have been a profitable arrangement.

[13] The correlation between slave mortality and crew mortality is +.3769.

TABLE 10.2
Average Slaves per Ton and Average Slave Mortality per Ship, by Ship Tonnage

Tonnage	Average slaves per ton	Average mortality (percentage)	Number of ships
Less than 100	2.36	14.5	173
100–149	2.43	13.7	157
150–199	2.31	17.2	180
200–249	2.11	13.7	128
250–299	1.84	14.6	75
300–349	1.50	18.6	29
Above 350	1.30	12.1	21
Total	2.21	14.9	763

slaves exceeded crew mortality.[14] The positive relationship, however, between the death rates of slaves and crew mortality, suggests the possible importance of similar factors in mortality. Apparently, the determinants of slave mortality, as affected by disease and by provisioning, had a similar impact upon the sailors in the crew as well.

MORTALITY AND VOYAGE LENGTH

As noted earlier, one of the important aspects of the middle passage, for which data are available (for some 441 of these ships), is the length of time at sea between the African port of departure and the New World port of arrival. It is to be expected that this would have an important effect on mortality. In the simplest case, of course, the longer the voyage, the greater the period of risk, and the higher the number of deaths expected. There are more important aspects, however, to the relationship between mortality and voyage length. Given the finite capacity of ships, there would be limitations upon the amount of provisions of food and water to be carried. The longer the time at sea, therefore, the more likely that shortage of provisions might

[14] The regression is

$$\text{Crew Mort} = 13.18 + .3718M \qquad R^2 = .1421$$
$$(.0437)$$

Strictly interpreted this suggests that about 70% (13.2/18.3) of the mortality of the crew occurred at times other than the middle passage, and about 30% during the middle passage. Direct data for a number of ships, which give crew deaths at various stages of the voyage, indicate that 34% of deaths occurred in the middle passage, whereas more than half occurred while the vessel was on the coast.

TABLE 10.3
Average Crew Mortality per Ship, by Slave Mortality per Ship

Range of slave mortality (percentage)	Average crew mortality (percentage)	Number of ships
.1– 1.99	13.3	47
2.0– 3.99	11.7	55
4.0– 5.99	13.7	51
6.0– 7.99	16.7	39
8.0– 9.99	18.0	42
10.0–11.99	19.6	28
12.0–13.99	17.4	24
14.0–15.99	20.8	19
16.0–19.99	19.3	32
20.0–29.99	26.8	49
30.0–39.99	19.9	22
40.0–49.99	28.9	19
Greater than 50.0	32.5	12
Total	18.3	439

occur. Similarly, given the possibilities for spoilage of water and food, as well as the incubation period for diseases, the longer the voyage, the greater would be the expected death rate.[15]

There was a clear positive relationship between slave mortality rates and the length of the middle passage.[16] The regression indicates, however, that overall only about 6% of the variation in the incidence of mortality is explained by the length of the voyage. As noted, there was a great variation from voyage to voyage for any given sailing time below a specified level, which accounts for the relatively low correlation overall. As seen in Table 10.4, the relationship between time at sea and mortality rates was heavily influenced by the difference between average sailing time from an African port, and the actual duration of a specific voyage. For not only was there some increased average mortality with sailing time, but generally the rate shifted up markedly for voyages that were atypically long. These patterns indicate the great importance of unexpectedly long sailing times on mortality, suggesting the role of provisioning rules and practices in explaining

[15] See the discussion in Klein and Engerman, "Shipping Patterns and Mortality."
[16] The regression is

$$M = 5.30 + .0874MP, \qquad R^2 = .057$$
$$(.0170)$$

where MP is the length of the middle passage.

TABLE 10.4
Slave Mortality Rates in Middle Passage in the Eighteenth-Century French Slave Trade

Time at sea in days	Guinée Percentage (ships)	Gold Coast Percentage (ships)	Angola Percentage (ships)	Unknown Percentage (ships)	Total Percentage (ships)
Less than 40	8.2 (15)	21.5 (2)	2.1 (4)	—	8.3 (21)
41–60	11.1 (28)	12.5 (8)	10.2 (34)	16.7((2)	11.0 (72)
61–80	10.4 (44)	21.4 (15)	10.3 (43)	10.3(2)	12.0(104)
81–100	10.6 (32)	13.0 (42)	14.4 (13)	10.1(2)	12.3 (89)
101–120	13.1 (31)	12.1 (39)	11.9 (6)	11.6(2)	12.5 (78)
121–140	20.7 (13)	16.7 (30)	56.1 (1)	12.5(1)	18.6 (45)
Over 141	18.8 (12)	22.8 (20)	—	—	21.3 (32)
Total	12.2(175)	15.6(156)	11.0(101)	12.2(9)	13.1(441)

mortality. Thus it would be expected that those factors that influenced the relationship between mortality and sailing time in this sample would also have held in other periods and national trades as well.

In this period differences in slave mortality among shipments from different African ports were not significant, once allowance is made for differences in sailing time. The higher mortality on shipments from the Gold Coast is explained, for the most part, by the longer sailing time in the middle passage.[17] In most studies, however, a significant difference in mortality experiences for the various African export areas has been shown, raising questions as to the nature of the disease environment in African supplying areas, the distance traveled to reach the coast, and the health conditions on the coast. The seeming absence of these differences in this

[17] It is worth noting that there is some variation in the eighteenth-century French designations of the Guinée and Gold Coasts. Some eighteenth-century maps bring the Guinée Coast up to Cape Mount (and thus include only the areas that the British called Senegambia and Sierra Leone). Other maps bring the Guinée designation down to the Cape of Three Points (or the Grain and Ivory and part of the Gold Coast as well). All charts agree in defining the border between the Gold Coast and Angola at Cape Lopez. Thus, even in its limited sense, the Gold Coast of eighteenth-century French designation includes what the British would call the Gold Coast and the Benin and Biafra areas, though both would agree on the designation of space for Angola. Turning again to the question of the limits of Guinée, we have coded the ships for both the larger and the smaller designations and it turns out that there is a difference of only eight ships which have no significant impact on the overall statistics. We have thus decided to adopt the Guinée designation as indicated by a 1756 listing of French trading ports in Africa that uses the limited Cape Mount designation. This list is reprinted in Marcel Cailley, *Histoire de l'Afrique Occidental Française, 1638–1959* (Paris, 1968), pp. 88–91. We would like to thank Professor Serge Daget who helped identify many of the eighteenth-century French place names for us.

eighteenth-century sample of the French slave trade remains a puzzle for further study.

DISEASE, SANITATION, AND PROVISIONS

The preceding analysis has cast doubt on the overcrowding argument as used to explain high slave mortality in the middle passage. As noted earlier, the slave ships did carry more people than did other vessels; but within the observed range of variation, there seemed no relationship between slaves carried per ton and mortality. The reasons for the relatively limited variation in slaves carried per ton might be explained by economic considerations, precluding the desirability of excessive crowding that might have led to substantial increases in mortality. In that case, where excessive crowding would have led to higher mortality, economic profits might be less than would be observed if ships had a more limited number of slaves and a lower mortality experience. Thus, to show that within a range there was no effect of crowding upon mortality does not necessarily mean that there were no economic limits on the number of slaves carried. Nor does it mean that there was an obvious correlation between profitability and crowding.

Another possible constraint on slaves carried is suggested by the importance of the effect of sailing time on mortality, for, based on expected voyage length, the magnitude of provisions desired would absorb a substantial part of the carrying capacity of the ship. Given that certain minimal daily needs of food and water were required to maintain slave health and to reduce susceptibility to disease, there were clearly demands for space for this purpose. Any increase in the number of the slaves put aboard would be at the expense of provisioning and storage space. The constraint here, it should be noted, was on space, and not on costs, for the bulk of the food-stuffs consumed by the Africans in the crossing were purchased on the African coast, with rice and yams serving as staples in the diet. The costs for these foods and for the water represented less than 5% of the total costs of outfitting the vessels and therefore offered little financial restraint on adding extra food.[18]

[18] The Nantes slave ship *Reine de France,* of 150 tons and a 47-man crew, transported 404 slaves from Guinée to St. Domingue in 1744. For this trip it purchased on the African coast 13,000 pounds of fresh foods including rice, chickens, and goats, for the approximate cost in trading goods of 2500 livres. This represented the approximate purchase cost of nine slaves in Africa. This same 2500-livres figure represented under 2% of the total value of goods carried by the *Reine* from France to purchase slaves and ivory on the coast. See Dieudonne Rinchon, *Pierre Ignace Lieven Van Alstein, Captain Négrier* (Mémoires of IFAN, no 71, Dakar, 1964), pp. 84–85.

In analyzing the causes of death in the eighteenth-century French slave trade, and in examining, also, the evidence of the British slave trade at the end of the century, it is evident that the primary killers were dysentery, yellow fever, and other unexplained "fevers," followed by communicable diseases such as measles and smallpox.[19] Given the relationship between food consumption and health conditions and the importance of amoebic dysentery as a cause of slave deaths, problems of sanitation and the maintenance of clean food and water were central to the reduction of mortality at sea. The importance of provisioning rules based upon expected sailing time is seen by the varying patterns shown by the different African ports of exit. For example, if the rate of water spoilage was based simply upon voyage duration, then all slave vessels should have suffered correspondingly similar rates of mortality after a common length of time at sea. As we have seen in Table 10.4, however, this was not the case. Equally, it is difficult to comprehend immediately the relationship between food spoilage and the increasing incidence of slave mortality. What does appear certain is that long voyages usually ended with both slaves and crew going on reduced rations, with subsequent increases in scurvy and related diseases. This would seem to support the idea that similar rules of provisioning operated in all trades, with captains provisioning for expected sailing times, plus some allowance for the possibility of longer voyages. Beyond some allowance for increased time at sea, however, provisioning would absorb too much space, and it was when this allowed time was exceeded, that the increasing risk of spoilage and unhealthy sanitary conditions meant sharply increased death rates for the slaves and the crew. It should be stressed that, occasionally, the sudden appearance of communicable diseases distorted this problem. Of these diseases, the one that seems to have been extremely difficult to control and that resulted in high deaths was measles. The incidence of smallpox should have been declining over the period, since French and British captains were already standardly inoculating their slaves by the second half of the eighteenth century.[20]

[19] The few published ships' logs constantly cite the "flux," or dysentery, as the single greatest malady suffered. In calculating the cause of death of the slaves shipped by Captain John Newton from Sierra Leone to Antigua in 1751–1752, 17 of 24 deaths were listed as due to the "flux," with 2 more listed as "fever and flux." Some of the flux deaths occurred several weeks after initial contagion, whereas the bouts of dysentery seemed to come in cycles. B. Martin and M. Spurrell, eds., *Journal of a Slave Trader (John Newton) 1750–1754* (London, 1962), pp. 29ff.; also see Alexander Falconbridge, *An Account of the Slave Trade on the Coast of Africa* (London, 1788), p. 25. The captain of the French slave ship *L'Economie* reported an outbreak of dysentery among his 217 slaves on his trip from the Congo to St. Domingue in 1753 after 2 weeks at sea. He reported that the majority of slaves who were buried at sea were killed by dysentery. Rinchon, "Van Alstein," p. 42.

[20] See, for example, Great Britain, Parliamentary Papers, *Accounts and Papers*, 1790, no. 29 (698), pp. 493–495; and Rinchon, "Van Alstein," p. 188.

CONCLUSIONS

The analyses we have attempted in this chapter have tested the thesis of overcrowding and of the effect of sailing time on slave mortality. We have argued that, based on the Rinchon compilations, the number of slaves per ton did not significantly influence the rate of slave mortality. This does not mean that extraordinary overcrowding would not lead to large-scale deaths. Instead, it means that the pattern of carrying slaves aboard ship did not lead to such densities at which a correlation between overcrowding and mortality could have occurred. From the analysis of the data relating to length of middle passage we have pointed out that time at sea was systematically related to slave mortality, most particularly on those voyages that greatly exceeded an expected normal sailing time. Many issues relating to mortality remain for further analysis as material becomes available, most important being the explanation of the variations in slave mortality from different parts of Africa, and the apparent long-term decline in mortality over the course of the eighteenth century, a decline greater than that expected on the basis of changing African supply areas and reduced sailing times.

ACKNOWLEDGMENTS

We would like to thank Professor Robert Stein of the University Centre of Guadaloupe for making available to us his manuscript notes on the Nantes trade, as well as Richard Bean, Philip Curtin, and Patrick O'Brien for comments on an earlier version. Some of this chapter also appeared in Herbert S. Klein, *The Middle Passage* (Princeton, 1978).

11

The Direction and Fluctuation of the Transatlantic Slave Trade, 1821–1843: A Revision of the 1845 Parliamentary Paper[1]

D. ELTIS

Despite the fact that it is only just over a century since the last slave ship crossed the Atlantic, historians are less certain of the details of the final period of the slave trade than they are of the traffic in earlier centuries. The obscurity is due to the immense controversy the subject generated amongst contemporaries, which confused rather than clarified issues, and to the related fact that during the first 30 years of the nineteenth century every importing nation in the Americas enacted abolition. Thus over half of the Africans landed in the Americas after 1800 were imported illegally, and there are few government or company records available of the kind used by Davies, Klein, Verger, Rinchon, and others for earlier years. Herbert Klein and Stanley Engerman have used reports of arrivals from Africa published in the Rio de Janeiro newspapers to construct a series for that city between 1825 and 1830,[2] but nothing further can be expected from this source for

[1] A grant from the Canada Council made possible the research upon which this chapter is based.

[2] H. Klein and S. Engerman, "The African Slave Trade to Rio de Janeiro, 1825–1830," paper read to the sixteenth annual meeting of the African Studies Association (Boston, November 1973).

the post-1830 period.[3] In that remarkable synthesis, *The Atlantic Slave Trade: A Census,*[4] Philip Curtin attempted to circumvent the problem in three ways. For Cuba and the French Caribbean he used census data coupled with birth and death rates in the receiving countries to derive decennial averages. For Brazil he relied on secondary sources and, in particular, Goulart's *Escrivadão Africana no Brazil.*[5] Finally, for all importing regions he incorporated information on the traffic, collected by the British Foreign Office and published in the sessional papers during the nineteenth century. The best of these papers and the one Curtin used most was the *Return of the Number of Slave Vessels Arrived in the Trans-Atlantic States since 1814* which appeared in 1845.[6] It is the purpose of the present chapter to point out problems in using this return, some of which were unknown to earlier writers, and to supplement it with data from the Foreign Office files on other slave voyages that the overworked clerks of the Foreign Office omitted from the list presented to Parliament.

STATISTICAL SOURCES

Since Curtin's book appeared, it has become apparent that British government correspondence together with dispersed and often fragmentary shipping records for individual ports form the only important sources for the statistics of the illegal portion of the nineteenth-century trade. L. M. Bethell has argued that the Brazilian governments of the time, and Brazilian historians ever since, used the British parliamentary papers previously referred to, in calculating the extent of the illegal traffic.[7] Furthermore, Brazilian census data, as the various British consuls pointed out, do not exist in a form that might support import estimates for any part of the Empire. A similar situation exists for Cuban imports after 1820, where D. R. Murray has shown the unreliability of official census figures used by Curtin.[8] The French Caribbean, which was the third area to receive significant numbers of slaves after 1807, is still an unknown quantity. The British Foreign Office had no representatives in these regions, which is why the 1845 paper

[3] Klein and Engerman, "African Slave Trade," p. 2.

[4] P. Curtin, *The Atlantic Slave Trade: A Census* (Madison, 1970).

[5] M. Goulart, *Escrivadão Africana no Brazil* (Sao Paulo, 1950).

[6] Great Britain, Parliamentary Papers (henceforth referred to as PP), vol. 49, 1845, pp. 593–633.

[7] L. M. Bethell, *The Abolition of the Brazilian Slave Trade, Britain, Brazil and the Slave Trade 1807–1869* (Cambridge, 1970), pp. 388–395.

[8] D. R. Murray, "Statistics of the Slave Trade for Cuba 1790–1867," *Journal of Latin American Studies,* vol. III, 1971, pp. 135–140.

contains little information on landings there, and perhaps also why historians have ignored the nineteenth-century French traffic. Work is presently underway on the port records of Nantes, Le Havre, St. Malo, and other centers, which may eventually yield import series for Martinique, Guadeloupe, and French Guiana. It is unlikely, however, that these imports made up a significant share of the traffic after the early 1820s, and French slavers disembarking cargoes at points outside the French Caribbean after 1820 would be just as likely as a non-French slaver to fall within the Foreign Office network. Thus, British government correspondence must be at the foundation of any estimate of the aggregate transatlantic traffic in the post-1820 period.

THE BRITISH FOREIGN OFFICE

The Foreign Office had an extensive reporting system. At its heart was the Slave Trade Department, which grew from one clerk in 1819 to five full-time officials by the late 1840s. This was in addition to Palmerston, whose command of detail and interest was such as to make him an additional member while he was in office. British consuls in Havana, Santiago de Cuba, Rio de Janeiro, Bahia, Pernambuco, Maranhão, and Pará, and the British legation at Rio de Janeiro supplied the department with reports on the state of the slave trade, in addition to their regular consular duties. Consuls on the eastern side of the Atlantic in Nantes, Lisbon, Cadiz, Barcelona, St. Jago in the Cape Verde Islands, and Santa Cruz were also expected to pass on information that might come their way. Most of these men were substantial merchants, familiar with local commerce and in a good position to report on ship movements and details of the organization of the trade. Some of them had their own informers paid for, as in the case of the Brazilian legation, with Foreign Office funds. Even more fertile sources of information were the Judges and Arbitrators of the Courts of Mixed Commission. Treaties between Britain on the one hand and Spain, Portugal, Holland, and eventually many more countries on the other, resulted in the establishment of tribunals with the power to condemn ships belonging to the contracting parties captured in the act of slave trading by authorized cruisers.[9] Between 1819 and 1842, Mixed Commission Courts sat in Rio de Janeiro, Havana, Paramaribo, and Sierra Leone, and the British Commissioners sent back volumes of reports on the slaving voyages that came to

[9] For the operation of the Courts of Mixed Commission, see L. M. Bethell, "The Mixed Commission for the Suppression of the Transatlantic Slave Trade in the Nineteenth Century," *Journal of African History*, 7, 1966, pp. 79–93.

their attention. The Admiralty completed the system by relaying to the Foreign Office extracts from the despatches of commanders in the Cape of Good Hope, Brazil, and Jamaica stations. The anti-slave-trade squadron varied between 5 and 21 ships in this period and regularly visited slave marts on the African coast and boarded slavers. Many other cruisers outside the squadron, however, carried the Admiralty instructions enabling them to search suspected vessels. Thus at any given point in the 1820s and 1830s, the British had dozens of well-placed and well-qualified observers collecting data on the transatlantic traffic.

AVAILABLE DATA

The 1845 Parliamentary Paper previously mentioned is the only readily available detailed output of this information network. It lists 2313 ships known to have landed slaves in the Americas between 1814 and 1843, giving where available the name, rig, nationality, armament, and tonnage of each ship, the master's name, the number of crew and slaves carried, deaths on the voyage, length of passage, and African point of departure. The lack of alternatives makes it an invaluable source of data, but it contains numerous omissions and anomalies that reduce its value. Fortunately, the 1845 Paper is not the last word on the subject. The Slave Trade Department clerks looked no further than the reports of the British representatives in Cuba and Brazil when preparing it. They ignored diplomatic sources on the eastern side of the Atlantic and even the navy, all of which knew something of imports into the Americas as well as exports from Africa. For the 1821–1843 period, the Parliamentary return lists 2185 voyages. Sixteen of these arrived without slaves or were listed twice, leaving a figure of 2169. Foreign Office correspondence yields data on 914 expeditions not included in the 1845 paper, many of them captured by the British navy, and additional information on 250 voyages that were included. Thus for the 1821–1843 period, we have data on 3083 slave voyages, representing a significant improvement in both quality and quantity over the data in the 1845 paper.

The additional data increase the likelihood of double counting. Different officials frequently report on different stages of the same voyage. The problem would be serious even if the trade had been legal, as merchants were dishearteningly unoriginal in naming their ships; a significant proportion of all the slaves carried across the Atlantic must have gone in the *Two Friends, Faithful, Mary,* or the Spanish, Portuguese, and French equivalents. Illegality, however, compounds the difficulties, as owners frequently concealed ship movements or changed flags, names of ships, and even crews and tonnage too, during the voyage, in order to escape the British navy. A ship could therefore be known by one name, nationality and tonnage to one observer and by a different set of facts to another, especially if the Atlantic separated the observers. The situation is not hopeless, however. Rigs, which slavers rarely changed once the voyage began, cargo size, dates, and other miscellaneous information often provide clues to the real identity of a ship. Moreover, flag changes occurred only in certain periods: The majority of Spanish ships importing slaves into Cuba did not begin assuming foreign identities until after the 1835 treaty between Britain and Spain made Spanish slavers without slaves on board liable to capture. Finally, slave ships that switched flags normally did so on the African coast. A ship landing slaves in the Americas was usually known by the same set of facts to all observers on the American side who recorded the event. Thus there is little risk of double counting in combining the data collected by American observers. This is not so for information from African and European sources on imports into the Americas, and accordingly the following import series include such information only when an observer in the Americas confirms the voyage. In summary, the present body of data probably includes a few voyages twice under different names of ships, flags, and other particulars; but overall, double counting is not a major factor in the series that follow.

SLAVE IMPORTS BY REGION

Figures 11.1–11.7 show annual slave imports by major importing regions. The six regions are, first, Southern Brazil from Bahia State to the Uruguay border; second, Bahia and Bahia State; third, Northern Brazil including the states of Pará, Maranhão, Pernambuco, and Algoas; fourth, the island of Cuba; fifth, the French possessions in the Caribbean and South American mainland; and sixth, all other parts of the Americas not included in the first five categories. Figure 11.7 is a consolidation of Figures 11.1–11.6. The size of the first region, Southern Brazil, is more apparent than real, for as long as the legal trade continued, all African imports into it were channeled through Rio de Janeiro; even during the illicit traffic of the 1830s, almost all the landings in this region occurred between Vitoria in the north and Santos in the south. It was only after 1838 that significant landings of African cargoes began in Paranagua and Santa Catharina further south.[10] Treating this large area as one, has the further advantage of making easier the allocation amongst regions of disembarkation points whose ap-

[10] G. Gordon to Palmerston, 19 January 1838, Foreign Office (FO) 84/252.

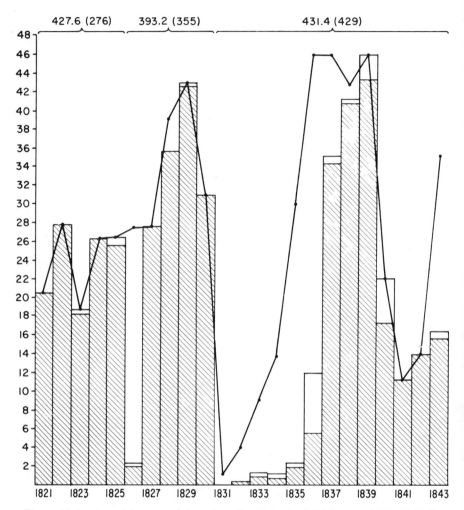

Figure 11.1. Annual imports of slaves into Brazil south of Bahia state, 1821–1843 (in thousands). For explanation of shaded bars and plain bars see text, pp. 278–279.

proximate geographic position is more obvious than their exact location.[11] The sixth category lumps together several very disparate regions and will be discussed more fully later.

There are three separate imports series for each region. The first, represented by the shaded areas of the histogram, simply includes slave imports

---

[11] Curtin miscoded the ports of arrival of 84 slave ships and assigned them to the wrong disembarkation zone. By reading the Foreign Office correspondence, I have been able to correct these and other errors.

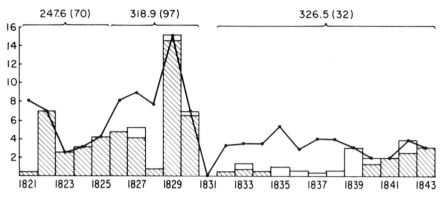

Figure 11.2.   Annual imports of slaves into Bahia state, 1821–1843 (in thousands).

known to the Foreign Office. These taken together with the unshaded blocks form the second series. The unshaded blocks are based on simple statistical inference. Of the 3083 voyages previously mentioned, the Foreign Office knew of only 2290 that ended in the disembarkation of slaves in the Americas, and in only 1683 cases did it know the number of slaves disembarked by each ship. Most of the 607 landings of unknown size were in Cuba. In the 1845 paper such listings have no entry in the "number of slaves carried" column. Curtin treated these ships as having arrived empty,[12] but there is no doubt that all but the 16 previously mentioned carried slaves. Those with cargoes of known size comprise 35% of the total estimated slave ship arrivals in Cuba, 53% of Bahian arrivals, 78% of Rio arrivals, and 25% of those arriving in North Brazil. They are spread evenly over the 23-year period. It is thus possible to derive an average cargo figure for 5-, 6-, or 7-year periods for each importing region and assign it to those landings of unknown size. These averages and the number of observations are shown at the top of each histogram.

Southern Brazil

The third series is the least reliable of the three and requires detailed explanation. It is composed of estimates, some by the group of officials already described and others by modern writers. For certain regions and periods, all three series have the same values. For Southern Brazil in 1821, for example, it is assumed that the British officials recorded almost every slave that arrived. The sample size of the first and second series is thus close to 100%. For most regions and periods, however, recorded arrivals were

[12] Curtin, *Census,* p. 37.

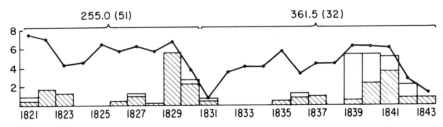

Figure 11.3. Annual imports of slaves into North Brazil, 1821–1843 (in thousands).

much less than actual arrivals. In Southern Brazil neither the commissioners, the consul, nor the British legation in Rio kept a record of individual arrivals in 1826, in the second quarter of 1828, or between mid-1830—when the legal trade ended—and October 1836. For 1826 and 1828, we can incorporate the Klein and Engerman figures into the series,[13] but for the other years we must rely on more dubious estimates. During 1831 and 1832 imports were no doubt very few, partly because of the glutted market created by massive inflows in 1829 and 1830 and partly because the slave dealers did not know how strictly abolition would be enforced. As the navy, however, reported trading activity in St. Paul de Loanda, a major Brazilian supply port,[14] some landings must have occurred. Early in 1883 at least one large estate owner was importing "considerable numbers,"[15] and by the end of the year slave arrivals were "increasing rapidly."[16] In 1834 "32 vessels sailed . . . from this port" (Rio de Janeiro) for the coast of Africa.[17] The Commissioners reported a "continued" and "uninterrupted" traffic in mid-1835 and approximately 45 departures in the second half of the year.[18] In the following year there were between 50 and 60 departures in the first 6 months.[19] All but a few would have returned with slaves, those that did not being counterbalanced by ships that landed slaves and returned to Africa without clearing out from Rio. Thus the official correspondence indicates a

[13] Klein and Engerman, "African Slave Trade," p. 3, Table 1. These data coincide exactly with the 1845 returns except for the years 1826 and 1828, as far as ships are concerned, but contain higher figures for slaves carried than the PP data. The reason is that the data are for slaves shipped from Africa and that slave deaths on the crossing should be subtracted to convert Table 1 into an import series. The figures for 1826 and 1828 in the third series have accordingly been adjusted downwards by 12% to allow for slave deaths.

[14] Admiralty to Palmerston, 12 December 1831, subenclosing Commander Harrison to Admiral Hayes, 23 September 1831, FO 84/126.

[15] W. G. Ouseley, Rio de Janeiro, to Palmerston, 5 June 1833, private, collection of Palmerston's papers in Broadlands Mss. EC/OU/26.

[16] Jackson and Grigg to Palmerston, 27 December 1833, FO 84/138.

[17] Jackson and Grigg to Palmerston, 23 March 1835, FO 84/174.

[18] Jackson and Grigg to Palmerston, 30 September 1836, FO 84/199.

[19] Jackson and Grigg to Palmerston, 30 September 1836, FO 84/199.

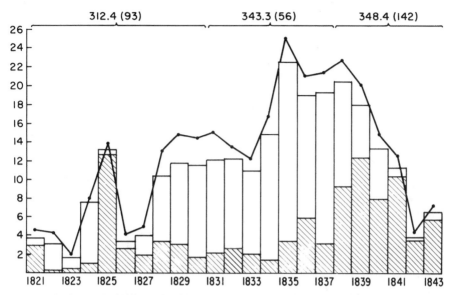

Figure 11.4.   Annual imports of slaves into the island of Cuba, 1821–1843 (in thousands).

steep upward trend in imports from 1833 to 1836. The actual figures in the third series from 1831 to 1833 are the result of a linear projection from 1834, when some data are available, to a very low figure, arbitrarily chosen at 1000, for 1831. The 1834 estimate is the product of ship departures from Rio and the average cargo landed between 1831 and 1843. The same technique produces a figure for the first three quarters of 1836, and to this may be added the inferred total from the second series, all of which arrived in the last quarter. The 1835 estimate is again a linear projection from the years 1834 and 1836. After 1836 British officials recorded individual landings that came to their attention and occasionally provided estimates for those that did not. Thus for 1837, 1838, and 1843 we have estimates of 46,000,[20] 42,970,[21] and 30,000–40,000,[22] respectively. Between 1839 and 1842, Foreign Office personnel in Brazil declined to make estimates of imports into Rio and noted only that actual imports greatly exceeded the arrivals listed in their despatches. British officials in Rio, however, as elsewhere, did not always cooperate with each other. Relations between Sir George Jackson, the commissary judge, and W. G. Ouseley, the chargé d'affaires, were particularly strained in these years. The commissioners, the

[20] Gordon to Palmerston, 28 February 1838, FO 84/252.

[21] Samo and Grigg to Palmerston, 17 July 1843, enclosing Report on 1838–1842, FO 84/454.

[22] Samo and Grigg to Palmerston, 20 February 1844, enclosing Report on 1843, FO 84/510.

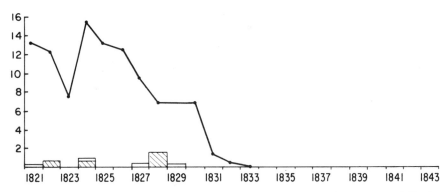

Figure 11.5. Annual imports of slaves into the French Caribbean, 1821–1843 (in thousands).

British minister at the Brazilian court, and the consul each appear to have used separate sources of information on the slave trade. Only the 1845 Parliamentary Paper consolidates these various sources,[23] and as a result the import series derived from the Paper is much greater than the annual figures supplied by anyone official in Rio.[24] Thus the second series in Figure 11.1 for the years 1839–1842 is probably a very large sample, though certainly less than 100%. In the absence of better information, however, we assume a sample size of 100%. For Southern Brazil over the whole period the second series has a sample size of 77% and for particular years ranges from 0 to 100%.

Bahia

The Foreign Office was not well represented in Bahia and Brazilian ports further north: Officials were both fewer in number and less diligent in their researches than their Rio counterparts. For Bahia, they returned neither detailed reports of landings nor estimates for the years 1821, 1828, 1831–1839, the last quarter of 1826, and the first and third quarters of 1827. Other sources fill the gaps, however. Pierre Verger has published two series from the Archivo Publico de Bahia, indicating ship departures to the coast of Africa, one of ships carrying tobacco, the other of passports issued.[25] Ship

[23] It consolidates in particular the monthly returns of the British legation and commissioners with a 5-year report on the years 1838–1842 prepared by the consul and the commissioners in 1843 (see Note 21).

[24] See for example Bethell's survey of the reports of individual officials in Rio (Bethell, *Abolition*, pp. 391–393).

[25] P. Verger, *Flux et reflux de la traite des négres entre le golfe de Benin et Bahia de Todos os Santos de 17e et 18e siècles* (The Hague, 1968), pp. 655–659.

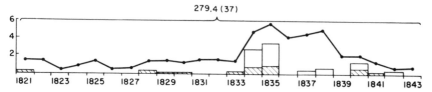

Figure 11.6. Annual imports of slaves into American regions not included in Figures 11.1–11.5, 1821–1843 (in thousands).

departures in 1821 were higher than in any other year for which records exist with the exception of 1827. A number of these would certainly have landed their return cargoes of slaves the following year, and accordingly, slave imports for 1821 are estimated to have been higher than in 1822 but below those of 1827. For 1826 and 1827, the years with missing quaterly reports, the estimates are derived by taking the proportion of annual imports into Bahia landed in each quarter for the years 1822–1825 and 1829, and assuming that the same proportion was landed in the missing quarters of 1826 and 1827. The results are confirmed by the upward trend in ship departures for those years apparent in Verger's series.[26] The Bahian archives contain no data for other problem years, and other methods must be used. Imports into Bahia averaged 22% of imports into Rio in 1822–1825 and 1829–1830, and the 1828 estimate is simply 22% of the 1828 Rio figure. Between 1832 and 1836 and in 1839, the third series is based on the returns of ships entering Bahia in ballast from the coast of Africa, compiled by the British consul. There is a strong presumption that these ships landed their slave cargoes outside Bahia. For the years 1837 and 1838, there is again little indication of the volume of imports; but for figures in these years and for support for other years in the series after 1830, we may rely on two independent contemporary sources. In 1835 a member of the British legation at Rio investigated the Bahian traffic in person and reported imports at 12–15 shiploads per year,[27] or 4000–5000 slaves; 8 years later the British consul at Bahia stated that "no regular copies of the returns were kept at this consulate up to the end of 1839 . . . but from the best information I have been enabled to obtain (imports) average about 4,000 annually.[28] From 1840, the series incorporates the lists of individual landings that the consul and the navy once more began to supply. As with the Rio figures for 1839–1842 we assume that the sample size of recorded arrivals is 100%.

[26] Verger, *Flux et reflux.*
[27] H. S. Fox to Palmerston, 8 November 1835, enc. W. G. Ouseley. Notes on the subject of the slave trade in the province and city of Bahia, September 1835, FO 84/179.
[28] E. Porter to Aberdeen, 30 July 1843, FO 84/470.

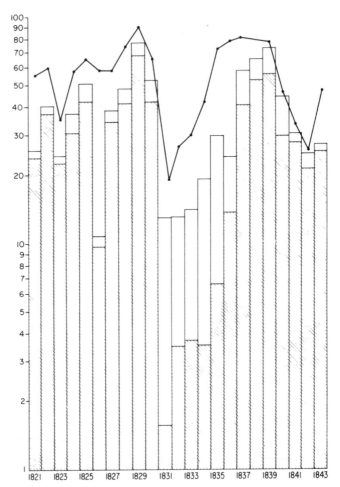

Figure 11.7. Annual imports of slaves into the Americas, 1821–1843 (in thousands).

For the whole period, the second series is a 61% sample of estimated actual arrivals in Bahia, with a range of 4–100% for individual years.

Northern Brazil

Information on arrivals in the states north of Bahia is rather slight. Maranhão, Pernambuco, Pará, and, for the last part of the period, Paraibo, each had British consuls, but the reports of the latter were infrequent. The Pernambuco consul listed arrivals in 1829, reported slaving activity in 1831, 1832, 1835, and 1836, but began listing individual landings again only from 1837. In the later years of the period under study, both the consul and the commander of the naval packet boat that served Pernambuco felt that the traffic rivaled that of Bahia in size,[29] and their belief is supported by the number of reported arrivals and by the fact that Pernambuco acted as entrepôt for Paraibo[30] and Rio de Janeiro.[31] For the years before 1829, however, data on imports into Pernambuco simply do not exist. Maranhão was the other significant northern importing centre. It received 8446 slaves between 1821 and 1828,[32] with the annual total declining steadily from a high of 1761 in 1821. After 1828 there were occasional landings only[33]; Ceará, Pará, and Paraibo received very few slaves direct from Africa, with the last two ports receiving no further shipments after 1835.[34] The third series for the region as a whole must be highly speculative. It is assumed that from 1821 to 1828, arrivals at Pernambuco were midway between those at Bahia and those at Maranhão, and that from 1830 to 1838 imports were similar to those into Bahia. It is also assumed that arrivals at ports other than Maranhão and Pernambuco, and to Maranhão after 1828, amounted to 1000 per year until 1830, and 500 per year for the illegal trade from 1832 to 1843. For the period as a whole, recorded arrivals amount to perhaps one-third of actual imports.

Cuba

The other major branch of the transatlantic traffic was to Cuba, and here the sample of slave imports is large. The British commissioners at the Havana Court of Mixed Commission sent returns on arrivals in the Havana area throughout the period. From 1833, David Tolmé, the British consul in Havana, also reported on slave imports, relying in part on sources of information separate from those of the Commissioners. In addition the British consul at Santiago, John Hardy, sent occasional reports on imports in the South after his appointment in 1832. The Havana officials were very thorough; in 1842, the British Commissioners gained access to the books of the Havana slave traders for the period 1835–1842 and found in them few landings about which they did not already know. It is likely that in every

[29] Admiralty to Palmerston, 25 May 1837, FO 84/228.

[30] B. Newcomen to Palmerston, 24 July 1843, FO 84/470.

[31] H. Hamilton to Palmerston, 24 December 1841, FO 84/367.

[32] R. Hesketh to Palmerston, 3 August 1831, enc. "Report of the State of the Slave Trade in the Northern Provinces of Brazil," FO 84/122.

[33] Hesketh to Palmerston, "Report," FO 84/122; John Moon to Palmerston, 27 May 1837, FO 84/223; William Wilson to Palmerston, 20 June 1839 and October 5, 1839, FO 84/289. Vice Admiral Colpoys to Admiralty, 22 May 1832, Admiralty (Adm) I/288.

[34] R. Ryan to Palmerston, 11 November 1843; B. Newcomen to Palmerston, July 24, 1843, FO 84/470.

year between 1821 and 1843 they recorded over 90% of all the landings
made by slavers that had any connections with the Havana area, including
those slavers owned or disembarking slaves in the outports but calling at
Havana for refit or for outward cargo. Inevitably, however, they missed
many landings at Santiago and Trinidad de Cuba. There are three indications of the scale of these missing landings. Between 1832 and 1835, John
Hardy reported eight or nine slavers per year, landing between 2 and 3
thousand slaves in the Santiago area.[35] Unfortunately, he gave details of the
landings in only a few cases, and it is not possible to check the data against
the Havana lists to eliminate those ships that subsequently entered Havana
and were spotted by the British officials there. It is thus not possible to
consolidate the two sources. A second indication is Tolmé's estimate that
20% should be added to his returns to take into account unrecorded arrivals
in the island as a whole.[36] Finally, the British Commissioners at Sierra Leone
reported all the Cuban slavers that came to their attention. About 30% of
these intended to land slaves in the outports.[37] Allowing for the fact that
some of the ships disembarking near the outports became known to British
officials in Havana, the Sierra Leone figures tend to support Tolmé's
suggestion for an addition of 20% to the Havana-based figures. As the
present body of data is larger than Tolmé's, it is reasonable to claim for it a
sample size of 90% for the period 1832–1843. For the years before
Tolmé's appointment a sample size of 80% seems likely, with the exception of the two years 1824 and 1825, when British cruisers reported from
the Santiago area and increased the sample to perhaps 95%. The third series
in Figure 11.4 incorporates these judgements. None of the Cuban series
allows for reexports, of which there were two kinds. Between December
1832 and October 1843, the Havana Court of Mixed Commission emancipated 7800 new arrivals and shipped them off to British Caribbean colonies,
mainly Trinidad and Demerara. A further undetermined number went to
Texas. This branch of the trade operated sporadically from 1835 to the end
of the period, and it was big enough for slave prices in Cuba to drop sharply
when General Santa Anna proclaimed the abolition of Texan slavery in
1836.[38]

[35] Hardy to Palmerston, 1 March 1833, FO 72/415; April 1, 1834, FO 72/431; 15 April
1836, FO 72/468; Clarke to Palmerston, 10 July 1835, FO 72/449.
    [36] Tolmé to Palmerston, 17 September 1839, FO 84/280; cf. J. Kennedy, Campbell J.
Dalrymple to Palmerston, 1 January 1841, FO 84/348.
    [37] The actual numbers for the years 1819–1837 are 40 to the outports and 98 to Havana.
The 138 ships are about 15% of all ships that arrived off Africa between these years with the
intention of shipping slaves to Cuba.
    [38] E. Schenley to Palmerston, 22 June, 1846, FO 84/195.

French Possessions in the Caribbean and South America

Imports into the Americas other than Brazil and Cuba are underrepresented in the Foreign Office data. As already noticed, information on the French Caribbean is particularly sparse. The British consul at Nantes reported very extensive French-owned slaving operations from that port in the 1820s,[39] and British naval officers repeatedly boarded French slave ships off the African coast; thus the Foreign Office data contain records of 210 French slavers in the period 1821–1831. These, however, form only a small fraction of the total French slaving ventures after 1820. Professor Daget, working from predominantly French sources, has collected data on 753 individual slaving voyages from French ports between 1814 and 1833, 556 of these after 1820.[40] Unfortunately, as most of this information comes from the eastern side of the Atlantic, and slaving captains were not disposed to publicize their real destination, it is very difficult to convert these data into a slave import series. The Ile de Bourbon attracted at least 53 of these ships, but the Americas undoubtedly accounted for the vast majority of the remaining 503 in the period 1821–1833. For most of these, the precise disembarkation point is not known. Once more, however, we may use the Foreign Office data as a guide, relying this time on their relative completeness for importing regions outside the French Caribbean rather than on their reports of actual arrivals. From the preceding paragraphs, it is clear that some American regions were much more likely than others to have received slaves from French ships. Such slavers did not go to Rio de Janeiro and very few could have gone to Bahia without the knowledge of British officials there. Some went to Cuba,[41] but the British Commissioner recorded all but 9 of those that, according to Daget's sources, disembarked in Havana, and several others besides that disembarked in the Cuban outports. Both the French sources and British naval reports indicate that French slave traders dominated the traffic to Santiago and the other outports sufficiently remote from the French consul in Havana, but this branch of the traffic

---

[39] Manderville to Canning, 30 May 1825, enc., FO 84/58. See also Commodore Bullen to Admiralty, 24 February 1824, enc., Adm I/1571.

[40] S. Daget, British Repression of the Illegal French Slave Trade: Some Considerations, Chapter 17 in this volume. In private correspondence with the author, Professor Daget generously supplied an annual breakdown of this total together with some information on destinations. Much of this will appear in a forthcoming publication. An alternative but less reliable series is provided in J. Vidalenc, "La traite négrière en France sous la Restauration, 1814–1830," *Actes du 91e Congrès National des Sociétés Savantes,* vol. 1, *Histoire maritime et coloniale,* 1969, p. 229.

[41] S. Daget, "Les navires français soupçonnables de traite négrière illégale à destination de Cuba, 1817–1830," Appendix A. Translated as the Appendix to this chapter, pages 299–301.

amounted, as we have seen, to only 20% of the total Cuban trade. French and British sources, combined, yield evidence of only 64 voyages to the Cuban outports between 1821 and 1831, and unless the preceding estimates to Cuban traffic are much too low it is likely that very few other French ships were involved.[42] Elimination of all the ships that visited Cuba, from Professor Daget's data, leaves us with a figure of 423. A few of these would certainly have carried slaves to Puerto Rico but the vast majority must have disembarked slaves in one of the two major blind spots of the British reporting system. One of these, Pernambuco, is not likely to have relied on the French for its slaves because in the two years, 1829 and 1830, for which the British consul there returned detailed reports, there is not a single reference to a French ship, and in earlier periods foreign traders had never taken a significant share of the Pernambucan traffic. Some French ships may have disembarked in Pernambuco and other north Brazilian ports, and if to these are added the French slavers plying the Puerto Rican trade and the few ships who disembarked undetected in Cuba, then it is possible that we can account for one-fifth of the remaining 423 slavers. We must conclude, however, that perhaps 338, or more than half of all French slave ships operating in the 1820s, went to the one remaining region that the British network did not cover, the French Caribbean. The third series in Figure 11.6 is the end result of this process of elimination; it is the product of Daget's annual series of known French slavers adjusted as described,[43] and average cargoes landed in Cuba between 1821 and 1830.[44] The total for the period 1821–1833, of 105,000 slaves imported, is slightly more than double Curtin's estimate.[45] The latter is based on population figures for the three French importing territories and an assumed rate of net natural decrease derived from the period immediately after the final demise of the traffic. As with the Cuban figures of the same period, it would seem that the census data are of doubtful accuracy.

Remaining Parts of the Americas

The remaining importing regions are grouped together in Figure 11.6. They include the Dutch West Indies, Puerto Rico, British colonies in the

[42] The British Commissioner noted in 1825 that French ships carried only a small proportion of the Cuban traffic, H. T. Kilbee to Canning, 1 January 1825, FO 84/39.

[43] An unresolved problem here is the fact that Daget's series is based on year of departure from the French port of origin, whereas all the port figures presented here are for year of arrival in the Americas.

[44] The average tonnage of Daget's French slavers is close to those disembarking in Cuba recorded by the Foreign Office, taking into account the different size of the French and Spanish ton.

[45] Curtin, Census, pp. 80–84.

Americas, and Montevideo. The British judge at the Court of Mixed Commission at Paramaribo in Surinam was the most underworked of all the Foreign Office officials in the Americas, slave imports after 1821 being very few. The Dutch islands were never major importing regions. Slaves arrived at Puerto Rico throughout the period though recorded arrivals are small. Reports from the Bahamas, Jamaica, Dominica, and other British-held territories, on the other hand, probably included all arrivals. British cruisers or bad weather brought nearly 7000 slaves to these areas, chiefly the Bahamas. None of these was en route to the United States as Curtin hypothesized.[46] Montevideo received a few thousand imports after 1834. Puerto Rico's population was approximately 10% of Cuba's. The third series in Figure 11.6 is thus the sum of 10% of the estimates in the Cuban import series, and imports into the other areas as observed by Foreign Office representatives. Finally, there are no reports of slaves being imported directly into the United States from Africa in this period, though before the Piracy Act was passed, there were probably some. One thousand has been added to the import estimates for 1821 and 1822 to cover such arrivals. Figure 11.7 is a consolidation of the data shown in the previous six diagrams.

ESTIMATE SERIES

Despite obvious shortcomings the estimate series for all regions except the French Caribbean is more detailed and better documented than previous estimates. It draws attention, first, to the very large annual fluctuations in the traffic, which previous attempts to calculate decennial averages have tended to obscure. More important, it suggests that previous estimates of the volume of the trade made by modern historians and some contemporaries are too low. For Brazil, Curtin's decennial figures amount to 637,000 for 1821–1843.[47] The combined third series in Figures 11.1–11.3 provides a total estimate of 829,100 imports for Brazil, which is about 30% greater than Curtin's total. The lowness of Curtin's figure is emphasized by comparison with the second series in Figures 11.1–11.3. This yields a total figure of 568,700, which means that for Curtin's figure to be credible we must accept the fact that the Foreign Office knew of 9 out of every 10 ships landing slaves in Brazil between 1821 and 1843. The obvious gaps in the records, such as the missing Rio de Janeiro figures for 1826 and 1828, make such a supposition implausible. Other modern writers attempting estimates include Klein and Engerman, whose figures for Rio for 1826 and 1828 are

[46] Curtin, *Census,* p. 236.
[47] Curtin, *Census,* p. 234.

incorporated into the third series,[48] and Bethell.[49] The latter cites estimates by Foreign Office representatives in Brazil for the post-1830 period, that are frequently lower than those given in the third series and indeed the first and second series for some years. Bethell, however, did not go behind the estimates and compare the shipping lists that these officials often returned. As long as the consuls and commissioners used different sources of information, one was always likely to discover landings unknown to the others. Thus, for years such as 1839 and 1840, the Foreign Office clerks consolidated the different Rio lists and obtained annual figures greater than the estimates of any one official.

Modern annual estimates of Cuban imports after 1820 are also scarce. Curtin's annual averages indicate 252,900 arrivals between 1821 and 1843.[50] The Figure 11.4 series is 14% greater than this, but the difference is small enough for the latter to be taken as confirmation of Curtin's data. Only Murray has made a modern attempt at annual figures for this period and his estimates are even further below the present figures than Curtin's. There are three reasons for this. First, his data for the 1830s are headed "British Consul Tolmé's Estimates of Slave Landings in Cuba" when in fact, as he correctly states in the text, this series is derived "from vessels which afterwards entered [Havana]."[51] As noted previously, 20% should be added to these figures to get an import series for the island as a whole. Second, both Tolmé and the British Commissioners in Havana based their estimates on average cargo sizes that were too low, 250 in the case of one commissioner and effectively less than 300 for Tolmé.[52] There is clear evidence that the actual average was closer to 350 for most of the period. Finally, neither Tolmé nor Murray include slaves and ships condemned at the Havana mixed court. Before 1833 such individuals, though nominally free, were quickly absorbed into the slave population.

Given the foregoing comments about Cuban and Brazilian imports, it is not surprising that the import series for the Americas as a whole in Figure 11.7 is larger than Curtin's estimates; indeed, it is larger than any for the period apart from the now discredited figures that James Bandinel, a former head of the slave trade department of the Foreign Office, presented to the

---

[48] Klein and Engerman, "African Slave Trade," p. 9.

[49] Bethell, *Abolition*, pp. 388–395.

[50] Curtin, *Census*, p. 234.

[51] Murray, "Statistics," p. 142.

[52] Tolmé assigned cargo to slavers on the basis of the ship's rig—200 for a schooner, 400 for a brig, and 600 for a ship. As most of the slavers were schooners or brigantines, which he seems to have classed as schooners, the effective overall average was less than 300. Tolmé to Palmerston, 17 September 1839, FO 84/280.

Commons select committee on the slave trade in 1848. More unexpected is the size of the third series relative to estimates of imports in the eighteenth century and earlier. The peak of the transatlantic trade is thought to have occurred between 1761 and 1780. Curtin depicts the traffic as declining steadily after this with a temporary and minor reversal of the trend in the 1820s.[53] In fact, the trade approached its previous peak in the 1820s, attaining an annual average of 61,500 compared to 65,500 before 1780; it is possible that in 1829 more slaves crossed the Atlantic than in any other year before and after. In the 1830s the annual 10-year average was only slightly lower than in the previous decade, with imports in 1837 just behind those in 1829. It is likely that another peak year of similar magnitude came about in the late 1840s, followed by another very sharp decline after 1850. Between 1821 and 1843 just under 1.3 million slaves disembarked in the Americas from Africa. This is about 30% more than Curtin estimated. The reasons for this discrepancy should be already apparent. An additional factor not yet discussed in this context, however, is the recognition that the present figures give to the French traffic in the 1820s. The validity of the aggregate import series, of course, depends on the validity of the individual series for the various importing regions.

DATA FOR OTHER VARIABLES: LOSSES IN TRANSIT AND SHIP TONNAGE

The slave import data in the Foreign Office records are incomplete but reliable. Data for several other variables in the listings must be treated with greater circumspection. Scholars have to some extent acknowledged this: Verger and Curtin, for example, have recognized that the normal African point of origin for most Bahian ships before 1831 was not south of the equator as given in the 1845 Parliamentary Paper, but the Bight of Benin. It was in fact illegal after 1815 to import slaves into Brazil from Africa north of the line, and slave ship captains would never admit to having embarked slaves from prohibited regions. It is not generally realized, however, that a very similar bias distorts the Foreign Office figures on losses of slaves in transit and slave ship tonnages.

Information on losses in transit is relatively abundant in the 1821–1843 period. The 1845 Parliamentary Paper has the figures for 734 voyages and the correspondence of the Foreign Office yields information on a further 71. Table 11.1 shows the average loss in transit on these voyages by African

---

[53] Curtin, *Census,* pp. 265–267.

TABLE 11.1

Loss of Slaves in Transit Known to the Foreign Office as a Percentage of Cargoes Embarked; American Importing Region by African Region of Embarkation, 1821–1843

	Senegambia	Bights of Benin and Biafra	Congo North and Angola	South East Africa	Africa unspecified	Total
Cuba	15.2 (22)[a]	16.1 (35)	13.8 (9)	29.5 (6)	45.0 (5)	19.1 (77)
Brazil	12.0 (3)	4.9 (47)	6.6 (500)	16.1 (161)	12.3 (13)	9.3 (724)
Total[b]	15.5 (28)	10.2 (83)	6.7 (509)	16.7 (167)	18.9 (18)	10.1 (805)

[a] Number of observations in parentheses.

[b] Total includes two slavers disembarking in the French Caribbean and two in Puerto Rico.

region of embarkation. The regions in these tables are as follows: Senegambia, Africa west and north of the Volta; the Bight of Benin, Volta to the Niger inclusive; the Bight of Biafra, the Niger to Cape Lopez; Congo North, Cape Lopez up to and including the Congo River; Angola, the Congo to Cape St. Martha; South East Africa, Africa north and east of the Cape of Good Hope. In addition to the Foreign Office records, the Rio de Janeiro newspapers list the deaths on the vast majority of the expeditions disembarking at that port between 1825 and 1830. Unfortunately much of this information, in newspapers and official records alike, is of questionable value. Treaties between Britain and Portugal in 1815 and 1817 restricted Portuguese and later Brazilian slavers to a cargo size of five slaves for every 2 measured tons until 1830. Despite the fact that port authorities allowed slave ship owners to register inflated tonnage figures, the British minister in Rio de Janeiro believed that captains of slavers frequently shipped more slaves than allowed in the expectation that deaths on the voyage would reduce the number carried to the permissible level. Thus "the number of deaths reported [to the Custom House] is very small."[54] During the 1820s the British consuls in Bahia and Rio relied exclusively on the Custom House returns for their reports as, apparently, did the Rio de Janeiro newspapers.[55] When the Brazilian traffic became illegal in 1830, this biased source disappeared. The number of observations, however, drops sharply too, with over 90% of the losses in transit recorded in the Foreign Office data occurring before 1830. There is thus a possible downward bias in the

[54] R. Gordon to Canning, 8 December 1826, enc., FO 84/56.

[55] As noted previously the newspaper figures in the consolidated form in which they appear in Klein and Engerman (pp. 9–12) are almost identical to the Parliamentary Paper data for 1827, 1829, and 1830.

mortality rates for the Brazilian traffic shown in Table 11.2 and calculated by Engerman and Klein,[56] and Curtin.[57]

Unfortunately the bias is not uniform. Rates reported on ships sailing from the Bights to Bahia seemed particularly susceptible to the downward bias. In the period 1821–1830 mortality on ships sailing this route was 4.4% (45 observations) according to the Foreign Office listings. Between 1821 and 1843, however, the British navy captured a number of fully loaded slave ships in the Bights and escorted them to Sierra Leone. Information about deaths on the voyage is available for 122 of these, 33 of which were actually bound for Bahia at the time of capture. The average loss rate from the various embarkation points to Sierra Leone was 12.9%. Bahia is much further away from the Bights than is Freetown, but the prevailing winds are such that a sailing ship might take the same time for the two voyages. The average passage to Bahia from the Bights in this period lasted 34.5 days (62 observations). Captured slave ships on the other hand took 32.7 days to reach Sierra Leone from the same range of embarkation points (106 observations), though if we count only vessels bound for Bahia the average rises to 40.5 (26 observations). Naval officers often provided less crowded accommodation for the slaves after capture and destroyed unseaworthy vessels, so it is unlikely that losses in transit to Bahia were any less than those to Sierra Leone. Clearly the 4.4% figure is much too low. Rates on more southerly branches of the trade, on the other hand, may be closer to the actual. Recent work by Joe Miller on the Foreign Office reports of ships disembarking in Rio de Janeiro before 1831 indicates that the mortality figures are consistent with long-run trends and do not vary markedly from those of earlier periods in ways that cannot be explained.[58] If, as seems likely, the bias is not uniform, then the Foreign Office data cannot even tell us much about relative mortality rates. Their main function is to establish a lower limit for estimates of actual losses in transit.

The Foreign Office records contain data on only 116 voyages that are definitely free of this downward bias. The Cuban sample is 8% and the Brazilian smaller still at 3–4%; neither is large enough to support generali-

[56] Klein and Engerman, "African Slave Trade," pp. 9–12.

[57] Curtin, *Census*, pp. 279–281. Curtin also assumed that the death column should be subtracted from the slave import column in the Parliamentary Paper to obtain actual imports. His mortality rate is therefore higher than it would have been had he calculated it against the sum of slave imports and deaths—the latter being necessary to find the number of slaves leaving Africa. I am indebted to Professor Herbert Klein for this information. In fact, Curtin's higher figure is still not high enough to offset the downward bias previously described.

[58] J. Miller, "Legal Portuguese Slaving from Angola, Volume and Direction," *Revue française d'histoire d'outre-mer,* vol. 62, nos. 226–227, 1975, pp. 135–176.

TABLE 11.2

Loss of Slaves in Transit Known to the Foreign Office as a Percentage of Cargoes Embarked, Excluding Those Subject to Treaty Bias; American Importing Region by African Region of Embarkation, 1821–1843

	Senegambia	Bights of Benin and Biafra	Congo North and Angola	South East Africa	Africa unspecified	Total
Cuba	15.2 (22)[a]	16.1 (35)	13.8 (9)	29.5 (6)	45.0 (5)	19.1 (77)
Brazil	23.9 (1)	23.2 (2)	16.9 (20)	23.1 (7)	12.5 (5)	18.6 (35)
Total[b]	16.1 (26)	16.5 (38)	16.1 (29)	25.9 (13)	26.1 (10)	19.0 (116)

[a] Number of observations in parentheses.

[b] Total includes two slavers disembarking in the French Caribbean and two in Puerto Rico.

zations. The distribution by African region of origin is shown in Table 11.2. Transatlantic voyages from South East Africa and the Bights took longer than those from Senegambia and Angola, in the case of South East Africa because of the distance involved, and in the case of the Bights because of adverse prevailing winds and currents that forced sailing ships far to the south before they could begin the western leg of their journey. Small as the sample is, Table 11.2 supports the expectation of greater losses on these routes. The overall loss in transit of 19.0% is higher than equivalent rates from earlier periods. The work of Gaston Martin and Dieudonné Rinchon on Nantes slavers, as processed by Curtin, yields loss rates of 16.2% for the 1715–1775 period (450 observations) and 15.2% for the years 1748–1792 (465 observations).[59] Johannes Postma has recently found a rate of 17.4% for 131 Dutch slavers trading between 1740 and 1795.[60] Substantially lower than any of these is the 9.5% figure that Herbert Klein calculated from 351 cargoes landed at Rio de Janeiro between 1795 and 1811,[61] though it is obvious that Brazilian data are seriously underrepresented in Table 11.2.

Losses in transit tended to go down with the passage of time during the eighteenth and early nineteenth centuries,[62] perhaps reflecting general im-

---

[59] G. Martin, *Nantes au XVIIIe siècle: L'ère des négriers (1714–1774)* (Paris, 1931), pp. 15ff.; D. Rinchon, *Le trafic négrier d'après les livres de commerce du capitaine gantois Pierre-Ignace Liévin von Alstein*, vol. 1 (Paris, 1938), pp. 248–302, as cited in Curtin, *Census*, pp. 276–279. The 15.2% rate is not strictly comparable because it includes all slaves who died before the sale of the cargo in the Americas, whereas all other rates cited in this study are for deaths in transit only.

[60] J. Postma, "The Dutch Slave Trade: A Quantitative Assessment," a paper presented at the Sixth International Congress of Economic History (Copenhagen, August 1974), p. 7.

[61] H. Klein, "The Trade in African Slaves to Rio de Janeiro 1795–1811: Estimates of Mortality and Patterns of Voyages," *Journal of African History*, vol. 10, 1969, p. 538.

[62] Curtin, *Census*, p. 277.

provements in ship design and navigation. A continuation of this trend through the second quarter of the nineteenth century would render the preceding eighteenth-century data irrelevant for the purposes of evaluating nineteenth-century experience. Most of the slave trade between 1821 and 1843, however, was illegal and subject to harassment from cruisers. Blockades could keep slaves confined to barracoons for months on end, reduce provisions to starvation levels, and cause overcrowding on slave ships built for speed rather than carrying capacity. The increased slave mortality rate associated with this activity was a major issue in the British Parliamentary debates of the 1840s on the effectiveness of the cruiser system. Almost all the figures in Table 11.2 are from the illegal phase of the nineteenth-century trade, whereas the data in Table 11.1 are mainly from the pre-1831 period. If the downward bias in this table is not very pronounced, then the difference between the actual pre- and post-1831 mortality rates may be wide. This would lend support to the popular contemporary belief that the illegal slave trade with its attendant cruiser activity was more lethal than the legal traffic, and that mortality rates at least in the Brazilian trade rose in the 1830s and 1840s. It is at least unlikely that losses in transit were any lower in this period than they were in the second half of the eighteenth century.

Slave ship tonnage figures in the Parliamentary Paper must also be used carefully. Many of the over 1000 records of tonnages are in fact useless. There are three reasons for this.[63] First, each country had its own method of measuring vessels despite the universal use of the terms ton and tonnage. The same ship might be measured at 100 Portuguese or Brazilian tons, 95 British or American tons, and 66 Spanish tons.[64] Second, the Portuguese and Brazilians allowed merchants to register slave ships at tonnage figures that were on average 60% in excess of the actual capacity of the ship.[65] The object, as we have seen, was to lessen the restriction imposed by Anglo–Portuguese treaties of 1815 and 1817. This subterfuge was no longer necessary after 1830, but the illegal nature of the traffic after that date brought a third complication neatly summarized by the Admiralty adviser in the Doctors Commons in 1840 when he wrote, "many . . . slave vessels

[63] E. Phillip LeVeen, "A Quantitative Analysis of the Impact of British Suppression Policies on the Volume of the Nineteenth Century Slave Trade," in Stanley L. Engerman and Eugene D. Genovese, eds., *Race and Slavery in the Western Hemisphere* (Princeton, 1975), p. 63, ignores these problems.

[64] J. Kennedy, C. Dalrymple to Aberdeen, 26 May 1843, FO 84/451. In 1835, the British ton became slightly larger as a result of adjustments to the admeasuring formula (5 and 6 W4 c. 56).

[65] H. Chamberlain to Canning, 18 September 1824, enc.; 11 December 1824, FO 84/31. Despite British protests the practice continued as long as the legal trade lasted.

have had fictitious and fraudulent papers on board . . . which . . . may specify a very different rate of tonnage to what the vessel really is, and these papers . . . are merely used to screen her from capture."[66] It is possible to manipulate the data to provide a basis for comparison but the results would be of questionable validity.

IMPACT OF BRITISH POLICY ON THE TRADE

The main aim of the present chapter is to establish the magnitude and the direction of the slave trade rather than examine the factors behind the fluctuations in the traffic. The questionable nature of the tonnage figures, however, and the size of the import estimates previously described, call into question a recent assessment of British suppression policy as a major influence over the trade. Phillip LeVeen has calculated the numbers of slave ships captured by British cruisers as a percentage of all slavers trading within regions subject to the influence of the navy. His figures are 15.3% for 1821–1830, 46.5% for 1831–1840 and 45% for 1841–1850.[67] LeVeen derived his estimate of the number of expeditions from Curtin's import data which he divided by the product of slavers per ton and the average tonnage of slavers taken from the 1845 Parliamentary Paper. The figures that result are much too low partly because Curtin's estimates are too low and partly, as noted, because the tonnage figures in the 1845 Paper have a pronounced upward bias. Even without these problems, however, his estimates would be too low on account of his assumption that the African coast south of the line remained outside the sphere of British influence until 1840. In fact, nearly 22% of all ships detained between 1832 and 1839 had traded or intended to trade south of the line. The risk of capture in this period was of course less to the south of the line than it was to the north, but it was much greater than zero. Moreover, after 1839 the relative incidence of risk between the two regions was reversed. It follows from this that the number of voyages taking place under British naval influence was much larger than LeVeen realized and therefore his detention rates are much too high.

Over 4000 separate slaving ventures reached Africa between 1821 and 1843. If we assume that one-third of the ships bound for Brazil other than Bahia State between 1832 and 1839 came within the coercive influence of the British, and make similar adjustments for slavers bound for the French Caribbean, we can estimate that 2800 of the total were liable to interference by the British. The Foreign Office records indicate that 661 of these were

[66] Treasury to Palmerston, 7 July 1840, enc. FO 84/335.
[67] LeVeen, "Quantitative Analysis," p. 68.

detained. The figure overstates British influence because several slavers were later released, and many others were sold for very little at Sierra Leone after condemnation and quickly reentered the trade.[68] Unlike the figure that LeVeen uses, it includes all ships that were destroyed prior to adjudication in the courts. The detention rates provided by these figures are 15% for 1821–1830, 25% for 1831–1840, and 31% for 1840–1843. In the latter period the cruisers operated under a British act that allowed them to capture Portuguese slave ships without slaves on board, and these years were the most successful experienced by the squadron. We may conclude that LeVeen's estimate of the shift to the left in the supply curve of slaves, brought about by the British navy, is too large, as is his estimate that "the number (of slaves imported) would have been about 50% larger without suppression"[69] at least for the 1821–1843 period.

It should now be possible to make a better quantitative assessment of the impact of British policies upon the slave trade, but we must not forget the nonquantitative judgements. One cannot go very far into the FO 84 and Admiralty I series at the Public Record Office without being impressed by the Sisyphean task taken on by the navy. Cuba and Bahia continued to draw almost exclusively from Africa north of the line before 1831, despite the fact that this was the very area where the navy concentrated its forces. Concentration is of course a misnomer; half a dozen warships, all of them dull sailers, and 20 or more major supply ports spread over several hundred miles of inhospitable coast obviously does not add up to much interference with trade. The navy certainly affected the traffic from particular zones in certain periods. Blockades were often 100% effective and, for example, contributed measurably to the decline of the trade in the Bight of Biafra in the late 1830s. Against the total traffic, however, the impact of the navy was much less noticeable. The leading Havana houses such as Martinez, Blanco and Carballo, and Forcade would often give their captains the option of trading at the Gallinas or the Bights and later Cabinda. A blockade at one port would simply mean increased trade at another.

CONCLUSION

Curtin has commented that the 1845 Parliamentary Paper is "the largest and most complete sample of the slave trade at any period in its entire history."[70] The present study revises that paper, adds additional data, and

[68] C. Fyfe, A History of Sierra Leone (London, 1962), p. 196.
[69] LeVeen, "Quantitative Analysis," pp. 72–73.
[70] Curtin, Census, p. 235.

utilizes qualitative evidence in a bid to make the 1821–1843 period a testing ground for hypotheses about the traffic. Despite the flaws in the tonnage and mortality figures, it is difficult to foresee any other period challenging the present one in the range and quality of its data. It should now be possible to move on to more precise studies of the market mechanism and policy questions.

APPENDIX
French Ships Bound for Cuba Suspected of Illegal Trading in Blacks (1817–1830)[a]

Year	Number	Ship	Tonnage of ship	Crew	Port	Captain	Shipowner	Site of trade	Number of blacks	Destination	Act of repression
1817	1	CAROLINE	428	33	Nantes	Gautreau	Soubzmain	—	—	Cuba	—
1818	2	CAROLINE	—	—	Bayonne	Pelleport	—	—	—	La Havane	—
	3	CHARLOTTE	159	17	Nantes	Blond	Ducoudray-B.	Bonny	—	Cuba	Acquitted
	4	GASTON	162	12	Nantes	Duhautcilly	Despecher	—	—	La Havane	—
	5	THEMIRE	152	11	Nantes	Gyuot	Haranchipy	—	—	Cuba	—
1819	6	ACTIF	143	18	Nantes	Dithurbide	Houssaye	Côte	—	La Nuevittas	—
	7	AMITIE	95	07	Bordeaux	Chrisiaens	—	Sierra Leone	—	Cuba	—
	8	CAROLINE	—	—	Bayonne	Pellport	Triarte	—	240	La Havane	Pursued
	9	CHARLOTTE	159	20	Nantes	Blond	Ducoudray-B.	Côte	—	La Havane	Pursued
	10	CINTRA	—	—	Bordeaux	Dupuis	Dooley/Baker	Sierra Leone	—	La Havane	Prescription
	11	IRENE	159	25	Nantes	Paqué	Ducoudray-B.	Bonny	150	La Havane	Pursued
	12	LEVRETTE	72	12	Nantes	Delecluze	Bournichon	—	105	Trinité Cuba	Pursued
	13	PENSEE	129	19	Bordeaux	Benoist	Pécarère	Bonny	—	Cuba	—
	14	TELEMAQUE	150	10	Bordeaux	Amanieu	Sangronis	Baie d'Yoff	75	Cuba	Condemned
1820	15	AFRICAIN	—	—	Sénégal	Quoniam	Mille/Ameline	Gallinas	170	La Havane	Pursued
	16	AFRICAIN	114	11	Nantes	Bureau	Bureau	Côte	204	Saint-Yago	No grounds
	17	ANGELIQUE	026	08	Le Havre	Daubin	Ferrand	Bissao	26	La Havane	Condemned
	18	ASTREE	98	20	Nantes	Leglée	Herbert/Sallier	Côte	—	Trinité-Cuba	Impeded
	19	CAROLINE	428	24	Nantes	Gautreau	Soubzmain	Cap Vert	240	La Havane	—
	20	CERES	87	—	Nantes	Le Merle	Bonfils	Cap Lopez	73	La Havane	Impeded
	21	CHARLOTTE	159	19	Nantes	Blond	Ducoudray-B.	Bonny	200	Trinité-Cuba	Seized on visiting G.B.
	22	CONFIANCE	—	—	Le Havre	Gauthier	—	—	350	La Havane	No grounds
	23	DAUPHIN	115	—	Bordeaux	Scolan	Audebert	Bonny	300	Saint Yago	Condemned
	24	ELIZA	150	12	Nantes	Gautreau	Soubzmain	—	—	Nuevittas	—
	25	ESPOIR	109	20	Nantes	Dennis F. C.	Dennis P. T.	Gallinas	200	Trinité-Cuba	Pursued
	26	ISIS	129	20	Nantes	Larriques	L. Bureau	Cap de Monte	—	Nuevittas	—
1820	27	LEVRETTE	72	14	Nantes	Delecluze	Sallentin	Grand Bassa	—	Nuevittas	—
	28	PETITE BETSY	139	24	Nantes	Blay	Jolin-Dubois	—	—	Nuevittas	—
	29	VALENTIN	—	—	Honfleur	Delomosne	Collin	Sénégal	300	Saint Yago	No grounds
1821	30	AFRICAIN	114	18	Martinique	Bureau E.	Vidal & Cᵒ	Gallinas	170	Saint Yago	Impeded
	31	AFRICAIN	92	—	Marseille	Quoniam	Mille	Casamance	bord	La Havane	Acquitted
	32	AIMABLE-HENRIETTE	138	22	Nantes	Bréaut	Chardonneau	—	246	La Havane	—
	33	AMITIE	147	—	La Rochelle	—	—	—	—	La Havane	Lost
	34	BONNE-AMELIE	105	20	Nantes	Pelletier	Chardonneau	Gallinas	100(+)	Saint-Yago	No grounds
	35	CAROLINE	113	—	Bordeaux	Pelleport	Simian	Gallin-Bonny	bord	La Havane	No grounds
	36	CONFIANCE	104	22	Nantes	Paqué	Dennis	—	320	Saint-Yago	Condemned
	37	CONSTANCE	120	21	Nantes	Olivier	Massien	Malaguette	bord	Saint-Yago	—

Year	Number	Ship	Tonnage of ship	Crew	Port	Captain	Shipowner	Site of trade	Number of blacks	Destination	Act of repression
	38	ELIZA	150	17	Nantes	Scheult	Vallée et f.	Gallinas	—	La Havane	Seized by U.S.N.
	39	ESPOIR	134	21	Nantes	Lempereur	Dennis P. T.	Gallinas	219	Saint-Yago	—
	40	ESPOIR	134	22	Nantes	Leray	Dennis P. T.	Gallinas	234	Saint-Yago	Condemned
	41	IRENE	159	23	Nantes	Blond	Ducoudray-B.	Bonny	288	La Havane	Annulment
	42	ISIS	129	20	Nantes	Savariau	L. Bureau	Bonny	218	Nuevittas	Pursued
	43	JULES-HYPPO.	129	20	Nantes	Delecluze	Sallentin	Grand Bassa	250	Saint-Yago	—
	44	LEGERE	194	28	Nantes	Salaun	Herbert/ Sallier	Bonny	bord	Trinité-Cuba	Seized on visiting G.B.
	45	PENSEE	129	20	Bordeaux	Courpon	Pécarère	Bonny	270	Saint-Yago	Condemned
	46	PHOENIX	320	22	Le Havre	Dupré	Martel	Gallinas	350	Saint-Yago	Pursued
	47	PILOTE	77	14	Nantes	Lavergne	Haentjens	Bonny	bord	Trinité-Cuba	No grounds
1822	48	ADOLPHE	169	26	St-Malo	Decaen	Surcouf	Gallinas	bord	La Havane	Seized on visiting G.B.
	49	CLAIRE	330		Le Havre	Dupuytren	Reilly	—	—	La Havane	Denounced
	50	COUREUR	151	24	Nantes	Verrier	Vallée et f.	—	—	La Havane	Pursued
	51	DAUPHIN	165	10	Nantes	Dumas	Rossel/Bondet	—	—	Saint-Yago	Pursued
	52	DEUX AMIS	182	15	Nantes	Mousnier	Lemarié	Sierra Leone	12	Saint-Yago	Seized on visiting G.B.
	53	DRYADE	152	22	Nantes	Devèze	Massion	Cap Vert	—	Saint-Yago	Suspect
	54	ELIZE	179	13	Nantes	Gauthier	Rossel/Bondet	—	—	La Havane	Suspect
	55	ELIZA	150	13	Nantes	Gautreau	Vallée et f.	—	—	Saint-Yago	Suspect
	56	FELICIA	128	22	Nantes	Thibaud	Massion	—	—	Saint-Yago	Suspect
	57	HENRIETTEAIMEE	105	23	Nantes	Gauthier M.	Chardonneau	—	—	La Havane	Pursued
	58	MARIE	73	17	Nantes	Guyot H.	Dennis	Gallinas	175	La Havane	Condemned
	59	MARIE-ANGEL.	—	—	Bordeaux	Menard	Fernandez	—	230	La Havane	Condemned
	60	PENELOPE	201	—	Bordeaux	Ducasse	Sangroniz	—	—	Saint-Yago	Pursued
	61	ROSE	138	22	Nantes	Thomas	Vallée et f.	Gallinas	bord	La Havane	Seized on visiting G.B.
	62	THEODORE	—	—	Honfleur	Clamard	Collin	Bonny	314	Cuba	Condemned
	63	VIGILANT	232	31	Nantes	Bouffier	Michaud	Bonny	344	pour Cuba	Condemned by G.B.
1823	64	AGILE	134	—	Nantes	Guyot H.	Dennis	—	—	La Havane	
	65	AIMABLE-HENR.	138	21	Nantes	Marsae	Chardonneau	—	—	Saint-Yago	—
	66	CLAIRE	139	24	Nantes	Danthon	Vallée et f.	—	—	Saint-Yago	—
	67	DEUX NANTAIS	201	16	Nantes	Pelletier	Ogereau	—	—	Cuba	
	68	ETINCELLE	95	17	Nantes	Jouanne	Massion	Doant Toro	—	Saint-Yago	Suspect
	69	HENRIETTE-AIM.	105	25	Nantes	Chesnel	Chardonneau	Mesurade	—	La Havane	Seen by G/B; F/
	70	JOSEPHINE	110	21	Nantes	Thomas	Vallée et f.	—	—	Saint-Yago	Denounced by G.B.
	71	VICTOR	151	25	Nantes	Verrier	Vallée et f.	—	—	La Havane	Suspect
1824	72	ACTEON	138	21	Nantes	Blond	Vallée et f.	—	—	Saint-Yago	Suspect
	73	ADOLPHE	169	—	St-Malo	Decaen	Surcouf	—	—	La Havane	No grounds
	74	AIMABLE-HENR.	138	17	Nantes	Brun	Chardonneau	Old Calabar	bord	Saint-Yago	Pursued
	75	ANGELINE	174	26	Nantes	Scheult	Vallée et f.	—	300	La Havane	Suspect
	76	BLUETTE	94	16	Nantes	Angaud	Wuilleaume	Cap de Monte	—	Saint-Yago	Suspect
	77	DEUX MANTAIS	201	30	Nantes	Mahe	Ogereau	Sherbro	483	Cuba	Condemned
	78	GASPARD	172	29	Nantes	Maillard	Vallée et f.	—	300	Cuba	Suspect

1824	79	GUSTAVE	165	27	Nantes	Héraud	Vallée et f.	—	400	Cuba	Suspect
	80	JULES	110	22	Nantes	Devarieux	Anthoine	Cap Trois Pointes	100	Saint-Yago	Condemned
	81	MARIE	150	22	Nantes	Soret	Dennis	—	—	La Havane	Suspect
	82	ORPHEE	352	37	Nantes	Coquard	François	Bonny	511	Saint-Yago	Suspect
	83	SOPHIE	128	16	Nantes	Goyeau	Wuilleaume	—	—	Cuba	Suspect
1825	84	AIMABLE CLAUD.	79	—	Bordeaux	Picaluga	Sangronis	—	34	Cuba	Condemned by G.B.
	85	AIMABLE-HENR.	138	24	Nantes	—	Chardonneau	—	—	Saint-Yago	Suspect
	86	ALCIDE	191	20	Nantes	Terrien	François	Cusco	387	Trinité-Cuba	Suspect
	87	CERON	250	—	Nantes	Métayer	Rives	—	—	Cuba	Suspect
	88	EUGENE	138	26	Nantes	Lavergne	Vallée et f.	Côte	—	Saint-Yago	Suspect
	89	FELICIE	131	16	Nantes	Berge	Anthoine	Bonny	300	Cuba	Suspect
	90	EUGENIE	125	21	Nantes	Gauthier	Wuilleaume	Côte	—	Saint-Yago	Suspect
	91	HYPPOLITE	153	23	Nantes	Drumel	Vallée et f.	Cameroun	284	Saint-Yago	Condemned
	92	JEUNE LOUIS	—	—	—	—	—	—	150	Cuba	Cf. Parl. Pap.
	93	MARIE	122	22	Nantes	Héraud	Dennis	Bonny	—	Saint-Yago	Suspect
	94	MARIE	122	22	Nantes	Roger	Dennis	Grand Bassa	—	Saint-Yago	Suspect
	95	ORPHEE	352	50	Nantes	Coquard	François	Old Calabar	698	Saint-Yago	Seized on visiting G.B.
	96	PAQUEBOT	—	—	Marseille	—	—	—	—	Saint-Yago	Suspect
	97	TELEMAQUE	173	24	Nantes	Savariau	Bouché j.	Côte	—	Saint-Yago	Seized by France
1826	98	CHARLES	151	22	Nantes	Blond	Vallée et f.	Douant Toro	265	Cuba	Seized by France
	99	DESTIN	106	12	Nantes	Cicquel	Massion	"Maroc"	—	Saint-Yago	Seized by France
	100	EPERVIER	201	—	Marseille	—	Bignoneau	Saint-Thomé	—	La Havane	Suspect
	101	ETIENNE	152	21	Nantes	Signoret	Dennis	Côte	—	Matanzas	Suspect
	102	EUROPE	166	12	Nantes	Dezaunay	Blanchard	Côte	—	Saint-Yago	Suspect
	103	FIRMINE	138	20	Nantes	Caharel	Loréal	Calabar	307	Saint-Yago	Condemned
	104	PAUL	164	—	Nantes	Tahet	Vallée et f.	—	—	Cuba	Suspect
	105	PHILEMON	198	26	Bordeaux	Bryhand	Peltier	—	—	Saint-Yago	Suspect
	106	FANNY	110	30	Guadeloupe	Lalande	Bonnassé	Côte	—	Saint-Yago	—
1827	107	FANNY	110	22	Guadeloupe	Lalande	Bonnassé: Larivière	Côte	252	Saint-Yago	Condemned by G.B.
	108	LINX	191	23	Nantes	Jarnou	Santerre & C°	Côte	300	Guantanamo	Suspect
1830	109	PAULINE	75	24	Guadeloupe	Martin	Laporte	Côte	151	Cuba	Seized on visiting G.B.

Sources: Prepared by Serge Daget. The sources from which part of this list was established are described in two articles:

1. "Le trafic négrier illégal français: Historiographie et sources," *Annales de l'Université d'Abidjan, Histoire III*, Abidjan 1975, 25 p.

2. "Long cours et négriers nantais du trafic illégal, 1814–1833," Numéro spécial, *Revue Française d'Histoire d'Outre-Mer*, 1975, I et II, Paris, 40 p.

a Notations relative to repression indicate the state of the case before the French authorities: ministerial, judicial, or port. *Suspect:* the position of the maritime authorities of the port of registry toward the ship cited. *Prevention:* administrative action exercised by the maritime ministers against a captain following a slave raid and to prevent another occurrence. *No grounds:* a negative judicial action—one that does not signify that the ship had not been a slave ship, but that indicates on the contrary the hesitation of French justice to sanction the shortcomings of the law. Without any indication to the contrary, notations relative to condemnations are the result of French judicial action. The notation *seized upon visiting Britain* implies a repressive British action. The same, with the letter F, implies a French intervention independent of the preceding one.

12

West African Consumption Patterns and Their Influence on the Eighteenth-Century English Slave Trade[1]

DAVID RICHARDSON

For many years it was widely assumed that West Africans played an essentially passive role in the Atlantic slave trade. For the most part they were seen as the innocent and unfortunate victims of a trading system over which they exercised little control. This picture derived in part from the abolition movement and partly from the fact that most of the surviving information about the trade was European in origin. It was further reinforced by the nineteenth-century image of Africa as an economically static and backward continent. The last notion appears to be no longer tenable, at least in its crude nineteenth-century form. Using new types of evidence such as African oral traditions and making imaginative use of the standard sources of information, recent generations of historians of West Africa have begun to revise very substantially our traditional ideas about West Africa during the era of the slave trade.[2] It is now coming to be appreciated that

[1] I am grateful to the British Social Science Research Council for providing financial assistance for some of the research upon which this chapter is based.
[2] See, for instance, A. G. Hopkins, *An Economic History of West Africa* (London, 1973); P. D. Curtin, *Economic Change in Pre-Colonial Africa: Senegambia in the Era of the Slave Trade* (Madison, 1975).

West African institutions and societies were more diversified and in some
ways more dynamic than most earlier authorities had suggested.

REASSESSMENT OF THE WEST AFRICAN ROLE
IN THE TRADE

The current reappraisal of West Africa's historical development suggests
that it may be necessary to reassess the part played by Africans themselves
in the operation of the Atlantic slave trade. It has always been recognized,
of course, that African merchants supplied most of the slaves delivered to
European and North American vessels stationed at coastal trading centers,
but it is increasingly obvious that African influences upon the trade were
felt in other ways too. It is the purpose of this chapter to focus attention
upon one of these other sources of influence, namely how Africans, in their
capacity as consumers of imported trade goods, affected trading relationships with Europeans. This is attempted by means of an analysis of English
exports to West Africa in the eighteenth century, when England's involvement in the slave trade was at its height. With only one or two notable
exceptions,[3] writers on the English slave trade have failed to pay much
attention to the composition of cargoes shipped out to West Africa. Discussion of these exports has usually been restricted to a cursory listing of
certain well-known trade goods, such as beads, firearms, liquor, and brightly
colored and exotically named Indian textiles, without any real attempt at
analysis.[4] This superficial approach has had unfortunate consequences, undoubtedly helping to create the impression that the peoples of West Africa
were unsophisticated and gullible, the easy prey of Europeans, and quite
incapable of exerting much influence on trading relationships with more
astute "outsiders." The following examination of English exports to
West Africa demonstrates that this view is not only an insult to the economic rationality of eighteenth-century West Africans but disguises important subtleties in West African consumption patterns. The latter are
significant in several ways. In conjunction with other evidence, they throw
light on the internal functioning of West African economies and societies,
helping in particular to bring out distinctions in the structure and level of
development of those economies. In the narrower context of the slave

[3] For example, K. G. Davies, *The Royal African Company* (London, 1957), pp. 165–179;
Conrad Gill, *Merchants and Mariners of the Eighteenth Century* (London, 1961), pp. 75–79.
[4] Eric Williams, *Capitalism and Slavery* (Chapel Hill, 1943), pp. 65–84, contains one of the
fullest discussions but the analysis is very limited. The recent book by Roger Anstey, *The
Atlantic Slave Trade and British Abolition 1760–1810* (Atlantic Highlands, N. J., 1975), p. 10,
simply contains the usual short list of trade goods.

trade, to which this chapter is confined, differences in West African consumption patterns appear to have had significant repercussions for the structure, organization, and even the profitability of English slave trading in the eighteenth century.

BRITISH EXPORTS TO WEST AFRICA, EIGHTEENTH CENTURY

Exports from England to West Africa grew substantially during the eighteenth century, reflecting the growth of demand for slaves in the New World and probable shifts in the net barter terms of trade in West Africa against English merchants. Table 12.1 provides data of the value of English exports to West Africa from 1701 to 1800 in both official (that is, constant) and current prices.[5] According to official values, exports increased over 10-fold between the first and last decades of the century, from an average of £76,750 per year between 1701 and 1712 to £794,580 annually from 1793 to 1800. With the exception of the 1790s, official values appear, on average, to have diverged from current prices by no more than 15%, and thus for most of the century the official and current price series of exports move quite closely together. Overall, West Africa's share of total English exports doubled during the course of the century, but even in 1800 the area took only about 4% of total English exports.[6]

The growth of exports to West Africa was by no means steady. They increased vigorously in three periods, from 1713 to about 1730, from 1763 to 1775, and from 1783 to 1792. In other years exports either grew much more slowly or even declined. Such fluctuations were hardly surprising during a century punctuated by numerous international wars involving the major slave-trading nations. War conditions brought forth large numbers of

---

[5] The problems of the official values are discussed in J. J. McCusker, "The Current Value of English Exports, 1697 to 1800," *William and Mary Quarterly,* 3rd series, vol. 28, no. 4, 1971, pp. 607–628. The data given in Table 12.1 understate the total volume and value of exports to Africa in English ships, though by what extent is uncertain. There appears to have been some underrecording of legitimate exports from England to Africa by the official figures themselves. In addition there is some evidence to indicate that trade goods were sometimes smuggled on to English slave ships at such places as Guernsey and the Isle of Man. Finally, some of the goods used by English merchants to buy slaves were shipped directly to Africa from foreign, particularly Dutch, ports. See Donald Woodward, "The Port Books of England and Wales," *Maritime History,* vol. 3, no. 2, 1973, pp. 160–161; J. E. Inikori, "Measuring the Atlantic Slave Trade: an Assessment of Curtin and Anstey," *Journal of African History,* vol. 17, no. 2, 1976, pp. 205–208.

[6] Total English exports in official and current values can be found in McCusker, "English Exports," pp. 620–622.

TABLE 12.1
English Exports to West Africa 1701–1800, Distinguishing British and Foreign-
Produced Goods, by Averages for Selected Periods

	Official values (£s)	Price Index	Current values 1701–1712 = 100 (£s)	Percentage of British	Percentage of foreign
1701–1712	76,750	100.0	76,750	60.7	39.3
1713–1720	90,950	93.4	84,590	54.6	45.4
1721–1729	194,420	92.5	179,840	40.0	60.0
1730–1738	195,910	86.7	169,850	42.4	57.6
1739–1747	141,550	90.3	127,820	42.2	57.8
1748–1755	215,960	88.4	190,910	58.7	41.3
1756–1762	240,490	96.0	230,870	70.1	29.9
1763–1775	626,220	101.2	633,730	66.0	34.0
1776–1782	261,100	109.0	284,600	64.7	35.3
1783–1792	805,600	114.0	918,380	66.0	34.0
1793–1800	794,580	141.4	1,123,540	54.8	45.2

Source: Public Record Office BT6/185, ff. 33–77, 79, Sir Charles Whitworth, *State of the Trade of England in Its Imports and Exports Progressively from the Year 1697* (London, 1776); David MacPherson, *Annals of Commerce,* 4 vols. (London, 1805), vol. 4, pp. 68, 99, 120, 137, 182, 198, 214, 231, 262, 288, 332, 370, 399, 438, 466, 491, 536. Price index based on J. J. McCusker, "The Current Value of English Exports, 1697 to 1800", *William and Mary Quarterly,* 3rd series, vol. 28, no. 4, 1971, p. 619.

enemy privateers, created great uncertainty in commodity markets, notably for New World staples, and disrupted supply channels of goods required for trade in West Africa. These war-induced problems were clearly reflected in statistics of exports to West Africa. The evidence suggests, however, that wars proved rather less disruptive for English, notably Liverpool, slave traders than their rivals on the continent. The slave-trading activity of French merchants collapsed during each of the major wars of the eighteenth century.[7] Despite the fact that English exports to West Africa fell sharply during the early 1740s and again between 1776 and 1783, the data indicate that English slave trading continued at sometimes remarkably high levels during other periods of international conflict, notably during the Seven Years' War and also the 1790s. Part of the explanation for this lay no doubt

[7] Gaston Martin, *L'Ere des Négriers 1714–1774* (Paris, 1931), Chapters 4 and 6. As the Dutch remained neutral during most of the eighteenth-century wars their trade was in general much less disrupted. Dutch trade was, however, severely dislocated by the Anglo–Dutch war of 1780–1782; after this, Dutch involvement in the trade almost completely ceased. Pieter Emmer, "The History of the Dutch Slave Trade, A Bibliographical Survey," *Journal of Economic History,* vol. 32, no. 3, 1972, p. 741.

in English naval supremacy and also in the westerly geographical position of Liverpool, the premier English slave trading port from the 1740s onward.[8]

Table 12.1 also demonstrates one other important feature of England's exports to West Africa: Throughout the century a significant proportion of these exports was of foreign origin. The proportion of foreign-produced goods rarely fell below one-third of total exports to West Africa in this period, and in some years, particularly before 1750 and again in the 1790s, it was near or even over one-half.[9] In resorting to foreign-produced trade goods for Africa, however, the private traders of the eighteenth century were only following the example of the earlier Royal African Company. About one-half of the Company's exports before 1698 consisted of foreign goods.[10] These included East Indian textiles and cowries and a wide range of continental European goods such as Swedish bar iron, German linens, sheets, beads, firearms, and gunpowder. Though many of these goods were obtained directly from producers overseas or, in the case of East Indian fabrics, from the English East India Company's warehouses in London, a major share of them were also supplied by Dutch middlemen at Amsterdam, much to the obvious political embarrassment of the Company. A determined effort by the Company's directors to reduce their dependence on Dutch supplies by encouraging home producers of certain trade goods such as annabasses met with some success, but English dependence on foreign suppliers was still evident in the early eighteenth century. Private traders based in London frequently resorted to Dutch ports to obtain trade goods in the 1730s,[11] and Bristol's rise as a slave-trading port in the first 30 years or so of the eighteenth century depended substantially upon access to trade goods produced abroad.

In view of the close relationship that is sometimes alleged to have existed between the growth of English industry, notably cotton textiles, and the emergence of English, particularly Liverpool, dominance of the slave trade, the continuing shipment of large quantities of foreign merchandise to West Africa by English merchants during the eighteenth century is perhaps surprising, but can be explained in several ways. During the first half of the century, prices of trade goods supplied by the Dutch seem to have remained very competitive. Contemporaries frequently asserted that England's only advantage in the supply of trade goods for Africa at this time lay in its

---

[8] In wartime Liverpool merchants often advised the masters of their ships to sail round the north of Ireland, thereby hoping to avoid enemy privateers operating in the English and Bristol channels and off Lands End.

[9] The official statistics probably underestimate the proportion of foreign goods included in English cargoes. See Note 5.

[10] Davies, *Royal African Company*, pp. 174–176.

[11] Gill, *Merchants and Mariners*, pp. 77–78.

woollen and worsted industries, and markets for the products of these industries in West Africa were naturally restricted. Thus in 1709 the Dutch were said to possess a general trading advantage over the English of about 30% in all goods except woollens, and such claims were being repeated as late as 1731.[12] The rapid increase, however, of Liverpool's share of English slave-trading activity during the 1730s and later may well have reduced Dutch trading advantages, for much less is heard about them from this time onward. Liverpool's rise was almost certainly attributable in part to its proximity to suppliers of textiles and a wide range of other trade goods in nearby Lancashire and the West Midlands. The expansion of Liverpool's commerce with Africa and the New World in turn allowed manufacturers in Manchester, Birmingham, and other places to extend their operations and increase their competitive strength in many sorts of trade goods previously obtained abroad. Yet for supplies of certain goods such as bar iron, beads, and many cotton and linen textiles, Liverpool merchants had to resort to overseas producers even at the end of the century. This was because competition among suppliers of trade goods was based not simply upon the price of goods but also on the design, texture, coloring, and finishing of goods, required to satisfy the discriminating tastes of the African consumer. The failure in certain cases by British manufacturers to reproduce the particular qualities in foreign goods, notably East Indian textiles, that Africans admired, meant that English merchants were forced to continue exporting large quantities of goods of foreign origin to Africa. In 1786–1787, for instance, over 36% of Liverpool's exports to Africa consisted of foreign goods, two-thirds of which were East Indian in origin.[13]

It is well known that England's exports to Africa in the eighteenth century consisted of a great assortment of goods. The East India Company supplied cowries, amber, and a great variety of cotton piece goods. Other foreign goods included Irish linen and tallow, German silesias, Swedish iron, Venitian beads, French brandy, Jamaican rum, and Virginia tobacco. The most notable British-produced goods were worsteds, Manchester checks and piece goods, Birmingham firearms, copper and brassware, gunpowder, and liquor.[14] If nothing else, such a listing of major exports indicates the

[12] PRO CO 388/12, K52; CO 388/30, V 75. As one might expect, worsteds such as perpetuanas and says formed a substantial part of English exports of woollens. PRO CO 388/12, K 53; CO 388/13, L 104; CO 388/15, M 148; CO 390/7, no. 36.

[13] PRO BT 6/7, Tarleton's calculations of the trade to Africa and the West Indies, 15 August 1788.

[14] Detailed lists can be found in W. Enfield, *An Essay towards the History of Liverpool* (1773), pp. 84–85, reprinted in Elizabeth Donnan, ed., *Documents Illustrative of the Slave Trade to America*, 4 vols. (Washington, 1935), vol. 2, p. 536; PRO BT 6/7, account of goods exported from Liverpool to Africa, 1787.

scattered origins of Africa-bound cargoes. In an era of uncertain communications and unstable international relations, however, the diverse sources of
these cargoes were bound to test the nerve and patience of those planning
and investing in slave-trading ventures. The total average real investment in
slave trading voyages was around £4000 in the 1730s and about £8000 by
the 1780s, of which approximately two-thirds usually consisted of trade
goods.[15] To assemble at any particular time and place a cargo of such value
from such diverse origins required sound organization, and especially the
cultivation of good economic and personal relationships with manufacturers
in order to ensure reasonable delivery times and, even more importantly,
credit if required. The relationship between English slave merchants and
their suppliers of trade goods is a neglected field of study, but it is often
suggested that Liverpool traders were very assiduous in establishing close
ties with Manchester manufacturers, in which task they had obvious geographical advantages over their Bristol and London rivals.[16] Assuming that
Liverpool merchants did form such close ties, the benefits that they derived
from them are somewhat uncertain. It is quite possible that they secured
preferences in the supply and terms of purchase of Manchester goods. The
importance of this should not be overrated, however, for Manchester goods
were by no means a major component of all Africa-bound cargoes, though
strong connections with Manchester were probably very useful in the event
of any disruption in supplies of East Indian textiles.[17] Whatever special
advantages Liverpool merchants may have possessed by way of supplies of
certain trade goods, the fact remains that the assembling of African cargoes
generally proved laborious and time-consuming for all merchants. On average the slave ships of Bristol and Liverpool spent 4 or 5 months in their
home port between slaving voyages;[18] and to judge from the sometimes
acrimonious correspondence between merchants and manufacturers, the
problems of putting together the outward-bound cargo contributed to such
delays.

Assembling a cargo for Africa was not just a test of the slave trader's
patience, however, but also of his judgment and skill, and the reliability of
his sources of information about market conditions in West Africa. A cargo
of trade goods had to be very carefully and precisely assorted to meet the

---

[15] Based upon my own calculations.

[16] Robert Norris, *A Short Account of the African Slave Trade* (Liverpool, 1788), p. 10; PRO
BT 6/9, p. 356.

[17] It is very difficult to say how far Lancashire cotton piece goods were an effective
substitute for East India goods. African middlemen appear to have drawn a clear distinction
between them, but in abnormal circumstances Manchester goods may have proved an acceptable substitute.

[18] Based upon my own calculations.

particular demands prevailing at the intended place of trade on the West African coast. Failure to assort cargoes with reasonable care could prove extremely detrimental to the overall success of voyages, causing lengthy delays on the African coast and the purchase of slaves only at high prices.[19] Historians of the English slave trade have long been aware of the need for merchants to assort cargoes to cater to African tastes, but they have tended to emphasize short-term and seemingly irrational fluctuations in demand on the coast. Beneath such short-term variations, however, there also existed quite definite longer-term interregional differences in African demands. Sometimes these had their origins in periods long before direct European commercial contacts with West Africa arose, and it was highly important for the success of slave trading ventures that English merchants appreciated these interregional differences in African tastes as much as the current fashion on the coast. Yet most of the literature fails to distinguish between short- and long-term influences on demand in West Africa, and so historians have generally missed the possible significance of African patterns of demand for the structure and profitability of the English slave trade.

Eighteenth-century travelers to West Africa, as well as factors resident on the coast, frequently commented upon the types of goods in demand at particular places and occasionally even made interregional comparisons. Among the many travelers, John Atkins was one of the most illuminating in his discussion of the state of demand at various West African trading centers. Writing of a voyage he had made in 1721, he pointed out that

> the Windward and Leeward Parts of the Coast are as opposite in their Demands, as in their distance. Iron Bars, which are not asked for to Leeward, are a substantial Part of Windward Cargoes. Crystals, Oranges [arrangoes], Corals, and Brass-mounted Cutlasses are almost peculiar to the Windward Coast; as are brass Pans from Rio Sestos to Apollonia. Cowreys (or Booges) at Whydah. Copper and Iron Bars at Callabar; but Arms, Gunpowder, Tallow, old Sheets, Cottons of all the Various Denominations, and English Spirits are every where called for.[20]

Much more recently, K. G. Davies in his book on the Royal African Company made some use of the surviving invoice books of the Company to suggest certain regional peculiarities of demand in the late seventeenth century. He found that one-quarter to one-half of the Company's exports to Gambia consisted of iron bars, but considerably fewer were dispatched to the Windward Coast and Gold Coast and none at all to Angola. East Indian textiles were essential for the trade at Angola but hardly found a market at Gambia at this time, while cowries were indispensable for the trade at

[19] John Newton, *The Journal of a Slave Trader, 1750–54*, Bernard Martin and Mark Spurrell, eds. (London, 1962), pp. 49–50.

[20] John Atkins, *A Voyage to Guinea, Brasil and the West Indies* (London, 1735), p. 159.

Whydah, Ardra, and the Bight of Benin but were in little demand elsewhere.[21]

Interesting and informative though such evidence is, it is still too impressionistic for a proper understanding of the economics of eighteenth-century slave trading; a more detailed analysis of a large number of invoices of cargoes shipped to the various West African trading centers is necessary. Few invoices of cargoes dispatched to West Africa by private traders before 1750 have survived, but quite a large number can be found for the half century after 1750. To date, invoices of cargoes for 93 English voyages to West Africa during the period from 1758 to 1806 have been discovered. Details of these can be found in Table 12.2, where vessels and their cargoes are arranged by years according to their intended place of trade in West Africa. Although invoices relating to all the major areas of English slave-trading activity in the second half of the eighteenth century have survived—and, indeed, include trading centers such as Old Calabar, Bonny, and the Cameroons that are not covered by Davies's work—the coverage of slaving areas by invoices is by no means even. In particular, an abundance of evidence has survived for trade at Old Calabar and the Cameroons, and relatively little for places such as Whydah, Benin, New Calabar, and Gabon. Fortunately the latter were some of the less important centers of English slave trading in the second half of the eighteenth century; the major areas of English activity at this time—the Windward Coast, the Gold Coast, the Bight of Biafra, and Congo–Angola—appear to be sufficiently well covered for present purposes.

Table 12.2 indicates the percentage of each cargo falling into each one of nine separate groups of trade goods; these are East India textiles, Manchester textiles, bar iron, hardware (i.e., items made of copper, brass, and pewter), beads, cowries, guns, gunpowder, and liquor. With only minor exceptions, these comprised the major sorts of trade goods sent to West Africa in the second half of the eighteenth century.

VARIATIONS IN AFRICAN CONSUMPTION PATTERNS

An examination of Table 12.2 reveals some significant variations in the composition of cargoes according to their intended destination in West Africa. Take, for instance, shipments of East India textiles, beads, guns, and gunpowder; cargoes bound for most places in West Africa included some of these goods but the proportions varied quite considerably. Very few India

---

[21] Davies, *Royal African Company*, p. 234.

TABLE 12.2
A List of Ships Destined for West Africa from Bristol (B) and Liverpool (L) from 1758 to 1806

Name of ship	Year	Cargo (pounds)[a]	Destination	Percentages of the total cargo									
				Textiles		Bar iron	Hard-ware	Beads	Cowries	Arms	Gun powder	Liquor	Total of nine commodities[b]
				East Indian	Man-chester								
William (L)	1764	1584	Gambia	—	21.5	7.5	.6	19.6	—	11.7	5.6	3.9	70.4
Aston (L)	1769	3825	Gambia	25.6	6.5	4.1	.9	17.1	—	14.1	5.9	.4	74.6
Aston (L)	1771	2787	Gambia	32.8	11.4	5.8	2.0	13.5	—	12.1	5.4	4.1	87.3
Aston (L)	1773	3330	Gambia	26.0	13.5	4.2	.8	10.3	—	16.1	5.4	5.4	81.7
Mermaid (B)	1792	3709	Gambia	25.8	—	3.6	—	14.3	—	19.3	3.5	8.3	74.8
Crescent (B)	1792	8297	Isle de Los	49.9	4.3	.9	8.1	.3	—	12.5	2.9	4.8	83.7
Ruby (B)	1788	3472	Sierra Leone	22.8	16.0	1.2	11.4	4.1	—	20.1	5.9	2.0	83.5
Ruby (B)	1790	3731	Sierra Leone	26.1	8.4	1.6	7.6	7.6	—	16.7	4.9	—	72.9
Fly (B)	1787	800	Sierra Leone	26.3	7.4	2.8	20.5	4.0	—	14.6	8.4	—	84.0
Fanny (B)	1792	5253	Bence Island	30.2	2.4	.8	9.2	7.2	—	16.3	3.9	6.4	76.4
Fame (B)	1790	2350	Banana Island	14.7	15.7	1.2	8.7	2.1	—	28.0	7.8	2.7	80.9
Eadith (L)	1760	2103	Windward Coast	11.4	17.7	2.4	12.5	1.7	—	19.5	8.8	8.3	82.3
Eadith (L)	1761	2071	Windward Coast	13.7	22.9	3.0	10.8	2.0	—	20.0	8.2	3.0	83.6
Plumper (L)	1762	2998	Windward Coast	9.5	19.6	1.1	14.4	1.8	—	18.4	12.7	2.3	79.8
Sally (L)	1768	2763	Windward Coast	6.8	22.1	1.8	8.1	.9	—	26.7	9.7	4.9	81.0
Tom (L)	1771	2575	Windward Coast	12.0	13.2	.8	11.0	1.0	—	23.5	9.6	5.2	76.3
Morning Star (B)	1792	3481	Windward Coast	51.1	11.9	.5	1.1	3.2	—	1.8	8.6	3.2	81.4
Sally (L)	1768	1829	Gold Coast	39.6	11.2	.4	6.7	—	—	1.8	5.3	2.2	67.2
Corsican Hero (L)	1771	5735	Annamaboe	42.0	12.5	1.7	5.0	—	—	4.6	7.3	1.2	74.3
Harlequin (L)	1782	5474	Annamaboe	31.2	6.6	1.9	4.1	.4	—	2.5	7.8	8.8	63.3
Ingram (L)	1783	7240	Annamaboe and Porto Novo	16.4	14.9	—	1.4	—	1.5	2.6	7.3	16.4	60.5

Golden Age (L)	1783	12660	Annamaboe and Whydah	15.4	6.7	2.8	.5	1.5	23.8	.7	.7	8.7	60.8
Little Britain (L)	1764	1529	Ardrah	20.7	15.4	3.6	5.3	—	10.7	4.1	4.9	8.8	73.5
Sisters (L)	1764	3984	Whydah	—	2.5	2.6	—	—	55.4	—	—	20.0	80.5
Blayds (L)	1782	7147	Porto Novo and Lagos	12.8	21.8	.7	.3	—	7.0	1.7	3.0	25.8	73.1
Plumper (L)	1768	3945	Benin	7.1	3.9	1.2	27.6	32.6[a]	—	2.3	.7	3.3	78.7
Plumper (L)	1769	4735	Benin	6.8	3.3	1.2	19.4	21.1[a]	—	2.2	.7	3.4	58.1
True Blue (L)	1770	6079	Benin	40.1	3.0	1.0	15.6	11.2[a]	—	2.9	.8	2.6	77.2
Plumper (L)	1771	5593	Bonny	13.0	22.7	5.8	15.1	4.0	—	6.3	13.0	8.2	88.1
Rodney (B)	1791	8102	Bonny	20.6	22.1	2.5	6.0	2.6	—	18.2	11.2	8.0	91.2
Trelawney (B)	1791	7564	Bonny	33.4	7.4	2.8	8.4	3.7	—	11.8	12.2	10.5	90.2
Langriche (B)	1793	5801	Bonny	29.1	10.2	6.9	13.7	10.0	—	4.8	—	14.0	88.7
Earl of Liverpool (L)	1797	5452	Bonny	18.4	16.4	2.9	5.8	4.8	—	7.8	22.2	10.2	88.5
Earl of Liverpool (L)	1798	5954	Bonny	37.5	5.8	3.5	6.7	4.5	—	8.1	17.0	7.0	90.1
Lottery (L)	1798	8327	Bonny	37.6	3.8	3.3	7.2	3.3	—	7.3	20.3	8.5	91.3
Lottery (L)	1802	6357	Bonny	46.0	7.3	4.6	3.9	4.6	—	5.2	13.3	7.2	92.1
Enterprise (L)	1803	8896	Bonny	35.9	8.0	4.0	3.6	4.7	—	5.4	12.3	7.0	80.9
Enterprise (L)	1806	7196	Bonny	38.0	12.1	3.6	—	4.1	—	7.0	17.5	8.4	90.7
Africa (B)	1774	4648	New Calabar	21.4	7.0	4.6	14.5	6.5	—	11.5	22.3	6.6	94.4
Chesterfield (L)	1757	3344	Old Calabar	17.6	18.4	11.7	23.0	5.8	—	6.7	6.6	5.0	94.8
Chesterfield (L)	1759	3514	Old Calabar	23.0	15.5	11.5	6.5	6.6	—	5.2	10.9	5.7	84.9
Dalrymple–Neptune (L)[c]	1768	4677	Old Calabar	8.3	24.9	14.0	14.9	6.7	—	6.9	6.4	4.8	86.9
Andromache–Hector (L)	1769	4738	Old Calabar	17.6	19.5	7.7	16.2	6.3	—	4.0	7.9	6.0	85.2
Dobson–Fox (L)	1769	5614	Old Calabar	11.7	24.7	13.5	15.3	6.6	—	5.2	4.6	4.9	86.5
Dobson–Fox (L)	1770	5608	Old Calabar	23.3	12.1	11.8	16.1	4.8	—	5.0	6.2	4.9	84.2
Dalrymple–Swift (L)	1771	5498	Old Calabar	16.3	19.5	10.2	18.1	5.2	—	6.3	6.9	5.9	88.4
Andromache–Hector (L)	1771	4905	Old Calabar	19.3	16.8	9.3	19.4	4.9	—	6.2	6.2	6.8	88.9
Lord Cassils–May (L)	1771	5280	Old Calabar	13.1	24.6	12.0	15.6	3.3	—	5.4	6.0	3.1	83.1
Dalrymple–Dreadnought (L)	1772	7336	Old Calabar	22.0	17.4	7.9	17.4	4.2	—	5.3	7.4	6.1	87.7
Swift (L)	1772	2184	Old Calabar	25.5	19.0	7.1	18.7	3.7	—	4.3	6.0	6.1	90.4
Andromache–Hector (L)	1773	6930	Old Calabar	20.7	18.4	7.1	17.6	3.6	—	5.1	6.4	7.9	86.8

TABLE 12.2 *(continued)*

Name of ship	Year	Cargo (pounds)[a]	Destination	Textiles East Indian	Textiles Manchester	Bar iron	Hardware	Beads	Cowries	Arms	Gun powder	Liquor	Total of nine commodities[b]
Dalrymple–Swift (L)	1773	6863	Old Calabar	21.6	17.2	7.9	15.9	4.4	—	4.9	6.2	6.9	85.0
Dreadnought (L)	1774	3110	Old Calabar	15.8	15.1	4.8	15.6	4.0	—	10.8	7.7	8.0	81.8
Lord Cassils–May (L)	1774	6042	Old Calabar	12.8	21.4	6.4	18.7	2.3	—	6.3	8.1	6.7	82.7
Dalrymple–Swift (L)	1775	6416	Old Calabar	30.2	14.7	4.8	17.9	2.1	—	5.9	5.8	8.7	90.1
Africa (B)	1776	3072	Old Calabar	26.9	16.1	—	13.8	5.5	—	10.5	—	8.5	81.3
Hector–Swift (L)	1776	6190	Old Calabar	25.1	15.2	2.7	19.2	2.0	—	7.4	9.9	5.8	87.3
Dreadnought (L)	1776	2448	Old Calabar	19.9	11.4	3.8	22.7	2.7	—	9.3	7.4	13.7	90.9
Dalrymple–Swift (L)	1777	5745	Old Calabar	21.0	13.6	3.1	18.3	2.2	—	8.6	8.7	10.5	86.0
Quixorte (L)	1783	3599	Old Calabar	18.7	21.6	6.0	11.7	—	—	9.8	8.1	6.7	82.6
Pearl (B)	1787	4582	Old Calabar	25.1	30.4	5.1	9.1	1.4	—	6.4	5.5	4.0	87.0
Pearl (B)	1790	9548	Old Calabar	45.2	13.8	6.7	7.7	3.1	—	6.2	4.2	3.6	90.5
African Queen (B)	1791	5106	Old Calabar	36.7	10.8	5.5	10.8	1.9	—	7.7	5.7	10.0	89.1
Sarah (B)	1791	4545	Old Calabar	15.8	24.2	3.0	15.1	3.9	—	14.0	12.2	8.8	97.0
Fame (B)	1792	2482	Old Calabar	61.2	—	4.1	6.7	1.2	—	10.0	3.5	6.7	93.4
Sarah (B)	1792	4103	Old Calabar	66.0	—	5.3	8.2	1.5	—	5.7	—	3.0	89.7
Calveley (L)	1758	914	Cameroons	—	2.9	25.7	23.5	17.0	3.5	3.2	1.9	2.3	80.0
Henry (L)	1765	1542	Cameroons	—	.9	23.5	24.4	21.6	12.1	5.8	1.2	2.0	91.5
William (L)	1766	1483	Cameroons	—	3.6	18.2	25.2	11.0	11.8	4.0	1.0	.5	75.3
King of Prussia (L)	1767	2141	Cameroons	—	.9	19.3	28.1	19.9	13.8	.5	.7	—	83.2
William (L)	1768	1500	Cameroons	—	3.2	16.5	33.3	18.7	14.6	4.5	—	1.5	92.3
William (L)	1769	1578	Cameroons	—	2.7	15.8	23.4	20.5	8.8	4.3	.7	.7	76.9
King of Prussia (L)	1769	2799	Cameroons	—	1.0	13.1	30.0	19.1	18.0	1.2	.6	1.2	84.2
Henry (L)	1769	1912	Cameroons	—	—	18.3	28.9	24.0	13.3	.5	.6	.6	86.2
King of Prussia (L)	1771	2332	Cameroons	—	2.3	17.3	28.0	6.6	15.5	3.3	1.3	.4	74.7

Percentages of the total cargo

Badger (L)	1772	2677	Cameroons	—	2.0	16.7	31.0	18.6	13.1	1.5	.8	.8	84.5
King of Prussia (L)	1772	2411	Cameroons	—	3.1	15.3	31.1	6.4	14.5	4.4	.7	1.0	76.5
Badger (L)	1774	3168	Cameroons	—	4.4	12.7	20.7	12.8	29.0	1.8	1.0	.8	83.2
Badger (L)	1775	3633	Cameroons	—	4.0	10.5	18.5	10.1	35.2	2.7	1.1	—	82.1
Badger (L)	1776	6885	Cameroons	3.9	—	10.0	12.7	7.3	50.3	2.3	1.0	.5	88.0
Hawke (L)	1779	3380	Cameroons	4.6	1.8	13.8	16.1	13.6	26.4	2.8	.9	1.4	79.6
Hawke (L)	1780	2757	Cameroons	8.2	1.8	9.2	14.8	12.2	19.9	5.5	2.2	.4	74.2
Preston (L)	1780	2226	Cameroons	6.2	—	10.5	15.8	15.1	24.7	3.0	1.3	1.5	78.1
Hawke (L)	1781	3459	Cameroons	11.1	1.1	10.2	14.3	12.6	19.7	5.9	4.3	2.2	81.4
Preston (L)	1781	2879	Cameroons	5.9	—	8.6	11.9	15.9	33.5	2.4	1.4	1.4	81.0
Preston (L)	1783	4198	Cameroons	9.2	6.3	10.9	19.0	11.0	20.4	5.4	3.4	2.5	88.1
Henry (L)	1767	967	Gabon	—	7.5	8.6	29.6	9.6	—	12.7	—	6.5	74.5
Earl of Liverpool (L)	1799	5599	Angola	52.9	13.0	.6		.6		6.5	4.5	4.8	82.9
Ranger (L)	1767	3791	Cabinda	68.0	—	1.1	.3			5.5	4.5	4.5	83.9
Madampookata (L)	1783	1521	Cabinda	11.4	58.5	1.6		.2		6.9	5.9	4.6	89.1
Spitfire (L)	1795	4881	Congo River	51.7	12.1	.8		.3		6.5	4.9	7.1	83.4
Fortune (L)	1805	7268	Congo River	59.9	8.5	.5		.2		5.7	4.3	5.7	84.8
Nancy (L)	1774	2378	Ambriz	62.0	8.5	.8				6.3	5.5	4.6	87.7

Sources: James Rogers papers, PRO C 107/1–15; Trading Accounts of William Davenport, Davies–Davenport manuscripts, The University of Keele Library, Keele, N. Staffs. (I would like to thank the University of Keele and especially Mr. I. H. C. Fraser, the University Archivist, for allowing me to use this material); miscellaneous Slave Trade Papers, Liverpool City Museum; accounts and papers of David Tuohy and the accounts of Thomas Leyland, Local History Collection, Liverpool Public Library; the Dumbell papers and the Peet papers, Harold Cohen Library, The University of Liverpool (I am indebted to Mr. Perkins, the Curator of Special Collections, for allowing me to consult both these sets of papers); Logbook of the *Africa*, Bristol City Museum.

[a] Normally between 40 and 50% of the trade goods shipped to West Africa by outport merchants were bought on credit. Prices of goods in invoices were thus a mixture of credit and cash prices. Adjusting for this presents many problems, as the length of credit and rate of discount for cash offered by individual suppliers of trade goods varied considerably. Consequently no attempt was made to convert credit prices into cash price equivalents in the following breakdown of cargoes. In any case it is very doubtful if such an adjustment would alter in any significant way the picture suggested by the raw data presented here.

[b] The proportion of the total value of each cargo accounted for by these nine groups of commodities was in fact greater than that revealed here. Cargo invoices usually included goods such as beans, peas, and rice, which were used, not for trading purposes, but for feeding slaves in the middle passage.

[c] Over 10% of the *Sister's* cargo consisted of "silesias" or linen cloths, which with cowries, liquor, and tobacco were the staple items of trade at Whydah. Brazilian tobacco could be obtained from Portuguese ships on the coast. See Simone Berbain, *Le Comptoir Français de Juda au XVIIIe Siècle* (Paris, 1942), Chapter 4.

[d] Includes some coral.

[e] Trade at Old Calabar was often conducted by two (or more) vessels in tandem, a small vessel acting as a tender to the larger, supply vessel. Hence the linking together of several Old Calabar vessels in the table.

cottons were dispatched to the Cameroons but about half of most cargoes bound for Angola consisted of such goods. By contrast, hardly any beads were sent to Angola but they formed between 10 and 20% of cargoes destined for the Cameroons. Guns and gunpowder formed only a small part of cargoes shipped to Whydah, Benin, and the Cameroons but comprised around 20% of cargoes intended for Gambia and Bonny and between one-quarter and one-third of those for New Calabar and the Windward Coast.

Interregional variations in African demand were usually more subtle, however, than this crude picture suggests. As an example one might briefly look at shipments of hardware. Copper, brass, and pewter goods were major items of trade at Sierra Leone and the Windward Coast and throughout the whole Bight of Biafra; yet significant differences in this hardware trade can be detected. A large proportion of hardware shipments to Bonny and Calabar in the Bight of Biafra consisted of copper rods whereas shipments to Sierra Leone, the Windward Coast, and the Cameroons and Gabon consisted largely of brass pans, basins, and copper kettles. One can discover similar interregional variations in other broad categories of goods, notably textiles as well as firearms and gunpowder. For instance, the number of kegs obtained from each barrel of gunpowder shipped from England varied widely from one area to another on the coast.

How does this broad picture of regionally related cargo assortments in the second half of the eighteenth century compare with earlier or later periods? Did cargo assortments change markedly or did they remain fairly constant over time?

Before attempting to answer such questions it is necessary to draw attention to some problems in making intertemporal comparisons. In the period before 1750, in particular, the information about interregional differences in African demand tends to be rather limited and therefore superficial. Furthermore certain areas of English slave-trading activity, such as the Cameroons, really developed only during the second half of the eighteenth century. The major difficulty, however, is that evidence gleaned from merchants' invoices is not strictly comparable with most of the other, often literary or archaeological, evidence of African consumption patterns. As this latter problem has an important bearing on later discussion, it is necessary to digress slightly at this point in order to consider it in some detail.

Invoices of cargoes shipped from Europe provide the best available estimate of eighteenth-century West African consumption patterns. It is worth emphasizing, however, that such invoices reflect African demands only imperfectly. Primarily they indicate the pattern of investments by merchants across a range of goods, and such investments were undoubtedly influenced by supply factors as well as African demands. Given the very diverse origins of trade goods shipped to West Africa, many factors on the supply side could affect merchants' investment decisions. A further and possibly even more significant complication arises from the fact that the size and proportion of merchants' investments in particular sorts of goods did not necessarily reflect the purchasing power of those goods in terms of slaves or other commodities in West Africa. African tastes clearly diverged in many vital ways from those in Europe, and consequently the valuations placed by Africans upon various sorts of goods could differ sharply from European valuations.

The last point can be illustrated to some extent by constructing sterling exchange rates for various trade goods bartered for slaves in West Africa. As is well known, slaves were usually paid for by bundles of goods, and in order to facilitate trade it was normal by the eighteenth century to value both slaves and the goods exchanged for them in some recognized local unit of account, such as the bar, the copper, the cloth, or the ounce trade. Where one has details about the prime cost of goods (as is the case with invoices) and their rating in local units of account, it is possible to ascertain rates of exchange for such goods in West Africa. In Table 12.3 the exchange rate in sterling for some trade goods selected from cargoes shipped to various parts of West Africa during the eighteenth century is given. It should be emphasized that Table 12.3 is only meant to be illustrative, but it suggests that due to differences in African and European tastes the purchasing power of trade goods shipped to West Africa was not necessarily identical to their relative weighting in merchants' invoices.

Two specific examples might be cited in order to reinforce this important point. At several places on the coast, including Gambia, the Windward Coast, the Gold Coast, and Bonny, gunpowder appears to have been a very advantageous trade good from the English point of view. The prime cost, calculated in sterling, of a bar or trade ounce of gunpowder was usually lower than that of most other goods at these places. It was hardly surprising, therefore, that the master of a Liverpool vessel should have reported from the Gold Coast in 1765 that gunpowder was "an Article on which there is the greatest Gains of any in the Trade."[22] By contrast, brass pans, copper kettles, and "neptunes" (large, fairly flat basins), which were also in quite regular demand, tended to be rather poor trade goods as far as the English were concerned. The prime cost in sterling per unit of account of such goods was normally relatively high in the eighteenth century and seems to have remained so even in the early nineteenth century, a fact that prompted John Adams to write in 1823 that brass pans, kettles, and neptunes "are

[22] PRO CO 388/53, L1 54.

TABLE 12.3

Prime Cost in Shillings[a] per Unit of Account of Some Selected Trade Goods at Various West African Trading Centers during the Eighteenth Century

1721 Angola		1728 Annamaboe		1773 Gambia		1773 Whydah		1774 New Calabar		1776 Old Calabar		1787 Windward Coast		1797 Bonny	
Goods	Piece	Goods	Ounce	Goods	Bar	Goods	Ounce	Goods	Bar	Goods	Copper	Goods	Bar	Goods	Bar
Brass pans	18.2	Buccaneer guns	48.0	Brass pans	4.2	Knives	52	Neptunes	8.5	Manchester photaes[b]	1.1	Virginia tobacco	3.5	Neptunes	9.2
Gunpowder	14.4	Perpetuanas	44.8	Blue bafts[b]	3.4	Linen	44	Manchester photaes	4.4	Romals[b]	.9	Bejutapauls[b]	3.3	Bar iron	4.5
Brawls[b]	11.0	Blue ells	40.0	Jamaica rum	3.2	Cowries	32	Copper rods	3.8	Copper rods	.9	Bar iron	3.2	Chelloes[b]	4.2
Photaes[b]	8.8	Brass pans	40.0	Bar iron	3.1	Gunpowder	31	Romals[b]	3.3	Pewter basins	.7	Pewter basins	3.0	Long cloths[b]	3.6
Trading guns	8.3	Trading guns	40.0	Guns	2.1	Handkerchiefs	30	Bar iron	2.8	Danish guns	.6	Romals[b]	2.5	Manilloes	3.3
Pewter basins	7.7	Chintz[b]	34.7	Irish linen	1.8	Bar iron	26	Rum	2.3	Brandy	.5	Brass kettles	2.3	Spanish guns	3.1
Blue bafts[b]	7.3	Bejutapauls[b]	34.0	Beads	1.1	Tobacco pipes	24	Muskets	2.2	Tobacco	.1	Brass pans	2.0	Bonny guns	2.1
Nicanees[b]	6.5	Tallow	32.0	Gunpowder	1.0	Siamoise[b]	17	Brandy	1.8	Arrangoes	.1	Brandy	2.0	Beads	1.7
Spirits	4.7	Gunpowder	22.5	Tobacco	.5	Brandy	15	Barley corn beads	1.7	Salt	.1	Gunpowder	1.1	Gunpowder	1.4

Sources: 1721, John Atkins, A Voyage to Guinea, Brasil and the West Indies (London, 1735), pp. 160–166, with some price data from the accounts of the King Solomon, July 1720, reprinted in Elizabeth Donnan, ed., Documents Illustrative of the Slave Trade to America, 4 vols. (Washington, 1935), vol. 2 pp. 244–246; 1728, from the accounts of the Judith, reprinted in Donnan, ed., Documents, vol. 2, pp. 362–383; 1773, Gambia, accounts of the Aston, Liverpool City Museum; 1773, Whydah, accounts of Le Roi Dahomet, in Berbain, Comptoir Français, Appendix 5; 1774, 1776, Logbook of the Africa, Bristol City Museum; 1787, accounts of James Cleveland with Richard Rogers, 19 February [1787], PRO C 107/1, with some price data derived from cargo invoices contained in the same volume; 1797, cargo abstract for the Earl of Liverpool, Peet papers, Harold Cohen Library, University of Liverpool.

[a] Except for Whydah in 1773, where prime costs are given in livres.

[b] Indicates East Indian textiles.

considered losing articles of trade"; but they were in such general demand that they were "highly necessary to complete an assorted cargo for Africa."[23] The very fact that the English had to trade in such articles is an indication perhaps of the major influence that Africans were able to exert over commercial relationships on the coast. In addition, the existence of differences in commodity exchange rates emphasizes the critical role that masters of slave ships had to play in the trade, for merchants were forced to trust in their ability to negotiate the most favorable terms of trade possible on the coast.[24]

The significance of African tastes and exchange rates for trade goods is something to which we must return later; but to take up first the question posed previously, how did interregional patterns of cargo assortments in the late eighteenth century compare with those of earlier or later years?

The number of points of continuity over often long periods of time in regional cargo assortments is perhaps surprisingly large in view of the quite common belief that eighteenth-century African consumers were fickle, irrational, and easily attracted to novelties. Only a few points of continuity can be mentioned here. Slave trading on the Loango Coast evidently required substantial quantities of Indian cottons throughout the eighteenth century.[25] On the Gold Coast, English half says and green long ells, popular in the early eighteenth century, were still major trade goods at least as late as the 1820s;[26] and spread-eagle dollars were apparently as much in demand among Africans at Gambia in the 1770s as they had been in the early 1730s.[27] Such evidence gives some support to the observation of one recent author that African traders "always preferred old and tried goods to new ones."[28]

Nevertheless African tastes were not immutable. For sometimes obscure reasons, shifts in demand occurred and were reflected in both coastal exchange rates for goods and cargoes shipped out from England. It was not unknown for articles with apparently secure markets to lose their appeal to Africans. Such was the case with the English serge called perpetuana, large

[23] John Adams, *Remarks on the Country Extending from Cape Palmas to the River Congo* (London, 1823), p. 263.

[24] The important role of the master is also discussed in my unpublished paper, "The Slave Merchants of the Outports," presented to the Organization of American Historians' Conference (Chicago, April 1973).

[25] Phyllis Martin, *The External Trade of the Loango Coast 1576–1870* (Oxford, 1972), p. 112.

[26] PRO CO 388/25, S 70; CO 388/45, Dd 56. Worsteds comprised part of the cargoes destined for the Gold Coast and Annamaboe listed in Table 12.2. On the 1820s see Adams, *Remarks,* p. 259.

[27] Francis Moore, *Travels into the Inland Parts of Africa* (London, 1738), p. 45. Spread-eagle dollars constituted between 5 and 7.5% of cargoes bound for Gambia listed in Table 12.2.

[28] K. Y. Daaku, *Trade and Politics on the Gold Coast 1600–1720* (Oxford, 1970), pp. 23–24.

quantities of which were exported to Africa in Bristol slave ships before 1730. By this time, however, the popularity of "perpets" was already declining, notably on the Gold Coast, and by 1750 they had largely disappeared from Bristol cargoes for Africa.[29] By contrast, demand for other sorts of traditional goods such as India textiles and gunpowder continued to expand in both old and new markets throughout the century. In addition new commodities such as Manchester goods, including imitations of Indian cottons, rum, and tobacco were successfully introduced into exchanges at several places on the coast. The net effect of such developments was to alter fundamentally the character of trade in some regions. It would appear, for instance, that the Gambia trade changed very noticeably between the end of the seventeenth century and the third quarter of the eighteenth. Whereas the Royal African Company shipped large amounts of bar iron and few India textiles to Gambia before 1700, a substantial part of the cargoes that the prominent Liverpool firm of John Knight and Company dispatched to the same place in about 1770 consisted of India and Manchester cottons (mainly India), with only small quantities of bar iron.[30] Likewise, the introduction of tobacco and rum into coastal transactions helped to bring about a transformation in the Gold Coast trade around 1750 and possibly also in the trade at Sierra Leone and the Windward Coast later in the century.

It is impossible in this chapter to attempt an explanation of either interregional differences in African consumption patterns or the shifts in them that evidently took place. Professor Curtin's recent study of Senegambia has demonstrated that any satisfactory explanation of African patterns of demand in the era of the slave trade can prove very problematical, even within a relatively confined region such as Senegambia.[31] Any explanation must look beyond obvious economic factors such as regional resource endowments, changes in incomes, or movements in relative prices of imports, and incorporate differences and adjustments in the internal social and political structure of West African "states." In view of the variety of resource endowments and inner structures of eighteenth-century African political entities, it would be misleading to offer highly generalized explanations of African consumption patterns. It may, nevertheless, prove useful to try to trace some of the possible implications of differences and changes in such consumption patterns for the eighteenth-century English slave trade.

---

[29] PRO Exchequer K. R., Series E 190, Bristol Port Books; Marion Johnson, "The Ounce in Eighteenth-Century West African Trade," *Journal of African History,* vol. 7, no. 2, 1966, p. 200.

[30] Davies, *Royal African Company,* p. 234; Curtin, *Economic Change,* p. 313; Miscellaneous Slave Trade Papers, Liverpool City Museum.

[31] Curtin, *Economic Change,* Chapter 8.

ENGLISH TRADING ACTIVITY

At the outset certain basic characteristics of eighteenth-century English trading activity on the African coast need to be emphasized. First, the eighteenth-century trade was carried out very largely by private "firms" which, unlike the earlier chartered companies, were not expected to represent national interests by maintaining some sort of permanent presence (e.g., forts) on any part of the coast. Eighteenth-century firms were thus probably more at liberty than their predecessors to pursue trade at whatever locality on the coast offered the best prospects for profit making. The number of partners in these firms varied considerably, and membership in them was by no means stable.[32] Second, English traders bought slaves in competition with traders of other countries. The intensity of this competition fluctuated greatly over time and between regions on the coast. Third, the English were usually active traders along the whole West African coast from Gambia in the north to the River Congo in the south and were responsible for developing some new sources of slave supply such as the Cameroons. Finally, substantial fluctuations seem to have occurred in the regional origins of slaves taken off the coast in English ships. Such fluctuations, however, could not disguise the significant fact that during the course of the eighteenth century the center of gravity of English activity on the coast tended to move intermittently but quite discernibly southward, away from Gambia, the Windward Coast and the Gold Coast—though these areas still remained suppliers of large numbers of slaves for English ships in the last quarter of the century—and toward the Bight of Biafra and the coast of Congo–Angola.

As with African consumption patterns, explaining shifts in the distribution of English trading activity on the West African coast presents many problems and requires an appreciation of many interrelated factors. It may be suggested, however, that part of any overall explanation of these movements may lie in variations in the level of international competition for slave supplies and differences in interregional prices of slaves, both of which

---

[32] One might expect that the fluid internal structure of slave-trading firms caused some problems in establishing stable relationships with suppliers of trade goods. The likelihood of such problems was considerably reduced, however, by the fact that during the eighteenth century much of the routine organization of slaving ventures became the responsibility of one of the partners, who was usually known as the "ship's husband." Within the whole group of ships' husbands at any one time there existed a small elite who regularly participated in the trade in a substantial way. It was through the person of the ship's husband, therefore, that steady contacts with manufacturers and suppliers of trade goods could be established and maintained.

were determined to some degree by the nature of African demands for trade goods. Combined with other factors, changes in the levels of competition and price differentials for slaves affected the profitability of slave trading in the various regions of West Africa, which in turn was reflected in the regional distribution of English commercial activity on the coast.

In order to develop this thesis more fully it is first necessary to understand how prices paid for slaves on the coast were determined. English merchants usually estimated the cost of slaves in terms of the prime cost of the goods traded for them. Looked at in this way the price of a slave was determined by the following variable factors:

1. The value of the slave expressed in terms of the prevailing local unit of account (e.g., ounce, bar, copper, piece)
2. The assortment or "basket" of goods exchanged for the slave
3. The rating of each item traded for slaves in terms of the local unit of account
4. The prime cost in sterling of each of the goods exchanged

Broadly speaking, the main determinant of the valuation placed by African middlemen on slaves was the general supply and demand situation for slaves at each market on the coast at any particular time. The cost of the slave to the English trader, however, depended also upon the prime cost in sterling of the local unit of account (i.e., the rate of exchange between sterling and bars, ounces, etc.). Contemporaries were well aware that this might fluctuate considerably from one series of transactions to another, and historians attempting to convert coastal units of account into their sterling equivalents have quite correctly tried to adjust exchange rates in accordance with the best evidence available.[33] The basic causes, however, of movements in exchange rates between sterling and coastal accounting units have not always been thoroughly explored, and so their wider significance for the economics of slave trading has usually been missed.

Obviously the prime cost in sterling of the ounce, bar, or whatever, might be affected by variations in the initial costs of trade goods in England. Exchange rates, however, also seem to have been influenced by African tastes as reflected in the assortment and rating of the goods exchanged for slaves. This is suggested by the prime cost in sterling of the ounce, bar, or copper value of various commodities listed in Table 12.3. A particular set of transactions might help, however, to illustrate the point more clearly. In 1728, the *Judith*, a London vessel, traded at Sestos, Bassam, and An-

---

[33] See Johnson, "Ounce," pp. 200–202; R. N. Bean, "The British Trans-Atlantic Slave Trade, 1650–1775," unpublished doctoral thesis (University of Washington, 1971), pp. 125–131.

TABLE 12.4
Purchases of Adult Male Slaves by the *Judith* at Sestos, Bassam, and Annamaboe, 1728

	Sestos	Bassam	Annamaboe
Cost per man (ounces, ackies)	3, 7	5, 7	6, 8
Total cost (shillings)	129.8	153.5	287.3
Prime cost (shillings) per ounce	39.4	29.6	44.1

namaboe.[34] At each place the *Judith* bought adult male slaves valued in ounces and ackies, the local unit of account. Three transactions, one from each place, are set out in Table 12.4. The crucial point about these three transactions is the notable difference in prime costs (sterling) per ounce or sterling–ounce exchange rates. As in this instance the commodities traded for slaves came from the same cargo, the explanation of this difference lies in the assortment of goods exchanged and their rating by local dealers in slaves.

Once it is recognized that African tastes could exert quite a substantial influence over prices paid for slaves it follows that the competitive position on the coast of any group of merchants depended upon its accessibility to low-cost supplies of standard trade goods or its ability to shift African consumption patterns to its advantage. It is widely assumed that Liverpool merchants possessed advantages over their domestic and overseas rivals in both these respects chiefly because of their close proximity to expanding industrial centers in Lancashire. The fact that even Liverpool merchants had to resort, to some extent, to foreign supplies of African trade goods throughout the century should make one wary of accepting this connection too uncritically. Nevertheless, on the question of cheap and well-assorted supplies of trade goods, English merchants may have secured advantages over some of their rivals by the end of the century. In 1790 William Roper, master of a ship owned by James Rogers and Company of Bristol, wrote to his owners from Sierra Leone that, though French vessels were paying £24–26 sterling for slaves, this "does not interfere with the Cargo's the English Vessels bring out in general as the Barr Trade is such an unfair trade[.] We can pay as many barrs with Eighteen pounds as they can with

[34] See Donnan, *Documents*, vol. 2, pp. 362–365, 373–378. For a discussion of sterling–bar exchange rates in Senegambia, see Curtin, *Economic Change*, Chapter 6. I should, perhaps, point out that I had reached my conclusions about the significance of coastal exchange rates before I had an opportunity to see Professor Curtin's valuable study.

Twenty Eight pounds Sterling."[35] Among English merchants those from Liverpool seem to have been able to obtain the best and cheapest assortments. Thus masters of ships owned by Rogers and Company of Bristol in the late 1780s frequently complained that the invoice prices of their trade goods were high compared to those obtained by Liverpool men, and that Liverpool ships also had more "small barrs."[36]

FOREIGN COMPETITORS

Even in the late eighteenth century, however, English merchants did not invariably possess superior access to supplies of trade goods for Africa. This is suggested, amongst other things, by the continued strength of French competition, in peacetime at least, on the Loango Coast, where the staple African demand was for India cotton piece goods or imitations of them. Periodic threats to supplies of Indian wares led to the growth of production of imitations in both England and France during the second half of the eighteenth century. Surprisingly perhaps, it would appear that French manufacturers based at Nantes and Rouen were able to produce imitations more satisfactorily and cheaply than their Lancashire rivals.[37]

More suggestive still was the expansion of Rhode Island's interest in the slave trade in the third quarter of the century. Recent research has indicated that the scale of Rhode Island's involvement in the slave trade and its significance for the colony's economy have both been exaggerated.[38] Despite this, however, even the limited participation of Rhode Island merchants may have had important repercussions for traders of other countries. It seems clear, for instance, that the growth of Rhode Island participation coincided with changes in the pattern of trading first on the Gold Coast and later in areas further to the west and north. Such changes included the exchange of gold for slaves on the Gold Coast and the emergence of rum and tobacco, notably Brazilian tobacco, as major articles of trade. It would be foolish to pretend that all these changes were occasioned by the intrusion of Rhode Island vessels into the trade, but the rise of the rum trade at least seems to have worked to the disadvantage of English merchants, and may have helped to render trading at the Gold Coast, Windward Coast, and Sierra Leone less profitable than it had been earlier.

[35] PRO C 107/5, bundle 14, 23 February 1790, William Roper to James Rogers.

[36] PRO C 107/13, 20 June 1786, Capt. Thomas Walker to James Rogers.

[37] Berbain, *Comptoir Francais*, p. 86.

[38] J. F. Shepherd and G. M. Walton, *Shipping, Maritime Trade and the Economic Development of Colonial North America* (Cambridge, 1972), pp. 49–50, 97.

The growth of Rhode Island's interest in slave trading is notable for several reasons. At present our understanding of the economics of Rhode Island slave trading is limited,[39] but certain features of this trade seem reasonably clear and are worth stressing in the context of this chapter. First, the expansion of Rhode Island's trade occurred mainly in the mid-eighteenth century when other groups of traders were already well established on the African coast. Second, Rhode Island merchants seem to have concentrated their trade at Sierra Leone, the Windward Coast, and the Gold Coast, areas normally thought of as producing slaves of the highest quality. Third, this trade was founded largely on the exchange of only one commodity—New England rum—in contrast to the assortments of goods that other traders exchanged for slaves. Thus, as the Rhode Island trade expanded, enormous quantities of New England rum found their way to the African coast; in 1791, for instance, the master of a Bristol slave ship reported from Sierra Leone that there were 80,000 gallons of rum for sale on that coast alone.[40]

Why Africans in areas frequented by Rhode Island ships developed such a partiality for New England rum is uncertain; it was possibly related to income changes brought about by the slave trade itself in coastal regions or to shifts in the power structure of the more remote inland areas that supplied most of the slaves shipped off the coast.[41] However one tries to explain it, African demand for New England rum along the Gold Coast and the Windward Coast seems to have become so great that it gave Rhode Island traders a marked competitive edge over their English rivals. This is attested by the accounts of the *Adventure* sloop of Rhode Island in 1774.[42] In March of that year the *Adventure* slaved at Cape Coast. Adult males cost 14 ounces 1 acky each, and for these the *Adventure*'s master paid 225 gallons of rum per head. As rum cost 15 pence sterling per gallon in New England, the sterling–ounce rate of exchange in these transactions was only 20.4 shillings. The sterling–ounce rate for English traders on the Gold Coast was thought to have been around 40 shillings at this time,[43] in which case African demand for rum provided Rhode Islanders with nearly 100% coastal bargaining advantage over English traders. To judge from the un-

[39] It is improving, however; see V. B. Platt, " 'And Don't Forget the Guinea Voyage': The Slave Trade of Aaron Lopez of Newport," *William and Mary Quarterly*, 3rd series, vol. 32, no. 4, 1975, pp. 601–618.

[40] PRO C 107/14, 18 December 1791, Thomas Walker to James Rogers.

[41] Cf. Curtin, *Economic Change*: "Rising brandy imports indicate a shift in power within Senegambian societies, as the ceddo and the military generally increased in wealth and power at the expense of the clerics and the Muslim peasantry [p. 323]."

[42] V. W. Crane, ed., *A Rhode Island Slaver: Trade Book of the Sloop Adventure 1773–1774* (Providence, 1922).

[43] *Journal of the Commissioners of Trade and Plantations, 1776–82* (London, 1938), p. 131.

happy reports from masters of Bristol slave ships on more northerly coasts in the 1780s a similar situation had arisen there also.

It would be premature to infer from such advantages in coastal bargaining that Rhode Island merchants must have made very substantial profits from their slave-trading ventures, for the financial outcome of slaving voyages depended also on many other factors, including shipping costs, the rate of slave mortality in the Atlantic crossing, and the ability to recover the proceeds of slave sales quickly and safely from the West Indies. It is quite conceivable that Rhode Islanders suffered from certain handicaps in these respects. Shipping costs were possibly high in view of the small size of Rhode Island slave ships and the high wage rates prevailing in the colonies. Furthermore, Rhode Island merchants seem to have experienced remittance problems in the West Indies largely because they did not possess the close ties with London financiers that Liverpool merchants had been able to establish and that proved so essential to the smooth functioning of the bill remittance system.[44] As a result of such difficulties it is not impossible that the merchants of the New England colony required some form of advantage in bargaining on the African coast in order to force a profitable entry into the trade in the first instance.

The favorable exchange rate obtained by Rhode Island traders in coastal dealings seems to have had important repercussions for English merchants. The increase of Rhode Island shipping on the Gold Coast in the third quarter of the century coincided with a large volume of English complaints about low profits or even losses in that sector of the trade.[45] It was alleged that this depression in profits was due to the rising price of slaves on the Gold Coast, which was attributable in turn to disruptions in the flow of slave supplies to the coast, changes in the character of the gold trade, and the illegal dealings of factors residing at the forts of the Company of Merchants trading to Africa. Although it would appear that contemporary allegations had some validity, the analysis earlier of coastal exchange rates suggests that shifts in the commodity structure of imports may also have had some relevance. Here one includes not only New England rum but Brazilian tobacco, which like rum became very popular on the Gold Coast and elsewhere after 1750 and seems to have acquired a very favorable rate of exchange.[46] As English merchants were less fortunately situated than their

---

[44] Some of these problems are raised in Platt, "Aaron Lopez."

[45] *Journal of the Commissioners, 1776–82*, p. 92.

[46] As early as 1754 Thomas Melvil, Governor at Cape Coast Castle, expressed fears about the possible repercussions for English trade of the introduction of Brazilian tobacco as a trade good on the Gold Coast. PRO CO 388/46, Ee 51. An Anglo–Portugese trade in Brazilian tobacco grew up in Senegambia, Upper Guinea, and the Gold Coast during the second half of the eighteenth century. PRO CO 267/13, 25 July 1766, Charles O'Hara to the Lords of the Committee of Trade and Plantations; BT6/6, f. 36.

Rhode Island and Portuguese rivals to secure supplies of these particular commodities, their ability to continue to pursue a profitable trade on the Gold Coast was thus impaired.[47]

ENGLISH EFFORTS AT EXPANSION

Events on the Gold Coast and adjacent areas, about mid-century, seem to have enhanced English interest in developing further the slave trading potential of other regions. Throughout the century there occurred fluctuations in the regional origin of slaves exported from Africa in English ships. Confronted at any particular center of trade by a reduction of slave supply or growing competition from other shippers, English, particularly Liverpool, merchants appear to have responded by attempting to open up new frontiers of slave supply or to improve the slave output from other existing channels. Thus, given the problems of the Gold Coast trade after 1750, it was probably more than a coincidence that some adjustment took place at this time in the regional distribution of English trading activity.[48] In the late 1760s and early 1770s there was a very pronounced growth of English shipping destined for the Windward Coast, one of the oldest centers of English slave trading in West Africa. This increase in interest in the Windward Coast proved short-lived, however, for by the 1780s English trade there had declined considerably. More significant in the long run were English efforts to expand the output of slaves from regions to the east and south of the Gold Coast. By 1750 English merchants had already established commercial contacts with the Bight of Biafra, but these were expanded further in the second half of the century. Trade at places such as Bonny and Old Calabar grew to unprecedented heights, and new and permanent relationships were developed with the Cameroons and Gabon. English advances further south beyond the Bight of Biafra tended, however, to be more spasmodic. In peacetime English slave trading on the

[47] It was possible, of course, to obtain supplies of rum and tobacco from Rhode Island and Portuguese ships on the coast. Such exchanges could not always be guaranteed, however, and in any case may only have been secured on payment of very high prices for either rum or tobacco. Berbain, *Comptoir français*, p. 68. The whole question of trade between non-Africans on the coast is in need of further detailed study.

[48] The following brief discussion of the regional distribution of English exports draws on P. D. Curtin, *The Atlantic Slave Trade: A Census* (Madison, 1969), p. 150; Roger Anstey, "The Volume and Profitability of the British Slave Trade, 1761–1807," in S. L. Engerman and E. D. Genovese, eds., *Race and Slavery in the Western Hemisphere: Quantitative Studies* (Princeton, 1975), p. 13. Curtin's data appear to underestimate the scale of English involvement in slave trading in the Bight of Biafra before 1730.

Loango Coast was generally limited in the face of powerful French and
Dutch competition, but with the sharp decline of French clearances for
Africa during general outbreaks of warfare in Europe it expanded
vigorously.[40]

In their efforts to expand commerce with these other regions the English
encountered difficulties apart from French or Dutch competition. The
tempo of trade on the Windward Coast was usually slow; here the slave
supply system was relatively unsophisticated, with cargoes being made up of
a large number of small and irregular consignments of slaves. Thus ships
engaged in this trade ran the risk of severe delays in gathering together their
cargoes. Merchants trading to the Bight of Biafra were confronted by other
sorts of problems. Slaves taken from the Bight of Biafra suffered on average
higher levels of mortality in the middle passage than those from other
regions on the west coast. Furthermore planters in the New World regularly
expressed their dislike of slaves brought from this region as well as from
Angola. Yet, despite these difficulties, it appears that at times levels of
profit could be earned from trading to these regions that compared favora-
bly with those achieved from the Gold Coast trade around 1770. This is
suggested by the trading accounts of William Davenport of Liverpool who
had extensive dealings with Old Calabar and the Cameroons during the
third quarter of the eighteenth century. Davenport's profits from his Old
Calabar and Cameroons ventures fluctuated widely from one voyage to
another, but they averaged 7% per annum from 37 Calabar voyages and
22% from 26 ventures to the Cameroons.[50] Achieved at a time of repeated
complaints about the Gold Coast trade, such profits, notably those from his
Cameroons voyages, were no doubt regarded with considerable satisfaction
by Davenport, particularly as he was one of the pioneers of English trade
with the Cameroons.

The causes of regional differences in profit margins and the intermittent
though discernible southward movement of English slave trading in West
Africa are very complex. Contemporaries sometimes suggested, however,
that slaves cost less in the Bight of Biafra and at Angola than elsewhere on
the coast but were sold in the West Indies at prices only slightly below those
received for "better" slaves from areas such as the Gold Coast. The extraordinary profits said to result from this situation were thought to have been a
major factor influencing the distribution of English trading activity along the

[49] PRO CO 388/43, Bb 88; British Parliamentary Papers (BPP), vol. 26, 1789, 646a,
Report on the Trade to Africa, evidence of James Penny; Martin, *External Trade,* pp. 83, 86.

[50] Based on calculations in my "Profits in the Liverpool Slave Trade: The Accounts of
William Davenport, 1757 to 1784," in Roger Anstey and P. E. H. Hair, eds., *Liverpool, the
African Slave Trade and Abolition* (for the Lancashire and Cheshire Historic Society, occasional
series, no. 2, Liverpool, 1976), pp. 60–90.

West African coast.[51] At present it is difficult to fully assess this argument. It is clear that profit margins were also affected by factors additional to those mentioned by contemporaries; these included investment levels, voyage times, slave mortality rates, and the credit requirements of planters in the New World. We lack detailed information over long periods of time about most of these factors. More information is perhaps available about slave prices in West Africa and the Americas, but it does not appear to be abundant or reliable enough to allow one even to establish the existence of regional differentials in slave prices, much less to estimate their extent and duration.[52]

Despite the unsatisfactory nature of existing price data, there are still some grounds for believing that contemporary claims about the existence of regional price differences were valid. One is persuaded to some extent by the fact that contemporaries were so consistent in their views on this matter. Even more significantly, it is now becoming possible to distinguish differences in commercial procedures at the various coastal trading centers, which may have contributed to the creation of price differentials. The earlier analysis of African consumption patterns suggests that they may have had some effect. There is also evidence to suggest that the efficiency of slave supply systems varied from one trading center to another. Information available for the 1790s, for instance, indicates that the supplying of slaves to vessels waiting on the coast was most efficiently carried out at Angola and certain places in the Bight of Biafra, notably Bonny, and was least efficiently conducted on the Windward Coast and at Sierra Leone.[53] On average over twice as many slaves were delivered each day to ships stationed at the former places compared to the latter. Moreover, other evidence gives the impression that the picture revealed by the data of the 1790s was probably not untypical of earlier periods.[54]

[51] PRO CO 152/27, 23 January 1751, Memorial of the Governor, Council and Assembly of Antigua to the Lords Commissioners for Trade and Plantations; BPP, vol. 26, 1789, 646a, Report on the Trade to Africa, Part 4, account no. 25. For supporting evidence of price variations in West Africa, based on levels of voyage investments and the intended numbers of slaves to be purchased, see PRO CO 388/45, Dd 4, which is discussed in my unpublished thesis, "The Bristol Slave Trade in the Eighteenth Century" (University of Manchester, 1969), p. 103.

[52] A considerable amount of price data is collected together in Bean, "Trans-Atlantic Slave Trade." Appendixes A and B. His price series for West Africa, however, is based heavily on information drawn from Upper Guinea and the Gold Coast; he has relatively little price data for the Loango Coast and, even more importantly, the Bight of Biafra.

[53] Based on data derived from a House of Lords return, order date 10 July 1799, House of Lords Record Office. I am very grateful to Professor Roger Anstey for allowing me to see his transcript of this valuable document.

[54] See, for instance, various comments on coastal trading methods in BPP, vol. 26, 1789, 646a, Report on the Trade to Africa, Part 1.

It is not inconceivable, therefore, that West African social mores and business institutions and procedures helped to establish regional differences in slave prices, and that these in turn affected the levels of profits to be derived from trade at the various commercial centers on the coast. In the present state of our knowledge it would be obviously premature and unwise to try to push such arguments too far. The relationship between prices paid for slaves and rates of profit attained was by no means as clear-cut as eighteenth-century observers implied: Given the well-recognized risk of higher slave mortality in the middle passage on ships that had traded in the Bight of Biafra, greater efficiency in the supply of slaves and lower slave prices were perhaps necessary before merchants could seriously consider pursuing trade in that region.

A NEW APPROACH

It is quite clear that the preceding analysis has raised many more questions than it has supplied answers. Nevertheless one point of some general significance does seem to have emerged. Until quite recently the study of the English slave trade tended to progress within a highly insular and aggregative analytical framework. This sort of approach had unfortunate consequences, for it proved especially conducive to the creation of a picture of the English slave trade that was both too simple and too static. Our brief examination of English exports to West Africa in the eighteenth century suggests that a different framework of analysis, using a more disaggregated and comparative approach, may prove more rewarding as a means of improving our understanding of the slave trade as a business enterprise. Central to such an approach is the need for greater awareness of regional differences and peculiarities in West Africa. At every place on the coast trade was subject to an almost unique combination of economic conditions which ultimately derived from variations in human and geographical circumstances. And in the last resort it is only through a proper appreciation of these variations and their economic significance that one can begin to comprehend not only the ever-changing character of eighteenth-century slave trading but the course of West African economic development in general.

ACKNOWLEDGMENTS

I wish to thank three of my colleagues at the University of Hull, Bernard Eccleston, Bernard Foley and Donald Woodward, for their perceptive and very helpful comments on an earlier version of this chapter. Three discussants at the Colby Conference, Dr. Joseph Inikori and Professors Patrick Manning and Walter Minchinton, offered useful criticisms. No blame can be attached to any of these for any remaining errors of fact or opinion.

13

The Triangular Trade Revisited

WALTER E. MINCHINTON

Recent research into the history of the transatlantic slave trade has tended to concentrate on the "numbers game," on the volume and direction and timing of the slave exports from Africa;[1] but there are also problems in the varied ways in which that trade was organized by different countries, between different destinations, and over time, which deserve to be investigated. One such question is the extent to which the slave trade was a triangular trade. Although the term "triangular trade" as attached to the African slave trade has acquired pejorative overtones—"this disreputable trade"—this would provide little reason for spending more time in discussing what meaning should be attached to it. It is worth further consideration because such an examination will cast light not only on the organization of the trade but on its profitability. First of all, however, it must be noted that there was nothing distinctive or unique in the fact that some parts of the Atlantic slave trade have been regarded as roundabout trades. Tramp steamers still engage in roundabout trades, while in the eighteenth and

---

[1] See, for example, Philip Curtin, *The Atlantic Slave Trade: A Census* (Madison, 1969).

nineteenth centuries the Atlantic was crisscrossed by a series of multi-lateral trades—England–Newfoundland–Portugal and back to England; England–South Carolina–Hamburg–Stockholm and back; and England–New England–West Indies and back, to mention only some of those trades originating in England. Triangularity is a consequence of physical imbalances in flows of goods.

How early the term *the triangular trade* was applied to the English African slave trade has not been ascertained definitively.[2] About 40 years ago, however, Charles MacInnes wrote in his *England and Slavery*[3] that "after the Restoration a great triangular trade developed between England, the West Coast of Africa and the West Indies or the continental colonies." Ten years later Eric Williams used the phrase in a chapter heading in his classic discussion *Capitalism and Slavery,*[4] although not quite in the same sense as MacInnes since Williams seemed little concerned with the actual organization of trade and had almost nothing to say about the third leg of the triangle as far as the slaving vessels were concerned. From monographs, moreover, the phrase found its way into the textbooks. Thus T. S. Ashton stated that "cloth, firearms, hardware and trinkets were sent to Africa and exchanged for slaves, who were shipped to the West Indies to pay for the luxuries and raw material which constituted the final cargo in this disreputable, triangular trade."[5] The same generation of historians in America held that the slave trade from New England was similarly conducted on a triangular basis.[6] Except for the Netherlands there has been little study of the question. In the case, however, of the Dutch Middelburgsche Commercie Compagnie, it has been shown that a cargo purchased with the proceeds of the slaves was always brought home.[7]

[2] The *Oxford English Dictionary* contains no reference to "the triangular trade" in this sense. The earliest American reference to the use of the word "triangle" in relation to this trade appears to be in Charles W. Taussig, *Rum, Romance and Rebellion* (New York, 1928). See Gilman M. Ostrander, "The Making of the Triangular Trade Myth," *William and Mary Quarterly*, 3rd series, vol. 30, 1973, p. 641.

[3] Charles MacInnes, *England and Slavery* (Bristol, 1934), p. 39.

[4] Eric Williams, *Capitalism and Slavery* (Chapel Hill, 1944), pp. 51ff.

[5] Thomas S. Ashton, *The Industrial Revolution* (Oxford, 1948), p. 47.

[6] See, for example, Edward C. Kirkland, *A History of American Economic Life* (New York, 2nd ed. 1933, 3rd ed. 1951); Melvin M. Knight, *Introduction to Modern Economic History* (Berkeley, 1940); Chester W. Wright, *Economic History of the United States* (New York, 1941, 2nd ed. 1949); Ross M. Robertson, *History of the American Economy* (New York, 1955, 2nd ed. 1964).

[7] Evidence from W. S. Unger, "Bijdragen tot de Geschiedenis van der Nederlandse Slavenhandel, II. De Slavenhandel der Middelburgsche Commercie Compagnie, 1732–1808," *Economisch–Historisch Jaarboek,* 1958, cited by Roger Anstey, "The Volume and Profitability of the British Slave Trade, 1761–1807" in Stanley L. Engerman and Eugene D. Genovese, eds., *Race and Slavery in the Western Hemisphere: Quantitative Studies* (Princeton, 1975), p. 21.

In 1958, however, the concept of the triangularity of the English slave trade was challenged by Richard Sheridan who argued that "the triangular trade was feasible only in the early stages of Caribbean economic development."[8] With the development of the guarantee system in the sugar trade, particularly after 1750, slave merchants, he argued, found it increasingly difficult to get return cargoes of sugar except at very high prices and accordingly were *often* forced to order their ships home in ballast.[9] Two years later J. E. Merritt, in an article entitled "The Triangular Trade," asserted that the physical transport of goods to Africa, slaves to the West Indies, and sugar to England in the same ships was, during the eighteenth century, the exception rather than the rule,[10] while, in 1973 David M. Williams wrote that "the popular view of the triangular trade . . . has little relevance for the end of the eighteenth century, for by then the majority of slave vessels returned to Britain with their remittances in the form of bills of exchange, and few carried cargoes of any significance."[11] More recently, C. Duncan Rice has argued that

> by the latter half of the eighteenth century, in fact, few vessels made genuine triangular voyages. Many ships were being forced to sail back to England from the West Indies in ballast, taking their payment in discounted bills of exchange, since the sugar crop was being shipped by commission merchants trading directly with the islands. The same was true of the French colonies, much of whose produce was latterly taken back to the mother country in bottoms sailing out of Nantes or Bordeaux but not directly involved in the slave trade at all.[12]

Gilman Ostrander has declared that one of the mainstays of American colonial commerce, the triangular trade in rum, slaves, and molasses between colonial New England, Africa, and the West Indies, was in fact a myth, for no such pattern of trade existed as a major factor in colonial commerce.[13]

[8] Richard Sheridan, "The Commercial and Financial Organisation of the British Slave Trade, 1750-1807," *Economic History Review*, 2nd series, vol. 11, 1958, pp. 249-250. Professor Sheridan's statement was intended to apply chiefly to trade with the Caribbean both by London and the outports, especially in terms of the financial organization that linked them, and not really to the Charleston and Chesapeake triangular trades.

[9] Sheridan, "Commercial Organisation," p. 252, emphasis added.

[10] J. E. Merritt, "The Triangular Trade," *Business History*, vol. 3, 1960, p. 1. This article is based on his unpublished Master's dissertation, "The Liverpool Slave Trade from 1789 to 1791" (University of Nottingham, 1959).

[11] David M. Williams, "Abolition and the Re-deployment of the Slave Fleet, 1807-11," *Journal of Transport History*, vol. 2, 1973, pp. 103-121.

[12] C. Duncan Rice, *The Rise and Fall of Black Slavery* (London, 1975), p. 106.

[13] Gilman Ostrander, "Triangular Trade Myth." It is perhaps worth pointing out that the argument that Ostrander attacks is not the triangularity of the pattern followed by New England slave vessels but the undue importance given to this trade in discussions of American

Whereas it is clear that some branches of the Atlantic slave trade such as
the trade between Angola and Brazil were bilateral[14] rather than triangular,
the new orthodoxy with respect to the English slave trade deserves reexamination. Two points, it should be stated at the outset, are not in question.
First, there is no reason to doubt that the voyage patterns of the vessels
employed in the trade were triangular (or more roundabout). Although
beads, liquor, or other merchandise might be collected from the Isle of Man
or the Netherlands on the voyage out to West Africa, and vessels might
move from island to island in the West Indies or from one American
mainland colony to another in search of a return cargo, essentially the pattern
was triangular—an outward voyage to West Africa, a middle passage across
the Atlantic, and a return sailing to England. Nor is there any dispute about
the first two stages, the export of trade goods to Africa for the purchase of
slaves who were then transported on the so-called "middle passage"—a
term that in itself implies triangularity—across the Atlantic for sale in the
New World. The debate turns on whether and to what extent, at any period
in time, English slave vessels carried cargoes of sugar, rice, tobacco, or other
products on the third leg of their voyages from the Caribbean or the
American plantation colonies back to England. To evaluate the proposition
as to whether the English Atlantic slave trade was "triangular" in this sense,
an examination will be made of the intentions of shipowners and merchants
and of the practice of the trade.

THE EVIDENCE

First, there is the evidence provided by mercantile correspondence
between English slave ship owners and their American and West
Indian agents and the letters of instruction received by masters of slave
vessels from the owners of such ships. Such material exists in relation to the

---

colonial commerce. As Gary Walton states in "New Evidence on Colonial Commerce," *Journal
of Economic History*, vol. 28, 1968, pp. 363–389, "some of the vessels to Africa may have
actually formed a triangle, either returning via the West Indies or the southern colonies. This is
not the point in dispute. What is important, is that when placed in a matrix of aggregate
tonnage flows, the African route is shown as an insignificant proportion of New England's
shipping activity [pp. 367, 369]." He also adds, however, in a footnote, "while the route was of
minor importance to New England, it was an important part of the commerce of Newport,
Rhode Island. For instance, in 1768, eighteen vessels comprising 704 tons cleared New
England for Africa. All of these vessels cleared from Newport [p. 369 n. 8]." See also Virginia
Bever Platt, " 'And Don't Forget the Guinea Voyage': The Slave Trade of Aaron Lopez of
Newport," *William and Mary Quarterly*, 3rd series, vol. 32, 1975, pp. 601–618.

[14] Herbert S. Klein, "The Trade in African Slaves to Rio de Janeiro, 1795–1811: Estimates
of Mortality and Patterns of Voyages," *Journal of African History*, vol. 10, 1969, pp. 533–549.

trade of the main English slave-trading ports, London, Liverpool, and Bristol, as well as for Lancaster, of which only a sample can be cited here.

In 1729, for example, Richard Assheton of Kingston, Jamaica wrote to Isaac Hobhouse, a Bristol merchant, of the arrival of his ship, the *Aurora*, with slaves and went on to add, "the ship will have good dispatch. She takes in sugars in two or three days and sailes in twenty more."[15] Then on 9 April 1740 Benjamin Satterthwaite wrote from Barbados to his stepfather in Lancaster, "Here is so many Guinea men in the bay that sugar is not expected to be under 20s 0d this year."[16] It is not necessary to document the pre-1750 situation further, for Sheridan's argument applies to the second half of the century. For this period some evidence is available for Bristol, London, and Liverpool. On her seventh slave-trading voyage in 1762 the journal of the *Black Prince* of Bristol[17] shows that she took on sugar, bread, water, wine, and some ballast at Antigua before settting sail on her return voyage. For the same year there exists a letter from a Liverpool merchant to the master of a slaving vessel that sets out the instructions on the return cargo most explicitly.

> Have the Ship Loaden in the Following Manner viz: about One Hundred Casks good Mus[covad]o Sugar for the Ground Tier, the Remainder with First and Second white Sugars, and Betwixt Decks with good Cotton and Coffee, and the Remainder of the neat Proceeds in Good Bills of Exchange.

If the slaves cannot be sold in Guadeloupe, Martinico, or the Leeward Islands, the letter continues, the master is to proceed to Jamaica and after the sale of the slaves the ship shall be

> Loaden in the Following Manner; as much Broad Sound Mahogany as will serve as Dunnage, the Hold filld with the very Best Mus[covad]o Sugar and Ginger and Betwixt Decks with good Cotton and Pimento and about Ten Puncheons Rum, the Remainder of the neat Proceeds of your Cargoe in Bills of Exchange.[18]

The expectation is not only that a return cargo can be obtained but that the proceeds from the sale of the slaves will exceed the return cargo that can be carried. Later that decade Edward Grace of London was concerned in three slaving voyages, by the *Charming Nancy* in 1767 and by the *Expedition* in 1768 and 1769. Though in this period Grace suffered unusually bad luck— for the *Charming Nancy* was lost at Senegal in 1767 while the *Expedition*

---

[15] Bristol Reference Library, Jefferies Manuscripts, vol. 13, p. 113.

[16] Maurice M. Schofield, "The Letter Book of Benjamin Satterthwaite of Lancaster, 1737–1744," *Transactions of the Historic Society of Lancashire and Cheshire*, vol. 113, 1961, p. 142.

[17] Journal of the *Black Prince*, Central Reference Library, Bristol.

[18] Gomer Williams, *History of the Liverpool Privateers and Letters of Marque, with an Account of the Liverpool Slave Trade* (London, 1897), pp. 487–488.

foundered at sea sometime before 8 February 1769, and thus only one of the three voyages was actually completed—Grace's intention on each occasion is clear: that the vessel concerned should sail to West Africa with trade goods to be exchanged for Negroes who were to be transported to the West Indies for sale by his agents "who will certainly provide a freight for the Vessel, and send her home with dispatch."[19] In the letter to the master of the *Expedition* on 25 July 1768, the matter is put most clearly.

> We therefore confirm our former directions to you on the return of the Sloop to proceed immediately with her Cargo to Barbadoes where Messrs John & Thomas Tipping will take up the Sloop, dispose of the Slaves and procure a freight home—but you are desired to remember that she is not of dimensions large enough to bring home Rum, wherefore her Freight must consist of Sugars &c.[20]

On 25 July 1782 David Tuohy wrote from Liverpool to the master of the ship *Blayds:* "You are not to bring produce on our own accounts but if possible get a freight which we have not a doubt of your doing (provided the House cannot get you one) as you have good connections."[21]

There is also some evidence from the colonial end. From South Carolina, Henry Laurens, the Charleston merchant, for example, reported on a number of occasions and in particular in 1755: "The engagements we enter into in the slave trade are these—to load the ship with such produce as can be got, pay coast commission and men's half wages and to remit the remainder as the payments become due."[22] And in the same year he reported to Thomas Easton of Bristol that he was sending him a bill of lading for the *Pearle* for 60 barrels of pitch and 288 barrels of rice "which is as much as Captain Jefferies [her master] could find room for."[23] Further, in 1788, Lieutenant General Matthew of Grenada reported that "some masters in the Africa trade from Liverpool receive payment for slaves in produce by which their ships return full-freighted."[24]

Among the considerations that affected the choice of West Indian agents

[19] Letter to Amable Doct, 27 October 1767. For the 1767 voyage see also the letters to Day & Walsh (Antigua) and John & Thomas Tipping (Barbados) of 20 October 1767; for the 1768 voyage see the letters to Day & Walsh, to John & Thomas Tipping, to James Berville and to the master (Captain Edward Williamson) all of 6 June 1768; and for the 1769 voyage see the letters to Amable Doct of 21 June, Day & Walsh of 22 June, and Stevenson & Went (Barbados) of 28 September in *Letters of a West African Trader, Edward Grace, 1767–70*, with an introduction by Thomas S. Ashton (Council for the Preservation of Business Archives, 1950).

[20] *Letters of a West African Trader*, p. 25.

[21] Liverpool Museum. This passage is quoted by permission.

[22] To Smith & Clifton (St. Christophers), 26 May 1755, printed in Philip Hamer, ed. *The Papers of Henry Laurens, Volume 1. Sept. 11, 1746–Oct. 31, 1755* (Columbia, 1968), p. 254.

[23] Hamer, *Henry Laurens,* vol. 1, p. 305.

[24] Public Record Office (PRO) Board of Trade (BT) 6/11.

by Robert Bostock, a Liverpool merchant, was their ability to secure local products for a return cargo quickly and at a reasonable price. No doubt it was easier for a large merchant firm such as Sattherwaite & Jones of Barbados, or Henry Laurens or Miles Brewton in South Carolina to have freight available. It may well be that minor firms did not have the necessary connections with planters, particularly in the interior in South Carolina, to enable them to fill the holds of vessels consigned to them, and so they could not freight vessels as quickly.[25]

For a number of merchants the critical factor with respect to a return cargo was the element of time. Thus, in 1761 the letter of instruction from William Davenport of Liverpool to the master of his vessel on 30 October stated "wherever you fix [South Carolina or Rappahannock] endeavour to get freight or load lumber on our accounts for this place and make what dispatch you can as it will not answer for a small vessel to lye long upon high wages, and if you cannot be dispatched in a month, come home in ballast."[26] A few years later in a letter to the West Indies on 6 March 1775, the Bristol merchant, John Chilcott, told Captain George Merrick, the master of his vessel, the *Africa*: "You are to make all dispatch possible as soon as your negroes are disposed of to proceed home unless a freight offers for Bristol worth staying a fortnight for: in that case you may take it in. We recommend dispatch and frugality."[27] Further, based on a study of 63 voyages made by Liverpool vessels between 1761 and 1784, Hyde, Parkinson, and Marriner state that "a ship might bring back West India produce for the venturers or for other merchants against freight charges: but time was a major consideration because of high overhead costs."[28] Then, in 1789, Robert Norris, a Liverpool merchant, told a Parliamentary committee that "African merchants would rather their ships return immediately than take freight, if obtaining it would cause delay,"[29] a statement on which the letters of

[25] I owe this general point to W. Robert Higgins (personal communication). For Bostock, see J. H. Hodson, "The Letter Book of Robert Bostock, a Merchant in the Liverpool Slave Trade, 1789–1792," *Liverpool Libraries, Museums and Arts Committee Bulletin*, vol. 3, 1953, pp. 37–59.

[26] Log book of brig *Edith*, Liverpool Museum.

[27] Walter E. Minchinton, "The Voyage of the Snow *Africa*," *Mariner's Mirror*, vol. 27, 1951, p. 193.

[28] Francis E. Hyde, Bradbury B. Parkinson, and Sheila Marriner, "The Nature and Profitability of the Liverpool Slave Trade," *Economic History Review*, vol. 5, 1953, pp. 368–377.

[29] Report of the Privy Council on the Slave Trade, *British Parliamentary Papers (BPP)*, 1789, vol. 24, pp. 26–27. In reply to the question of whether it did not frequently happen that an African vessel took a West India cargo on her return, Norris replied "It does sometimes, not generally." When asked to be more specific, however, whether it happened once in three times, or once in ten times, Norris replied evasively "I do not know how often." (I am indebted to Professor Sheridan for this reference.)

instruction of another Liverpool merchant provide a gloss. On 17 May 1789 Robert Bostock wrote to Captain Williams, one of his masters: "if you arrive at time produce can be had without detention you are to take it, if more can be had on freight and you can get some on my own account at a fair market price such as an assortment of rum, sugar &c you may fill the vessell."[30] On 28 November 1792 he told another of his masters, Captain Fryer: "You are to proceed to Montego Bay and put your cargo of slaves into the hands of Messrs Barrat & Parkinson of that place . . . and if you can have your ship fill'd with produce on my account you must purchase such sugar, rum &c and be dispatched as soon as possible."[31]

If the descriptive evidence of correspondence and letters of instruction provides some evidence of both the intention and the practice of triangularity for London and Liverpool after 1750 and for Liverpool as late as the 1780s, particularly provided account was taken of the time factor, what of the quantitative evidence of the practice offered by the naval office shipping lists?[32] As has already been mentioned, attention has been focused on the extent to which slave vessels were able to secure return cargoes. To assess this issue, three main questions will be examined: how many vessels returned in ballast, how long slave vessels spent in the West Indies or the plantation colonies and what the composition was of their return cargoes. Certain subsidiary issues will also be discussed.

First, how many vessels returned in ballast? Sheridan draws on the analysis of the Davenport papers by Hyde, Parkinson, and Marriner which, though it may not be typical, show that of the 63 ventures examined only 9 revealed the return of West India produce for the Liverpool venturers.[33] Sheridan's statement, however, that "by the second half of the eighteenth century slave merchants, who formerly exchanged slaves for sugar in the West Indies, were often forced to order their ships home in ballast" appears to be based largely on evidence before the Parliamentary investigation of 1788–1790. To this inquiry, Sheridan reports, "masters of slave vessels, sugar planters and island governors testified that few slavers returned to

[30] Letter Book of Robert Bostock, Liverpool Museum.

[31] Hodson, "Letter Book of Robert Bostock," p. 58.

[32] These shipping lists, compiled by the naval officers in colonial ports and sent quarterly to England, give details of vessels and their cargoes that entered and cleared. The surviving returns, which contain some gaps, are to be found mainly in the Colonial Office Papers in the Public Record Office, London. In the following discussion I have been able to draw on statistical work done by a number of my research students, Roger Dancey, Christopher French, John Gould, D. Gareth Rees, and Peter Waite.

[33] Hyde, Parkinson, and Marriner, "Nature and Profitability," p. 369, n. 3. These voyages took place between 1761 and 1784 and may have been affected by war conditions.

England with sugar."[34] In particular Sheridan cites Captain William Mackintosh who, when asked whether the ships in the Africa trade generally returned from the West Indies fully laden with West Indian produce, replied that they seldom or never brought produce home.[35]

An examination of the naval office shipping lists, however, reveals a somewhat different picture. For this purpose the southern plantation colonies as well as the West Indies will be considered. For Virginia during the whole of the period from 1698 to 1769 for which evidence is available, only 6 out of a total of 226 vessels that brought slaves to Virginia cleared in ballast and, of these 6, 2 cleared for other mainland colonies (for Philadelphia and Maryland) probably in search of return cargoes.[36] For Jamaica in the later eighteenth century, moreover, the evidence is almost as overwhelming. Of the 300 slave vessels that cleared from Jamaica during 1782–1787, the period immediately before the Parliamentary inquiry, and 1803–1807, the last 5 years of the slave trade, less than a dozen cleared from Jamaica in ballast.[37] On this evidence, few vessels cleared from either the West Indies or the southern plantation colonies in ballast.

The second issue is the length of stay of slave vessels in colonial ports. It has recently been argued that slaving vessels found it difficult to secure return cargoes because of the need to avoid a long waiting period in the Caribbean.[38] Certainly there were arguments against a long stay. The longer vessels stayed in colonial ports, the greater the cost of such a stay. While there, not only had the wages of the crew to be met but the vessel was exposed to the ravages of the teredo worm—"Worms eating the bottom, men the top" in a pungent contemporary phrase.[39] The length of stay in colonial ports appears to have been influenced by two factors: First, the availability of a return cargo was to a considerable extent determined by the relation of the arrival time to the time when a cargo of sugar or tobacco was available. A return cargo, moreover, was obviously easier to obtain if there were few ships and an abundant harvest than if there were many ships and a

[34] Sheridan, "Commercial Organisation," p. 252. In his Footnote 3, Sheridan refers to the examination of Charles Spooner, agent for St. Christopher; Stephen Fuller, agent for Jamaica; John Matthews and James Penny, Liverpool merchants; and Governor Parry of Barbados.

[35] Sheridan, "Commercial Organisation," p. 252.

[36] Calculated from PRO Colonial Office (CO) 5/1441–50.

[37] Calculated from PRO CO 142/13–25. On the load factor, see Note 48 to follow. Slave ships trading with Jamaica had greater opportunities to secure freight than those trading with other British West India islands because Jamaica was larger, had a more diversified economy, and also had a logwood and mahogany trade with Honduras.

[38] Anstey, "Volume and Profitability," p. 15.

[39] Cited by Richard Pares, *Yankees and Creoles: The Trade between North America and the West Indies before the American Revolution* (London, 1956), p. 110.

TABLE 13.1
Average Length of Stay of Liverpool Vessels at Jamaica

	1718–1722	1742–1748	1752–1757	1762–1769
Number of vessels	6	71	66	57
Average length of stay (days)	79	113	86	93

Source: PRO CO 142/13-19.

poor harvest. Second, since the profitable operation of a slave vessel employed as a constant trader depended on its being able to maintain a rough 12-month timetable for the complete triangular voyage, the length of stay on the West African coast was also of consequence. Nevertheless, if the evidence of the naval office shipping lists is of significance, the desire for a return cargo seems to have been of more importance than a strict 12-monthly voyage pattern. Between 1718 and 1769 the average length of stay of Liverpool vessels at Jamaica, tabulated in Table 13.1, was never less than 2 months. An analysis of the length of stay of Bristol vessels during the same period follows approximately the same pattern (see Table 13.2). For these years very similar lengths of stay are recorded for all slave vessels trading to Virginia (see Table 13.3). Finally, the average length of stay of slave vessels in Jamaica in the 1780s (1782–1787) was comparatively short, amounting to only 55 days, whereas by the last years of the slave trade, 1803–1807, the length of stay had increased to 102 days.[40] Other factors such as the activities of naval vessels and privateers in time of war, the need for repairs and refitting, and the nature of the winds were of some significance in determining the length of time spent in a colonial port. On occasion time was needed for rest and recuperation and to obtain crew replacements. The attempt to secure a return cargo, however, was clearly also of importance. Indeed, may it not be argued that if a return cargo was of no consequence for slave vessels, they would have spent as little time in colonial ports as possible once they had unloaded their slaves and would have cleared quickly for their English home ports?

Thus, accepting on this evidence that slave vessels endeavored to secure return cargoes, with what products did they return? Here the discussion will concern first Virginia and then Jamaica. Based on the naval office shipping lists, Table 13.4 shows the composition of the average cargoes carried by slave vessels on the voyage home to England and the changes that occured between 1698–1701 and 1764–1769. Of these items, tobacco provided the most valuable freight, whereas the other goods—iron, pitch, tar, and staves—served as much as ballast as freight-earning cargo. It will be seen,

[40] Calculated from PRO CO 142/13-25.

TABLE 13.2
Average Length of Stay of Bristol Vessels at Jamaica

	1710–1719	1740–1749	1750–1759	1760–1769
Number of vessels	49	45	48	36
Average length of stay (days)	56	108	89	82

Source: PRO CO 142/13-19.

TABLE 13.3
Average Length of Stay of All Vessels Trading to Virginia

	1698–1701	1702–1706	1725–1738	1739–1748	1749–1755	1756–1763	1764–1769
Number of vessels	8	12	79	38	28	25	7
Average length of stay (days)	97	89	72	78	78	81	89

Source: PRO CO 5/1441-50.

moreover, that by and large the average lading of tobacco declined in the course of the eighteenth century. Of the 191 slave vessels that cleared from Virginia for England between 1698 and 1769, 145 carried tobacco.[41] Slave ships continued to return to England with some lading of tobacco because the slave-importing merchants were also tobacco-exporting merchants.[42]

The situation regarding the sugar trade from Jamaica over more than a century, from 1686 to 1804, is set out in Table 13.5. From 1719 to 1804 the proportion of slave vessels to sugar ships fell from 38% to 7% and of slave tonnage from 36% to 5%. Thus slave vessels were smaller as well as less numerous. The share of the sugar trade enjoyed by slave ships, however, fell more sharply than either numbers of vessels or tonnage would suggest and the decline was especially marked from the 1760s. While slave ships always carried less sugar proportionately (in terms of hogsheads per ton) than sugar vessels, the disparity increased from the 1760s, as Table 13.6 shows. Table 13.6 also indicates, however, that the lading of sugar ships varied and that they had more difficulty in securing a full lading in 1804 than in 1764 and earlier. Although slave vessels never held more than a modest share of the total trade in sugar, sugar continued to provide a

[41] Calculated from PRO CO 5/1441–50. Similar information for South Carolina has not yet been calculated but of the 25 London slave vessels that cleared from South Carolina during 1717–1767, 23 returned to London with 5998 barrels of rice and 2924 barrels of pitch (derived from PRO CO 5/508–11).

[42] Jacob M. Price, "The Economic Growth of the Chesapeake and the European Market, 1697–1775," Journal of Economic History, vol. 24, 1964, p. 498.

TABLE 13.4
Average Cargoes of Slave Vessels from Virginia to England, 1698–1769^a

Years	Number of vessels	Hogsheads of tobacco	Tons of iron	Barrels of pitch	Barrels of tar	Number of staves
1698–1701	7	209	—	—	—	—
1702–1706	12	154	—	—	—	—
1725–1738	79	54	7	24	61	3819
1739–1748	37	116	12	13	52	5067
1749–1755	28	114	5	6	132	8279
1756–1763	22	99	9	—	27	9426
1764–1769	6	62	19	17	15	2807

Source: PRO CO 5/1441-50.

^{a} It should be noted that this table includes only those vessels for which both the entry and clearance returns are available.

TABLE 13.5
Quantity of Sugar Transported from Jamaica by English Slave Vessels and English Sugar Vessels, 1686–1807 (Selected Years)

Year	Category of vessel	Number of vessels	Total tonnage	Average size of vessel (tons)	Total hogsheads carried	Average lading (hogsheads)	Total hogsheads carried as percentage of total sugar exports
1686	Slave	11	1075	98	1447	131.6	13
	Sugar	32	2751	86	9688	302.8	87
1719	Slave	26	2780	107	3117	119.9	25
	Sugar	42	5020	119	8958	213.3	75
1744	Slave	25	2040	82	2672	106.9	16
	Sugar	56	8355	149	14,318	255.7	84
1754	Slave	41	4215	103	3696	90.2	18
	Sugar	101	15,375	152	16,461	162.9	82
1764	Slave	32	4376	137	2304	72.0	9
	Sugar	98	18,527	187	24,473	249.7	91
1784	Slave	34	5860	172	1270	37.4	2
	Sugar	182	40,131	220	65,020	357.3	98
1804	Slave	19	4612	243	1020	53.7	1
	Sugar	246	83,669	340	99,491	404.4	99

Source: PRO CO 142/13–25.

TABLE 13.6
Lading of Slave and Sugar Vessels from Jamaica 1686–1804 (Hogsheads per Ton)

		1686	1719	1744	1754	1764	1784	1804
a	Slave vessels	1.35	1.12	1.31	.88	.53	.22	.22
b	Sugar vessels	3.52	1.78	1.71	1.07	1.32	1.62	1.19
$\frac{a}{b} \times 100$		38	63	77	82	40	14	18

Source: PRO CO 142/13–25.

sizeable cargo for slave vessels until the 1760s. Even after that decade, however small the cargoes carried by slave vessels sometimes were, nevertheless when opportunity offered slave vessels continued to bring back some sugar from Jamaica, and the separation of the sugar and slave trades was never complete before abolition.[43] While the evidence on quantity is clear enough, it does not enable the quality of the consignments to be analyzed to see whether the vessels in the direct trade carried back the best quality sugars while the slave ships got the leavings.[44]

Such was the overall picture, but the naval office shipping lists allow the changed position during the eighteenth century to be documented in more detail. In Tables 13.7 and 13.8 the information relating to all the slave vessels trading with Jamaica is summarized for 1710 and 1787. No significance attaches to these particular years, but since the lists are not complete for every year, two years—one at the beginning and one toward the end of the century—have been chosen. In Table 13.7 it can be seen that two vessels, the *Richard & James* and *Macclesfield Gally*, returned heavily laden, while six other ships, the *Raper Gally*, the *Dover Gally*, the *Alexander Gally*, the *Honvill*, the *Berkeley Gally* and the *Dolphin*, carried sizable cargoes of sugar. The table also indicates the range of time needed to carry out other activities and to secure a return cargo, from the 2 weeks taken by the *Richard & James* to the more than 13 weeks taken by the *Neptune*, with an average length of stay for the 15 vessels of 40 days. Vessels took on average longer to clear from Port Royal than from Kingston. All the vessels in 1710 came from Bristol and London (except 1 from Boston) and there were no Liverpool vessels.

[43] Roger Anstey, *The Atlantic Slave Trade and British Abolition, 1760–1810* (London, 1975), where Professor Anstey writes, "my own study of the Jamaica naval office lists, the most significant of those which survive, and even they are not complete, confirms Minchinton's conclusion about part cargoes [p. 42, n. 13]."

[44] I owe this point to Professor Sheridan. It should be noted, however, that in 1790 Robert Bostock of Liverpool instructed his captain to load "carefully sorted sugar" (Hodson, "Letter Book of Robert Bostock," p. 55).

TABLE 13.7
Slave Ships at Jamaica, 1710: Inward and Outward Cargoes

Entered	Vessel	Negroes	Cleared	For	Length of stay (days)	Cargo
(a) Kingston						
3 January	*Expedition* Gally	145	4 March	Bristol	60	40 hhds sugar, 3 tons logwood
30 January	*Fanteen* Gally	280	7 April	London	67	70 hhds sugar, 13 tons logwood, 13 tons fustick, 6 tierce pimento, 2 casks indigo, 2200 lbs wild cinnamon, 19 bbls snuff
10 March	Sloop *Neptune*	120	13 June	Bristol	95	59 hhds sugar, 3 tons logwood, 2 tons fustick
27 March	Brigantine *Martha*	158	10 April	Bristol	14	60 hhds sugar, 7 tons fustick, 3 hhds pimento, 4 bbls indigo, 3 bags cotton, 1 hhd lime juice
27 March	*Raper* Gally	290	10 April	London	14	110 hhds sugar, 3 bbls sugar, 15 tons fustick, 3 tons logwood, 10 bags ginger, 25 bags wild cinnamon, 4 bbls indigo, 2000 lbs elephants teeth
31 May	*Richard & James*	352	13 June	London	13	410 hhds sugar, 9 casks pimento, 16 tons fustick, 6 tons logwood, 7 casks indigo
13 June	Sloop *Union*	113	21 July	Bristol	38	27 tons logwood
25 August	*Dover* Gally	245	2 October	Bristol	38	147 hhds 3 bbls sugar, 3 pipes 1 half pipe and 7 bbls pimento, 4 tons nicolago wood
14 September	*Grewold* Gally	186	6 October	London	22	74 hhds sugar, 7 tons fustick, 32 elephants teeth, 15 bags chania root
22 September	Brig *Martha*	148	7 October	Bristol	15	77 hhds sugar, 6 tons fustick, 30 bags ginger
11 November	*Dolphin*	270	7 December	London	26	164 hhds sugar, 403 bags ginger, 14 tons fustick, 12 tierce pimento, 4 bbls indigo

(b) Port Royal

5 April	9 May	Macclesfield Gally	360	London	34	315 hhds sugar, 111 casks pimento, 52 casks cocoa, 3 seroons cocoa, 8 casks indigo, 24 bbls gum, 18 boxes and trunks sassapirilla, 2 casks 1 seroon Anota, 139 bags ginger, 1 hhd madeira wine, 21 tuns 18 cwt fustick, 70 bags pimento
3 May	18 June	Alexander Gally	136	Boston	46	113 hhds sugar, 59 hhds 1 bbl 25 seroons cocoa, 2? bbls indigo, 256 bags ginger, 50 bags sassapirilla, 10 tons logwood, 2 bbls pimento, 1 bbl tortoiseshell
7 October	5 December	Ship Honvill	186	Bristol	59	122 hhds sugar, 21 tons camwood
25 November	18 January 1711	Berkeley Gally	370	Bristol	54	112 hhds sugar, 5 tons logwood, 2 casks 4 seroons Cashazilla, 4 casks indigo, 2 casks rum, 1 cask tortoiseshell, 4 casks pimento, 2 casks 10 seroons cocoa, 150 hides, 12 casks lime juice, 1000 gallons rum

Source: PRO CO 142/14.

TABLE 13.8
Slave Ships at Jamaica, 1787: Inward and Outward Cargoes

Entered	Vessel	Tons	Built	Negroes	Cleared
(a) Kingston					
27 January	Ship *Vulture*	100	Prize	641	3 April
23 February	Ship *Venus*	130	1783	285	7 April
15 March	Snow *John*	100	Prize	180	7 April
16 March	Ship *Gregson*	120	1769	430	22 May
8 June	Ship *Antonetta*	274	1773	290	25 July
9 June	Ship *Ingram*	150	Prize	520	24 July
26 June	Ship *Elizabeth*	150	1784	540	31 July
26 September	Ship *Tom*	180	1771	310	4 February 1788
4 October	Ship *Brooks*	297	1781	596	15 December
9 November	Ship *Preston*	100	Prize	195	16 January 1788
5 December	Ship *King Pepple*	323	1785	495	26 February 1788
5 December	Sloop *Fortitude*	44	1787	40	15 March 1788
15 December	Ship *Bettey*	200	1783	444	8 February 1788
29 December	Ship *King George*	278	Prize	410	29 January 1788
(b) Montego Bay					
2 February	Bring *Alert*	100	Prize	300	20 March
(c) Savannah LaMar					
5 April	Ship *Alfred*	150	1777/ 1757	300	11 May

Source: PRO CO 142/20

For	Length of stay (days)	Cargo
Liverpool	66	101 hhds sugar, 45,11 casks sugar, 66 puncheons rum, 2 casks rum, 9 bbls molasses, 33 bags pimento, 157 bags cotton, 14 tons logwood and fustick, 29 planks mahogany, 2 casks coffee, 1 box 1 bbl indigo, 12 tons nicaragua wood, 8 elephants teeth, 8 hhds Calcavella wine
London	43	7 hhds sugar, 16 puncheons rum, 16 bundles sassaparilla, 108 bags cotton, 7 tons logwood and fustick, 93 planks mahogany, 5 casks coffee, 30 cwt 1 qtr 15 lbs molasses, 3 bbls tortoiseshell, 13 hhds bbls and kegs tamarinds, 3 trunks and boxes Chian pepper, 5 bbls gum, 158 elephant and seahorse teeth, 10 boxes indigo
London	23	24 puncheons rum, 35 bags cotton, 28 casks coffee, 47 cwt 3 qtrs 10 lbs molasses, 5 elephants teeth
Liverpool	67	143 hhds sugar, 61,6 casks sugar, 24 puncheons rum, 322 bags ginger, 50 bags cotton, 10 tons logwood and fustick, 61 casks coffee, 39,865 lbs molasses, 1 cask shell, 7 tons nicaragua wood
London	45	8 puncheons rum, 191 oz gold dust, 179 bags cotton, 232 planks mahogany, 1 pipe madeira wine, 50 tons nicaragua wood, 627½ tons lignum vitae, 270 lbs elephants teeth
Liverpool	45	73 hhds sugar, 30,9 casks sugar, 101 puncheons rum, 1 cask rum, 161 bags cotton, 1 cask coffee, 184 casks molasses
Liverpool	36	4 casks sugar, 15 puncheons rum, 3 casks rum, 23 bags ginger, 10 kegs gum, 83 bags cotton, 27 tons logwood and fustick, 25 planks mahogany, 1 pipe 2 hhds madeira wine
Liverpool	131	19 hhds sugar, 11 casks sugar, 46 puncheons rum, 13 bbls gum, 2 puncheons pimento, 252 bags cotton, 18 tons logwood and fustick, 142 planks mahogany, 2 hhds 11 tierce coffe = 9260 lbs, 11½ tons nicaragua wood, 140 hides
Liverpool	72	142 hhds sugar, 36,6 casks sugar, 90 puncheons rum, 24 casks rum, 40 casks ginger, 69 bags pimento, 102 casks pimento, 49 bags cotton, 12 planks mahogany, 1410 lbs coffee, 1 hhd madeira wine, 4 tons old iron, 573 bbls 10 kegs gum, 1 bbl wrought iron, 1 bbl indigo, 1462 hides, 1 bbl glass
Liverpool	68	30 puncheons rum, 1 bag cotton, 23 tons logwood and fustick, 80 planks mahogany, 1258 lbs ivory, 10 bbls pepper, 5 puncheons palm oil
Liverpool	83	124 hhds sugar, 4,2 casks sugar, 54 puncheons rum, 12 puncheons pimento, 1227 bags cotton, 11 tons logwood and fustick, 430 casks coffee = 17,203 lbs, 2 casks 13 bags indigo, 3 elephants teeth
Honduras	100	1 bottle oil, 1 puncheon rum, 1 large copper, 2 screws, 2 casks corn, 3 boxes candles, 4 negroes, 161 boxes pepper
Liverpool	55	45 hhds sugar, 11 casks sugar, 39 puncheons rum, 1 cask rum, 94 bags pimento, 10 bags cotton, 283 tons logwood and fustick, 27 planks mahogany, 15 casks coffee, 8 casks molasses, 8740 lbs cocoa, 4 bbls indigo
Bristol	31	14 tons logwood and fustick, 12 elephants teeth, 26 logs
Bristol	46	101 puncheons rum, 335 elephants teeth, 3 [?] Guinea grain, 1 pipe Madeira wine
Bristol	36	92 tons logwood and fustick, 8 tons ebony, 2 bbls beads, 4 cwt elephants teeth

Table 13.8 shows the situation toward the end of the century when 16 vessels were involved as compared with 15 in 1710. Most of the vessels belonged to Liverpool (9) whereas London and Bristol were represented by 3 vessels each. Thus this table documents the shift of the slave trade to Liverpool, which dominated it at the end of the century. The length of stay ranged from 23 days for the snow *John* to 131 days for the ship *Tom* with an average of 63 days, 23 days longer than at the beginning of the century. Further, although no ship returned in ballast, only the *Gregson* and *Vulture* (in relation to their size) obtained sizable cargoes of sugar and three others had a fair lading, whereas the remainder carried a negligible quantity or no sugar at all. All were able, however, to secure some kind of return cargo.[45] This table therefore serves as a commentary on the question asked by the Lords of the committee of enquiry in 1788, "Are the ships which bring negroes to the British Islands employed in carrying back the produce of those Islands to Europe?" The reply given was that "the ships bringing negroes from Africa are not generally employed in transporting the produce of the West Indian Islands, and that the number of such vessels which are employed in transporting produce bear little or no proportion of the whole."[46]

During the French wars many ships sailed from the West Indies in convoy. Accordingly it has been suggested that because their stay in the West Indies was prolonged while they waited for convoys to form, slavers may have availed themselves of the opportunity to secure a return cargo.[47] Evidence for 1805 shows that 56 Liverpool slave vessels returned to their home port with a calculated load factor of 60% compared with a similar load factor of 70% for a sample of 20 out of the 148 Liverpool vessels in the direct trade with the West Indies. By volume the slave vessels carried 8100 tons or 22% of the total amount of West Indian produce imported into Liverpool in that year.[48] Thus, on the eve of abolition, it can still be argued that the separation of the West Indian and slave trades had not completely

[45] Measured by hogsheads per ton, the *Gregson* obtained 1.19, the *Vulture* 1.01, the *Ingram* .49, the *Brooks* .48 and the *King Pepple* .38. This measurement takes no account of any other cargo carried.

[46] *House of Commons Accounts and Papers,* 1789, vol. 26, Part 4, no. 1, cited in Merritt, "The Triangular Trade," p. 7.

[47] F. E. Sanderson, "Liverpool and the Slave Trade: A Guide to Sources," *Transactions of the Historic Society of Lancashire and Cheshire,* vol. 124, 1972, p. 160.

[48] Bryan Drake, "Continuity and Flexibility in Liverpool's Trade with Africa and the Caribbean," *Business History,* vol. 18, 1976, pp. 89–90. The load factor was calculated as a relationship of measured cargo tonnage to registered tonnage. It should be noted that the market share is by volume and not by value. On the sample evidence provided by Mr. Drake of actual cargoes, the slave vessels appear to have had a limited share of the sugar trade, probably the most lucrative trade.

taken place and that slave vessels continued to be engaged in a triangular trade.

In the debate concerning the triangularity of the slave trade, two subsidiary arguments have been arrayed relating to the vessels and to the trading partnerships. As far as the first issue is concerned, Sheridan wrote that "slave vessels were not well suited for the carriage of sugar"[49] and in support cited again from the Parliamentary enquiry of 1789 the views of a ship master who said that "the West India merchantmen are built for burthen, full; and in general, I believe, the African ships are built for sailing, sharp built," while another view was that "the African ships are not esteemed equal to the others after a Guinea voyage, for the protection and safety of the cargo."[50] In a similar way, it was held that tobacco planters were prejudiced against sending their produce to England in slave vessels.[51] Certainly, as previously cited, Captain Grace considered his vessel suitable to bring home sugar but not rum, whereas Robert Bostock thought his vessel could return with both.[52] Slave vessels were in fact able to carry substantial cargoes of sugar or tobacco on a return voyage when they could obtain them.

A further charge has been that the slave ship "was said to be often in a leaky, worm-eaten condition."[53] Again the evidence is largely circumstantial. In the opinion of William Hutchinson of Antigua "as very few [Guinea] ships leave the coast of Africa before their bottoms are become worm-eaten they are thought to be unsafe vessels for West India cargoes."[54] On the truth of this statement the foregoing information casts little light, though if age is a contributing factor to the condition of a vessel, it can be observed from Table 13.8 that although some ships were old, some were comparatively new.[55] We know also from other evidence that ships were built especially

[49] Sheridan, "Commercial Organisation," p. 252.

[50] Sheridan, "Commercial Organisation," pp. 252–253. In correspondence, Professor Sheridan has suggested further that planters did not like shipping sugars in slave vessels and also that slave vessels were more difficult to insure than sugar vessels. According to Laurens, insurance on furs freighted on a slave vessel was impossible to obtain (Hamer, *Henry Laurens*, vol. 1, p. 266).

[51] Elizabeth Donnan, *Documents Illustrative of the History of the Slave Trade to America*, 4 vols. (Washington, Carnegie Institution, 1935 and New York, 1969) vol. 4, p. 203, n. 30; Arthur Pierce Middleton, *Tobacco Coast: A Maritime History of Chesapeake Bay in the Colonial Era* (Newport News, 1953), p. 141. Robert Carter was willing to do so, however, provided the freights were low. See Louis B. Wright, ed., *Letters of Robert Carter, 1720–1727: The Commercial Interests of a Virginia Gentleman* (San Marino, Calif, 1940), p. 77.

[52] See Note 20.

[53] Merritt, "The Triangular Trade," p. 4.

[54] PRO BT 6/10, 1788.

[55] Of the 69 Liverpool vessels that cleared in the Africa trade from that port in 1788, 10 were new-built vessels, a further 26 were less than 10 years old, and of the remainder, 18 were prizes (*BPP Accounts and Papers,* 1789, vol. 82).

for the trade.[56] There is evidence, moreover, that slave vessels from time to time underwent extensive refits.[57] Further, slave owners were amongst the first to copper-bottom their vessels to protect them from the ravages of the teredo worm.[58] The first known Liverpool vessel to be copper-bottomed was the slaver *Hawke,* 140 tons, in 1777;[59] and by 1786, according to *Lloyd's Register,* 124 vessels in the Africa trade, probably the majority of the vessels in that trade, were coppered, accounting for 45% of the total vessels so protected.[60] So effective was this that Thomas Williams, MP, reported to a Parliamentary Committee in 1799 that a Liverpool coppered slaver had made 15 voyages between England, Africa and America in 14 years with almost no repair bills.[61] Finally, such an argument makes little economic sense. The slave trade involved merchants in a heavy investment both on capital and on current account. As rational business men they were hardly likely to risk their investment in unsuitable vessels.

A further factor that, it has been argued, led to the separation of the slave trade from the West Indies trade was that the latter generally was "built upon a foundation of trust and knowledge of West Indian affairs which formed a bond between the planter and the merchant." According to this view no such bond would have been possible, to any large extent, between the West Indian planter and the Liverpool slaver "because many of the slave trade firms were comparatively short-lived."[62] Here the available evidence seems to point in the opposite direction. The firm founded by Bryan Blundell lived on through his sons and son-in-law, with various Liverpool partners, from at least 1745 to 1758, while a group that began in Lancaster and transferred to Liverpool lasted in various combinations of five or six partners from 1759 to 1773.[63] The roll call of Liverpool slave traders includes many of the great Liverpool merchants—Foster Cunliffe, George Campbel, John Knight, John Welsh, Richard Gildart, William Whalley, Edward Forbes, and Richard Nicholas.[64] As for Bristol, it appears

[56] PRO BT 6/7, "Dimensions of the Following Ships in the Port of Liverpool Employed in the African Slave Trade." The document ends with the statement, "about six ships are building for the trade." Robert Bostock began building a vessel for the trade to carry 210 slaves in 1791 (Hodson, "Letter book of Robert Bostock," p. 57).

[57] See Minchinton, "Snow *Africa,*" p. 190.

[58] Gareth Rees, "Copper Sheathing: An Example of Technological Diffusion in the English Merchant Fleet," *Journal of Transport History,* vol. 1, 1971–1972, pp. 85–94.

[59] Rees, "Copper sheathing," p. 94, n. 10.

[60] Rees, "Copper sheathing," p. 89.

[61] *Papers presented to Parliament,* 1799, cited in Rees, "Copper sheathing," p. 92.

[62] Merritt, "The Triangular Trade," pp. 3–4.

[63] I am indebted to Maurice Schofield for this information and for other help with this chapter.

[64] List taken from William Enfield, *An Essay towards the History of Liverpool Drawn up from Papers Left by the Late G. Perry and from Other Materials* (Liverpool, 1774), p. 43.

that all of her men of great or considerable fortune in the eighteenth century, such as William Miller, John Brickdale, Joseph Percivall, Henry Hobhouse, Michael Atkins, Jeremiah Ames, Henry Tonge, John Bright, James Read, Stephen Nash, and John Curtis, were deeply involved in slaving.[65] These were not short-lived merchant houses but well-established businesses. In both Bristol and Liverpool the slave traders could perform just the functions that were required and were able to meet not only the trade demands but also the personal needs of the planters.

CONCLUSIONS

The results of this reexamination of the English Atlantic slave trade on the basis of evidence provided by mercantile correspondence, other documents, and the naval office shipping lists are modest. Throughout the eighteenth century, there were separate bilateral trades for the carriage of sugar, rum, rice, and tobacco from the Caribbean and the American mainland colonies to England; but vessels that had gone out from England to West Africa with trade goods, which they had exchanged for slaves that they carried to the Americas, often succeeded in bringing back some freight to England. By and large such a course of action was easier before 1750, for from the middle of the eighteenth century, with the development of the guarantee system, slave ships found it more difficult to obtain return cargoes and therefore made a smaller contribution to the transport of these commodities to England.[66] Such changes affected all the ports—London, Liverpool, and Bristol—engaged in the slave trade.

The picture given by recent commentators, however, needs modifying in some respects. First, evidence has been presented to show that although some may have moved from one colonial port to another in ballast, few slave vessels returned to England in ballast. Thus the great majority were able to secure some kind of return cargo, the variety of which is illustrated in Tables 13.7 and 13.8. Therefore the statement that in the eighteenth century the physical transport of goods to Africa, slaves to the West Indies, and sugar to England by the same ships was the exception rather than the rule,[67] as well as the assertion that the triangular trade was feasible only in the early stages of Caribbean economic development,[68] are generalizations that require some modification. Until the abolition of the slave trade it is

---

[65]Lawrence P. Gipson, *The British Empire before the American Revolution*, vol. 3 (New York, 1960), pp. 271–272.

[66] Sheridan, "Commercial Organisation," p. 252.

[67] Merritt, "The Triangular Trade," p. 1.

[68] Sheridan, "Commercial Organisation," pp. 249–250.

clear that some English slave merchants at least intended their vessels to operate in a triangular trade and were frequently able to translate such intentions into practice. Moreover, the evidence relating to the time that slave ships spent in colonial ports suggests that the view that such stays were comparatively short is ill founded.[69] Rather, lengthy stays were made in order to secure return cargoes. Thus, if the carriage of freight-earning cargoes on the three legs of a venture, one leg of which was devoted to the transport of slaves across the Atlantic, constituted a triangular trade, then the English slave trade in the eighteenth century was such a trade. If this, moreover, is agreed to be the case, then the earnings on the return voyage need to be taken into account in any discussions of profitability.[70] Finally, it must be noted that although at the end of the eighteenth century the West Indies trade was much more important as an employer of vessels and men and in its demand for credit, this bilateral trade could not have existed without the services supplied by the African slave trade.

[69] See pp. 339–340 in this chapter.

[70] Compare Anstey in "Volume and Profitability": "Since our concern is with the slave trade and its profits we can ignore what was a possible and marginal profit in the operation of a slave based economy [p. 17]."

14

The Dutch Participation in the Atlantic Slave Trade, 1596–1650[1,2]

ERNST van den BOOGAART
PIETER C. EMMER

THE BEGINNINGS OF THE DUTCH SLAVE TRADE IN THE ATLANTIC

The Dutch began to acquire a major share in the Atlantic slave trade only after they had achieved control over the sugar-growing areas in Pernambuco, Itamacá, and Paraíba in northeastern Brazil. Before then their participation in this field of business was very small indeed, as far as can be deduced from the scarce evidence available.[3]

---

[1] Ernst van den Boogaart contributed the first sections of the chapter and would like to express his gratitude to the Netherlands Organization for the Advancement of Pure Research (Z. W. O.) for its financial assistance. Pieter C. Emmer contributed the last section.

[2] Abbreviations:

Ara   Algemeen Rijks Archief, Den Haag (General State Archives, The Hague)
WIC   West Indian Company
OWIC   Old West Indian Company
SG   Staten Generaal (Estates General)
GAA   Gemeente Archief Amsterdam (Municipal Archives Amsterdam)
NA   Notarial Archives

[3] See for the beginnings of the Dutch slave trade in the Atlantic: W. S. Unger, "Bijdragen tot de geschiedenis van de Nederlandse slavenhandel," *Economisch Historisch Jaarboek*, vol. 26, 1956, pp. 133–144; K. Ratelband, ed., *De Westafrikaanse Reis van Piet Heyn, 1624–1625*

From the notarial archives in Amsterdam it can be shown that Dutch skippers participated in the slave trade to Europe and America on behalf of merchants in Lisbon and Portuguese Jews in the Netherlands. In 1596, Cornelis Jansz. Boer from Amsterdam brought 58 blacks from São Thomé to Lagos in the Algarve on his ship the *Fortuyn,* by order of Anthonio Soares del Mego in Lisbon. Another notarial deposition and a Portuguese document cited by K. Ratelband show that Diego Nunes Belmonte and other Portuguese Jewish merchants in Amsterdam were partners in the slave trade between Luanda and the West Indies.[4] According to the Portuguese document, they even went so far as to bring some Negroes to Holland to be trained as interpreters. Similar instances could perhaps be unearthed in the notarial archives of other cities, but as yet there is no reason to suppose that the Dutch infiltrated the Portuguese slave trade to any great extent.

Only two cases are known of Dutchmen carrying slaves to the West Indies on their own account before the founding of the Dutch West India Company (WIC) in 1621. The unidentified author of an English manuscript, edited by V. Harlow, states that Spaniards on Trinidad ordered Negroes from Dutch merchants in 1605 and that 470 were duly delivered next year by Isaac Duverne. In that same year a ship from Middelburg called at the River Wiapoco with slaves for the English colonists, who had recently settled there.[5] As far as we know the WIC organized only one slaving voyage between 1621 and 1636, that of the Chamber of Zeeland for the benefit of a Dutch settlement on the Wild Coast.

('s-Gravenhage, 1959), pp. 50–61; C. C. Goslinga, *The Dutch in the Caribbean and on the Wild Coast, 1580–1680* (Assen, 1971), pp. 340–355. The literature on the Dutch slave trade has been reviewed by P. C. Emmer, "The History of the Dutch Slave Trade, a Bibliographical Survey," *Journal of Economic History,* vol. 32, 1972, pp. 728–747. The data collected by Wätjen on the Dutch slave trade to Brazil are to be found scattered over two articles and in a few pages of his book on the Dutch in Brazil: H. Wätjen, *Das Holländische Kolonialreich in Brasilien; ein Kapitel aus der Kolonialgeschichte des 17. Jahrhundert* (Gotha, 1921), pp. 310–314; H. Wätjen, "Zur Geschichte des Tauschhandels an der Goldküste um die Mitte des 17. Jahrhunderts," *Forschungen Dietrich Schäfer dargebracht,* 1915, pp. 557–560; H. Wätjen, "Der Negerhandel in Westindien und Südamerika bis zur Sklavenemanzipation," *Hansische Geschichtsblätter,* vol. 19, 1913, pp. 425–426, 431–432. Some additional information is to be found in J. A. Gonsalves de Mello, *Tempo dos Flamengos; Influência da Ocupacão Holandesa na Vida e na Cultura do Norte do Brasil* (São Paulo, 1947), pp. 209–214; and in C. R. Boxer, *The Dutch in Brazil, 1624–1654* (Oxford, 1957), pp. 138–139 and Appendix 2 (pp. 277–279); and in C. R. Boxer, *Salvador de Sá and the Stuggle for Brazil and Angola, 1602–1686* (London, 1952), pp. 232–233.

[4] Ratelband, *Westafrikaanse Reis,* Appendix F. GAA, NA 83, ff. 165–165 v. and NA 258, f. 81 v. (29 March 1613). Biographical information on Diego Nunes Belmonte (Jacob Israel Belmonte) in Wilhelmina C. Pieterse, *Livro de Bet Haim do Kahal de Bet Yahacob* (Assen, 1970), pp. 183–184. Another important merchant trading to West Africa, among other regions, is discussed in E. M. Koen, "Duarte Fernandes; Koopman van de Portugese Natie te Amsterdam," *Studia Rosenthaliana,* vol. 2, 1968, pp. 178–193.

[5] V. T. Harlow, ed., *Colonising Expeditions to the West Indies and Guiana, 1623–1667* (London, 1925), p. 125; J. A. Williamson, *English Colonies in Guiana and on the Amazon, 1604–1668* (Oxford, 1923), p. 38.

On the other hand, the Dutch profited from the Portuguese slave trade by privateering. Two cases before 1621 have been traced by historians: the Negroes brought to Middelburg in 1596 and the delivery to Virginia in 1619.[6] These chances of profit and of inflicting loss on the Spanish Empire were not lost on the WIC. According to one of the Company directors, Johannes de Laet, 2356 slaves were captured and sold for an average price of ƒ250 in America between 1623 and 1636.[7]

Two complementary explanations of this very minor role of the Dutch in the Atlantic slave trade before 1636 have been offered, one economic, the other cultural. As Ratelband remarked, the Dutch had insufficient access to selling markets; or, as we would rephrase it, smuggling slaves to Spanish America, in which Brazil was included at the time, was too chancy to be risked with purchased instead of captured cargoes. Apart from this economic barrier Ratelband and Goslinga claim that there was a strong popular opposition to the slave trade, shared by a majority of the WIC board.[8] This certainly strains the available evidence. Goslinga derives popular condemnation from one line in a play by the poet Bredero; this is shallow. In the far more influential writings of Jan Huyghen van Linschoten and Dierick Ruiters, in which the commercial opportunities in the Atlantic are discussed, no marked disapproval of the slave trade appears.[9] It is true that Usselincx, the *auctor intellectualis* of the WIC, had been opposed to slavery on economic ground in 1608 but by 1620 he had modified his position to allow for some slavery in the projected colonies in the West Indies.[10] Moreover, in the

---

[6] L. C. Vrijman, *Slavenhalers en Slavenhandel* (Amsterdam, 1943), p. 16. The Estates of Zeeland prohibited the auction of the hundred Negroes on the grounds that they were all baptised Christians. The resolution of the Estates of Zeeland (15 November 1596) called upon the citizens of Middelburg to employ the Africans as free apprentices or servants. There is some new information on the slaves brought to Virginia in 1619 in W. F. Craven, *White, Red and Black. The Seventeenth Century Virginian* (Charlottesville, Virginia, 1971), pp. 77–81.

[7] Joh. de Laet, *Iaerliick Verhael van de Verrichtingen der Geoctroyeerde West-Indische Compagnie,* (S. P. l'Honoré Naber and J. M. C. Warnsinck, eds., 's-Gravenhage, 1937), vol. 4, p. 287.

[8] Ratelband, *Westafrikaanse Reis,* pp. L–LXI; Goslinga, *The Dutch in the Caribbean,* pp. 341–342.

[9] Jan Huyghen van Linschoten, *Itinerario, Voyage ofte Schipvaert naer Oost ofte Portugaels Indien, 1579–1592,* vol. 3 (C. P. Burger and F. W. T. Hunger, eds., 's-Gravenhage, 1934). Dierick Ruiters, *Toortse der Zeevaert, 1623* (S. P. L'Honoré Naber, eds., 's-Gravenhage, 1914). Ruiters professes some scorn for the treatment of the slaves by the Portuguese, but he does in no way condemn slavery or the slave trade.

[10] W. Usselincx, *Vertoogh hoe nootwendich, nut ende profijtelick het sy voor de vereenighde Nederlanden te behouden de vrijheyt om te handelen op West Indien* (Amsterdam?, 1608); W. Usselincx *Politicq Discours over den welstant van dese vereenichde Provincien etc.,* (Amsterdam, 1622); W. Usselincx *Octroy ofte Privilege soo by den Alderdoorluchtigste Grootmachtige Vorst ende Heer Gustaeff Adolph aen de nieuw opgerichte Zuyder Compagnie . . . onlangst genadigst gegeven,* (Amsterdam, 1627). In 1644 Usselincx stressed once again some of the moral defects of slavery and the slave trade in an address to the Estates General. See also C. Ligtenberg, *Willem Usselincx* (Utrecht, 1914), pp. 60–74; O. van Rees, *Geschiedenis der koloniale politiek van de Republiek der Vereenigde Nederlanden* (Utrecht, 1868), vol. 2, pp. 320, 384–408.

Dutch East Indies both slave trading and slavery had become accepted institutions without causing a moral outcry in the mother country.[11]

Neither do the records of the WIC show that a majority of the directors had to be talked into an enterprise they were at first strongly opposed to. The evidence bearing on the issue is patchy but suggests a rather different conclusion. The committee that had been appointed by the WIC board to look into the matter of the slave trade from Angola advised negatively in 1623. Their first argument was the economic one previously referred to; only the second one testifies to some moral doubts: "It appears that this trade ought not to be practised by Christians." The committee was asked to take a second look at the moral question. More evidence on their deliberations is no longer extant, but the absence of any discussion over the slaving voyage organized in 1626 seems to indicate that the matter was settled without much ado.[12] When the Company had achieved a prominent position in the Atlantic slave trade, not all qualms of conscience had disappeared. In a report on the Congo in 1641, F. Capelle discussed in a few lines the morality of the slave trade. According to him, opponents thought that the slave trade encouraged the heathen in their total disregard of the sacred ties of kinship. They supposed that parents sold their children, a husband his wife, a brother his sister. This was strongly denied by Capelle. Though without knowledge of the True Religion, the Africans recognized the obligations to their relatives and in-laws. Slaves were born as such or became slaves as prisoners of war. He added the standard argument of the seventeenth-century advocates of the trade, namely, that it could be only beneficial to the heathen to be brought to a country where they could become acquainted with the Word of the Lord.[13]

These scarce data allow for the following conclusions. Doubts as to the morality of the trade existed from the start and lingered on later in the century.[14] We do not have sufficient evidence to attribute these doubts to any specific social or religious group. The attitude of Usselincx and the Chamber of Zeeland indicate that the Orthodox certainly were not unanimous in opposing the slave trade. Exactly what aroused the misgivings can only be guessed. As far as we know the sufferings of the Africans were not

[11] J. A. van der Chijs, Nederlandsch Indisch Plakkaatboek, 1602–1642 (Batavia–'s-Gravenhage, 1885), pp. 99–100, 171–173, where two ordinances of 1622 and 1625 concerning the trade and the treatment of slaves are printed. See also C. R. Boxer, The Dutch Seaborne Empire, 1600–1800 (London, 1965), pp. 239–240.

[12] Resolutions of the Heeren XIX, 24 July 1623, 3 August 1623, 10 September 1624, Ara, OWIC 1.

[13] March 1642, Ara, OWIC 46.

[14] Cf. G. de Raad, Bedenckingen over den Guineeschen Slaefhandel der Gereformeerden met de Papisten (Vlissingen, 1665), pp. 2–3. His main objections to the slave trade were that the Africans were sold to the Catholic Spaniards and thus enlarged the army of the Antichrist.

discussed. This probably was due to an element in the contemporary European culture that was of prime importance in shaping the attitudes toward the slave trade, namely, the widely held idea of the African's inferiority. In the travel literature of the period the Negroes are generally described as wild, cruel, voluptuous barbarians.[15] For Usselincx this justified enslavement: "Some people were so vile and slavish by nature that they were of no use either to themselves or to others and had to be kept in servitude with all hardness."[16] It is a safe assumption that in a time when cultural relativism was practically beyond the grasp of the imagination, this ethnocentrism was shared by the opponents of the slave trade. We would suggest that the doubts at this time were aroused primarily by the discomforting feeling that participation in the trade meant adapting to the ways of Catholics and Jews, for all that compassion with the misfortunes of the African might play a role at a later stage.

THE BEGINNINGS OF THE SLAVE TRADE
TO DUTCH BRAZIL

During the first 6 years of the Dutch conquest in Brazil only one cargo of a captured slaver was sent ashore in Recife. In June or July 1630 Dirck Symonsz. delivered 280 Negroes from Angola to the Council of the colony. They were immediately claimed as property of the Company. It soon became apparent, however, that they were more a burden than an asset, since food was scarce and little employment was available apart from heavy labor on the fortifications of the beleaguered city for some of the men, and prostitution (not approved of by the Council) for the women. After a few months the majority of these slaves were sent to the island of Fernâo de Noronha, where they were supposed to grow their own food and were held in store for the time they really should be needed.[17]

In 1635–1636 the river valleys of Pernambuco, Itamaracá, and Paraíba

---

[15] We hope to deal elsewhere with the image of the Negro in Dutch seventeenth-century travel literature. Negative stereotypes abound in the writings of Van Linschoten, Pieter de Marees, Nicolaes van Wassenaer, and others. Later on in his play *Moortje,* from which Goslinga quoted the condemnation of slavery, Bredero alluded to the voluptuousness of the blacks. Cf. G. J. Knuttel, ed., *Werken van G. A. Bredero,* vol. 2 (Amsterdam, 1924), p. 167.

[16] Usselincx, *Octroy.* The attitude toward slavery of the Dutch Calvinist Church is discussed by G. F. de Jong, "The Dutch Reformed Church and Negro Slavery in Colonial America," *Church History,* vol. 4, 1971, pp. 423–436. In his *Vertoogh* of 1608 Usselincx refers to some people in the Republic who thought that the moral rectitude of the Dutch was threatened by their venture in the tropics.

[17] De Laet, *Jaerlyck Verhael,* vol. 2, p. 148; P. van der Hagen to the *Heeren XIX,* 26 July 1630, 23 September 1630; Ara, OWIC 49.

were sufficiently pacified to allow for a resumption of sugar production. The shortage of Negroes in these parts was immense. Many owners of sugar mills and cane fields had fled to Bahia taking their Negroes with them. Many slaves had escaped from their masters into the backlands; a number of them joined the already existing *quilombo* of Palmares. Since the landing of the Dutch, the import of slaves (estimated at 3000–4000 per year before 1630) had come to a standstill. Already from the end of 1634 officials and private persons in Dutch Brazil had urged the WIC board to organize a supply from Africa. It was some time before the measures taken by the *Heeren XIX* were effective. In the spring of 1635 the *Eendragt* was sent by the Chamber of Zeeland on a slaving trip to Guinea, as was the *Halve Maen* by the Chamber of Amsterdam. In January 1637, Zeeland despatched the *St. Michiel* to Sonho with two Portuguese, João de Sousa and Manuel Pinto, as agents. These were ships of circa 375 tons, manned with 40–50 sailors. They arrived in Recife in June 1637 and September 1638, respectively.[18] The orders of the *Heeren XIX* to intensify the pursuit of Portuguese slave ships produced quicker results. In the last months of 1636, 1046 slaves were captured at sea.[19] At the same time preparations were made for an attack on the main Portuguese fort on the Guinea coast, leading to the capture of El Mina in 1637.

The supply of slaves from Guinea and Sonho did not satisfy the needs of the planters in Pernambuco, Itamaracá, and Paraíba. Therefore the Dutch attacked Luanda, the other center of the Portuguese slave trade, which was conquered in 1641 along with the sugar-producing island of São Thomé, despite the alliance between the Dutch Republic and the newly restored Portuguese Monarchy, both then at war against Spain.

In 1642, the *Heeren XIX* divided their African possessions into a northern district, governed from El Mina and controlling the trade north of Cabo Lopez; and a southern district, to be ruled from Luanda. El Mina and Luanda now became centers of Dutch trading activities ranging from Senegambia to Benguela.[20] An estimate of the revenues to be expected from the African

---

[18] The *Heeren XIX* to Pompeius de la Salle, 12 November 1635, Ara, OWIC 9; Resolutions Chamber Zeeland, 22 October 1635, 2 and 19 November 1635, 13 February 1636, Ara, OWIC 22.

[19] Generale Missiven 6 November 1636 and 18 December 1636, Ara, OWIC 57.

[20] See for the Dutch in Guinea: K. Y. Daaku, *Trade and Politics on the Gold Coast, 1600 to 1720* (Oxford, 1970); K. Ratelband, ed., *Vijf Dagregisters van het Kasteel São Jorge da Mina aan de Goudkust, 1645–1647* ('s-Gravenhage, 1953); A. F. C. Ryder, "Dutch Trade on the Nigerian Coast during the 17th Century," *Journal of the Historical Society of Nigeria*, vol. 3, 1966, pp. 195–210; H. Terpstra, "Nederlands Gouden Tijd aan de Goudkust," *Tijdschrift voor Geschiedenis*, vol. 73, 1960, pp. 340–362; W. S. Unger, "Nieuwe Gegevens betreffende het begin der vaart op Guinea," *Economisch Historisch Jaarboek*, vol. 21, 1940, pp. 194–217.

trade of the WIC, probably dating from 1645, lists four main articles besides slaves: gold, ivory, copper, and dye wood. Furthermore, it indicates that gold from Guinea was still believed to be the major source of income, but that the slave trade, in which the Dutch had by now achieved preeminence, was supposed to be in a good second position. Data on the export of Guinea gold by the Dutch in this period make it very likely that, in fact, the value of the gold exports surpassed the value of slave exports from both Guinea and Angola.[21] Many ships bringing slaves to Brazil carried gold and other articles also.

BUYING SLAVES IN GUINEA

The three slave-trading areas in the northern district were the Gold Coast, Ardra, and the region of the Calabari, Rio del Rey and Cameroon. Table 14.1 specifies the region of embarkation of 10,053 slaves bought in Guinea (74% of the total exported between 1637 and 1645).[22]

The slaves were exchanged for a great variety of goods. In the accounts of Nicolaes van Yperen we find that 874 slaves, acquired between 27 September 1636 and 6 April 1637, were bartered for 16 different articles: 329 for copper arm rings, 288 for cowry shells, 91 for white cotton cloth, 38 for Guinean gold, and quantities varying from 2 to 21 slaves for the other articles (iron bars, textiles, beads, large knives). As becomes clear in the accounts of August 1644 to January 1647, the assortment grew to 30 different articles. At that time, most of the slaves were bought for bars of iron or copper and for luxury products like damask or Cyprian rugs; cowry shells had been largely replaced by "fijn corael." The average price of a slave varied considerably between the three regions and probably went up through the years, mainly because of the growing competition of the Eng-

[21] Ara, Collectie Sweers, 8, pp. 115–122, contains the following lists of yearly exports:

Guinea		Angola	
50,000 pounds tusks	ƒ 100,000	4800 slaves	ƒ600,000
3600 marc gold	1,044,000	40,000 pounds tusks	80,000
1200 slaves	150,000	20,000 pounds red copper	7600
		30,000 pounds dye wood	6000

An equal mortality of 14% for the slaves transported from Guinea and Angola was reckoned with in this estimate. Maxima are given rather than averages. The average gold export in 1630–1640 was circa 2000 pounds, cf. Wätjen, "Zur Geschichte des Tauschhandels," pp. 549–551. See also Richard Bean, "A Note on the Relative Importance of Slaves and Gold in West African Exports," *Journal of African History*, vol. 15, no. 3, 1974, pp. 351–356.

[22] It is not certain that all slaves taken on board in El Mina were bought at the Gold Coast. The castle may also have served as a transit station for slaves bought at Cabo Verde.

TABLE 14.1
Distribution of Slaves Bought in Guinea According to Region of Embarkation,
1637–1645

Region	Slaves	Region	Slaves
Gold Coast	238	Bight of Benin	611
Mouree	285	Calabari	2461
El Mina	1059	Rio del Rey ⎱	
Accra	139	Cameroon ⎰	432
Total	1721	Total	3504
		Ardra	4828

Sources: The data are gleaned from numerous letters from agents on the African coast to the
Council in Brazil, and from the Council in Brazil to the Heeren XIX; the daily resolutions of the
Council in Brazil; and sales accounts in Ara, OWIC 51–71.

lish.[23] In 1640 the average prices for El Mina were given as $f64$ and $f75$,
for Ardra $f44$ in 1630 and $f38$ in 1640; for Calabari $f12$ and $f17$ in 1640–
1642.[24] The accounts of 1644–1646 indicate the relative price of men,
women, and children in Calabari and the Bight of Benin (see Table 14.2).

In onshore trading posts like El Mina or Ardra, it was customary to hand
over a number of goods to African middlemen, who carried them into the
hinterland and traded them for slaves. In Ardra debts in slaves to be
delivered ran up to 20 per trader, or in the case of two "nobles," even 100.
In March 1643 the king owed 345 slaves to the Company. By this time the
frictions over the delivery became so severe that the trading post in Ardra
was discontinued.[25] In spite of this almost half of the slaves bought in
Guinea were acquired in Ardra. This system had the advantages that the
slaves could be better taken care of onshore and that the ship bringing the
slaves to Brazil could collect its cargo in a relatively short time, provided the
middlemen delivered.

In dealings with places without onshore trading posts, small ships called,
bartered the required number of slaves, and then sailed on to a meeting
place, usually Cabo Lopez, where their cargo was transferred into a larger
ship, which made the crossing. To give an example, J. Foullon left El Mina

[23] The account of W. van Yperen in Ara, OWIC 52; the accounts of 1644–1647 in OWIC
11. English competition in the slave trade is referred to in T. Willekens to Council in Brazil, 21
May 1641, Ara, OWIC 56; and Generale Missive, 30 April 1642, Ara, OWIC 57. The
accounts give the impression that the slaves were bartered for with one single item and that
slaves were not exchanged for an assortment of trading goods.

[24] Wätjen, "Negerhandel," pp. 425–426.

[25] Willem van Mekeren to the Council in Brazil, 10 January 1642, Ara, OWIC 57; J.
Ruichaver to the Council in Brazil, 1 February 1643, Ara, OWIC 58; Joh. Ter Weyden to the
Council in Brazil, 2 March 1643, Ara, OWIC 58.

TABLE 14.2
Relative Prices of Men, Women, and Children

| | Copper arm rings | | | |
	1644	1646	Copper bars	Iron bars
Male, age 20–40	100	105	23	6
Female, age 20–40	83	93	18	4
Boy, age 7–15	80	83	16	4
Girl, age 7–15	—	—		—

Source: Accounts in Ara, OWIC 11.

on board the *Gulden Ree* on 14 May 1643. Between 1 and 6 June he bought 78 slaves and some tusks on the Rio del Rey; between 6 and 13 June, 12 slaves on the "High Land of Ambrosius"; and between 13 and 16 June, 116 slaves on the Rio Cameroon. He arrived 2 July at Cabo Lopez, where "on 9 July the *Noort Holland* delivered us of the black scum."[26]

Through this commercial organization the Dutch were able to export yearly from Guinea an average of 1300 slaves between 1637 and 1644. After 1643, however, the Guinea trade lagged behind the trade from Angola.

BUYING SLAVES IN CONGO AND ANGOLA

In Guinea the trade depended on the cooperation of the local men in power on the coast; the larger political units were still being established.[27] Increasingly, English competition had to be reckoned with. In the southern district the Dutch had to take into consideration the balance of power between African rulers, like the King of Congo and his vassal the Count of Sonho, who possessed more or less effective sovereignty over a vast territory, and the relations between these rulers and the Portuguese in Luanda. After the Dutch had conquered that town, the course of war and the alliances it created determined the supply of slaves. These factors explain the fluctuations in the slave exports from the Congo–Angola region. Between 1637 and 1639 the Dutch were able to export a mere 876 slaves from Sonho. In 1640 there was a complete standstill. During the first year and a half after the conquest of Luanda the supply was low but rose sharply to 5000 in 1643 and 1644 to fall markedly again in 1645. A summary account

[26] J. Foullon to the Council in Brazil, 15 July 1643, Ara, OWIC 58.
[27] J. F. A. Ajayi and M. Crowder, eds., *History of West Africa,* vol. 1, (London, 1971), Chapters 8–10.

of the short-lived attempt by the Dutch at gaining a foothold in Angola will elucidate the matter.

The relative failure of slave exports from Sonho was due in the first place to the Portuguese and, second, to the King of Congo.[28] During the first 6 months after their arrival the Company agents could establish onshore trading posts at Mpinda, the port of Sonho, and in Zarry, upstream on the right bank of the river Congo. From March 1638 the Portuguese put pressure on the Count of Sonho through his lord Alvaro VI of Congo to expel the Dutch and English who were trading in Mpinda. The Count and especially the local middlemen did not readily comply. The Count asked for armed assistance from Brazil. When it was not forthcoming, however, he could not prevent the Dutch from being forced to leave their trading post in Mpinda and take refuge on the island of Kimy, twice in 1640. At the end of that year the King of Congo emphatically refused to tolerate Dutch trading any longer. The Company agents then gave up the trading posts on the Congo and took the rest of their wares and a number of slaves to Recife.

One agent, Hendrick Cornelisz. Ouman, returned with the Jol's fleet, which succeeded in capturing Luanda in August 1641. Ouman had trouble restarting the export of slaves. He was able to send several hundred slaves, seized from the defeated Portuguese on the *Orpheus, Sloterdijk,* and *Over-ijssel,* and to establish friendly relations with the new King of Congo, Garcia II, and with other African rulers. All this was to no avail. The Portuguese had fortified themselves in the inland stronghold of Massangano and managed to block the supply of slaves from Matamba, the region that had long been the main provider. The Dutch had to be satisfied with the smaller amounts offered up for sale in Sonho and Loango. The directors in Luanda thought it wiser not to attempt collecting slaves as customary dues from the chiefs around Luanda, as the Portuguese had done before them.[29]

The situation improved considerably after the armistice with the Portuguese in June 1642.[30] More than 1000 slaves were now sent to Luanda by

---

[28] L. Jadin, "Rivalités luso-néerlandaises au Sohio, Congo, 1600–1675," *Bulletin de l'Institut Historique Belge de Rome,* fasc. 37, 1966, pp. 143–152. A French translation of the reports by F. Capelle and P. Segers is printed on pp. 215–244. The 600 slaves taken to Brazil, according to the translation (p. 220) are not mentioned in the original document, Ara, OWIC 46.

[29] P. Mortamer and C. Nieulant to the Council in Brazil, 24 January 1642; H. C. Ouman, to the Council in Brazil, May 1642, Ara, OWIC 57; The *Heeren XIX* to the Directors in Luanda, 19 June 1642 and 9 August 1643, Ara, OWIC 9.

[30] The following paragraph is based on D. Birmingham, *Trade and Conflict in Angola. The Mbundu and Their Neighbours under the Influence of the Portuguese, 1483–1790* (Oxford, 1966), pp. 100–110; and Jan Vansina, *Les anciens royaumes de la savane* (Léopoldville, 1965), pp. 104–110, whose accounts differ in detail. There is also some problem with the identification of the several "Jaga" bands. Cf. Jan Vansina, "More on the Invasions of the Kongo and Angola by the Jaga and the Lunda," *Journal of African History,* vol. 7, 1966, pp. 421–429; Joseph Miller,

Portuguese middlemen. The Portuguese governor Don Pedro de Menezes even provided food for this rapidly increasing number of bondsmen, from the plantations on the Bengo, to which he and his countrymen had returned. The news of the rebellion against the Dutch in the Maranhão and São Thomé, which reached Angola in May 1643, reversed the situation once again. The Dutch raided the camp on the Bengo. A number of Portuguese managed to escape to Massangano. There they were beleaguered by the Dutch and their allies the King of Congo and Queen Nzinga, who had established her rule over Matamba around 1620 but also claimed the lordship over Ndongo. The alliance of the Portuguese and Ngola Ari of Ndongo and the "Jaga" Kabuku Kandonga provided only temporary relief, and the Portuguese were forced, by an acute shortage of food, to renew the armistice. The Dutch now asked for an inordinate number of slaves in exchange for the small quantities of food they delivered to Massangano, thereby compelling the Portuguese to undertake raids, "wherever the risk of defeat seemed smallest."[31] Queen Nzinga also provided an increasing number. Taking advantage of the defeat of the Portuguese and their allies, she had established a camp on the Dande. Probably with no other reason than to capture slaves she conducted raids in southeastern Congo. This might be the explanation of the spectacular increase in exports from Luanda in 1644.

At Benguela there was apparently no regular supply of slaves, but the Africans around the fort invited the Dutch to join them in slave-catching expeditions. The captives were to be shared equally and the Dutch could barter for the other half. The *Heeren XIX* thought this procedure morally wrong and we have no evidence that any slaves from Benguela were exported for whatever reason.

Information in Dutch sources on the events in Angola between 1646 and 1648, when the Portuguese reconquered Luanda, is meager. Those few data available suggest that the slave trade by the WIC in this region had practically come to a standstill, because the *Heeren XIX* were no longer able to send supplies.[32]

The account of the slaves bought for the cargo of the first slave ship to the

"Requiem for the 'Jaga'," *Cahiers d'études africaines*, vol. 13, 1973, pp. 121–149. There is information on the slave trade by the Dutch in C. Nieulant to the Council in Brazil, 30 October 1642, 17 December 1642, 17 February 1643, 10 June 1643, Ara, OWIC 58. The attack on the camp at the Bengo is described in a deposition of Portuguese prisoners and in a letter of John Maurits to the Estates General, 31 August 1643, both in Ara, OWIC 58.

[31] Birmingham, *Trade and Conflict*, p. 107.

[32] Extracts from the Resolutions of the Directors in Luanda, 23 January 1642, Ara, SG 5761¹; the *Heeren XIX* to the Directors in Luanda, 9 August 1643, Ara, OWIC 9; Resolutions of the Council in Brazil, 29 May 1647, Ara, OWIC 71.

Congo, the *St. Michiel,* is the only one surviving on the trade in this region. It shows that 230 slaves were bought for 44 different articles: 60 for woolen cloth; 67 for different types of linen; the others, in small quantities, for stockings, swords, mirrors, etc. This is consistent with P. Mortamer's comment, that the Congolese merchants wanted to have an assortment of goods. One slave was acquired for an amount of powder. There is, however, no indication that this should be taken as a beginning of a guns–slave cycle. Only 3 slaves were bought at this time for African goods like takula wood, Anba cloth, and Nzimbu shells. According to Mortamer and Segers a few years later, Loango palmcloth and Nzimbu shells were indispensable for the slave trade in Congo and Angola. We could not determine whether the amount of African goods did in fact increase.[33]

In 1643 the average price for a slave was given as *f*38 by Segers, and as *f*50 by Mortamer and Rasenberg. Mortamer also mentioned the relative prices in Portuguese currency of men, women, and youths: 21–22 *milreis* for a man, age 18–24; 16–18 *milreis* for older men and women; 8–10 *milreis* for boys between 7 and 15.[34]

The slaves were brought to Luanda in long chains from 200 miles inland. There were no adequate installations for housing them before they were sent to Brazil. First they were kept in the small fortress *Tijger,* but as they succeeded in escaping regularly, they were stored in ships lying in the harbor. We do not know if Mortamer's advice to build barracoons was heeded. There was also a shortage of food in Luanda. A number of slaves were sent to the Bengo to grow corn. Dutch troops in Benguela raided the kraals of nonallied Negro communities to obtain meat for themselves and for the slaves in the city. From Brazil a quantity of third-rate tobacco was sent over, because—as Director Nieulant wrote from Luanda—"it appears that these people [the slaves] cannot live or remain healthy without smoke. They cut rope into pieces and suck at it, if they cannot get tobacco."[35]

---

[33] Account of *St. Michiel,* Ara, OWIC 56. The Dutch did send some firearms to the King of Congo and the Duke of Bemba as presents.

Resolutions of the Directors in Luanda, 21 April 1643, Ara, SG 12564, 7–15; Phyllis Martin, "The Trade of Loango in the Seventeenth and Eighteenth Centuries," in R. Gray and D. Birmingham, eds., *Precolonial African Trade. Essays on the Trade in Central and Eastern Africa before 1900* (London, 1970), pp. 139–161.

[34] S. P. l'Honoré Naber, ed., "Nota van Pieter Mortamer over het gewest Angola, 1642," *Bijdragen van het Historisch Genootschap te Utrecht,* vol. 54, pp. 1–42. There is a second version of this document, not used by Naber (Ara, OWIC 58), that contains some interesting variants. From this version it appears that Mortamer drew his information about the Portuguese slave trade from an ex-slave, who had made several voyages from Brazil to Angola with his Portuguese master. J. van Rasenberg to the Council in Brazil, 6 November 1643, Ara, OWIC 58.

[35] Resolutions of the Directors in Luanda, 2 and 6 May 1643, Ara, SG 12564, 7–15; report of a delegate of the Estates General in the Council of the *Heeren XIX,* October 1644, Ara, SG 5757; C. Nieulant to the Council in Brazil, 17 December 1642, Ara, OWIC 58. The Council in Brazil to the Directors in Luanda, 15 March 1644, Ara, OWIC 59.

THE SEX RATIO AND AGE COMPOSITION OF THE SLAVES FROM GUINEA AND ANGOLA

The *Heeren XIX* did not send any instructions on the age and sex composition of a slave cargo to West Africa; neither did the Council in Brazil express any preferences. The Company agents were apparently more or less free to buy whatever was offered. The data on 16 cargoes from Guinea (1636–1637, 1641–1643, 1645) and 7 cargoes from Angola (1636, 1642–1643) suggest that there might have been a considerable difference in sex and age composition between the slaves offered up for sale in the two regions (see Table 14.3). In the shipments from Guinea 13% were children and the sex ratio was almost 3:2, compared to 33% children and an almost balanced sex ratio in the shipments from Angola.

THE MIDDLE PASSAGE AND MORTALITY

Only two documents give indications as to how the slaves were treated during the middle passage: a note of Joost Beyendaels to the Council in Brazil (4 January 1639) and Pieter Mortamer's report on Angola (29 June 1643).[36] Beyendaels had made three slaving trips to Guinea with the *Eendracht* of Zeeland, when on the request of the Council he gave his opinion on how to keep mortality low during the crossing. Enough food and drink were of primary importance, he stated. Insufficient water rations had often caused the slaves to drink sea water. More water casks and pigskins should be supplied to the African coast. One or two times a day (the text is not very clear on this point) the slaves should be given a hot pot of beans, gruel, or barley porridge with some palm oil added. The decks should be washed regularly. Mortamer, one of the Directors in Angola, made the same general points. He advised the Council also to construct bunks in order to prevent the slaves from sleeping on the decks, and to provide some cassava meal, which they could eat with their hands, some palm wine for the sick, and some rags to cover themselves with. The fact that Beyendaels and Mortamer concurred in their advice shows that the shortcomings were not much remedied between 1639 and 1643. The shortage of food should not cause surprise, since neither the Brazilian nor the African colonies could at any time subsist on the foodstuffs locally produced; and even when sufficient quantities were sent from Holland, the quality was generally very poor and the deterioration during the transport to the tropics enormous.[37]

[36] Ara, OWIC 55; see also Note 34.
[37] Gonsalves de Mello, *Tempo dos Flamengos,* pp. 42–46. Wätjen, *Kolonialreich,* p. 305. J. Ruichaver to the Council in Brazil, 12 August 1642, Ara, OWIC 58; Adriaan Slechmam to Chamber of Zeeland, 10 June 1643, Ara, OWIC 58.

TABLE 14.3
Division of Slaves Bought in Guinea and Angola According to Sex and Age

		Guinea	Angola	Total
Male		1587	706	2293
Female		1107	672	1779
Children	boys	190	—	—
		14	580	944
	girls	160	—	—
Babies		28	106	134
Total		3086	2064	5150

Source: See Table 14.1

In the sales accounts and the daily resolutions of the Council in Brazil the number of deaths among the slaves during the crossing up to the auction day was usually registered. As is shown in Table 14.4 mortality varied considerably both from year to year and within any one single year. A closer analysis and a further interpretation of these figures is hampered by the small number of voyages (57 from Guinea in 1637–1645 and 45 from Angola in 1638–1645) and by insufficient data on the route, sailing time, and tonnage of each ship. The mortality that was registered in Brazil included in most cases the number of deaths that had occurred after the slaves were handed over by the Company agents on the African coast to the skipper, who made the crossing. Thus, when the slaves were taken in at Cabo Lopez or were transferred from an entrepôt ship in the harbor of Luanda, the mortality during the coastal voyage does not show in the figures. It is clear, from the few instances we know, that the mortality during the coastal trip could be considerable. Seventy-two slaves of the 847 bought by Van Yperen in 1637, 17 of the 100 bought by P. Pyters, and 10 of the 206 acquired by J. Foullon in 1643 died.[38] It is clear, however, that Gonsalves de Mello's statement that a mortality of 20–30% during the middle passage was common is incorrect. It refers rather to the exceptions.[39]

The difference in mortality of the slave cargoes from Angola and from Guinea is not so obvious as one would expect considering the difference in sailing time: 3–4 weeks from Luanda to Recife compared to 3–4 months from Guinea. Using a Kolemogorov–Smirnov test, the difference was not

[38] The account of slaves bought by W. van Yperen, Ara, OWIC, 52; J. Foullon to the Council in Brazil, 15 July 1643; P. Pyters to the Council in Brazil, 16 July 1643, Ara, OWIC, 58. For two cases of losses through resistance see D. Gerlofsen to the Council in Brazil, March 1641, Ara, OWIC, 56; J. Ruichaver to the Council in Brazil, 18 November 1642, Ara, OWIC, 58.

[39] Gonsalves de Mello, *Tempo dos Flamengos,* p. 210.

TABLE 14.4
Mortality of the Slaves from guinea and Angola during the Middle Passage[a]

Year	Taken aboard in Guinea	Deaths	Percentage	Taken aboard in Angola	Deaths	Percentage
1637	1299	88	7	—	—	—
1638	1439	172	12	68	2	—
1639	1758	365	20	353	27	8
1640	1537	221	14	—	—	—
1641	1306	244	19	341	44	13
1642	2121	505	24	892	130	15
1643	1867	314	17	3242	781	24
1644	1507	396	26	5096	742	15
1645	787	193	25	3864	685	18

Source: See Table 14.1.
[a] Mortality on land until the auction is included.

statistically significant ($X^2 = 3.66$, $p < .20 < .10$). This is the more remarkable, in that, during 1642–1643, the mortality on the trips from Guinea increased because of smallpox epidemics, whereas no such contagious disease was reported for the slaves from Angola. Most of the shipments from Angola contained a considerably greater number of slaves than did those from Guinea.[40] A correlation of the mortality and the size of the cargo in the Angola trade produced the low coefficient $r = .19$, which indicates that this element was only of minor importance in raising mortality.[41] Other explanations can only be guessed at. It should be noted that the high figure for 1643 was caused by the great number of deaths among the 700 slaves

[40] The sizes of slave cargoes are listed in the table below.

Number slaves	Number of ships	
	Guinea 1638–1645	Angola 1641–1645
Less than 125	4	6
126–175	5	3
176–225	15	2
226–275	4	2
276–325	15	5
326–375	8	4
376–425	—	3
426–475	—	7
476–525	—	4
More than 525	—	3

Source; See Table 4.1
[41] We gratefully acknowledge the assistance of Dr. Robert Ross in analyzing these data.

described as very young and weak, who were offered as a gift by the King of
Congo to the Council in Brazil. Our data on age composition show that
more children may have been exported from Angola than from Guinea.
This could have been a factor in raising the mortality of Angolan slaves, but
since no age-specific mortality was recorded, factual evidence to prove this
is lacking.

THE SELLING OF SLAVES IN RECIFE

During the fortnight between arrival in Recife and the day of the auction
the slaves stayed on board ship. Only in 1643 was a barracoon built in
Mauritsstad, a section of Recife. A few times the Council ordered the killing
of a cow and the distribution of the meat among the starved Africans. In
September 1644, a Portuguese was engaged to look after the Negroes, who
were too sick to be sold; f25 was to be paid for every sick Negro restored to
health. Because there were no positive results, the contract was canceled in
November 1645.[42]

To prevent smuggling the ship was visited by the officials immediately
after arrival, and the master had to hand over a sworn statement listing the
numbers imported and the losses during the trip. At auction day, the slaves
were brought ashore in lots of 5 guarded by two sailors, who had to deliver
them to an official in exchange for a receipt. In Recife they were brought
into a room, where they were sorted in lots suitable for the sale.[43] From
there they were taken to the market, where after inspection by potential
buyers they were auctioned off in lots of 5 or 10.

Only two or three times were attempts at smuggling slaves reported in
the daily resolutions of the Council. By itself this does not tell us much
about the actual occurrence, since the Councillors may have been involved.
It is revealing, however, that in the pamphlets, severely critical of the
Company officials in the colony, taking bribes for illegal imports of slaves
was one of the few charges not brought against them. Neither was the
landing of slaves in other sections of Dutch Brazil ever reported. Thus, we
believe that the figures, presented in Table 14.5, give a fair picture of the
total slave imports into the *capitanías* under Dutch rule.

The Council in Brazil expected that the costs of administering and policing the conquests in Africa and the New World could be paid out of the
profits of the slave trade.[44] It is difficult to determine how much wishful

---

[42] Resolutions of the Council in Brazil, 12 February 1643, Ara, OWIC 69.

[43] Antwoordt opt Rapport gedaen by Pieter Zeldeman, s.d., 1643, Ara, OWIC 58.

[44] Council in Brazil to the Directors in Luanda, 15 March 1644, Ara, OWIC 59.

TABLE 14.5
Imports of Bought and Captured Slaves in Dutch Brazil, 1630–1653

Year[a]	Imported from Guinea[b]	Imported from Angola[b]	Other[b]	Total
1630	—	280	—	280
1636	—	1046	—	1046
1637	1211	346	—	1557
1638	1267	66	Bahia 419	1752
1639	1393	326	Cacheu 77	1796
1640	1316	—	—	1316
1641	1062	297	—	1359
1642	1616	762	—	2378
1643	1553	2461	—	4014
1644	1111	4354	—	5465
1645	594	3179[c]	—	3773
1646	24	251	—	275
1649	290	200	—	490
1651	—	785	—	785
Total	11,437	14,353	456	26,286

Source: See Table 14.1

[a] In the years 1631–1635, 1647–1648, 1650, 1652–1653, no imports were reported.

[b] A blank indicates no importes reported. The few slaves brought on Company ships for private accounts are included.

[c] Of these, 592 were later transported to the West Indies.

thinking went into these expectations. Letters from the *Heeren XIX* to the Council in Brazil and to the Governor of El Mina show that even as late as 1644, they had no clear idea of the real costs of the slave trade.[45] Since only fragments of the financial records of the OWIC are left, it is now impossible to make an accurate calculation. An estimate, however, of the profits to be expected of the slave trade, drawn up by the Council in Brazil in 1641, gives some indication about two important cost components. The costs of feeding slaves were set at *f*5 per slave per month, a sum equivalent to the food money handed out to the Negro and Indian Company soldiers in Brazil. The estimate assumes further that the Company would have to feed the slaves for a period of 6 months, which seems a long time, especially for the slaves imported from Angola. Twenty guilders per slave were indicated as

[45] *Heeren XIX* to the Council in Brazil, 24 October 1643; *Heeren XIX* to J. Ruichaver, 17 January 1644, Ara, OWIC 9; Generale Missive, 13 February 1645, Ara, OWIC 60. In the last letter the Council in Brazil voiced its doubts about the profitability of the slave trade from Guinea. The losses were too high and the Negroes from Guinea were less in demand than those from Angola, they stated.

transport costs. This probably referred only to the costs of the trip from West Africa to Brazil, so that the voyages from Europe to West Africa and from Brazil to Europe would have to be paid out of the proceeds from the sales of African gold and ivory and Brazilian sugar. Since the slaves were bought for an average of *f*43, the additional *f*20 for transport and *f*30 for food would bring the cost price of a slave to *f*93. The allowance for food seems rather high, and most of the slaves were under the care of the Company for less than 6 months; thus the *f*93 figure may be somewhat exaggerated even when certain other overhead costs, generally small, are added.

Between 1643 and 1645, the Company officials in Recife started to sell slaves for credit again whenever the price fell below *f*60 per slave. Assuming that this was done because they would rather take the chance of a loss in the future than an actual loss, it seems reasonable to suppose that that the average cost price of a slave sold in Recife was between *f*60 and *f*93.[46]

The prices for which slaves sold in Recife between 1636 and 1645 were much higher than these estimated cost prices (see Table 14.6). The Company could have made a large profit on the slave trade, had not 60% of the slaves been sold on credit. When the *moradores* began their "Revolt of Divine Liberty" they owed the Company *f*4,642,193, most of which was an unpaid debt for slaves. It seems very probable that, instead of making a profit, the Company lost substantially on the slave trade in this period.[47]

---

[46] The estimate of the costs and profits to be expected from the Angola slave trade in Ara, OWIC 56. Food money for the black and Indian soldiers: Daily Resolutions of the Council in Brazil, 7 November 1645, Ara, OWIC 70; and Resolutions, 14 January 1642, Ara, OWIC 69. Decision to sell slaves on credit: Daily Resolutions of the Council in Brazil, 30 May 1644, Ara, OWIC 70; and the sales account of the slaves of the *Leeuwinne*, 9 May 1644, Ara, OWIC 59. On cost accounting methods of the WIC see Ratelband, *Vijf Dagregisters*, p. XCIV.

[47] A Portuguese translation of the list of debtors from the original in the collection of the Historical Society of Pennsylvania has been published in Adriaen van der Dussen, *Relatório sôbre as Capitanias Conquistadas no Brasil pelos Holandeses, 1639* (Rio de Janeiro, 1947), pp. 149–157. The years 1642–1643 excepted, the prices do bear out the preference for Angola slaves noted by contemporary authors. From 1636 to August 1643, practically all the slaves were sold on credit. Most of the time, it was stipulated that they were to be paid for within 6 months. In 1643, 1644, and 1645 (until August) the percentages of slaves sold for cash were, respectively, 41, 78, and 100. During these three years, only from July to September 1644 was there any interest charged on credit sales, namely, 6% for the 6 months in which they had to be paid. This percentage seems to have corresponded with the interest rate the Portuguese had to pay whenever they bought slaves through an intermediary (Ara, OWIC 70, Daily Resolutions of the Council in Brazil, 15 July 1645). On all the other occasions the Company was apparently content with the high sales prices, which were, in 1638–1642, 150–200% or even more of the sales prices for slaves before the Dutch occupation. Before 1630 the prices were said to have been 60–100 patacas = *f*144–200 (Artichewsky to the *Heeren XIX*, 7 April 1639, Ara, OWIC 54, and E. Hercmans to the *Heeren XIX*, 8 September 1640, Ara, OWIC 55.

TABLE 14.6
Average Prices of the Slaves Sold in Recife, 1636–July 1645

Year	Slaves from Guinea (price in guilders)	Slaves from Angola (price in guilders)
1636	—	161,52
1637	251,26	228,34
1638	457,49	639,27
1639	530,88	581,85
1640	375,20	—
1641	427,03	470,17
1642	449,83	384,52
1643	280,74	228,14
1644	99,44	172,12
1645	236,53	244,49

Source: The sales accounts in Ara, OWIC 51–61.

THE SHIFT OF THE DUTCH SLAVE TRADE FROM BRAZIL TO THE WEST INDIES

By the end of the 1640s the WIC had lost to the Portuguese its predominant position in the Atlantic slave trade. Though a few forts in Pernambuco and the neighboring *capitanías* remained in Dutch hands until 1654, the Company never regained control over the sugar-growing areas and was thus deprived of its outlet for slaves. In 1648 the main supply harbor, Luanda, was surrendered to Salvador de Sá. The Company's position was further affected by the growing competition of the English. During the years 1645–1647 the estimated yearly average of slave imports into the British Caribbean could well have been carried by British ships only, according to the reports of the governors of Dutch El Mina.[48] The foreign-based, but

---

[48] Philip D. Curtin, *The Atlantic Slave Trade: A Census* (Madison, 1969), p. 119, estimates that during the second quarter of the seventeenth century around 800 slaves per year were imported into the British Caribbean. The Dutch governors of El Mina detected 19 English slaving vessels during the period between February 1645 and January 1647. These ships were generally small (100–300 tons) and capable of carrying an average of 100 slaves. See Ratelband, *Vijf Dagregisters,* pp. 9, 11–12, 20, 23–24, 29–36, 40–41, 54, 56, 73, 75, 80, 90, 94, 115, 117, 165–166, 169, 195, 211, 230, 232, 234–236, 242, 248, 264–265, 283–285, 292, 294, 297. Another strong indication that the English were ahead of the Dutch in bringing slaves to the Caribbean is to be found in a letter by Jacob van der Wel to the *Heeren XIX,* 2 April 1646, Ara, OWIC 11. Van der Wel told the board that the English had shown that the slave trade to the Caribbean, with small vessels capable of carrying 100–150 slaves, could make profitable voyages in spite of the mortality. According to Van der Wel, the English sold their slaves for 2000 pounds of cotton or 1600–1800 pounds of tobacco. Mr. Franz Binder,

Dutch-financed slaving companies in Sweden, Brandenburg, Courland, and Denmark became additional competitors.[49] Moreover, the *Heeren XIX* partly relaxed the monopoly by issuing licenses to private merchants for the trade to the north and the south of the Gold Coast, and partly lost it through the activities of the Dutch interlopers, who took advantage of the near bankruptcy of the WIC.[50]

It is indicative of the minor importance attached by the Company to the Caribbean during the first half of the seventeenth century that, after 1645, the *Heeren XIX* choose São Thomé as a new outlet. Between 1646 and 1648 the Company sold 2300 slaves, purchased at the Guinea Coast, to the Portuguese on that island.[51] Although in 1641 the *Heeren XIX* had ordered that slaves captured in the Caribbean were to be sold on Curaçao for ƒ65 and had allowed some slave exports from Dutch Brazil to the Lesser Antilles and New Netherland after 1645, it was only around 1650 that they decided to redirect the slave trade to the Caribbean.[52]

One of the reasons for this slow process of reorientation of the Company slave trade is obvious: There was no Dutch-owned colony in the Americas, where slaves were in great demand. Unlike the English and French colonies the Dutch Caribbean possessions could not at that time be developed for sugar, tobacco or coffee growing.[53] New Netherland, situated in North America, was geared to the trade in hides and to subsistence farming, and

---

graduate student at the Department of History of the University of Vienna, brought to our attention the fact that in the period between 1652 and 1656, 25 English slavers were detected by the Dutch on the Gold Coast, and another 50 English slavers during the years 1656 and 1657. Binder's data appear in his article "Die Zeeländische Kaperfahrt, 1654–1662," *Archief Zeeuwsch Genootschap der Wetenschappen*, 1976, pp. 40–92.

[49] E. Donnan, ed., *Documents Illustrative of the History of the Slave Trade to America*, vol. 1 (Washington, D. C., 1930–1932), pp. 73–121. It is clear that both the Danish and the Swedish slave-trading companies were mainly financed by Dutch merchants hoping to avoid problems with the monopoly of the Dutch West India Company. See G. W. Kernkamp, "Een contract tot slaafhandel, 1657," *Bijdragen en Mededelingen van het Historisch Genootschap*, vol. 22, 1901, pp. 444–459. The same was true for the Courland-based company (Goslinga, *The Dutch in the Caribbean*, p. 442) as well as for the "Churfürstliche Afrikanisch–Brandenburgische Compagnie" (Albert van Dantzig, *Het Nederlandse aandeel in de slavenhandel* [(Bussum, 1968)], pp. 50–52).

[50] The Dutch interloper slave trade to the Caribbean was mentioned by Director Nieulant in Luanda as early as October 1642 (C. Nieulant to Council in Brazil, 30 October 1642, Ara, OWIC 58). See for the partial abolition of the monopoly, *Heeren XIX* to Directors in Luanda, 26 June 1648 and *Heeren XIX* to Director in El Mina, 8 August 1652 in Ara, OWIC 10, as well as the new charter for the Dutch West African Trade, dated 25 April 1648, Ara, SG, 5760.

[51] Sales accounts in Ara, OWIC, 11.

[52] Resolutions, Chamber of Zeeland, 14 February 1641, Ara, OWIC 23; Resolutions of the Council in Brazil, 29 December 1645–January 1646, 11 October 1648, 5 November 1648, 1 April, 1649, 19 July, 1649, 21 December 1649, Ara, OWIC 71–74.

[53] Goslinga, *The Dutch in the Caribbean*, p. 260.

was very sparsely populated. A few slaves were introduced before 1650 as farm and household hands and as servants to the Company, but there was never a demand comparable to that of the plantation areas in the south of North America or in the West Indies. The last governor of this Dutch colony, Pieter Stuyvesant, asked the directors of the Dutch West India Company for more slaves, but the actual imports were very small indeed; from Curaçao 5 slaves were sent to New Netherland in 1659, 39 slaves in 1660 and 40 slaves in 1661. Because the Company wanted to grow more tobacco, two cargoes of slaves were brought in directly from Africa, one consisting of 290 blacks.[54]

Foreign colonies then seemed to be a more promising market for Dutch slaves. As early as 1641 the directors of the Dutch West India Company were advised by some company employees to use Curaçao for the transit trade in slaves to Spanish America. At that time the Company was afraid that Curaçao would not be able to provide the slave ships with suitable return cargoes. Also, there might not be enough victuals on the island to feed large numbers of slaves in transit. In addition, the directors of the Company were afraid that, if they stimulated slave imports, the Spaniards in nearby Venezuela would attempt to reconquer Curaçao.[55]

Only in the 1650s did Curaçao become the main center of the Dutch slave trade in the New World. At that time the Spanish government had discontinued its custom of importing slaves into Spanish America only via *asiento* treaties, since after 1640 the customary Portuguese *asentistas* from Lisbon had to be regarded as rebels. Illegal but tolerated imports into Spanish America were the only answer to this situation, and the Dutch governors of Curaçao were induced by the Company to turn Willemstad into the main transit harbor for this trade. Both before and after the *asiento-interregnum* Dutch slavers used Curaçao as their final destination, because vessels from Spanish America arrived with great regularity to buy slaves.[56] The English and French colonies also became important markets after the exodus from Dutch Brazil stimulated sugar production there.

The influence of these changes in the demand and supply of the Dutch slave trade on the quantities of slaves transported by the Dutch became evident after 1650. These quantitative aspects are presently being re-

[54] E. B. O'Callaghan, ed., *Voyages of the Slavers St. John and Arms of Amsterdam, 1659, 1663; Together with Additional Papers Illustrating the Slave Trade of the Dutch* (Albany, 1867), pp. 140, 141, 176, 177, 178, 179, 181, 183.

[55] Goslinga, *The Dutch in the Caribbean*, p. 352.

[56] The connections between Spanish America and Curaçao have been studied in P. C. Emmer, "De slavenhandel van en naar Nieuw-Nederland," *Economisch-en Sociaal-Historisch Jaarboek*, vol. 35, 1972, pp. 94–147.

searched.[57] As yet the only indication as to the volume of the Dutch slave trade to Spanish America is that between 1662 and 1668, 2000 slaves were contracted to be delivered yearly at Curaçao, and from 1668 until 1675, 4000 slaves per year. The figures for the earlier imports into the British and French Caribbean were not put into trading contracts. The only way to discover how many slaves were actually imported in both Spanish America and the British and French Caribbean by the Dutch consists of a ship-by-ship reconstruction of the Dutch slave trade for the years 1650–1675.[58]

In this reassessment of the early Dutch participation in the Atlantic slave trade it is argued that two current assumptions on the role of the Dutch need to be revised. First, the Dutch attempt to supersede the Portuguese in the Atlantic slave trade was even less successful than Curtin supposed, because he did not take sufficient account of the effects of the Dutch–Portuguese struggle in Angola and Brazil. Between 1630 and 1636 the Dutch blocked slave imports into Pernambuco, Itamaracá, and Paraíba and seriously hampered the trade to Bahia. Between 1636 and 1645 the imports in the *capitanías* under Dutch rule came up to previous Portuguese levels only in the years 1643–1645, and were negligible during the last 8 years. The war in Angola must have put a serious brake on the exports to Bahia in the 1640s. The assumed yearly average of 4000 slaves imported into Brazil during the second quarter of the seventeenth century is certainly too high for the years 1630–1650.[59]

Second, it is doubtful whether the Dutch hegemony in the slave trade to the Caribbean, taken for granted by Curtin and Davies, lasted until the

[57] Mr. Franz Binder is undertaking research in the archives pertaining to the Dutch possessions on the West Coast of Africa as well as in the Amsterdam municipal archives. The authors want to express their warm thanks to Mr. Binder for supplying them with some preliminary information.

[58] The period thereafter has been researched by Johannes Postma, "The Dimension of the Dutch Slave Trade from Western Africa," *Journal of African History*, vol. 13, 1972, pp. 237–248, based on a more extensive unpublished doctoral dissertation: Johannes Postma, *The Dutch Participation in the African Slave Trade; Slaving on the Guinea Coast, 1675–1795* (Michigan State University, 1970).

[59] Curtin, *The Atlantic Slave Trade*, pp. 119, 125, 126. The declining imports of Angolan slaves into Bahia might have been compensated by rising imports of Cabo Verde slaves. This is suggested by the observations of a Dutch mission to Bahia in 1645. They did not notice a shortage of slaves, but they only visited the city (Johan Nieuhof, *Gedenkweerdige Brasiliaense Zee-en Lantreize* (Amsterdam, 1682), pp. 59–60). On the other hand, there are some indications in Dutch sources that the Portuguese were short of slaving ships and had to resort to overcrowding. In 1644 they had to charter a Dutch ship *Het Lant van Belofte* to carry 300 slaves from the island of Principe to Bahia (Generale Missive, 13 February 1645, Ara, OWIC 60). Mathias van den Broecke, a Dutch prisoner in Bahia during 1646, reported the arrival of two Portuguese ships each carrying 1000 (!) slaves. See M. van den Broecke, *Journal ofte Historiaelse Beschrijvinge* (Amsterdam, 1651), p. 31. In 1651 the Dutch captured the *Salvador do Mondo* carrying 1300 slaves (Deposition of Pierre Rodrigues, 8 June 1651, Ara, OWIC 66).

1660s, if it ever existed.[60] Present research shows that British ships were already involved in the slave trade to the Lesser Antilles as early as the 1640s. In our opinion the English are not to be treated as *quantité négligeable* in supplying the Caribbean with slaves, since before 1650 the Dutch West India Company preferred to sell its slaves elsewhere; the presumed hegemony would thus have been the preserve of Dutch interlopers and privateers. An already substantial English share in the slave trade to the Caribbean would explain why in 1663 the two Genoese *asentistas* Lomelin and Grillo contracted the newly founded British Company of Royal Adventurers to deliver 3500 slaves per year to Barbados and Jamaica for transshipment to the Spanish American possessions.[61] If the British expertise in the Atlantic slave trade were more extensive than has been assumed previously, the Dutch "monopoly" of slave imports into Spanish America also deserves closer scrutiny. From the financial involvement of the Dutch West India Company in the *asiento* treaties, whether these were semiofficial (1662–1684) or official (1684–1687), it should not be argued that the Dutch were in complete control of slave transport to Spanish America. Instead, the relative shares of the British and the Dutch in the slave trade to Spanish America need closer examination.

ACKNOWLEDGMENTS

Both authors are indebted to Ms. Dr. M. E. van Opstall, Dutch National Archives (Algemeen Rijksarchief), The Hague, as well as to Dr. S. Hart and Ms. Dr. Chr. W. Pieterse, Municipal Archives, Amsterdam, The Netherlands, for assistance in archival research, and to Dr. Joseph Miller, University of Virginia, for his searching criticisms of an earlier draft of this chapter.

[60] Curtin, *The Atlantic Slave Trade,* pp. 55, 62; and K. G. Davies, *The North Atlantic World in the Seventeenth Century* (Minneapolis–London, 1974), pp. 124, 125.
[61] K. G. Davies, *The Royal African Company* (London, 1957), p. 43.

15

The Adoption of Slave Labor in British America

RICHARD N. BEAN
ROBERT P. THOMAS

During the seventeenth century a fundamental shift in the source of field labor occurred in the plantation colonies of British America. In both the British West Indies and the continental region of the Chesapeake, European indentured servants were replaced by African slaves. This transition occurred rapidly in both areas but did not occur simultaneously. In the West Indies slaves replaced indentures during the middle decades of the century, whereas the same transition in the Chesapeake was delayed until the end of the century.

The purpose of this chapter is to offer an explanation for the timing of this transition. We shall first examine the historical context of this problem and then review and analyze the existing hypotheses for the switch. We will examine these within the framework of contemporary economic theory. None, as it turns out, will prove acceptable. Then we will present an alternative explanation that we feel is consistent both with economic theory and with the historical evidence.

THE NATURE OF THE PROBLEM

The West Indies and the Chesapeake were settled by Europeans during the first decades of the seventeenth century. Both areas relied initially upon the growing of tobacco as their staple crop, employing in the main European indentured servants as field labor. These Europeans signed a contract of indenture in return for passage to America and "freedom dues" paid at the end of the term. The indentured servant bound himself to labor for the owner of his contract for a specified period, usually 3 or 4 years. Working conditions, term, and the severance pay called "freedom dues" were set by a combination of contract, custom, and law. The majority of the Europeans coming to the Chesapeake and the British West Indies came as indentured servants in the seventeenth and eighteenth centuries.

During the decade of the 1640s, planters in the West Indies shifted from tobacco to sugar as their primary export crop and then began to import African slaves as field labor instead of European indentured servants. During this process the size of West Indian plantations increased, the number of Europeans in the islands fell, and by 1670 Africans made up more than half of the population.

The area of the Chesapeake meanwhile continued to rely upon tobacco as its staple and upon European indentured servants as its main source of new field labor. The average size of plantations remained small. This situation continued until the last decade of the seventeenth century when African slaves began to replace indentures. The transition was then fairly rapid but it was not until the middle of the eighteenth century that blacks actually outnumbered whites in the population. The average size of plantations in the Chesapeake remained far smaller than the ones in the West Indies throughout the colonial period.

The transition from European indentured servants to African slaves thus took place substantially earlier in the West Indies than it did in the Chesapeake and under quite different circumstances. Slaves began to replace indentures in the West Indies in the 1640s; a similar shift began in the Chesapeake a half century later. Whereas the rise of slavery in the West Indies was accompanied by the establishment of relatively large plantations organized to produce a different staple, tobacco in the Chesapeake continued to be grown on approximately the same scale that had existed prior to the switch to slaves.

The problem of explaining the transition from indentures to slaves in the two areas of British America has not escaped the attention of historians. In fact, there are several competing explanations. Aside from vague statements about the shortage of labor or that slavery was the "more profitable," the existing explanations can be roughly grouped into three categories. One explanation claims that organizing agriculture on plantations required slavery;[1] another that planters discovered Africans to be superior to Europeans because they were better able to withstand tropical climates;[2] a third explanation suggests that over the course of the seventeenth century mortality rates fell for both whites and blacks and this change favored the selection of slaves who were forced to serve for life over the shorter term indentures.[3] The comparison of these competing explanations requires a framework of analysis.

ANALYTICAL FRAMEWORK

The implications of each of the three existing categories of explanations can be easily considered and compared with reference to contemporary economic theory. A planter who was interested in doing as well as possible would choose the combination of factors of production that would maximize his profits. He would in the process behave as if he equated the ratio of the marginal physical product of the input and its price between all factors of production.

$$\frac{MPP_L}{P_L} = \frac{MPP_C}{P_C} = \frac{MPP_S}{P_S} = \frac{MPP_I}{P_I} = \frac{MPP_N}{P_N}$$

Should either the marginal physical product or the price of the factor of production change, thus altering the ratio, the planter would adjust by changing the quantity of the factor he used which was subject to diminishing returns until the equality between ratios was again restored.

Slaves and indentures were two sources of labor that were good substitutes for each other. The choice between the two would depend upon which ratio was the larger. Thus the important variables affecting the planters' choice between slaves and indentures was the marginal physical product of both and their relative prices. A change in any of these four variables could affect the decision as to how much labor to employ and which kind, slaves or indentures.

This framework allows us to consider in turn each of the existing expla-

---

[1] The "technological determinism" approach can be found in Eric Williams, *Capitalism and Slavery* (New York, 1966), p. 23; or E. E. Rich, "Colonial Settlement and Its Labour Problems," in E. E. Rich and C. H. Wilson, eds., *The Cambridge Economic History of Europe*, vol. 4 (Cambridge, 1967), p. 340.

[2] The old "African superiority in the tropics" belief is exemplified by George Louis Beer, *The Old Colonial System, 1660–1754*, vol. 1 (New York, 1933), pp. 321–322.

[3] Edmund S. Morgan, "The Labor Problem at Jamestown, 1607–18," *The American Historical Review*, vol. 76, no. 3, June 1971, p. 611.

nations. An acceptable explanation for the transition from indentures to slaves requires that either the price of slaves fell relative to the price of indentures at the time of the switch or that the relative productivity of slaves increased.

The marginal physical product of labor of either kind in the colonies depended upon the extent of skills, the level of technology, the availability of other factors of production, the legal environment, and life expectancy over the period of the employment contract. Many of these conditions were identical between types of labor and hence could not lead to differences in productivity between the two sources. Others however could. The marginal productivity of slaves relative to indentures, for instance, would certainly differ according to differential skill levels and life expectancy between the two competing groups. The price that a planter would be willing to pay for labor would reflect these differences.

The price of labor, on the other hand, depended upon the supply and demand for labor in the colonies. The price of indentures in any one colony depended upon the opportunity cost of labor in the Old World and upon transport costs between the Old World and the New World. The price of slaves in any colony was a function of their world market price plus transport costs between regions. The price of either slaves or indentures was beyond the control of any single planter. The existing explanations for the transition from indentures to slaves can each be evaluated within this economic framework.

EXISTING EXPLANATIONS

Each of the three existing explanations for the transition from indentures to slaves fails to account for the timing of the shift. Each concentrates upon differences in the productivity of slaves relative to indentures and, in the process, ignores the relative prices of the two types of labor.

Those historians that suggest that organizing agriculture via plantations requires slave labor are suggesting that the ratio of the marginal physical product of slaves and the price of slaves was and will always be greater on plantations than the ratio for alternative sources of labor. This occurs, so the argument must go, because the nature of the production function of a plantation makes slave labor always more productive than other types of labor. In fact, for the argument to hold true under all circumstances would require that organizing production in a plantation made slaves so much more productive than alternative sources of labor that no change in the relative prices of labor could ever induce planters to consider any other source of labor. No explanation is offered as to why the plantation form of operation should have this effect on the relative productivities of labor. Nor is it obvious why this would be so, since the methods for managing gangs of indentures must have been little different than the methods used for slaves.

The usual context in which this explanation is offered is that the introduction of sugar and the plantation to the West Indies provides the reason for the replacement of indentures by slaves. It is true there were technical economies of scale in sugar production that tended to make the optimum size of a sugar production unit fairly large. It is also true that for a period of centuries sugar plantations were usually manned by slave labor. These facts are normally interpreted as meaning that slave labor is always preferred by sugar planters. If this interpretation were correct, we would expect to find that the Barbadians would have imported slaves when they imported the technology of sugar planting from Dutch Brazil. The fact is that the replacement of indentures by slaves in Barbadian sugar production lagged by 5 or more years behind the adoption of sugar as the main staple crop. The available population data for the British West Indies indicates that more European indentures than African slaves were being imported until 1650 or later.[4] By that time sugar had been the primary crop grown for export for several years.[5] The Dutch West India Company dominated the Atlantic slave trade in the 1640s by virtue of the Company conquests in West Africa. We know that the Company sold one shipload of slaves in Barbados as early as the end of 1645.[6] A recent study of Company records shows, however,

---

[4] The slave population of Barbados rose from a maximum of 1000 in 1640 to 5000 or 6000 in 1643–1645, to 20,000 in the 1650s, and on to 40,000–80,000 in the 1660s. The white population grew very rapidly through the late 1640s, starting at about 10,000 in 1640, rising to nearly 40,000, and falling back to about 25,000 by 1655 and down further to about 20,000 by the late 1660s. Great Britain, *Calendar of State, Papers, Colonial, 1661-68,* vol. 5, no. 1657; Beer, *The Old Colonial System,* vol. I, p. 320n; K. G. Davies, *The Royal African Company* (London, 1957), p. 300; J. Harry Bennett, "Peter Hay, Proprietary Agent," *Jamaican Historical Review,* vol. 5, November 1965, pp. 12–13; V. T. Harlow, *A History of Barbados, 1625–1685* (Oxford, 1926), pp. 310n and 338; and C. S. S. Higham, *The Development of the Leeward Islands Under the Restoration, 1660–1688* (Cambridge, 1921), p. 4.

[5] In 1640 there was effectively no sugar grown in Barbados. In 1645, 40% of the cultivated land has been said to have been in sugar—with the proportion rising to 80% by 1667. David Lowenthal, "The Population of Barbados," *Social and Economic Studies,* vol. 6, no. 4, December 1957, p. 451. A sugar output of 6950 tons is reported for 1655. This is only slightly less than the 7538-ton average for 1701–1710. Noel Deerr, *A History of Sugar,* vol. I (London, 1949), p. 193.

[6] The ship, *Tamadare,* dispatched in December 1645 from Brazil, sold 207 Negroes on Barbados. Ernst van den Boogaart, "The Dutch Participation in the Atlantic Slave Trade, 1596–1648," paper circulated at Mathematical Social Science Board Conference (Colby College, Maine, August 1975), p. 17 (Chapter 14 in this volume).

that there could not have been a significant number of slaves sent by the Company to Barbados until 1648 or 1649 at the earliest.[7]

There is, of course, the possibility that English planters were slow learners—that it took them half a decade to learn that slaves and sugar went together. This does not seem very probable, however, since slaves were not new to Barbados. Slaves had been used on the island in small numbers from the first year of settlement.[8] Furthermore, we know that slaves and indentures were employed side by side in the same fields during the transition period. This suggests that, for a while at least, productivity–price ratios were equal for slaves and indentures on West Indian sugar plantations.[9] An alternate possibility is that slave suppliers waited that long before awakening to the opportunity. This long a lag is hard to credit to even as ponderous an organization as the Dutch West Indian Company, especially in light of the urgent need for an outlet to replace Brazil after that slave market collapsed in 1645.[10] It is even harder to credit such a slow response to opportunity to the numerous interlopers that we know to have been poaching upon the Dutch monopoly in Africa.[11]

In the Caribbean, if a half-decade lag in response by planters or slavers is credible, then the shift in crops to sugar, and thus to large plantations, may explain the replacement there of indentures by slaves. In the case of the Chesapeake the argument that it was the establishment of the plantation system that caused the introduction of slavery simply has no explanatory power at all. The production of Virginia tobacco was not characterized by large plantations in the period either before or after indentures were replaced by slaves. At the same time that the transition from indentures to slaves occurred the average size of the work force on a tobacco plantation remained small and effectively constant, as shown in Table 15.2. Slave imports to Virginia were trivial prior to the last quarter of the century in comparison to the number of indentured servants being imported. It was not until the 1690s when the number of indentured servants entering Virginia drastically declined that the number of slaves being imported grew substantially. The timing of the transition is suggested by the available

---

[7] Van den Boogaart, "Dutch Participation" (Chapter 14 in this volume).

[8] Harlow, *History of Barbados,* p. 329.

[9] In 1646 a plantation in Barbados is noted with "50 Negroes and 40 men." J. H. Bennett, "The English Caribbees in the Period of the Civil War, 1642–1646," *The William and Mary Quarterly,* 3rd series, vol. 24, no. 3, July 1967, p. 372. Indentured servants and slaves being used together as field labor is mentioned about 1650 and as late as 1667. Richard Ligon, *A True and Exact History of the Island of Barbados* (London, 1657), pp. 44–45; and Harlow, *History of Barbados,* p. 309.

[10] Van den Boogaart, "Dutch Participation," p. 17 (Chapter 14 in this volume).

[11] *Ibid.*

evidence on population,[12] slave import data,[13] and the headright lists[14] (see Tables 15.1–15.3).

A second explanation for the prevalence of slaves over indentures is based upon the higher life expectancy of Africans relative to Europeans when introduced into a tropical or semitropical climate. Whether the new colonials were of European or African origin they faced a new disease environment when introduced into America. Blacks seem to have fared less badly than whites in adjusting to this new climate.[15]

This fact suggests one reason why the marginal product of slaves might differ from that of indentures. In itself, however, it does not provide an explanation for the transition unless blacks suddenly in the 1640s fared better than whites in the West Indies, and similarly in the Chesapeake at the turn of the century. So far, no evidence that this was true has been presented by the expositors of this explanation.

The explanation then fails because it does not consider all the variables that affect the ratio of the marginal physical product of labor and its price. Any advantage or disadvantage of one type of labor relative to another can generally be compensated for by a difference in price. If one type of labor is more productive than another but has proportionally an even higher price then it is not more but less efficient.

The third explanation relies upon a general decline over time in mortality for both colonial whites and blacks. This explanation suggests that as mortality due to "seasoning" declined, slaves would become relatively more desirable as an investment. Slaves were owned for life, indentures for a fixed term of usually 4 or 5 years. The planter would benefit more from slaves if their life expectancy increased than he would from a similar occurrence affecting indentures. The planters would, after all, enjoy the product of longer-lived slaves but would not gain similarly from indentures whose term of service had expired.

This argument, like the others, also suffers from difficulties in explaining the timing of the transition. Unless the decline in mortality occurred at different periods in the West Indies than in the Chesapeake, this explanation cannot account for the timing.

---

[12] U. S. Bureau of the Census, *Historical Statistics of the United States, Colonial Times to 1957*, (Washington D.C., 1960), series Z 1–19; and Beer, *Old Colonial System*, vol. I, p. 367.

[13] *Historical Statistics of the United States, Colonial Times to 1957*, series Z 294–297.

[14] Evidence from Charles Co., Maryland, and Northumberland Co., Virginia, reported in Russell R. Menard, "Immigration to the Chesapeake Colonies in the Seventeenth Century: A Review Essay," *Maryland Historical Magazine*, vol. 68, no. 3, Fall 1973, p. 327, indicates that servant imports may have had a brief revival in 1698 and 1699 but collapsed thereafter.

[15] Philip D. Curtin, "Epidemiology and the Slave Trade," *Political Science Quarterly*, vol. 83, June 1968, pp. 190–216.

TABLE 15.1
Surry County, Virginia, Slave Holdings

Size of slave holding	1674	1684	1694	1703
1–3	10	23	26	52
4–6	2	4	7	12
7–9	1	3	2	4
10–12	—	—	2	1
13–15	—	—	2	—
16–18	—	—	—	2
19 +	—	—	—	—

Source: Surry County Records: Deeds and Will Book 1652–1703.

Furthermore, it would take quite a large shift in life expectancies to have much of an impact upon a planter's profit calculations. The relative value of a slave and of the same man bound by an indenture contract can be calculated if we know the time period of the indenture, the discount rate, and life expectancies. Indenture terms averaged 4 to 5 years in the seventeenth century, and the opportunity cost of capital to the planter was a minimum 8% per year.[16] Life expectancies for migrants to the Chesapeake were extremely low and were even worse in the Caribbean. The one relevant life table available is for Maryland in the seventeenth century. Life expectancy for a 22-year-old migrant from Europe who already had survived the first deadly year of "seasoning" was only 22.7 more years.[17] It is reasonable to assume that at least 15% of the migrants died in the initial seasoning period.[18] If we further assume that labor productivity and maintenance costs remain constant through age 70, then discount to a present value the expected stream of labor services for a 5-year indenture and, for a slave for life, the slave turns out to be worth only 238% as much as the

[16] For indenture terms see Harlow, *History of Barbados,* p. 301n. For interest rates see Ward Barrett, "Caribbean Sugar-Production Standards in the Seventeenth and Eighteenth Centuries," in John Parker, ed., *Merchants and Scholars* (Minneapolis, 1965), p. 152.

[17] Lorena S. Walsh and Russell R. Menard, "Death in the Chesapeake: Two Life Tables for Men in Early Colonial Maryland," *Maryland Historical Magazine,* vol. 69, no. 2, Summer 1974, pp. 211–227. See also Richard S. Dunn, "The Barbados Census of 1680: Profile of the Richest Colony in English America," *The William and Mary Quarterly,* 3rd series, vol. 26, no. 1, October 1969, p. 26; Great Britain, *Calendar of State Papers, Colonial, 1708–9,* vol. 24, no. 94; Frank Wesley Pitman, "Slavery on the British West Indian Plantations in the Eighteenth Century," *Journal of Negro History,* vol. 11, no. 4, October 1926, p. 645.

[18] More than 40% of a group of seventeenth-century Maryland servants do not appear in the records as free men. Some of these had moved on, but most had probably died. Russell R. Menard, "From Servant to Freeholder: Status Mobility and Property Accumulation in Seventeenth Century Maryland," *William and Mary Quarterly,* 3rd series, vol. 30, no. 1, January 1973, p. 39.

TABLE 15.2
Average Titheables per Household in Virginia by Counties

Year	Surry	Accomack	Lancaster	Northampton	Northumberland	Henrico
1655	—	—	3.95	—	—	—
1658	—	—	4.13	—	—	—
1663	—	3.27[a]	5.10	3.11	—	—
1668	2.38	2.44	4.90	2.22	—	—
1673	1.94	2.25[b]	3.79	2.08[b]	—	—
1678	2.12	2.55	3.47	2.27[c]	3.06[d]	2.73
1683	1.86	2.07	2.62	—	—	—
1688	1.88	2.19	2.98	—	—	—
1693	1.75	2.16	2.62	—	—	—
1698	1.87	—	2.55	—	—	—
1703	2.06	—	3.49	—	—	—

Source: Virginia County Records, Virginia State Library.
[a] In 1665.
[b] In 1674.
[c] In 1677.
[d] In 1679.

indentured servant. A 22-year-old man for life was worth only a little more than twice as much as a 5-year indenture contract on the same man. High mortality and a high discount rate made claims on labor services more than a few years in the future nearly valueless (see Table 15.4).

The relative value of a lifetime contract and a 5-year contract probably differed by even less than this implies. Mortality for servants and slaves was doubtless higher than for the migrants that supplied the data for the Walsh–Russell life table. The opportunity cost of capital was higher than 8% in seventeenth-century British America.

The fact that slaves would have children may at this time have narrowed rather than increased the gap between the value of slaves and indentures, because in the seventeenth century children probably cost more to raise than could be realized by their sale as adults even when the value of their productivity as adolescents was netted out.[19] In the British West Indies

[19] Lowell Joseph Ragatz, The Fall of the Planter Class in the British Caribbean, 1763–1833 (New York, 1928), p. 337, shows, at least, that the costs of raising slaves in the West Indies at the end of the eighteenth century was very high indeed. The general price level rose much slower through the eighteenth century than did the price of slaves; thus the discrepancy between the cost of buying Africans or raising Creoles should have been even larger in the seventeenth century. Even in the Southen states in the nineteenth century, when slave prices were much higher as a result of the ending of importations from Africa, the net value of children was very low in comparison to the value of the mother's labor services. Robert William Fogel and Stanley L. Engerman, Time on the Cross, vol. 1 (Boston, 1974), p. 83.

TABLE 15.3
Virginia and Maryland Headrights by Decade

| | Virginia | | Maryland |
Decade	White	Black	White
1635–1639	6356	140	622
1640–1649	4769	105	1096
1650–1659	18,836	317	2938
1660–1669	18,369	609	8138
1670–1679	13,867	421	8639
1680–1689	10,401	629	5047[a]
1690–1699	9388	1847	5252[a]
1700–1709	—	6936	—

Source: Virginia: W. R. Craven, *White, Red and Black: The Seventeenth Century Virginian* (Charlottesville, 1971); Maryland: Gust Skordas, ed, *The Early Settlers of Maryland, 1633–1680* (Baltimore, 1968).

[a] Adjusted at the ratio of Maryland–Virginia headrights in 1670–1679 to fill in missing decades.

slaves were not encouraged to have children until the late eighteenth century when the price of slaves increased substantially.[20]

Even a dramatic reduction in mortality could have had little impact upon the relative prices of indentures and slaves. If seasoning deaths fell by one-third (to 10%) and life expectancies rose by one-third (from 23 years to 34 years for a seasoned 22-year-old), a life term would be worth 266% of a 5-year term instead of 238%.[21] There is no reason to believe such a drastic increase in life expectancies occurred, and even if it had, it would have resulted in only a 10% increase in the relative value of a slave. Rising life expectancy can be eliminated as a likely cause of planters substituting slaves for indentured servants.

[20] Planters during this period strenuously attempted to prevent births to indentured women because of the risk of death and the lost labor time entailed by motherhood. The courts cooperated by increasing the terms of indentured women who gave birth to illegitimate children. Harlow, *History of Barbados,* p. 305n; and William Wallace Hening, *The Statutes at Large . . . of Virginia . . . from 1619* (New York, 1823), vol. 1, pp. 252–253 and 438–439, vol. 2, pp. 114–115 and 167–168; vol. 3, p. 452.

[21] A life expectancy of 34 years for a 22-year-old is closely approximated in the "Level 25" table in United Nations, *Methods of Population Projection by Sex and Age,* United Nations Population Studies no. 25 (New York, 1956), p. 76. Calculated in the same manner as in Table 15.4, the present equivalent of discounted expected future man-years of work would have been 3.81 years for a 5-year term, and 10.12 years for life.

TABLE 15.4
Present Value of Bound Labor (Seventeenth-Century Maryland)

Age	Percentage alive at year end	Present equivalent of work year, 8% discount	Cumulative present equivalent work years
22	85.0	.85	.85
23	83.2	.77	1.62
24	81.5	.70	2.32
25	79.7	.63	2.95
26	78.0	.57	3.52 Fifth year
27	76.2	.52	4.04
28	74.4	.47	4.51
29	72.7	.42	4.93
30	71.0	.38	5.31
—	—	—	—
40	50.0	.13	7.54
—	—	—	—
50	25.4	.03	8.18
—	—	—	—
60	12.2	.007	8.33
—	—	—	—
70	5.3	.001	8.36

AN ALTERNATIVE EXPLANATION

The colonial historians who were most vague about explaining the switch from indentures to slaves, confining themselves to a statement that slaves were "more profitable," were correct. "More profitable," however, is simply a truism without substance unless we can specify why slaves were more profitable and why they suddenly became so at the times that they did. We rejected the other explanations that we have examined on the basis of their failure to explain the timing of the events, so that timing must be the first basis for judging the alternative explanation that we are presenting.

When we formulated the analytical model we showed that the choice between alternate inputs would be made on the basis of relative productivities and relative prices. A plantation manager would switch from indentures to slaves when

$$\frac{MPP_S}{P_S} > \frac{MPP_I}{P_I}$$

Thus, a change in any one of four variables—marginal physical product of slaves, marginal physical product of indentured servants, price of indentures, or price of slaves—could cause the transition. If both marginal products or both prices changed, then it was the relative changes that were important. Economic theory thus suggests what to look for in the historical records by specifying which variables could have been important. A reliable time series of prices and of the relative productivities of the two types of labor would easily resolve our question. Regrettably, such data series do not exist. It is possible, however, to infer the timing, direction, and even general magnitude of shifts in relative prices and/or productivities from other evidence that is available. In the next sections we shall investigate the prices and productivities of both factors to see if and when there were changes.

THE PRODUCTIVITY OF LABOR

We have seen in the preceding that existing explanations have focused upon the relative productivity of slaves compared with that of indentures in their attempt to explain "Why slaves?" These explanations failed because there was no evidence that the productivity of slaves increased relative to that of indentures at the time of the transition. The productivity of labor at any point in time depended upon the existing technology, the skill level of labor, the availability of other factors of production, and the legal environment. We have found no evidence to suggest that any such changes occurred in a manner that would result in substantially increasing the productivity of slaves relative to indentures.

Certainly there were no changes in the legal environment with respect to slavery that could explain the transition. There is a debate of long standing among social historians on the date that chattel slavery was established in British America.[22] Both sides of this debate seem to be agreed, however,

[22] Among those who have argued that Negroes were really indentured servants in Virginia until mid-century are Oscar and Mary Handlin, "Origins of the Southern Labor System," *William and Mary Quarterly,* 3rd series, vol. 7, no. 2, April 1950, pp. 199–222; Paul C. Palmer, "Servant Into Slave: The Evaluation of the Legal Status of the Negro Laborer in Colonial America," *South Atlantic Quarterly,* vol. 65, no. 3, Summer 1966, pp. 355–370; George M. Fredrickson, "Toward a Social Interpretation of the Development of American Racism," in Nathan Huggins, Martin Kilson, and Daniel Fox, eds., *Key Issues in the Afro-American Experience,* vol. 1 (New York, 1971), p. 244. Evidence that Negroes were being treated as slaves before chattel slavery was codified into law can be found in Carl N. Degler, "Slavery and the Genesis of American Race Prejudice," *Comparative Studies in Society and History,* vol. 2, no. 1, October 1959, pp. 55–58; Winthrop D. Jordan, "Modern Tensions and the Origins of American Slavery," *Journal of Southern History,* vol. 28, no. 1, February 1962, p. 25; and Alden

that the latest dates are 1636 for Barbados and 1670 for Virginia. These are the years when laws were instituted in those colonies specifying perpetual slavery for Negroes imported without contracts of indenture.[23] These dates precede the transition from indenture to slave labor in the two colonies, thus eliminating changes in legal institutions as a possible cause for the shift in labor forms.

Neither were there significant differences over time in the skill levels of the two potential immigrant groups or in the availability of other factors of production. In both areas slaves replaced indentures and little else changed. The scale of operation of a Chesapeake tobacco plantation remained small and more or less constant throughout the transition. Prior to the 1680s a Virginia or Maryland planter tilled his field aided by one or two indentures. Increasingly after 1680 he tilled his field with the aid of one or two slaves.

The changes in the West Indies, first replacing tobacco with sugar as the staple and then replacing indentures with slaves as the main source of field labor, were accompanied by an increase in the average size of plantations. The small tobacco farm was absorbed into a larger sugar plantation. Even then a sugar plantation was not large in size, covering 100–200 acres. This was the area necessary to support the processing equipment. The consolidation of sugar plantations was a lengthy process taking much longer than the transition from white to black labor. Nevertheless there exists evidence that during the transition both indentures and slaves were used together in the fields, suggesting that the ratios of their respective productivities to their price were, for a time at least, equal even on a large sugar plantation.[24]

Whereas it is impossible to state precisely the relative productivity of slaves compared to indentures, there is little need, for our purposes, to do so. The important consideration is the ratio of the productivity of each to their prices. When we observe both types of labor being simultaneously employed we can infer that the ratios are equal. Since we do not find evidence of significant and timely changes in the productivity of slaves

T. Vaughan, "Blacks in Virginia: A Note on the First Decade," *William and Mary Quarterly,* 3rd series, vol. 29, no. 1, January 1972, pp. 469–478. Our own opinion is that Negroes who were brought to the British colonies as slaves were treated as slaves from the beginning. The legal terminology was laggardly, probably because the number of Negro slaves was so small. The free blacks either had entered the colonies as nonslaves or had been voluntarily emancipated.

[23] For Barbados see Winthrop D. Jordan, "The Influence of the West Indies on the Origins of New England Slavery," *William and Mary Quarterly,* 3rd series, vol. 18, no. 2, April 1961, p. 248. For Virginia see W. W. Hening, ed., *The Statutes at Large . . . of Virginia,* vol. 2 (New York, 1823), p. 283.

[24] Ligon, *True and Exact History,* pp. 44–45, notes the simultaneous use of white indentured servants and Negro slaves as field labor on the same plantations in the early days of Barbados sugar culture. See also Bennett, "The English Caribbees," p. 372.

relative to indentures we must now look at their relative prices to ascertain whether changes occurred that would explain the transition.

PRICES OF LABOR

Our information about the prices of slaves and indentured servants is unfortunately not too much better than our information on relative productivities. Price series for neither slaves nor indentured servants exist in either area for the entire seventeenth century. It is possible, however, to infer the pattern of these prices from related data.

The assembling of pertinent information for the mid-1600s poses the greatest problem. This was an era of turmoil and disruption in the American slave trade, a period when the Dutch West India Company at least partially replaced the Portuguese in most of the African slave traffic. Spain halted legal slave imports to her colonies with the Portuguese revolt of 1640, while at the same time British and French Caribbean demand for slaves increased. War and conquest in Brazil surely caused significant fluctuations in demand. There is no direct evidence telling us whether the total volume of the slave trade or the prices paid for slaves in Africa rose or fell. This was also a period of monopoly. Unfortunately there is no direct evidence as to the proportion of the slaves imported into the British West Indies that were supplied by the Dutch West India Company. Thus we cannot be certain that there was enough competition in the British West Indian slave trade to ensure that the Dutch West India Company did not dictate prices.

This last point is of some significance. We do have Dutch West India Company slave prices in Pernambuco for 1636–1645 (see Table 15.5). These data show drastic falls in slave prices in 1643 and 1645. If the movement in slave prices in Dutch Brazil was a reflection of market conditions for the entire Atlantic trade then they are a good proxy for movements in British West Indian slave prices. If the Dutch West India Company, however, was significantly exercising its monopoly power in Brazil alone, or if it also had such power in the British West Indies and exercised that power differentially in Brazil, then Pernambuco prices may not tell us anything about Barbados prices. In summary, the fall in Brazilian slave prices is suggestive but is unfortunately not conclusive.

There is even less direct evidence on the prices of indentured servants in the mid-1600s than there is for slaves. A large part of the problem results from the nature of imported labor itself. Both slaves and indentured servants varied in price due to age, sex, and health differences. Indenture prices were also affected strongly by skill differentials whereas Africans were almost entirely homogeneous in this respect. Finally, indentures were

TABLE 15.5
Pernambuco Slave Sales 1636–1645

Year	Number of slaves sold	Price per capita in decimalized florins	Price per capita in decimalized sterling[a]
1636	1031	162.31	15.57
1637	1580	243.41	23.60
1638	1711	436.97	40.88
1639	1802	482.96	44.15
1640	1188	335.49	30.03
1641	1437	430.15	36.72
1642	2312	454.66	39.75
1643	3948	246.26	20.54
1644	5565	155.03	13.03
1645	2589	247.62	20.98

Source: H. Wätgen. Das Holländische Kolonialreich in Brasilien (Haag, 1921), p. 311.

[a] The Wätgen data are expressed as total revenue in florins. These were converted to sterling by the Amsterdam exchange rate and divided by the number of slaves to get the decimalized sterling price. The exchange rates used are from N. W. Posthumus, Inquiry into the History of Prices in Holland, vol. 1 (Leiden, 1946), pp. 579, 638.

mostly freely entered contracts. These contracts could and did differ considerably in their provisions.

An individual signed an indenture as the only method for a poor man to raise the capital to transport himself (and sometimes his family) to the potential riches of the New World. In practice it was the only way for a person without cash who wished to emigrate, to borrow on his major asset—his future labor. There were, of course, debtors, felons, and, on occasion, political prisoners who were sold by some arm of government and thus had no voice in the terms of the contract; but ordinarily the prospective indenture could negotiate his own terms. The time periods seem to have usually been about 4 years of service for an adult, but much longer and shorter terms frequently occurred.[25] The articles of indenture were often quite complex, specifying not only the length of service but also the type of work, the colony, diet, clothing, wages, and a termination settlement in cash and/or kind. These complications make the compilation of a meaningful price series for indentures practically impossible since so many factors other than the time period and the price paid could be varied.

It is possible, however, to look at the conditions affecting the supply of indentures. The decision of an Englishman (or Irishman, Welshman, or

[25] Harlow, History of Barbados, p. 301n, says that the usual term of service was 5–7 years before the Restoration but fell to 3 or 4 years thereafter.

Scotsman) to emigrate would be mainly a matter of comparing expected income in Great Britain with expected income in the colonies. Expected income in America would be determined most importantly by the terms of indenture, life expectancy in the colony, and economic opportunity once the indenture had been served out. For example, in the 1640s the numbers of ex-indentured servants who left Barbados grew rapidly. The desirable arable land there was already occupied and the same thing happened rapidly thereafter in the Leeward Islands. A large part of these departures were for North America. High death rates from tropical diseases and declining economic opportunities for new arrivals should have combined with the gradual spread of information about the true state of affairs in the British West Indies to raise the offer price of indentured labor to the West Indies above that to the Chesapeake.[26]

At least as important as colonial conditions, and much more easily quantifiable, were employment opportunities in England. There is quite strong evidence of rising money wages between 1640 and 1645 (see Table 15.6 and Figure 15.1). This rise was, in fact, the most rapid indicated by the English wage data for more than a century before and more than a century after that time.

This evidence suggests that the substitution of slaves for indentures as field labor in the British West Indies during the 1640s is consistent with changing relative prices. There is at the same time no evidence for changing relative productivities to counter this influence. The decline of economic opportunity for time-served indentures in the British West Indies must have raised their offer price. The increase in wages in England for potential indentures certainly also raised the supply price of indentures. Furthermore, there is some scanty evidence that the price of slaves may have fallen in the British West Indies, and really no evidence exists indicating a price rise in the 1640s. This evidence suggests that European labor rose in price

---

[26] A. E. Smith, *Colonists in Bondage: White Servitude and Convict Labor in America, 1607–1776* (Chapel Hill, 1947), p. 57, discusses the preference of indentured servants for North America; and Harlow, *History of Barbados,* p. 301 ff., discusses the increasing difficulty of acquiring indentured servants after 1650. The poor treatment sometimes meted out to indentured servants by their Barbadian masters aroused demands among planters that these servants be given better protection under the law. Here is a classic case of external costs. Knowledge of cruelty by a few planters spread back to Europe and made it more difficult and expensive for all the planters to acquire European laborers. No such externalities were perceived by the planters for cases of poor treatment of African slaves and no demands were made by them for the protection of slaves from harsh masters. Actions by the colonial governments to mitigate the lot of slaves were not taken until late in the eighteenth century when the colonists perceived that the supply of slaves could also be influenced by tales of harsh treatment. In this case the mechanism was through British public opinion and its control over laws governing the slave trade.

TABLE 15.6
Index of Building Wages in Southern England 1655–1686 = 100

Year[a]	Index	Year	Index
1625	68	1685	100.1
1630	75.3	1690	103.3
1635	76.7	1695	106.7
1640	85.3	1700	111.3
1645	94.7	1705	118.3
1650	96.7	1710	121.3
1655	98.7	1715	123.3
1660	100	1720	123.3
1665	100	1725	123.3
1670	100	1730	126.3
1675	100	1735	130.3
1680	100	—	—

Source: E. H. Phelps-Brown and S. V. Hopkins, "Seven Centuries of Building Wages," *Economica,* vol. 22, no. 87, August 1955, p. 205. These are the middle values of the ranges given for "craftsmen" and "labourers" averaged annually and then averaged by 5-year periods.

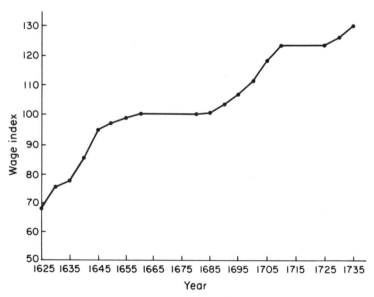

Figure 15.1. Index of building wages in southern England, 1655–1686 = 100. (Data are from Table 15.6.)

relative to African labor, which is theoretically consistent with the shift from indentures to slaves in Barbados in the late 1640s.

As a final note it should be realized that the replacement of European indentured servants by African slaves as field labor on plantations does not imply the complete halt of importation of indentured servants. It does imply a drastic reduction in their numbers, but white indentures entered the production function of a plantation in ways other than just as field labor. Indentures were also valued as skilled labor, supervisors, foremen, and security guards for the plantation owners, but the use of indentures as field labor in the Caribbean was to be increasingly unusual after the late 1640s.

If the relative rise in the price of indentures is why Barbados replaced servants with slaves, why did the planters at the Chesapeake wait for nearly a half century more before going through the same transition? Some slaves, it should be noted, were used in Virginia as early as 1619. The basic techniques of tobacco cultivation established by 1640 were not substantially altered for at least another century. The institutional arrangements of Virginia did not differ from those of Barbados in a way that raised the relative costs of slave labor in Virginia. The rising wages in England, which probably caused the switch to slaves in the West Indies, also raised the cost of indentures in Virginia, and yet Virginia planters did not substitute slaves for indentures in mid-seventeenth century.

The explanation for this phenomenon again lies in relative supply prices of labor. Geography alone would have caused the relative prices of slaves and indentures to differ between Virginia and the West Indies. The offer price of each type of labor in the colonies was a function of their cost in the Old World plus the cost of transporting them to the New World. These transport costs for slaves, which certainly differed substantially between regions, differed less than those for indentures. The passage rates are measurable. The costs of passage for an indenture from England to America did not differ substantially between North America and the West Indies because the passage times did not vary appreciably. Also, since there was excess capacity on the Western leg of both routes, passage could be obtained at marginal cost. In contrast, the passage time between Africa and Virginia was considerably longer than the passage time between Africa and Barbados. Barbados was actually only slightly off the fastest route for sailing ships between West Africa and Virginia. This meant that both the per-slave operating costs of the ship and mortality rate of slaves during the passage were higher for slaves destined for Virginia.

The price of slaves in Virginia seems to have been for these reasons consistently £3–4 sterling higher than in Barbados. This is a 15–20% increase over the usual Barbados price. The evidence for this differential is three-fold. Freight rates for a slave from the West Indies to North America ran about £3 per slave.[27] Second, we have the Royal African Company agreement of 1672 which set North American slave prices £3 above the Barbados level.[28] Finally we have the direct comparison of a large number of actual transaction prices from the later seventeenth century through the eighteenth century. The average of these differences was £4.72 (decimalized sterling) and the median difference was £3.91.[29] Since the price of an average slave in Barbados was at this time a little less than £20, African labor cost substantially more on a percentage basis in Virginia than Barbados.

If the cost of indentured servants was approximately the same in both areas but the cost of slaves significantly higher in the Chesapeake, then the relative prices of the two sources of labor obviously differed between regions. It was therefore possible under certain conditions for slaves to be both the lowest cost source of labor in the West Indies and the highest cost in the Chesapeake.

A more formal diagrammatic exposition in the form of an economic model will aid our explanation of this situation. Let us begin with the assumption that European indentured servants and African slaves are perfect substitutes as plantation field labor. Thus, the vertical axis will be price in pounds sterling and the horizontal axis will be units of labor. Further, let us assume that the supplies of slaves and of indentures were perfectly elastic at the market price in the long run to any British colony. This assumption appears realistic for slaves because all of the British colonies together took only a small fraction of Africa's total slave exports in the seventeenth century and the market for slaves in Africa was highly competitive. In the case of indentures the assumption of perfect elasticity is also apt to be fairly realistic because annual immigration during the seventeenth century was always small relative to the labor force in Britain and even to the numbers of people moving long distances in England.

The model graphically depicted in Figure 15.2 demonstrates how it is possible to go from a situation (1640) where slave labor is relatively more expensive in both colonies, hence is not used, to a situation (1650–1670)

[27] Darold Duane Wax, "The Negro Slave Trade in Colonial Pennsylvania," unpublished doctoral dissertation (University of Washington, 1962), pp. 23, 24, 99, 104, 106. These rates are for the West Indies to Pennsylvania but should not differ appreciably from the rates to Virginia. The rates tend to overstate the Virginia–West Indies slave price differentials because they include transshipment costs but tend to understate the differential by omitting losses due to increased mortality of the longer trip.

[28] Great Britain, *Calendar of State Papers, Colonial, 1669–1674*, vol. 7, no. 985.

[29] These price observations come from too many different sources to list here. For a complete tabulation see Richard Bean, *The British Trans-Atlantic Slave Trade, 1650–1775* (New York, 1975), Appendix B.

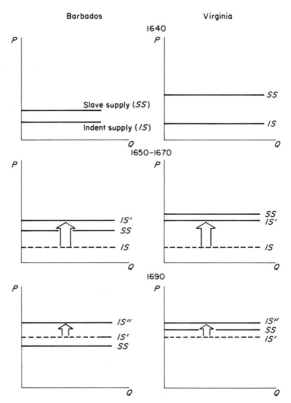

Figure 15.2. The model of labor supply, demonstrating a transition from indentured to slave labor.

where slave labor is relatively cheaper, hence used, in Barbados but not in Virginia, and finally to a situation (1690) where slave labor is relatively cheaper in both colonies and indentures are no longer used.[30] If we continue our search for an explanation for Virginia's belated transition to slaves, we need to explore what actually happened to the relative prices of slaves and indentures during the period of changeover. Fortunately, we have more and better evidence for this period than we possessed for the 1640s. The evidence on the price of slaves in the last quarter of the

[30] This model can be complicated with added "realism" without altering our conclusions. If the indenture supply function were not perfectly elastic the results would be unchanged except for the possibility of a less than 100% substitution of slaves for indentures. If we relax the assumption that African and European labor had the same relative productivities in tobacco and sugar production, our earlier conclusions would still hold so long as indentures are relatively more efficient than slaves in tobacco cultivation, or if less efficient, are not sufficiently so to offset the £4 freight advantage that Barbados had in the purchasing of slaves.

TABLE 15.7
Slave Prices in Jamaica (Decimalized Pounds)

Mid-year of 5-year averages	Davies, average prices (currency)	Bean, price of men (sterling)	n
1665	—	21.14	15
1670	—	21.14	20
1675	21.37	21.92	19
1680	16.65	19.32	29
1685	16.70	19.95	10
1690	20.15	23.85	5
1695	20.67	26.02	9
1700	20.95	23.68	26
1705	24.83	26.37	26
1710	25.75	24.37	24

Sources: K. G. Davies, The Royal African Company (London; 1957), p. 364; and a series compiled by R. N. Bean, Tables Z1865–1868, U. S. Bureau of the Census, Historical Statistics of the United States, Colonial Times to 1972 (Washington, D. C., 1975). n in the Bean series is the number of different prices that were averaged to get the figure given. Many of the observations were themselves averages of the prices of a large number of slaves.

seventeenth century is much more reliable than it was for the middle of the century. We have two alternate slave price series which move closely together[31] (see Table 15.7). The absolute level of slave prices in Virginia was higher than in Jamaica by a constant amount so price movements in the two areas should have been very similar. Although for much of this period there was a chartered monopoly over the importation of Africans into the British Empire, there was no restriction on the trading of slaves between colonies within the Empire. Thus free traders would have arbitraged out any inter-colonial price differentials that were not reflections of true cost differences.

Both of these price series indicate that the slave prices in Virginia may have fallen by as much as 20% in the 1680s and returned to their previous level in the 1690s. Meanwhile the price of indentures as measured by wages in England began to rise and had increased by 10% by 1700, and as much again by 1710. The indenture supply function facing Virginia thus shifted up relative to the slave supply.

Also, with the opening of North Carolina and Pennsylvania to large-scale

[31] In many ways the better of the two comes out of K. G. Davies's compilations from the Royal African Company Records. This series is expressed as an average in colonial currency for large groups of slaves. The other series is compiled from a large number of sources and is not completely independent of the Davies series because it probably includes many of the same transactions. The prices in this second case are in sterling per adult male.

settlement in the 1680s, the productivity of indentures was reduced. The lure of these new frontiers and their relative lawlessness raised the costs of enforcing the indenture contract. Successful escape for a bond servant was made both more attractive and easier.[32] The desirability of indentures relative to slaves may have been further reduced with the onset of war with France in 1689 because slaves were not liable for military service whereas European indentured servants were—and their masters were not compensated for labor or lives thus lost.

It is impossible to provide weights to ascertain whether the relative increase in price of indentures or their reduced productivity was more important in causing Chesapeake tobacco planters to turn to slaves. Both changes reinforced one another. The changes in the relative supply prices of slaves and indentures are, however, consistent with the timing of the large-scale introduction of slaves into the British West Indies and later into Virginia. In the 1640s a substantial rise in English wages drove up the price of indentures in the colonies at a time when the price of slaves appears to have been constant or falling. This rise was sufficient to cause the planters in the West Indies to shift to slaves but, because of transport cost differentials, slave labor remained more expensive than indentured labor in Virginia. The increase in the cost of indentures during the 1640s was not enough to cause a similar shift in Virginia. Both English wages and slave prices remained effectively static until the 1680s, when the price of slaves began to fall. At this point Virginian planters began to substitute slaves for indentures. Slave prices rose in the 1690s but were more than matched by rising wages in England. It was at this point in time that slaves became cheaper than indentures in the Chesapeake. Thereafter slaves increasingly replaced indentures as the primary source of field labor. The transition was complete.

---

[32] Complaints are frequent in the official correspondence of Virginia from 1681. See Great Britain, *Calendar of State Papers, Colonial, 1681–85,* vol. 2, p. 155; *1706–8,* vol. 23, pp. 598, 679; and John Spencer Bassett, *Slavery and Servitude in the Colony of North Carolina* (Baltimore, 1896), p. 79.

16

The Economic Considerations behind the Danish Abolition of the Negro Slave Trade

SVEND E. GREEN-PEDERSEN

By an edict of 16 March 1792, the Danish slave trade was to be abolished in 1803. As Denmark thus became the first European colonial power to issue a ban on slave trading, Danish historians have often assigned a prominent place to this edict in the Danish reform legislation of the late eighteenth century. The basic account of the writing of the edict is a turn-of-the-century treatise by C. A. Trier.[1] Trier's view of the Danish slave trade abolition in many ways resembled Reginald Coupland's view of the British abolition.[2] His view has been commonly accepted in broader surveys of Danish history, just as it was repeated in the German historian Christian Degn's recent monograph about the Schimmelmann family.[3] As is known,

[1] C. A. Trier, "Det dansk-vestindiske negerindførselsforbud af 1792," *Historisk Tidsskrift,* 7th series, vol. 5 (Copenhagen, 1904–1905), pp. 405–508.

[2] Reginald Coupland, *The British Anti-Slavery Movement,* 2nd ed. (London, 1964, first published 1933).

[3] See for instance Edvard Holm's account in *Danmark-Norges Historie fra Den store nordiske Krigs slutning til rigernes Adskillelse (1720–1814),* vol. 6, no. 2 (Copenhagen, 1909), Chapter 15; Axel Lindvald's in Aage Friis, A. Linvald, and M. Mackeprang, eds., *Schultz Danmarkshist-*

Reginald Coupland has been sharply criticized, not least by Eric Williams. Although this criticism is exaggerated, it has, however, helped draw a number of factors apart from the humane abolitionist movement into the debate on the abolition of the slave trade.[4]

The purpose of this chapter is, first and foremost, to call attention to the economic considerations of the Danish Negro Trade Commission of 1791 as to the possibility of maintaining the slave population on the Danish sugar islands without new supplies of Negroes. Furthermore, it will show how abolition connects with the structure of the Danish Negro slave trade.

STRUCTURE OF THE TRADE

In my article "The Scope and Structure of the Danish Negro Slave Trade,"[5] I have endeavored to show that the Danish slave trade at the end of the eighteenth century may be broken down into three, only partially interdependent, main branches. One main branch involved the import of slaves to St. Croix. The number of Negroes imported to this island exceeded by several times the number of those exported. The slaves that arrived at Christiansted (the main port of St. Croix) came mainly from Africa. During the period 1778–1792, these imports seem to a large extent to have been carried on Danish ships, whereas a large part of the import during the years 1764–1777 and after 1792 seems to have been carried on foreign ships. The greater part, however, of trade to the other port of St. Croix, Frederiksted, came from the West Indies, mostly from the British Leeward Islands. The import of slaves for use on St. Croix was the part of the Danish slave trade that was least subject to market fluctuations, since a steady import of fresh slaves was a necessary prerequisite for Danish sugar production and the sugar trade.

The second main branch of the Danish slave trade was the transit trade at St. Thomas. Before 1733, when the West India–Guinea Company pur-

---

orie, vol. 4 (Copenhagen, 1942), p. 185ff; and Jens Vibæk's in John Danstrup and Hal Koch, eds., [*Politikens*] *Danmarks Historie,* vol. 10 (Copenhagen, 1964), pp. 116ff; Christian Degn, *Die Schimmelmanns im atlantischen Dreieckshandel: Gewinn und Gewissen* (Neumünster, 1974), pp. 281ff. and passim.

[4] Eric Williams, *Capitalism and Slavery,* 2nd ed. (London, 1964, first published 1944); Roger T. Anstey, "Capitalism and Slavery: A Critique," *The Economic History Review,* 2nd series, vol. 21 (Cambridge, 1968), pp. 307–320; Roger T. Anstey, *The Atlantic Slave Trade and British Abolition 1760–1810* (London, 1975); Seymour Drescher, *Econocide: British Slavery in the Era of Abolition* (Pittsburgh, 1977).

[5] Sv. E. Green-Pedersen, "The Scope and Structure of the Danish Negro Slave Trade," *The Scandinavian Economic History Review,* vol. 19, 1971, pp. 149–197.

chased St. Croix from the French, the soil of St. Thomas was already exhausted by the cultivation of sugar cane. Its slave trade therefore came to depend on the possibility of transit trade via the natural harbor of the island. The transit slave trade depended heavily on favorable wartime conditions, and during the period of company rule (until 1755) the greater part of the slaves in transit were brought to the island on foreign ships. According to the figures from the West Indian customs accounts, the transit slave trade of St. Thomas at the end of the eighteenth century seems to have been a part of inter-West Indian commerce.

The third main branch of the Danish slave trade involved exports from Africa. The present investigation concentrates on the three concessionary companies: the West India–Guinea Company, the Bargum Trading Society, and in particular the Baltic–Guinea Company. It has been found that this branch of the Danish slave trade also depended on favorable wartime conditions, and that all three companies were from time to time subjected to severe crises.

It has been shown that during the colonial wars, Denmark carried on a transit slave trade and slave export from Africa that were, in Danish terms, considerable; but under peacetime conditions these branches of the trade were of much more negligible dimensions. In contrast, the French slave trade suffered badly during the colonial wars. In times of both war and peace Denmark needed a relatively constant import of slaves to St. Croix; the slaves, however, were in large measure delivered by foreign ships. Thus, Denmark and her African and West Indian colonies do not appear to have constituted a closed, mercantilistic commercial system. Presumably, the Danish possessions were too small for this. A related view is held by Ole Feldbæk with regard to the Danish colonies in the East Indies. Outward-bound, the Danish East Indiamen often supplemented their cargoes with foreign goods, and return cargoes were often picked up outside the Danish possessions; frequently the capital involved in the ventures was English. Like the Danish slave trade, the Danish East India trade was subject to market fluctuations. For instance, the American War of Independence gave it a certain upward turn. Incidentally, both Danish colonial trade and the Danish slave trade were concentrated in Copenhagen. In 1782 a West Indian trading company was formed in Århus, but it merely considered entering into the slave trade.[6]

[6] Gaston Martin, *l'Ère des Négriers 1714–1774* (Paris, 1931), pp. 173–175 and pl. 7; Emanuel Sejr, "Århus vestindiske Handels Selskab," *Erhvervshistorisk Årbog 1962*, vol. 13, 1962, pp. 47–72; J. Everaert, "Les fluctuations du trafic négrier–nantais (1763–1792)," *Cahiers de Tunisie*, vol. 43, 1963, pp. 37–62; Ole Feldbæk, *India Trade under the Danish Flag 1772–1808* (Odense, 1969).

DANISH ATTITUDES TOWARD SLAVERY

When viewing the intellectual attitude of eighteenth-century Denmark toward the system of Negro slavery, it is readily apparent that there was no organized antislavery campaign comparable to the British Abolition Society or the French Société des Amis des Noirs.[7] During the years before 1792, however, a more differentiated attitude toward slavery appeared in Danish literature, and individual critics such as P. E. Isert made their mark; but the debate was limited and to a great extent carried on in periodical articles, translated from French and English.[8] It may be mentioned in passing that no Danish verdict prohibited the export of Negro slaves from Denmark as did the Somerset case in Britain in 1772. As late as 1802 the prominent Danish legal expert A. S. Ørsted helped pass a verdict that permitted the export of a Negro slave from Denmark.[9] Of importance was the fact that the slave question roused the interest of influential men such as Ernst Schimmelmann, Minister of Finance from 1784. The 1792 volume, however, of the leading periodical *Minerva* contains extracts from the Representation of the Negro Trade Commission as well as reports of the Sierra Leone Company and of the antislavery movement in Britain.[10]

The abolitionist sentiment in Denmark did not attain the same dimension and character as in Britain, due partly to the different political tradition. During the eighteenth century Denmark was an absolute monarchy with no parliament, and the important political decisions were thus made within a very narrow circle. In addition, the West Indian "sugar money" seems to have had great economic importance, especially for Copenhagen. Even though the data that Richard Willerslev and Christian Degn have brought to light are not always systematic, it is clear that both the import and export of sugar were of great importance for Copenhagen's trade. Furthermore, it is undeniable that many of the city's large merchant houses

---

[7] On these movements, see for instance George R. Mellor, *British Imperial Trusteeship 1783–1850* (London, 1951), Chapter 1; David Brion Davis, *The Problem of Slavery in Western Culture* (New York, 1969, first published 1966); David Brion Davis, *The Problem of Slavery in the Age of Revolution 1770–1823,* (New York, 1975).

[8] Sv. E. Green-Pedersen, "Negro Slavery and Christianity. On Erik Pontoppidan's preface to L. F. Roemer, *Tilforladelig Efterretning om Kysten Guinea* (A True Account of the Coast of Guinea), 1760," *Transactions of the Historical Society of Ghana,* vol. XV, 1974, pp. 85–102. Moreover, see an unpublished MA-thesis by Henning Højlund Knap, "Negerslavedebatten i Danmark til 1807 belyst gennem de i tidsskriftartikler og bøger udtrykte holdninger" (University of Aarhus, 1975). I am indebted to H. H. Knap, MA from the University of Aarhus, for allowing reference to his thesis.

[9] Knud Waaben, "A. S. Ørsted og negerslaverne i København," *Juristen,* vol. 46, 1964, pp. 321–343.

[10] Trier, "Det dansk-vestindiske negerindførselsforbud," pp. 447ff.

had something to do with sugar or slaves. The most striking example is the Schimmelmann family, on whom a good many commercial records have been preserved. Many of these merchants were at the same time leading figures in the Danish Enlightenment. Chr. D. Reventlow and Ernst Schimmelmann were both directors of the Baltic–Guinea Company. Reventlow's name, however, is chiefly remembered in connection with the great agrarian reforms, and Schimmelmann supported a number of poets, such as Adam Oehlenschläger and Friedrich Schiller.[11]

THE NEGRO TRADE COMMISSION

The background for the work of the Great Negro Trade Commission has been mentioned. According to its mandate, dated 5 August 1791, the Commission was "set up in order to improve the structure of the Negro trade on our West Indian Islands and the Coast of Guinea;" the mandate said nothing about abolition. The periodical *Politisches Journal,* however, which had connections with A. P. Bernstorff, the Danish Foreign Secretary, cautiously informed its readers that the purpose of the Commission was to improve the condition of the Negroes but not, on the other hand, to give them full liberty. In addition to Ernst Schimmelmann, the Commission consisted of some high-ranking civil servants, who in Trier's opinion "scarcely contributed much to the main views expressed in the Report of the commission [p. 425]." Secretary of the Commission was Ernst P. Kirstein. Trier believed Schimmelmann was the main author of the report. The Representation, dated 28 December 1791 is in German and fills 102 foolscap pages. Its principal idea, namely, that the central problem concerning the abolition of the slave trade was the maintenance of West Indian sugar production without new supplies of slaves, accorded with Schimmelmann's views written in the summer of 1791. In the Report of the Danish Commission, references were made to a corresponding British report; to the debates on the question in the British parliament; to works by Falconbridge, Clarkson, and Frossard; as well as to the missionary history by Oldendorp.[12]

[11] P. P. Sveistrup and Rich. Willerslev, *Den danske sukkerhandels og sukkerproduktions historie* (Copenhagen, 1945), Chapters 5–6 and 9–11; Degn, *Die Schimmelmanns im atlantischen Dreieckshandel;* Aage Rasch, *Niels Ryberg 1725–1804. Fra bondedreng til handelsfyrste* (Århus, 1964); Sv. E. Green-Pedersen, "The History of the Danish Negro Slave Trade 1733–1807," *Revue française d'histoire d'outre-mer,* vol. 62, 1975, pp. 196–220.

[12] The mandate, Schimmelmann's review, and the Representation (*Allerunterhänigste Vorstellung an ihro königliche Majestät*) are preserved in the National Archives in Copenhagen among the papers of the West Indian–Guinean Exchequer and Central Customs Department in the file labeled "Dokumenter vedk. kommissionen for negerhandelens bedre indret-

THE REPRESENTATION

The Representation of the Danish Commission may be divided into two main sections. First, the Danish slave trade was analyzed, and second, its importance for the West Indian sugar production was discussed.

In the introduction, reference was made to the earliest opposition to slavery (for instance, the work of Morgan Godwyn, John Woolman, and Anthony Benezet), to the debates of the British parliament on the slave trade, and to the British report. Then the Representation went on to deal with the harmful effects on Africa of the slave trade. These alone sufficed to make the slave trade inadmissible; in addition conditions on the slave ships were discussed. The analysis of the volume and structure of the Danish slave trade was based on limited and one-sided material, from concessionary Danish slave-trading companies. This material proved to the Commisssion that the Danish slave trade was subject to market fluctuations, that in Africa many slaves were purchased from foreign establishments and some sold to foreign ships, and that many slaves were sold to foreign islands in the West Indies. The material did not, however, show the importance of foreign slave imports into the Danish West Indies, nor discuss the transit slave trade at St. Thomas. Further, the Report mentioned that more foreign and East Indian goods were sold in the Guinea trade than goods from the European realms of the king. In addition, experience showed that the Negro trade yielded no profit; on this point reference was made to a commission set up in November 1786.[13] A maximum of 1400 Negroes were exported from Africa each year. This export necessitated the maintenance of four forts and three factories, which entailed an annual expenditure of 30,000 Rix-Dollars (*Rigsdaler*). The sale of domestic products was estimated at an annual figure of 42,830 Rix-Dollars. The Negroes fetched lower prices in the Danish

---

ning og ophævelse, samt efterretninger om negerhandelen og slaveriet i Vestindien, 1783–1806." On p. 6 of the Representation reference is made to the report of the British commission; on p. 3f. to the debates of the British parliament; on p. 12ff. to Alexander Falconbridge, *An Account of the Slave Trade on the Coast of Africa* (London, 1788); on pp. 47ff. to Thomas Clarkson, *An Essay on the Impolicy of the African Slave Trade* (London, 1788); on p. 50 to M. Frossard, *La cause des esclaves nègres et des habitants de la Guinée, portée au tribunal de la justice, de la religion, de la politique*, vols. 1–2 (Lyon, 1789); on p. 77 to C.G.A. Oldendorp, *Geschichte der Mission der evangelischen Brüder auf den caraibischen Inseln S. Thomas, S. Croix, und S. Jan*, vols. 1–2 (Barby, 1777). In addition to this edition, there were extracts published in German (1782) and in Danish (1784). Cf. Trier, "Det dansk-vestindiske negerindførselsforbud," pp. 416ff. Another copy of the Representation is preserved among the same papers in the file "1788–1847. Negerslavehandelens afskaffelse betræffende (korrespondance med kommissionen, etc.)."

[13] On this, see Georg Nørregård, *Danish Settlements in West Africa 1658–1850* (Boston, Mass., 1966), p. 172ff.; and Degn, *Die Schimmelmanns im atlantischen Dreieckshandel*, pp. 213ff.

islands than in the other islands, and not even the export of Negroes to the French islands had any notable advantages. Nor was the slave trade very important to Danish shipping. At the most, two or three ships were occupied with it every year, and it entailed an extraordinarily high rate of mortality among the sailors. The latter argument is familiar from the abolitionist literature; thus Thomas Clarkson maintained that the British slave ships were not nurseries but graves for sailors. The Danish commission thus concluded that Danish slave trade on its own was not worth maintaining. It is interesting to note that there was no tradition in Denmark, as opposed to England, for considering the slave trade particularly profitable. The Commission's conclusion regarding the economic importance of the slave trade to Denmark was the same as that of modern historians (e.g., Stanley Engerman), who contest its importance for England.[14]

The Commission then turned to the importance of the slave trade for West Indian sugar production, "the most important and most difficult aspect of this whole case [p. 28]." It would be too circumstantial to find out "whether it was at all possible that the West Indian colonies could be cultivated without negroes, or at least without negro slaves [p. 29]." It was not believed feasible to give up the cultivation of sugar in the West Indies; but the Representation nevertheless stressed the desirability of a *speedy* abolition of slavery. The Commission, however, did not dare tell the public that it wished to go so far. In the semiofficial extract, for instance, published in the influential periodical *Minerva* in April 1792 by Ernst P. Kirstein, the text was manipulated so much that the Commission's wishes concerning slavery were obscured. C. A. Trier had already observed this and also pointed out that the previously mentioned review, written by Schimmelmann before the Commission was set up, demonstrated that he had no intention of consulting the planters. Whereas Jens Vibæk has failed to comprehend the degree of manipulation in Kirstein's extract, Christian Degn followed Trier on this point.[15] The Commission then reviewed the question of the possibility of creating conditions for the Negro population

---

[14] The Commission's Representation, pp. 1–28. Stanley L. Engerman, "The Slave Trade and British Capital Formation in the Eighteenth Century: A Comment on the Williams Thesis," *Business History Review*, vol. 46, 1972, pp. 430–443. It is not possible to compute the contribution of the slave trade to the Danish gross national product (GNP), since this has not been computed for the eighteenth century.

[15] Ernst P. Kirstein, "Udtog af forestillingen til kongen angående negerhandelens afskaffelse," *Minerva*, vol. 2, 1792, pp. 56ff.; Trier, "Det dansk-vestindiske negerindførselsforbud," pp. 429ff.; Jens Vibæk, "Dansk Vestindien 1755–1848," in Johannes Brøndsted, ed., *Vore gamle Tropekolonier*, 2nd ed. (Copenhagen, 1966, first published 1952–1953), pp. 179ff.; Degn, *Die Schimmelmanns im atlantischen Dreieckshandel*, p. 287. Kirstein's extract was printed in German in C. U. D. von Eggers, ed., *Deutsches Magazin*, vol. 3, 1792, pp. 626–684.

that would enable it to sustain or even increase itself. The Central Customs Department tax roll figures, for the number of Negroes on St. Croix between 1780 and 1790, fluctuated between 21,000 and 23,000. Whereas the annual rate of mortality was 1 in 28, the corresponding figure for fertility was 1 in 51. If the three years in which epidemic diseases, including smallpox, had occurred, were excluded, the mortality rate was only 1 in 34. The Commission was especially worried about the low fertility rate and pointed out a number of reasons for it. There were more men than women, matrimonial relations were unstable, married couples could be separated in sale, children could be separated from their parents, expectant mothers were not particularly cared for during pregnancy, nor were the children cared for, and there were too many house Negroes. On the Schimmelmann Estates, however, humane treatment of the Negroes had raised the fertility rate to 1 in 35, and the mortality rate there was 1 in 27. Even here the mortality rate exceeded the fertility rate, and the reason was thought by the Commission to be the disproportionate number of male and female slaves, the ratio being 100 : 90. From the works of Clarkson and Frossard more examples were quoted of the fruitful results of humane treatment of the Negroes, examples that proved that the fertility rate might be increased to exceed the mortality rate. The commission thus concluded that a steady supply of Negroes from external sources was unnecessary, provided that certain conditions were fulfilled. As may be seen, this optimistic conclusion was reached by a primitive quantitative method. The 21,847 Negroes on St. Croix were not judged to be a sufficient basis for the future population. The Commission believed that 30,000–45,000 Negroes were needed for a proper base. Since the concessionary Danish slave-trading companies had failed to export a sufficient number of slaves to St. Croix after 1778, the Commission suggested a completely unrestricted import of slaves for a period of 10 years, with permission for the planters to export a certain quantity of sugar for each slave purchased. Normally the sugar had to be exported to Copenhagen. Further, it was proposed that government loans be made available to the planters for purchasing slaves during the transition.[16]

Finally, the Commission turned to the social measures that were to ensure the future maintenance of the Negro population. Cautious mention was made of statutory regulation of the planters' treatment of the Negroes. Without the goodwill of the planters, the enforcement of such legislation

[16] The Commission's Representation, pp. 28–62. In Thomas Clarkson, *Essay on the Impolicy,* 2nd ed., p. 89, mention is made of Schimmelmann's experiments on increasing Negro fertility through better treatment.

was deemed difficult. In order to relieve the disproportion in numbers between the two sexes, the commission suggested that the poll tax on adult female Negroes be lifted as of 1795 and transferred to the men; and in order to diminish the number of house Negroes, it was proposed that the poll tax on them be increased. As the missionary work of the Moravian Brethren had demonstrated that Christian Negroes were the best slaves, the Commission wished to encourage the work of the Christian missions. Further, it wished to promote Negro marriages. Finally, it desired a ban on the export of Negroes from the Danish islands, and a ban on their import after a period of 10 years. It might be mentioned at this point that the attempt to raise the fertility rate of the Negro population above the mortality rate after the abolition of the slave trade met with failure. The Commission's Representation terminated with a reference to the settlements in Guinea and mentioned that the king had the right to demand the restitution of these from the merchants Duntzfelt, Meyer & Co., who were at that time conducting the Guinea business. The Representation stated that before the abolition of the Negro trade in 10 years' time, decisive facts must show whether the settlements could become remunerative. The Commission mentioned the new, rare African woods that had by then been introduced to Britain, and referred to the British activities in Sierra Leone. The Commission refrained, however, from recommending a possible sale of the forts, as it was known that the king was having this investigated.[17]

The royal resolution on the Representation was dated 24 February 1792, and most of the items were left to be dealt with by the Central Customs Department. The edict itself, issued 16 March 1792, was very soberly worded.[18] The preamble stated that enquiries had been carried out as to whether the Danish West Indies could manage without supplies of new Negroes from Guinea. The enquiries had shown not only the possibility but even the advantage of terminating the supplies, when the plantations had been stocked with a number of Negroes sufficient for their future propaga-

---

[17] The Commission's Representation, pp. 62–102. L. Rothe, *Om populationsforholdene i de danske vestindiske kolonier og fornemlig på St. Croix* (Copenhagen, 1847), now in the Manuscript Collection vii D 5 in the National Archives in Copenhagen, quotes from the tax rolls and census figures for the slave population of St. Croix, which prove that the mortality rate was larger than the fertility rate during the years 1816–1831. From 1832 to 1844 it was higher, except for 3 years.

[18] An English translation of the edict is printed in Elizabeth Donnan, *Documents Illustrative of the History of the Slave Trade to America,* vol. 2, reprint (New York, 1965, first published 1931), pp. 616ff. The administrative process preceding the edict is discussed by F. Thaarup, *Udførlig vejledning til Det danske Monarkis statistik,* vol. 6 (Copenhagen, 1819), pp. 659–698. Cf. Trier, "Det dansk-vestindiske negerindførselsforbud," pp. 441ff.

tion. The provisions of the edict were contained in six paragraphs. The first paragraph banned all participation in Negro trade after the beginning of 1803, for the king's subjects outside the West Indies. After that time, no Negroes were to be purchased on the Coast of Guinea or anywhere else, by or for the king's subjects, nor carried on their ships; "neither must they be brought to our West-India Islands for Sale." This formula later enabled the Central Customs Department to allow the transit slave trade of foreign citizens on foreign ships via the free port of St. Thomas to continue, after 1803. The West Indian customs accounts, which were revised in Denmark, give the figures for this trade until the British occupied the islands at Christmas 1807.[19] The second paragraph allowed all foreign nations to import slaves into the Danish West Indies till the end of 1802. The third paragraph allowed the export of a certain clearly defined quantity of sugar (also to foreign parts) within 1 year of the import of each Negro. The fourth paragraph abolished the import duty on female Negroes. The fifth paragraph abolished the poll tax on Negro females used for field work while doubling it on the males. The sixth paragraph prohibited the export of slaves from the Danish West Indies.

From this survey of the Commission's Report it can be seen that the explanation that Eric Williams has given for the British abolition of the slave trade, that is, that it was caused by a surplus production crisis for sugar, probably cannot be applied to the corresponding Danish legislation. The Report mentioned nothing of a Danish sugar crisis. On the contrary, the commission assumed that West Indian sugar production must be maintained; moreover, the figures brought to light by Richard Willerslev concerning Danish sugar production and sugar trade do not seem to suggest that Danish West Indian sugar in 1791 was faced with a crisis due to overproduction. Thus, the Danish slave trade—like the British—does not seem to have been abolished for the sake of economic gain.[20]

SCHOLARLY ACCOUNTS

C. A. Trier's 1905 article on the Danish West Indian ban on Negro imports was a thorough and meticulous account of the ideological back-

[19] Green-Pedersen, "The Scope and Structure," pp. 160ff.

[20] Williams, Capitalism and Slavery, pp. 149ff. and 209ff.; Anstey, "Capitalism and Slavery: A Critique"; Sveistrup and Willerslev, *Den danske sukkerhandels og sukkerproduktions historie*, Tables 28, 31–32, 37, 41–42, Chapter 11 and *passim;* the Commission's Representation, pp. 28ff. and *passim.*

ground and political execution of the edict of 1792.[21] He undertook a careful study of the British abolitionist literature as well as extensive studies of unprinted records, in attempts to throw light on the work of Ernst Schimmelmann. Trier supplied lavish documentation of his view of Schimmelmann, referring to the latter's private correspondence. For instance, Trier characteristically stressed that already in 1782, in a letter to Charlotte Schubart, his fiancée, Schimmelmann expressed uneasiness at having become director of a slave-trading company. Trier's view may be summarized thus: that Denmark abolished the slave trade as early as 1792 because Schimmelmann—under the influence of the abolitionist movement and in cooperation with other Danish reform politicians—wished this reform for humane reasons. Trier emphasized that, despite all obstacles, Schimmelmann never abandoned his "great idea" of the abolition of the slave trade. It was typical of Trier's account that he paid very slight attention to the economic considerations of the Commission, just as he did not endeavor to clarify the volume and structure of the Danish slave trade.

The earliest criticism of Trier's view of Schimmelmann came from Emil Gigas who showed, 2 years after the appearance of Trier's treatise, that Ernst F. Walterstorff, later governor–general of the Danish West Indies, as well as Professor D. G. Moldenhawer, D. D., were sent to Spain in 1786–1787 by Ernst Schimmelmann on a secret mission to obtain, among other things, the right for the Baltic–Guinea Company to deliver slaves to the Spanish colonies. Gigas marveled that this was the same Schimmelmann to "whom we owe the abolition of the slave trade in Denmark in 1792."[22]

A more extensive criticism of Trier's view appeared in Jens Vibæk's chapters on the Danish West Indies, 1755–1848, in the first edition of *Vore gamle Tropekolonier* in 1952–1953. Vibæk stressed that the edict of 16 March 1792 rested "on a double basis: a humanitarian and an economic [p. 162]." By economic basis he meant that the slave trade was unprofitable as a business and that a gradual abolition was desirable in order that the islands be supplied with a sufficient number of slaves. A rational population policy,

---

[21] What prompted Trier to write his treatise was that H. Lawaetz (*Brødremenighedens mission i dansk Vestindien 1769–1848* [Copenhagen, 1902], pp. 112–114) had expressed doubts as to whether the edict had any connection with the Danish reform legislation of the eighteenth century. Later, Lawaetz (in *Peter von Scholten* [Copenhagen, 1940], pp. 136–138) endorsed Trier's view. Before Trier, Louis Bobé (in *Efterladte papirer fra den reventlowske familiekreds*, vol. 5 [Copenhagen, 1902], pp. LXIV–LXVIII) maintained that Schimmelmann alone originated the idea of the abolition of the Negro trade. Later, Bobé, (*Efterladte papirer*, vol. 8 [Copenhagen, 1917], pp. XVI–XVII), gave his full support to Trier's article.

[22] E. Gigas, "En theologisk professors diplomatiske mission," *Historisk Tidsskrift,* 8th series, vol. 1 (Copenhagen, 1907–1908), pp. 185–253. The quotation is from p. 188.

if instituted, would ensure the propagation of the Negro inhabitants. Vibæk also spoke of the influence of the abolitionist movement on Schimmelmann and his circle. Vibæk underlined, however, that Schimmelmann was not only "a well-informed versatile intellect with a humane outlook, he was also tied to the problem economically with double strings." Here Vibæk was alluding to the fact that Schimmelmann was a large plantation owner in the Danish West Indies as well as having economic interests in the Danish slave trade. Vibæk most sharply criticized Schimmelmann in connection with a discussion of a postponement of the enforcement of the ban on Negro imports, a discussion that began in 1802. In July 1802 some West Indian planters petitioned the king for a 3-year postponement of the ban. The matter was submitted to the Negro Trade Commission. Here, Schimmelmann proposed a plan that had originally been devised by the West Indian school headmaster Hans West. The state was to purchase some plantations, cultivate them as model operations, and set the planters a good example in humane treatment of the Negroes. The population surplus from these plantations (Vibæk called them Negro stud farms) was to be placed at the planters' disposal on favorable terms. The plan depended on new supplies of Negroes from Africa, and this transport was to be undertaken by the state. The prospects of returning to Africa, when no more new Negroes (Vibæk called them breeding animals) were needed, could be held out to the Negroes. Schimmelmann's proposition engendered the opposition, on the one side, of the West Indians E. F. Walterstorff and P. L. Oxholm, who simply wanted a postponement of the ban, and, on the other, of Rosenstand-Goiske of the Central Customs Department, who wanted the ban to come into force. On this occasion, Vibæk characterized Schimmelmann as having "a problematic nature." The commission accepted Schimmelmann's proposal and forwarded it to the Council of State. The Council, however, asked for new information about the Negro population from the West Indies. This did not come forth until 1805–1806, and at that time Britain was once more about to abolish the slave trade; so no postponement of the ban was possible. Thus, the development in Britain once more had a decisive influence on Danish policies regarding the question of the Negro trade. Jens Vibæk's account of the economic aspects of the Danish abolition of the slave trade was superior to that of earlier authors. On the other hand, he has underestimated the humane aspects. As mentioned previously, he has simply failed to understand that the Commission wished in principle to see slavery abolished. Nor was his criticism of Schimmelmann's attitude during the deliberations about the postponement of the enforcement of the ban on Negro imports reasonable. In using words such as "Negro stud farms" and "breeding animals" he applied modern moral standards, forgetting that the political conditions after 1800 were different from those of 1791–1792. Contrary to expectations, Britain had not abolished her slave trade. The political reaction in Denmark and the different composition of the Danish government should also be taken into account. Axel Linvald maintained that Walterstorff had persuaded the Prince Regent to postpone the ban on Negro imports. For these reasons Schimmelmann's proposal of model plantations may be interpreted as a preventive measure. In a private letter of 22 May 1804, Schimmelmann referred to the Council of State's treatment of the planters' petition for a postponement of the ban's enforcement. The way in which the reference was made supports the interpretation noted previously. The present author agrees, however, with Jens Vibæk in not regarding Schimmelmann as an ardent abolitionist. He is better described as a politician, friendly toward abolitionism, who wanted to bring about reforms, but who also let his attitude be dictated by whether reform could be afforded and whether it was practically possible. That Schimmelmann and his circle were interested in the slave question for humane reasons is seen, among other ways, from many private letters published by Louis Bobé, to which Vibæk made no reference. Both in 1791–1792 and after 1802, however, the Minister of Finance took the view that there had to be a sufficient number of Negroes, and that a rational population policy would have to be enacted, before a definitive abolition of the slave trade could take place.[23]

In his section on the Gold Coast in *Vore gamle Tropekolonier* from 1952–1953, Georg Nørregård saw a connection between the edict and the nascent interest in plantations in Africa. He mentioned that a couple of plantations were abandoned and then wrote, "All the efforts lavished on these plantations bore no fruit. In the meantime, reports reached Copenhagen that it was possible to cultivate the African soil. This information profoundly influenced the renewed discussions of the slave traffic between Africa and America." Nørregård's views have been adopted by René Pélissier and by the Danish geographer Henrik Jeppesen. The latter wrote of the African plantations, "The plans of establishing plantations and colonies should be viewed in connection with the efforts towards the abolition of the slave trade. The first attempt was made in 1788, the intention being to eliminate the slave traffic by growing such products in West Africa as

---

[23] Jens Vibæk, "dansk Vestindien 1755–1848," pp. 162–189. In the first edition of *Vore gamle Tropekolonier*, the chapter is found in vol. 2, pp. 248–262. For private letters, see for example Bobé, *Efterladte papirer*, vol. 4, 1900, pp. 14, 120ff., 129, 133ff.; vol. 5, 1902, p. 304; vol. 7, 1906, pp. 65–67; vol. 8, 1917, pp. 287–292, 340–341: Axel Linvald. *Kronprins Frederik og hans regering 1797–1807*, vol. 1 (Copenhagen, 1923), p. 327. Cf. Bobé, *Efterladte papirer*, vol. 7, 1906, p. 382.

were produced in the West Indies by imported slaves [p. 73]." It appears, however, from Jeppesen's article that the Danish plantations on the Gold Coast were of negligible importance when compared to the plantations in the Danish West Indies. Even though the notion of moving the plantations from the West Indies to Africa was not foreign to the Danish debate, it played no role in the political decision. Nor were the political experiments with plantations in Africa used in the Representation of the Negro Trade Commission as an argument in favor of the abolition of the slave trade; but they were mentioned in connection with the question of the Danish retention of the African possessions after the abolition of the slave trade.[24]

The latest account of the Danish abolition of the Negro slave trade has been given by Christian Degn in his monograph on the Schimmelmann family. Degn, who has brought to light much new material for the elucidation of the Schimmelmann family through extensive study of unpublished records, stressed, as did Trier, the humane personality of Ernst Schimmelmann. He also documented extensively his view of Ernst Schimmelmann through references to his private correspondence. It is thus typical that he too called special attention to Ernst Schimmelmann's letter from 1782 to his fiancée Charlotte Schubart. Jens Vibæk was sharply criticized, in general for having doubted the meritorious efforts of Ernst Schimmelmann in bringing out the edict, and in particular for having pictured Schimmelmann's model plantations as Negro stud farms with breeding animals. On the other hand, Degn concurred with my opinion that the government's situation was forced upon it from abroad, as it would be difficult not to follow suit when the expected British abolition of the slave trade took place. Among the most valuable parts of Degn's account was his publication of some hitherto unknown material that threw light on Ernst Schimmelmann's reform plans for more humane treatment of the plantation Negroes. The plans would permit the maintenance of the Negro population by natural reproduction without constant slave import. Degn did not, however, suggest that these calculations determined Schimmelmann's attitude. He

[24] Nørregård, *Danish Settlements in West Africa*, pp. 172ff. This book is an English translation of "Guldkysten," in Johannes Brøndsted, ed., *Vore gamle Tropekolonier*, vol. 8, 2nd ed. (Copenhagen, 1968, first published 1952–1953). René Pélissier, "Les danois en Afrique," *Genève–Afrique*, vol. 6, 1967, pp. 9–32; Henrik Jeppesen. "Danish Plantations on the Gold Coast," *Geografisk Tidsskrift*, vol. 65, 1966, pp. 48–88. The quotation from Nørregård is slightly difficult to understand in this context. On the one hand it is seen from the two sources to which he refers that Schimmelmann received two applications (dated 16 and 18 Sept. 1790, respectively) from merchants N. Lather and P. Meyer for support for plantations, and that Lather's application represented an optimistic picture of the possibilities of running plantations in Africa. On the other hand, the plantations of these merchants were abandoned as early as 1793 (cf. Jeppesen, "Danish Plantations," p. 53).

thus wrote, "Such a calculation is rejected by Schimmelmann himself, what matters to him is humaneness [p. 261]."[25]

It was stated in the introduction to this chapter that its purpose was, first and foremost, to call attention to the economic considerations of the Danish Negro Trade Commission as to the possibility of maintaining the slave population by natural reproduction without new slave imports. Ernst Schimmelmann developed his previously mentioned reform plans in a large scheme at the end of the 1780s. In it, he spoke of the desirability of the maintenance of the slave population solely by natural reproduction, and he was in favor of such humane reforms for the Negroes as a school education, statutory measures to prevent arbitrary treatment by the masters, a voice in the management, and even a share of the profit. The basic views embodied in this scheme reappeared in the previously mentioned review, written by Schimmelmann in the summer of 1791, which dealt with the problems surrounding the abolition of the Negro slave trade. They also reappeared in the Representation of the Commission. Because of the considerable space allotted to these demographic calculations in the Representation, it looks much more like a politico–economic reform programme for Danish colonialism than a declaration of human rights for the Negro slaves. Debates about, and experiments with, the possibility of enabling the Negro population to sustain itself solely by natural reproduction are known in Denmark as well as abroad.[26] As mentioned, Schimmelmann's attempts at reform were noted by Thomas Clarkson, and the Negro Trade Commission, in turn, noted in its Report Clarkson's and Frossard's references to other experiments. As has been pointed out by Richard Sheridan among others, the slaves seemed in general to receive better treatment in the decades preceding the American Revolution than earlier. Planters such as Samuel Martin on Antigua, Thomas Mills on St. Kitts and Nevis, and John Pinney on Nevis experimented by giving the slaves better medical care and a better

[25] Degn, *Die Schimmelmanns im atlantischen Dreieckshandel,* pp. 194, 210, 217, 256ff., 281ff., 346ff. My quotation from Degn is in the middle of a long Schimmelmann quotation, concerned with the calculations of other planters on the subject of the reproduction of the negroes. The latter indicates that Schimmelmann fully appreciated that such calculations on their own were insufficient for an appraisal of the issue of abolitionism; but it does not indicate that Schimmelmann totally rejected that kind of calculation as unnecessary—as Degn infers from the quotation. Hence Degn's quotation becomes an example of his exaggerated interpretation of the economic and moral aspects of the issue of abolitionism as being mutually exclusive rather than compatible.

[26] Peder Paludan, "Udsigter til slavehandelens ophævelse," *Magazin for lidende eller underholdning, råd og trøst i sorg,* vol. 1, 1790, Part 1, pp. 152–169 and Part 2, 171–177, thus maintained that in plain economic terms it did not pay for the planters to work their slaves to death. Paludan's article is, via a German article, a paraphrase of a British polemical contribution. I am indebted to H. H. Knap for this information.

diet. These attempts at reforms should be viewed as stemming in part from the rising prices of slaves.[27]

PRAGMATIC ASPECTS OF ABOLITION

As far as the present author is able to judge, the importance of these demographic considerations has not been sufficiently emphasized in connection with the Danish abolition of the Negro slave trade. C. A. Trier thus spoke of "a calculation of slight import," whereas Vibæk had a certain understanding of the problem. Degn accredited these considerations too much to humane wishes. It seems evident to me that the economic aspects ought to be given more attention, and I concur with Magnus Mörner, who has written about the problem in another and more general context: "Slave owners had to make up their minds whether they were willing to depend on continuous purchase of new slaves or preferred to promote natural reproduction instead. It was a basic economic decision [p. 3]." In conclusion, I cannot refrain from mentioning once more the Commission's statement, that precisely this was the most important and most difficult aspect of the abolition of the slave trade. The primitive calculation, made by the Commission in considering the possibility of the Negro population sustaining itself by natural reproduction, enabled the government to afford humaneness.[28]

[27] Degn, *Die Schimmelmanns im atlantischen Dreieckshandel,* pp. 261ff.; Richard B. Sheridan, "Africa and the Caribbean in the Atlantic Slave Trade," *American Historical Review,* vol. 77, 1972, p. 27ff.; Richard B. Sheridan, "Samuel Martin, Innovating Sugar Planter of Antigua 1750–1776," *Agricultural History,* vol. 34, 1960, pp. 126–139; Richard B. Sheridan, "Mortality and the Medical Treatment of Slaves in the British West Indies," in Stanley L. Engerman and Eugene D. Genovese, eds., *Race and Slavery in the Western Hemisphere: Quantitative Studies* (Princeton, New Jersey, 1975), pp. 285–310; D. W. Thoms, "Slavery in the Leeward Islands in the Mid Eighteenth Century: A Reappraisal," *Bulletin of the Institute of Historical Research,* vol. 42, 1969, pp. 76–85; Richard Pares, *A West-India Fortune* (London, 1950), pp. 126ff.; Philip D. Curtin, "Epidemiology and the Slave Trade," *Political Science Quarterly,* vol. 83, 1968, pp. 190–216; Magnus Mörner, "Das vergleichende Studium der Negersklaverei in Anglo-und Lateinamerika," *Jahrbuch für Geschichte von Staat, Wirtschaft und Gesellschaft Lateinamerikas,* vol. 5, 1968, pp. 418ff.; Elsa V. Goveia, *Slave Society in the British Leeward Islands at the End of the Eighteenth Century* (New Haven and London, 1965), pp. 194ff.

[28] Magnus Mörner, "Approaches to the History of Black Slavery in Latin America," manuscript edition of a revised and enlarged version of "Der historische Hintergrund der sozialen Situation des Afroamerikaners in Lateinamerika," in Jürgen Gräbener, ed. *Klassengesellleschaft und Rassismus,* (Bielefeld, 1971), pp. 17–35. I am indebted to Professor Mörner for access to this manuscript edition. That it was a basic economic decision is not altered by the fact that new research (e.g., Michael Craton, *Searching for the Invisible Man: Slaves and Plantation Lives in Jamaica,* 1978, p. 85) has demonstrated that slaveowners' import of slaves was made necessary by the excess of death over birth. The very point is, however, what planters thought to be economically possible. Incidentally, I am working on a more detailed account of the question of natural reproduction as an introduction to an edition of the Commission's Representation.

I also wanted to discuss the abolition in light of the structure of the Danish slave trade. The structure of the Danish slave trade did to a large extent connect it with the slave trade of other countries. It is also natural to view Danish abolitionary policies in conjunction with the policies of other countries, especially Britain. It is known that the Danish Negro Trade Commission, like some authors of abolitionist literature, was also familiar with the corresponding British report from 1788 (printed in 1789). Its aim was to survey slave imports, not only to the British West Indies but also to the rest of the West Indies. It contained a wealth of statistical information, not only about Britain's own slave trade but also about the slave trade of France, Portugal, the Netherlands, and Denmark. It appears from the report that inquiries had been made to the Danish authorities in order to obtain information about the Danish slave trade, but no answer had been received. We also know that the British Prime Minister William Pitt supported joint abolition of the slave trade by Britain, France, Spain, and the Netherlands. The British thus realized the interdependence of the slave trades of the different countries and worked towards multinational abolition. Pitt's attempt foundered and in April 1791, the House of Commons rejected a bill to abolish the slave trade immediately.[29]

The summer of 1791 might thus seem an unpropitious time for Danish consideration of the abolition of the Danish slave trade. Among the Schimmelmann papers there was, however, a German translation of the British parliamentary debates on the slave question as reported in a British newspaper. His review showed a difference in his appraisal of the situation. He wrote that the latest parliamentary debate on the abolition of the slave trade could only arouse the greatest attention in all other slave-trading nations, that the leading politicians of both parties and the greater and worthier part of the British nation were in favor of abolition, and that if the bill were to be passed, a transitional period should be fixed. According to Schimmelmann, the main problem was that the value of the West Indian Islands lay in sugar production, which was managed in such a way as to require fresh supplies of

---

[29] *Report of The Lords of the Committee of Council Appointed for the Consideration of all Matters Relating to Trade and Foreign Plantations* (London, 1789). The purpose of the Committee is mentioned in the report, pp. 2–6. Part IV, "The Slaves Exported from Africa," No. 14, gives figures for the annual Negro export from Africa by Britain, France, Portugal, the Netherlands, and Denmark. The inquiry to Denmark is mentioned in Part VI. The British report is preserved in the National Archives in Copenhagen in the spuriously labeled file "Det engelske parlaments forhandlinger angående slavers transport til Amerika (trykt 1789)." Cf. J. Bloch, ed., *Vejledende Arkivregistraturer*, vol. 2 (Copenhagen, 1892), p. 298; Coupland, *The British Anti-Slavery Movement*, pp. 87ff., 92ff.; *Wilberforce*, 2nd ed. (London, 1945, first published 1923), pp. 84ff, 114ff.; Williams, *Capitalism and Slavery*, pp. 146ff.; F. J. Klingberg, *The Anti-Slavery Movement in England: A Study in English Humanitarianism* (New Haven, London, and Oxford, 1926), pp. 88ff., 97ff.; Anstey, *The Atlantic Slave Trade*, pp. 323ff. Cf. pp. 380ff. on later attempts to secure international abolition.

Negroes. His review was partly in the form of a number of questions that he desired the commission to examine.

> Will all nations be able to agree on abolishing the slave trade? If they cannot agree on it, will there not soon arise a market for negroes in the West Indies created by those, who cannot import them from Africa themselves? . . . Do Britain and France, if they agree on it, have the power to force their colonies into compliance? . . . If France and Britain agree on it, will Spain, Portugal, the Netherlands and North America take the same measures?

Apparently, in Schimmelmann's opinion the slave question had not suffered an irreparable setback in Britain, and he even considered the possibility of the abolition of the whole of the Atlantic slave trade.[30]

In the period between June 1791 and the Commission's Representation of 28 December 1791, news was received of the rebellion on Saint Domingue. The massacre of the white planters by the Negroes made the cause of the Negroes unpopular. It is with this background that one should read the Representation's attempts to belittle the Saint Domingue rebellion. It set forth the British attitude:

> It is familiar that the abolition of this trade has already been attempted with the greatest fervour in the latest sessions of parliament. Although the party that wishes to maintain it—without doubt because of economic interest—has so far gained the upper hand, the ferment is still so strong that the case cannot be regarded as settled. Wilberforce, the most prominent antagonist of the trade, stated in the latest session of parliament that the public has already abolished the trade, and as regards the fate of the present proposal, he will further it with incessant zeal. The leaders of both parliamentary parties have declared themselves in favor of the abolition with such emphasis and fervour that one cannot— without entertaining the very lowest opinion of their characters—doubt their sincerity. It is thus most likely that the previous rejection of the abolition bill should only be regarded as a postponement and not as a final decision, and that perhaps this course has been chosen deliberately in order to give those who have economic interests in it the time to adjust themselves to it; otherwise, if the change was brought about abruptly, it would be harmful to their economic interests. But if the case be so, then this alone would merit the attention of all nations with interests in such trade, as it would probably be very difficult to neglect an example, once given [pp. 3–4].

[30] The copy of the British Parliamentary debates is in the National Archives in Copenhagen, E. Schimmelmann's private papers, old deposit file no. 11. Schimmelmann's review (see N. 12) is found in two fair copies, one with an accompanying letter of 18 June 1791 to a high dignitary. According to Trier ("Det Dansk-vestindiske negerindførselsforbud," pp. 416ff.) and Bobé (*Efterladte papirer,* vol. 5, p. LXVI) this was probably J. E. Skeel, Director of the Central Customs Department. The other copy is dated 16 July 1791, and was, according to Trier, forwarded to the Commission. From the letter accompanying the first copy it is seen that Schimmelmann had talked to A. P. Bernstorff, the Foreign Secretary, about the matter, and that the latter seemed willing to lend his support. An appraisal of the debates of the British Parliament, similar to Schimmelmann's, was given by the Danish ambassador in London (National Archives in Copenhagen, Department for Foreign Affairs, 1771–1848, England 2, Depecher 1791, no. 32). Cf. Anstey (*The Atlantic Slave Trade,* p. 318ff.) who thinks that abolition might have been possible in 1791–1792, if the abolitionists had used better tactics.

In this quotation from the Representation, one recognizes important aspects of Schimmelmann's review. In his publication of the Representation, Kirstein mentioned that in April 1792 Britain had decided to abolish the Negro trade. In the French colonies, on the other hand, he believed the unrest was too widespread to permit any similar prophecy. Kirstein's comment must have been written at a time when it was known that the House of Commons had voted for British abolition of the slave trade as of 1 January 1796, but before it was known that the House of Lords would veto the bill.[31]

There may have been two sets of reasons for the Representation's assertion that it would be very difficult to neglect an example, once given, of abolition of the slave trade. Either humane reasons would force the Danish to follow the British example, or, it was believed, there would be practical problems involved in maintaining a Danish slave trade, if other countries abolished their trade. The humane example, which it was assumed Britain would offer, did play a role. It does not however, explain everything since the leading members of the commission, among them Schimmelmann, did not seem at all ready to support the abolition on humane grounds if it would entail serious economic problems. The reason that interdependence between the Danish slave trade and the foreign slave trade was not analyzed in every possible detail in the Representation may have been that it was self-evident to the Commission. It thus seems reasonable to assume that Danish maintenance of the slave trade was considered. Would it be practically possible and economically worthwhile for her to do so alone, without any cooperation with other nations in Africa and the West Indies as they had prohibited the slave trade? Denmark must also have considered whether other nations would allow her to continue the slave trade alone. If Denmark of 1791–1792 believed that the slave trade would not be continued by other nations, a transitional period of 10 years would seem quite long. Given the importance of the influence of the other countries' policies, there are many indications that the Danish edict was passed in 1792, largely because leading Danish politicians were convinced that Britain was about to abolish her trade, and they believed this would imply negative consequences for the Danish slave trade.

[31] On Saint Domingue, see Coupland, *The British Anti-Slavery Movement,* pp. 96ff.; Williams, *Capitalism and Slavery,* pp. 145ff.; C. L. R. James, *The Black Jacobins: Toussaint L'Ouverture and the San Domingo Revolution,* 2nd ed. (New York, 1963, first published 1938). In the autumn of 1791, the Danish ambassador in London reported that the rebellion in Saint Domingue harmed the cause of the slaves (reference to the same depeches as in n. 30, nos. 86–91). See also Commission's Representation, p. 3f., 70ff., 96f.; Kirstein, "Udtog af forestillingen til kongen angående negerhandelens afskaffelse," p. 43ff.; Mellor, *British Imperial Trusteeship,* pp. 49ff.

To summarize briefly the economic background of the Danish abolition of the slave trade: Under the impression that Britain was about to abolish her slave trade and desiring to abolish the Danish slave trade, the Danish Minister of Finance, Ernst Schimmelmann, caused a slave-trading commission to be established in the summer of 1791. This Commission reached the conclusion, first, that the Danish slave trade was not in itself profitable. Second—and more decisively—a primitive quantitative demographic analysis seemed to demonstrate that the Negro population of the West Indies, after a transitional period and after the introduction of certain social improvements, would be able to sustain itself without new supplies of slaves.

17

British Repression of the Illegal French Slave Trade: Some Considerations

SERGE DAGET

(translated by Charles Ferguson)

Research by English-speaking historians in the British Parliamentary Papers and the FO 84 Series in the Public Record Office has provided almost all the information thus far concerning repression of the slave trade in the nineteenth century. In one particular instance, however, one piece of information from these sources is not complete, as Dr. Eltis has brilliantly argued in his Chapter 11: This is the list of slave ships published by order of the House of Commons in 1845,[1] on the basis of which Professor Curtin made the landmark computer study familiar to us all.[2]

QUESTIONS RAISED BY THE 1845 LIST

If by some fluke a historian of the illegal trade were to limit himself to this analytical tool alone, the material concerning France—a slave-trading nation

[1] Archives nationales, Section d'Outre Mer (referred to in the following as Arch. nat. SOM), Paris, *Généralités (Gén.)*, 166/1344, Répression de la traite des Noirs, "Returns of Cases adjudged under Slave Trade Treaties . . . ordered, by the House of Commons, to be printed, 25 February 1845," 45 pp. It is significant that we find this list among official French papers, for this shows that it was studied by the government of a nation involved in the slave trade.

[2] P. D. Curtin, *The Atlantic Slave Trade: A Census* (Wisconsin, 1969).

and a potential slave-owning colonial power—would suggest that England's abolitionist campaign had met with success. This impression would be reinforced by two observations. On the one hand, the 1845 list, a basic source, "knows of" 2313 slavers of various nationalities: Spanish, Portuguese, and Brazilian; some Dutch, Swedish, Danish, North or South American; and even one Russian. On the other hand, it records 31 French slavers between 1814 and 1845, or 1.34% of the total. Here is where we detect an unreliable source. Before proceeding, we must comment on this finding. In producing a fact contrary to the implication of the official list, we most assuredly do not claim the dubious distinction of proving the existence of an illegal French slave trade. The omissions in the Foreign Office list, however, distort the calculations made by historians, and part of their argument as well. It is therefore worthwhile to entertain a few questions in this regard.

1. Let us assume that from 1814 on, the French slave trade dwindled to those 31 slavers over a period of about 30 years. Such a trade would indeed be negligible, sporadic, or occasional, lacking solid historical significance because of its slight overall effects, and lacking genuine statistical meaning, whether economic, social, demographic, or political. In the realm of attitudes, however, the limited activity recorded would suggest that proslavery Frenchmen became favorable toward putting humanitarian interests into practice. Thus we would have the success of abolitionist ideas and of English policy:[3] a fallacious argument that can be ignored. From the economic standpoint, these 31 ships would never have mobilized an investment worth entering in a record of French seaport activity. In the social context, compared with the employment market for the coastal population, these ships would have represented very low wages for their crews; whereas between 1814 and 1831, ships from Nantes alone employed more than 5000 sailors in the slave trade, and they were the best-paid in France.[4] Compared with the population drain from Africa, these 31 ships would have removed only a few thousand persons—about 6000—a tiny percentage in comparison with the hundreds of thousands usually thought to have been deported to slave-owning centers by the international trade in the

[3] This was not the case. Compare the bitterness of the proslavery arguments in the debates of the *Chambre des Deputés* in 1827 and again in 1841. See also Petit de Baroncourt, quoted in S. Daget, "Les mots esclave, nègre, noir, et les jugements de valeur sur la traite négrière dans la littérature abolitionniste française, 1770–1845," *Revue française d'histoire d'outre-mer,* vol. 60, no. 221, 1973, pp. 511–548. Slave trading is merely "transporting Blacks from one shore of the Atlantic to the other [p. 533]."

[4] S. Daget, "Long cours et négriers nantais du trafic illégal, 1814–1833," special issue of the *Revue Française d'histoire d'outre-mer* on the slave trade, vol. 62, nos. 226–227, 1975, pp. 90–134.

nineteenth century. In other (abolitionist) words, France would have "clean hands," just like England.

2. So limited a participation on the part of the French would make it impossible to understand the long-lasting, intense pressure applied by the English. This pressure definitely had its causes. In the economic sector, for example, faced with the uncertainty of French abolition, England neither took punitive action on French purchases of production equipment, nor did she refuse to secure English labor trained to operate machinery; such coercion would have run counter to her industrial and capitalist development. Still bound up with traditional principles and relationships between sovereign states, the pressure was at first diplomatic and psychological. Nevertheless, its influence on the French political context must not be overlooked: Rather extensively supported by England, the Bourbon regime had to take England into account, abroad as well as at home. Obligation created contradictory attitudes, varying between touchy autonomism and necessary deference to the leading world power. During the 30 months that followed the treaties of Paris and Vienna, slave trading was merely *discouraged*[5] by the restored monarchy. In 1817 and 1818, once it had become official, the illegality of the slave trade was clearly determined by the political and diplomatic situations: on the one hand, acquisition of the colonies grudgingly restored by England, Sweden, or Portugal; and on the other hand, the liberation of French soil from foreign occupation. Its being explicitly outlawed does not automatically imply that slave trading disappeared all at once. Concrete proof is found in 1827, and finally in 1831, in the new, harsh antitrade laws. During these 17 years of slave trading, English pressure never relented, and it went beyond diplomatic means.[6] The list of the British Parliamentary Papers seems to indicate that French sanctions, together with British pressure, produced good results, since only 31 French slave ships are mentioned. This is a distortion of political, diplomatic, legal, and maritime realities, as quantitative reality clearly shows.

3. In quantitative terms, the official list quite abbreviates the French situation. Our research has enabled us to list 763 ships that may reasonably be suspected of being slavers. They set out from Le Havre, Honfleur, Nantes, Bordeaux, Bayonne, and Marseilles; from ports in the French

---

[5] Arch. nat. SOM *Gén.* 152/1272: Ferrand, Interim Minister of the Navy, to Talleyrand, Paris, 30 September 1814.

[6] S. Daget, *La France et l'abolition de la traite des Noirs, de 1814 à 1831. Introduction à l'étude de la répression française de la traite*, unpublished doctoral dissertation in History, (mimeographed, Paris, 1969, 358 pp.). By the same author, "L'Abolition de la traite des Noirs en France," *Cahiers d'Etudes Africaines*, vol. 41, no. XI, 1971, pp. 14–58.

Antilles, Sénégal, and the Isle Bourbon (la Réunion) in the Indian Ocean. The port of Nantes alone handled 47% of the trade, 261 ships at least, between 1814 and 1833; there were probably 353. With French activity considerably increased, the 1845 list should be raised from 2313 to 3033 slave ships, an increase of one-third, transforming the statistical data now available.

4. All the conditions of the traditional slave trade are still present in this period, scarcely diminished by illegality and repression. I say "repression," for, just like England, France exerted repression on the west coast of Africa or in colonial waters. Created a few months after the law of 1818, the French squadron had no positive action during its first 4 years of duty. This lack of effectiveness led the English to accuse it of "desertion" and then to criticize "the ruling house," in other words, Louis XVIII himself.[7] Between 1822 and 1831, spurred on in various ways, it was more active, but never on the scale of slave trading by French nationals. All during this time, the Royal Navy took action against slavers flying the white (Bourbon) flag, until 1830.

5. What we have just said raises legitimate questions as to why so few French are listed in 1845, and why no others are mentioned. Four working hypotheses are possible. Was it a breakdown of the well-orchestrated intelligence service that England maintained in the other slave-trading countries? This is unlikely, for the worldwide network, a worthy precursor of today's Intelligence Service, supplied very exhaustive reports on the French slave trade. Sometimes the reports show more concern for French activities than those of other countries, so threatening did the former appear. Sources are British consuls,[8] abolitionists on missions,[9] and especially naval squadrons and joint enforcement commissions acting as courts of law, at Sierra Leone and elsewhere.[10] Since they confiscated the records of captured ships,

[7] Arch. nat. SOM *Gén* 154/1286, Thirteenth Report of the African Institution of London, Appendix A, 12 January 1821; Arch. nat. SOM, *Gén*. 152/1273, Report to the Council of Ministers, 29 September 1821.

[8] Public Record Office (PRO), FO 84/59, f° 158; Arch. nat. SOM, *Gén*. 166/1342.

[9] Ministère des Affaires étrangères, Paris (referred to as Aff. ét), Afrique 24, Traite des Noirs 1817–1820, Baron Séguier to Portal, Minister of the Navy, concerning the trip of Zachary Macaulay, former Governor of Sierra Leone, to Honfleur, where he witnessed preparations for the slave trade.

[10] PRO/FO 84, but see also PRO/FO 315. The Public Archives of Sierra Leone Contain some information in this connection that was not forwarded to London: cf. Archives of Sierra Leone, Fourah Bay College, Stack 4, shelves 23–25, *Sierra Leone Duplicate Dispatches,* 1822–1839, 23 vols., especially the interrogation of Captain Ferrand, master of the *Jules.* See S. Daget, "Les Archives de Sierra Leone et la traite illégale française," *Annales de l'Université d'Abidjan,* Série I, Histoire III, pp. 23–53. A serial analysis of these data may be undertaken on the basis of R. Meyer-Heiselberg, *Notes from Liberated African Department, in the Archives at Fourah Bay College, Freetown . . .,* research report no. 1 (Scandinavian Institute of African Studies, Uppsala, 1967), mimeographed, 67 pp. Less useful in this connection is J. U. J. Asiegbu, *Slavery and the Politics of Liberation, 1787–1861. A Study of Liberated Emigration and British Antislavery Policy* (London, 1969).

these commissions had at their disposal firsthand information on the status of the trade, coming from the traders' private papers. Therefore, England was very well informed, much better than France, at least during the first decade of repression.

The second hypothesis is that of David Eltis in his fine chapter: Are the lacunae in the list the result of careless work or weariness on the part of the few clerks charged with the endless, boring job of checking lists? In our opinion, this explanation is too facile a reduction to chance event, whereas the mass of omissions and their consequences are quite significant, as we shall see.

The third hypothesis implies poor communications among the official bureaus. In fact, England "knew" (that cautious, biblical verb is used in the list) many more French slavers than the list includes. Now, lack of communication between the Admiralty or the Colonial Office on the one hand and the bureaus of the Foreign Office on the other hand resulted in the almost complete suppression of French data, *but only and especially those data*!

The last hypothesis is perhaps more promising. Is it not plausible that in 1845 English political authorities made a deliberate omission, with the sole purpose of making political circles at home and abroad forget Great Britain's posture from 1815 to 1830? During that time, England deliberately remained outside the bounds of international law where France was concerned. Above all, as we shall see, in 1845 Franco–British negotiations on the elimination of the slave trade appeared to be reaching the point of decision.

For each of these hypotheses, the complete answer comes not from economic analysis but from political science. This kind of explanation makes little use of solutions through economic factors. In that case, does it belong in this volume? Of course our answer is yes. Indeed, political science can contribute to the study of the French slave trade opportunities for bringing it partly up to date, while clearing the way for future economic analyses and econometric models. We shall not address the latter, and we shall but touch upon the former. We shall go little beyond the objective terms of English repression against French slavers, showing a few consequences hidden by the 1845 list. Let us briefly review this in the international context, before we take up the specific subject.

THE INTERNATIONAL SITUATION

For England, eliminating the slave trade lay in reciprocal rights of search by warships of contracting nations aboard merchant vessels suspected of carrying slaves. In order to develop an international system, Lord

Castlereagh called a major conference in London in August 1816, a few months after the war. His action was too ambitious and premature, as English naval hegemony on the high seas was considered a threat to the sovereignty of the nations involved. The London discussions lasted until the eve of the negotiations at Aix-la-Chapelle, and apparently they failed.[11] An international antislaving league with unlimited search rights was not to be. Rather than give up, London made the best of failure by settling problems through bilateral negotiation.

As to search rights, international reaction was mixed, varying between accords, reticence, opportunism, and great flexibility. Whatever motives she had—humanitarian, political, or economic—England spared no effort to attain her repressive and abolitionist goal, and those efforts were most stringent, convincing, and questionable. Faced with the various forms of English pressure, other nations reacted ambiguously; there was neither cooperation nor explicit statement, but there was similarity. England stated the issues of repression and abolition in terms of a universal moral obligation. Economists may smile at this, but let us remember that the spirit of the time was not yet one of economic rationality. Faced with a humanitarian position, governments can but commit themselves in one way or another. So today, few nations would avoid taking a position publicly if it would prevent their being labeled as racist. At that time, an essentially similar reason led them to accept, willy-nilly, contractual obligations with the outstanding abolitionist "leader." These obligations took the forms of national laws; reciprocal search rights; or unilateral, autonomous repression, in the case of the United States[12] and France. These two nations agreed on search rights as the best way to do away with the slave trade.[13] Both refused them, however, as an infringement of their sovereignty. They also considered themselves powerful enough to prevent England from yielding to any inclination to force. On the other side, Portugal, Spain, and Holland, then Sweden and Brazil, agreed to reciprocal search rights with England, because their initial positions were to a certain degree those of dependency. Eco-

[11] Aff. ét, Afrique 15, TdN 1815–1844, and Afrique 23, TdN 1814–1816, the minutes of the conference, particularly the fourth.

[12] De l'état actuel de la traite des Noirs (London, 1821), cf. "Classe D: Etats-Unis," the debate at the conference and the address to the Chairman. For France, see Arch. nat. SOM, Gén. 166/1342, report of Baron Séguier, French Consul, to the Minister of the Navy, 15 January 1818. This opinion was still accurate in 1826 (see Arch. nat. SOM Gén. 191/1473, the preliminary work for the law of 1827).

[13] It is interesting to note here that the patrol sent by the United States to the coast of Africa between 1821 and 1823 seized French slavers. The Hornet and the Alligator captured seven or eight ships. One of them, the Pensée, was to cause serious problems, as the American captain, Robert Stockton, behaved like a genuine pirate. The Alligator's midshipman thought his captain had lost his self-control or gone mad.

nomically, they depended on England for continental or tropical markets; politically, for internal support; and diplomatically, as in the case of the new Brazilian Empire, for recognition as a nation in the world at large as well as at home, her chief concern at first.[14] The results of this situation were not merely theoretical; as early as 1813, international commissions were at work, supplied with slave traders by the (Royal) Navy's repression squadrons. The latter grew from three ships to seven, and then to nine off the west coast of Africa in 1822.[15] As for reciprocity, it was practically nil. Anti-slave-trade coercion was brought to bear on several hundred ships by sentences from international courts[16] or national jurisdictions, but the latter were by far the less frequent.

Now it must be emphasized that none of these arrangements forbade the slave trade to continue, or even to reach dimensions during the illegal period that it had seldom reached during the previous era of legal, government-sanctioned trading. Economic factors, of course, were undeniably the chief cause of this state of affairs. In the absence of substantial data on repression, however, it would be interesting to include the hypothesis of *national resistance,* by virtue of inertia and conscious inhibitions *vis-a-vis* the leading power, which was both envied and hated. As we have shown elsewhere, this was clearly the case in France. Her chief concern, quite apart from any economic interests, was not to appear in the eyes of the world as subordinate or subject to England.

BRITISH POLICY TOWARD FRENCH SLAVE TRADE

In dealing with France, England was much more subtle than with other nations, particularly in regard to European policy. Where maritime policy was concerned however, her attitude became openly arbitrary. In violation of maritime law, she searched vessels, although in principle search was tolerated only on neutral ships and in time of war. In violation of international law, since there was no Franco–British repression treaty, England seized French ships. In violation of the law of nations, she ignored the old definition given by Grotius that the oceans are free. English repression was then arbitrary in both phases of a first period between 1814 and 1831. After

[14] L. Bethell, *The Abolition of the Brazilian Slave Trade. Brazil, Britain, and the Slave Trade Question, 1807–1869* (Cambridge, 1970).

[15] C. Lloyd, *The Navy and the Slave Trade,* 2nd ed. (London, 1968), Appendix C, does not show that these patrols operated before 1819. Nevertheless, his book remains a basic reference. See our Appendix, a list of English repression cruisers.

[16] Cf. R. Meyer-Heiselberg, *Notes, passim.*

the signing of search agreements in 1831 and 1833, there was a period of repression by contract, also in two phases.

The first phase (of the first period), from 1814 to 1817, was fraught with ambiguities: The French accepted the Declaration of the Powers of Vienna, Napoleon decreed the abolition of the slave trade to appease England, the second Restoration rejected that action (and substituted a personal promise of Louis XVIII to the Prince Regent). The only results were a few circulars, mildly restrictive in tone, but without any lasting effect. There were economic ambiguities, for French traders and shipowners were counting on peace to pull them out of the stagnation caused by 25 years of revolutionary and imperial wars. Slave trading was to play a role in the resumption of activity, and shipowners lost no time in applying for clearance to sail. Officially, no clearances were issued after July 1815. Victorious England was herself ambiguous, for she delivered at least one safe-conduct for slave trading, whereas through her ambassador in Paris, she voiced strong abolitionist demands. The military situation did nothing to clarify the abolition issue, for in about 15 months peace, then war, then peace again disrupted the flow of news overseas, where slave-holding French colonies were occupied. As a result, French ships that had set out by virtue of the Additional Act of the Treaty of Paris in 1814, allowing slave trade south of the Formosa (Cape) Straits, were stopped by English ships on account of the war of 1815, even though it was over. Other ships sailed at their own risk, with the warning that international considerations did not theoretically allow shipping slaves from Africa.

Five French ships started slaving as early as 1814, 12 in 1815, and 10 in 1816, for a total of 27 trading ships. Of these, 2 encountered English cruisers off Africa, whereas 10 reached the Caribbean or Isle Bourbon (Réunion) with their cargoes and returned to France without difficulty Seventeen were taken by the English to Antigua, Sierra Leone, or Mauritius; tried; and condemned.[17] Table 17.1 presents the results.

So we see 19 British acts of repression against French slavers during this first phase; 2 searches or charges were made, 17 condemnations, and 2 unspecified actions. One ship was returned after the blacks were released, one ship was paid for upon the owner's complaint, and one was acquitted in London on appeal, after condemnation at Sierra Leone. Now let us distinguish.

1. The first slave traders were not condemned as such, but as war prizes, just as if the peace regulations of the British Admiralty had not been sent overseas. Thus it was for the *Belle* and the *Bonne Mère* in 1814, and for the *Jenny* and "four ships of unknown name" in 1815; so 7 slavers were

---

[17] Table 17.3 will later list all ships.

TABLE 17.1
Fates of French Slavers, 1814–1816

Year	Total number of French slavers	English searches or charges	Seized by the Royal Navy	Condemned by English courts
1814	5	1	2	2
1815	12	—	9	9
1816	10	1	4	6
	27	2	15	17

punished on a military pretext. On these grounds, the owner of the *Belle* appealed in 1817, claiming damages of 268,475 francs from the English. This is a sizable sum, for the ship displaced 334 tons; she was to carry 500 blacks, and they were actually boarded.[18] We do not know whether the military pretext was used intentionally as camouflage for illegal repression. The award was unusual, and the London administration upheld the decision of its colonial bureau.

2. Starting in 1815, of 15 ships seized, 8 were condemned at Sierra Leone or Mauritius. Six of these arrests brought about official protests from the French government in support of those from the owners, but only the owner of the *Cultivateur,* a ship of 351 tons captured by *HMS Telemachus* near Bonny with 507 blacks on board, was compensated by the Prince Regent for illegal activities.[19] The most significant case, however, is that of the *Louis.* Under the command of Jean Forest, she loaded 12 blacks at New Sestros, near Cape Mesurado. She was sighted on 1 March 1816, 12 leagues from the coast, by *HMS Queen Charlotte.* The two ships engaged in combat, and the slaver "killed and wounded many of His Majesty's subjects." Seized and taken to Sierra Leone, she was tried and condemned. Her owners appealed, and in a new trial before the High Court of the Admiralty in London, Judge Scott gave his celebrated verdict: The *Louis* was definitely a slave ship, but Scott acquitted her nonetheless, for England has no right at all "on any pretext whatever" to seize a French ship in peacetime. This judgment might have set precedent, but the English Navy took little note of it. On several occasions, the Admiralty reprimanded its squadron officers, though nothing enabled them to bring a foreign vessel to British justice,[20]

[18] PRO/HCA 42: 382 *148B;* PRO/FO 83/2264, *Law Officer's reports.* Arch. nat. SOM, *Gén.* 154/1288, 152/1273, and 166/1340. Aff. ét. Afrique 15, TdN 1814–1844.

[19] Arch. nat. SOM, *Gén.* 152/1273 and 154/1288, according to *Parliamentary Papers,* 1817–1821, Class C.

[20] Arch. nat. SOM, *Gén.* 204/1505, Twelfth Report of the African Institution of London, the Scott verdict.

unless she was a pirate. This was one reason for the years London would spend trying to make seagoing nations consider slave trading as piracy. Theoretically, the United States legislated this idea first, in 1819–1820, Commons came to it in 1824.

It remains impossible to interpret these actions. Was there merely contradiction between English orders and their execution? Or was there a rather devious strategy to give credit to French denunciations of "British machiavellianism?"[21] Were the French responses not also dictated by strategy? The Restoration's first Royal Order abolishing the slave trade, in January 1817, was the result of political opportunism much more than humanitarian ideology: The Bourbon government wanted to get the colonies back, in the spirit of Aix-la-Chapelle. Giving England a token of abolitionist good faith was cheap and made good sense. Besides, the slave trade in this phase did not have the numerical significance it was to have in the second phase.

Between 1818 and 1831 was the phase of pretense and strategy, against a backdrop of opportunism. First came the law of 1818, soon followed by the Royal Order creating the repression squadron.[22] Then came a series of delaying tactics and maneuvers whereby the French governments parceled out to England what England demanded from slave-trading countries: measures that were powerless to put an end to the trade but enabled England to suspend her frequent, urgent recriminations.[23] England used the carrot-and-stick method: diplomatic flexibility and strict repression. This phase can be broken down into three parts. In the two French abolitionist campaigns, of 1820–1822 and 1826–1827, England discerned the seeds of support from within, on her opponent's home ground. Certain influential persons in positions of power, the Duc de Broglie and the author, Benjamin Constant, to name but two, made substantial contributions to humanitarian practices. To a great extent, this brought about the third part of this phase, a slow but steady progress towards a reciprocal agreement. In 1828, with Charles X's government, joint action by the two powers was hardly likely. In 1829, the tone of ministerial exchanges sometimes resembled collaboration. Around the time of the 1830 Revolution, a decisive moment that ushered in mutual understanding, the idea of joint repression was germinating. It would ripen in November 1831 in the first mutual search agreement, to be improved

[21] This attitude was felt and expressed as early as 1815, but it endured far into the century. It was a factor in shaping the approach to historiography shown in contemporaneous literature.

[22] The law dates from 15 April, and the Royal Decree from 24 June.

[23] There was a Royal Decree in 1823, forbidding shipowners to engage in slave trading; a few months later, general mobilization of the French Navy against slavers; a Royal Decree in 1825 offering a bounty to the patrol for each black captured; in 1826, a judicial repression in the city of Nantes, led by a former patrolman; etc.

upon in March 1833. Louis-Phillippe's government needed British support, French abolitionists were in power, and the French economy had left behind its former structure and became autonomous, at least in Rostow's terms. These, however, are considerations involving the entire continent.

On the western coast of Africa, the prospect of the first *Entente Cordiale* was less obvious. During the years from 1818 to 1831, England was agressively searching, seizing, trying, and condemning French slave traders. One of the consequences, moreover, was that the French repression squadron was driven to take action against French nationals, in the name of dignity, honor, and respect for French law. Men like Massieu de Clairval and Villaret de Joyeuse, squadron commanders, finally gave meaning to the term, "repression of slave traders." Without much enthusiasm, courts in France as well as in the colonies followed the new trend. The French Admiralty was "liquidating" slave traders.

As for British repression, during this second phase it achieved the results found in Table 17.2.

This second table emphasizes the varying intensity of English repression. The changes correspond to certain outside influences: changes of govern-

TABLE 17.2
Fate of French Slavers, 1817–1831

Year	Total French slave ships	English charges or seizures	Seizure by English squadrons	Condemnations by English or international courts
1817	14	3	3	2
1818	29	4	7	7
1819	52	7	1	—
1820	71	10	4	4
1821	76	19	1	1
1822	76	8	8	8
1823	46	9	1	1
1824	76	10	4	4
1825	70	10	8	3
1826	59	9	4	2
1827	42	4	2	2
1828	30	9	9	9
1829	31	2	2	2
1830	34	4	4	3
1831	12	—	—	—
Total	718	108	58	48

Source: Serge Daget, *Analytical List of French Ships Suspected of Engaging in the Illegal Slave Trade from 1814 to 1867,* from archives in France, England, Sénégal, and Sierra Leone (Paris, 1976).

ment, the French expedition in Spain (London was opposed, and the trade fell off during the war, but British sanctions did not take advantage of the circumstances), and a new law (then England came to the rescue, and search was followed by seizure, but condemnation was not automatic). In addition, this policy was reversed between 1828 and 1830. Then, sanctions completely disappeared with the preliminaries of the 1831 agreement. During this second phase, the English took action 108 times, in one or another of the three ways making up the repression system, that is, search, seizure, or condemnation.

Adding up the results of both phases of the first period, we find that 110 French ships were searched, 70 seized, and 65 condemned. Among these, 2 were awarded damages, 3 were returned, and 1 was acquitted on appeal. One or 2 condemnations were overturned, and we do not know what the practical outcome was. Thus 1 slave ship out of every 7 had difficulties with the British Admiralty. Table 17.3 enunciates the French slave ships condemned by British tribunals, during this period. Another unanswered question is that of the influence of this conflict situation on the French navy's frame of mind, at a time when the conquered nation was growing even more bitter over the treaties of 1815, and the myth of the vanished Emperor was everywhere. Concerning the official list of 1845, it is a fact that England knew of four times as many French slavers as the list contains, and the repression was twice as active, ignoring the Scott judgment 48 times although it was recognized by the higher jurisdictions in London. We can answer a few questions concerning the exact methods of repression.

Searches were seldom made on the high seas, where the slave ship was usually faster than her pursuer. They were made near the great trading sites, where patrolling was easy: around the *mirador* of Sierra Leone (Rio Pongo, Rio Nuñez, Sherbro, and especially Gallinas), or much farther east, in the Bight of Biafra near the mouths of the rivers in the Niger Delta (Brass, Bonny, Calabar), all located north of the Equator and thus theoretically prohibited by various bilateral accords from trading in slaves. Sent out from the cruisers, launches mounting cannon and carrying a sizable detachment of marines went upriver to identify and count the merchant vessels awaiting their cargoes of blacks. Along the banks and sometimes in the harbors, the slave ships would often wait several weeks for their turn to load. This was done in a few hours once the cargo, previously ordered and paid for in advance, became available. The ship, however, might also leave the trading site empty ("on ballast"), only to return at the time appointed for delivery.[24] Searches took place at the mouth of the river. The ship was full, for so long as the "equipment clause" was not in effect, with its financial implications for the Navy's sailors, the latter had no interest in capturing a

[24] PRO/FO 315/55 and 315/58; Archives Nationales, Marine, BB⁴ 436, *Campagnes.*

TABLE 17.3
French Slave Ships Condemned by British Tribunals[a]

Year	Ship's name	Tonnage	Number of blacks	Remarks
1814	*Belle*	334	501	Military operation
	Bonne Mère	203	—	Military operation
1815	*Actif*	143	—	Condemned
	Cultivateur	315	507	Compensation
	Hermione	120	On board	Condemned
	Jenny	65	On board	Military operation
	Parisienne	—	On board	Condemned
	Unknown	—	On board	Military operation
	Unknown	—	On board	Military operation
	Unknown	—	On board	Military operation
	Unknown	—	On board	Military operation
1816	*Eléonore*	—	137	Condemned
	Helène	—	154	Condemned
	Louis	—	12	Condemned–acquitted
	Marie	—	—	Condemned
	Nueva Amable	—	—	Condemned
	Thérentia	—	—	Condemned
1817	*Reine Caroline*	73	18	Condemned
	Rôdeur	200	32	Condemned
1818	*Cintra*	—	124	Condemned
	Elize	42	1	Condemned
	Jeune Adolphe	—	—	Condemned
	Marie	98	106	Condemned
	Sylphe	153	388	Condemned
	Virginie	—	32	Condemned
	Marie	160	2	Condemned
1820	*Catherine*	—	50	Condemned
	Industrie	—	130	Condemned
	Marie	98	88	Condemned
	Succès	204	340	Condemned
1821	*Industrie*	—	300	Condemned
1822	*Aurora*	—	180	Condemned
	Caroline	—	85	Condemned
	Deux Amis	182	12	Condemned
	Légère	—	63	Condemned
	Petite Betsy	139	230	Returned
	Suzanne	—	—	Condemnation void
	Ursule	100	216	Condemned
	Vigilant	232	344	Returned
1823	*Légère*	186	352	Handed over to the Dutch
1824	*Cécile*	—	—	Condemned
	Deux Nantais	201	483	Condemned–returned
	Deux Soeurs	—	132	Condemned
	Vénus	82	74	Condemned

(continued)

TABLE 17.3 (*continued*)
French Slave Ships Condemned by British Tribunals

Year	Ship's name	Tonnage	Number of blacks	Remarks
1825	*Aimable Claudine*	79	34	Condemned
	Charles	198	247	Condemned
	Philibert	223	—	Condemned
1826	*Entreprise*	—	28	Condemned
	Fourtuneé	—	125	Condemned
1827	*Lynx*	112	251	Condemned
	Fanny	110	253	Condemned
1828	*Adeline (Fourmi)*	130	—	Condemned
	Coquette (Vénus)	90	182	Condemned
	Elisabeth	—	—	Condemned
	Henriette	190	306	Condemned
	Hirondelle	105	48	Condemned
	Jeune Eugénie	68	45	Condemned
	Jules	147	191	Condemned
	Persévérance	—	—	Condemned
	Vénus	—	—	Condemned
1829	*Laure*	278	255	Condemned
	Louise	125	—	Condemned
1830	*Caroline*	—	47	Taken to Senegal
	Potose	128	—	Condemned
	Virginie	39	91	Condemned and taken to Senegal

[a]Most condemnations were handed down at Sierra Leone. Three were made in the Old Bailey.

ship that was not laden with blacks. The bonus was paid on the basis of the number of blacks taken. This situation was later changed.

Theoretically, nothing could result from these searches on board French vessels. That being the case, we might be tempted to see in the abolitionist callings of certain officers making seizures a desire to give tangible evidence of repressive activity. On the crew lists of a few ships, we find reports of searches, written in English and signed by all parties present. These unusual annotations are rare. They give the place and the date of the operation and the exact number of blacks actually shipped, and this information is attested to by the captain of the slave ship himself. The *Orphée* out of Nantes, 352 tons, carried 698 "slaves."[25] The *Pauline* out of Guadeloupe, 75 tons, was

[25] PRO/FO 84/43, Granville to Damas, 10 December 1825; Archives départementales de la Loire-Atlantique, Nantes, Inscription maritime, 2455, côte provisoire. The next-to-last page of the ship's log reads, "Boarded by HBMS Maidstone, Commodore Bullen, OB, on the 4th Sept. 1825 after a chase of upwards of ten hours, and firing several shots to make him leave to do which he did not till the shot reached him he was aboard of me. His cargo consisted of 698 slaves. Extremes of Princes Island. Bullen [*sic*]."

carrying 151 Africans to Cuba.[26] It may readily be seen how valuable these figures would be, if there were more of them. In sum, although searches were the lightest of the repressive methods, they were a violation of international law, and the French were inclined to consider them outright piracy. If no further steps were taken, however, the slave trader got along despite searches; he grew accustomed to them and tried to elude them. They became another aspect of the "sport," and some captains, "in full dress uniform," took delight in showing search parties around their professional facilities and invited them to dinner. The officers were furious, and they complained to the Foreign Office.

Seizure had a quite different repressive value. The French authorities were hampered in their protests against seizure, for it always involved a ship carrying its black cargo, and therefore in open violation of French law. The only avenue of protest was through a foreigner's taking the place of French law. The English, however, were not random in selecting ships or times for seizure. The action could occasion serious errors on the part of the captors. For example, in November of 1822, the searching officer from HMS *Cyrene* took offense at the tone of voice used by Captain Baron, commanding the slaver *Caroline,* and shot him dead with a pistol. The homicide was acknowledged by the Foreign Office, and damages of 10,000 francs were offered to the widow, who accepted.[27] Often, the slavers made armed and deadly resistance to the British Navy (remember the *Louis*). The example furnished by four ships, the *Petite Betsy,* the *Vigilant,* the *Théodore,* and the *Ursule,* is both spectacular and significant. A cannon-shot away from Bonny while trading with a Spaniard as another Spaniard and an Englishman awaited their turn, these four ships were attacked by nine English launches from the frigate *Iphigenia* and the corvette *Myrmidon.* Twenty men in each launch, "all armed with guns, sabers, and pistols, and each boat mounting a . . . bronze deck gun," joined battle. The Spaniards replied. Caught among the combatants, the *Petite Betsy* tried to escape. Her maneuver drew heavy fire from the British. Of the four vessels seized, two were laden with blacks. At Sierra Leone, 230 Africans were freed from the *Petite Betsy,* and 298 from the *Vigilant* were turned over to the *King's Yard.*[28] On board the latter ship, between the Niger and Freetown, 46 died. The ships were condemned. The rest of the incident is of still greater interest. The British

---

[26] Bibliothèque municipale, La Rochelle, Manuscript 2268, release of the ship *Pauline,* owner Laporte, 75 tons, crew of 24. On the back, "Boarded by His Majesty Schooner Speed off the coast of Cuba with 151 slaves on board from the Coast of Africa to some port in Cuba."

[27] PRO/FO 84/58, especially folio 52 verso; PRO/FO 83/2243, *Law Officer's Reports;* Arch. Nat. Justice, BB[18] 1009 (1822), case of widow Baron.

[28] A dozen sources agree on this point. The least known are the Archives départementales Charente-Maritime, *Papiers Fleuriau;* Service Historique de la Marine, Cherbourg, 3[P3] 102. See in PRO/FO 84/19 the naval battle plan, taken from the *Sierra Leone Advertiser.*

experts had to admit that even if two English sailors were killed in the engagement, European Admiralties might well consider it a fine example of self-defense on the part of the French sailors, and civil or criminal proceedings would be impossible.[29] An amicable settlement with Paris, which had already requested that the ships be returned in order to strengthen French pursuit, brought the *Vigilant* and the *Petite Betsy* back to Cherbourg, where they were taken into custody by French maritime authorities and, finally, the courts. This case clearly shows that seizure usually was the result of armed resistance. Then, in Sierra Leone, the Vice-Admiralty Court had jurisdiction, freeing the blacks and condemning the ship.

In more involved cases, however, an international court had jurisdiction; these commissions were set up in accordance with the treaties. Now during the period under discussion, 1814–1831, there was no Franco–English treaty of repression. Therefore only special conditions enabled the English to bring ships before an international tribunal. These conditions were clearly analyzed by Leslie Bethell,[30] and by Dr. Pieter C. Emmer. Their origins lie in a slave trader's ruses to elude maritime repression. The trader secured forged sailing papers, which documents were required and stated the nationality of the ship. They were secured from the authorities in St. Thomas, a Danish Caribbean colony, or in Dutch St. Eustatius, and sometimes even from the colonial authorities in Martinique, from what level we do not know. French cruisers were shown the Danish or Dutch papers, and thus lawsuits were avoided, since there existed no organization for repression between those countries and France. English cruisers were shown the French papers, in hopes of the same results for the same reasons. If the French, however, were understanding, the English were less so. Searches were taken to extremes on ships laden with blacks. The double set of papers was easy to find; and if it was not found, the suspicion of fraud was enough to warrant seizure, in the eyes of the international commission at Sierra Leone. As Pieter C. Emmer has clearly shown, most of the ships condemned at Sierra Leone as "Dutch" were Frenchmen carrying duplicate papers.[31] Operating on the borders of maritime law, like England, they were also on the borders of piracy, as the French said of the English cruisers. They were nevertheless condemned and sold as slave ships, and they were often bought back by their former owners, or by their captains on the owner's behalf.

The fact remains that if the three elements of the British repressive

[29] PRO/FO 83/2243 and 83/2266.

[30] L. Bethell, "The Mixed Commissions for the Suppression of the Transatlantic Slave Trade in the Nineteenth Century," *Journal of African History*, vol. 7, no. 1, 1966, p. 79–93.

[31] P. C. Emmer, *Engeland, Nederland, Afrika en de Slavenhandel in de Negentiende eeuw* (Leiden, 1974), 215pp.

system were enforced with varying degrees of severity, the official doctrine was capable of evolving. Along with the activities they reported to London, the authorities at Freetown received the order to rid themselves speedily of the French ships left on their hands after the blacks were freed, by sending them beyond the "limits of [their] jurisdiction," or later, by escorting them to the French authorities at Goree.[32] They obeyed these orders, but only once they felt well enough supplied with maritime equipment. Until then, they did not hesitate to buy condemned ships, sometimes fine, brand-new vessels, at prices well below "their value."[33]

In fact, seizure and condemnation, and the confiscation of French property and capital, aroused some protest in an effort to save face; but as to the fundamental issue, nothing could bring about a break in relations. Also, in economic terms, the losses were hardly significant, even in their short-term effects. From this standpoint, unfortunately, the general conditions of the illegal trade complicate the analyst's task. Outlaws are seldom talkative about their activities. As research now stands, we have little information concerning investment in the illegal trade, and this shortage leads to artificial and sometimes awesome assumptions. Nevertheless, on the basis of a small set of data interpreted through elementary arithmetic, we have proposed a few hypotheses appropriate to the French slave trade in the nineteenth century. For a slave ship of 145 tons—the average of several hundred ships—the investment would have been about 100,000 francs. This figure includes the cost of the new ship, the original cargo, 2 months' pay for the crew, their food and that of the blacks, and insurance at 20%.[34] In order to set even an approximate figure for losses to French shipping as a result of English repression, the first step is reducing the total cost to cost per ton, or about 700 francs. We have precise data for 29 ships seized: For 3975 tons, the investment required would have been 3,000,000 francs. Applying this to the 65 ships seized we have the figure of 6,500,000 francs. Extrapolating to the 763 ships suspected of trading, we find an investment in the French illegal trade of about 75,000,000 francs; the gross loss incurred by French shipowners is then 8%.

Hypotheses are even more fragile when they attempt to measure the loss of the anticipated sale price of new blacks in the Americas. On the one hand, the number of Africans shipped is still relatively unknown; but here we have precise data concerning 38 seizures. These ships were carrying 5885 individuals, for an average of 155 per ship. Applied to the 65 seizures, this average gives 10,075 individuals. On the other hand, a financial esti-

---

[32] Arch. publiques de Sierra Leone, Fourah Bay College, Stack 1, shelf 5, *Secretary of State Dispatches,* 1808–1839, *Sylph* case, 29 July 1819.

[33] Cf. S. Daget, "Les Archives de Sierra Leone."

[34] S. Daget, "Long cours et négriers nantais."

mate would require knowing the sale price of these blacks. All indications are that local market prices fluctuated widely, from 400–500 francs per head to 3000–4000; the latter figures are unlikely before the end of the trade, at around 1865. A certain number of sources agree on a sale price for new blacks of about 1500 francs, and this is the figure we use. In 38 known cases, the losses incurred indicate a deficit of about 9,000,000 francs. Applied to the 65 English seizures, the figure is 15,000,000 francs. A fleet of 763 slavers could transport 118,000 blacks, whose sale price would be about 175,000,000 francs.

If French shipowners invested 75,000,000 francs in the trade and anticipated sales of 175,000,000, and if the total loss due to English seizures comes to 22,000,000 francs, the loss is 8.8% of the real and anticipated financial movement. Let us not push our hypotheses so far as to estimate the return voyages as included in that loss. Spread over 17 years of activity and divided among the number of French shipowners involved in the trade, the damage may be considered minor. If a few shipowners failed during that period, it was not the fault of England, but rather, as we have shown elsewhere, because of delinquent accounts in America. Therefore, English repression did not seriously hamper the economics of the French slave trade, and it was even less of a threat to the shipping trade in general.

These various approximations, which an economist will judge with severity, have at least the qualitative advantage of showing that the French slave trade possessed a certain dynamic character, despite the risk of repression on its capital. Individual investments in the 8.8% of shipping lost were a trifling contribution to humanitarian interests, hardly more than offerings for the poor and for charity, after the Sunday sermon. From the government's viewpoint, the loss also explains why there were not more vigorous reactions directed to the authorities in London; during debate on the repression law of 1827, the Duke of Fitz James said the loss was the interest on the Restoration's debt to England, for having restored the monarchy.

Let us now take a much briefer look at the second period, in which the two phases are defined by the 1845 Franco–English conference in London, held by the repression specialists. We shall deal here only with the first phase, divided into two parts: 1831–1840 and 1840–1845. It includes the time when the search agreements were in full force, including the "equipment clause" whereby a ship could be seized on the mere suspicion that she was a slaver, and without black cargo actually aboard. To a specialist, a ship's design, fitting, and even her odor, were sufficient indication of her function.[35]

The first years of official, cooperative repression went by with none of the

[35] The special repression commission at Nantes in 1826 took as its criteria these routine observations by professionals. See also PRO/FO 84/59 folios 61–62.

difficulties apprehended by the authorities at the time of the preliminary discussions. A key figure in this phase, L.-E. Bouët-Willaumez, commander of the squadron, governor of Senegal, a shrewd tactician and talented author who was later to be an Admiral, states categorically: "English and French never met on the coast but we shook hands cordially and exchanged invitations to dinner, etc."[36] That was at the beginning. The good feeling is easy to explain, for the severity of the 1831 French law, together with the search agreements, made slaving a dangerous trade. Not that it disappeared permanently, but its scope was greatly reduced in comparison to the previous period. Therefore, search rights were seldom used, and as a result, the relations between the two squadrons were indeed those of friendly colleagues. This good feeling did not banish caution, however, for despite its smaller numbers, the French squadron always strove to outdo English repression; they succeeded, particularly in the straits of Mozambique in 1832, when they seized four slave ships bound for Isle Bourbon (la Réunion).[37]

As things now stand, we cannot draw up a satisfactory table comparing the activity of the traders with that of the cooperative repression. Heavy suspicion fell upon 17 ships between 1832 and 1845, and on 16 more by 1862. Among them was the *François I*[er] in 1858, a screw-driven three-master said to have landed 1600 blacks in Cuba. The information is vague and contradictory, and it involves two new aspects: "indirect trade" through sale of merchandise to coastal traders without loading blacks, and "free contracts" or trade disguised as an official contract. The role of English repression is hard to evaluate, and it became so discreet as to appear suspicious. Here again, the 1845 list does not tell all. It names the *Clémentine* in 1831 and the *Réparateur* in November 1834. The same year, it cites the freeing of the 390 blacks on board the *Formidable* at Havana; and the 484 Blacks on board the *Phoenix,* at Sierra Leone in 1836, without mentioning their nationality. It mentions the notorious affair of the *Marabout* in 1841, which greatly agitated French opinion and contributed to a deterioration of relations as well as the "public image" of search rights. But the list says nothing of the "collisions," "dangerous maneuvers," "intimidations," or "harassments" perceived and reported as such by the French, regarding the *Henri,* the *Sénégambie,* and the *Niger,* avowed slavers and known as such by England.[38] This official silence may offset the errors of Royal Navy officers

---

[36] Journal officiel de la Martinique, 10 August 1842, Letter by Bouët-Willaumez, dated 30 June, reprinted in this paper from *Le Courrier,* a Paris paper.

[37] Archives Nationales du Sénégal, 1 B[20], folio 26 verso, on the *Algaé.* See also H. Gerbeau, "Quelqùes aspects de la traite interlope à Bourbon au XIXe siècle . . .", *Congrès de l'Association Historique de l'Océan Indien* (Saint-Denis de la Réunion, September 1972), 67 pp.

[38] Arch. nat. SOM, *Gén.* 143/1213, 90/835, 175/1405, 208/1518, etc.

in acting too violently on five or six occasions against less suspicious vessels. It could also be explained otherwise.

The reciprocal search agreements were open to other nations. Sweden, Sardinia, and the Hanseatic ports adopted them, as did others, and the internationalization so long sought was thus partly achieved. England would have made an error in giving the impression to possible member states that a lack of true reciprocity allowed her to coerce merchant ships. These incidents were best kept quiet. Two decisive events occurred on a higher plane. The Oriental Question nearly caused a breakdown in Franco–English relations. When some kind of settlement was reached, England took advantage of the decreased tension to mobilize international opinion once again concerning the repression of the slave trade. In December of 1841, an abolitionist treaty was signed by the Powers, including France. If the French Parliament refused to ratify the treaty,[39] the explanation must be sought in a questionable desire for revenge, after the failure of its jingoistic stance in 1840. Let us consider this as an example of patriotic resistance, reinforced by the *Marabout* incident. The second event afforded a compromise solution. In 1842, abandoning a policy followed for 20 years, the United States in turn subscribed to the international program of repression. In comparison with earlier accords, the chief clause of the Webster–Ashburton treaty, found in Articles 8 and 9, is quite peculiar. No mention is made of reciprocal search rights (enabling the British to board a ship, in other words, to enter foreign territory); the legitimacy of the flag flown by the vessel is merely verified. This scheme would safeguard national sovereignty and dignity, while enabling the squadrons to perform their repressive duties on nationals who were in violation of the international treaty. France seized on this idea and made of it the central issue in the discussions at the 1845 London conference.[40]

The American precedent no longer allowed England a valid defense for maintaining the "traditional" right of search. The conference drew up a new rationale for repressive action:Fifty-two vessels from both navies, a sizable number, would patrol the west coast of Africa, but their authorization to intervene went no further than determining the nationality of the ship

---

[39] See *Le Moniteur Universel,* 1841, vol. 2, for the harangues of *Despute* Billault, a dyed-in-the-wool partisan of slavery.

[40] Arch. nat. SOM, *Gén.* 166/1340. France is officially advised by the American government of the conclusion of this treaty, as well as of "her policy regarding the abolition of the slave trade." See Guizot to the Minister of the Navy, 31 October 1842. France could follow the progress of negotiations, especially in the text of the "Tucker–Paine agreement" of March 1840, whereby the two patrol commanders agreed on the detention of captured slavers, a private act denounced by the respective governments, but the origin of the official exchanges to follow. The chief texts were accessible to the Guizot cabinet, which therefore had three years to study them and observe their effectiveness.

challenged. There was an end to military repression. A few ships were reported by the British squadron, but penalties were treated as French internal matters.[41] The year 1867 may have seen the end of an Atlantic slave trade carried on illegally by France for 53 years.

The contents of the 1845 list, names of slave ships and numbers of blacks shipped or freed, suggests that if repression was not triumphant, it was not the failure openly denounced by certain M.P.'s, first of all T. F. Buxton. Rather than fatigue or oversights on the part of records clerks—who are assumed to have "overlooked" more than 700 ships (by chance, all of the same nationality!); rather than breakdowns in communication among the officers concerned—again following the same pattern—we believe British pragmatism is the cause of the omissions in this list concerning the extent of the French slave trade. By 1845, the French trade had been impossible to measure statistically for 15 years. Raising the issue again would have stirred up memories of general conditions and specific practices, and these memories were still quite fresh; moreover, England's conduct had not always been beyond criticism. By making judicious omissions, the British Parliament spared the sensibilities of an ally who was ever ready to take offense, thus keeping her in reserve for future battles, abolitionist or other; and she took defensive measures against her possible reaction to the forthcoming 1846 decisions on sugar, which would inevitably lead to a revival of the slave trade by Portugal, Spain, and Brazil.

CONCLUSIONS

We can no longer afford to overlook one of the chief aspects of the illegal slave trade in the nineteenth century; its relationship with the history of international relations. As in other fields of study, we find here that politics and diplomacy thrive on forgetfulness when it suits them, and deny that events may have been otherwise than described. The House of Commons' list deliberately reduces the French slave trade and its repression to the role of a mere "micro-phenomenon."[42] The list is therefore an excellent example of a historic fact deformed and made to serve the needs of contemporary history. It is a model for political science.

French historiography need not attempt to hide its delay compared to slavery studies in English, for this delay is common knowledge. At present,

---

[41] We must not confuse these ships with those which transported "indentured servants." On this point, see F. Renault, *Libération d'esclaves et nouvelles servitudes* (Abidjan-Dakar, 1976).

[42] The term comes from Professor J. B. Duroselle, who uses it to establish the typology of the "underlying forces" that determine international relations. See J. B. Duroselle *et al.*, *Mélanges Pierre Renouvin* (Paris, 1966), pp. 1–15.

French research is emphasizing the correlations and parallels among the attitudes and responses of slave-trading nations to pressures from the leading world power. These concepts have already been studied by English-language historiographers. However, reading those studies shows them to be very poorly documented or informed concerning Franco–English relations over the slave-trade issue. French research is striving to analyze the situation without partiality, nationalism, or ethnocentrism. Its methods are not ambitious, and it seeks uncomplicated structures. When the first phase of political science analysis has been completed, research can proceed to complex models, for instance, econometric, but only if we have enough sources concerning the economic factors in the illegal trade. Almost nothing is available in this field. As for measurements, we are still in the quantitative and serial phase. The basis chosen for this chapter, a British source that has already undergone masterful computer analysis, has been further clarified and interpreted by traditional or qualitative, and even subjective methods. We submit our findings for discussion.

APPENDIX. NUMBER AND SIZE OF BRITISH REPRESSION PATROLS

Historians always concentrate exclusively on the list published by Christopher Lloyd, *The Navy and the Slave Trade* (London, 1949, 2nd ed. 1968), Appendix C), to enumerate the English ships engaged in repression on the west coast of Africa. The latest example to our knowledge is the highly interesting viewpoint expressed by William A. Green in "The West Indies and British West African Policy in the Nineteenth Century—A Corrective Comment," *Journal of African History*, vol. 15, no. 2, 1974, pp. 247–259. Citing Lloyd, p. 248 and n. 12, the author states that a British patrol was one "normally comprising six vessels," and that from 1821 to 1830, it varied between five and eight ships. This is not entirely accurate.

We find the following information in the *British Parliamentary Papers, Colonies, Africa*, no. 50: West Africa General, Sessions 1812–1874 (Shannon, Ireland, pp. 132–133 [pp. 94–95 of the original]):

Return of the Number of Vessels of every Class in His Majesty's Service which have been employed on the West African Station, in each year since the Year 1815.

1816	1817
Inconstant, 245 tons	*Inconstant*
Bann, 115 tons	*Cherub*
Cherub, 115 tons	*Semiramis*, 245 tons

1818
Semiramis
Cherub
Tartar, 245 tons
1819
Tartar
Erne, 110 tons
Pheasant, 100 tons
Morgiana, 100 tons
Myrmidon, 110 tons
Snapper, 50 tons
Thistle, 50 tons
1820
Tartar
Pheasant
Morgiana
Snapper
Thistle
Myrmidon
1821
Tartar
Pheasant
Morgiana
Thistle
Iphigenia, 245 tons
1822
Driver, 100 tons
Cyrene, 110 tons
Snapper, 50 tons
Thistle, 50 tons
Iphigenia
Pheasant
Morgiana
Myrmidon
Bann
1823
Owen Glendower, 246 tons
Pheasant
Bann
Driver
Cyrene
Snapper

Thistle
Victor, 100 tons
Swinger, 50 tons
1824
Owen Glendower
Maidstone, 245 tons
Thetis, 255 tons
Bann
Driver
Cyrene
Victor
Atholl, 150 tons
Swinger
1825
Maidstone
Atholl
Bann
Victor
Esk, 112 tons
Swinger
Redwing, 104 tons
Conflict, 50 tons
Brazen, 129 tons
1826
Maidstone
Brazen
North Star, 160 tons
Esk
Redwing
Swinger
Conflict
Clinker, 50 tons
1827
Maidstone
Sybille, 275 tons
North Star
Eden, 135 tons
Esk
Redwing
Conflict
Clinker
Primrose, 115 tons
Plumper, 50 tons

1828	*Primrose*
Sybille	*Conflict*
North Star	*Clinker*
Eden	*Plumper*
Esk	

The document is signed, James Lance. With the exception of the first 3 years, we note that the English patrol is larger than is generally stated. Characteristically, the reinforcement in 1819 corresponds to the setting up of international tribunals at Sierra Leone. We must, therefore, correct the data given by Lloyd and used by W. A. Green.

ACKNOWLEDGMENTS

Since the version submitted to the Symposium, this chapter has been revised to include the comments made during the discussion by Pierre H. Boulle, David Eltis, Pieter C. Emmer, and Professors Curtin and Rottenberg. We most gratefully acknowledge their contributions.

Index

A

Abolition of slave trade, 171, 275–276, 280, 292, 295, 399–418, 420, 421, 422, 423, 428
Abomey, 107, 108, 131, 175
Adamu, Mahdi, 7–8, 9, 163–180
Aja, 112, 125, 127, 129, 131, 134
Akinjogbin, I. A., 108, 111, 112, 113, 116, 120, 127, 132, 133
Algeria, 37–43, 51, 65, 67
Alkali, Nur, 177
Amin, Samir, 30, 44
Angola, 77–106, 140, 232, 245, 247, 250, 251, 252, 269, 292, 294, 310, 311, 316, 318, 321, 328, 329, 334, 356, 357, 359, 361–369, 371, 374
Anstey, Roger, 7, 11, 14, 118, 138, 343
Anti-slave trade squadron, 79, 276, 419–442
Arada, 126, 127, 129

Ardra, 6, 114, 121, 122, 125, 126, 135, 138, 139, 311, 359, 360
Asante, 222, 223, 224, 231, 232
Asiento, 258, 373, 375
Atkins, John, 120, 130, 131, 132, 310
Austen, Ralph, 4, 23–76, 171

B

Badagry, 116, 120, 123, 127, 133, 136, 173, 175
Bahia, 79, 80, 81, 83, 86, 100, 101, 103, 135, 137, 138, 164, 175, 277, 278, 279, 282, 283, 284, 285, 287, 291, 292, 293, 296, 297, 358, 374
Baikie, W. B., 172
Baltic–Guinea Co., 401, 403, 409
Baqt, 32, 65
Barbados, 335, 336, 337, 375, 381, 382, 389, 390, 392, 394, 395, 396

Barbot, John, 6, 110, 119, 125
Bargum Trading Society, 401
Barth, Heinrich, 6, 151, 152
Beads, 307, 308, 311, 312–315, 316, 334, 359
Bean, Richard, 7, 15, 16, 156, 165, 215, 234, 377–398
Benguela, 77, 78, 80–86, 90, 92, 98, 102, 103, 358, 363, 364
Benin, 107–141, 175, 186, 202, 316
Benue River, Valley, 9, 153, 217, 225, 230
Bethell, L. M., 274, 290, 434
Beyendaels, Joost, 365
Bight of Benin, 5, 6, 7, 9, 107, 109, 118, 119, 121, 124, 125, 126, 127, 129, 133, 134, 135, 136, 140, 141, 163–180, 217, 221, 224, 232, 291, 292, 293, 294, 311, 360
Bight of Bonny (Biafra), and hinterland, 9, 197, 205, 217, 228, 232, 292, 293, 294, 297, 311, 316, 321, 327, 328, 329, 330, 430
Black servile military forces, 51–58
Boahen, A. Adu, 29, 68
Bonny, 225, 226, 227, 229, 230, 311, 316, 317, 318, 327, 329, 427, 430, 433
Borno, 170–171
Bosman, William, 6, 110, 119, 151
Brazil, 5, 14, 15, 18, 77–106, 118, 122, 123, 124, 129, 136, 138, 224, 231, 232, 274–280, 284–296, 324, 326, 334, 353, 355, 357, 358, 359, 360, 364, 365, 366, 368, 369, 370, 374, 381, 382, 390, 424–425, 439
Bristol, 307, 309, 312–315, 320, 324, 325, 326, 335, 336, 337, 340, 341, 343, 344, 345, 347, 348, 350, 351
British America, adoption of slave labor in, 377–398
British Foreign Office, 273–298, 423, 433
British Parliamentary Report (1845), see Parliamentary Paper of 1845
British trade, 12, 13, 14, 265, 303–330
British West Indies, 286, 371, 377, 378, 381–385, 390, 392, 394, 398, see also specific island names
Burton, Richard, 110, 131
Buxton, Thomas F., 29, 439

C

Cairo, 27, 47, 50, 63
Calabar, Calabari, 197, 202, 226, 227, 228,

229, 230, 310, 311, 327, 328, 359, 360, 430
Cameroons, 153, 311, 316, 320, 327, 328, 359, 360
Central Sudan, 45, 59, 63, 64, 65, 67, 163–180, 182
Chamber of Zeeland, 354, 356, 358, 365
Chesapeake, Bay, region, 16, 377, 378, 382, 383, 384, 389, 392, 394, 395, 398
Christiansted, 400
Clapperton, Captain, 174
Clarkson, Thomas, 403, 405, 406, 413
Colby College, 1, 11
Competition for slaves, 213–225
Congo, King of Congo, 292, 294, 311, 321, 356, 361, 362, 363, 364, 368
Consumption patterns, 303–330
Cooper, F., 191, 211
Copenhagen, 2, 401, 402, 406
Copper, copper bars, see Hardware
Costa da Mina, 107, 136, 137
Cowries, 134, 135, 138, 158, 307, 310, 311, 312–315, 359
Craton, Michael, 17
Credit arrangements, 5, 6, 229, 230–231, 233, 360
Crowding of slaves during passage, 249, 250, 260, 261–265, 293, see also Slaves per ton
Cuba, 124, 129, 140, 141, 274, 276, 277, 279, 281, 285–290, 292, 293, 294, 297, 433, 437
Curaçao, 251, 252, 257, 258, 259, 372, 373, 374
Curtin, Philip, 2, 3, 5, 6, 7, 11, 18, 23, 26, 27, 28, 29, 62, 69, 116, 118, 119, 121, 129, 138, 141, 150, 155, 156, 157, 158, 160, 164, 183, 214, 247, 274, 279, 289, 290, 291, 293, 294, 296, 297, 320, 374, 419

D

Daget, Serge, 17, 118, 287, 288, 299–302, 419–442
Dahomey, 6, 9, 107–141, 153, 165, 174, 179, 186, 197, 205, 206, 208, 222, 223, 224, 232, 242
Dalzel, Archibald, 6, 108, 110, 112, 131, 132, 135
Danish Negroe Trade Commission, 17, 400,

402, 403, 404, 406, 407, 410, 412, 413, 414, 415, 416
Dapper, O., 109, 110, 124
Davenport, William, 328, 337, 338
Davidson, Basil, 30, 43, 69, 71, 164, 214
Davies, K. G., 111, 118, 138, 273, 310, 311, 374, 397
Degn, Christian, 399, 402, 405, 412, 414
Demerara, see Guiana; Guiana Coast
Denmark, Danish trade, 16–17, 119, 372, 399–418
Domestic African slavery, 18, 181–212
Dondo, 84–85
Ducasse, Jean-Baptiste, 119, 121
Duignan, P., 144
Dutch Brazil, see Brazil
Dutch trade, 6, 14, 15, 118, 120, 122, 135, 139–140, 239–260, 288, 294, 332, 353–375, 415
Dutch West India Company (WIC), 242, 243, 244, 245, 247, 249–258, 260, 354, 355, 356, 358, 359, 363, 369, 371, 372, 373, 375, 381, 382, 390

E

East India Company (English), 307, 308
Economic costs, and benefits of slavery, 143–161
Economic welfare, 145–148
Edrisi, 4, 32
Egypt, 32–36, 42, 45–47, 50–51, 56, 58, 62, 64, 67, 69, 71
Elmina, 242, 243, 358, 360, 369, 371
Eltis, David, 11, 12, 17, 62, 69, 118, 119, 121, 136, 141, 273–298, 419, 423
Emmer, Pieter C., 12, 14, 15, 353–375, 434
Engerman, Stanley, 11, 249, 261–273, 280, 289, 293, 405
Epidemiology, see Mortality
Export of slaves, and routes of export, 163–180, 213–225

F

Ferguson, Charles, 419
Fernão de Noronha, 357
Fisher, Allan and Humphrey, 167, 214
Fon kingdom, 126, 127, 131
Forbes, Frederick, 110

Frederiksted, 400
French slave trade, 261–272, 275, 287–288, 291, 323, 324, 401, 415, 419–442
French West Africa, 8, 182, 183, 187–199, 201, 205
French West Indies, 274, 275, 277, 282, 287, 288, 292, 294, 296, 405, 422, 434, see also specific island names
Frossard, M., 403, 406, 413

G

Gabon, 311, 316, 327
Gambia, 187, 310, 316–321
Gann, L. H., 144
Gemery, Henry A., 1–19, 143–161, 165, 215, 234
Geniza documents, 27, 28
Gold, 69–71, 158, 219, 347, 359, 360
Gold Coast, 9, 151, 173, 202, 217, 221, 224, 232, 242, 269, 310, 311, 316, 319, 320, 321, 324, 325, 326, 327, 328, 359, 360, 372, 411, 412
Green-Pedersen, Svend E., 16–17, 399–418
Guianas, Guiana Coast, 247, 252, 257, 258, 275, 286
Guinea, Guinea Coast, 9, 140, 151, 199, 217, 222, 231, 241, 243, 245, 246, 247, 250, 251, 252, 269, 349, 358, 359, 360, 361, 365, 366, 367, 368, 369, 371, 372, 403, 404, 407, 408
Guns and gunpowder, 159, 307, 308, 310–318, 320, 364

H

Hardware (copper, brass, pewter), 305–316, 318, 359, 361
Hardy, John, 285, 286
Hausa, Hausaland, 7, 125, 126, 127, 134, 163–180, 190, 218, 220, 224, 230
Havana, 275, 285–286, 287, 290, 297, 437
Heeren XIX, 358, 363, 369, 372
Herskovits, Melville, 112, 131, 132
Hogendorn, Jan S., 1–19, 143–161, 165, 183, 213–235
Hopkins, A. G., 30, 44, 154, 178, 200
Hueda, 126, 127

I

Ibn Battuta, 4, 32
Illegal slave trade, 419–442
Imports into Africa, *see* particular goods
Identured servants, 377, 378, 380–385,
    387–392, 394, 395, 397, 398
Inikori, J. E., 11
Iron, iron bars, 307, 308, 310, 312–315, 320,
    340, 342, 347, 359, 361
Itamoracá, 353, 357, 358, 374
Ivory, 359, 360
Ivory Coast, 9, 217, 231

J

Jamaica, 276, 289, 335, 339–344, 346, 347,
    375, 397
Jeppesen, Henrik, 411, 412

K

Kano, 152, 153, 170, 171, 172, 175, 183
Katsina, 152, 171
Kilson, Marion D. de B., 164, 214
Kingston, 343, 344, 346
Kirstein, Ernst, 403, 405, 417
Klein, Herbert, 8, 11, 249, 261–272, 273,
    280, 289, 293, 294
Klein, Martin A., 181–212
Koelle, 129, 154, 155
Kopytoff, Igor, 181–182, 183, 184, 190,
    199, 207, 208, 212

L

Labat, Jean Baptiste, 110, 120, 126, 127
Labor, price of, 390–398
Lagos, 107, 116, 120, 122, 123, 127, 133,
    134, 136, 173, 175, 196, 222, 224, 230
Lake Chad, 9, 217, 220
Lancashire, Lancaster, 308, 323, 324, 335,
    350
Leeward Islands, 335, 392, 400
Le Herissé, 130, 131
Lesser Antilles, 372, 375
LeVeen, E. P., 6, 7, 151, 156, 158, 159, 165,
    215, 296, 297
Lewicki, Tadeusz, 44
Libya (Tripoli), 29, 36–37, 42, 51, 62, 67,
    68

Liquor, 311–315, 318, 320, 324, 325, 326,
    334
Liverpool, 306, 307, 308, 309, 312–315,
    317, 320, 323, 324, 326, 327, 335, 336,
    337, 338, 340, 343, 347, 348, 350, 351
Loango, Loango Coast, 78, 140, 245, 319,
    324, 327–328, 362
London, 309, 335, 338, 343, 344, 345, 347,
    348, 351
Lovejoy, Paul A., 8–9, 165, 181–212, 213–
    235
Luanda, 77–106, 354, 358, 361, 362, 363,
    364, 366, 374
Lumber, 344, 345, 347, 364, 407

M

Maghreb, 28, 36, 47, 51, 58, 65, 69, 71
Maize, 151
Manchester, 308, 309, 311, 320
Manning, Patrick, 4, 5, 6, 107–141
Maranhão, 275, 277, 284, 285, 363
Marginal physical productivity of labor,
    379–380, 382, 383, 384, 387–388
Martin, Gaston, 17, 111, 118, 294
Massangano, 362, 363
Mauny, Raymond, 29, 30, 68, 69
Meade, James, 148
Meillassoux, C., 181, 183, 190, 191, 193,
    201, 202, 208, 212
Merritt, J. E., 333
Mettas, Jean, 17, 111
Middelburg, 354, 355
Middlebursche Commercie Compagnie
    (MCC), 244, 245, 260, 332
Middle passage, duration of, 240, 245, 246,
    251, 334, 365, 367, *see also* Mortality in
    the slave trade
Miers, S., 181–184, 190, 199, 207, 208, 212
Miller, Joseph, 2, 4, 5, 77–106, 293
Millet, 150, 151, 152
Minchinton, Walter E., 12, 14, 331–352
Minimum physiological level of living, *see*
    Subsistence
Miracle, Marvin, 6, 149, 151, 156, 157, 160
Monopoly factors in slave markets, 213–225
Morgan, E. S. and Pugh, J. C., 16, 156
Mörner, Magnus, 414
Morocco, 29, 37–43, 51, 56–57, 62–63, 67
Mortality, in the slave trade, 10, 11, 15, 100,
    101, 102, 155–157, 239–272, 276, 292,

293, 294, 295, 330, 365, 366, 367, 379
age and sex ratios, 254–256, 258
crew, 259–260, 263, 266, 268, 276
Mortamer, P., 364, 365
Mpinda, 362
Murray, D. R., 274, 290

N

Nantes, 17, 262, 263, 275, 294, 324, 333, 420, 421, 422, 432
Netherlands, see Dutch trade
New Netherland, 372, 373
Nieboer, H. J., 15, 16
Nigeria, Niger Delta, Niger River, 8, 153, 166, 194, 225, 226, 227, 228, 230, 231, 232, 242, 292, 430, 433
Nilotic Sudan, 29, 32–36, 45, 46, 59, 62, 64, 65, 67
Nørregård, Georg, 411
Nupe, 125, 179, 183

O

Old Calabar, see Calabar
"Open resource" hypothesis, 15
Oroge, E. A., 170, 183
Ostrander, Gilman, 333
Ouidah (Whydah), 6, 107, 108, 114, 119, 120, 121, 122, 123, 126, 127, 133, 134, 135, 138, 139, 175, 242, 310, 311, 316, 318
Ouman, Hendrick, 362
Oxholm, P. L., 410
Oyo, 9, 122, 123, 126, 127, 129, 132, 133, 173, 175, 176, 179, 186, 202, 204, 205, 206, 222, 223, 224, 225

P

Paraíba, Paraibo, 284, 285, 353, 357, 358, 374
Parliamentary Paper of 1845, 12, 17, 273–298, 419–422, 430
Pernambuco, 79, 80, 81, 86, 101, 103, 275, 277, 284, 285, 288, 353, 357, 358, 371, 374, 390, 391
Piloti, Emmanuel, de Crete, 4, 32
Plantations, demand for labor, 16, 378–381, 389
Polanyi, Karl, 108, 113, 132, 133, 202, 210

Porto-Novo, 116, 120, 122, 123, 124, 127, 133, 136, 175, 222
Port Royal, 343, 345
Portugal, Portuguese trade, 77–106, 123, 135, 164, 265, 292, 327, 354, 362, 363, 371, 390, 415, 421, 424, 439
Postma, Johannes, 6, 10, 11, 111, 118, 138, 139, 140, 239–260, 294
Productivity of labor, 388–390
Provisioning of ships, 270, 365

Q

Quantitative research, 2–3
Queen Nzinga, 363

R

Ratelband, K., 354, 355
Recife, 357, 358, 362, 366, 368, 370, 371
Red Sea–Indian Ocean trade, 28, 46, 68
Rhode Island, 324, 325, 326, 327
Rice, 334, 336, 351
Rice, C. Duncan, 333
Richardson, David, 12–13, 303–330
Rinchon, D., 118, 262, 263, 272, 273, 294
Rio de Janeiro, 79, 80, 81, 83, 86, 100, 101, 273, 275, 277, 279, 280, 281, 282, 283, 285, 287, 289, 290, 292, 293, 294
Rio del Rey, 359, 360
Robinson, C. H., 172
Ross, David, 111, 112, 134
Royal African Company, 5, 6, 118, 119, 138, 139, 307, 310, 320, 395

S

Saharan slave trade, see Trans-Saharan slave trade
St. Croix, 400, 401, 406
Saint Domingue, 416
St. Eustatius, 251, 252, 257, 258, 434
St. Thomas, 400, 401, 404, 408, 434
Santiago, 275, 285, 286, 287
São Thomé, 354, 358, 363, 372
Schimmelmann, Ernst, 399, 402, 403, 405, 406, 409, 410, 411, 412, 413, 415, 416, 417, 418
Seasoning of slaves, 383, 384, 386
Senegal, Senegal River, 8, 219, 220, 232, 235, 422, 437
Senegambia, 9, 59, 150, 154, 182, 183, 189,

199, 206, 217, 218, 231, 232, 246, 292, 294, 320, 358
Sertanejos (caravan operators), 5, 89–95, 98, 100, 104
Shepperson, George, 166
Sheridan, Richard, 333, 335, 338–9, 343, 349, 413
Sierra Leone, 129, 141, 217, 224, 231, 275, 286, 293, 296, 297, 316, 320, 323, 324, 325, 329, 402, 407, 422, 426, 427, 428, 433, 434, 437, 442
Slave acquisition, original, in Africa, 167–169
Slave Coast, 107, 223, 242
Slave delivery system, in Africa, 163–180, 213–225
Slave marketing, in Africa, 213–225
Slavery in West Africa, 181–212
Slaves per ton, 261–262, 264–267, 270, see also Crowding of slaves
Snelgrave, Capt. William, 110, 131, 133
Social saving, 143–144
Sonho, Count of, 358, 361, 362
South Atlantic slave trade, 77–106
South Carolina, 336, 337
Staudinger, P., 172
Stein, Robert, 263
Subsistence, 149–153, 157, 200
Sugar, 15, 333, 334, 335, 336, 339, 341, 342, 343, 344, 345, 347, 349, 351, 353, 358, 360, 372, 378, 381, 389, 400, 401–406, 408, 439
Supply curve for slaves, 395
Surinam, 247, 251, 252, 257, 258, 289

T

Tambo, D., 214
Terms of trade, 305
Texas, 286
Textiles, 307, 308, 309, 311–316, 318, 319, 320, 359, 363
Thomas, Robert P., 15, 16, 165, 215, 234, 377–398
Tight-packing, see Crowding of slaves during passage
Tobacco, 308, 318, 320, 334, 339, 340, 341, 342, 349, 351, 364, 372, 378, 382, 389, 394, 398
Tolmé, David, 285, 286, 290

Transport of slaves, and costs of transport, 7, 8, 9, 163–180, 213–225
Trans-Saharan slave trade, 4, 5, 18, 23–76, 172, 183, 186, 199, 218, 225
Triangular trade, 13, 14, 331–352
Trier, C. A., 399, 403, 405, 408–9, 412, 414
Trinidad, 286, 354
Tunisia, 37–43, 45, 51, 56, 65, 67

U

Units of account, 317, 318, 322, 323, 325
Usselincx, W., 355, 356, 357

V

van den Boogaart, Ernst, 12, 14, 15, 353–375
Vansina, Jan, 129
Verger, Pierre, 5, 111, 112, 118, 136, 138, 164, 178, 273, 282, 283, 291
Vibæk, Jens, 405, 409, 410, 411, 412, 414
Virginia, 16, 339, 340, 341, 355, 382, 384, 385, 386, 389, 394, 395, 396, 397, 398
Voltaic people, 125, 127, 129, 153

W

Walterstorff, E. F., 409, 410, 411
Western Sudan, 8, 59, 63, 67, 193, 196, 203
West Indian–Guinea Co., 400, 401
West Indies, 18, 331–352, 354, 403, 404, 405, 408, 412, 415, 426, see also British West Indies; French West Indies; specific island names
Whydah, see Ouidah
Williams, David. M., 333
Williams, Eric, 16, 18, 332, 400, 408
Windward Coast, 310, 311, 316, 317, 318, 320, 321, 324, 325, 327, 328, 329

Y

Yoruba, Yorubaland, 112, 125, 126, 127, 129, 134, 170, 174–179, 183, 187, 197, 224

Z

Zaire, 78, 83, 97, 103
Zango (rest stop), 8, 176–178
Zaria, 7, 170, 172, 183

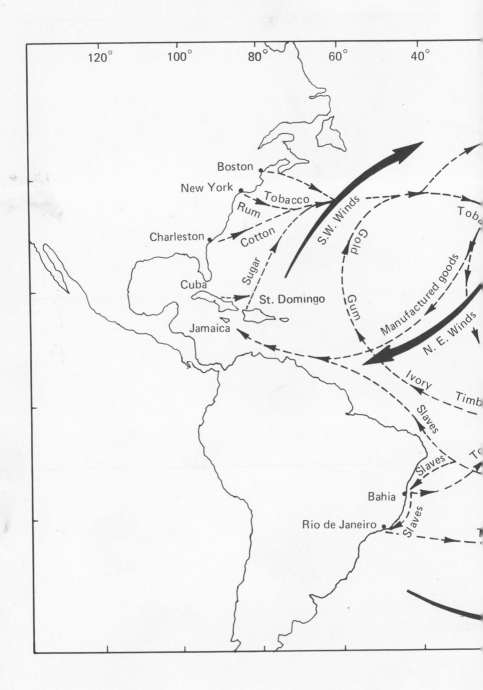